MODELLING SCENERY

THE KIRTLEY WAY

PETER SMITH

ISBN 13: 978-1494282028

ISBN 10: 149428202X

CHAPTERS

CHAPTER 1 - INTRODUCTION

The scenery on a model railway demands totally different skills from tracklaying, electrics or baseboard building; they are crafts, things that can be taught. To do the scenery, though, that's on the opposite side of the coin, the artistic side. You can teach anyone how to wire up a point motor or make a leg for a baseboard, but you can't teach someone how to paint a backscene. You can either do it or you can't and if you can't no number of lessons is going to turn you into John Constable.

Looking around at layouts at exhibitions, most people can't! That includes me, by the way; I'm hopeless. The trouble is that a backscene done badly can ruin an otherwise good layout...so can poor trees, unrealistic contours on the hills or water that looks like painted plaster.

This book is for those who find scenery difficult, to whom it does not come naturally. The gifted will learn a trick or two as well, hopefully, but for the majority who don't instinctively know what to do without thinking about it, this is for you. If you follow my techniques you will find that you can produce realistic scenery, without needing to do anything difficult or complicated, and with no need of expensive tools either despite what some would have you believe, (mostly those trying to sell you the tools!)

If you follow my guidelines you will be able to create a model landscape using the simplest of materials and techniques; cover the ground surface so that it looks realistic and convincing; add a backscene that gives depth to the layout and looks utterly believable; model water that looks like water; and finally add all those little details that bring a layout to life. You'll be able to create scenes like these....

This book is illustrated using layouts representing British, American, German, French and Austrian prototypes; don't be put off by that thinking that because you only model British outline much of it won't be of interest.

Naturally the scenic techniques described apply to any prototype and to any scale....I have worked in all scales from 2mm up to 16mm and I do things the same way in all of them.

The scenery needs to be planned into the layout from the very beginning, perhaps even on the back of that beer mat when inspiration first struck! It's no good trying to put in a river bridge after the track has been laid, it needs to be thought about right from the start before the baseboards have been built.

When you have drawn out your track plan and fitted it all onto the baseboards, think about what else you want to feature as well as the track and buildings. What is there room for? Water always looks good but it can make the baseboard more complicated to construct. Do you need a scenic break where the line leaves the layout? Where will the station approach road come in? If there is a level crossing, how will you continue the road onto the backscene?

Make your mistakes on paper; that's the time to keep trying new things until the whole plan starts to come together and looks like what you have in your minds eye. Only when your plan is settled can you think about cutting wood to make the baseboards, with allowance for any sunken sections below track level. These do look good, but they also add complication.

An alternative to lowering sections of baseboard is to raise the whole of the trackbed or to use open framed baseboards, although when I have used these I have found that they solve some problems but create others just as irritating. I prefer a flat surface on which to work if at all possible, the blank canvas on which our creation will arise.

I like to draw everything onto the baseboard surface with a marker pen; track, buildings, bridges, everything that will be on the finished layout. Then you can see that they all fit, whether board joints are in awkward places and whether the planned buildings might be too big. You can also stand back and look at it and visualise the finished layout of course which is very satisfying!

I am going to assume that you have your baseboards, you have laid and wired your track, tested everything and then ballasted it. Only then are you ready to start your scenery. Let the fun begin!

CHAPTER 2 THE BACKSCENE

I think a backscene is essential if it is possible to include one; the only time when it isn't is when you need to be able to access the boards from both sides, perhaps because they are too wide to reach across.

Here's why you need a backscene:

The picture is ruined by the pile of cloth in the background. It would be possible to add a sky using Photoshop but

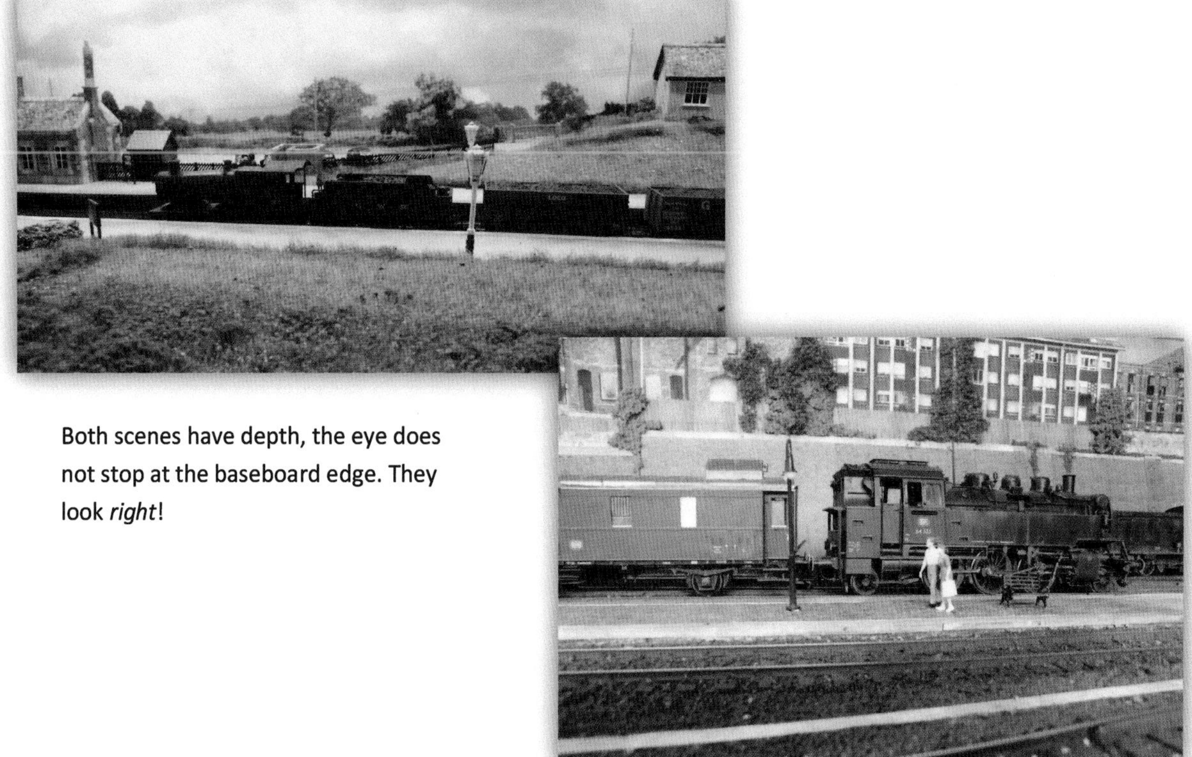

Both scenes have depth, the eye does not stop at the baseboard edge. They look *right*!

I have tried every method under the sun to produce backscenes over the years, and I've finally settled on one that suits me.

Here are the ones that didn't work.

Painting them—I'm not a good enough artist. Without wishing to be rude, neither are you!

Using printed paper ones stuck on with wallpaper paste—they crinkle, crease, tear, and generally get in a right mess. If you try to sponge the surface to spread them out the image comes off, if you don't they stay crinkled. Air bubbles form and you can't get rid of them for the same reason.

Using printed paper ones stuck with aerosol adhesive—you only get one chance, and if it's not right, too bad because it won't come off again. You'll still get air bubbles, it will still crease……… forget it.

Using printed ones with repositionable aerosol adhesive—they don't stay stuck.

I've found one way that works for me. Here it is.

An American firm called Backdrop Junction produce printed backscenes on self adhesive vinyl. Because there is no glue involved they are clean to apply. Because they are on plastic, any mess that gets on the surface can be wiped off with a damp cloth. If they don't go on straight you can pull them off and try again.

Even better, they are custom printed so that you can specify the size you want….28' long by 18" high in 4' long sections, for instance.

I know what you're saying….they're all American.

They're not —they do UK scenes as well, and European. However, it doesn't matter because we're going to adapt them.

The backscene itself is part of the baseboard structure, 6mm plywood so it stays straight and doesn't need any bracing on the back. My local timber merchant cuts it to the exact size I want, far more neatly than I could ever do.

The height will vary; for a fixed layout as high as you can manage really, for a portable layout it will depend on transport, having to lean over to uncouple, etc. but as a rule of thumb I try to use around a foot high if possible. The lower the backscene the harder it is to take photo's without getting the top edge in the picture.

Backdrop Junction (by the way I've no connection other than as a satisfied customer), produce a wide variety of scenes, and to me the most useful are the fairly non specific ones with lots of sky and not too much landscape. It will depend on where your layout is set, of course. To me the perfect backscene is one that you don't notice. You should be looking at the trains, perhaps the scenery, but if you find your self looking at the backscene it's not doing its job. A bad backscene draws the eye, you can't miss it...a really bad one is like a magnet! The backscene should be there but not noticed, like the backdrop in a theatre.

There was a an O gauge layout on the circuit a while ago on which the owner had spent hours meticulously painting a high backscene. It was awful; sadly you didn't notice the layout, it was totally dominated by this dreadful backscene. If he'd had plain boards behind it or a simple sky, the layout would have looked fantastic.

So, the first thing to do is order a fairly plain backscene to the size of your boards. When it arrives it can be stuck directly to the plywood; I varnished my first ones but in fact the vinyl sticks better to the plain plywood. Smooth it with a cloth as it goes on to get rid of any air bubbles and unroll it as you go—easy!

That's a Backdrop Junction backscene on my On30 layout; just some hills and the sky, a general scene that doesn't draw the eye but adds depth and atmosphere to the overall view.

However, now it's time to be a bit more creative!

Here the backscene is the sky and the wooden hillside, but the house has been added afterwards. It looks like part of the model, yet it's just a flat picture on the backscene. Adding buildings like this enables you to customise the backscene to suit exactly what you want, to make it individual and unique. It's also fun and very rewarding.

Look how the two dimensional pictures fit in with the three dimensional models, making it look as though the scene continues right into the distance. It's all about fooling the eye, of course. The angled front of the coaching inn disguises the corner of the layout.

You are going to need a computer for this—if you haven't got one, this might encourage you to you out and get one, it's a really valuable modelling tool.

You need a selection of pictures of buildings in the locality of your layout. You can go out and take your own, as I did here:

I used my own digital photographs of Scrayingham in Yorkshire to print off my own images for use on the backscene. As a way of locating the model in particular place you can't beat it. I use Serif PagePlus software to get the picture just as I want it, perhaps flipping an image to get the shadows on the right side, before printing it off onto gloss photo paper. I then cut it out with my scalpel on a cutting mat before going round the edges with a black marker pen to get rid of the white line. A spray with Testor's Dullcote to seal the image and get rid of the shine and it can be stuck onto the backscene with Evostic.

However, it's not so easy if your layout is set in the past, or in another country. Then I turn to the internet; on **www.flickr.com** are millions of photographs, and copying them once for your own use is not a problem. Put in the search box 'Yorkshire Church', or 'Swiss Chalet' and up will come hundreds of photographs from which you can take your pick. You just save the images you want to use, and then treat them in just the same way as your own digital photo's.

If your layout is set in an earlier time, try visiting places such as Beasmish, Ironbridge or the Black Country Museum. There you will find restored buildings with no modern items as satellite dishes or PVC windows to spoil the effect. If you go one weekday when it's not a school holiday with luck it won't be too busy and you can get all the pictures you'll need. A day that's dry and bright but a bit cloudy is best, then the shadows won't be too strong.

Once the buildings are stuck to the backscene (just stand them in front to begin with until you like the arrangement), you can add foliage or a tree to hide any edges or other things that need covering up. A half tree can be a useful space saver, with the trunk against the backscene and the full branches only on the layout side.

Avoid any items such as vehicles or people on the backscene; keep it simple and fairly plain and it will be doing it's job.

One problem with backscenes is how to lose a road which is heading straight for the back of the layout.

Here's how to do it; the level crossing gates hide the join from the normal viewing angle, and the buildings on either side cover the edges of the picture. In a rural setting trees could do the same job just as well. Instead of the crossing gates a vehicle or two can hide the join between vertical and horizontal.

A river can cause the same problem; here on the left you can see the picture on the backscene where it meets the actual river.

However from the normal viewing angle you don't notice it because the bridge is in the way ands the eye focuses on that.

CHAPTER 3 FORMING THE LANDSCAPE

The first thing to remember is that the landscape was there before the railway, so it should look as though the railway was inserted into the landscape and not the other way round. The railway builders tried as far as possible to create a straight and level platform the width of the tracks across whatever landscape features already existed. They followed valleys if they could rather than crossing them because that was easier and therefore cheaper, although we are in the happy position of not having to worry about spending shareholders money so if we fancy a nice viaduct or tunnel, we can have one.

If your baseboard is complete with the track laid, wired and working you are ready to begin being creative!

If you have your buildings already made as these were you can stand them in place and check for clearances; otherwise a simple cardboard box the same size does just as well. Then the contours of the landscape can be drawn round them. The buildings and turntable deck are just standing loosely, it is far to early to fix them down as a lot of messy work is still to come.

If you are incorporating a bridge that needs to be placed in position as well, though not necessarily fixed down at this stage:

Ideally the baseboard should already have the backscene fixed in place as here; it is much easier to do it now as part of the structure rather than adding it later on, though for portable layouts it may need to be removable of course. Here I cut the top of the backscene in a wavy line as I thought that might look more natural than a straight edge but in the end I put a piece of straight beading along it to match the rest of the layout. It doesn't really matter what sort of top edge the backscene has, because you don't want anyone to notice it!

The landscape will be built up from pieces of corrugated cardboard glued together with a hot glue gun. It's quick, easy and light, the card is easy to cut and is cheap or even free if you chop up old boxes as I do. I cut the shaped pieces first, one at a time, holding them on place on the layout and trimming them until they look right; the first one is glued in place, then one or two spacers about 10cm wide, then the next former and so on. In the sample above they are standing on a piece of card but on the layout you glue them directly onto the baseboard.

You don't need to use anything stronger than card; on a portable layout weight is important and you're not going to be standing on the scenery....card is plenty strong enough. If you are concerned about strength laminate two pieces together with the corrugations at right angles; it's nearly as strong as wood then.

Next to form the ground surface itself I cut lengths of thin card (bought in packets of 50 A4 sized from the local stationers) and glue them in place with the glue gun one at a time, one layer in one direction and then a second layer at right angles to them. .

It's an extremely robust and light construction which will support any features such as buildings. However, on the example above I have stuck a length of plastic tube in place which will support a tree trunk; as they are top heavy trees need a bit more help to stay upright. The tube is kept in place by the former....if you want to add a tree later on the tube can easily be added afterwards and glued in place from above simply be cutting a hole through the card. Once the ground surface had been completed the tree trunk is simply pushed into the tube.

The beauty of this system of landscape construction is that the formers can easily be altered with a Stanley knife if they don't look like you want them too.

I use a dark coloured card for the top surface, usually black, so that if any shows through the ground cover it won't look wrong.

Here a rock face has been built up (we'll deal with that later on), and the card pieces have been glued in place above it. It looks a mess, but as it's never going to be seen it doesn't matter.

In this picture the upper baseboard has been added and now the landscape is being built up around it:

In most instances, unless there is a feature such as a rock face, the landscape should flow, with gentle curves and no sudden changes. Blending together two separate baseboards like this is important as when the work is finished it should look like one single scene with no obvious division between the two. Keep steep slopes for where man has been involved, for cutting sides as here or embankments; nature works with more subtle curves and gradients.

Fitting the landscape around the railway was easier on this 00 layout of Berkeley Road and as it's a real place I just copied what was really there. However, it still had to be got right; notice how gently the fields slope, the different greens and browns in the fields rather than all being one colour, and how the backscene blends in to become part of the layout. That join in the backscene will be hidden by a nice large tree!

Here is a similar approach on an O Gauge layout, with the fields rising from track level to give a nice backdrop for the trains. All the scenery was done with card formers exactly as described.

The next job is to cover them with the ground surface, but before we do that I like to do the ballasting; I'll explain why and how in the next section.

CHAPTER 4 BALLASTING

Ballasting is one of those jobs that can make or break a layout; it's not one I enjoy, but it has to be done so let's get on with it. Done well, it does make all the difference:

As with everything in this book, the technique I am going to describe is simply the one that years of experience has taught me is the best....others will disagree, but this works for me.

I don't use an underlay; I have found that they cause more trouble than they're worth, soaking up the glue when it should be sticking the ballast together and so on. I may put down as layer of self adhesive cork floor tiles, but nothing more. I like to use Woodland Scenics ballast in the large jars; it comes in a range of colours and grades and doesn't change colour when it is glued unlike real granite. It is actually made from ground up fruit seeds, so it is lighter than real stone, and it does the job very well.

Before any ballast is put down the track needs to be painted - I use a spray can of Railmatch sleeper Grime or Track Colour, with other cans of rust colours for sidings. Spraying the track is far easier than brush painting it. When the paint is dry, brushes can be used to highlight areas such as dry brushing in white and fawn on the sleepers of lightly used sidings, rust colours on the rails and chairs in similar places and so on. Heavily used track though is a pretty uniform colour, it just depends on what sort of line you are modelling. The busy urban station above has track that looks totally different from my On3-0 American layout.

I pour the ballast over the track and then use a 2" wide paint brush to level it off. A smaller paintbrush removes it from the point blades and tie bar area. Again, how it looks will depend on your railway...in the Victorian period they ballasted right over the sleepers whereas on a light railway there might be almost no ballast at all. I like to mix the shades, perhaps light grey with brown or brown with buff, it gives some variation to the tone of the ballast which can look effective if it is not going to be painted heavily once it is laid.

Once it all looks like it should I soak it in diluted PVA glue, the cheap own brand stuff because it's going to use a lot. I use a 50/50 glue and water mix with a few drops of washing up liquid to help it soak right in where we want it. You read of people putting it on a drop a at time from an eye dropper........personally I use a large plastic PVA bottle and put it straight on from that, putting on plenty and keeping on until the ballast turns white. That's when you know it's soaked right in and it's got enough on.

The layout will look awful –the temptation is to fiddle with it. Don't—leave it well along until all the ballast is rock hard. Then you can enjoy yourself chipping it away from all the point blades!

It is only now that the ballast really becomes part of the scenery. Let's assume that you've chipped all the bits from the points and the inside of the rails, all the points have been freed up and the layout is working as it should. Now the fun part can begin.

What you do next will depend on what sort of railway you are building, so I'll go though them in stages.

BUSY MAIN LINE STATION. The track and ballast will be dirty, and very much one colour all over as in the picture at the start of this chapter. I spray the whole of the track & ballast with Railmatch spray cans, mainly sleeper grime & track colour, and that's really all it needs. Clean the rail heads, and off you go.

MAIN LINE OUT IN THE COUNTRY. This will be a lot cleaner, depending on the age of the ballast and track of course. I might give it a mist of spray paint but really it's probably best left alone as long as the rails themselves are painted.

BRANCH LINES AND LIGHLY USED LINES. The ballast will be clean so leave that alone, but the colour of the rails should be lighter so dry brush them with Railmatch light rust and dark rust, highlighting the chairs. The sleepers can be dry-brushed with greys and light browns, followed by white which picks out the sleeper grain.

SIDINGS. On seldom used sidings the ballast will be clean, and the rails a much lighter rust colour so use Railmatch light rust here, and give the buffer stop the same treatment.

GRASS GROWN TRACK. This one is the most fun the model—the hard part is knowing when to stop, before the whole layout disappears under a sea of green!

You might just want a few clumps between the tracks, or to go the whole hog as below.

In both cases I use Noch static grass fibres, which come in lengths up to 12mm which is very useful.

The first thing to do is forget about that expensive Static Grass applicator you were sold—you don't need it. I should stick it on Ebay, you might get your money back!

The only tools you'll need are the packs of grass, some PVA and your fingers.

For lightly grass grown track, I brush on a little PVA between the sleepers, with increasing amounts where the grass is to be longer such as the end of a siding. I do around 10cm of track at a time.

I then take a small clump of the fibres in my fingers and simply press then into the glue, varying the lengths and the colours as I go along. When no more PVA can be seen I blow the fibres from four directions, one after the other, and they stand up in the glue as if by magic. Some strands will be going off at odd angles, but so does real grass. Doing it like this you get thick clumps of fibres, it's much quicker and you can see at once how it looks. More can be added as required. You can use the same technique to spread the grass out from the track towards the scenery—we'll deal with that in a later chapter.

Before the PVA dries make sure no clumps of grass are stuck to the inside of the rail, and that's all there is to it. It won't interfere with the trains, and it looks superb.

Something you can also do with the shorter strands is to sprinkle them onto the track when the glue on the ballast is still wet; it will soak into the grass fibres so that they become part of the ballast and look very effective as short grass growing in the track. For longer stuff though, do it in clumps, it looks great.

If you want to add a few wild flowers give it a spray over with repositionable Photomount aerosol adhesive and sprinkle on the flowers (I use ones from Greenscene), and then clean off the rail heads.

CHAPTER 5 GROUND COVER

This Summer I did the scenery on a Gauge 3 model of St Ives, some 80 feet long and four feet wide. That's a lot of static grass. If I'd used one of the applicators we're told are necessary I'd still be there doing it now!

I didn't, I used my fingers.

This is how it looks. I think it's OK, it looks like grass to me.

You don't need expensive equipment to do scenery. If someone tells you that you do, they are probably trying to sell you some of it!

When we left the landscaping chapter, we had out hillsides covered in strips of black card. What we do next depends on what we are going to cover them with.

I use three grass mats made by Busch and sold as 'Wildgrass', in light green, dark green and cornfield. The strands are about 5mm long and they look superb, for long grass in 4mm and moist grass in 7mm. The dark green is a bit too dark and regular for my liking, and the cornfield is fine if you're making a cornfield, but the light green, reference 7216 is superb. It comes in a square 80cm by 80cm, and it's not cheap, but if you've a big area to cover quickly and easily you can't beat it. The strands of grass a various colours, it's really convincing. I wouldn't want to cover 80 square centimetres with static grass; this can just be stuck straight down onto the black card with the glue gun, starting in one corner and doing a bit at a time until it is all in place. It can be cut to shape with scissors of course. You'll see it in a lot of the photographs, like this one....

For smaller areas of course I use static grass fibres, usually Noch and bought in the 4mm, 6mm and 12mm lengths and various colours. These are another excellent product, though of course other makes are available...Heki are very good too though less easy to find.

Before applying it I paint a layer of neat PVA over the card to give a smoother surface and help bond it all together, and the same for any other surface I am covering with grass. I let that dry before going nay further.

As described in the ballasting chapter, I then simply spread a good thick layer of PVA glue over the area to be covered and plant the grass in it with my fingers a clump at a time, varying the lengths and the colours. It settles into the PVA, and a blow from each direction makes the fibres stand up. That's all there is to it. As I said, I did 80 feet of St Ives like that. It used a lot of grass but it really looked the part. When the glue us dry I vacuum off the loose stuff; if you're careful you can do this while the glue is wet which also helps the fibres stand up straight.

Quite apart from saving a lot of money, this is a much more controllable method than sprinkling it on from an applicator; along the bottom of a wall, say, or between the rails, you want to be able to put the grass in just the right place and using your fingers you can. The results can be fantastic:

Weeds and flowers can then be added from scraps of commercial foliage material , (Heki and Woodland Scenics ideally), and smaller flowers sprinkled onto a spray of Photomount aerosol glue.

Long strands of dead grass for Summer scenes can be modelled using the straw coloured static grass from Noch; the 12mm long fibres are good for this.

Lots of different types of scenic materials have been used here, all blending together to create the scene. The trees are by Anita Décor, the best ready made trees on the market by a country mile. The grass on the bank here is the darker grass mat from Busch.

The static grass here gets longer as it approaches the buffer stop, and some Heki foliage around the timbers finishes things off nicely.

The grass is the Busch matting with static grass around the edges; the rock face is made using Sculptamold as described later on.

The foliage on the trees uses Seamoss covered in foliage scatter, glued directly onto the backscene to get away from the flat look. The Seamoss is quite weak and brittle but used like this it doesn't matter.

International Models sell these trees ready made, much less messy than making them yourself.

Two pictures from a similar viewpoint showing how effective the static grass can look, especially on the overgrown siding in the foreground. The same grass has been used right across the area beyond the siding so it all blends in together.

In the lower picture a baseboard join runs across from under the tender; loose Woodland Scenics foliage is pressed into the join to disguise it each time the layout is erected.

Here's our sample bank covered with two different pieces of grass matting ,in this case with short strands more suited to a 4mm scale layout, though they are good for lawns and the like in the larger scales. The grass mats were simply stuck down with the hot glue gun, a little at a time; no mess and no waiting for it to dry.

The area still in black card will be covered with static grass, then I'll detail it with hedges, undergrowth, flowers etc.

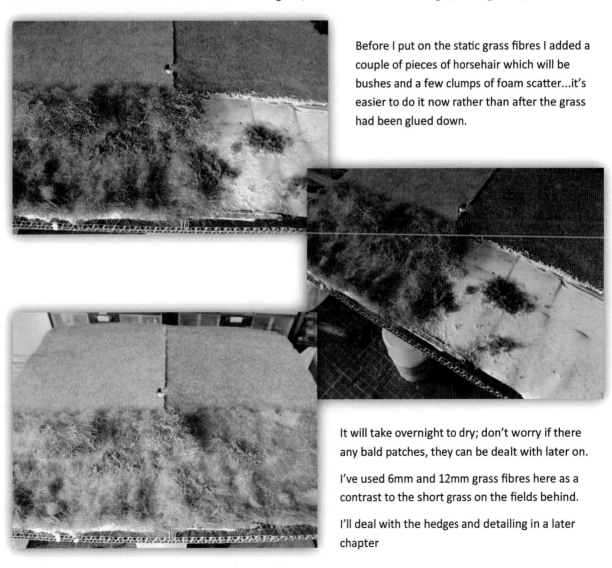

Before I put on the static grass fibres I added a couple of pieces of horsehair which will be bushes and a few clumps of foam scatter...it's easier to do it now rather than after the grass had been glued down.

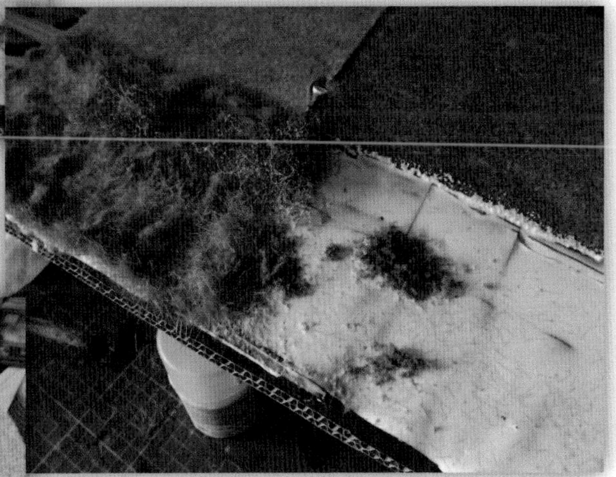

It will take overnight to dry; don't worry if there any bald patches, they can be dealt with later on.

I've used 6mm and 12mm grass fibres here as a contrast to the short grass on the fields behind.

I'll deal with the hedges and detailing in a later chapter

Of course, not everywhere is covered in grass, so it's time to look at some other surfaces.

Soil and mud are generally best done with either plaster or Sculptamould – for those not familiar with this it is a papier-mâché based product that you simply mix with water like plaster and then put in place with a palette knife or something similar...actually fingers are as good as anything. There are ready made scenic sheets for things such as ploughed fields that do have their uses as well though they can be expensive.

I use either Railmatch spray cans for painting or if using a brush Tamiya acrylics....both ranges have plenty of mud and soil like colours in a flat finish. The paint soaks into the surface a little when applied which helps if it gets chipped or knocked. Brush painting is best for small areas or where there are items such as puddles that need to be kept clean, but for a large rock face for instance I would always use a spray can. If spraying or brush painting it's best done before grass or undergrowth are added.

You do need to be aware of the colour of the underlying rock in the area you are modelling as this is reflected in the colour of the soil; the red of Devon looks very different from the grey of the Peak District.

You can use loose scatter for soil quite effectively; I find Woodland Scenics brown and buff ballast very good for this, particularly in the fine grade. It can be sprinkled onto PVA or put on loose and fixed down in the same way as ballast.

****

Man made surfaces are a different matter. They all have a texture of course, but when it's scaled down to 7mm or 4mm scale it's so fine it just disappears. That being the case I use printed papers for as much as possible; roads, pavements, platforms, even a gravel surface as it is much cleaner and easier than sticking down loose material which is almost always overscale. If you work out the size of a piece of gravel in 4mm scale it's not very big, you'd have to be using powder to get the right scale size.

I use printed papers because I produce them; I produce them because no one else did what I wanted when I began and of course I was able to produce exactly what I wanted for my models. Now other firms make good sheets as well, so this is not just a plug for my own products, but I do believe that using papers for many aspects of modelling, not just buildings, is an excellent idea that very few people make use of.

On the next page there are some examples of the sheets I produce, followed by some pictures of them on layouts. Clearly the image is flat, but because they are taken from photographs the shadows make them look three dimensional and the colours of course are spot on. The are easy to use, clean and free from mess, and can be stuck down with a tube adhesive such as Evostick, UHU or Bostick. They don't need painting, you don't have to wait for them to dry and if you don't like how it looks you just stick another piece over the top. It really is that easy!

Being printed on paper from artwork on the computer, of course, these sheets can be resized to any scale, and if you take the master copy down to the local print shop they will do you as many copies as you want, all exactly the same.

They can be produced from your own digital photograph of the surface, or from a picture found on the internet (as it's for your own use there is no issue with Copyright). I use Serif PagePlus software to adjust the image and then copy and paste it to fill a sheet of A4 paper.

There are limitations; curved roads are difficult though not impossible. However, for most applications printed papers work really well. Could you paint worn tarmac to look like the picture on the previous page? I couldn't.

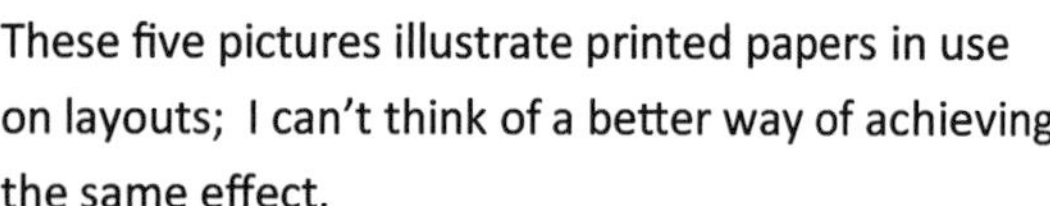

These five pictures illustrate printed papers in use on layouts; I can't think of a better way of achieving the same effect.

CHAPTER 6 TREES AND UNDERGROWTH.

If you are expecting a long chapter on how to craft the finest model trees from basic materials, then my apologies….I have found a better way of adding trees to my layouts.

I buy them.

I can't make big trees that look like trees. I've tried; I just can't do it. I can do little trees, and I'll come onto that in a minute, but the big ones defeat me.

A scale tree is huge; it's usually as wide as it is tall, and that means it could take up half the width of a baseboard. That's why nearly all the trees we see on layouts are far too small, but because we are so used to it we accept them as correct. The best place for a scale sized tree is on the backscene; on there we can have hundreds of them and they don't take up any space at all; they look realistic too!

Small trees are a different matter; they're easy. Real trees are made of wood, not twisted wire or any of the other things people use for trunks, so it seems to me sensible to use real wood as the basis for the model so I find a small piece of a real tree or bush that looks about the right size and shape. I plant it on the layout, usually using the hot glue gun which dries almost at once and holds it in place really firmly if a small hole is made in the scenery for the lower inch or so of the trunk. I then stick teased out pieces of foliage, either Heki or Woodland Scenics ideally, over the branches of the new tree until it looks right. Let's face it, we all know what a real tree looks like, so we should be able to tell when a model one looks the part.

You wouldn't think so though looking around some shows; without naming names there are some professional builders who never seem to have looked at a real tree.

The trick—and this is where they get it wrong—is to use a small amount of foliage and let the light show through it. If it looks like a green lollipop, you've used too much.

The Silver Birch was bought from Anita Décor, the other trees are home made with natural twigs and Heki foliage. Look how the light shines through the Birch, it's superbly done. It was expensive, but worth every penny.

Making small trees isn't difficult then, and it doesn't need any fancy equipment or tools either. If you are making several use different shades of foliage, as the real thing are not all the same shade of green, and if you can find some with smaller leaves that's a good thing too.

Some of the time you don't really need to model the tree at all as such, as if a lot are clumped together all you really see are the tops, maybe not the trunks at all. They are very useful for hiding things, such as the line disappearing into the fiddle yard as here:

Notice how some of the trees are just pieces of Seafoam glued to the backscene, and that they all blend in together to form the whole scene with the trees on the backscene itself adding to the effect.

Seafoam is very useful, it can be extremely realistic, but it is fragile and gets brittle as it ages so if it can be used where something can help support it then that's a good thing; here's it's the backscene but it might be a building, a hedge or whatever. I use a lot of it; International Models sell it ready made with very realistic foliage so I don't bother making my own which can be a very messy business. It can be used as trees or undergrowth on the ground; if a different shade of green is required a dusting over from a spray can does the job nicely. This is a good way of introducing Autumnal tints as well.

As long as you choose carefully, some of the cheaper ready to use trees can be effective as seen here—it was sold as HO but the layout is in O, after all a tree is a tree, in O scale it's just a smaller one.

Sooner or later though, you're going to want something a bit more special, either because it will be right at the front or because it's going to be big and impressive. Let's face it, you're not going to want dozens like that unless you've got a very big layout indeed, so my advice is to invest in a ready made model that will be really eye catching.

I've only found one firm that produces ready made trees that I would consider having on my layout, and that's Anita Décor, sold in the UK by International Models. This is why I think they're the best....

That looks like a real tree, standing behind the locomotive and to the left of the station building. It's superb. I couldn't make that. I wouldn't waste time trying; it was expensive but it makes that scene for me.

If you recall, I mentioned in the first section about gluing a length of tube into the scenery to support a large tree; this is the sort of tree I was talking about. It's 30cm high, about 15cm across, and quite heavy.

One or two trees like that are probably enough; these on the same layout are just Seamoss and they look fine. One or two really special trees, though, make an impression.

Here there are Birch and Fir trees form Anita Décor, home made trees from twigs and foliage and Seamoss trees as well; nothing looks out of place, they all sit together well to create the overall scene.

Undergrowth, bushes and hedges use mainly the same materials. Rubberised horseshair is very useful; pull it into clumps, spray it with Photomount adhesive, sprinkle on your choice of scatter for foliage and you have a bush ready to plant on the layout. I don't like it for trees, but for ground cover it works really well. Woodland Scenics make a number of good products that can be used such as clump foliage which makes realistic hedges if they are not supposed to have been too well trimmed.

Do jobs such as making the horsehair bushes over a cardboard box, then all the loose scatter will fall into the box and can be used again. Put the piece of horsehair on a stick when you spray it with glue, then your fingers don't get sprayed as well.

Hedges are useful for hiding joins in the grass mat, or for running along the gap between the layout and the backscene. As mentioned Woodland Scenics clump foliage is good for a fairly overgrown hedge, but for a neatly trimmed one a length of Woodland Scenics foliage cut with scissors into a long rectangle can then be folded over along its length to double the thickness and then glued in place; it is strong enough then to retain it's shape.

Wild flowers always add a splash of colour; Greenscene produce a useful selection as scatter. You simply give the area a spray with Photomount and sprinkle on the flowers; the grass will be sticky for a day or two but then it goes off. For longer flowers Mini Natur produce some excellent products in a wide variety of colours.

I'm not a great fan of the Noch plastic flowers; they are incredibly fiddly to assemble, and they look like....well, plastic!

The undergrowth here is largely made from Rubberised horsehair; it's really useful stuff. The scatter comes from Greenscene, as does the Horsehair. For large areas such as to the left of the bridge in the picture below it's great stuff, it covers big area quickly and easily. I generally stick in place with the hot glue gun as it sets almost at once and there's no waiting.

The ground cover here is Busch grass matting, with Seamoss bushes and some wild flowers from Mini Natur. The foliage hanging over the stone retaining wall is Woodland Scenics.

Let's get back to our grass bank.....

I've sprinkled some scatter foliage onto the two horsehair bushes; to get it onto the sides lower down just blow gently as your drop it. You can make the bushes away from the layout and glue them in place ready made, of course.

Next the hedges will be added; the lower one is made from two strips of Woodland Scenics light green foliage; I run a strip of Evostick along one edge and then fold it over to double the thickness before sticking it in place with more Evostick. This makes a neatly trimmed hedge such as you might see along a railway.

The darker hedge along the middle is made from Woodland Scenics clump foliage, this time dark green. Again it is simply glued in place with Evostick.

Along each side of the hedge I put a strip of PVA glue and into this are pressed more clumps of static grass as was used on the front section. Fields are never trimmed right up to the hedge, so the grass needs to be longer

Next I have sprinkled on some flowers, coloured scatter made by Greenscene, done by spraying the grass lightly with Photomount adhesive and just dropping the flowers on from my fingers. On the darker hedge I have put on some lighter scatter to vary the tone and lighten the overall colour; this was done with the spray glue as well. Using a small can it is quite controllable so it doesn't go everywhere and before long the stickiness goes off.

The field on the right has some patches of weeds, just small amounts of foam foliage stuck to blobs of PVA. This gives some texture to the field, getting away from the mowed lawn look.

That plastic tube that I glued in place when the card structure was first made now has a tree standing in it, just a twig from my back garden. Because it is real wood the colour is perfect, of course.

The left hand field has gained some cow pats, blobs of Evostick Impact glue painted with Tamiya flat brown.

The foliage on the tree is simply Woodland Scenics light green foliage teased out into very thin pieces and draped loosely over the branches with just a little glue to hold it in place.

The scenery on this piece of hillside took about an hour, excluding waiting for things to dry. Scenic modelling doesn't need to take hours, in fact if you are too careful and methodical it can look wrong because everything has been too carefully placed. The way I do it, the flowers largely end up wherever they happen to fall, so it looks natural.

CHAPTER 7 PUDDLES

Puddles are such a part of everyday life in Britian that we barely notice them. They are just there....but when did you last see any on a layout?

You occasionally see a blob of gloss varnish at the side of a road, but that is not a convincing way to model a puddle.....it just doesn't look right. Here's how to do it properly.

Puddles need to be included in the planning stage....I know it sounds silly but they do because they cannot be added after everything else is done, they need to be included as part of the scenery or the ballasting.

You'll need some grey or brown card or paper , some Plastruct square section rod or stripwood and a sheet of 3mm thick clear plastic, (I use 'Ariel Clear Polystyrene', bought from B&Q in 4' x 2' sheets. It's got loads of uses, you won't need much for your puddles).

The first thing to do is draw where your puddles are going to be on the baseboard with a marker pan, allowing roughly twice the area of the finished puddle. You don't need dozens, just a few look more effective because then they draw attention in their own right.

Then stick two lengths of the wood or plastic to the card like this, as spacers, with the clear plastic on top:

Next, glue a piece of thin black card with a hole cut out in the shape of the puddle, but slightly larger, onto the clear plastic like this:

Glue this whole construction to the baseboard in the position of the puddle, and then finally you can build up the ground surface around it, using loose scatter or ballast fixed in place with dilute PVA glue, or plaster for a muddy track or maybe grass mat or strands of static grass. The effect should look like this (just a sample with the scatter poured on loose)

Try to keep the surface of the puddle clear of stray scatter, glue or any other substances of course. That's all there is to it, and the finished result should look like this with the puddle level with the ground surface:

CHAPTER 8 ROCKS & CLIFFS.

On a portable layout, you do not want to make that cliff face out of plaster or to use real rocks as the Americans tend to do on their basement layouts. Portable means you can actually lift the baseboards!

I model rocks and cliffs in two ways, either with cork bark or with Scupltamold. Both are light, easy to use and look very effective.

Let's start with cork bark. Obviously this is a natural product, just lumps of bark and it's surprisingly tough stuff to break into smaller pieces. In colour it is a fairly non-descript brown, just the job for our needs, and it has patterns which look like the lines on a rock face. As with all these things, it's how you use it that counts.

First a tip—don't buy it in small plastic bags from a model shop. There is an importer in Birmingham called Charles Cantrill who sell it in large sacks and it's far cheaper (see the 'Suppliers' page for their website). The model shops all buy it from them anyway, and then double the price.

I like to put the various lumps of cork that come out of the sack on a surface near to where I'll be working—the next baseboard perhaps—so that I can see them all. Then it's like doing a jigsaw, choosing the piece that will best fit in the gap made by the previous piece. You glue them in place one by one with the hot glue gun, starting at the base of the cliff or rock face, and building it up until it is the right height. There will be lots of gaps, but don't worry about that at the moment.

Here the pieces of cork have been stuck in place, with the lines running in the same direction as they would do on a rock face. The flat ground above had been crudely sketched in with a piece of card. It won't carry any weight so it's plenty strong enough. The rocks go along the railway as well as though the trackbed has been blasted out of them.

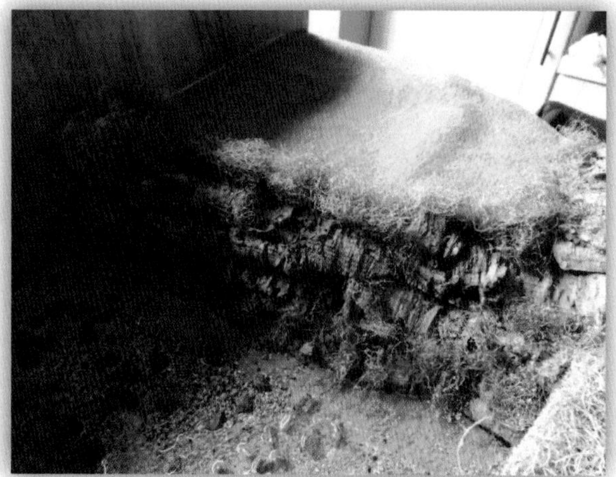

Now I have begun to push pieces of rubberised horsehair into the gaps between the pieces of cork.

On the finished layout a lot of the cork is covered up, but that's just as it should be, with outcrops of rock showing through the grass and the undergrowth. The grass is simply static grass stuck down with PVA as already described which helps stick all the cork pieces firmly together, and the undergrowth is made from all sorts of odds and ends of scenic materials. I think it looks very effective.

On Johannesorf, though, the cork was a bit too large for using along the river, so we used cork along the back and Sculptamold nearer the front.....

Here there are three ways of modelling rocks; the mountains on the backscene, cork for the cliff behind the train, and Sculptamold in the foreground. They all blend is together surprisingly well.

Sculptamold is an American product but it can be bought in the UK; it is basically dry papier-mache which you mix with water to form a paste. This is then put in place wherever you want bare rocks to show. It is easier to use for smaller areas than cork, but of course it has to be coloured as the paste is white. The beauty of it is that when it dries it forms rocky patterns as in the picture above all on it's own....we didn't carve that rockface, that's just how the stuff looks when it's dried. It's great if you're in a hurry, as we were. Because it is paper based rather than a plaster it's light too.

We painted it by spraying it with Railmatch spray cans and then brushing on some other tones to vary things a bit but to be honest it didn't need much, it looked like rock as soon as it was painted. It's a remarkable product.

The rocks along the right hand side are cork, all the others were done using Sculptamold.

CHAPTER 8 RIVERS, STREAMS, PONDS AND THE SEA.

There is something about water; it always makes an attractive feature on a layout. It's not always done well though, and it can look pretty unconvincing.

Let me talk you through the saga of the river on my American On30 layout Grass Valley. I wanted a trestle bridge to cross a nice wide river with lots of rocks in the river bed.

I prepared the baseboard, 15cm lower than the rest of the layout. The trestle bridge was built and put in place to see how it looked and to make sure the tracks each side would line up as they should:

I began to build up the rocks along each side using lumps of cork bark, which is lovely stuff...it's ready coloured, light, and it looks like rock. Perfect. I stuck it down using a hot glue gun.

With the bridge fixed in place I used real gravel and stones to make the river bed and then soaked the lot in dilute PVA in the same way as ballast; once the glue is dry it sets like concrete and forms a water tight surface which is obviously important. Sand was used along the edges under the cliffs, built up higher to contain the water.

I then finished off the cliffs, began to build up the landscape on either side and put on the backscene, including a picture of a similar river disappearing into the distance.

I then poured on a lot of Woodland Scenics EZ Water. It looked fantastic!

A couple of days later it didn't look so good—all the water had cracked like a broken pane of glass. I then found out that the EZ Water sets rock hard, and because wooden baseboards are by their nature slightly flexible this causes the rigid water to crack if the board is moved at all, even just under the influence of changes in temperature or humidity.

I had to chisel out the whole lot, without damaging the bridge. It's tough stuff; in the end I removed what I could and simply put down a new river bed over the remains. This time I used another product, 'Magic Water'. It's expensive, I spent over £40, but again it looked good. Magic Water is slightly flexible, so I was confident that it would be OK this time.

The following morning all the water had gone, it had soaked into the surrounding scenery and the river bed and hardly any remained where it should be. Then I did what I should have done in the first place; I went down to my local timber merchants and bought a big can of gloss Polyurethane varnish and poured the lot over the river bed.

It took a week to dry, but it stayed where it was meant to be, it won't crack, it look great and it was only £13 for the tin!

I am telling you this sorry tale for two reasons; one, we all make mistakes and we're always learning, however much experience we've got. Two, expensive products aren't necessarily better than cheaper, simpler alternatives.

I got a really nice looking river in the end, but that baseboard now weighs a ton because it's effectively got two river beds on it! When I look at it though, I don't mind, it was worth it in the end.

Using real stones adds weight, but they look good because they are the real thing, as is the sand and the gravel....the latter comes from the pet shop, it's used for cage birds. A little green weathering powder streaked into the varnish before it dries looks good, it makes the water look as though it is flowing, and strands of foliage can be used in the same way.

With varnish, you can also add more layers if you want to build up a greater depth of water.

Not every river you make will be as wide as that one, of course:

Here the actual water depth is minimal, the painting of the river bed giving the illusion of depth while the standing figures have had their legs shortened to make them look as though they are standing in deeper water. The beach is real gravel, and the green weathering powders in the water streaked along the direction of the flow imply that the water is moving.

Of course, sometimes you want a river that is a bit more fast flowing:

This is John Smith's 0 Scale Austrian narrow gauge layout 'Johannesdorf'. Here we did use 'Magic Water' for the river to build up some depth, and then on top of that Deluxe Materials 'Making Waves', a white paste used for creating ripples and waves. This is stippled on using a paintbrush and as it dries it gradually goes clear, but not totally. Some whiteness is a good thing; we drybrushed the wave tops with white paint once the paste had hardened. The one thing you cannot achieve is actual movement of course, but it's as close as you'll get.

We used 'Sculptamold' for the cliffs on Johannesdorf, spray painted brown and then brush painted to add some variation before the grass and other scenery were added. The river bed was painted a light blue/green shade as a fast flowing mountain stream isn't the dirty brown colour of a slow moving sluggish river, and again some real stones were added with patches of gravel where the current would be less fast. The backscene is another one from Backdrop Junction; they are actually the Rocky Mountains but they look very like the Alps!

Sometimes a much smaller, narrower stream is all you need as here where the water is still and a family are enjoying an afternoon fishing. I did use EZ Water for this as the layout is fixed and the area of water is much smaller.

That just leaves us with the sea. There is one big problem with the sea—it is never still, and for that reason on a model it just never looks right, frozen in time. This is a model of Dawlish in 7mm scale:

It looks OK in a picture because you don't expect the waves to be moving.

You can use tricks like cutting off the legs of the figure to suggest depth, but you can't do anything about the lack of movement.

I used real sand for the beach, fixed in place with dilute PVA; I then painted the sea onto it with spray cans. I put on a coat of gloss varnish before adding the waves from the Woodland Scenics paste and highlighting them with white paint. It looks good, but............it doesn't move.

My advice is to avoid having the sea on your layout, unless it's perhaps in the distance on the backscene; that can be very effective indeed.

Finally, a canal, easy to model because there is no current. This is just a sheet of 3mm thick clear plastic sheet fixed about 10mm over a piece of ordinary plastic card on which the canal bed was painted ...then a few ripples were added using the Making Waves paste.

CHAPTER 9 THE URBAN SCENE

Scenery does not just mean chocolate box villages and dramatic moorland vistas, a bit of urban grot is just as applicable if that is the setting of your layout.

In these instances it is usual for there to be a lot more track and a lot less scenery, so this is where the backscene really comes into it's own.

The railway in a busy town or city has usually been inserted onto a pretty confined site, hemmed in with buildings and using every available space for the station facilities, loco sheds, goods yards and so on. Our layouts need to reflect this, and of course it is very much the situation we are in ourselves with out restrictions on available space.

My German O Gauge layout Schwachhausen faced this problem; all I had room for were some vertical retaining walls with the backscene above, the rest of it was track. The challenge then is to convince the viewer that this is just a part of a wider scene, that the world does not finish at the top of the retaining walls. The colours are different too, more subdued and dirty due to the smoky environment, and more likely to be plastered with advertising posters.

Again, I used lots of printed papers.

Width was at a premium; the red brick factory building was three dimensional but the blue one is only 5mm thick, glued onto the backscene. The windows are printed paper, photo's of real factory windows so they have realistic reflections, etc. The retaining walls all used printed papers for the brickwork, and then above them were pictures of large city buildings to build up the urban environment beyond the railway. The sky was only glimpsed in a few places between the buildings. The only greenery on the whole layout was a few patches of scruffy grass and some foliage on the backscene, mainly to cover gaps where the boards joined.

It all looked quite effective; buildings such as these would be far too big to model in three dimensions, and doing it this way they were still very much part of the layout.

Look at the concrete wall behind the steps; this is a photo of a real wall...it would be very difficult indeed to reproduce that by painting.

These are a few examples of building papers useful for a scene like this....

CHAPTER 11 ADDING THE DETAIL.

To me, this is the most important part of all. This is when the basic scenery begins to finally look like a real place, the only problem I find being knowing when to stop because the temptation is to keep on adding more bits and pieces, and you can overdo it. The trade spoil us with a range of accessories that would have been unthinkable a few years ago, but as always it's not what you use, it's how you use it.

Here are some ideas.....

A garden in front of a cottage, much more effective than just putting the cottage right next to the road. This is 7mm scale; the vegetables came from Scenic Express in the USA, the hedge is made from Woodland Scenics foliage, and the flowers are a mixture of Mini Natur and Greenscene. Making the path twist and turn makes it more interesting, as does the curve of the road.

The milk float is from Duncan Scale models, a lovely little kit.

A bit further along the road the postman is delivering, an everyday scene that brings the cottage to life. The figures are Phoenix and Omen Miniatures and the bike is Phoenix. The dry stone wall came from Jarvis, and the lovely rose arch is from Scenic Express as are the flowers in the garden. The ones growing by the wall are Mini Natur.

This is the top cottage from a different angle. The Silver Birch is by Anita Décor.

A different cottage garden, again in 7mm scale. The soil is a sheet of HO scale ploughed field.....if something looks right, then use it! The vegetables are from Noch; they are also meant for HO but are pretty big in that scale and I think they look fine here. Plants vary in sixe after all. The other plants are a variety of foliages with flowers from Mini Natur.

Something different—a family of bears playing by a river. The bears are by Woodland Scenics, and the river was described in a previous chapter.

The flowers on the platform at Berkeley Road are from Mini Nature, and the piece of trellis is an offcut from a Scalelink etching.

Here the lamp is meant for HO, but if it looks right on an O gauge layout then I'll use it. The etched fence is my product, and the children looking over it are from Preiser. Small details like the cable trunking, the line-side phone and the signs all add to the scene and none are difficult to add.

Here a picture has been used to imply that the scene continues through the arch, and the vehicles distract the eye from the joint where the road meets the pictures. All the vehicles are die cast models, but have had they correct number plates fitted (just printed on paper and stuck on) and drivers added. It's amazing how many cars drive around on layouts with no one inside!

The figures are Presier, the lamp is by Viessmann and meant for HO but it look fine.

The road surface and pavements use my own building papers.

Figures should look natural; ideally standing or sitting in relaxed poses. Nothing looks worse than a figure frozen in mid run, it immediately destroys the realism of the scene. The people at the bus stop in the picture above are ideal, because you don't expect them to move.

The same applies to animals, perhaps even more so.

Here the people look natural; one taking a photo, a group standing together by the building, and one being given a parking ticket by a Policeman! None of them are animated, so it looks right.

The flowers are by Mini Natur, and the tree came from Derby Trees.

The building is the Mairie from Torcy le Grand in Normandy, on John Smith's HO layout.

This man is walking which looks fine in the photograph but it's not so good on the layout itself because he's frozen in mid stride.

The posters were home made on the computer, and the flowers are by Mini Natur. The layout is O Scale.

Introducing signs, advertising posters and such like to a layout not only adds colour, it sets the model in a particular period and location as well. Even if the station on your layout is imaginary, a road sign pointing to the nearest large town to your fictitious location immediately sets it firmly in that place. You can buy kits for the actual signposts, though they are not difficult to make yourself from plastic card....whichever way you do it, print 'BRISTOL 10 MILES' or whatever, cut it out and glue it to the arm of the post and your layout cannot be anywhere but Gloucestershire or Somerset.

Advertising can do the same; my German layout had a poster advertising a special beer made by Becks purely for sale to the FC Bremen supporters club, so the layout couldn't have been anywhere else. I'm sure no one ever noticed it, but at least I knew!

Enamel advertising signs were generally more widespread in their use, indeed most were national, but some were more localised; breweries again, or local newspapers, made use of them. Whatever the type, they add interest to a building—once they are cut out, draw round the white edge with a black marker pen before sticking them in place. Use the ones that are made from a photograph of an actual sign (like the ones I sell!) because then you get the rust and wear and tear as well so they look more realistic.

Station poster boards again need to be correct for the period and the location; in 0 Gauge certainly you can recognise the posters so they need to be correct. An SR layout set in the 1920's shouldn't have a Bullied Pacific on one of the posters.

Business signs are another trap for the unwary but they can be very effective too. I use the computer to produce them...one good trick is to slightly fade the lettering as though it has been there for some time. There are plenty of books of old photographs to give you an idea of what local firms looked like during your period, and for foreign layouts the internet is very useful of course.

On this American depot building I have put a poster advertising a picnic; you can read in in 0 Scale. I found it in a book, scanned it, resized it and printed it off—just the job!

Here's another easy home made accessory that you can tailor exactly to your layout. I needed some fruit boxes for my On30 layout; all the pictures I needed were on the internet, so I made up these little kits....

The original picture is on the left, the kit to make up the box is on the right. Pretty soon I had dozens of them to put by the depot and in some box cars. You can see some by the depot building in the previous picture.

CHAPTER 10 MATERIALS & SUPPLIERS

Let me make it clear that I have no connection with any of these suppliers; I simply use their products because I think they are the best on the market for doing a particular job.

Here are the main glues and paints that I use:

All the contact details for the suppliers are on the next page.

Here are some of the scenic materials that I recommend....

The packaging of the Noch static grass is very clever as the bags stand up even once they have been opened.

This is just a selection that just happened to be in my box when I wanted to take the picture; there are lots of other makes, some of which are just as good as these.

These are the glues, paints and other items that I use and recommend:

Evostock Impact tube adhesive; I use this for just about everything. Brilliant stuff!

PVA glue; I use the cheapest own brand stuff for all scenic work, it does the job perfectly well. Buy it in 1 litre bottles, it works out much cheaper.

Bostick Fast-tak photomount adjustable spray adhesive; ideal for adding foliage, flowers, etc. Don't use the permanent stuff, it's too powerful and just makes a gooey mess over everything. Use the small can, it's more controllable.

Tamiya acrylic paints for all brush painting.

Railmatch spray cans for painting track and other large areas, especially Track Dirt, Sleeper Grime, Light & Dark Rust among others.

Deluxe Materials Making Waves for creating ripples, waves and other moving water. Woodland Scenics so a similar products which works well too.

Tester's Dullcote matt lacquer, for killing any sheen on printed papers.

These are some of the products and suppliers of the actual scenic materials I recommend:

Woodland Scenics foliage, clump foliage and many other products, all of which are widely available.

Noch static grass. *www.howardscenicsupplies.co.uk*

Heki foliage and static grass. As above, and also *www.elmetimages.co.uk*

Greenscene flowers, horsehair, scatter and many other excellent products. *www.green-scene.co.uk*

Cork bark *www.charlescantrill.com* Much cheaper than buying it from the model shop!

Sculptamould & Dullcote EDM Models *www.ngtrains.com*

Printed papers *www.kirtleymodels.com*

Deluxe materials *www.deluxematerails.com*

Anita Décor trees, Mini Natur flowers and many other products *www.internationalmodels.net*

Backscenes Backdrop Junction *www.backdropjunction.com*

Small accessories and a huge range of other products -Scenic Express *www.sceneryexpress.com*

(However, note that this is a US firm so you will be charged VAT and import duty when the items arrive).

American Academy of Pediatrics

Dear EMS Professional:

Continuing education is one of the cornerstones of the American Academy of Pediatrics. We are delighted and proud to introduce another quality pediatric educational program: *Pediatric Education for Prehospital Professionals* (PEPP). This exciting new program is the first of its kind—designed specifically for prehospital professionals.

The American Academy of Pediatrics invited representatives from eight national organizations concerned with EMS for children and formed the PEPP Steering Committee. The Steering Committee's goal was to create a comprehensive program to enhance and expand the knowledge and skills of prehospital professionals who care for ill and injured children across this country. As a result of their hard work and dedication, they have created a program that is certain to have a profound impact on the field of EMS education.

On behalf of the board of directors of the American Academy of Pediatrics I applaud the efforts of all of the EMTs, paramedics, nurses, and physician volunteers who have participated in the development of the PEPP materials. A very special thanks goes to Ron Dieckmann for his leadership, tireless efforts, and extraordinary vision.

I would also like to thank you personally for your dedication to improving the emergency health care of children throughout this country. Working together we can really make a difference.

Sincerely,

Joe M Sanders, Jr, MD, FAAP
Executive Director
American Academy of Pediatrics

The PEPP course is designed to give prehospital professionals the education and confidence they need to effectively treat pediatric patients. This textbook is the core of the PEPP program with features that will reinforce and expand on the essential information. These features include:

Procedure buttons: These buttons tell students to refer to the Procedures section at the end of the book for more information on how to perform a specific procedure.

Learning objectives: Learning objectives are placed at the beginning of the chapter to highlight what students should learn from that chapter.

Case study: Each chapter opens with a case study to start students thinking about what they might do if they encountered a similar case in the field and to prepare them for key concepts. Additional case studies can be found within the chapter, and answers can be found in the chapter resources section at the end of the chapter.

Glossary terms: These terms are comprehensively defined in the glossary at the end of the book, and pronunciations of terms are available at www.PEPPsite.com, so that students can listen to the proper pronunciations of difficult terms.

Web links: Web links direct students to helpful pediatric sites on the Internet that can be accessed through the PEPP website. Web links reinforce and expand on important information from the chapters.

Chapter 8 Trauma

PROCEDURE 19

Spinal Immobilization
The spinal column is made of 33 articulating bones, and its structure changes significantly during childhood growth. The age of the child, the developmentally appropriate behaviors, and the physical state of spinal growth are important factors in the incidence and types of pediatric spinal injuries. Cervical spine injuries are the most dangerous, but whenever the mechanism of injury, signs, or symptoms suggest possible spinal injury, immobilize the entire spine. For a step-by-step explanation of this procedure see page 295.

Breathing
Breathing is the second priority. Injuries to the airway, chest wall, lungs, or abdomen, as well as gastric distention due to air swallowing, may negatively affect breathing. Head and cervical spine injuries will sometimes depress the brain's instinct to breathe or diminish the protective airway reflex. Pulmonary aspiration of gastric contents is a common and potentially serious complication of head injuries. Aspiration will cause extreme hypoxia and increased work of breathing.

Look for soft-tissue or penetrating injuries of the chest or back. Listen for quality and symmetry of breath sounds with the stethoscope. Feel the chest wall for crepitus, pain, or instability. Use pulse oximetry to assess the degree of hypoxia, especially when there is no change of skin color.

Actions. If breathing is inadequate, position the child and assist ventilation. Pull the jaw into the mask. Pushing the mask onto the face to make a seal may cause cervical spine flexion. The E-C clamp technique (Figures 8-12a, 8-12b, 8-12c, and 8-12 d) will help with proper hand placement for good mask-to-face seal. Consider inserting an airway adjunct to help maintain an open airway.

Give 100% oxygen through a nonrebreathing mask or BVM. There is no nonrebreathing mask size for infants, so use a properly fitted oxygen mask on these patients. Airway management for the trauma patient is similar to airway management for the ill patient. Provide assisted ventilation with BVM, based on respiratory effort and level of neurologic disability. Use the "squeeze-release-release" timing technique to keep the right breathing rate. Allow a brief pause between each breath to minimize the chance of gastric distention. The AVPU score and pupillary reactions are the best guides for rate of ventilation in the comatose child, as outlined in Table 8-6.

! Tip
Pulmonary aspiration of gastric contents is a common and potentially serious complication of head injuries.

CASE STUDY 2

A neighbor calls 911 about a 2-year-old boy who has fallen from an open third-story window onto a patch of grass. On scene, you find a boy who is alternating between crying and sleeping. He will not interact or fix gaze with you. He has no abnormal airway sounds, retractions, or flaring. His color is pink. Respiratory rate is 25 breaths/min, heart rate 130 beats/min. Skin is warm with capillary refill time of 2 seconds. Blood pressure cannot be obtained on one attempt. You find no other obvious injuries.

What is this child's greatest threat to life?
Is endotracheal intubation indicated on scene?

Chapter 8 Trauma

Learning Objectives

1. Explain the unique anatomic features of children that predispose them to injuries.
2. Sequence the initial assessment of the injured child.
3. Integrate the essential trauma interventions in the ABCDEs.
4. Distinguish ... manageme...
5. Discuss assessment and treatment of pediatric burn patients.
6. Describe priorities in managing a child and family in a multicasualty incident.
7. Apply appropriate assessment techniques and treatment plans to case studies presenting a variety of trauma situations.

130 Fatal Injury Mechanisms

Introduction

Half of the children who require EMS services have an acute injury. Fortunately, the most common injuries are minor problems, such as lacerations, burns, mild closed head injuries, and extremity fractures. In these cases, the role of the prehospital professional is straightforward: perform a scene size-up, assess for physiologic or anatomic problems, and transport to the ED. Treatment usually entails only wound care, immobilization, and splinting when necessary.

Multisystem trauma, in contrast, provides the prehospital professional with great challenges and rewards, and demands a disciplined and child-specific approach. Usually, principles of adult trauma management can be effectively and safely applied to the assessment and treatment of children, with modifications related to differences in mechanisms of injury, anatomy, and physiologic response.

Between infancy and adulthood, injuries are the most common cause of death. Most injuries are unintentional. However, intentional injuries, primarily child maltreatment and violent assaults, are the leading mechanisms of traumatic death in infants and are a significant cause of injury and death in children and adolescents. Intentional injuries from maltreatment are easily overlooked, as discussed in Chapter 12. About 80% to 90% of pediatric trauma involves a blunt mechanism. This differs from the adult population, where there is a much higher incidence of penetrating injuries. Handgun injuries, however, are on the rise in children and are now the most common cause of penetrating injuries in adolescents.

The emotional response of prehospital professionals to an injured child can be intense. They often see the patient as a friend or relative and can be impaired in their professional duties. Experience and education will help the prehospital professional develop an efficient and emotionally neutral approach. Critical incident stress debriefing is often valuable to the prehospital professional after treating a seriously injured child.

www.PEPPsite.com

Fatal Injury Mechanisms

Table 8-1 summarizes the most frequent fatal mechanisms of injury in children and adolescents. Vehicular trauma (including automobile occupant, pedestrian, and bicyclist injuries) is the leading specific mechanism in all age groups. Drowning is the second leading cause. House fire is a significant cause of death, especially in the eastern United States. Falls are common but rarely cause major injury unless the length of the fall is greater than the child's height.

Tips: Tips are placed throughout the chapter to help students remember important items.

Blips: Blips are placed throughout the chapter to warn students about things they should not do.

Controversies: Controversies highlight issues that may be under debate in the EMS community.

ALS boxes: These colorful headers alert students that the information is for advanced life support (ALS) personnel.

PAT triangle: The patient assessment triangle (explained fully in Chapter 3) represents the essence of the PEPP patient assessment method. It reminds students when to assess a patient's appearance, work of breathing, and circulation to skin.

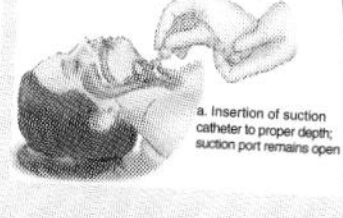

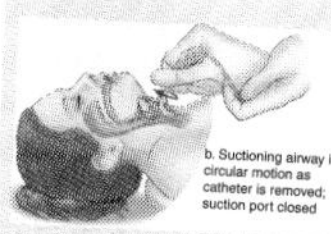

Patient assessment flowchart: The flowchart provides a quick, visual reference for the patient assessment process.

Chapter resources: This section provides answers to the case studies and suggests additional resources that may supplement the chapter content.

There are 21 Procedures in the textbook. Each procedure provides a step-by-step guide to the most critical prehospital skills. Specific features include:

Indications, Contraindications, Equipment, and Complications: These items are highlighted for quick and easy reference.

Introduction and Rationale: These sections tell the student why the procedure is useful in emergency care situations.

Preparation and Procedure: These sections guide the students step-by-step through the actual process. Tips and Blips alert the students to do's and do not's.

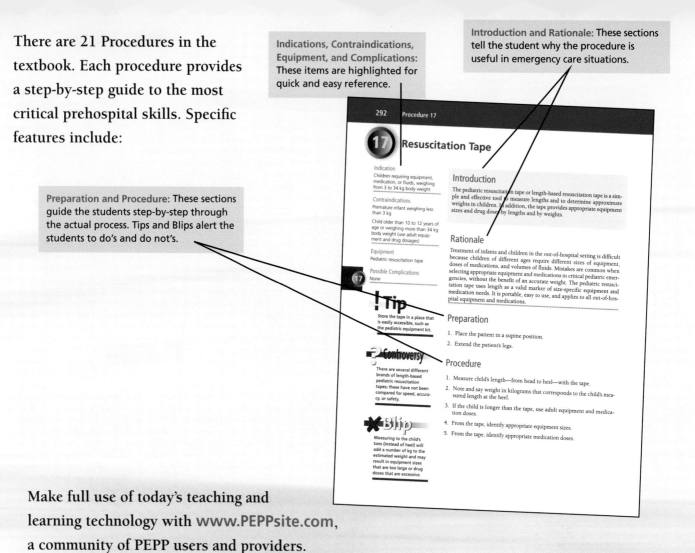

292 Procedure 17

17 Resuscitation Tape

Indication

Children requiring equipment, medication, or fluids, weighing from 3 to 34 kg body weight

Contraindications

Premature infant weighing less than 3 kg

Child older than 10 to 12 years of age or weighing more than 34 kg body weight (use adult equipment and drug dosages)

Equipment

Pediatric resuscitation tape

Possible Complications

None

! Tip

Store the tape in a place that is easily accessible, such as the pediatric equipment kit.

? Controversy

There are several different brands of length-based pediatric resuscitation tapes; these have not been compared for speed, accuracy, or safety.

✖ Blip

Measuring to the child's toes (instead of heel) will add a number of kg to the estimated weight and may result in equipment sizes that are too large or drug doses that are excessive.

Introduction

The pediatric resuscitation tape or length-based resuscitation tape is a simple and effective tool to measure lengths and to determine approximate weights in children. In addition, the tape provides appropriate equipment sizes and drug doses by lengths and by weights.

Rationale

Treatment of infants and children in the out-of-hospital setting is difficult because children of different ages require different sizes of equipment, doses of medications, and volumes of fluids. Mistakes are common when selecting appropriate equipment and medications in critical pediatric emergencies, without the benefit of an accurate weight. The pediatric resuscitation tape uses length as a valid marker of size-specific equipment and medication needs. It is portable, easy to use, and applies to all out-of-hospital equipment and medications.

Preparation

1. Place the patient in a supine position.
2. Extend the patient's legs.

Procedure

1. Measure child's length—from head to heel—with the tape.
2. Note and say weight in kilograms that corresponds to the child's measured length at the heel.
3. If the child is longer than the tape, use adult equipment and medication doses.
4. From the tape, identify appropriate equipment sizes.
5. From the tape, identify appropriate medication doses.

Make full use of today's teaching and learning technology with www.PEPPsite.com, a community of PEPP users and providers. Features of the site include:

Web links: Web links direct students to pediatric sites on the Internet. Web links reinforce and expand on important information from the chapters.

Glossary terms: Pronunciations of glossary terms found within the chapters help students learn difficult terms.

Administrative forms: Roster sheets, course coordinator applications, and administrative forms are available to help the coordinator.

Class schedules: Students can access the web to see what classes are available in their area.

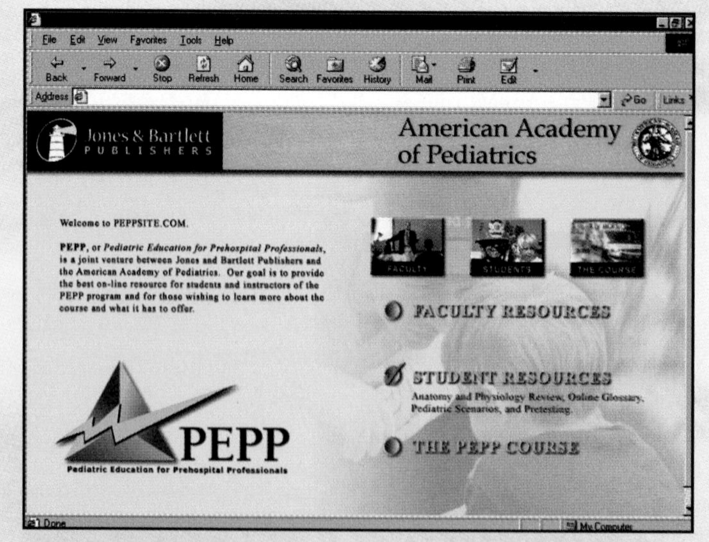

The PEPP program is supported by a complete teaching and learning system. This system includes the textbook plus the following resources:

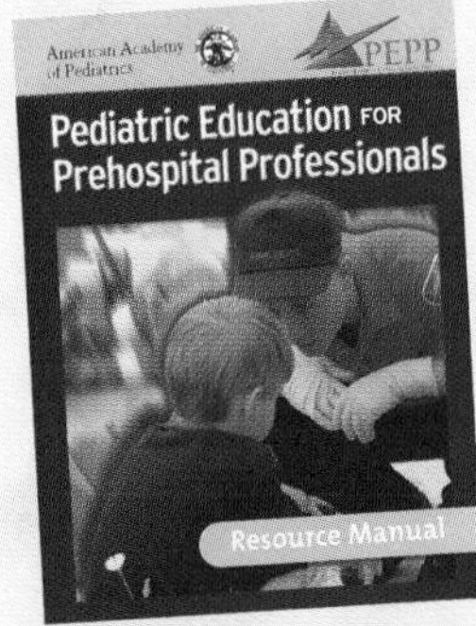

Resource Manual: This indispensable manual contains lecture outlines that are keyed to the slides and PowerPoint presentations, skill station strategies that are tied to the book's Procedures, scenarios to use in class that will keep your students interested, guidelines for how to become a coordinator and teach a course, and administrative forms.

ISBN: 0-7637-1259-0

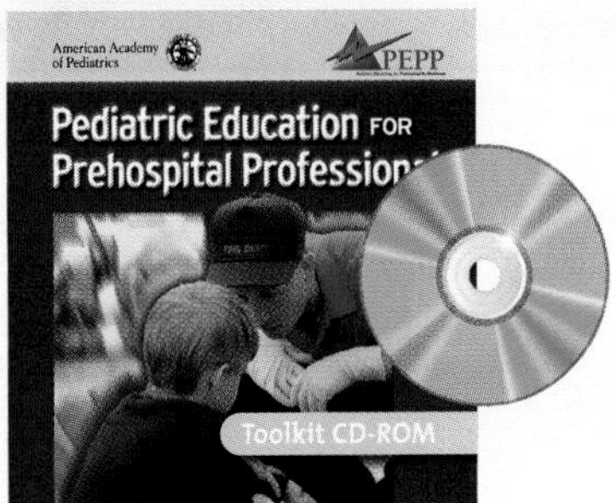

ToolKit CD-ROM: Preparing for class is easy with these PowerPoint presentations that are keyed to the lecture outlines in the Resource Manual. Screen shots from www.PEPPsite.com are also included to allow faculty to go over web links in class with their students, without the hassle of a live Internet connection.

ISBN: 0-7637-1256-6

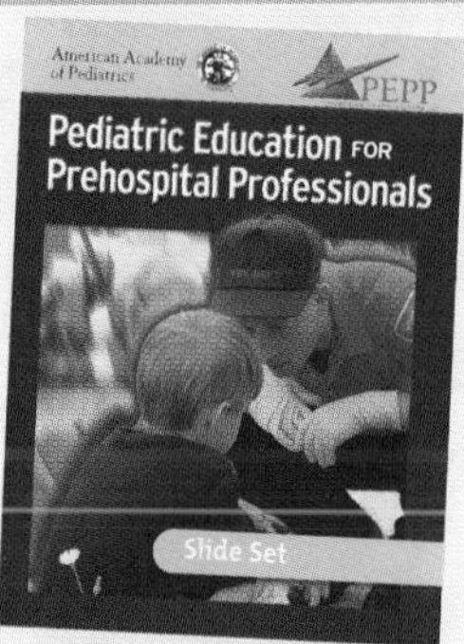

Slide Set: These dynamic and informative slides are keyed to the lecture outlines in the Resource Manual for the faculty's convenience. Both BLS and ALS slides are included.

ISBN: 0-7637-1258-2

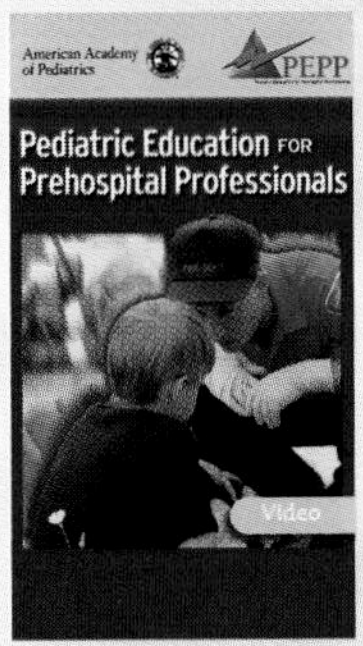

Videos: Containing real-life footage of the field, emergency departments, and operating rooms, these videos will captivate students and show them skills they could only learn from watching a "real" procedure.

BLS ISBN: 0-7637-1257-4
ALS ISBN: 0-7637-1414-3

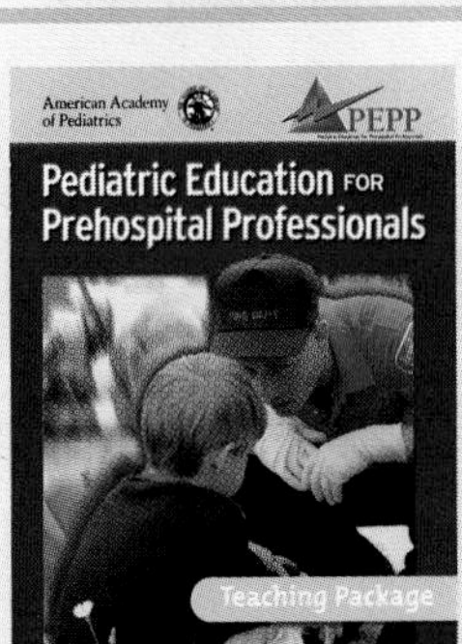

Teaching Package: The teaching package combines the Textbook, the Resource Manual, ToolKit CD-ROM, or slide set, and videos in one convenient box.

ISBN: 0-7637-1260-4

Brief Contents

Contents

13 Medicolegal Considerations 220

Procedures

Preface

The Pediatric Education for Prehospital Professionals (PEPP) Course has a rich history. It is the product of ten years of collaboration, brainstorming, review, revision, and re-revision by many dedicated physicians, nurses, paramedics, EMTs and EMS educators interested in improving the quality of prehospital care for children. The course is the culmination of the best and most recent educational efforts in prehospital pediatrics, including the pediatric components of the National Standard Curricula for EMT-basics, intermediates, and paramedics.

The PEPP Course began in 1990 as a distant vision of the California Pediatric Emergency and Critical Care Coalition and the California EMSC Project, funded by the California EMS Authority.* In 1992, the coalition's Pediatric Education for Paramedics (PEP) Task Force joined with the American College of Emergency Physician's Pediatric Emergency Medicine Committee and published Pediatric Education Guidelines for Paramedics. These guidelines were the first national consensus curriculum on prehospital pediatrics. Subsequently, a National PEP Task Force was formed which brought together representatives from the Florida Technical Advisory Panel for EMSC, the California PEP Task Force, and several other pediatric prehospital education groups. The new National PEP Task Force was funded by the Florida Emergency Medicine Foundation, who assumed a major leadership role in the project, and by the California EMS Authority.

In 1995, the National PEP Task Force produced its first course, the PEP Course, which built upon the outstanding work of several state EMSC projects, especially The Washington Pediatric Prehospital Care Project headed by Dena Brownstein and The California Pediatric Airway Project by Marianne Gausche-Hill.

In 1998, the American Academy of Pediatrics (AAP) established a national steering committee to restructure and expand the course. The AAP entered into a key partnership with Jones and Bartlett Publishers—a publisher with experience and a strong commitment to quality EMS education—to produce the materials. The goal was to create a comprehensive, innovative and highly visual pediatric course for both BLS and ALS providers.

Over the last two years, the AAP's national steering committee has completely revised and upgraded the PEP Course with the latest educational concepts and clinical advances for prehospital professionals. The committee chose the new name, the PEPP Course (Pediatric Education for Prehospital Professionals), to reflect the wider audience—all BLS and ALS prehospital providers. In developing PEPP course recommendations, the National PEPP Steering Committee carefully reviewed the most current data on the efficacy, safety, and feasibility of pediatric prehospital interventions. Where scientific research is not definitive, the recommendations derive from expert opinion and clinical experience in hospitals, emergency departments, and pediatric ambulatory settings. The PEPP Course emphasizes careful assessment and BLS care, and supports prudent use of ALS interventions.

The PEPP Course is a dynamic EMS teaching tool that will be subject to ongoing review and modification, in concert with changes in the science of emergency pediatrics and advances in EMS educational design and methodology. The National PEPP Steering Committee is committed to continual course improvement and dissemination to a national and international audience.

Ronald A. Dieckmann, MD, MPH, FAAP, FACEP
San Francisco, CA

*Funding for original PEP course development provided by the State of California Emergency Medical Services (EMS) Authority under Special Project Grant #EMS-2045 and #EMS-4067.

Authors

Ronald A Dieckmann, MD, MPH, FAAP, FACEP
Pam Baker, RN, BSN, CEN, CCRN
Dena Brownstein, MD, FAAP
David J. Burchfield, MD, FAAP
Arthur Cooper, MD, FACS, FAAP, FCCM
Susan Fuchs, MD, FAAP, FACEP
Karen Frush, MD, FAAP
Marianne Gausche-Hill, MD, FAAP, FACEP
Susan McDaniel Hohenhaus, RN
Deborah Mulligan-Smith, MD, FAAP, FACEP
Michael Panté, NREMT-P
Steve Strawderman, NREMTP, BBA
Robert A. Wiebe, MD, FAAP, FACEP
George A. Woodward, MD, MBA, FAAP, FACEP

Reviewers

Michael R Anderson, MD, FAAP
Attending Physician, Pediatric Critical Care
Rainbow Babies and Children's Hospital
Cleveland, OH

M. Douglas Baker, MD, FAAP
Professor of Pediatrics/Chief, Pediatric Emergency Medicine
Yale University
New Haven, CT

Tod Baker, EMT-P
EMS Coordinator
University Hospitals Health System - Geauga Regional Hospital
Chardon, OH

DeAnn Barnson, BSN, ADN, EMT
President
EMEDCO
Salt Lake City, UT

Brian A Bates, MD, FAAP
Director, Children's Emergency Center
Methodist Children's Hospital
San Antonio, TX

Jan Berger, MD, FAAP, MJ
Assistant Medical Director
Caremark
Northbrook, IL

John G Brooks, MD, FAAP
Professor of Pediatrics
Dartmouth Medical School
Lebanon, NH

Mark S Brown, EMT-P, MA
EMS Educator
Point La Jolla Media
San Diego, CA

Patrick L Carolan, MD, FAAP
Medical Director
Minnesota Sudden Infant Death Center/Children's Hospitals and Clinic
Minneapolis, MN

Nancy N Dodge, MD, FAAP
Developmental Pediatrician
Texas Scottish Rite Hospital for Children
Dallas, TX

Kathleen L Fernbach, RN, BSN, PHN
President, Association of SIDS & Infant Mortality Programs
Minnesota Sudden Infant Death Center, Children's Hospitals and Clinics
Minneapolis, MN

George Foltin, MD, FAAP, FACEP
Director, Center for Pediatric Emergency Medicine
Associate Professor of Clinical Pediatrics, New York University School of Medicine
Director of Pediatric Emergency Medicine Program, Bellevue Hospital Center/New York University Medical Center
New York, NY

Karen Frush, MD, FAAP
Director, Pediatric Emergency Medicine
Duke University Medical Center
Durham, NC

Mary Beth Gibbons, MA, EMT-3 [Flight], RN, ENC
Sunnybrook Health Science Centre
Toronto, ON, Canada

Peter W Glaeser, MD, FAAP, FACEP
Professor of Pediatrics, Director Ped. Emergency Med.
University of Alabama at Birmingham
Birmingham, AL

James Green, RN, CEN, EMT-P
Paramedic Division
San Francisco Fire Department
San Francisco, CA

J. Alex Haller, Jr, Ped. Surg., FAAP
Professor of Pediatric Surgery, Emeritus
Johns Hopkins
Baltimore, MD

Jacqueline Holmes, EMT-P
Senior Paramedic
Durham County EMS
Durham, NC

Carl E Hunt, MD, FAAP
Professor of Pediatrics
Medical College of Ohio
Toledo, OH

Donna O Janen Thomas, RN, MSN
Director Emergency Department & Rapid Treasures Unit
Primary Children's Medical Center
Salt Lake City, UT

Carden Johnston, MD, FAAP, FACEP
Emeritus Professor of Pediatrics
University of Alabama School of Medicine
Birmingham, AL

John Kattwinkel, MD, FAAP
Professor of Pediatrics
University of Virginia
Charlottesville, VA

Brian M Kelly, CEP, NREMT-P
Instructional Faculty
Pima Community College
Tucson, AZ

Desmond Kelly, MD, FAAP
AAP Section on Developmental & Behavioral Pediatrics
Greeneville, SC

Marian Kummer, MD, FAAP
AAP Committee on Children with Disabilities
Billings, MT

Jeff Linzer, MD, FAAP
AAP Section on Emergency Medicine
Atlanta, GA

Thomas Loyacono, NREMT-P, MPA
National Association of Emergency Medical Technicians
Baton Rouge, LA

Robin L Mazzuca, RN, BSN, CEN, EMT-P
Safe Communities Contractor
NHTSA Region V Office
Olympia Fields, IL

Susan McDaniel Hohenhaus, RN
EMS-C Coordinator
North Carolina Office of EMS
Raleigh, NC

Jeff McDonald, EMT-P
Coordinator—Emergency Medical Technology Program
Tarrant County College
Hurst, TX

Reviewers, continued

Robert Negri, RN
EMS Coordinator
Hayward Fire Department
Hayward, CA

Steven Neish, MD, FAAP
Division Head, Pediatric Cardiology
University of Wisconsin Children's Hospital
Madison, WI

Michael O'Brien, EMT-P
St Vincent Hospital
Indianapolis, IN

Kelley L Pastor, EMT-P
Critical Care Transport Paramedic
University Hosp. Of Cleveland
Cleveland, OH

Pamela Poore, RN
Clinical Supervisor, Emergency Department
Little Co of Mary Hospital
Torrance, CA

William S Proctor, NREMT-P, CCEMT-P
MICU paramedic
Med Flight of Ohio
Columbus, OH

Mike Rains, CEP
Firefighter/Paramedic
Scottsdale Fire Department
Scottsdale, AZ

Robert M Reece, MD, FAAP
Clinical Professor of Pediatrics
Tufts University School of Medicine
Boston, MA

Breck Rushton, RN, BSN
Utah EMSC Deptment of Health, EMS
Salt Lake City, UT

James S Seidel, MD, PhD, FAAP
Chief, Division of General and Emergency Pediatrics/Harbor-UCLA Medical Center
Professor of Pediatrics/UCLA School of Medicine
Torrance, CA

Steven M Selbst, MD, FAAP, FACEP
Professor and Vice Chairman, Department of Pediatrics
Thomas Jefferson University/duPont Hospital for Children
Wilmington, DE

John Todaro, REMT-P, RN
Senior Coordinator, Medical Quality Assurance and Education
Seminole County Department of Public Safety
Sanford, FL

Michael Tunik, MD, FAAP
Assistant Director, Center for Pediatric Emergency Medicine
Assistant Professor of Clinical Pediatrics, New York University School of Medicine
Associate Director of Pediatric Emergency Medicine Program, Bellevue Hospital Center/New York University Medical Center
New York, NY

Robert K Waddell II, EMT-P
Director—EMS Systems
Emergency Medical Services for Children National Resource Center
Washington, DC

The PEPP Course was piloted in North Carolina in September 1999 and California in October 1999. Many thanks to the pilot participants for their review and critique of all of the course components which resulted in further improvement and refinement of the PEPP course materials.

North Carolina Pilot Participants

Jennifer L. Andrews, Josh Barr, Megan Bernard, Robin Best, Will Boden, Allan Cantrell, Angie Clark, Michael Crater, Ricky Denning, Mike Dymes, Patricia Eifler, Maurice Gundrum, John Harrington, Deane Hodde, Jacqueline Holmes, Wanda Jackson, Dale Johnson, Erika Jones, Mark Keller, Mike Keller, Jonathan Kelly, John Laughter, Kent McKenzie, Debbie Messer, Jason Neal, Chris Neal, Matt Osborne, Bryan Phillips, Erin Powell, Rachel Price, Jeff Reed, Heather Reichlen, Deborah Stein, Anne Thomas, Charlotte Younge

California Pilot Participants

Jon Borer, Jeff Brown, James Charron, Alan Coffield, Frank Culhno, Jim Doersam, Erin Dorsey, Cathy Gagnon, Chris Giatras, Dave Grate, Susan Hayward, Joe Ingram, Jerry Koyama, Marcel Melanson, Ray Navarro, Dale Nordberg, Kathy Ord, Liz Palmas, Phil Peck, Dave Perusse, Marcus E Pierce, Dwayne Preston, Kevin Reed, Andy Reno, Jon Thompson, Bob Trevett, Linda Verraster, Dean Viana

A special note of thanks and recognition goes to the original National PEP Task Force and the California PEP Task Force (1997). Without the dedication of these individuals the PEPP course would not have been possible.

National PEP Task Force
Ronald A Dieckmann
Dena Brownstein
Joan Burg
George Foltin
Marianne Gausche-Hill
Joan Hu
Ramon Johnson
Robert Luten
Janet Jones
Deborah Mulligan-Smith
Robert Negri
Lou Romig
Robert Schafermeyer
Joseph Simon

The California PEP Task Force
Ronald A Dieckmann
Joan Burg
Marianne Gausche-Hill
Ramon Johnson
Angie Mendoza
Patricia Murrin
Eika Reich
James Schneider
Joanne Stonecipher
David van Stralen

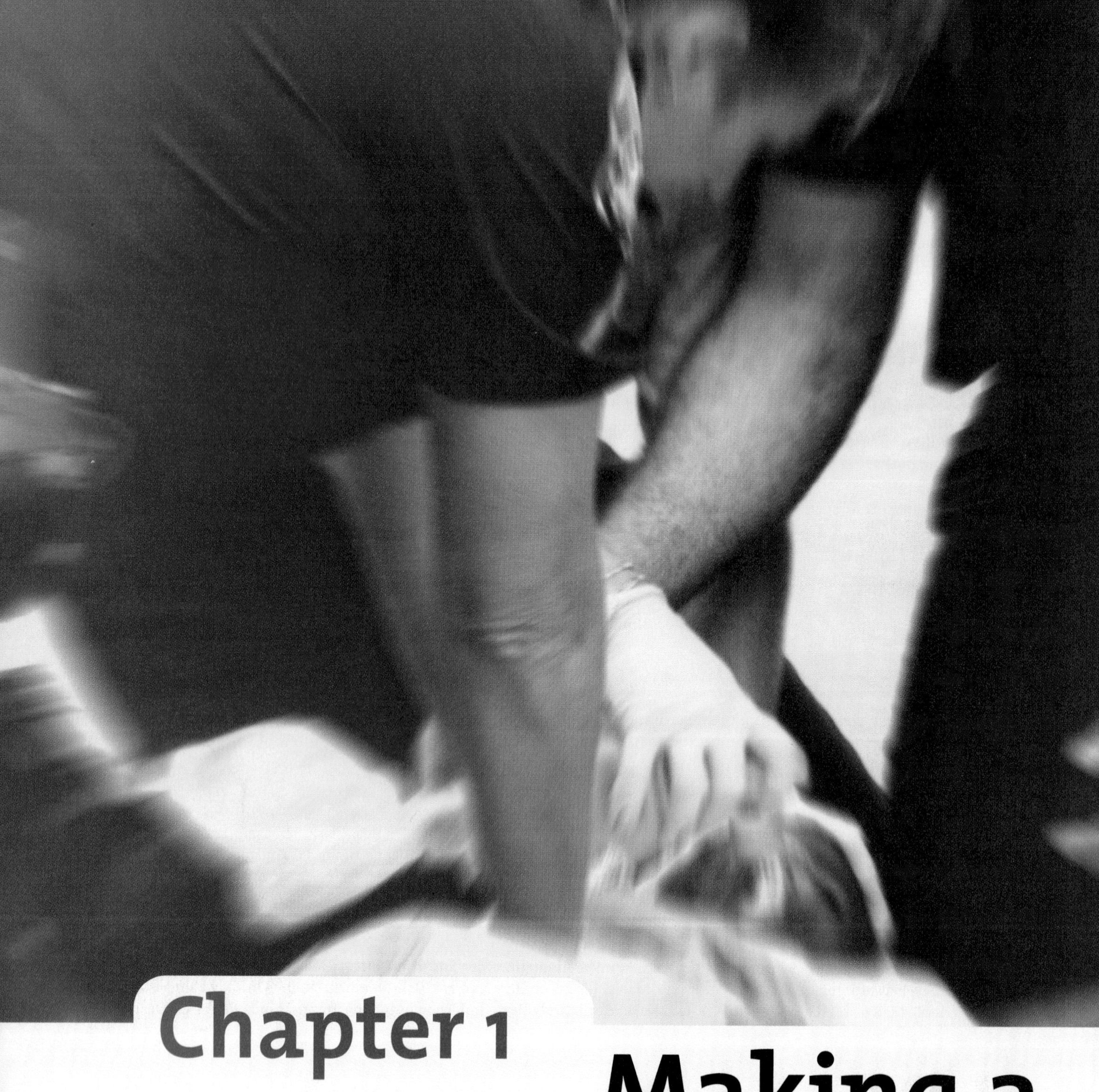

Chapter 1

Making a

Learning Objectives

1. Describe Emergency Medical Services for Children (EMSC).
2. Discuss why injuries are not accidents.
3. Recall possible community roles for the prehospital professional in prevention of childhood illness and injury.
4. State how a prehospital professional can be an advocate for EMSC within EMS.
5. Distinguish the special needs of children in disasters.
6. Apply principles of injury prevention to case studies.

You have been called to the scene of a bicycle versus motor vehicle crash. A 9-year-old girl was hit by a truck. She is unconscious and has no spontaneous movement. There are no abnormal airway sounds, retractions, or flaring. Her skin is pale. Respiratory rate is 35 breaths/min, heart rate is 60 beats/min, and blood pressure is 50 mm Hg/palp. Her pupils are fixed and dilated. You intervene with appropriate treatment and transport her quickly to the emergency department. The child dies 24 hours later.

How could this injury have been prevented?
What role do you have in preventing this type of injury for other children?

Difference

Introduction

"We must hurry,
There is no time to dally.
Do we build a fence on the cliff,
Or put another ambulance in the valley?"

Effective emergency care for children involves many professionals, both inside and outside of the community's hospitals. Two important concepts for professionals who want to provide high-quality emergency care are teamwork and prevention. Teamwork involves professionals working together to develop and implement comprehensive clinical services and administrative structures specifically for children. Prevention involves professionals recognizing the limitations of an emergency care system oriented only toward treatment *after* an illness or injury occurs. Of all community activities that can improve children's overall health and well-being, prevention of acute injury and illness is by far the most cost-effective. "Making a difference" means prehospital professionals getting involved in injury and illness prevention in many new ways, both as part of their professional day-to-day duties and as part of their activities as community leaders and health advocates. This includes supporting emergency medical services for children (EMSC) and programs within local emergency medical services (EMS) systems.

Emergency Medical Services for Children (EMSC)

Children are a unique group of EMS patients. They have special needs and problems that are different from those of adults. They require equipment and tools designed for smaller bodies and different physiology. They have to be approached and treated as children. Altogether, children under 18 years of age make up about 10% to 20% of out-of-hospital care. However, evaluating, treating, triaging, and transporting this group causes a lot of stress to prehospital professionals.

EMSC stands for emergency medical services for children. EMSC requires policies, processes, and resources that the EMS system uses specifically for children. Many EMS systems have recognized the special needs of children and have made important changes to adapt to their needs. For example, some systems have pediatric triage, treatment, and transport policies. Others require that children with serious injuries be transported to identified trauma centers or critically ill children be transported to **pediatric critical care centers**. An EMS system plan that specifically addresses children's needs might also require changes in the ways of delivering care. One example of this would be a pediatric base hospital contact policy for prehospital professionals that is different from adults. Another example would be a refusal policy that recognizes the legal issues surrounding provision of care to unaccompanied minors, to address the needs of children who need to be treated and/or transported without their parent or guardian on scene.

The EMSC plan might require changes or improvements in clinical services with pediatric-specific treatment methods, pediatric procedures such as **intraosseous** infusions and rectal **diazepam** administration, and pediatric equipment. In all of these EMS clinical and operational activities, EMSC is best viewed as a subsystem, not a separate system. *EMSC is fully within and completely dependent on the overall EMS system for safe and effective treatment of children.*

Because there are only a few specialized pediatric centers (i.e., **pediatric trauma centers**, pediatric critical care centers, and **general trauma centers**) in the United States, the type of emergency department (ED) locally available to over 90% of children with acute illness and injury is still the general hospital ED. Hence, universal standards for pediatric emergency care for all EDs, urban and rural, is an important part of EMSC development in the new millennium.

EMSC programs bring together out-of-hospital and in-hospital health care to fortify the chain of survival for children. This organized group of services and operations is more appropriately named the **EMS-EMSC continuum** (Figure 1-1). This term reflects the key concept of teamwork in the **chain of survival**—the organized interface between the EMS system and the community's child health services and personnel. The five major phases in the EMS-EMSC continuum include (1) prevention, (2) primary care (the child's medical home), (3) out-of-hospital care, (4) hospital care, and (5)

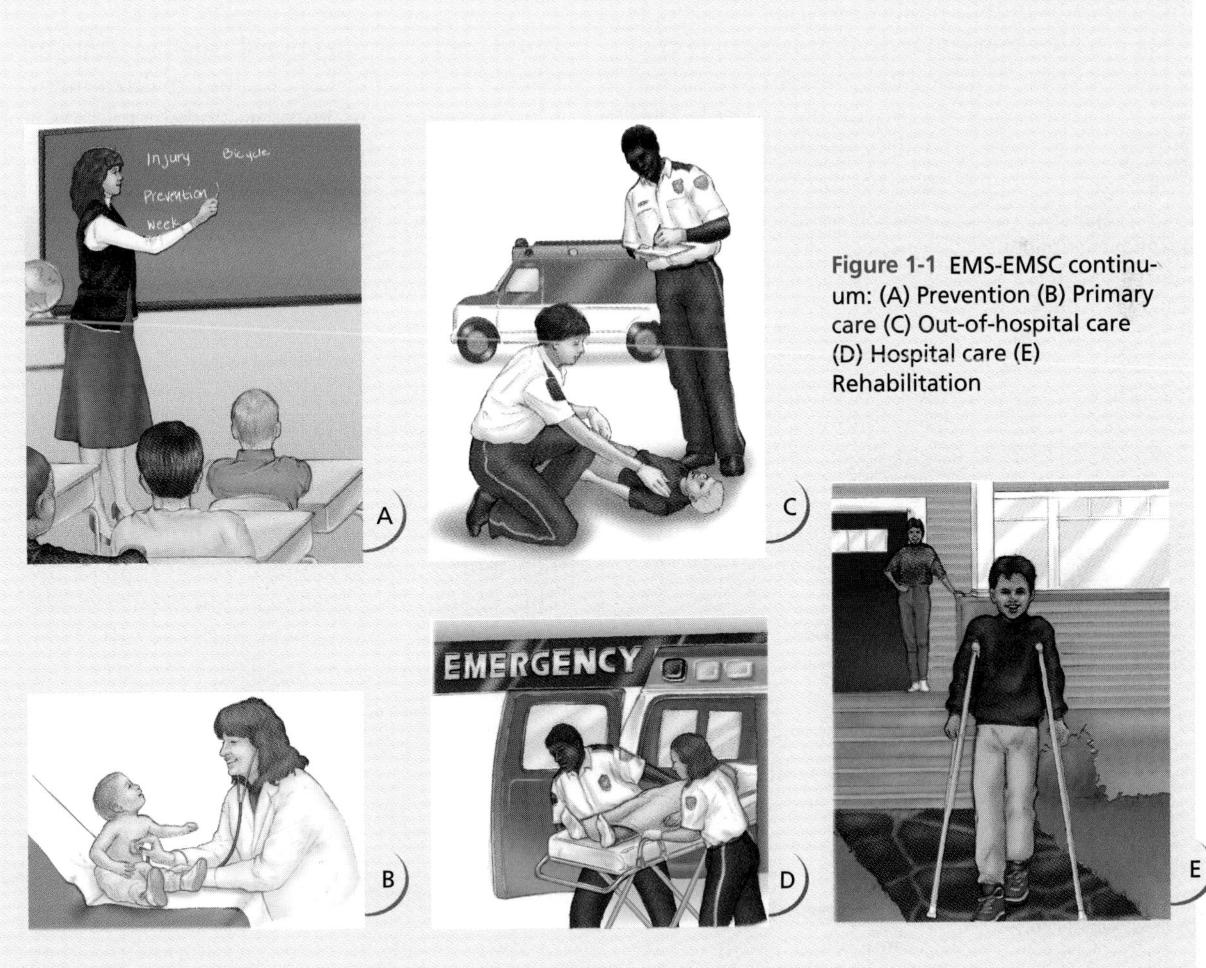

Figure 1-1 EMS-EMSC continuum: (A) Prevention (B) Primary care (C) Out-of-hospital care (D) Hospital care (E) Rehabilitation

rehabilitation. The prehospital professional may play an important role in two of these phases: prevention and out-of-hospital care. Primary care, hospital care, and rehabilitation do not usually involve the prehospital professional.

Injury and Illness Prevention

Many ill and injured children die in every community each year, despite receiving optimal medical care. There is a scientific discipline that is even more effective at saving lives than optimal medical care: injury and illness prevention. Prevention is an essential feature of all EMS systems. It is an opportunity for prehospital professionals to greatly affect the health and safety of their own children and every child in their community.

Prevention is the first phase of the EMS-EMSC continuum. While prevention does apply to both illness and injury, out-of-hospital services have concentrated primarily on injury control. Table 1-1 lists the eight identified elements of injury control. These elements make injury control an objective and scientific effort. For the prehospital professional, injury control involves understanding how and why injuries occur, knowing how to identify the risks in the environment, and doing something in the community to stop injuries from happening.

! Tip

EMSC is not a separate out-of-hospital emergency system for children. It is a subsystem, fully within and completely dependent on the overall EMS system for safe and effective treatment.

? Controversy

An important controversy in EMSC is the unknown effect of specialized centers for children on outcomes of illness and injury events. While it seems logical that pediatric trauma centers and pediatric critical care centers will improve care and reduce morbidity and mortality, outcome data from such centers have not been widely compared to general hospitals and general trauma centers.

Table 1-1 Elements of Injury Control

1. Recognize injury as a disease process.
2. Maintain a reliable database.
3. Identify problem injuries and high-risk groups.
4. Identify the factors in injury causation.
5. Practice appropriate injury assessment.
6. Formulate injury prevention strategies.
7. Select efficient, practical countermeasures.
8. Reevaluate selected countermeasures for the desired effects.

Injuries are not accidents

When injury patterns are carefully studied, it is clear that injuries, like illnesses, vary with the seasons, can occur in epidemics, and often have local trends and demographic distributions. In other words, injuries are largely predictable, whether they are unintentional (such as drowning) or intentional (such as handgun assaults). Chapter 12, on child maltreatment, addresses intentional injuries and the role of the prehospital professional in recognizing and reporting them. Whether they are intentional or unintentional, injuries are predictable. If injuries are predictable as to when and how they occur, they are potentially preventable.

Injuries are not accidents. Accidents are flukes of nature, or rare events that occur at random. True accidents that cause injuries are rare. Even apparently random events, such as lightning strikes or earthquakes, have predictable features and can be anticipated. For example, homes may be equipped with lightning rods and their foundations reinforced for earthquake stability. Automobile crashes are almost never accidents. Crash injuries usually result from predictable and preventable factors; the most common mistakes are driving while intoxicated, speeding, or improper use of child seats.

Remember: Injuries are predictable. They are not accidents. They can be prevented.

Components of an injury event

Part of understanding how injuries occur involves looking at the three components of an injury event: the host, the agent, and the environment (Figure 1-2).

The **host** is the person who is the recipient of the injury. An injury occurs when a delivery of energy is too much for the host to tolerate. Human hosts have different levels of tolerance. Children, because of their unique **anatomic** and **physiologic** features, are particularly vulnerable to highly destructive energy transfers. Their smaller body size means they are more likely to be injured.

The **agent** is a form of energy. The major agents of injury are types of energy: kinetic, thermal, chemical, electrical, and radiation. Most injuries are associated with these types of energy. Kinetic energy is the most common injury agent in circumstances that involve prehospital professionals. For example, falls, auto-passenger injuries, pedestrian versus auto and bicyclist versus auto events all involve a human as the host and kinetic energy as the agent. Burns involve a human host and thermal, chemical, or electrical energy.

The **environment** is the setting where the agent meets the host. The environment causes or influences the injury event. Some examples are an unfenced swimming pool, a poorly maintained road, or an open upper-story window without a protective barrier. Any of these may provide the environment for an injury event to occur that might involve a young child as a host and kinetic energy as the agent.

Looking at injury events, the prehospital professional can consider what can be modified to prevent injuries. Modifying the host to prevent drowning or head injury, for example, may involve education in swimming skills or driving techniques. Modifying the agent may include providing bicycle helmets (Figure 1-3) or installing soft stopping surfaces in playgrounds (Figure 1-4). Modifying the environment may include fencing of swimming pools or setting up window bars.

Phases of injury

Just as there are three components in every injury event, there are also three separate phases of every injury that need to be considered when devising control strategies: the pre-event period, the event itself, and the post-event period (Figure 1-5).

Prevention is an essential feature of all EMS systems and represents an opportunity for prehospital professionals to affect profoundly the health and well-being of their own children and every child in their community.

Pre-event factors are conditions in the host, the agent, or the environment that make an injury more or less likely to occur. For example, riding a bicycle without a helmet is a pre-event factor that might increase the probability of injury. Event factors are conditions that increase

Figure 1-2 Components of an injury event: the host, the agent, and the environment. The child is the host, the heat from the boiling water is the agent, and the dangerously placed handle is the environment for a burn injury.

Figure 1-3 When worn correctly, bicycle helmets can significantly reduce complications and death from closed-head injuries. This helmet is being worn too far back on the girl's head. Prehospital professionals have an important community role in teaching simple injury control strategies.

Figure 1-4 Absorbent surfaces in playgrounds are an effective method of modifying the environment for injury control.

or decrease the effect of the agent on the host. An event factor that would decrease the risk of injury in a vehicle crash would be lower speed of the automobile at the time of the crash. Post-event factors are conditions that increase or decrease the effect of the agent on the host after the injury event. An example of a post-event factor that would affect the outcome in a severely head-injured child might be on-scene airway management by the prehospital professional.

Traditionally, out-of-hospital care has focused almost exclusively on the post-event period, or medical care and transport after the injury has occurred. Prehospital professionals must now recognize their potential to influence the pre-event and event phases of injury by acting as community educators and advocates. Table 1-2 provides examples of injury control strategies aimed at modifiable factors in different phases of injury. The prehospital professional can have an important role in all of these prevention strategies.

Prevention does not require advanced technical skills and may have a profound impact on children's health and well-being, but until recently prehospital professionals may not have been taught injury or illness prevention. Therefore, bringing prevention into the prehospital professional's scope of practice is new and exciting; however, what the prehospital professional should do differently at the scene, at the hospital, or in the community is not yet clear.

Injuries are not accidents.

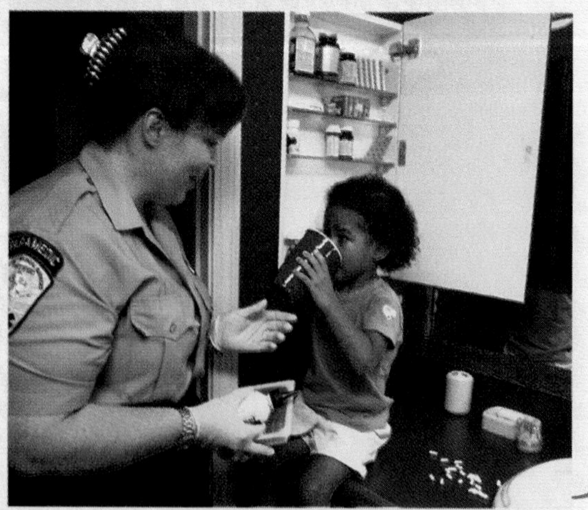

Figure 1-5 Phases of an injury: (A) The pre-event period. An unlocked medicine cabinet invites an adventurous toddler. (B) The event itself. A toddler will put anything into her mouth, including dangerous medications. (C) The post-event period. Activated charcoal is a treatment option for many poisons.

Summary of EMSC and Injury Control

Creation of EMSC within EMS involves developing pediatric-specific services and programs with a team approach that includes primary care, prehospital, and in-hospital professionals. Injury and illness prevention is a key feature of EMSC. Injuries are not "accidents" and are almost always predictable. Prehospital professionals have a unique role in community injury control. They are at the scene and able to assess accurately the principle components in an injury or illness event. This includes assessing the child or host, the energy type or agent of injury, and the environment, as well as understanding the pre-event, event, and post-event phases of injury.

Prevention: The Prehospital Professional's Role

Prehospital professionals can have a valuable role in community illness and injury prevention. They can have a greater impact in reducing illness and injury through prevention than they can through treatment. In order to be effective in this new role, prehospital professionals need education and training. Recognizing the many ways that injuries can be avoided is the first step in developing a plan for becoming involved in prevention activities in the community.

Role on scene

Prevention actions of the prehospital professional begin during the "scene size-up" and include (1) ensuring scene safety, and (2) performing an **environmental assessment**. Ensuring scene safety involves prevention of injury and illness to the prehospital professional herself and to other medical and law enforcement personnel. This includes identification of possible communicable diseases in the child, such as **chicken pox** (**varicella**) (Figures 1-6a and 1-6b) or **meningococcemia** (Figures 1-7a and 1-7b). Both of these infectious diseases can be transmitted to unwary scene personnel unless proper body substance precautions are observed. Ensuring scene safety may also prevent an injury to the child herself or to her caregiver.

! Tip

Prehospital professionals can have a greater impact in reducing the incidence and impact of illness and injury through prevention than through treatment.

Table 1-2 Modifiable Factors in Different Phases of an Injury

Phase	Examples of modifiable factors
Pre-event	Maintaining child restraint seats
	Installing proper fencing around pools
	Assuring that smoke detectors work in homes
Event	Properly using child restraint seats
	Deploying of front and side airbags
	Wearing bicycle helmets
Post-event	Performing pediatric airway management skills
	Using pediatric ambulance equipment properly
	Ensuring safe and rapid hospital transport of injured children

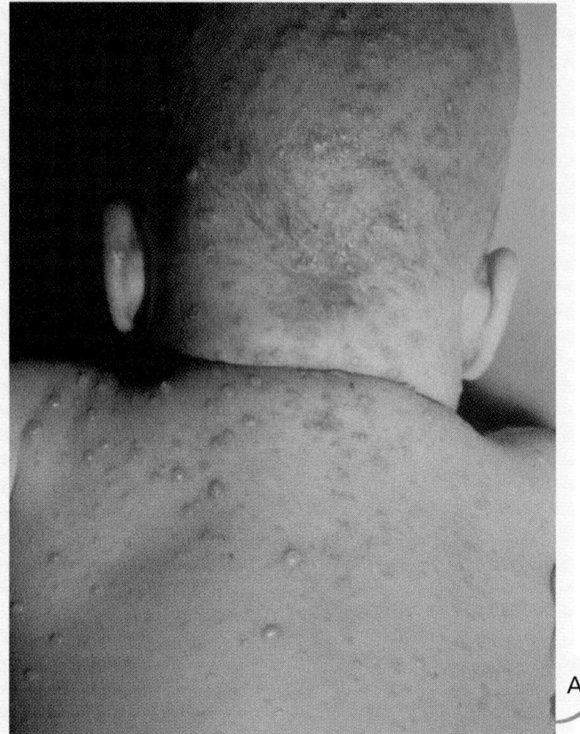

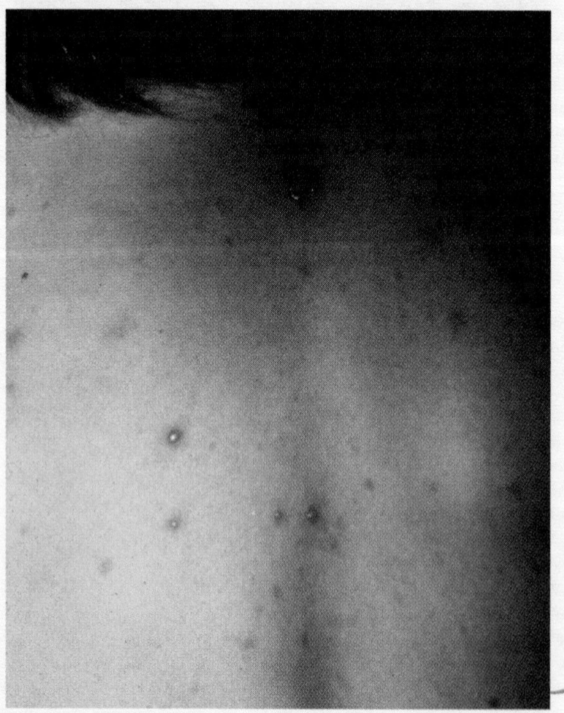

Figure 1-6 Children can pass on infectious diseases to the prehospital professional, who needs to recognize this potential. The highly infectious chicken pox rash is characterized by red dots and blisters.

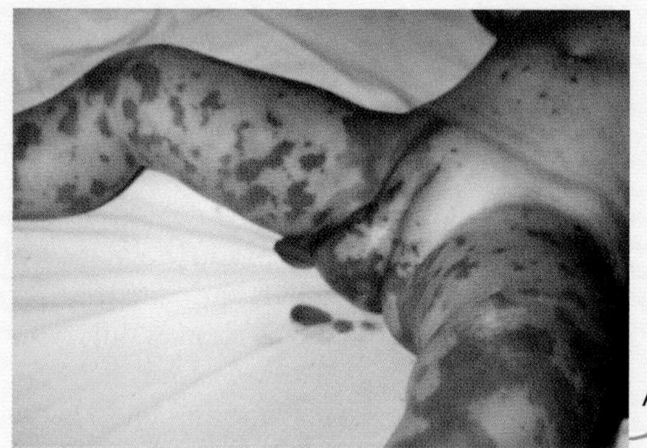

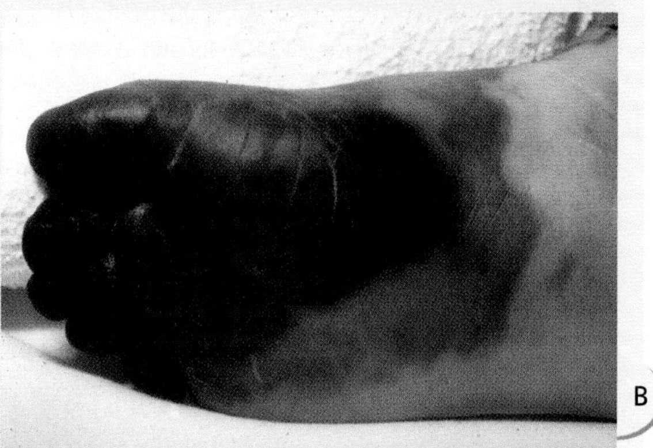

Figure 1-7 Meningococcemia is highly infectious. The meningococcemia rash looks like extensive bruising and usually involves the extremities.

Performing an environmental assessment adds a crucial piece to the overall picture at the scene. ED providers cannot do environmental assessment. Observation and documentation of the physical and interpersonal environment by the prehospital professional may provide the basis for important prevention actions. Such actions may include providing advice directly to the caregiver on obvious safety hazards in the home. Table 1-3 lists the stages of the STARR Program, developed by the National Highway Traffic Safety Administration (NHTSA). The STARR Program is a general strategic approach to home and community prevention actions for the prehospital professional.

Another type of environmental assessment involves observing and noting any evidence of possible maltreatment by the caregiver, then communicating these concerns to the ED physician. This preventive action may be lifesaving to the child, as explained in Chapter 12.

Role in the community

Detailed and accurate observations at the scene may serve to start or support community-wide strategies for injury and illness control. For example, in Europe and Australia prehospital professionals played a key role in recognizing the relationship between sleep position and **sudden infant death syndrome (SIDS)**. Scene observations were part of the scientific studies that confirmed the increased risk of SIDS in babies who slept **prone** and assisted in the campaign that has decreased SIDS **mortality**. Chapter 11 discusses SIDS in more detail.

Prehospital professionals can help in the understanding of community injury and illness patterns. They can do this by documenting the mechanism and scene circumstances of an acute event in the prehospital record and by assisting in other local data collection efforts. Table 1-4 lists some specific community injury prevention activities that prehospital professionals might consider in their expanded roles as community advocates, public educators, and teachers (Figure 1-8).

! Tip

Scene observations were part of the scientific studies that confirmed the increased risk of SIDS in babies who slept prone.

Table 1-3 The Prehospital Professional's Role in Illness and Injury Prevention: The STARR Program (National Highway Traffic Safety Administration)

See problems with safety
Talk to family to get history and obtain permission to survey the house
Assess adverse home-caregiver-environmental conditions at the scene
Remedy situation by discussion with family; educate family; demonstrate to family as needed (e.g., proper placement of child in car seat); document findings and discuss
Review and monitor over time

CASE STUDY 2

A 12-year-old girl calls 911 when her parents find a 3-year-old next-door neighbor at the bottom of their swimming pool. The child had been missing for only 15 minutes. On your arrival, you notice there is no fence. Several adults are frantically trying to do CPR. The child is unconscious, with no spontaneous movement, respirations, or pulse. The pupils are fixed and dilated. You continue CPR, initiate bag-valve-mask (BVM) ventilation, and perform endotracheal intubation on scene. On the way to the ED, you place an intraosseous line and administer epinephrine. A pulse returns. Three days later the child dies.

What simple safety measure could have prevented this tragedy?
How might you help inform your community about drowning prevention?

Table 1-4 Examples of Common Injuries and Possible Prevention Strategies

Vehicle Trauma	Infant and child restraint seats Seat belts and air bags Pedestrian safety programs Motorcycle helmets
Cycling	Bicycle helmets Bicycle paths separate from vehicle traffic
Recreation	Appropriate safety padding and apparel Cyclist/skateboard/skater safety programs Soft, energy-absorbent playground surfaces
Drowning	Four-sided locked pool enclosures Pool alarms Immediate adult supervision Caretaker CPR training Swimming lessons Pool/beach safety instruction Personal flotation device
Poisoning and Household	Proper storage of chemicals and medications Child safety packaging
Burns	Proper maintenance and monitoring of electrical appliances and cords Fire/smoke detectors Proper placement of cookware on stove top
Other	Discouragement of infant walker use Gated stairways Baby-sitter first aid training Child care worker first aid training

Appendix 1 provides some hints from the American Academy of Pediatrics (AAP) about ways for the prehospital professional to help in public education about prevention. The AAP website offers numerous handouts to assist with this important outreach education.

Role in safe transport

Another important injury control action for the prehospital professional is safe restraint and transport of the child in the ambulance itself. For a child who requires spinal immobilization, use a spinal board secured to the ambulance gurney to package the child safely, as described in Chapter 8. If the child is critically ill, treat and transport the child in a **supine** position on a gurney. This position will allow the prehospital professional to manage and monitor the airway, breathing, and circulation most easily. Secure the child to the gurney. *Never allow any infant or child to ride in the ambulance on a caregiver's lap.*

For a child with mild to moderate illness or injury not requiring spinal immobilization or a supine position, use an age-appropriate and locally approved approach to restraint. For some children with respiratory problems, an upright position of comfort is important, as explained in Chapter 4. The child with cardiopulmonary or neurological disabilities may require a specialized child seat to breathe effectively, as described in Chapter 10. Some EMS regions allow prehospital professionals to use child restraint seats for pediatric transport, but the safety and efficacy of these devices in ambulances are not known. *A child restraint seat that has been involved in a vehicle crash may be damaged and unsafe for transport use.*

Advocacy for EMSC within EMS

There are many ways that the prehospital professional can help EMSC and the EMS system. These include possible roles as a policy maker on EMS committees, an educator at school, a CPR trainer, or a community resource on injury control and children's health issues.

Another way for prehospital professionals to promote children's issues in EMS is through advocacy for EMSC programs and services at the local, state, and national levels. Appendix 2 provides a pediatric survey for state EMS offices. These questions are intended to help evaluate EMSC development at the state level during statewide EMS system assessments and to highlight available pediatric resources. Such a comprehensive EMSC survey should include organizations and providers involved in the EMS-EMSC continuum, such as pediatricians, emergency physicians, prehospital professionals, and EMS experts.

Figure 1-8 Use advocacy to help prevent injuries.

Children appear to sustain predicable patterns of physical and psychosocial injury and illness after natural disasters.

There has been much attention directed at disaster management but until recently the special issues for children in disasters have been largely overlooked.

Children in Disasters

Disasters may be natural or man-made. Examples of natural disasters are earthquakes, hurricanes, tornadoes, and floods. Man-made disasters include mass shootings, fires, mass transportation incidents, toxic spills, and riots. Mass casualty incidents are events causing a large number of injuries, such as train wrecks.

While there has been much attention directed at disaster management, until recently the special issues for children in disasters have been overlooked. Recent school shootings, however, have revealed the profound psychological effects of such events on children (Figure 1-9). The impact of recent wars and natural disasters on children has now been documented, and children appear to suffer severe physical and psychosocial injury and illness in predictable patterns. Significantly, the psychosocial impact of disasters on children may last much longer than the physical impact.

Following natural disasters, injuries to children can be minor to life threatening, but most do not come immediately to medical attention. As with adults, *the vast majority of injuries are seen after the disaster*, during the recovery phase. Also, environmental disturbances from disasters tend to cause increases of **chronic** respiratory ailments, especially asthma. **Bronchospasm** is the most frequent pediatric illness seen after an environmental disaster.

The EMS system can play a key role in preparing the community for an organized, coordinated pediatric response to a disaster. The first step is to evaluate the potential disaster risks in the community. The next step is to identify local hospital facilities and field medical operations with pediatric capabilities that can respond to anticipated needs. Using this information, the last step is to develop prehospital pediatric protocols involving community leaders from key organizations. Stakeholders might include community emergency response teams (CERTs), local emergency management agencies, local health department, schools, primary care professionals, the media, and hospital staff.

! Tip

Bronchospasm is the most frequent pediatric illness after a disaster.

Pediatric EMS policies that address expected disaster situations involving children include consent for care and transport, designation of hospital destination, and refusal of care or transport. Chapter 13 addresses these and other medicolegal issues in detail.

Another role for the prehospital professional is that of community educator for family participation in disaster preparedness. In the first 72 hours following a disaster, responsibility for emergency response usually falls on the shoulders of the family and neighbors. For this reason, careful advance planning to address the unique needs of children in disasters is imperative, including both provider and community preparedness. Table 1-5 provides a checklist for disaster preparedness at home.

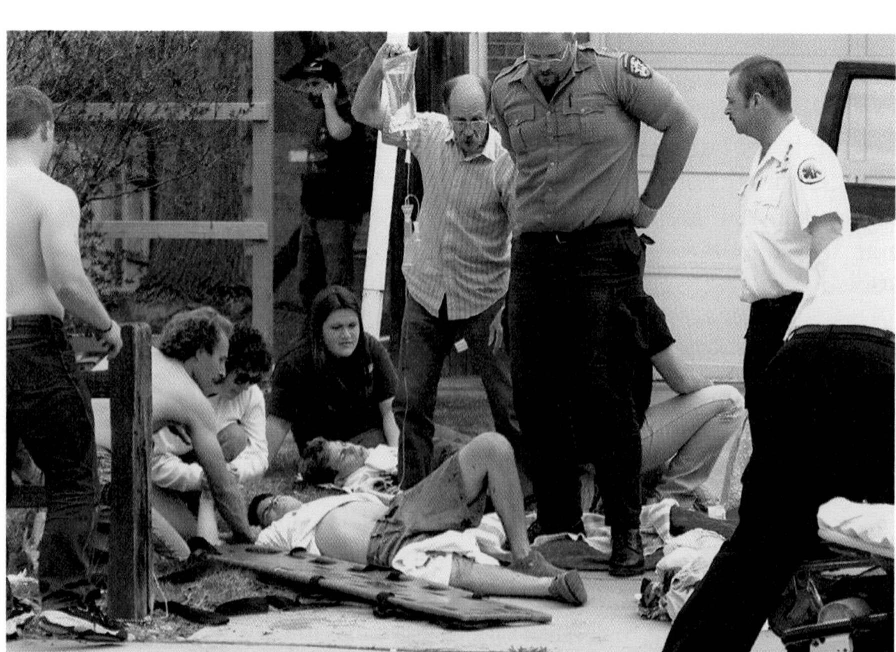

Figure 1-9 Children have special needs during and after disasters, such as these adolescents who were involved in the shooting at Columbine High School in Colorado in 1999.

Summary of the Role of the Prehospital Professional

Prehospital professionals play a key role with pediatricians, emergency physicians, and EMS experts in community injury and illness prevention and in disaster preparedness. The scene size-up includes specific prevention actions. Careful observation and documentation by the prehospital professional are crucial to general community illness and injury prevention strategies. Advocating for injury and illness prevention and for EMSC within the state EMS system are significant actions by the prehospital professional.

Table 1-5 Family Disaster Preparedness

First aid/CPR training
Emergency phone numbers
Home structural preparedness (e.g., cellar in tornado-prone areas)
Emergency supplies (e.g., water, food, first-aid supplies, flashlight)
Identification of the safest place in the home
Storage of personal identification, health records, insurance policies, and medications
Location of shelters prepared to assist children with special health care needs
Shelters for family pets
Emergency personal contacts

CASE STUDY 3

You live in a community that anticipates a flood with the winter rains. A number of plans have been proposed to meet the needs of the community in a disaster, but none specifically addresses the children, who make up 25% of the population.

What specific recommendations can you make to help community leaders meet the needs of children in disasters? What groups can assist you in this process?

Case Study Answers

See page 1

Factors that may have helped prevent or modify this injury include: a bicycle helmet, bicycle safety education in schools, reduced vehicle speed, better signs for drivers, and established crosswalks.

For the prehospital professional, the first prevention step in this case is to do the scene size-up and document important conditions, provide appropriate on-scene care, and rapidly transport the child to a pediatric-ready emergency department. Documenting the mechanism and informing hospital professionals of the preventable aspects of the injury (unhelmeted rider) has many benefits. While it would not be good timing for the prehospital professional to counsel the family on scene about injury prevention in the middle of an acute injury event, these opportunities may be available to hospital personnel at a time when the family will be receptive. Reinforcement of simple safety practices by multiple professionals may not only improve this family's compliance with helmet use but also help turn this family into advocates for injury prevention with their neighbors and friends.

The prehospital professional's careful documentation will contribute to vital data collection and help define patterns of injury within the community. The prehospital professional can also become a community advocate for injury prevention at home, at school, and in the community.

See page 9

This injury may have been prevented with appropriate fencing of the pool. This strategy for drowning prevention is known to be highly effective.

Effective out-of-hospital care is a phase of the EMS-EMSC continuum and requires the appropriate equipment, personnel education, and system support. The prehospital professional must participate as a learner and, whenever possible, as a teacher of EMSC.

The prehospital professional also has an important role as a community advocate for injury and illness prevention. By identifying that these injuries are occurring in your community and that they are preventable, you can help to educate parents and community lawmakers about the problems and the solutions.

There are many other ways the prehospital professional can be a prevention advocate in the community:

- Obtain support and resources for primary injury-prevention activities.
- Learn about injury risk identification and role-modeling prevention methods.
- Network with other local organizations.
- Be an advocate!

CHAPTER RESOURCES

See page 13

First, determine the likely types of acute pediatric injuries and illnesses after disasters such as the anticipated flood in your community. Identify local facilities (hospitals, schools, clinics) and field medical operations with pediatric capabilities and explain these resources to disaster planners in the community. Ensure that there is a plan for pediatric care that includes specific equipment and supplies at EDs.

Involve the community emergency response teams (CERTs), local emergency management agencies, health department, schools, primary care professionals, the media, and hospital staff to assist in providing anticipatory guidance.

Suggested Educational Resources

1. American Academy of Pediatrics Committee on Pediatric Emergency Medicine. The pediatrician's role in disaster preparedness. *Pediatrics* 1995;99:130–133.
2. Dieckmann RA, Athey J, Bailey B, Michaels J. *A Pediatric Survey for the National Highway Traffic Safety Administration Emergency Medical Services System Re-Assessments.* (In press.)
3. Dieckmann RA. *Pediatric Emergency Care Systems: Planning and Management.* Baltimore, MD: Williams and Wilkins; 1992.
4. Garrison H, Foltin G, Ecker LR, Chew JL, Johnson M, Madsen GM, Miller DR, Ozmar BH. Consensus statement: The role of emergency medical services in primary injury prevention. *Prehosp Emerg Care* 1997;1(3):156–162.
5. Quinn B, Baker R, Pratt J. Hurricane Andrew and a pediatric emergency department. *Ann Emerg Med* 1994;23(4):737–741.

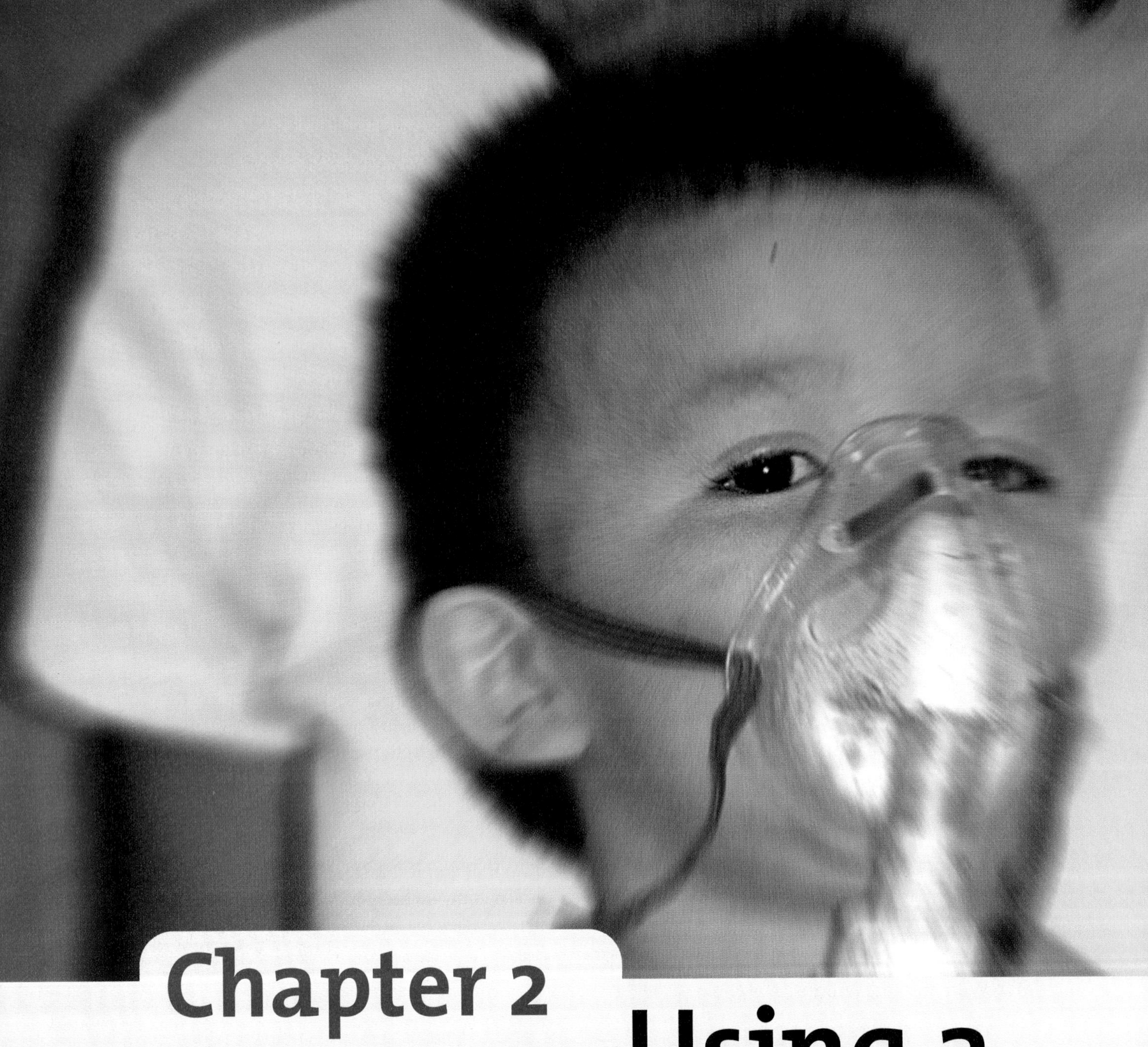

Chapter 2 Using a Developmental

Learning Objectives

1. Discuss the common responses of the family with a child who is ill or injured.
2. Describe key growth and development characteristics for each of the following groups: infants, toddlers, preschoolers, school-aged children, adolescents, and children with special health care needs.
3. Distinguish different techniques for successful assessment of each group.
4. Apply age-appropriate assessment techniques to case studies involving ill or injured children.

You are called for a 23-month-old boy who is having trouble breathing. When you arrive, the child is sitting on his mother's lap and starts to cry when he sees you. He has wheezing that you can hear from the doorway and exhibits visible intercostal retractions. His skin is pink. His mother states he has had a runny nose for 2 days and has a history of asthma. When you approach to get vital signs, he yells "Go away!" and tries to hit, kick, and bite you.

Is this "normal appearance" for a 23-month-old?
How can you facilitate the assessment?

Approach

Introduction

Children are special! There are many unique features in the anatomy, physiology, and psychosocial development of the child that will affect the assessment and treatment. Each age requires different considerations. Unlike the adult, who is usually reassured by the arrival of the prehospital professional, the infant or toddler will probably be afraid. This is especially true if the stranger is touching the child, coming between the child and other family members, or removing the child's clothing.

In addition to knowing the growth and developmental characteristics of these age groups, you must also be aware of exceptional considerations when assessing a child with special health care needs (CSHCN). Sometimes the age of a CSHCN does not correspond with his developmental stage and his physical growth may be ahead of, or behind, his emotional maturity.

Caring for a child includes caring for the family. Often, in addition to parents, other caregivers and siblings may be present. Each family member may have a different response to the child who is ill or injured. For this reason, the prehospital professional must have good communication skills and be prepared to care for the entire family. This is especially important in the event of a mass casualty incident or natural disaster.

This chapter will address growth characteristics and assessment techniques for physiologically stable children in age groups from infant to adolescent and for CSHCN. Chapter 9, on emergency delivery and stabilization, focuses on newborn characteristics and assessment techniques. Chapter 10, on children with special health care needs, talks more about this pediatric population.

Responses to Illness and Injury

Every family responds differently to a child's being ill or injured. Some of the factors that might determine how a family responds are the child's development level, the family's previous experience with the health care system, **coping strategies**, **culture**, availability of support systems, and the nature of the emergency. Table 2-1 summarizes some of the common ways in which adults behave under stress.

While some caregivers' responses in emergencies may seem too emotional or illogical, listen carefully to their concerns. They are "experts" on the child and usually know what works best.

The ill or injured child may respond to a stressful situation in a variety of ways, often by acting younger than he actually is. It is helpful to tell caregivers that this is a common temporary response. An adolescent may exhibit responses similar to the caregiver's.

Infants

www.PEPPsite.com

Growth and development characteristics

Infants are vulnerable creatures, with a limited number of behaviors. Infants less than 2 months of age spend most of their time sleeping or eating. They are not yet able to tell the difference between parents and other caregivers or strangers. They need to be kept warm, dry, and fed. They experience the world through their bodies. Being held, cuddled, or rocked soothes the infant. Hearing is also well developed at birth, and calm and reassuring talk is often helpful.

Infants between 2 and 6 months of age are more active, which makes them easier to evaluate. They spend more time being awake, they begin to make eye contact, and they recognize caregivers. Healthy infants in this age group will have a strong suck, active **extremity** movement, and a vigorous cry. They may follow a bright light or toy with their eyes, or turn their heads toward a loud sound or the caregiver's voice.

A family's response to a child's illness or injury will be influenced by the child's developmental level, previous experience with the medical system, coping strategies, culture, availability of support systems, and the nature of the emergency.

Between the ages of 6 and 12 months, most infants learn to talk or babble, sit unsupported, reach for toys, move objects from one hand to another, and put things in their mouths. At approximately 1 year of age, most infants start to scoot or crawl, pull to a stand, "cruise" furniture, and may start to walk.

At 7 to 8 months, infants are afraid of separation from their parents or caregivers and at 9 to 10 months develop stranger anxiety. They are

Table 2-1 Common Responses of Caregivers to Acute Illness or Injury in a Child

Disbelief: Caregivers may be struggling with the child's illness or injury. They may seem too calm or unconcerned.
Guilt: Caregivers may be horrified that they were unable to recognize the serious nature of their child's condition or because they were unable to prevent an injury. They may focus their attention on what should have been done, rather than on the child's immediate situation.
Anger: Caregivers may show their consternation as anger, and they may direct their anger at the prehospital professional. Caregivers may become hostile when the prehospital professional makes efforts to stabilize the child. They may attempt to refuse transport.
Physical symptoms: Caregivers may have tachycardia, nausea, headache, chest pain, sweaty palms, dry mouth, or hyperventilation.

able to sense anxiety in their caregivers and react to being separated from them. Their caregiver or a familiar adult most easily comforts them.

Table 2-2 summarizes anatomic and physiologic differences that are important in the assessment and care of the infant.

Infants' capacity to interact with their environment is limited, and the signs and symptoms of illness are not always easy to see. Because of these factors, the caregiver's perception that "something is wrong" must be taken seriously. An infant who is reported as fussier than usual, feeding poorly, or sleeping excessively, or who has a temperature greater than 38°C must be seen by a physician. Be especially concerned about an infant under 3 months who has a fever. It is important to find out if there has been a recent history of trauma, how the infant was acting prior to the event, and if the infant has been healthy since birth. Find out if the infant was born at term and if there were any problems during pregnancy, labor, delivery, or immediately after the birth.

Excessive irritability or sleeping, fever, and poor feeding may be symptoms of a very serious

Table 2-2 Anatomic and Physiologic Features of Infants

Infants are nose breathers for the first several months of life. Obstruction of the nose from secretions, blood, or edema may cause respiratory distress.
The muscles of the infant's chest wall are not yet developed, and the abdominal muscles are the main muscles used for breathing. "Belly breathing" is normal in infants and may become exaggerated as breathing becomes more rapid.
Retractions are easily seen in the infant with respiratory distress.
A faster metabolic rate increases the need for oxygen and nutrients.
Temperature regulation is immature.
The head is large (Figure 2-1) and may be a potential source of significant heat loss.

CASE STUDY 2

You respond to a call to help a 2-week-old girl reported to have stopped breathing. On arrival at the house, you find a tiny infant who lies in the crib with eyes open, moving her arms and legs, and crying loudly. Her abdomen rises and falls with each breath, and there are no abnormal airway sounds, retractions, or flaring. Her skin is pink centrally, but her hands and feet are slightly blue. The baby-sitter tells you that the child was born after a full-term pregnancy and has done well since birth. Over the last 2 days the infant has fed poorly but has had no fever. This morning, she turned pale and went limp for a few seconds. The infant revived rapidly when the baby-sitter "blew in her face."

What are the normal behaviors of a 2-week-old?
How sick is this infant?

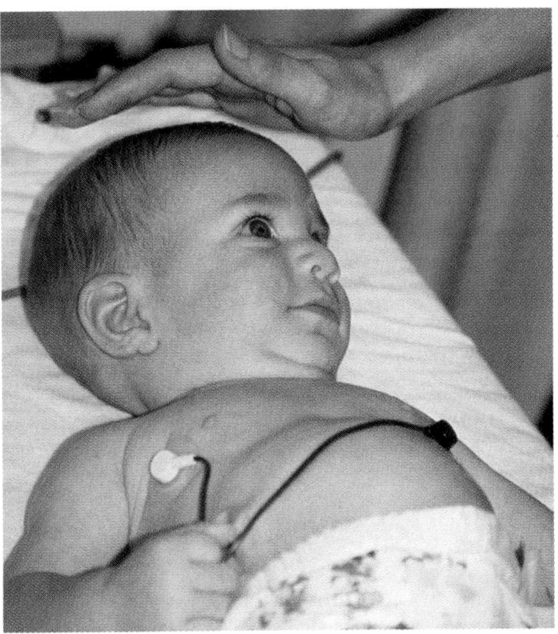

Figure 2-1 The infant's head is disproportionately large compared to older children and adults. The head may be a source of significant heat loss.

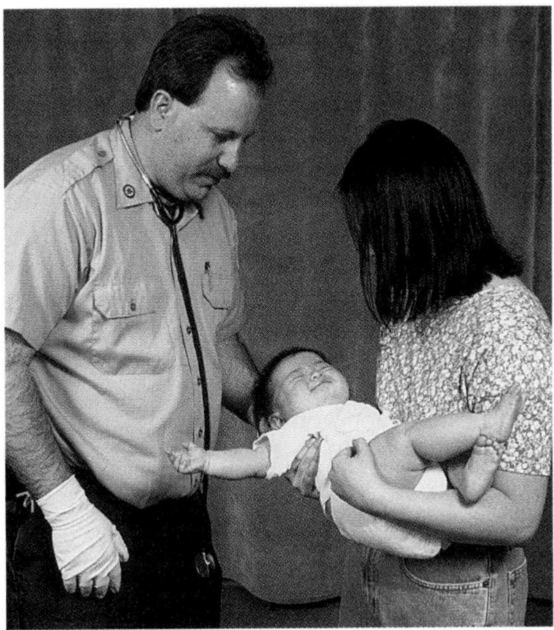

Figure 2-2 Approaching an infant: Observe the infant in the caregiver's arms before palpating or auscultating.

illness, such as **sepsis** or **congenital heart disease**. **Apnea** is a common chief complaint in the infant period. Apnea may be a sign of infection, heart disease, seizure activity, head injury, or a metabolic problem such as **hypoglycemia**.

Assessment of the infant

Conduct the assessment of the infant using the following principles:

- Ask the caregiver the infant's name and use it.
- Observe, **auscultate**, and **palpate** in this order to get the most information with the least amount of stress to the infant (Figure 2-2).
- Approach the infant slowly and calmly because loud voices and quick movements may frighten him.
- Squat down or sit at "baby level."
- Observe the interaction of the infant with the caregiver(s). It is often helpful to assess the infant while the caregiver is holding him. This is especially true for the infant older than 6 months, who may have stranger anxiety. An infant who is happily snuggled in a caregiver's arms may become fussy and cry when unwrapped and placed on cold sheets.
- If the infant begins to cry, a pacifier, blanket, or favorite toy may help to calm him. Avoid feeding the infant who is seriously ill or injured.
- Perform the assessment based on the infant's activity level. For example, if the infant is calm, get the respiratory rate and auscultate lung sounds at the beginning of the assessment.
- Make nonthreatening physical contact first, such as touching an extremity to assess warmth and **capillary refill**. Perform the most upsetting parts of the exam last.
- Use a warmed stethoscope and warm hands, and handle the infant gently. Talk in a monotonous, soothing voice.
- Avoid doing anything potentially painful or distressing until after the assessment is completed. It is difficult to assess heart and lung sounds

The older infant is fearful of separation and develops stranger anxiety. Approach slowly and assess the infant while he is being held by the caregiver.

or to palpate the abdomen when the infant is crying.

- Consider offering the infant a toy as a distraction.
- Have the caregiver remove the infant's clothing if needed because this is less threatening to the infant. Remove one item of clothing at a time, then replace it, if possible, before moving on to the next body area.
- Show respect for the caregiver by praising the infant's appearance and behavior.

Toddlers

Growth and development characteristics

Toddlers experience rapid changes in growth and development. By about 18 months of age, the toddler is able to run, feed himself, play with toys, and communicate with others. The toddler begins making his own decisions and asserting his independence. The "terrible two" stage actually begins at about 1 year of age and often lasts into the third year. Toddlers are mobile, opinionated, and may be terrified of strangers. Most toddlers also resist logic, and they cannot be reasoned with. They are very curious and have no sense of danger. They are playful, magical thinkers, and are tremendously self-centered. They understand ownership and will label things (toys, etc.) as their own.

Do not separate the older infant or toddler from the caregiver.

Toddlers think very concretely. They are able to solve problems by trial and error. Their negative behavior is based on their need for independence. Language capabilities are different depending on the toddler; some toddlers will utter only single words while others may speak in paragraphs. They often understand what is being said, even if they cannot respond with words. Older toddlers may remember earlier experiences with doctors or nurses, such as vaccinations or stitches, and be fearful about being examined.

The toddler's anatomy and physiology are much like the infant's, notably the large head and the use of abdominal muscles to breathe. **Thermoregulation** is better, and limb muscles are more developed.

Assessment of the toddler

Conduct the assessment of the toddler using the following principles:

- Approach the toddler slowly and keep physical contact to a minimum until he is familiar with you. Watch the toddler's activity level and behavior as you approach him.
- Sit down or squat next to the toddler and use a quiet, soothing voice.
- Allow the toddler to remain on the caregiver's lap.
- Use play and distraction tools, such as a penlight or teddy bear, to help with the assessment (Figure 2-3). Introduce equipment slowly and encourage him to hold it.
- Talk to the toddler, preferably about himself. Admire his shoes; ask about pets or recent events. A toddler is the center of his universe.
- Give him limited choices, such as "Do you want me to listen to your belly or feel your

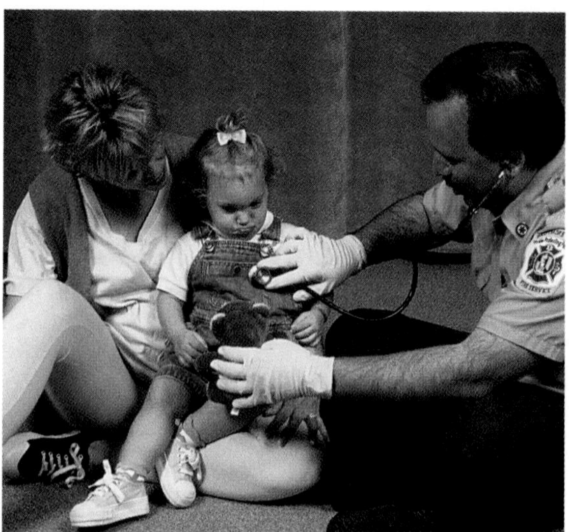

Figure 2-3 Approaching a toddler: Offer a toy or distraction tool to gain the child's attention and to assess neuromotor function.

pulse first?" This provides the toddler with a sense of control.

- Avoid questions that the toddler can answer with no.
- Praise the toddler to get cooperation.
- Use simple, concrete terms. Provide a lot of reassurance.
- Perform the most critical parts of the assessment first—"toe-to-head," with the head and neck last.
- Ask for caregiver assistance with the assessment. The toddler is often less upset if the caregiver removes his clothes or administers oxygen.
- If necessary, you may need to ask the caregiver to gently palpate the toddler's extremity to test for pain.
- Do not expect toddlers to sit still and cooperate. Be flexible but thorough.

In certain situations, the toddler may be extremely difficult to examine. If he is alert but resists the exam, determine the need for transport based on history. Use of lights and sirens during transport may increase the toddler's level of fear.

Preschoolers

Growth and development characteristics

Preschoolers are magical and illogical thinkers. They aren't always able to know the difference between fantasy and reality, and they have many misconceptions about illness, injury, and bodily functions. For example, a preschooler might think of a cut as "my insides leaking out." If you tell a preschooler you are going to take his pulse, he may ask "Where are you going to take it and will I get it back?" Common fears for this age group include body mutilation, loss of control, death, darkness, and being left alone. Attention span is short.

Assessment of the preschooler

Conduct the assessment of the preschooler using the following principles:

- Use simple terms to explain procedures. Choose words carefully, using language that is age-appropriate. Clarify any apparent misconceptions.
- Use dolls or puppets, if available, to explain what you are doing.
- Allow the child to handle equipment. Ask for his help (Figure 2-4).
- Set limits on behavior; for example, "You can cry or scream, but don't bite or kick."
- Praise good behavior.
- Use games or distraction tools.
- Use dressings or bandages freely.
- Focus on one thing at a time.
- Play games with the immobilized preschooler to distract him from squirming and complaining.

Preschoolers are magical thinkers who fear loss of control. Explain procedures in simple terms, allow them to handle equipment, and assess from toe to head.

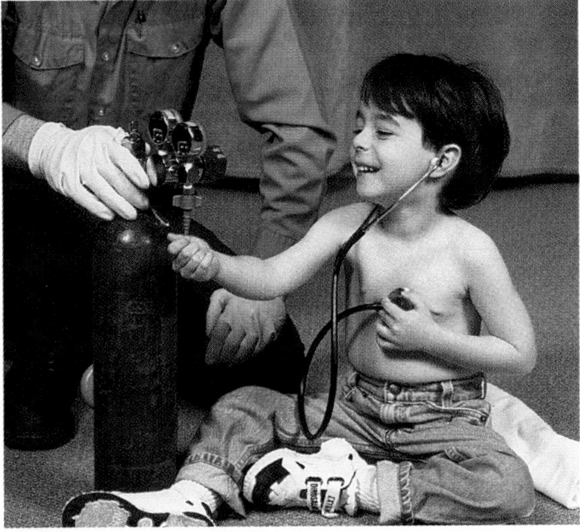

Figure 2-4 Approaching a preschooler: Allow the child to handle the equipment.

School-Aged Children

Growth and development characteristics

School-aged children are talkative, analytical, and able to understand the concept of cause and effect. They feel a sense of accomplishment as they get new skills. They still have some wrong ideas about how their bodies work. They also do not always understand what it means to have a particular illness or injury. They may misunderstand certain words and phrases. By 9 years of age, they usually understand simple explanations about their bodies and like to be involved in their own care.

! Tip

School-aged children fear separation from caregivers, loss of control, pain, and physical disability. Explain procedures and anticipate questions, provide privacy, and conduct assessment from head to toe.

Common fears include separation from parents and friends, loss of control, pain, and physical disability. They are often afraid to talk about their feelings and usually hide their thoughts or they may not be able to put their feelings into words. As they become more mobile and more independent, they begin to take more risks. They live in the present. Belonging and peer group support are important.

Offering choices that aren't really there violates the child's sense of trust. Tell the school-aged child what you are going to do, and do it!

The anatomy and physiology of a child is similar to an adult's by about 8 years of age.

Assessment of the school-aged child

Conduct the assessment of the school-aged child using the following principles:

- Speak directly to the child, then include the caregiver.
- Anticipate the child's questions and fears and discuss them immediately. Explain in simple terms what is wrong and how it will affect them. For example, when speaking to a 5-year-old, you may explain "Your arm-bone is broken, but the doctor will be able to fix it good as new. We'll give you some medicine in your arm to help stop it from hurting so much."
- Be careful not to offer too much information.
- Explain procedures immediately before doing them. Never lie to a child, telling them that something won't hurt, or that you are almost finished, if this is not true. Remember that the child may not ask questions or admit not knowing something.
- Ask the older school-aged child if he would like to have the caregiver present.
- Provide privacy. Children in this age group are modest. Uncover areas when necessary and cover them up when done.
- If physical restraint is necessary to complete a procedure or to guarantee the safety of the child or crew, tell the child what is going to happen and then do it.
- Don't negotiate unless the child really has a choice. For example, it is okay to ask the child if he would like the IV in the right or left hand but not to ask if it is okay to start an IV when it must be done.
- Let the child be involved in the care. Children in this age group are afraid of being out of control (Figure 2-5).

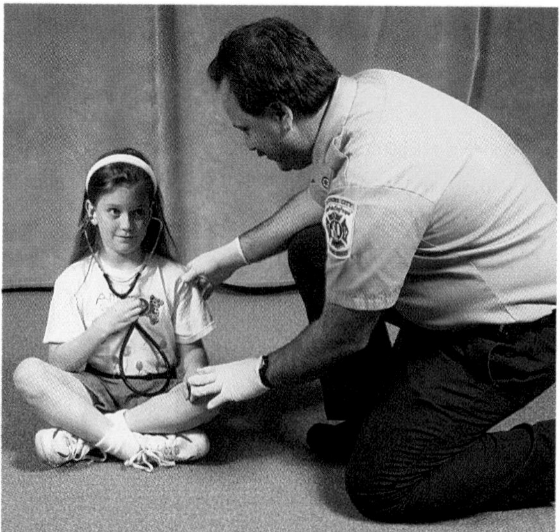

Figure 2-5 Approaching a school-aged child: Let the child be involved in her own care.

- Reassure the child that being ill or injured is not a punishment.
- Praise the child for cooperating. Be careful not to be irritable if he is unable to cooperate.
- The physical assessment can usually be done in the head-to-toe format.

Adolescents

Growth and development characteristics

Adolescents are something like toddlers in that they are very mobile but may lack common sense. Adolescents, however, are more rational, understand cause and effect, and are able to express themselves with words. Adolescence is a time of experimentation and risk-taking behaviors. Adolescents often feel that they are free from danger, that they are "indestructible." They gradually shift from relying on family to relying on friends for psychological support and social development.

Adolescents struggle with independence, loss of control, body image, sexuality, and peer pressure. Anything that makes them different from their peers causes anxiety. **Psychosomatic** complaints are common in this age group. They have mood swings, depression, and occasionally go back to earlier developmental levels. When ill or injured, their maturity level might drop, leaving a scared child in an adult body.

Assessment of the adolescent

Conduct the assessment of the adolescent using the following principles:

- Provide good information about the illness or injury, normal body functions, and **interventions**. Explain what you are doing and why.
- Encourage him to ask questions and to be involved in his own care.
- Show respect. Speak directly to the teen. Do not turn to the caregiver for initial information (Figure 2-6).
- Respect the adolescent's privacy and confidentiality unless it places him at risk.
- Be honest and nonjudgmental.
- Don't be misled by the patient's size, and don't overestimate his intelligence level. He may not be able to understand the seriousness of the situation. Teens may also have many fears about permanent injury, disfigurement, or "being different" as a result of the illness or injury.
- Avoid becoming frustrated or angry if the teen does not talk or is uncooperative.
- Talk to the teen about care and decision making, when appropriate.
- Ask his friends to help comfort or persuade him.

Adolescents struggle with independence, loss of control, body image, sexuality, and peer pressure. Provide concrete information, respect their privacy, and speak to them directly.

Children with Special Health Care Needs

Growth and development characteristics

Children with special health care needs (CSHCN) can be any age. It is important to consider developmental age, rather than chronological age, when working with this population.

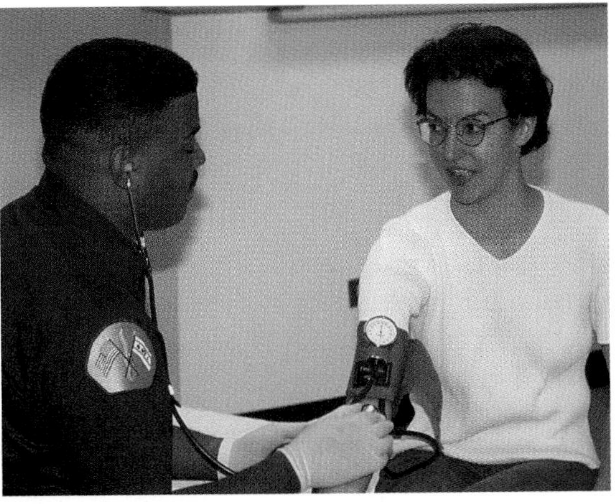

Figure 2-6 Approaching an adolescent: Speak directly to the teen and respect confidentiality.

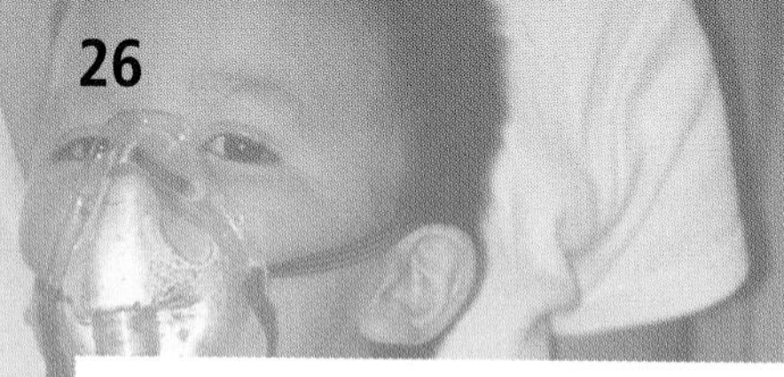

Assessment of a CSHCN

CSHCN are children who have any type of condition that may affect normal growth and development. This may include physical disability, **developmental** or **learning disability**, technologic dependency, and chronic illness. The child who is technology dependent may have a home ventilator, **tracheostomy**, **gastric** feeding tube, or long-term intravenous access device. The developmental or learning disability may include mental retardation, difficulties in communication, sensory impairment, or limitations in physical activity. Chapter 10, on CSHCN, discusses specific categories of patients and methods of assessment and treatment.

Blip

Don't assume that a child with physical disability is cognitively impaired. Always ask the caregiver to clarify the normal level of functioning and interaction of a CSHCN.

Tip

Even if a disabled child cannot talk or interact, show your respect by introducing yourself, explaining what you are doing, and providing verbal reassurance.

The number of children in the community with special needs is growing. Prehospital professionals must be familiar with the conditions and types of technology used in assessing and treating CSHCN. These children may require transport and care for exacerbation of their illness or for an unrelated illness or injury.

Conduct the assessment of the CSHCN using the following principles:

- Get a careful history from the caregiver. He can provide detailed information about the child's medical history, medications, and current complaints. He is also aware of what works best and of typical responses and behaviors.
- Ask the caregiver what he thinks of the child's condition, activity, and behaviors. Find out if the caregiver feels that the child is "not acting right."
- Include the impressions of the caregiver in chart documentation.
- Approach the child with a developmental delay gently and using techniques appropriate to his developmental level, not his chronological age. Use understandable language and techniques to communicate with the child.
- Do not assume that the child with a physical disability is mentally impaired (Figure 2-7). Ask the caregiver about the child's level of functioning, thinking, and interaction with others.
- Use polite, professional behavior, acknowledge the caregivers' expertise, and take their concerns seriously. Families of chronically ill children have usually had extensive experience with the medical system. If most of their experiences have been good, they will very likely perceive the prehospital professional as an ally. However, if they have had bad experiences, they may be difficult or want to be in control.

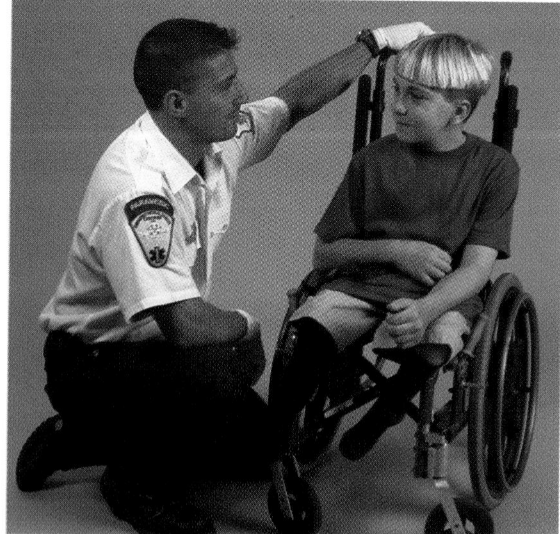

Figure 2-7 Approaching the child with special health care needs: Obtain a thorough history and identify approaches that work best with the child.

- Keep in mind the amount of stress that the caregiver of a CSHCN may be experiencing and be sympathetic.

Summary

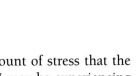

www.PEPPsite.com

Understanding the characteristics of growth and development for each age group is essential to accurate assessment and treatment of the child in the out-of-hospital environment. Good field care requires good communication with the child and family. The family may include a large number of people, which may expand the number of patients being cared for. CSHCN pose additional challenges to performing assessment and care, but the caregivers of CSHCN can be especially important in getting accurate information.

CASE STUDY 3

You are called to the scene of a 16-year-old boy who has rolled his Jeep. He is standing by the vehicle, examining the crumpled front end. He is obviously intoxicated. He becomes immediately hostile when you begin to talk to him. His work of breathing appears normal, and his skin is pink. He starts to cry when he realizes that he is bleeding from a scalp wound and asks you "Am I going to die?"

Is this young man's appearance normal?
What are the special challenges you face in assessing a teen?

Case Study Answers

See page 17

A normal toddler is likely to be afraid of strangers and will cry, try to get away, and seek "safety" in a caregiver's arms when you attempt to do an exam. Hitting, kicking, and biting are not unusual responses to a perceived threat. On the other hand, a toddler who is too quiet and cooperative should concern you.

Observe the toddler's activity, behavior, color, and work of breathing from across the room. Allow the child to remain on his mother's lap for your exam, and sit or squat to get "eye-to-eye" with the patient. Ask the mother to remove his shirt, and observe his chest and abdomen for retractions and respiratory rate. Touch him first on the feet to assess circulation to the skin, then conduct a toe-to-head assessment.

Provide a toy or exam tool, such as a penlight, that he can play with. Allow him to touch the stethoscope before you place it on his chest. Explain what you are going to do in simple terms, remembering that he understands more than he is able to say in words. Praise him when he cooperates with the exam or procedures. Allow the mother to assist with administering oxygen or **nebulizer** therapy.

See page 20

A normal 2-week-old has a very limited range of behaviors. She will spend most of her time sleeping, awaking to feed, and will have only brief "quiet, alert" periods. She will not yet make eye contact or track faces, and cannot differentiate between a parent and a stranger. She should be easily comforted by being cuddled, having her diaper changed, and being fed.

Ask the caregiver how the infant's current activity level compares to normal. Because infants less than 2 months of age have such limited ability to interact with their environment, signs and symptoms of illness may be very subtle. Any infant in this age group who is reported to have been unusually fussy, feeding poorly, sleeping excessively, or having had a fever needs to be seen immediately by a physician.

Regardless of the infant's appearance or current activity level, an infant who has had an episode of loss of consciousness, loss of muscle tone, or change in skin color must be urgently evaluated by a physician. Such an episode is called an apparent life threatening event (ATLE) and may be a sign of underlying infection, heart disease, seizure activity, or head injury. Be prepared to administer oxygen or assist ventilation if the episode occurs again during transport.

See page 27

Adolescents, like toddlers, are mobile and risk taking and tend to believe themselves invulnerable. These characteristics lead them into situations where self-harm may result. Teens have a great fear of losing control and a horror of being "different" from their peers. This may lead them to overestimate the consequences of an illness or injury.

While capable at baseline of sophisticated thought and communication, an ill or injured teen may fall apart, so that you are dealing with a child's emotions packaged in an adult's body. Communicate respect to the teen by speaking to him directly, rather than to his parents. Provide concrete explanations and reassurance, and never belittle the teen for his fears. A hostile, intoxicated, or uncooperative teen can be provocative and a challenge to your ability to maintain a professional attitude. Preparing yourself for this possibility may minimize its impact.

Suggested Educational Resources

1. Engel J, ed. Preparation for examination. In: *Pocket Guide to Pediatric Assessment.* 3rd ed. St. Louis, MO: Mosby–Year Book; 1997: 46–51.

2. Henderson DP, Brownstein D, eds. *Pediatric Emergency Nursing Manual.* New York, NY: Springer Publishing; 1994: 253–293.

3. Seidel JS, Henderson DP. Approach to the pediatric patient in the emergency department. In: Barkin RM, ed. *Pediatric Emergency Medicine: Concepts and Clinical Practice.* 2nd ed. St. Louis, MO: Mosby–Year Book; 1997: 1–7.

Chapter 3

Pediatric

Learning Objectives

1. Summarize the purpose of prearrival mental preparation and scene size-up for pediatric assessment.
2. Differentiate the three elements of the Pediatric Assessment Triangle (PAT).
3. Describe the important pediatric assessment features for each step in the hands-on ABCDE sequence of the initial assessment.
4. Discuss how to decide whether to stay on scene and treat or immediately transport an ill or injured child.
5. Contrast the special anatomic considerations in the focused and detailed exams of a child and an adult.
6. Apply the Pediatric Assessment Triangle, AVPU scale, and other age-appropriate assessment techniques to case studies.

You are called to the home of a 6-month-old boy who has had constant vomiting for 24 hours. The infant is lying still and has poor muscle tone. He is irritable if touched, and his cry is weak. There are no abnormal airway sounds, retractions, or flaring. He is pale and mottled. The respiratory rate is 30 breaths/min, heart rate is 180 beats/min, and blood pressure is 50 mm Hg/palp. Air movement is normal and breath sounds are clear to auscultation. The skin feels cool and capillary refill time is 4 seconds. The brachial pulse is weak. His abdomen is distended.

What are the key signs of illness in this infant?

How helpful are respiratory rate, heart rate, and blood pressure in evaluating cardiopulmonary function?

Assessment

Introduction

Acute assessment of a child with an acute illness or injury requires special knowledge and skills. For patients of all ages, the evaluation includes four steps: (1) pre-arrival preparation; (2) scene size-up; (3) initial assessment; and (4) additional assessment. The initial assessment and additional assessment both have well-defined components that follow the same sequence that the prehospital professional uses for adult patients. However, all four steps in physical assessment have important pediatric modifications.

www.PEPPsite.com

! Tip

On the way to the scene, begin the assessment mentally by preparing for approaching and treating an infant or child and for interacting with a caregiver or family.

Assessment Flowchart

The chapter flowchart reflects the required sequence of pediatric assessment and reinforces the relationships of the different parts of the sequence. In the child with a life- or limb-threatening problem, the focused history and physical exam, and the detailed physical exam are not necessary. Ongoing assessment is required in every case to monitor response to treatment, to guide further interventions and to assist with transport and triage decisions.

Prearrival Preparation

The pediatric assessment begins at the time of the initial dispatch. On the way to the scene, prepare mentally for approaching and treating an infant or child and for interacting with a family. This means planning for a pediatric scene size-up, pediatric equipment requirements, and a pediatric physical assessment. The information from dispatch on age and gender of the child, location of the scene, and chief complaint or mechanism of injury (or both) will help in this important process of prearrival mental preparation.

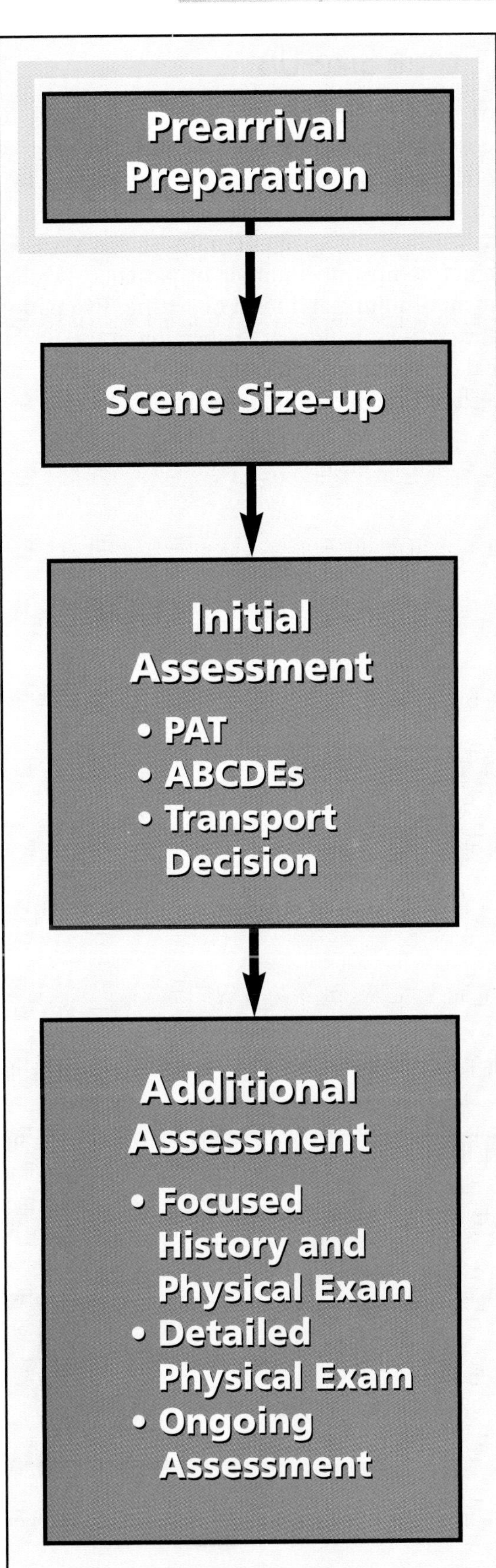

Scene Size-Up

At the scene, begin the size-up by looking for possible safety threats to the child, caregiver, or prehospital professionals. After that, do the environmental assessment. The environmental assessment will give important information on chief complaint, number of patients, mechanism of injury, and kind of setting. Evaluating the setting includes an inspection of the physical environment and watching the family-child and/or caregiver-child interactions.

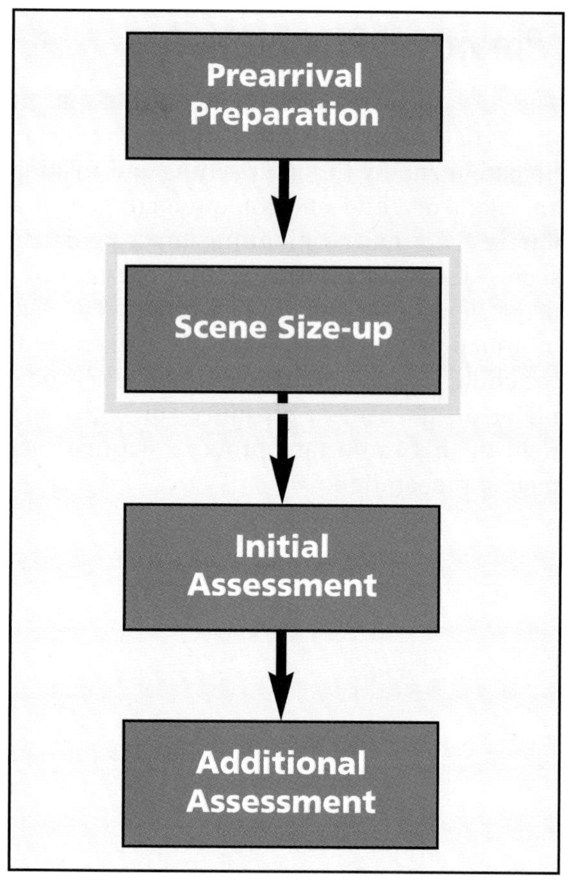

Figure 3-1 **Developing a General Impression: The Pediatric Assessment Triangle (PAT)**

Appearance
Work of Breathing
Circulation to Skin

The three components of the PAT are appearance, work of breathing, and circulation to skin. Together, these physical characteristics provide an excellent picture of the child's underlying cardiopulmonary, neurologic, and metabolic status. While the PAT is not intended to diagnose, it will usually identify the general category of physiologic problem, and establish urgency for treatment and/or transport. The PAT does not replace traditional vital signs and the ABCDEs. It precedes and complements them.

None of the three individual components of the PAT is new or original. Experienced health-care providers instinctively use these characteristics to form their first "general impression" of ill or injured children. What is unique about the PAT is the integrated way that the key physical findings are molded together into a simple and easy-to-remember format.

Use the PAT with every encounter with every child. Over time, it will become a comfortable method of organizing assessment of injured or ill children of all ages.

Initial Assessment

After the scene size-up, begin the initial assessment of the child. The initial assessment must have a developmentally appropriate approach. It has three parts: (1) the visual and auditory general impression (the PAT); (2) the "hands-on" assessment of the ABCDEs; and (3) the transport decision.

Speedy assessment is essential to determine urgency for treatment and transport. For *injury*, the assessment is sometimes straightforward because there is usually a known cause or mechanism of injury, and the child's pain or tissue deformity may identify the problem. The child still needs careful evaluation for less obvious injuries that may be serious and for possible physiologic problems. For *illness*, the assessment may be much trickier. The prehospital professional must find out when the illness began, what the symptoms are, and how long they have lasted. Whether the child has an injury or an illness, the PAT will help to identify physiologic instability. It should also help with resuscitation, general support, specific treatment, and timing of transport.

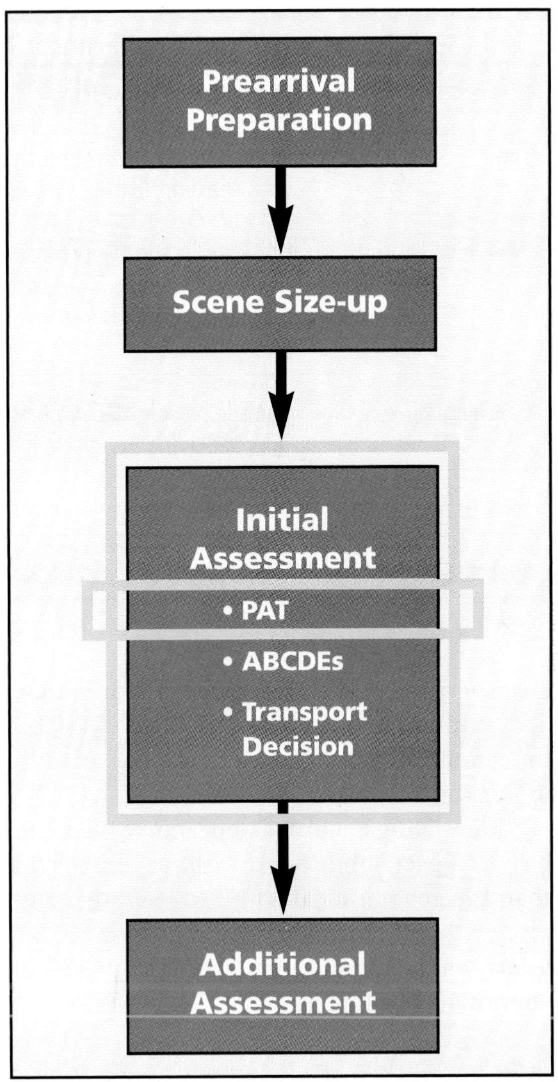

Developing a general impression: The pediatric assessment triangle (PAT)

The PAT is an easy way to do a rapid, initial assessment of any child (Figure 3-1). It allows the prehospital professional, using only visual and auditory clues, to develop a first general impression of the child. By using the PAT at the point of first contact with the patient, the prehospital professional will immediately *establish a level of severity, determine urgency for life support*, and *identify key physiologic problems*. Continued use of the PAT gives the prehospital professional a way to keep track of response to therapy and timing of transport. It also allows for communication among medical professionals and for accurate radio reporting about children.

The three components of the PAT reflect the child's overall physiologic status: (1) appearance, (2) work of breathing, and (3) circulation to skin. It is based on listening and seeing, and does not require a stethoscope, blood pressure cuff, cardiac monitor, or **pulse oximeter**. The PAT can be completed in 30 to 60 seconds. In reality, the PAT is designed to systematize the "across the room assessment"—an intuitive process for experienced pediatric providers.

! Tip

Use the PAT at the point of initial contact with every child, regardless of age or presenting complaint.

Appearance

Characteristics of appearance.

The child's general appearance is the most important thing to consider when determining how severe the illness or injury is, the need for treatment, and the response to therapy. Appearance reflects the adequacy of ventilation, oxygenation, brain **perfusion**, body **homeostasis**, and central nervous system (CNS) function. There are many

Table 3-1 Characteristics of Appearance: The "Tickles" (TICLS) Mnemonic

Characteristic	Features to look for
Tone	Is she moving or resisting examination vigorously? Does she have good muscle tone? Or is she limp, listless, or flaccid?
Interactiveness	How alert is she? How readily does a person, object, or sound distract her or draw her attention? Will she reach for, grasp, and play with a toy or exam instrument, like a penlight or tongue blade? Or is she uninterested in playing or interacting with the caregiver or prehospital professional?
Consolability	Can she be consoled or comforted by the caregiver or by the prehospital professional? Or is her crying or agitation unrelieved by gentle reassurance?
Look/Gaze	Does she fix her gaze on a face? Or is there a "nobody home," glassy-eyed stare?
Speech/Cry	Is her speech or cry strong and spontaneous? Or is it weak, muffled, or hoarse?

characteristics of appearance; the most important are summarized in the "tickles" (TICLS) mnemonic: tone, interactiveness, consolabilty, look/gaze, and speech/cry (Table 3-1).

Identifying abnormal appearance is a better way to detect subtle abnormalities in behavior than the conventional **AVPU scale**. Most children with mild to moderate illness or injury are "alert" on the AVPU, although they may have an abnormal appearance.

! Tip

The elements of the PAT are auditory and visual clues obtained from "across the room" without threatening an anxious child.

In assessing patients with mild to moderate illness or injury, numerical illness and injury "scoring" methodologies and severity scales for levels of consciousness are rarely useful.

Techniques to assess appearance. Assess the child's appearance from the doorway. This is Step 1 in the PAT. Techniques for assessment of a conscious child's appearance include observing from a distance, allowing the child to remain in the caregiver's lap or arms, using distractions such as bright lights or toys to measure interactiveness, and kneeling down to be on eye level with the child. An immediate "hands-on" approach may cause agitation and crying, and may confuse the assessment. Unless a child is unconscious or obviously critically ill, get as much information as possible by observing the child *before* touching the child or taking vital signs.

One example of a child with a normal appearance might be an infant with good muscle tone, good eye contact, and good color (Figure 3-2). An example of an infant with a worrisome appearance might be a toddler who makes poor eye contact with the caregiver or prehospital professional and is pale and listless (Figure 3-3).

Abnormal appearance may be due to lack of oxygen, ventilation, or brain perfusion. It may be the result of systemic problems such as poisoning, infection, or hypoglycemia. In another child, it may be due to acute brain injury from **hemorrhage** or **edema**, or to chronic brain injury from **shaken baby syndrome**. Regardless of what might be the cause, a grossly abnormal appearance establishes that the child is seriously ill or injured. Immediately begin life support efforts to increase oxygenation, ventilation, and perfusion while completing the hands-on ABCDE assessment.

While an alert, interactive child is usually *not* critically ill, there are some cases where a child may be critically ill or injured without looking that way.

Toxicologic or traumatic emergencies are good examples:

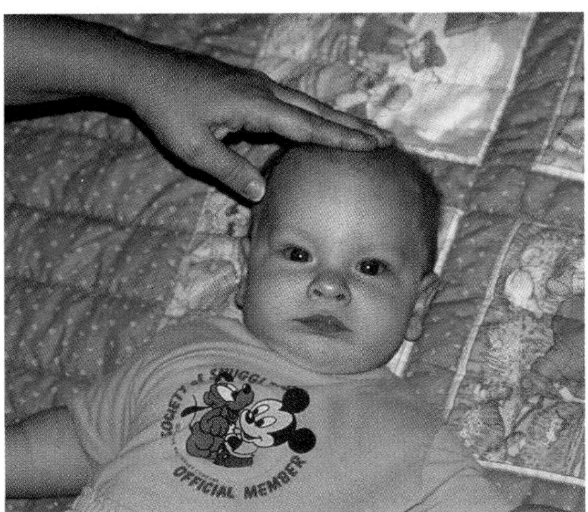

Figure 3-2 A child making good eye contact is not very sick.

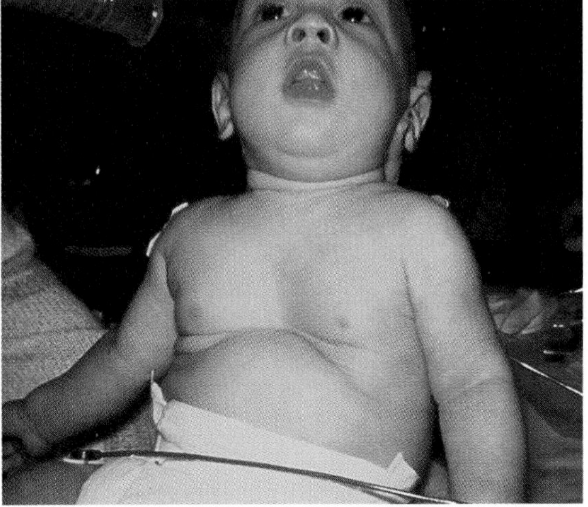

Figure 3-3 A limp, pale child unable to make eye contact or a child with retractions may be critically ill or injured.

1. A child with a dangerous intoxication, such as from **acetaminophen**, iron, or **cyclic antidepressants**, may not show symptoms immediately after ingestion. Despite her normal appearance, she may develop deadly complications in the coming minutes or hours.
2. A child with blunt trauma may be able to maintain adequate core perfusion despite internal bleeding by increasing cardiac output and systemic vascular resistance and may appear normal. When these compensatory mechanisms fail, she may acutely "crash," with rapid progression to decompensated shock.

A benign appearance should never justify a denial of transport. However, a normal appearance usually means that "lights and siren" are not necessary.

Age differences are associated with important developmental differences in psychomotor and social skills. Therefore, "normal" or expected appearance and behavior varies by age group, as discussed in Chapter 2. Children of all ages engage their environment. For newborns, this occurs by energetic sucking and crying. For older infants, it occurs through smiling or tracking a light. For toddlers, it is by exploring and touching their surroundings. And for most adolescents, it is by talking. Knowing what normal development is for children of different age groups will guide the approach to children of all ages and will result in more accurate judgments about appearances.

While appearance reflects real illness or injury, it does not always show the *cause* of injury or illness. Appearance is the "screening" portion of the PAT. The other elements of the PAT—work of breathing and circulation to skin—provide more specific information about the physiologic derangement. They help to show the likely cause of system dysfunction while also providing additional clues about *severity*.

! Tip

The child's general *appearance* is the single most important feature when assessing severity of illness or injury, need for treatment, and response to therapy.

While an alert, interactive child is usually *not* critically ill, there are some exceptions to the reliability of general appearance as an indicator of stable cardiopulmonary and neurologic function.

Work of breathing

Characteristics of work of breathing. **Work of breathing** *is a more accurate quick indicator of oxygenation and ventilation than respiratory rate or chest sounds on auscultation*—the traditional measures of breathing in adults. Work of breathing reflects the child's attempt to make up for difficulties in oxygenation and ventilation. Assessing work of breathing requires listening carefully for abnormal airway sounds and looking for

Table 3-2 Characteristics of Work of Breathing

Characteristic	Features to look for
Abnormal airway sounds	Snoring, muffled or hoarse speech, stridor, grunting, wheezing
Abnormal positioning	Sniffing position, tripoding, refusing to lie down
Retractions	Supraclavicular, intercostal, or substernal retractions of the chest wall; head bobbing in infants
Flaring	Nasal flaring

signs of increased breathing effort. It is another "hands-off" evaluation method. Table 3-2 summarizes the key characteristics of work of breathing.

Abnormal airway sounds. Examples of abnormal airway sounds that can be heard without a stethoscope are snoring, muffled or hoarse speech, stridor, grunting, and wheezing. Abnormal airway sounds provide excellent anatomic and physiologic information about breathing effort and type and anatomic location of the breathing problem. Snoring, muffled or hoarse speech, and stridor suggest *upper airway obstruction*. Snoring, or gurgling, occurs if the **oropharynx** is partially obstructed by the tongue and soft tissues. Altered speech is an expiratory sound when the child attempts to talk. **Stridor** is an inspiratory, high-pitched sound. These abnormal sounds reflect abnormal airflow across partially obstructed upper airway structures, such as the oropharynx, **vocal cords**, **trachea**, or **bronchi**. Obstruction of upper airway passages can occur in a variety of illnesses and injuries, including **croup**, foreign body **aspiration**, and bacterial upper airway infections, or as a result of bleeding or edema.

! Tip

Abnormal airway sounds provide excellent anatomic and physiologic information about breathing effort, type and anatomic location of the breathing problem, and degree of hypoxia.

Grunting is a way to keep lower respiratory air sacs or **alveoli** open for maximum gas exchange. Grunting involves exhaling against a partially closed **glottis**. This short, low-pitched sound is best heard at the end of the exhalation. Grunting is often present in children with moderate to severe hypoxia, and it reflects poor gas exchange because of fluid in the lower airways and air sacs. Conditions that cause hypoxia and grunting are **pneumonia**, **pulmonary contusion** (bruising of the lungs), and **pulmonary edema** (fluid in air sacs).

Wheezing is the movement of air across partially blocked small airways. At first, wheezing may occur during **exhalation** and can be heard only by auscultation. As the airway obstruction increases and breathing requires more work, wheezing is present during both inhalation and exhalation. With more obstruction, wheezing is audible without a stethoscope. Finally, if respiratory failure develops, work of breathing may diminish and the wheezing may not be heard at all. The most common cause of wheezing is **asthma**, although **bronchiolitis** and lower airway foreign body aspiration can also cause it.

Visual signs. There are several useful visual signs of increased work of breathing. These signs reflect increased breathing effort by the child to improve oxygenation and ventilation. The presence or absence of certain physical features shows how severe the overall illness or injury is. Examples of visual signs are abnormal positioning, retractions, and nasal flaring.

Abnormal positioning is immediately evident from the doorway. There are several types of posture that show the child's efforts to increase airflow. A child who is in the **sniffing position** is trying to line up the axes of the airways to open the airway and increase airflow. This position is

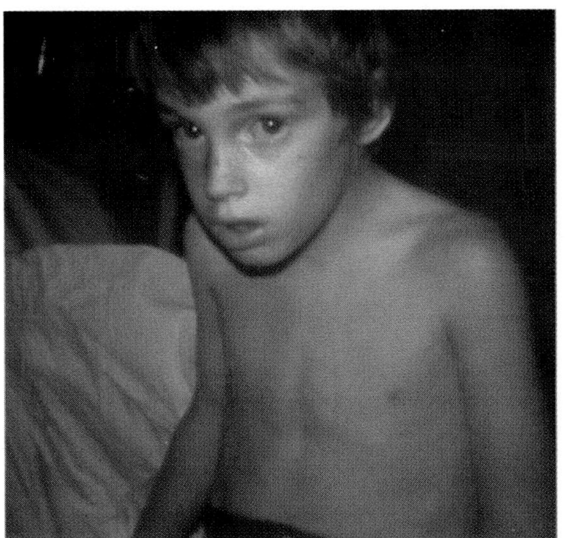

Figure 3-4 The sniffing position is an abnormal position and reflects upper airway obstruction.

usually the result of severe upper airway obstruction (Figure 3-4). The child who refuses to lie down or who leans forward on outstretched arms (**tripoding**) is trying to use accessory muscles to improve breathing (Figure 3-5). The sniffing position and tripoding are abnormal and indicate increased work of breathing and severe respiratory distress.

Retractions are physical signs of increased work of breathing. They represent use of accessory muscles to help breathing. Retractions are easily missed. The prehospital professional must look specifically for them after the child is properly exposed. Retractions are a more useful measure of work of breathing in children than in adults. This is true because a child's chest wall is less muscular and thinner, and the inward excursion of skin and soft tissue between the ribs is visually more apparent. Retractions are a sign that the child is using extra muscle power to move air into the lungs. They may be in the **supraclavicular** area (above the clavicle), the **intercostal** area (between the ribs), or the **substernal** area (under the sternum), as illustrated in Figure 3-6. One form of retractions that is seen in infants is **head bobbing**—the use of neck muscles to help breathing during severe hypoxia. The child extends the neck as she inhales, then allows the head to fall forward as she exhales.

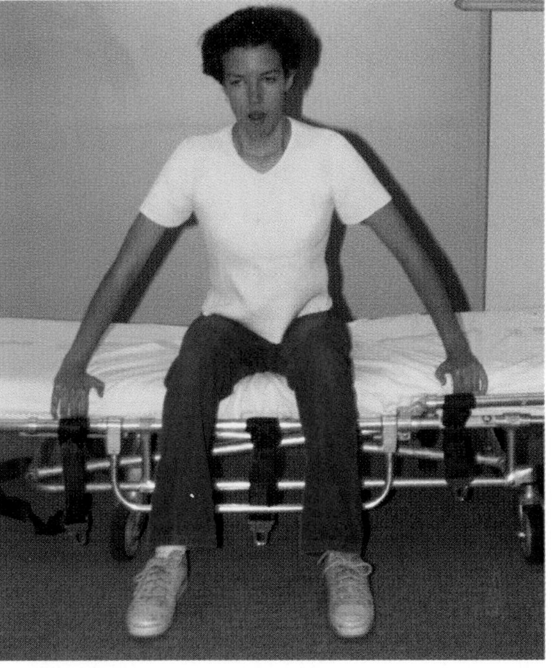

Figure 3-5 The abnormal tripod position indicates the patient's attempts to maximize accessory muscle use.

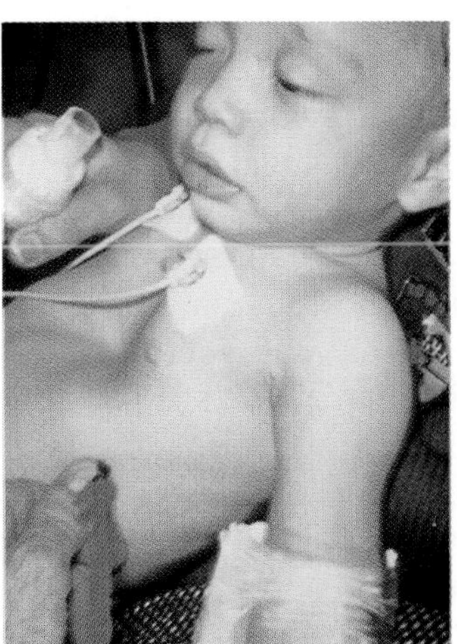

Figure 3-6 Retractions indicate increased work of breathing and may occur in the supraclavicular, intercostal, and substernal areas.

Nasal flaring is another form of accessory muscle use that reflects significantly increased work of breathing (Figure 3-7). **Flaring** is the exaggerated opening of the nostrils during labored inspiration and indicates moderate to severe hypoxia. The prehospital professional must inspect the face specifically to detect flaring.

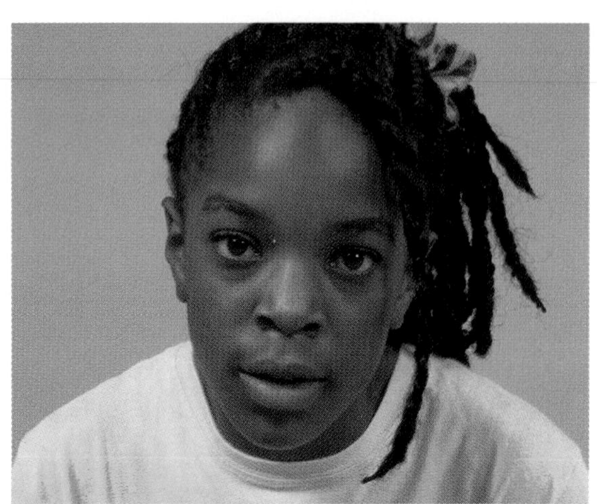

Figure 3-7 Nasal flaring indicates increased work of breathing and moderate to severe hypoxia.

! Tip

Head bobbing is a form of retractions or accessory muscle use that is specific to infants.

Techniques to assess work of breathing. Step 2 in the PAT is assessing work of breathing. Begin by listening carefully from a distance for abnormal airway sounds then looking for key physical signs. From the doorway, try to hear abnormal airway sounds. Then, note if the child has abnormal positioning, especially the sniffing posture or tripoding. Next, have the caregiver uncover the chest of the child for direct inspection or have the child undress on the caregiver's lap. Look for intercostal, supraclavicular, and substernal retractions and note if there is head bobbing in infants. After examining for retractions, inspect for nasal flaring.

Children may have increased work of breathing because of abnormalities anywhere in their airways, air sacs, **pleura**, or chest wall. However, assessing these auditory and visual characteristics together helps to show the type of problem and the degree of distress. *The type of abnormal airway sound gives an important clue to the anatomic location of the illness or injury process, whereas the number and type of visual signs of increased work of breathing helps in determining the degree of physiologic stress.*

Combining assessment of appearance and work of breathing can also help establish the severity of the child's illness or injury. A child with normal appearance and increased work of breathing is in respiratory distress. Abnormal appearance and increased work of breathing suggests respiratory failure. Abnormal appearance and abnormally decreased work of breathing implies impending respiratory arrest.

Circulation to skin

Characteristics of circulation to skin. The goal of rapid circulatory assessment is to determine the adequacy of cardiac output and core perfusion, or perfusion of vital organs. The child's appearance is one indicator of brain perfusion, but abnormal appearance may be caused by conditions other than decreased core perfusion. For this reason, other signs of perfusion must be added to the evaluation of appearance to assess the child's circulatory condition.

An important sign of core perfusion is circulation to skin. When cardiac output is too low, the body shuts down circulation to nonessential anatomic areas such as skin and mucous membranes in order to preserve blood supply to the most vital organs (brain, heart, and kidneys). Therefore, circulation to skin reflects the overall status of core circulation. Pallor, mottling, and cyanosis are key visual indicators of reduced circulation to skin and

Table 3-3 Characteristics of Circulation to Skin

Characteristic	Features to look for
Pallor	White or pale skin or mucous membrane coloration from inadequate blood flow
Mottling	Patchy skin discoloration due to vasoconstriction
Cyanosis	Bluish discoloration of skin and mucous membranes

mucous membranes. Table 3-3 summarizes these characteristics.

Pallor may be the first sign of poor skin or mucous membrane perfusion and may be present in compensated shock. It may also be a sign of anemia or hypoxia. **Mottling** is caused by constriction of blood vessels to the skin and is another sign of poor perfusion (Figure 3-8).

Cyanosis is blue discoloration of the skin and mucous membranes. Do not confuse **acrocyanosis**—or blue hands and feet in a newborn or infant less than 2 months of age—with true cyanosis. Acrocyanosis is a normal finding when a young infant is cold, and it reflects **vasomotor** instability rather than hypoxia or **shock**. True cyanosis is a late finding of respiratory failure or shock. A hypoxic child is likely to show other physical abnormalities long before turning blue. These abnormalities may include abnormal appearance with agitation or lethargy and increased work of breathing. A child in shock will also have pallor or mottling. Never wait for cyanosis to begin care with supplemental oxygen. *Cyanosis is always a critical sign that requires immediate intervention with breathing support.*

Abnormal circulation to skin in combination with abnormal appearance suggests shock. However, the abnormal appearance in early compensated shock may be subtle. Some children may seem remarkably alert. However, careful observation will detect at least mild abnormalities, such as restlessness or listlessness. Another clue for the presence of shock is **tachypnea** without signs of increased work of breathing; this is called **effortless tachypnea**, and represents the child's attempt to blow off extra carbon dioxide to correct the **acidosis** generated by poor perfusion. Effortless tachypnea is different from the rapid and labored respirations and increased work of breathing that are present with illnesses and injuries associated with primary oxygenation and ventilation problems.

Techniques to assess circulation to skin. Step 3 in the PAT is evaluating circulation to skin. Be sure the child is exposed enough for visual inspection, but not cold. Cold may cause false skin signs. In other words, the cold child may have normal core perfusion, but abnormal circulation to skin. *Cold circulating air temperature is the most common reason for misinterpretation of skin signs.*

Inspect the skin and mucous membranes for pallor, mottling, and cyanosis. Look at the face, chest, abdomen, and extremities. Then, inspect the lips for cyanosis. In dark skinned children, circulation to skin is sometimes more difficult to assess. The lips and mucous membranes in the mouth may be the best places to look.

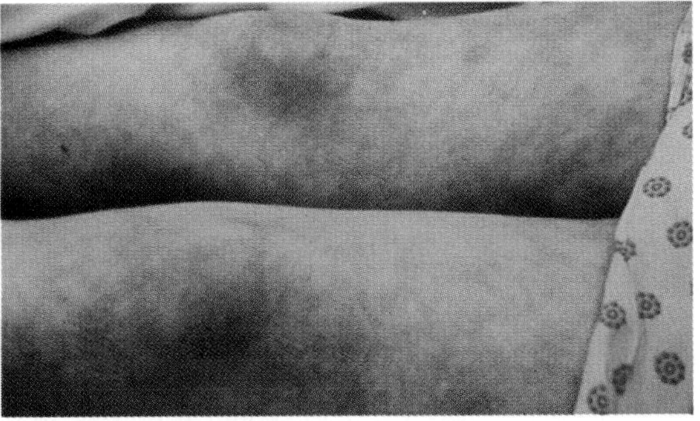
Figure 3-8 Mottling is the result of constriction of blood vessels to the skin and may indicate poor perfusion.

! Tip

By combining the three components of the PAT, the prehospital professional can answer two critical questions: (1) How sick or injured is the child? and (2) What is the most likely physiologic abnormality?

Using the PAT to evaluate severity and illness or injury. By combining the three components of the PAT, the prehospital professional can answer two critical questions: (1) How severe is the child's illness or injury? and (2) What is the most likely physiologic abnormality? This information will help the prehospital professional select her most important actions: how fast to intervene and what type of general and specific treatment to give.

The three elements of the PAT work together and allow rapid assessment of the child's *overall* physiologic stability. For example, if a child is interactive and pink, but has mild intercostal retractions, the prehospital professional can take time to approach the child in a developmentally appropriate manner to complete the initial assessment. On the other hand, if the child is limp, with unlabored rapid breathing and pale or mottled skin, shock is likely. In this case, the prehospital professional can move rapidly through the initial assessment, and begin resuscitation based on the ABCDEs, because abnormal appearance and decreased circulation to skin means shock. A child who has abnormal appearance, but normal work of breathing and normal circulation to skin, probably has a primary brain dysfunction or a major metabolic or systemic problem, such as **postictal** state, **subdural hemorrhage**, brain **concussion**, intoxication, hypoglycemia, or sepsis.

Blip

Never ignore the pale infant, the "nobody home stare," or the infant who doesn't respond appropriately to stimulation.

The PAT has two important advantages. First, it lets the examiner quickly get critical information about the child's physiologic status before touching or agitating the child. This is important because it may be difficult to identify abnormal appearance, increased work of breathing, or decreased circulation to skin when a child is agitated and crying. Second, the PAT helps set priorities for the rest of the hands-on initial assessment. The PAT only takes seconds, it identifies need for life-saving interventions, and it blends into the next phase of hands-on physical assessment.

The three components of PAT—appearance, work of breathing, and circulation to skin—can be assessed in any order. Unlike the PAT, the ABCDEs of resuscitation discussed below must be done in a specific order.

Assessing the pediatric ABCDEs

The initial assessment has two main parts: the general impression, or PAT, and the hands-on physical assessment of the ABCDEs. The PAT provides the general impression of the pediatric patient. The PAT uses pediatric-specific observations in combination with the scene size-up and chief complaint to evaluate the efficacy of cardiopulmonary function, to establish a level of severity, and to determine urgency for care. The intent is to provide an objective overview of the child and an instant picture of the child's physiologic status.

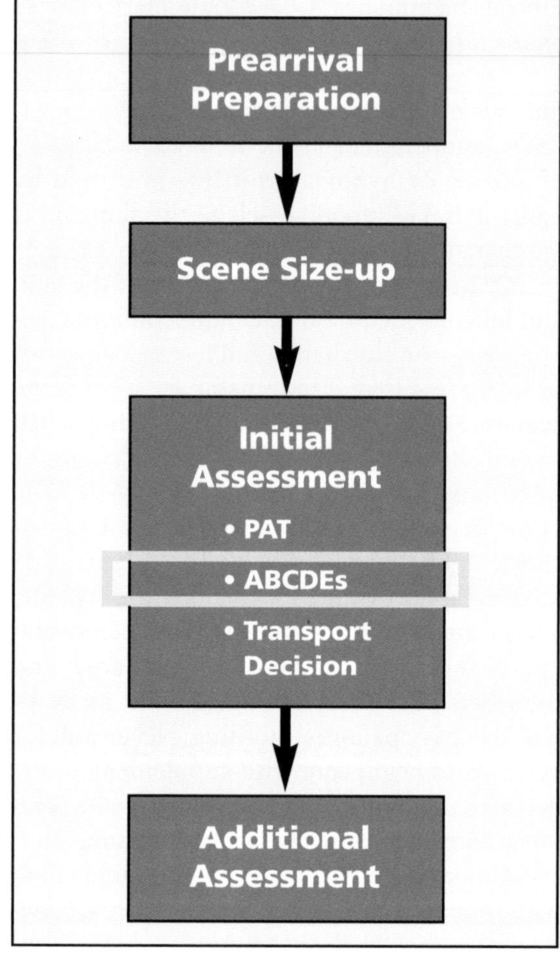

The second part of the initial assessment is an ordered, hands-on, first physical evaluation of the ABCDEs. It provides a prioritized sequence of life-support interventions to reverse organ failure. As in adults, there is a specific order for treating life-threatening problems as they are identified, before moving to the next step. The steps are the same as with adults, but there are important pediatric differences in anatomy, physiology, and signs of distress. ABCDE assessment involves the following components:

1. Airway
2. Breathing
3. Circulation
4. Disability
5. Exposure

Airway

The PAT will usually identify the presence of airway obstruction. However, the loudness of the stridor or wheezing is not necessarily related to the amount of airway obstruction. For example, asthmatic children in severe distress may have little or no wheezing. Similarly, children with an upper airway foreign body below the vocal cords may have minimal stridor. Abnormal airway sounds tell whether there is *any* amount of upper or lower airway obstruction.

If the airway is open, ensure that there is chest rise with breathing. If gurgling is present, this means there is mucus, blood, or a foreign body in the mouth or airway.

Breathing

Respiratory rate. Determine the respiratory rate per minute by counting the number of chest rises in 30 seconds, then doubling that number. *Interpret the respiratory rate carefully.* Normal infants may show "periodic breathing," or stopping and starting breathing for less than 20 seconds. Therefore, only counting for 10 to 15 seconds may obtain a respiratory rate that is too low.

Respiratory rates may be difficult to interpret. Rapid respiratory rates may simply reflect high fever, anxiety, pain, or excitement. Normal rates, on the other hand, may occur in a child who has been breathing rapidly with increased work of breathing for some time and is now becoming fatigued. Finally, interpret respiratory rate based on what is normal for age. Table 3-4 shows the range of normal respiratory rate for age.

Several recorded respiratory rates may be especially useful and the trend is sometimes more accurate than the first documented respiratory rate. A sustained increase or decrease in respiratory rate is often significant. Use respiratory rate in conjunction with other information about breathing.

Pay close attention to extremes of respiratory rate. A very *rapid* respiratory rate (more than 60 breaths/min for any age), especially with abnormal appearance or marked retractions, indicates respiratory distress and possibly respiratory failure. An abnormally *slow* respiratory rate is always worrisome because it might mean respiratory failure. Red flags are respiratory rates of less than 20 breaths/min for children under 6 years old and of less than 15 breaths/min for children under 15 years old. A normal respiratory rate alone never determines that there is adequate oxygenation and ventilation. The respiratory rate must be interpreted with appearance, work of breathing, and air movement.

Cold may cause falsely positive skin signs that look like signs of shock.

Auscultation. Listen with a stethoscope over the **midaxillary** line to hear abnormal lung sounds, in inhalation and exhalation, such as **crackles** and

Table 3-4 Normal Respiratory Rate for Age

Age	Respiratory Rate (breaths/min)
Infant	30–60
Toddler	24–40
Preschooler	22–34
School-aged child	18–30
Adolescent	12–16

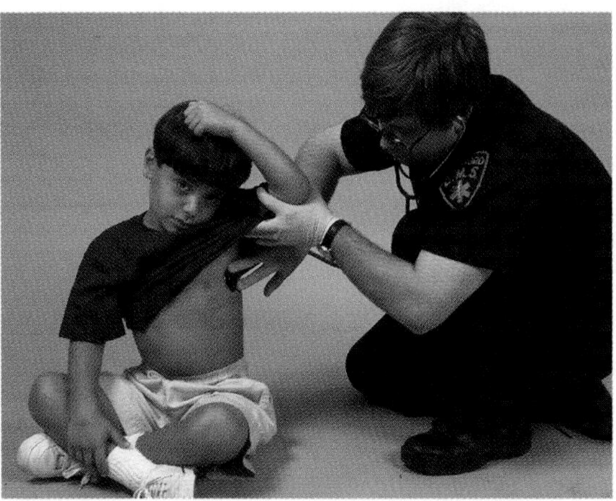

Figure 3-9 Listen for air movement over the midaxillary line.

Table 3-5 Interpretation of Abnormal Breath Sounds

Sound	Cause	Examples
Stridor	Upper airway obstruction	Croup, foreign body aspiration, retropharyngeal abscess
Wheezing	Lower airway obstruction	Asthma, foreign body, bronchiolitis
Expiratory grunting	Inadequate oxygenation	Pulmonary contusion, pneumonia, drowning
Inspiratory crackles	Fluid, mucus, or blood in the airway	Pneumonia, pulmonary contusion
Absent breath sounds despite increased work of breathing	Complete airway obstruction (upper or lower airway) Physical barrier to transmission of breath sounds	Foreign body, severe asthma, hemothorax, pneumothorax Pleural fluid, pneumonia, pneumothorax

wheezing (Figure 3-9). Inspiratory crackles indicate disease in the air sacs themselves. Expiratory wheezing points to lower airway obstruction. Also evaluate air movement and effectiveness of work of breathing. A child with increased work of breathing and poor air movement may be in impending respiratory failure.

Table 3-5 lists abnormal breath sounds, their causes, and common examples of associated disease processes.

! Tip

Rapid respiratory rates may simply reflect high fever, anxiety, pain, or excitement and not any real physiologic or anatomic problem.

Oxygen saturation. After determining the respiratory rate and performing auscultation, obtain **pulse oximetry**. Pulse oximetry is an excellent tool to use in assessing a child's breathing (Figure 3-10a). Figure 3-10b illustrates the technique of placing a pulse oximetry probe on a young child. A pulse oximetry reading above 94% saturation indicates that oxygenation is probably good. A reading below 90% in a child on 100% oxygen by nonrebreathing mask is an indication for assisted ventilation. Be careful not to underestimate respiratory distress in a child with a reading above 94%. A

CASE STUDY 2

A young mother calls 911 because her 11-month-old daughter awoke fussy, and she thinks the child has "infection on her brain." A cousin had been hospitalized in the last few days with that condition, she tells you.

When you arrive, the child is standing, screaming in the crib. The mother is anxious and demanding immediate hospitalization for the child. The infant turns pink and becomes agitated whenever you approach. There are no abnormal airway sounds, retractions, or flaring. The respiratory rate is 50 breaths/min, and she vigorously fights when you touch her to perform the physical assessment. You are unable to obtain a heart rate or blood pressure.

How useful is the Pediatric Assessment Triangle (PAT) in evaluating severity of illness and urgency for care?

Is the PAT different than the ABCDEs in the initial assessment?

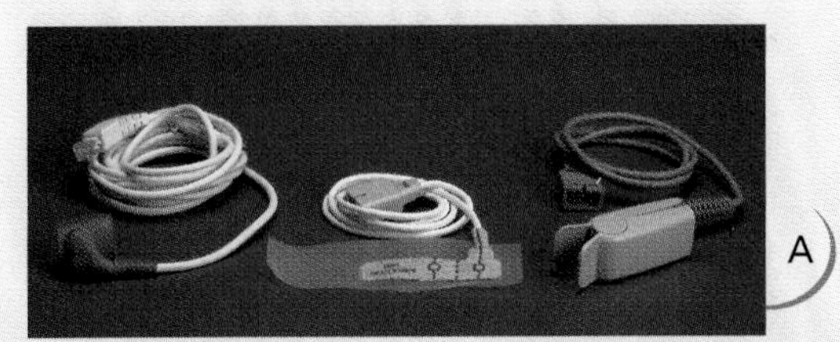

Table 3-6 Normal Heart Rate for Age

Age	Heart Rate (beats/min)
Infant	100–160
Toddler	90–150
Preschooler	80–140
School-aged child	70–120
Adolescent	60–100

child in respiratory distress or early respiratory failure may maintain her oxygen level by increasing work of breathing and respiratory rate. This child may not appear to be ill by pulse oximetry alone. *Interpret pulse oximetry together with work of breathing.*

Circulation

The PAT provides important visual clues about circulation to skin. Add to these observations with more information from the hands-on evaluation of heart rate, pulse quality, skin temperature, capillary refill time, and blood pressure.

Heart rate. Guidelines often used to assess adult circulatory status—heart rate and blood pressure—have important limitations in children. First, normal heart rate varies with age, as noted in Table 3-6. Second, tachycardia may be an early sign of hypoxia or low perfusion, but it may also reflect less serious conditions such as fever, anxiety, pain, and excitement. Like respiratory rate, heart rate should be interpreted within the overall history, PAT, and entire initial assessment. A trend of increasing or decreasing heart rate may be quite useful, and may suggest worsening hypoxia or shock, or improvement after treatment. When hypoxia or shock becomes critical, heart rate falls, leading to frank bradycardia. **Bradycardia** means critical hypoxia and/or ischemia. When the heart rate is above 180 beats/min, an electronic monitor is necessary to accurately determine heart rate.

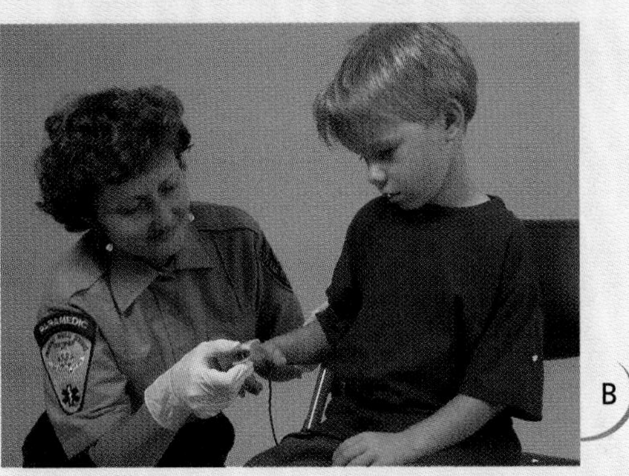

Figure 3-10 (A) Various pulse oximeter probes wrap around or clip onto a digit or earlobe. (B) Pulse oximetry is an excellent tool for assessing the effectiveness of breathing.

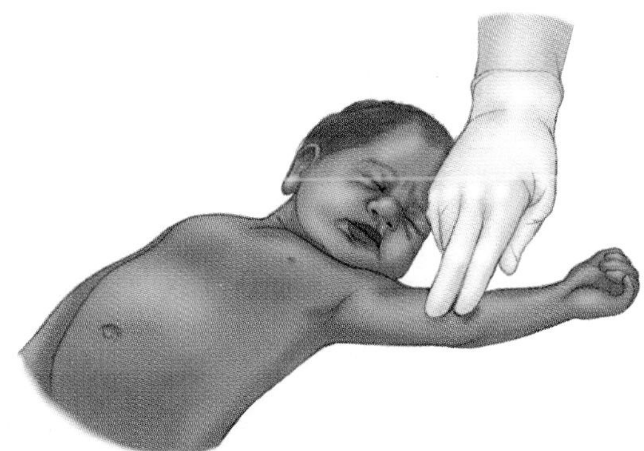

Figure 3-11 The anatomic position of the brachial pulse is medial to the biceps muscle.

Pulse quality. Feel the pulse to obtain heart rate. Normally, the brachial pulse is palpable inside or medial to the biceps (Figure 3-11). Note the quality as either weak or strong. *If the brachial pulse is strong, the*

Be careful not to underestimate respiratory distress in a child with a pulse oximetry reading above 94%.

Figure 3-12 (A) There are several different BP cuff sizes: neonatal, infant, child, and adult. (B) To obtain an accurate BP reading, use a cuff that is two-thirds the length of the child's upper arm.

! Tip

Interpret heart rate in the context of the overall history, PAT, and entire initial assessment.

? Controversy

The value of capillary refill time is controversial. Peripheral perfusion may be variable in some children, and environmental factors such as ambient temperature may have a strong influence on capillary refill time.

child is probably not hypotensive. If a peripheral pulse cannot be felt, attempt to find a central pulse. Check the femoral pulse in infants and young children, or the carotid pulse in an older child or adolescent. If no pulse is felt, listen for heart tones with a stethoscope over the heart, then count heart rate. Absence of a central pulse is an indication for CPR.

Skin temperature and capillary refill time. Next, do a hands-on evaluation of circulation to skin. Feel if the skin is warm or cool. With enough perfusion, the child's skin should be warm near the wrists and ankles. With decreasing perfusion, the line of separation from cool to warm advances up the limb.

Check capillary refill time at the kneecap or forearm. These are good anatomic locations to feel for capillary refill time. Be sure the child is not cold from exposure, because skin signs will be deceptive. Normal capillary refill time is less than 2 to 3 seconds. The value of capillary refill time is controversial. Peripheral perfusion may vary in some children, and environmental factors such as cold room temperature may affect capillary refill time. Also, it may be difficult for the prehospital professional to accurately count seconds under critical circumstances. The capillary refill time is just one element of the assessment of circulation. It must be evaluated in the context of the PAT and other perfusion characteristics such as heart rate, pulse quality, and blood pressure.

Signs of circulation to the skin (skin temperature, capillary refill time, and pulse quality) are tools to assess a child's circulatory status, *especially when performed consecutively on a child who is not cold.*

Blood pressure. Blood pressure determination and interpretation may be difficult in children because of lack of patient cooperation, confusion about proper cuff size, and problems remembering normal values for age. Figure 3-12a depicts the different sizes of blood pressure cuffs, and Figure 3-12b demonstrates the technique for getting a correct blood pressure in the arm or thigh. Always use a cuff with a width of two thirds the length of the upper arm or thigh. *For patients 3 years of age or less, technical difficulties reduce the value of a blood pressure in the field.* When shock is suspected in this age group based on other guidelines (e.g., history, mechanism, PAT), consider attempting blood pressure once on scene, but do not delay treatment or transport. For a child older than 3, always try once.

Blood pressure may be misleading. Although a low blood pressure definitely indicates decompensated shock, a "normal" blood pressure *frequently* exists in children with compensated shock. For children above one year of age, an

Table 3-7 Normal Blood Pressure for Age

Age	Minimal Systolic Blood Pressure (mm Hg)
Infant (birth–12 mos)	>60
Toddler (1–3)	>70
Preschooler	>75
School-aged child	>80
Adolescent	>90

easy formula for determining the lower limit of acceptable blood pressure by age is: minimal systolic blood pressure = 70 + 2 × age (in years). For example, a 2-year-old toddler with a systolic blood pressure of 65 mm Hg is probably in decompensated shock. Table 3-7 shows approximate normal systolic blood pressure for age. High blood pressure is not a clinical problem for children in the field.

Disability

Assessment of disability or neurologic status involves quick evaluation of two main parts of the central nervous system: the **cerebral cortex** and the **brain stem**. Assess neurologic status (controlled by the cortex) by looking at appearance as part of the PAT and at level of consciousness with the AVPU scale (Table 3-8). Evaluate the brain stem by checking the responses of each pupil to a direct beam of light. A normal pupil constricts after a light stimulus. Pupillary response may be abnormal in the presence of drugs, ongoing seizures, hypoxia, or impending brain stem herniation. Next, evaluate motor activity. Look for symmetrical movement of the extremities, seizures, posturing, or flaccidity.

AVPU scale. The AVPU scale is a conventional way of assessing level of consciousness in all patients. It categorizes motor response based on simple responses to stimuli. The patient is either alert, responsive to verbal stimuli, responsive only to painful stimuli, or unresponsive.

For patients less than 3 years of age, there is little value in obtaining a blood pressure in the field.

Abnormal appearance and the AVPU scale. The PAT and the AVPU scale are not the same. A child with altered level of consciousness on the AVPU scale will always have abnormal appearance in the PAT. Assessing appearance using the PAT may give an earlier indication of the presence of illness and injury. A child with a mild to moderate illness or injury

Do not depend on blood pressure readings. A "normal" blood pressure *frequently* exists in compensated shock.

Table 3-8 AVPU Scale

Category	Stimulus	Response Type	Reaction
Alert	Normal environment	Appropriate	Normal interactiveness for age
Verbal	Simple command or sound stimulus	Appropriate Inappropriate	Responds to name Nonspecific or confused
Painful	Pain	Appropriate Inappropriate Pathological	Withdraws from pain Sound or motion without purpose or localization of pain Posturing
Unresponsive	No perceptible response to any stimulus		

may be alert on the AVPU scale but have abnormal appearance.

The application of the AVPU scale is controversial. It has not been well tested for effectiveness in children. However, there is no other easy way to assess disability in children in the field. The more complicated Pediatric Glasgow Coma Scale for neurologic injury, involves memorization and numerical scoring—tasks that may be hard to accomplish in critical situations.

Exposure

Proper exposure of the child is necessary for completing the initial physical assessment. The PAT requires that the caregiver remove part of the child's clothing to allow careful observation of the face, chest wall, and skin. Completing the ABCDE components of the initial assessment requires further exposure, as needed, to fully evaluate physiologic function and anatomic abnormalities. Be careful to avoid rapid heat loss, especially in a cold environment with infants and children.

Summary of initial assessment

The initial assessment includes the general impression and the hands-on physical assessment of the ABCDEs. The pediatric assessment triangle (PAT) is the basis for the general impression. It includes characteristics of appearance, work of breathing, and circulation to skin, and uses listening and looking clues obtained from across the room. The rest of the initial assessment includes an evaluation of pediatric specific indicators of cardiopulmonary or neurologic abnormalities. Although vital signs can be useful in the initial assessment, they can also be misleading. They must be examined carefully and looked at together with other parts of the initial assessment. Interventions may be necessary at any point in the ABCDE sequence.

The transport decision: Stay or go?

After completing the initial physical assessment and beginning resuscitation, the prehospital professional must make a crucial decision: Should she immediately transport the child to the ED, or should she continue with additional assessment and treatment on scene? This decision process will be different for each child and for each EMS system.

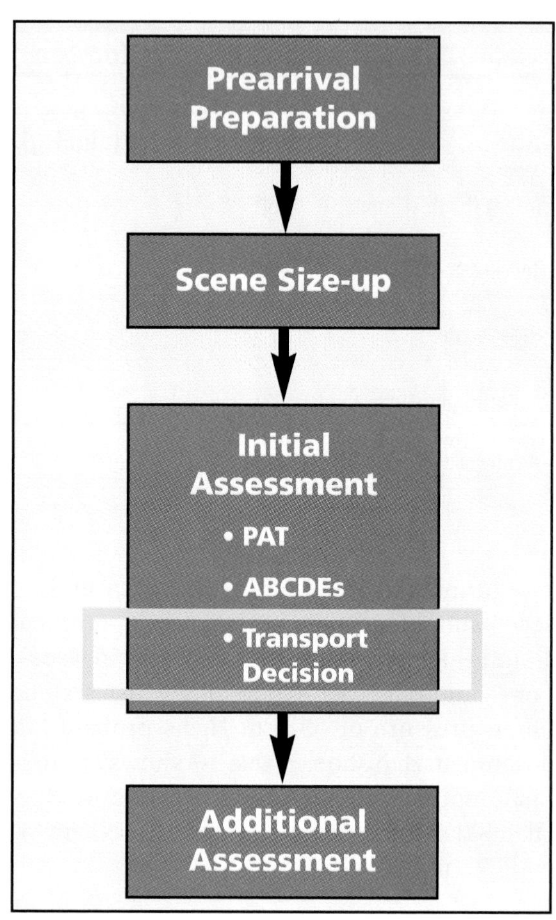

In a BLS system, field treatment options are limited. A request for ALS backup or early transport is appropriate if the scene is unsafe for the child, caregiver, or prehospital professional or when a child has:

- a serious mechanism of injury
- a history compatible with serious illness
- a physiologic abnormality noted on initial assessment
- a potentially serious anatomic abnormality
- significant pain.

The transport decision

In an ALS system with more extensive treatment options, the transport decision is often complex. Major factors to consider include:

- the type of clinical problem (injury versus illness)
- the expected benefits of ALS treatment in the field
- local EMS system treatment and transport policies
- the ALS provider's comfort level
- transport time.

The clinical problem

If the 911 call is for trauma, and if the child has a serious mechanism of injury, a physiologic abnormality, a potentially significant anatomic abnormality or if the scene is unsafe, immediate transport is imperative. In these cases, immobilize, manage the airway and breathing, stop external bleeding, then transport. Attempt vascular access on the way to the ED. Examples of such patients include a child with an abnormal appearance after a closed head injury from a fall, or a child struck by a car who has a painful, deformed femur.

If the 911 call is for illness, the decision to stay or go is less clear cut and depends on the next set of factors.

Expected benefits of treatment

Time to operative care in the hospital has a major effect on the outcomes of children with serious injuries. Therefore, rapid transport after initial stabilization is extremely important. Time to hospital care may also significantly effect the outcomes of certain children with medical illnesses. For example, a child in cardiogenic shock will benefit most from rapid transport to definitive care, because the hospital is the best place for life-saving treatments of this rare and complex condition.

On the other hand, some critically ill children, such as a child who is seizing, will benefit from ALS treatment on scene. Such children, if treated with a benzodiazepine drug right away, will probably stop seizing sooner and have less need for ED interventions such as additional anticonvulsant administration and endotracheal intubation. Another example might be an unconscious diabetic child with hypoglycemia, who may have less chance of brain injury if she receives sugar in the field.

EMS system regulations

The decision to stay or go will often be defined by EMS system regulations about treatment and transport. For example, some systems allow prehospital professionals to treat a child in cardiopulmonary arrest with ALS interventions until either the resuscitation is successful or death is declared. Other systems require transport after initial resuscitation is underway, with the decision to discontinue efforts left to the ED staff.

Deciding when to go and when to stay is different for each child and for each EMS system.

Comfort level

Whenever a prehospital professional feels that the illness or injury requires a higher level of care, it is best to initiate transport quickly. Moreover, whenever the prehospital professional feels uncomfortable with a critical intervention, it is best to transport and attempt the intervention on the way to the ED, rather than on scene. For example, a child with decompensated hypovolemic shock usually deserves one attempt at vascular access on scene, then fluid administration on the way to the ED. But if the prehospital professional feels that the vascular access attempt will not be successful and an ED is nearby, it is prudent to transport and try on the way.

Transport time

The time to the nearest ED is another key factor. A briefer transport time will ordinarily support a shorter scene time. For example, if a child has ingested a potentially lethal poison, immediate transport is prudent if the ED is close by because of the complications of delay to definitive care. However, if transport time is long, consider initiating treatment on scene.

Additional Assessment

Focused history and physical exam

The focused history and physical exam has three objectives:

1. To obtain a complete description of the main complaint
2. To determine the mechanism of injury or circumstances of illness
3. To perform additional physical exam of specific anatomic locations

After the initial assessment, if the prehospital professional decides to transport immediately, defer the focused history and physical exam and the detailed physical exam, until the child is on the way to the hospital. But if the child is stable and the scene is safe, perform the focused history and physical exam and detailed exam on scene, and transport afterward. These parts of the additional assessment are optional in the physiologically distressed child.

To obtain the focused history, use the SAMPLE mnemonic, as suggested in Table 3-9.

After getting the focused history, reassess the physical findings based on the additional information. Focus the physical exam on the anatomic areas of concern after obtaining the history from the child or caregiver (or both). After the focused exam, reconsider the need for immediate transport.

If a child has an apparently minor condition—such as low-grade fever, feeding difficulties, fussiness, or minor trauma—be careful not to overlook clues to possible serious underlying conditions. Child maltreatment, ingestions, and early systemic infections in infants, toddler, or preschoolers are examples of conditions when the child may not have any acute signs or symptoms or when the child has physical findings not logically related to the complaint or history.

If the child is physiologically unstable, it is usually best to defer or omit the focused history and physical exam and the detailed exam.

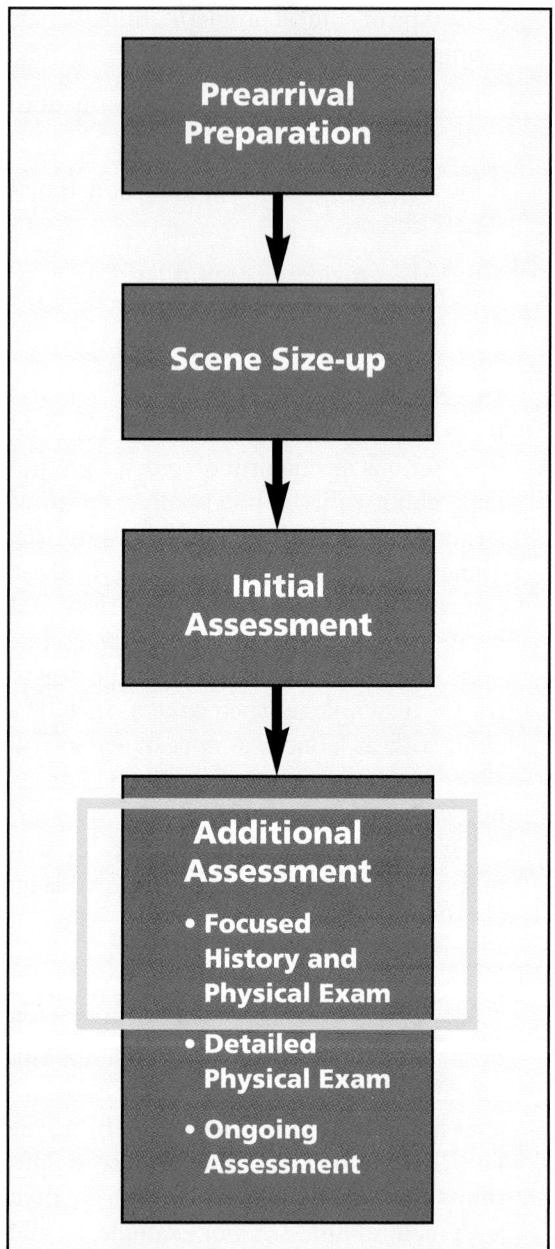

Detailed physical exam

If the child is stable on scene and does not need treatment after the focused history and exam, or if she is on the way to the hospital but does not require ongoing treatment, perform a detailed physical exam if possible. This physical evaluation must include all anatomic areas. It differs from the focused exam by building on the findings of the initial assessment and focused exam.

Often this portion of the assessment is not possible because of transport and treatment priorities. Sometimes, it is unnecessary because the problem has been fully evaluated in earlier phases of the assessment or the complaint and history are minor and in a specific location (e.g., an earache, twisted ankle).

Use the toe-to-head sequence for the detailed physical examination of infants, toddlers, and preschoolers. This approach allows the prehospital professional to gain the child's trust and cooperation and will increase the accuracy of the physical findings. Get the assistance of the caregiver in the detailed exam.

Note the following special anatomic characteristics of children when performing the detailed examination.

- **General observations** Observe the clothing for any unusual odors or for stains that might suggest a poison. Remove soiled or dirty clothing and save, and wash the skin with soap and water when there is time. If the infant or child vomits, save some of the vomit to give to the emergency department. **Bile** may suggest obstruction, and blood may suggest occult abdominal trauma or stomach bleeding.

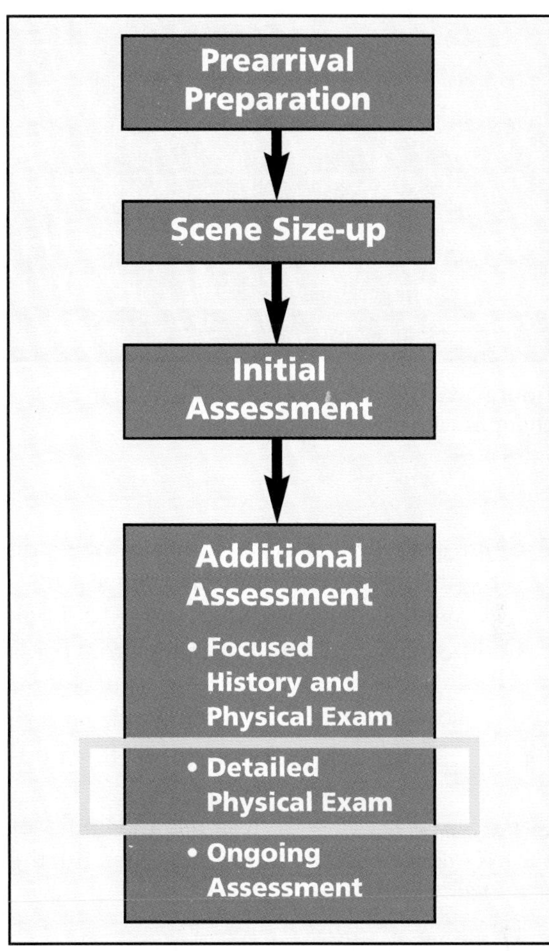

Table 3-9 Pediatric SAMPLE Components

Component	Explanation
Signs/Symptoms	Onset and nature of symptoms or pain or fever Age-appropriate signs of distress
Allergies	Known drug reactions or other allergies
Medications	Exact names and doses of ongoing drugs Timing and amount of last dose Timing and dose of analgesic/antipyretics
Past medical problems	History of pregnancy, labor, delivery Previous illnesses or injuries Immunizations
Last food or liquid	Timing of the child's last food or drink, including bottle or breast feeding
Events leading to the injury or illness	Key events leading to the current incident Fever history

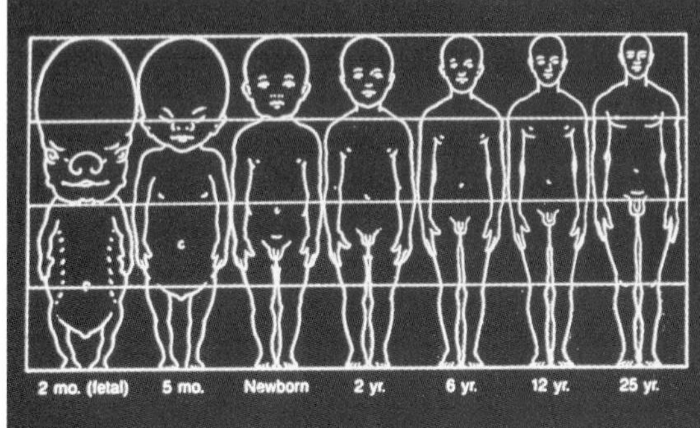

Figure 3-13 The relationship of the head to body changes with advancing age.

- **Skin** Observe the skin carefully for rashes and for bruising patterns that may suggest maltreatment, as discussed in Chapter 12. Look for bite marks; straight line marks from cords or straps; pinch marks; or hand, belt, or buckle pattern bruises. Inspect for nonblanching **petechiae** or **purpuric** lesions, and look for any new lesions during transport.

Blip

Do not look in a child's mouth if she has stridor.

- **Head** The younger the infant or child, the larger the head in proportion to the rest of the body (Figure 3-13). In the infant, the large head sits atop a small and weak neck. Because of this, the head is very easily injured when deceleration occurs (such as in motor vehicle crashes). Look for bruising, swelling, and

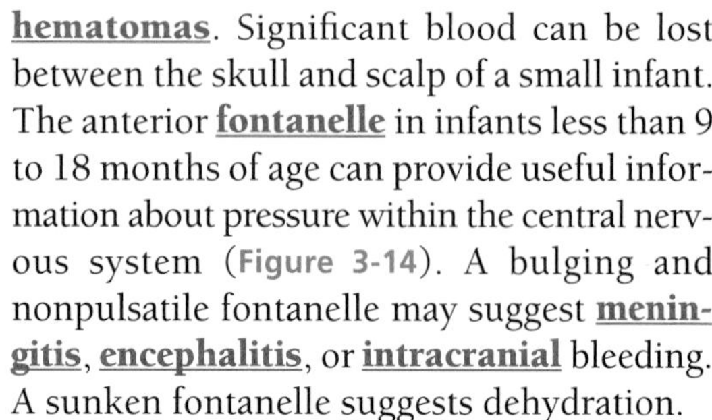

hematomas. Significant blood can be lost between the skull and scalp of a small infant. The anterior **fontanelle** in infants less than 9 to 18 months of age can provide useful information about pressure within the central nervous system (Figure 3-14). A bulging and nonpulsatile fontanelle may suggest **meningitis**, **encephalitis**, or **intracranial** bleeding. A sunken fontanelle suggests dehydration.

- **Eyes** A thorough evaluation of pupil size, reaction to light, and symmetry of extraocular muscle movements may be difficult to perform in infants. Gently rocking infants in the upright position will often get them to open their eyes. A colorful distracting object can then be used to look at eye movements.
- **Nose** Many infants need to breathe through their nose, as well as through their mouth, and when the nose is plugged with mucus, they are unable to breathe unless they are crying. The most common cause of respiratory distress in small infants is nasal obstruction from mucus. Gentle bulb or catheter suction of the nostrils may bring relief. In the toddler, foreign bodies are often the cause of nasal obstruction or unilateral discharge. Peas, beans, paper, plastic toys, and a myriad of small objects find their way into the toddler's nostrils. Leaking blood (**cerebrospinal fluid [CSF] rhinorrhea**) suggests a **basilar** skull fracture.
- **Ears** Look for any drainage from the ear canals. Leaking blood (**CSF otorrhea**) suggests a basilar skull fracture. Check for bruis-

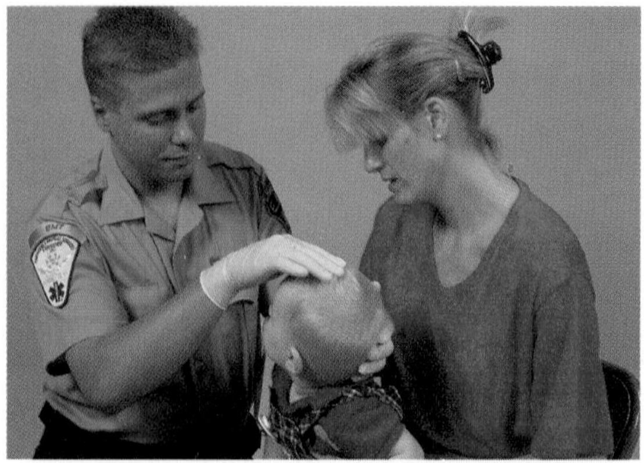

Figure 3-14 The anterior fontanelle of the infant is a window to the central nervous system.

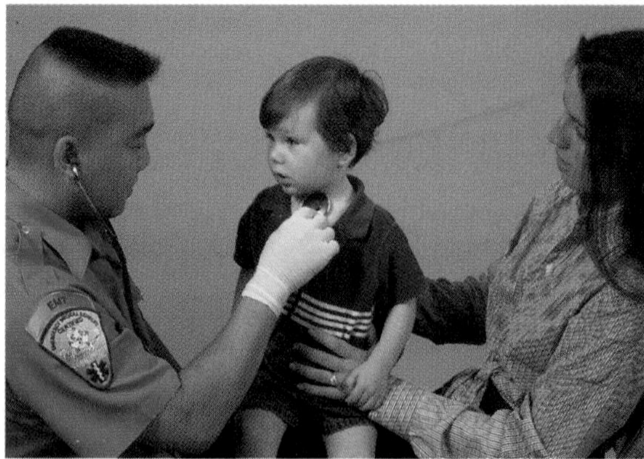

Figure 3-15 Listen at the trachea to distinguish the origin of upper airway sounds.

es behind the ear or **Battle's sign**, another sign of basilar skull fracture. The presence of **pus** may indicate an ear infection or perforation of the ear drum.

- **Mouth** Avoid looking in the mouth if the child has stridor. A partially obstructed airway in a child with stridor can become completely obstructed if touched. In the trauma patient, look for active bleeding and loose teeth. Note the smell of the breath. Many types of ingestions have specific odors, especially hydrocarbons. Acidosis may impart a sweet smell to the breath.
- **Neck** Locate the trachea for midline positioning. Listen with a stethoscope over the trachea at the midline (Figure 3-15). This is a quick and easy way to tell the difference between the sounds of mucus in the mouth, nose, and pharynx and wheezing and stridor.
- **Chest** Reexamine the chest for penetrations, bruises, or rashes. If the child is injured, feel the **clavicles** and every rib for tenderness and/or deformity.
- **Back** Inspect the back for penetrations, bruises, or rashes.
- **Abdomen** Inspect the abdomen for **distention**. Gently palpate the abdomen and watch closely for guarding or tensing of the abdominal muscles, which may suggest infection, obstruction, or intraabdominal injury. Note any tenderness or masses.
- **Extremities** Assess for **symmetry**. Compare both sides for color, warmth, size of joints, and tenderness. Put each joint through full range of motion while watching the eyes of the child for signs of pain.

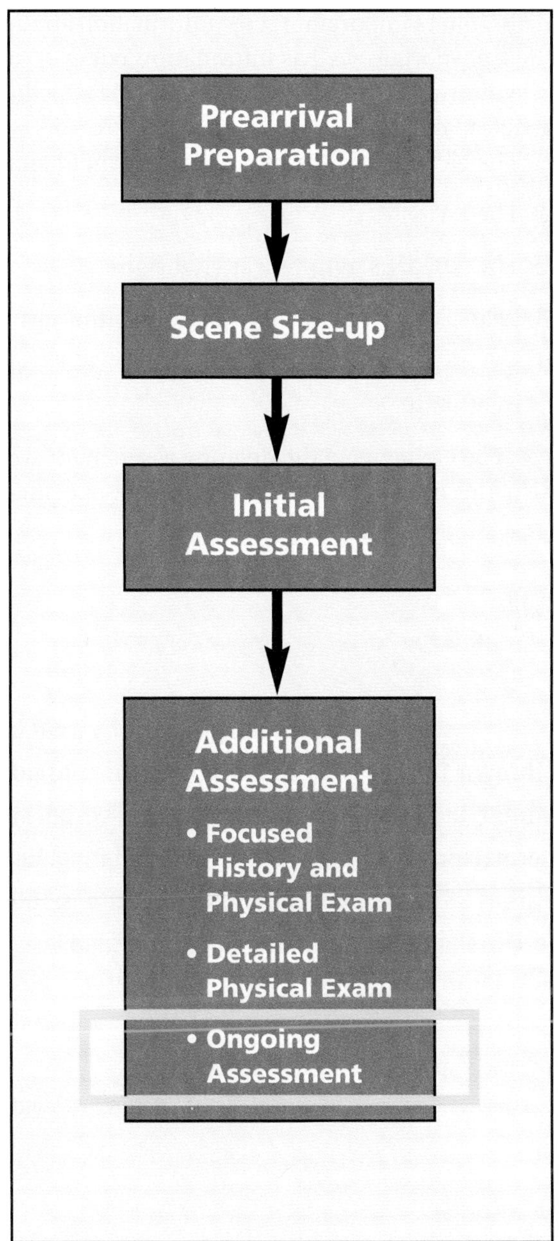

Ongoing assessment

Perform ongoing assessment of all patients while in transport to the hospital. Use the ongoing assessment to observe response to treatment and to track the identified physiologic and anatomic problems from moment to moment. Sometimes ongoing assessment identifies new problems. The ongoing assessment provides necessary guidance about continuing and modifying treatment.

Tip

Always do the ongoing assessment to track problems and monitor response to treatment.

It also offers important **triage** information about the transport, as well as information relevant to selection of an ED with the appropriate pediatric capabilities.

The elements in the ongoing assessment are:

1. The PAT
2. The ABCDEs with repeat vital signs
3. Reassessment of positive anatomic findings
4. Review of the effectiveness and safety of treatment

The elements in the ongoing assessment are also the basis for accurate, pediatric-specific, radio or telephone communications with medical oversight or with the ED.

Radio Reporting

Proper radio reporting integrates efforts from all emergency care professionals—EMTs, nurses, and doctors—and helps ensure that vital data is transmitted completely and concisely. Pediatric-specific reporting techniques will assist appropriate age-related modifications in assessment, treatment, triage, and transport. For a step-by-step explanation of this procedure, see page 233.

CASE STUDY 3

A 5-year-old girl is hit by a car in the crosswalk on the first day of kindergarten. She is thrown 10 feet and has a brief loss of consciousness. On your arrival, she is lying motionless in the street, but opens her eyes with a loud verbal stimulus. She will not speak or interact. There are no abnormal airway sounds, retractions, or flaring. Her skin is pink. Respiratory rate is 20 breaths/min, heart rate is 95 beats/min, and blood pressure is 100 mm Hg/palp. The chest is clear with good tidal volume. The skin feels warm, capillary refill time less than 2 seconds, and her brachial pulse is strong. She has a large frontal hematoma.

Does this child's appearance suggest serious injury?
How does the AVPU scale complement appearance in assessing brain function in this child?

Summary of Additional Assessment

After the initial assessment and resuscitation, the prehospital professional must decide how severe the problem is and what the timing of the transport will be. If additional assessment beyond the initial assessment is appropriate either on scene or on the way to the ED, perform a focused history and physical exam, and a detailed exam. These additional phases of assessment are not indicated if there is an acute life-threatening or limb-threatening problem. The focused and detailed exams are more for detection of anatomic problems than for evaluation of physiologic abnormalities. Last, always perform ongoing assessment to observe response to interventions and to guide changes in treatment, transport, and triage.

Case Study Answers

See page 31

This infant is severely ill. The PAT indicates poor appearance with diminished tone, poor interactiveness, and weak cry. These are important signals of weakened cardiopulmonary and/or neurologic function in an infant. Work of breathing is normal, but circulation to skin is poor. The PAT establishes this child as a critical patient that requires resuscitation and rapid transport. However, the respiratory rate, heart rate, and blood pressure are possibly within the normal ranges for age. Therefore, vital signs in this child could be deceptive, unless correlated with the PAT and the entire initial assessment. In this case, the PAT tells you that the child has an abnormal appearance and decreased skin circulation, which suggest shock.

The hands-on ABCDE phase of the assessment shows poor skin signs and diminished brachial pulse. These important physical findings confirm the PAT impression of shock. Furthermore, when you review the vital signs in the context of the initial assessment, you may identify that this child has "effortless tachypnea," a physiologic attempt to clear acidosis generated by shock.

See page 44

The PAT is a good way to get a general impression of this child and to judge degree of illness and urgency for care. Many other conventional assessment methods such as history taking, auscultation, and blood pressure determinations would be frustrating to attempt and possibly inaccurate in the first few minutes. The child's appearance is reassuring, with good tone, comfort in the parent's arms, and a vigorous cry. There are no abnormal airway sounds, retractions, or flaring, so work of breathing is normal in spite of a respiratory rate in the highest range for age. Circulation to skin is normal. With these PAT findings, it is highly unlikely that the child has a serious illness. The PAT provides the impression of a relatively well child and allows you to stand back and gain the confidence of the child and mother before rushing to a hands-on evaluation. Place this child in mother's arms and allow the mother to keep the girl on her lap while you proceed with the evaluation. When the child is less agitated, approach gently to complete the initial assessment. Use a "toe-to-head" sequence.

The PAT is the important first phase of the initial assessment. It does not replace the hands-on assessment of the ABCDEs and vital signs. The PAT for this child should reassure you. Treatment and transport are not urgent, and a focused history and physical exam and detailed physical exam can be performed first.

See page 54

This child's appearance is grossly abnormal. The scene size-up indicates a serious mechanism of injury. The girl's lethargic appearance with no increased work of breathing or abnormal skin signs on the PAT suggests a possible intracranial injury. This could be a concussion, hemorrhage, or brain edema. The appearance indicates an unstable patient who needs rapid treatment on scene and transport. Complete the ABCDEs and immobilize the child. Provide 100% oxygen by mask.

ALS: Fluid Administration

Use the resuscitation tape to determine her length, endotracheal tube size, weight, volume requirements, and other information relevant to drug doses. Transport immediately. Get vascular access during transport and give 20 ml/kg of crystalloid. Reassess. Repeat crystalloid if necessary.

There are many methods of determining neurologic function in this child in order to guide treatment decisions, minimize differences among different observers, and provide for consistent exams. Different EMS systems use different methods such as the Glasgow Coma Scale or the Pediatric Glasgow Coma Scale. Some of the problems with these numerical neurologic scoring systems in children include the following: they require memorization or written prompting; they may not be easily adapted to children because of difficulties evaluating speech in nontalking or frightened youngsters; they may only apply to injury cases; and there is no validated national standard.

The AVPU scale is a basic approach for children adapted from adult disability assessment. It has not been validated in children. The AVPU scale is easily linked to abnormal appearance in the PAT, which may identify more subtle signs of early neurologic dysfunction. The AVPU scale divides brain response into general categories that are simply remembered, seem to remain consistent among different observers, and provide good information for prehospital treatment decisions.

Suggested Educational Resources

1. Barkin RM. *Pediatric Emergency Medicine: Concepts and Clinical Practice*. 2nd ed. St. Louis, MO: Mosby; 1997:3–10.
2. Dieckmann RA, Fiser DH, Selbst SM. *Illustrated Textbook of Pediatric Emergency and Critical Care Procedures*. St. Louis, MO: Mosby; 1997:10–20.
3. Grimes J, Burns E. *Health Assessment in Nursing Practice*. 3rd ed. Sudbury, MA: Jones and Bartlett; 1992.
4. Simon JE, Goldberg AT. *Prehospital Pediatric Life Support*. St. Louis, MO: Mosby; 1989: 1–14.
5. Henderson DP, Brownstein D, eds. *Pediatric Emergency Nursing Manual*. New York, NY: Springer; 1994:253–293.

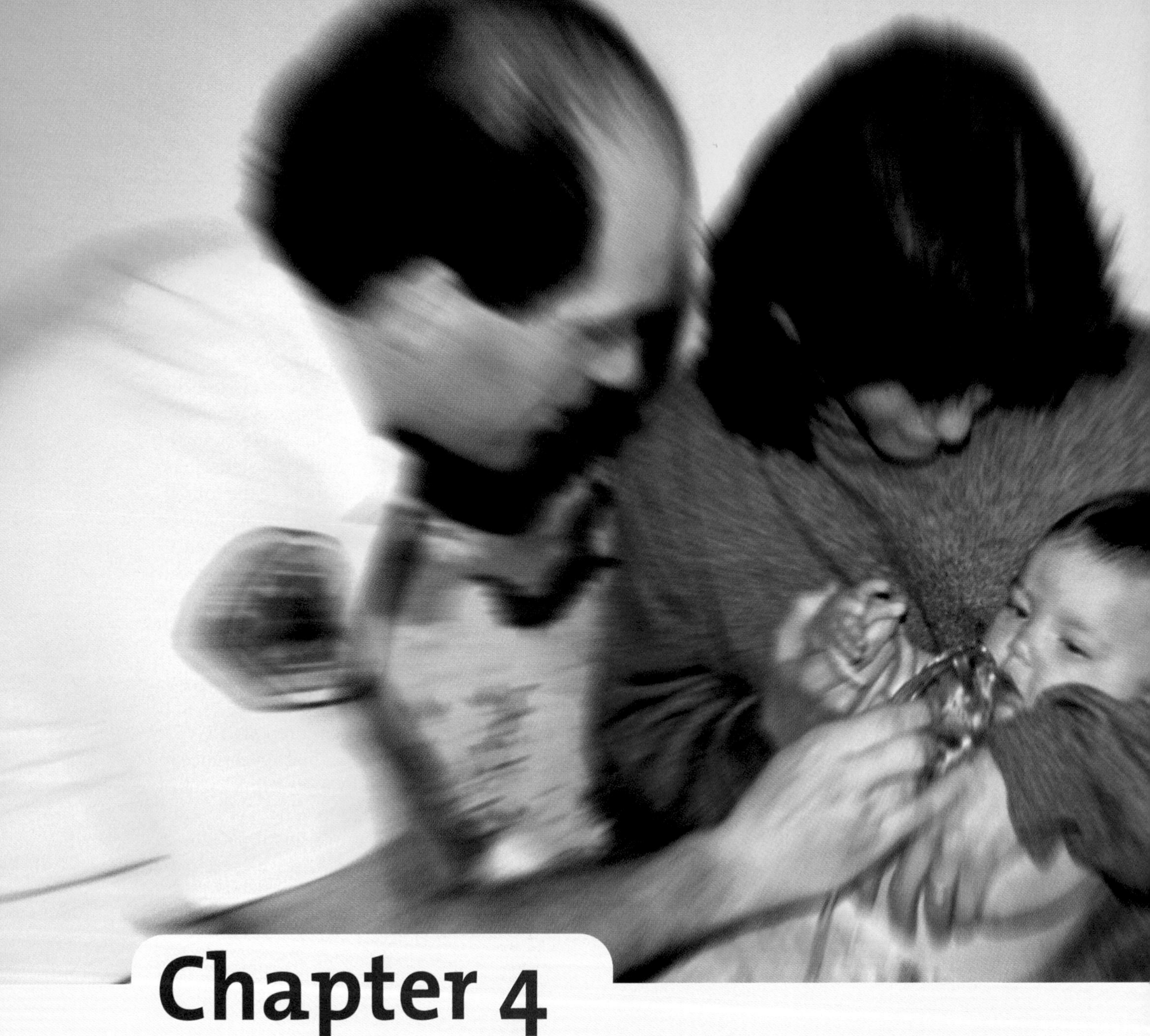

Chapter 4 Respiratory

Learning Objectives

1. Differentiate between respiratory distress, respiratory failure, and respiratory arrest.
2. Outline a general treatment strategy, going from the least to the most invasive, for children with respiratory compromise.
3. Contrast the key signs and symptoms of upper airway obstruction versus lower airway obstruction.
4. Describe the similarities and differences in the management of upper and lower airway disease.
5. Discuss possible complications of assisted ventilation, and outline strategies to identify and correct them.
6. Apply appropriate assessment and treatment techniques to case studies presenting patients with respiratory emergencies.

You are called to the scene of a 9-month-old boy who is having difficulty breathing. His mother tells you that he has had a fever and has been "wheezing" for 2 days. He has been getting worse over the last few hours. The child has no prior history of wheezing.

The child is sitting on his mother's lap, but does not make eye contact and cries weakly when you approach. You can hear wheezing without a stethoscope. His color is pink, but he has marked intercostal and subcostal retractions and nasal flaring. Respiratory rate is 80 breaths/min, heart rate is 180 beats/min. The blood pressure is not obtained. His skin is warm, and he has strong pulses and normal capillary refill time. He has good air movement and wheezes on auscultation.

How sick is this child?
How will you manage him in the field?

Emergencies

Introduction

Respiratory disease is the most frequent medical emergency in out-of-hospital pediatrics. Of all conditions causing respiratory disease in children, asthma is the most common. Good assessment and care of pediatric respiratory problems are important for the prehospital professional because serious illness and death can be avoided by early intervention.

There are several important physical signs and symptoms that reflect the effectiveness of gas exchange in the lungs and help distinguish respiratory distress from respiratory failure. Using the PAT to rapidly evaluate breathing is an important first step in determining the severity of the disease, localizing the physiologic problem, and beginning treatment. Appearance reflects overall brain oxygenation. Work of breathing reflects hypoxia and hypercarbia (carbon dioxide retention). Cyanosis reflects severe hypoxia.

The initial breathing assessment also includes respiratory rate, hands-on chest auscultation, and pulse oximetry. Respiratory assessment not only provides a picture of respiratory function but also helps prioritize general and specific treatments, as well as invasive interventions. This chapter explains how to use recognizable signs of pediatric respiratory dysfunction to determine the right field treatment and to time transport to the emergency department properly.

Respiratory Distress and Failure

Respiratory distress is an abnormal physiologic condition identified by increased work of breathing. The physical signs of increased work of breathing represent the patient's attempt to make up for decreased gas exchange in the lungs and to maintain oxygenation and ventilation. The child in respiratory distress is effectively compensating.

Respiratory failure occurs when the infant or child exhausts his energy reserves, can no longer maintain oxygenation and ventilation, and begins to decompensate. Respiratory failure may occur when chest wall muscles get tired after a long period of increased work of breathing (e.g., a tight asthmatic condition) or when there is failure of central respiratory drive (e.g., a child with a severe closed head injury). Respiratory failure must be treated immediately to restore good oxygenation and ventilation, and to prevent respiratory arrest.

Respiratory arrest means absence of effective breathing. If ventilation and oxygenation are not adequately supported, respiratory arrest will rapidly progress to full cardiopulmonary arrest, with a low probability of survival.

Evaluating the Presenting Complaint

On arrival at the scene, find out the nature of the presenting complaint by asking several directed questions, as suggested in Table 4-1. In patients with mild distress, there is time to get a more complete SAMPLE history (see Table 4-8) on scene, but this should be done later, as part of the focused history.

Assessment of respiratory status

The PAT

Begin the assessment with the PAT, as discussed in Chapter 3. Carefully evaluate appearance and work of breathing. These parts of the general impression will determine whether the child is in respiratory distress or in respiratory failure. The key to making this clinical distinction is *observation* of the child's appearance, as defined in Table 3-1.

Appearance

Assess appearance to determine urgency of BLS versus ALS treatment, as discussed below. Appearance reflects the adequacy of oxygenation and ventilation in a child with difficulty breathing.

ALS Advanced LIFE support

Use of appearance to determine urgency of BLS vs. ALS treatment

Example 1: A child who has stridor and retractions, but is running around the room and has a normal appearance requires general noninvasive treatment and transport. The child is compensating effectively and is in respiratory distress.

Example 2: A child who is agitated or inconsolable, with wheezing and increased work of breathing, has an abnormal appearance, and is probably hypoxic. The child is decompensating and is in early respiratory failure. In addition to general noninvasive treatment, this child requires specific ALS treatment with a **bronchodilator** and rapid transport to an emergency department (ED).

Example 3: A child who has been working hard to breathe and is now sleepy or poorly responsive has an abnormal appearance. His altered level of consciousness is the result of severe hypoxia or hypercarbia, reflecting late respiratory failure and impending respiratory arrest. He requires immediate assisted ventilation with bag-valve-mask (BVM), and possibly endotracheal intubation.

Work of breathing

Look for four signs of increased work of breathing:

1. Abnormal positioning
2. Abnormal airway sounds, such as snoring, stridor, wheezing, or grunting
3. Retractions
4. Nasal flaring

The significance of each of these findings is discussed in Chapter 3. These indicators of breathing effort will help to identify the anatomic location of the problem, the severity of the physiologic dysfunction, and the urgency for treatment.

Circulation to skin

Last, evaluate skin color. Cyanosis is an ominous sign, signaling profound hypoxia and the need for assisted ventilation. However, a child may have severe hypoxia without an obvious change in skin color. Skin color is not a helpful indicator of respiratory distress or failure in noncritical children.

Table 4-1 Key Questions about Presenting Complaint

Key Question	Possible Medical Problem
Has your child ever had this kind of problem before? Is this the first time that he has had trouble breathing?	Asthma, chronic lung disease
Is your child taking any medications?	Asthma, chronic lung disease, congenital heart disease
Has your child had a fever?	Pneumonia, bronchiolitis, croup
Did your child suddenly start coughing/choking/gagging?	Foreign body aspiration or ingestion
Has your child had an injury to his chest?	Pulmonary contusion, pneumothorax

The ABCDEs

After the PAT, perform the hands-on ABCDE assessment. There are three parts:

1. Respiratory rate
2. Air movement and abnormal lung sounds
3. Pulse oximetry

Respiratory rate

In the noncritical patient, determine respiratory rate by sitting the child in his caregiver's lap and exposing his chest. Count the rise and fall of his abdomen over 30 seconds, then double that number. Normal respiratory rate varies in children of different ages (see Table 3-4). Always think about respiratory rate in the context of the PAT and the overall clinical assessment. Respiratory rate may be affected by level of activity, fever, anxiety, and metabolic state.

A respiratory rate of greater than 60 breaths/min is abnormal in a child of any age and should be a signal for careful evaluation for other signs of respiratory or circulatory problems. Even more dangerous is a rate that is too slow for age. A respiratory rate of less than 20 breaths/min in a sick child under 6 years of age, or a rate of less than 15 breaths/min in a sick child between 7 and 14 years of age is a sign of respiratory failure and the need for immediate intervention. A child who has normal appearance and good color, without increased work of breathing, has good breathing regardless of his respiratory rate.

Air movement and abnormal lung sounds

Assess air movement by placing the stethoscope at the midaxillary line and listening for the amount of air movement with each breath (see Figure 3-9). Poor air movement may exist in children with respiratory problems for many reasons, as outlined in Table 4-2.

Assessing air movement, or the volume of air exchanged with each breath, allows clinical estimation of **tidal volume**. Tidal volume is one of two factors that determines **minute ventilation**— the volume of air exchanged per minute. Minute ventilation is the basis for gas exchange in the lungs.

$$\text{Minute Ventilation} = \text{Tidal Volume} \times \text{Respiratory Rate}$$

This equation shows the connection between tidal volume and respiratory rate. A child may not have enough gas exchange if tidal volume is low, even with a normal or fast respiratory rate. Also, a normal or increased tidal volume does not mean there will be enough gas exchange if the respiratory rate is too slow.

While listening for air movement, also listen for abnormal breath sounds. Table 3-5 summarizes the types and causes of abnormal breath sounds.

Pulse oximetry

Pulse oximetry is a useful tool for detecting and measuring hypoxia. Figure 3-10 illustrates possible sites for placement of the oximetry probe. When properly applied, if there is a good arteri-

Table 4-2 Causes of Poor Air Movement in Children

Functional Problem	Possible Causes
Obstruction of airways	Asthma, bronchiolitis, croup
Restriction of chest wall movement	Chest wall injury, severe scoliosis or kyphosis
Chest wall muscle fatigue	Prolonged increased work of breathing, muscular dystrophy
Decreased central respiratory drive	Head injury, intoxication
Chest injury	Rib fractures, pulmonary contusion, pneumothorax

al tracing, a reading above 94% saturation means normal blood oxygen saturation. A value of 94% or less on room air is abnormal and is a signal to give supplemental oxygen. A reading of less than 90%, with the patient on 100% nonrebreathing mask oxygen, usually indicates respiratory failure. Begin immediate ventilatory assistance to correct the hypoxia and possible hypercarbia.

Be careful not to overanalyze low oxygen saturation. Pulse oximetry is an adjunct to physical assessment. *Falsely low readings are common with pulse oximetry*. Check probe placement, the quality of the tracing, and the child's clinical state before treating.

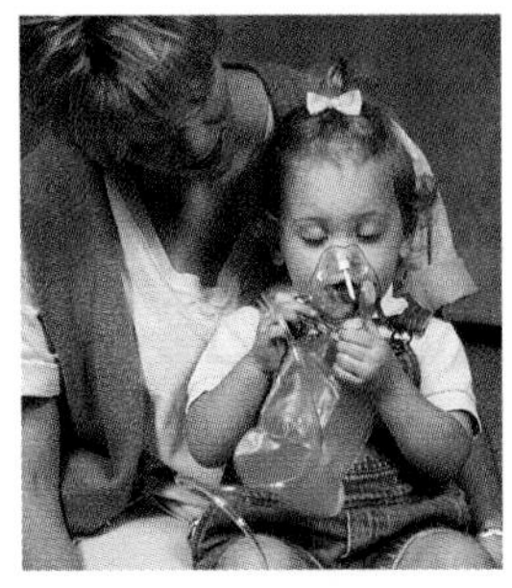

Figure 4-1 Always keep a child with respiratory distress in her position of comfort.

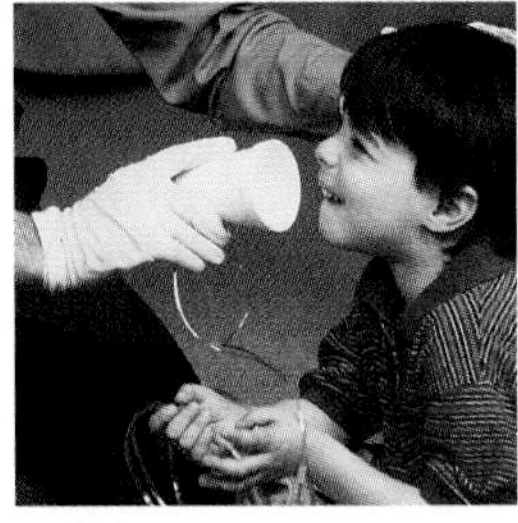

Figure 4-2 If the child resists application of a mask or nasal cannula, administer oxygen through a nonthreatening object such as a paper cup.

General Noninvasive Treatment

For every child in respiratory distress, begin general noninvasive treatment. If the child is in respiratory failure, provide assisted ventilation. The general noninvasive treatment of every noncritical patient is the same—allow him to assume a position of comfort (Figure 4-1) and supply oxygen, if tolerated. This is the only treatment for patients in respiratory distress *without* upper or lower airway obstruction.

Positioning

A child in respiratory distress will naturally move into the position that gives him the best air exchange—his "position of comfort." For example, a child with severe upper airway obstruction may get into the "sniffing position" (see Figure 3-4) to straighten the airway and open the air passages. A child with severe lower airway obstruction may voluntarily take the "tripod" posture—sitting up and leaning forward on outstretched arms—to help accessory muscles (see Figure 3-5). Infants and toddlers may be most comfortable in their caregiver's arms or lap. Do not move a child from his position of comfort. This might worsen his respiratory distress.

Oxygen

Treatment with high-flow oxygen is usually safe. Unlike adults with chronic lung disease, children rarely lose their respiratory drive after oxygen administration. However, the prehospital professional must weigh the possible benefits of giving oxygen against the risks of agitating the child and worsening his respiratory distress. This is a special concern in a child with an unstable airway.

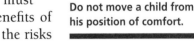

Blip

Do not move a child from his position of comfort.

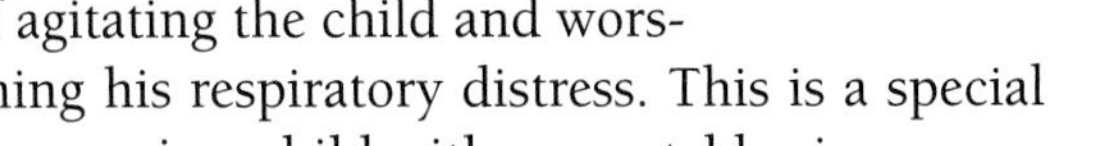

PROCEDURE 2

Oxygen Delivery

Give oxygen to any child with clinical signs of cardiopulmonary distress or failure, or with a history suggesting possible abnormalities in gas exchange. The delivery method should give the concentration of oxygen most appropriate for the child's condition, degree of cooperation, respiratory effort, and age. For a step-by-step explanation of this procedure, see page 237.

Most children will accept oxygen therapy, especially if the prehospital professional is creative in the approach. This often means getting the help of the caregiver. If a child resists the use of a mask or **nasal cannula**, have the caregiver give blow-by oxygen from the end of the oxygen tubing or from tubing inserted into a cup (Figure 4-2). *When treating children, it is better to overuse oxygen than to underuse it.*

! Tip

Applying oxygen to an infant or young child may cause agitation and increase respiratory distress.

Summary of Initial Respiratory Assessment and General Noninvasive Treatment

The PAT is a good tool for determining the effectiveness of gas exchange, based on observation of appearance and work of breathing. If the PAT suggests respiratory distress, begin general noninvasive treatment with oxygen and keep the child in his position of comfort. The PAT will also identify the critical child in respiratory failure who requires immediate assisted ventilation. Obtaining respiratory rate, listening for air movement, and determining oxygen saturation by pulse oximetry will work in concert with the PAT. The initial assessment should allow an evaluation of severity and urgency for treatment, and establish if specific treatment for upper or lower airway obstruction is indicated.

Specific Treatment for Respiratory Distress

After completing the initial assessment, consider specific treatment for airway obstruction. The PAT and ABCDE assessment will help determine whether the child has upper or lower airway obstruction. *Snoring or stridor indicates upper airway obstruction; wheezing indicates lower airway obstruction.* It can be difficult to separate true stridor from upper airway noise due to nasal congestion. Breath sounds may also make it difficult to tell the difference between upper airway noise and true wheezing. Listen for breath sounds in the second or third intercostal space at the midaxillary line bilaterally (see Figure 3-9). At this location, it is easier to distinguish upper airway congestion from lower airway obstruction. When abnormal airway sounds are loudest with the stethoscope held near the child's nose rather than over the lungs, nasal congestion is the likely cause.

Upper airway obstruction

Proximal airway obstruction

In a patient with neurologic impairment, loss of oropharyngeal muscle tone may cause upper airway obstruction due to the tongue and **mandible** falling back and partially blocking the **pharynx**. The head-tilt/chin-lift (Figure 4-3) or jaw thrust (Figure 4-4) may relieve this proximal airway obstruction.

Sometimes secretions, blood, or foreign bodies block the **proximal** upper airway. This is an important concern in the child with closed head injury or seizures. Suctioning alone will often relieve the upper airway obstruction caused by fluids or occluding objects in the mouth, pharynx, or nose.

Suctioning

Suctioning is a basic technique to maintain an open airway. Children have tiny airways that are easily obstructed by secretions, vomitus, pus, blood, or foreign bodies. Children of different ages, with different clinical problems, need different types of suction devices and suctioning procedures. For a step-by-step explanation of this procedure, see page 241.

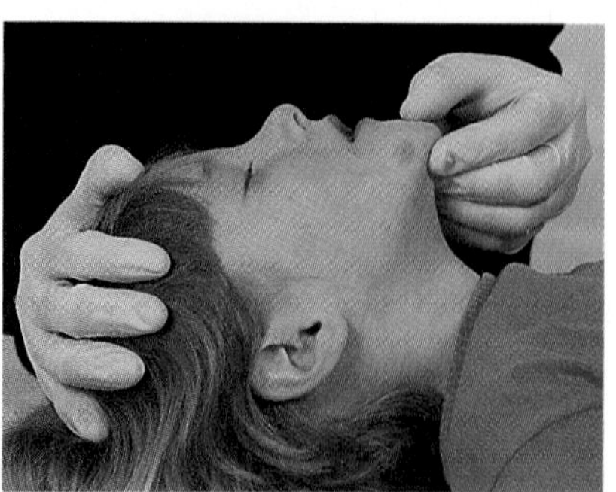

Figure 4-3 Use the head-tilt/chin-lift maneuver to place the airway in a neutral position.

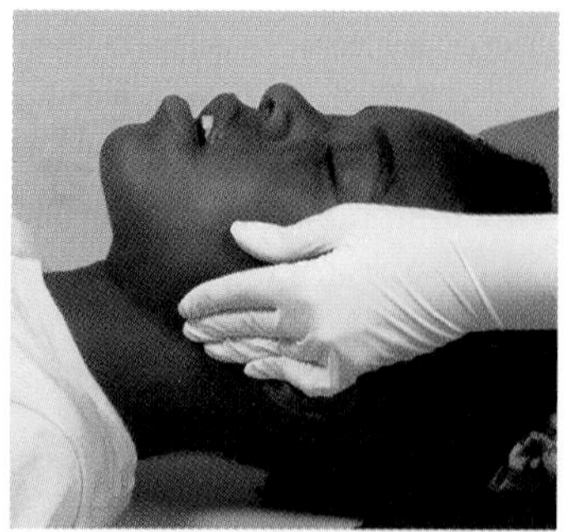

Figure 4-4 Use the jaw thrust maneuver in a child with possible spinal injury.

Maintenance of an adequate airway may require placement of an oropharyngeal airway, **nasopharyngeal** airway, or an endotracheal tube.

Airway Adjuncts
Adjuncts may immediately improve the child's spontaneous ventilation. In addition, they may allow more effective BVM ventilation, reduce gastric inflation, and avert the need for endotracheal intubation. For a step-by-step explanation of this procedure, see page 244.

Croup

In an awake, alert child, upper airway obstruction is usually due to *croup*, a viral disease with inflammation, edema, and narrowing of the larynx, trachea, and bronchioles. Croup usually affects infants and toddlers. Most children with croup have had several days of cold symptoms. The cold symptoms are followed by the development of a barking or "seal" cough, stridor, and various levels of respiratory distress. There is usually a fever, and symptoms are often worse at night. The severity of symptoms will vary widely among patients, but they usually progress over days, rather than hours.

Treatment. Treat children with apparent croup with cool mist—either in the form of humidified oxygen or nebulized saline. Use the caregiver to assist (Figure 4-5). The cool water vapor will help reduce the inflammation and obstruction of croup.

ALS Advanced LIFE support **Pharmacologic treatment of croup**
Nebulized epinephrine is a specific treatment for the upper airway inflammation associated with croup. Epinephrine is a potent alpha and beta **agonist**, and works through vasoconstriction to decrease the upper airway edema causing partial obstruction. If local EMS protocols permit nebulized epinephrine therapy, consider this specific treatment for children with stridor, increased work of breathing, poor air movement, blood oxygen saturation less than 94%, or altered appearance.

Nebulized epinephrine has two formulations:

- **Racemic** epinephrine, 2.25% solution for inhalation: Dose: 0.5 ml mixed with 4.5 ml of normal saline, nebulized, every 20 min based on clinical response
- Epinephrine 1:1000 solution for injection: Dose: 3–5 mg (3–5 ml) nebulized, every 20 min based on clinical response

Side effects of nebulized epinephrine include tachycardia, tremor, and vomiting. Another concern about out-of-hospital administration of epinephrine for croup is longer time in the ED. Children who receive nebulized epinephrine may need observation in the ED for 4 to 6 hours because of possible rebound effects after the medicine wears off.

Position of comfort, humidified oxygen, and avoiding agitation are the best treatments for suspected croup.

Very few children with croup will require assisted ventilation in the out-of-hospital setting. In the rare case of a child with croup and respiratory failure, begin assisted ventilation and reassess.

ALS Advanced LIFE support **Invasive airway management for croup**
Perform endotracheal intubation only in the unusual case of the child with respiratory failure who does not respond to BVM ventilation. Preparation for intubation includes choosing an endotracheal tube one or two sizes *smaller* than normal for age or length. Inflammation of the trachea at the **subglottic** level makes it difficult or impossible to use an endotracheal tube of normal size.

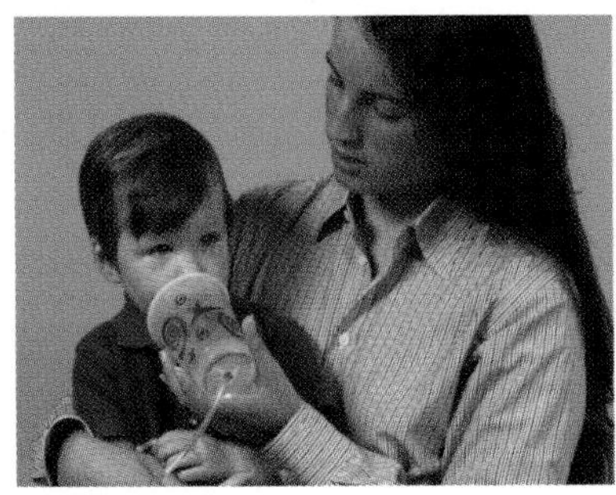

Figure 4-5 Use the caregiver to assist in the administration of oxygen or nebulized saline.

Bacterial upper airway infections

Bacterial infections may also cause upper airway obstruction in children. Unlike viral croup, these infections tend to progress rapidly with severe respiratory compromise developing over hours. The child with a bacterial upper airway infection usually is older than 12 months, appears ill or toxic, and has pain on swallowing. Stridor may be present, but the child will not have the barking cough that is common with croup.

There are several possible but even less common causes of bacterial upper airway infections. **Epiglottitis**, inflammation of the **epiglottis**, is now *extremely rare* due to widespread vaccination of infants against the bacteria *Haemophilus influenzae*, type B. Peritonsillar abscess, retropharyngeal abscess, **tracheitis**, and **diphtheria** are other possible causes of upper airway infection.

Treatment. When a bacterial upper airway infection is suspected, give only general noninvasive treatment with high-flow oxygen and position of comfort. Avoid agitating the child by trying to place an IV or attempting another maneuver, and quickly transport. If the child is in respiratory failure, initiate BVM ventilation and consider endotracheal intubation.

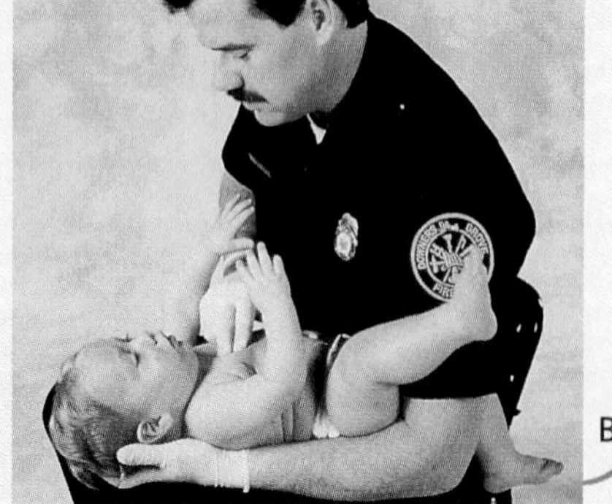

Figure 4-6a (A) Use five back blows (B) followed by five chest thrusts in infants with complete airway obstruction.

Foreign body aspiration

Foreign body aspiration may cause mechanical obstruction anywhere in the airway, from the pharynx to a bronchus. A retained esophageal foreign body can also cause respiratory distress in an infant or young child. This happens because the trachea is pliable and can be compressed by the adjacent distended **esophagus**. A typical history of foreign body aspiration is the sudden onset of coughing, choking, gagging, and shortness of breath in a previously well child without a fever. Older infants and toddlers, who explore their world by placing things in their mouths, are at highest risk.

Treatment. If the child can still cough, cry, or speak, the airway is only partially obstructed. Stridor is typical. Immediately transport such children, who have *incomplete* upper airway obstruction. Use only general noninvasive treatment and avoid agitating the child.

If the child has severe respiratory distress and is at risk for getting worse during transport, be prepared to perform foreign body airway obstruction maneuvers for complete obstruction, as illustrated in Figures 4-6a and 4-6b and Figures 4-7a and 4-7b. Table 4-3 summarizes these maneuvers. Consider these foreign body airway obstruction maneuvers if the child cannot cough, cry, or speak. *Never* perform foreign body airway obstruction procedures if the child has incomplete obstruction (i.e., can cough, cry, or speak).

Table 4-3 Foreign Body Airway Obstruction Maneuvers

Age	Technique
Infant (<12 months)	Five back blows followed by five chest thrusts
Child (>1 year)	Five abdominal thrusts

Airway Obstruction/Foreign Body Removal
In the setting of complete airway obstruction, prehospital professionals can make the difference between life and death. Immediate removal of an airway foreign body can often be achieved using BLS procedures. Sometimes basic maneuvers are unsuccessful and using Magill forceps along with direct laryngoscopy may be the only option for removal. For a step-by-step explanation of this procedure, see page 247.

ALS Advanced LIFE support

Foreign body airway obstruction maneuvers
If the child has complete obstruction and BLS maneuvers fail to dislodge the foreign body to the mouth where it can be easily removed, consider direct **laryngoscopy**. If the foreign body can be seen at or above the level of the larynx, remove it using pediatric Magill forceps. If the child has complete obstruction, and neither foreign body airway obstruction maneuvers nor direct laryngoscopy relieve the obstruction, attempt BVM ventilation. If BVM ventilation fails to achieve chest rise, perform endotracheal intubation.

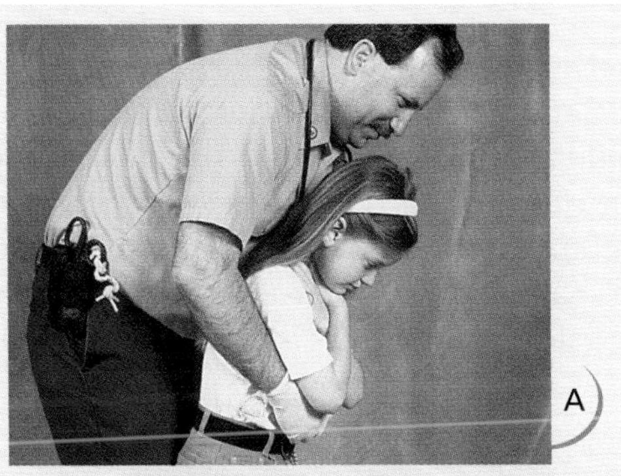

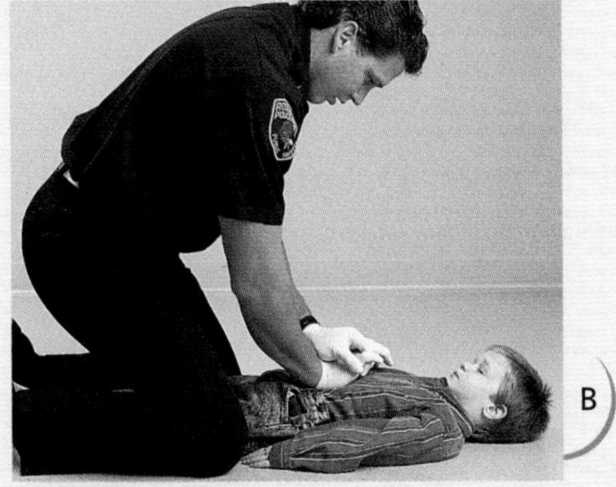

Figure 4-7 (A) Use five abdominal thrusts to treat complete airway obstruction in the conscious child in the standing position. (B) For the unconscious child with a suspected airway obstruction, use five abdominal thrusts with the patient in the supine position.

Specific treatment of upper airway obstruction

When transporting any child with suspected incomplete upper airway obstruction, have airway equipment immediately available. Consider transporting the caregiver with any conscious child with airway obstruction, as this may keep the child calm. Also, the caregiver can help administer oxygen (Figure 4-8).

Blip
Never perform airway obstruction procedures if the child has only incomplete obstruction and can still cough, cry, or speak.

Lower airway obstruction

Bronchiolitis and *asthma* are the most common conditions causing lower airway obstruction in children. Foreign body aspiration is much less common and usually occurs in toddlers, who may have suddenly started choking, then coughing or wheezing. *Wheezing is the clinical hallmark of lower airway obstruction* of any cause. A specific diagnosis for lower airway obstruction in the field is not necessary, and many times it is impossible to tell which of the three main conditions the child is experiencing: bronchiolitis, asthma, or foreign body aspiration. Fortunately, treatment for all forms of **bronchoconstriction** is similar and will help reverse the common pathophysiology of these conditions.

Tip
Attempt BLS maneuvers *first* in a child with suspected foreign body aspiration and critical airway obstruction.

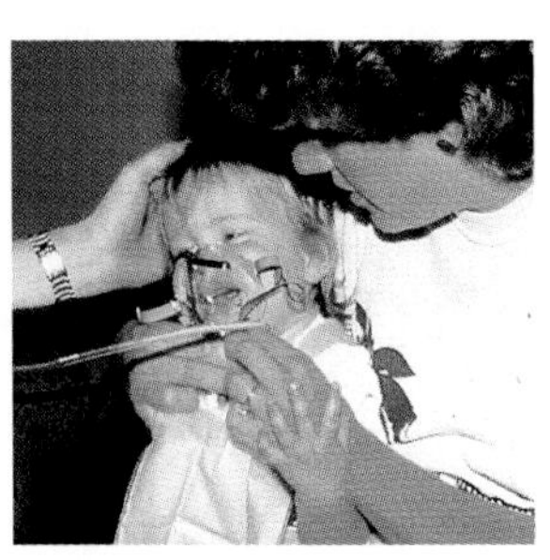

Figure 4-8 A nebulized bronchodilator can also be given without a mask using a blow-by technique.

Bronchiolitis

Bronchiolitis is a viral lower respiratory infection, which usually affects infants and children less than 3 years of age. Often caused by the respiratory syncytial virus (RSV), this disease is widespread in the winter months. The infection leads to destruction of the lining of the bronchioles, profuse secretions, and bronchoconstriction. Infants are particularly likely to catch the disease because of their small airway size, high resistance to airflow, and poor airway clearance.

Controversy

Specific field treatment of infants with wheezing may include bronchodilation with nebulized beta agonists or nebulized epinephrine. The relative effectiveness of these treatments is unknown.

Tip

When a child has history of increased work of breathing, but now has altered appearance and a slow or normal respiratory rate without retractions, THINK RESPIRATORY FAILURE.

Presenting complaints of bronchiolitis include upper respiratory infection symptoms, fever, cough, vomiting, poor feeding, poor sleep, and trouble breathing. Assessment shows variable degrees of increased work of breathing, tachypnea, diffuse wheezing, inspiratory crackles, and tachycardia.

Historical risk factors for respiratory failure in infants with suspected bronchiolitis include age less than 2 months, history of prematurity, underlying lung disease, congenital heart disease, and immune deficiency. Table 4-4 lists important clinical predictors of respiratory failure in children with suspected bronchiolitis.

Table 4-4 Predictors of Respiratory Failure in Suspected Bronchiolitis

Respiratory rate >60 breaths/min with increased work of breathing
Respiratory rate <20 breaths/min with decreased work of breathing
Heart rate >200 beats/min or <100 beats/min
Poor appearance
Blood oxygen saturation <90% on supplemental oxygen

Asthma

Asthma is the most common chronic disease of childhood, affecting almost 5 million children in the United States. The hospital admission rate for asthmatics under 5 years old is more than twice the national average for all ages, and the mortality rate for children is rising. Half of all pediatric

CASE STUDY 2

A school principal calls 911 because a 13-year-old asthmatic "can't breathe." The boy is on daily treatments with a metered dose inhaler (MDI). His physician prescribed oral steroids yesterday for worsening asthma symptoms. He tells you that he was up all night, using his albuterol MDI every 1 to 2 hours.

The boy is sleepy and pale and has audible wheezing. He is in the tripod position. There are suprasternal, intercostal, and substernal retractions and nasal flaring. The respiratory rate is 45 breaths/min, the heart rate 160 beats/min, and the blood pressure is 120/70 mm Hg. Blood oxygen saturation is 83% on room air. On auscultation you hear minimal air movement and a prolonged expiratory phase.

What is this child's physiologic status?
What is the most important treatment?

asthma deaths occur in the out-of-hospital setting. The length of the final attack is less than 1 hour in many children, and less than 2 hours in half of asthmatic children who die. Common reasons for an asthma attack include upper respiratory infection and exercise, although exposure to cold air, emotional stress, and passive exposure to smoke may trigger attacks as well.

Asthma is a disease of small airway inflammation. The inflammatory reaction leads to bronchoconstriction, mucosal edema, and profuse secretions. These three factors in combination cause severe airflow obstruction and **ventilation-perfusion mismatch**. Clinically, children having an asthma attack will show different degrees of tachypnea, tachycardia, increased work of breathing, and wheezing on exhalation. Pulse oximetry may be normal or low.

Carefully assess air movement by auscultation. The asthmatic complaining of shortness of breath, but without wheezing on auscultation, may have too much airway obstruction to wheeze. Aggressive bronchodilator treatment may improve airflow and increase audible wheezing. Beware of the following features of the initial assessment, which suggest severe bronchospasm and respiratory failure:

- altered appearance
- exhaustion
- inability to recline
- interrupted speech
- severe retractions
- decreased air movement

In the focused history, several things suggest that a severe or potentially fatal attack is to come. These include:

- prior intensive care unit admissions or intubation
- more than three ED visits in a year
- more than two hospital admissions in past year
- use of more than one metered dose inhaler (MDI) canister in the last month
- use of steroids for asthma in the past
- use of bronchodilators more frequently than every 4 hours
- progressive symptoms despite aggressive home therapy

Home therapy of asthma has several goals: preventing and controlling asthma symptoms, reducing the number of attacks and the severity of each one, and reversing existing airflow obstruction. Some children with a history of severe or frequent asthma attacks are on daily medications, but most children receive treatment only during serious attacks. Table 4-5 lists the frequent drugs for use in home asthma therapy for quick relief.

Table 4-5 Asthma: Common Home Therapy Quick-Relief Medications for Acute Asthma Attacks

Class of Drug	Medication	Mechanism of Action
Beta-2 agonists	Inhaled bronchodilators	Relax bronchiole smooth muscle; prevent bronchospasm; rapid onset of action
Anticholinergics	Inhaled anticholinergic agents	Relax bronchiole smooth muscle; decrease secretions; rapid onset of action
Anti-inflammatory drugs	Oral corticosteroids	Block allergic response; reduce airway hyper-responsiveness; improve response to bronchodilators; delayed onset of action (2–12 hours)

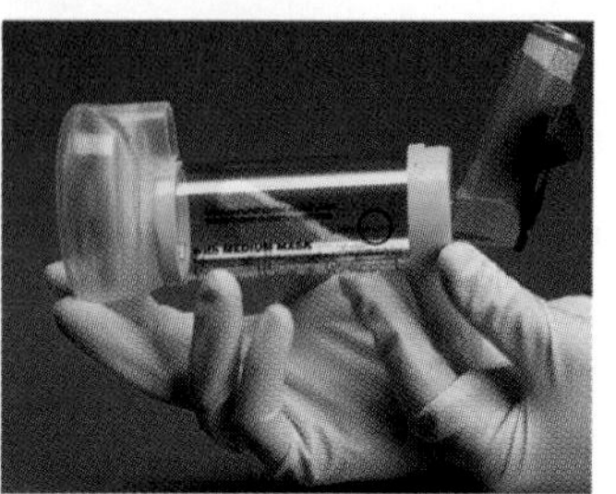

Figure 4-9a A metered dose inhaler and spacer can be used with or without a mask.

Figure 4-9b An MDI with spacer and mask can be used in children as young as 6 months old.

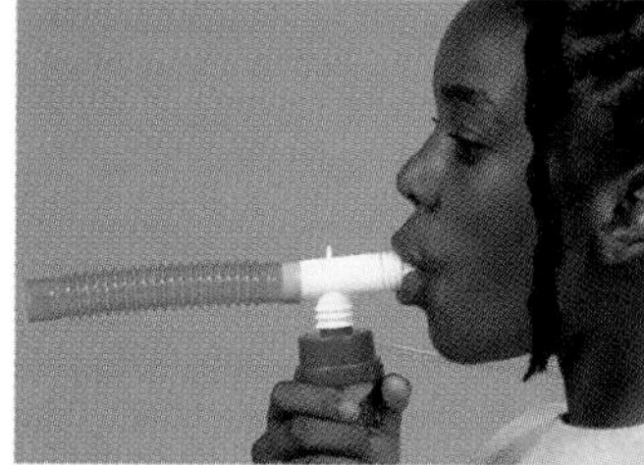

Figure 4-10 The most common method for delivering a bronchodilator is with an oxygen-powered nebulizer.

Treatment of lower airway obstruction

For all children with lower airway obstruction, give general noninvasive treatment as the first field action.

ALS Advanced LIFE support

Asthma treatment

Specific field treatment of wheezing is limited to inhaled bronchodilators or subcutaneous (SQ) epinephrine. Figures 4-9a, 4-9b, and 4-10 illustrate the different techniques for administration of inhaled bronchodilators.

Bronchodilators

Early bronchodilator therapy, on the scene and on the way to the ED, helps immediately open airways, relieve respiratory distress, and improve oxygen delivery. In unstable or critical patients, continuous inhaled treatment with a beta agonist is the preferred approach, although SQ bronchodilators may be needed in some patients. For a step-by-step explanation of this procedure, see page 250.

IM and SQ Injections

Intramuscular (IM) or SQ administration allows the medication to absorb slowly but steadily. The SQ route (e.g., for SQ epinephrine in bronchospasm) has few complications because it avoids contact with tendons, nerves, and blood vessels. The IM route may result in nerve damage, particularly if the injection is in the buttocks of infants and small children. For a step-by-step explanation of this procedure, see page 252.

Pharmacologic treatment of wheezing

Albuterol is the most popular inhaled bronchodilator. Because of its selective action on the bronchiole smooth muscles and its minimal effect on cardiac rate, the drug has a high margin of safety. In a "sick" child with wheezing, treat with the highest dose (0.5% albuterol undiluted) and give continuous treatment. If a child cannot tolerate nebulized drug therapy, or is moving air so poorly that the drug is not being inhaled, give SQ epinephrine. Transport with cardiac monitoring if frequent nebulized treatments or SQ epinephrine is necessary. Table 4-6 summarizes the drugs and doses for field bronchodilator therapy.

Assisted ventilation. Because of the severe air trapping associated with bronchospasm, assisted ventilation is associated with many complications and death. Positive pressure ventilation requires very high inspiratory pressures and may result in pneumothorax or **pneumomediastinum**. *Consider BVM ventilation and endotracheal intubation of a wheezing child only if the child is in respiratory failure and has failed to respond to high-flow oxygen and maximal bronchodilator therapy.*

Summary of Specific Treatment for Respiratory Distress

After identifying respiratory distress or failure and beginning general supportive measures, find out whether the anatomic level of the respiratory problem is in

Table 4-6 Management of Wheezing: Bronchodilator Treatment

Albuterol, 0.5% (5 mg/ml solution for inhalation)	<15 kg: 2.5–5.0 mg (0.5–1.0ml) diluted to 3 ml with normal saline, nebulized; May repeat every 20 min × 3 doses or use continuously in critical patients >15 kg: 5–10 mg (1–2ml) diluted to 3 ml with normal saline, nebulized; May repeat every 20 min × 3 doses or use continuously in critical patients
Albuterol metered dose inhaler (90 micrograms per puff)	4 to 8 puffs every 20 min × 3 doses; administer with mask or spacer device
Epinephrine 1:1000 (1 mg/ml solution)	0.01 mg/kg SQ injection, deltoid muscle or anterior thigh (infants); may repeat every 20 min × 3 doses; maximum single dose = 0.3 mg (0.3 ml)

the upper or lower airway, using both the PAT and the hands-on ABCDEs. Stridor is the hallmark of upper airway obstruction, and wheezing is the hallmark of lower airway obstruction. The common causes of upper airway obstruction are croup and foreign bodies lodged at or above the vocal cords, conditions most common in infants and toddlers. Specific treatment of croup includes cool mist and nebulized epinephrine. Frequent causes of lower airway obstruction are bronchiolitis—a disease of infants—and asthma. Asthma is the most likely reason for wheezing in all children from infancy to adulthood. A nebulized bronchodilator—delivered continuously if necessary—is the specific treatment for all causes of wheezing.

Management of Respiratory Failure

Regardless of the cause, initially treat every cooperative child in respiratory failure with general noninvasive measures. If upper or lower airway obstruction is present, attempt specific treatment. On the other hand, if the child has altered appearance or altered level of consciousness and has signs of increased or decreased work of breathing (e.g., flaring, grunting, gasping, apnea, or cyanosis), or if the child has a documented blood oxygen saturation of less than 90% on 100% nonrebreathing oxygen mask, the child is in respiratory failure or respiratory arrest. For this child, bypass general noninvasive treatment and immediately begin assisted ventilation.

! Tip

High dose, continuous albuterol nebulized therapy is as effective as SQ or IV administration of bronchodilators.

Deliver assisted ventilation or **positive pressure ventilation** using either BVM ventilation or endotracheal intubation. BVM will often be the best method for providing oxygenation and ventilation during stabilization and transport. Use an age-appropriate rate of 30 breaths/min in infants and 20 breaths/min in older children. Saying the words, "Squeeze, release, release" will help time the ventilations to avoid a rate that is too rapid. Ensure that there is good chest rise. Good BVM technique will decrease the risk of gastric distention—a common complication leading to elevation of the **diaphragm**, decreased lung compliance, and increased risk of vomiting and aspiration of gastric contents.

BVM Ventilation

BVM ventilation is one of the prehospital professional's most useful skills in pediatric out-of-hospital care. While the technique does not provide the definitive airway control that endotracheal intubation does, in most cases BVM ventilation will be the best technique for providing oxygenation and ventilation during resuscitation and transport. For a step-by-step explanation of this procedure, see page 257.

When a child requires ongoing BVM, placement of an orogastric (OG) or nasogastric (NG) tube can relieve gastric distention and improve ventilation.

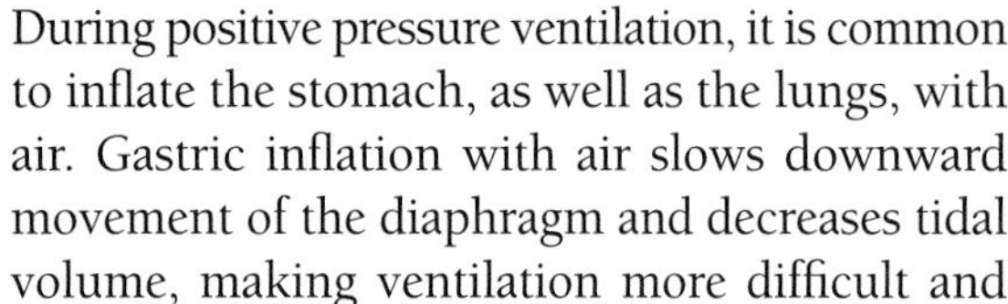

Nasogastric/Orogastric Intubation

During positive pressure ventilation, it is common to inflate the stomach, as well as the lungs, with air. Gastric inflation with air slows downward movement of the diaphragm and decreases tidal volume, making ventilation more difficult and necessitating higher inspiratory pressures. In addition, inflation of the stomach with air increases the risk that the patient will vomit and aspirate. Gastric intubation with an NG or OG tube takes air from the stomach and helps positive pressure ventilation. For a step-by-step explanation of this procedure, see page 260.

! Tip

Minimize gastric distention during BVM ventilation with good bagging technique.

Beware of assisted ventilation of asthmatics.

If the child does not respond to BVM ventilation, or if there is a long transport time with a critically ill or injured child who has an unstable airway, consider endotracheal intubation.

Endotracheal intubation

Successful endotracheal intubation allows optimal oxygenation and ventilation, provides a tube for medication delivery, and decreases the risk of aspiration and loss of airway control. A properly placed and secured endotracheal tube is a good tool for managing critical patients, but the procedure can take a long time, and there can be frequent and serious complications. For a step-by-step explanation of this procedure, see page 263.

Management with endotracheal intubation

The indications for endotracheal intubation of a child in the out-of-hospital setting are controversial. Potential advantages of intubation include definitive airway control, decreased risk of aspiration, and ease of assisted ventilation. Potential complications include transient hypoxia and hypercarbia due to prolonged intubation attempts, elevation of intracranial pressure, mechanical trauma to the airway, and failure of ventilation due to unrecognized misplacement of the tube (mainstem bronchus or esophageal intubation).

Dislodgment of the tube from the trachea during patient movement or transport is common and may be catastrophic. If an intubated patient fails to respond with improved color, oxygen saturation, heart rate, and appearance, the DOPE mnemonic may help to identify potential technical problems (Table 4-7).

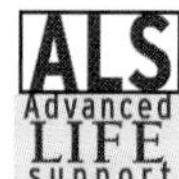

Confirmation of endotracheal tube placement

Several products are currently available for confirming proper placement of the endotracheal tube. These include quantitative end-tidal carbon dioxide monitors that read out the blood carbon dioxide tension ($PaCO_2$); colorimetric end-tidal carbon dioxide detectors that give a qualitative reading; and syringe devices that distinguish tracheal from esophageal intubation based on positive aspiration of air from the tube. The syringe device is currently approved only for children greater than 15 kg because the pliable trachea in young children may collapse, like the esophagus, with aspiration of air through the esophageal detector device.

The optimal method for tube confirmation in children in the out-of-hospital setting is not known. Because the child's airway is so short, even slight movement of the endotracheal tube can lead to extubation or mainstem intubation. If the end-tidal carbon dioxide monitor gives a low or negative reading or if the detector fails to change color with ventilation, extubate the child, do BVM, and reintubate. The only exception to this is the patient in full cardiopulmonary arrest, where

Table 4-7 Troubleshooting the Endotracheal Tube: DOPE

	Problem	Assessment	Intervention
Dislodgment	Esophageal intubation	End-tidal carbon dioxide monitor/detector reads no carbon dioxide or no color change Oxygen saturation <90% Bradycardia Lack of chest rise with ventilation Auscultation of bubbling over the stomach	Extubate BVM Reintubate
	Mainstem bronchus intubation	Asymmetric chest rise Asymmetric breath sounds	Pull tube back until breath sounds and chest rise are symmetric
	Accidental extubation	End-tidal carbon dioxide monitor/detector reads no carbon dioxide or no color change Oxygen saturation <90% Bradycardia Lack of chest rise with ventilation Poor or absent air movement on auscultation	BVM Reintubate
Obstruction	Tube blocked with blood, secretions, or kink	Decreased chest rise Decreased breath sounds bilaterally Oxygen saturation <90% Increased resistance to bagging	Suction Extubate BVM Reintubate
Pneumothorax	Tension pneumothorax, spontaneous or induced, compromises air exchange and may lead to decreased cardiac output	Asymmetric chest rise Asymmetric breath sounds Shock Oxygen saturation <90% *Jugulovenous distention *Tracheal deviation	Needle thoracentesis
Equipment	Big air leak around tube Activated pop-off valve on resuscitator Oxygen tubing disconnected Oxygen tank empty	Check equipment "patient-to-tank"	

* Not easily assessed in young children

pulmonary circulation may be too low to generate detectable expired carbon dioxide.

If the monitor shows a negative end-tidal carbon dioxide reading *in the setting of ongoing CPR*, observe for chest rise, auscultate bilaterally for air movement, and attempt to visualize the tube passing through the vocal cords via direct laryngoscopy. If the endotracheal tube appears to be in proper position, leave the tube in place.

Confirmation of endotracheal intubation

Tracheal insertion of an endotracheal tube makes it possible to oxygenate and ventilate children with critical illnesses or injuries. Esophageal placement of an endotracheal tube can be deadly. Fortunately, several mechanical adjuncts are available to help confirm correct tube placement in the trachea. For a step-by-step explanation of this procedure, see page 271.

Summary of Management of Respiratory Failure

Respiratory failure or respiratory arrest can result from many different insults to the airway, mechanics of breathing, or gas exchange. Infection, trauma, and bronchospasm are important causes in children. Think respiratory failure when initial assessment reveals a child with altered appearance in the setting of significantly increased or decreased work of breathing.

! Tip

When a child fails to respond to assisted ventilation with improvement in clinical status, quickly assess your equipment from the oxygen tank to the patient for mechanical failure.

The relative value of BVM and endotracheal intubation in the child with respiratory failure or arrest is unknown. However, recent studies suggest that endotracheal intubation provides little advantage and has many associated complications.

Bradycardia, poor air movement, and low oxygen saturation are key supportive findings. In a child with respiratory failure or respiratory arrest, immediately begin assisted ventilation with BVM at an age-appropriate rate. Add specific treatment for airway obstruction if indicated. Perform endotracheal intubation cautiously and be alert for the frequent "DOPE" complications in the intubated child who suddenly worsens or fails to respond.

The Transport Decision: Stay or Go?

When a child has respiratory distress, begin general noninvasive treatment and consider specific treatment on scene whenever possible. Never transport a child who is in respiratory failure without assisted ventilation. Also, never transport a child with an obstructed airway until after performing foreign body obstruction maneuvers. Immediate on scene care to support breathing will improve the outcomes of children with respiratory emergencies. After opening the airway and providing assisted ventilation when necessary, or after simply giving general treatment, the prehospital professional must decide whether to stay on scene to assess further and treat specifically, or to go.

If the PAT and ABCDEs are normal and the child has no history of serious breathing problems, the child does not usually require urgent treatment or immediate transport. Take the time to get a focused history and focused exam and perform a detailed examination on the scene if possible.

If the child has respiratory distress without signs of upper airway obstruction, transport is usually indicated after general noninvasive treatment. Consider specific treatment of suspected croup with cool mist and a dose of nebulized epinephrine on the way to the ED, if available. On the other hand, if the child has lower airway obstruction with wheezing, begin specific treatment with a bronchodilator *on scene*, then transport.

Additional Assessment

If the child has minimal respiratory distress and there are no immediate safety concerns for the child or prehospital professional, consider obtaining the focused history and performing focused and detailed exams on scene. Use the SAMPLE mnemonic to find important features of the complete respiratory history. Table 4-8 gives examples of a focused history in a child with a breathing problem.

Do vigilant ongoing assessment of all children with respiratory distress or failure while on the way to the ED. Use the PAT to recall observational indicators of effective gas exchange, and watch respiratory rate, heart rate, and pulse oximetry. Be prepared to increase the level of respiratory support, or to correct complications of therapy, if the child worsens or fails to respond.

Table 4-8 SAMPLE Components in a Child with Respiratory Distress

Component	Explanation
Signs/Symptoms	Onset and nature of shortness of breath Presence of hoarseness, stridor, or wheezing Presence and quality of cough, chest pain
Allergies	Known allergies Cigarette smoke exposure
Medications	Exact names and doses of ongoing drugs, including metered dose inhalers Recent use of steroids Timing and dose of last dose Timing and dose of analgesics/antipyretics
Past medical problems	History of asthma, chronic lung disease, or heart problems Prior hospitalizations for breathing problems Prior intubations for breathing problems Immunizations
Last food or liquid	Timing of the child's last food or drink, including bottle or breast feeding
Events leading to the injury or illness	Evidence of increased work of breathing Fever history

CASE STUDY 3

A grandmother calls 911 because her 4-month-old granddaughter is "not breathing right." The baby has had a fever, cough, and runny nose for 2 days. The grandmother says that the child's symptoms seem to get worse at night.

The baby will smile at her grandmother, and has good color and tone. She has a frequent barking cough, slight stridor only when agitated, and minimal intercostal retractions. There is no nasal flaring. Respiratory rate is 70 breaths/min, heart rate is 170 beats/min. Her blood pressure is not obtained. Blood oxygen saturation is 96% on room air. Her skin is warm, and she has good pulses and capillary refill time. On auscultation, she has good air movement and clear lungs.

Is this child in respiratory distress or respiratory failure?
What are the general and specific treatments for this condition?

Case Study Answers

See page 59

This child is in respiratory failure. He has an abnormal appearance (not interactive, weak cry) and increased work of breathing (retractions, abnormal audible airway sounds). His elevated heart rate, respiratory rate of 80 breaths/min, and diminished air movement support this assessment.

Wheezing signifies lower airway obstruction. In obstructive airway disease, bronchoconstriction, edema of the lining of the small airways, and increased mucus all contribute to narrowed airway caliber, which leads to increased work of breathing. In an infant less than 2 years old with no prior wheezing history, the most likely cause of lower airway obstruction is bronchiolitis. Although foreign body aspiration is also a possibility in this age group, focal wheezing (in just one lobe) would be more typical of that condition.

Provide general treatment with supplemental oxygen as tolerated, and keep him in a position of comfort. In an alert toddler, placing a face mask or nasal prongs may lead to the child becoming upset and worsened respiratory distress. Permit his mother to administer blow-by oxygen—usually the method best tolerated.

ALS Advanced LIFE support Give nebulized albuterol as specific treatment on scene. If a nebulizer is used for albuterol administration, use blow-by method. Because this child is in repiratory failure, give continuous nebulized undiluted albuterol and reassess the effectiveness of each nebulizer treatment during transport.

See page 68

This child is in respiratory failure. He has poor appearance (sleepy), poor color (pallor), and increased work of breathing (retractions, audible wheezing, flaring, tripod position). His tachypnea, tachycardia, documented hypoxia, and poor air movement support this assessment.

Further, he is being treated aggressively at home, with worsening symptoms despite steroids and utilization of his albuterol MDI far more frequently than is recommended for patient self-administration. The fact that he was up all night indicates that he was in too much respiratory distress to recline or sleep.

Asthma is a chronic disease, involving inflammation of the small airways. Although bronchoconstriction, airway edema, and increased secretions all contribute to lower airway obstruction, the only part of this pathophysiology that can be reversed in the short time frame of a field response is bronchoconstriction.

General noninvasive treatment includes administration of high-flow oxygen through a nonrebreathing mask, and position of comfort. Support ventilation with BVM if his condition deteriorates. Positive pressure ventilation will require high peak inspiratory pressures and may be associated with worse air trapping and **barotrauma**.

ALS Advanced LIFE support Specific treatment includes continuous high-dose nebulized albuterol, using 10 mg per dose, and "back-to-back" nebulizer treatments. Consider giving SQ epinephrine if he does not respond to the first nebulizer treatment or if his condition worsens. If transport is long and assisted ventilation is required, consider endotracheal intubation.

See page 75

This child has minimal respiratory distress with normal appearance and color and very mild increased work of breathing (mild intercostal retractions, intermittent stridor), and no flaring. However, her initial vital signs show significant tachypnea and tachycardia and probably are not good indicators of degree of distress. A trend of sustained tachypnea and tachycardia would be more worrisome. If this child gets angry or upset during the exam, her respiratory distress is likely to worsen, with marked retractions, prominent stridor, and decreased air movement.

The presence of stridor indicates upper airway obstruction. An infant with stridor in conjunction with cold symptoms and barking cough that get worse at night most likely has viral croup. Although a tracheal foreign body could also cause stridor, the age of this child makes that unlikely. A 4-month-old does not yet sit or crawl and has poor fine motor coordination. It is not likely that she will locate, pick up, and eat or inhale a foreign body small enough to get stuck in her airway. Because agitation will make this child worse, limit her treatment to general noninvasive measures with supplemental oxygen as tolerated and position of comfort, then transport.

ALS Advanced LIFE support

If her work of breathing increases, she develops fixed stridor in transport, or she becomes hypoxic, consider specific treatment with nebulized epinephrine. Nebulized epinephrine causes vasoconstriction, and rapidly decreases the swelling that obstructs airflow in croup.

Suggested Educational Resources

1. *Airway Management of the Pediatric Patient* [videotape]. Irving, TX: National American College of Emergency Physicians; 1994.

2. Aijian P, Tsai A, Knopp R, et al. Endotracheal intubation of pediatric patients by paramedics. *Ann Emerg Med* 1989;18:489-494.

3. American Heart Association. *Textbook of Pediatric Advanced Life Support*. Dallas, TX: American Heart Association; 1997.

4. Bhende MS, Thompson AE, Orr RA. Utility of an end-tidal carbon dioxide detector during stabilization and transport of critically ill children. *Pediatrics* 1992; 89:1042-1044.

5. Brownstein D, Shugerman R, Cummings P. Prehospital endotracheal intubation of children by paramedics. *Ann Emerg Med* 1996;28:34-39.

6. Kellner JD, Ohlsson A, Gadomski AM, et al. Efficacy of bronchodilator therapy in bronchiolitis—a meta-analysis. *Arch Pediatr Adolesc Med* 1996;150:1166-1172.

7. Washington Emergency Medical Services for Children Project. *Respiratory Distress in Infants and Children* [videotape]. Seattle, WA: Emergency Services, Children's Hospital and Regional Medical Center; 1990.

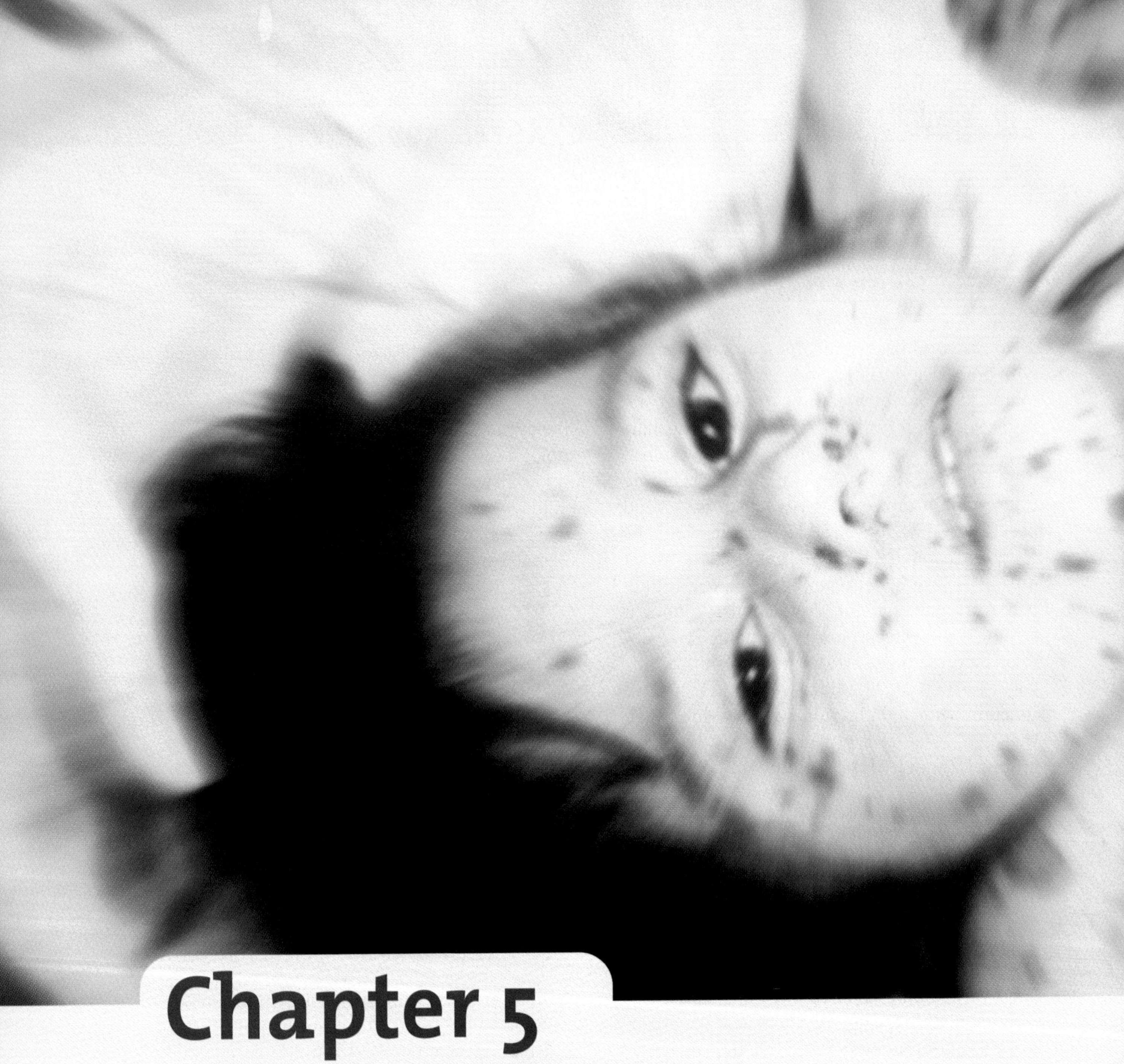

Chapter 5
Cardiovascular

Learning Objectives

1. Explain the relationship between shock and blood pressure.
2. Describe how to assess circulation.
3. Differentiate between early (compensated) and late (decompensated) hypovolemic shock and discuss appropriate management.
4. Explain when to treat tachycardia and bradycardia and discuss management.
5. Sequence the steps in the management of cardiopulmonary arrest.
6. Apply appropriate assessment and treatment techniques to case studies presenting patients with cardiovascular emergencies.

You are called to evaluate a 15-month-old girl with fever of 12 hours duration. The child is listless and does not wake up to your voice. She allows you to touch her without response. She has a hemorrhagic rash of the face, trunk, and legs. There are no abnormal airway sounds. Breathing is rapid without retractions or flaring. The brachial pulse is faint, the skin is warm to touch, and capillary refill time is greater than 3 seconds. Respiratory rate is 60 breaths/min, and blood pressure is not obtained. Cardiac monitor shows a heart rate of 180 beats/min.

What type of shock is present?

What differs in the management of this case from treatment of hypovolemic shock?

Emergencies

Introduction

Serious pediatric cardiovascular problems are unusual in the out-of-hospital setting. Loss of fluid or hypovolemia is the main cause of pediatric cardiovascular distress. Bleeding from injury is the most common specific pediatric cause of severe hypovolemia. Water losses from gastroenteritis (vomiting and diarrhea) and sepsis are important etiologies as well, especially in infants and children under the age of 3 years. This is different from adults, where primary heart problems are usually the reason for cardiovascular emergencies.

The child's young, healthy cardiovascular system makes up for volume loss by increasing heart rate and reducing blood flow to non-essential anatomic areas (peripheral vasoconstriction or "clamping down"). These functions protect core perfusion to the key organs—brain, heart, lungs, and kidneys—until the disease or injury process causes profound ischemia and the child can no longer compensate. The physiologic process of clamping down of circulation to non-essential anatomic areas, such as the skin, provides important physical signs of hypoperfusion.

Children may also develop distributive shock, especially in infants and toddlers, or cardiogenic shock, although it is rare. The assessment and management of these types of shock have important differences which will be discussed in this chapter. Shock from any cause, if unrecognized or inadequately treated, may advance to cardiopulmonary arrest—which is extremely difficult to reverse in children.

www.PEPPsite.com

Shock

Shock, or *hypoperfusion*, is decreased effective circulation, with inadequate delivery of oxygen to tissues. Shock may be present in its compensated stage well before its decompensated stage when hypotension is detectable. Shock may exist with normal, high, or low blood pressure. When **hypotension**, or decreased systolic blood pressure occurs, the body's built-in functions to make up for fluid loss have failed and the child is in decompensated shock.

Shock is not hypotension.

Studies of hypovolemia—the most common type of shock—have allowed researchers to determine the relationship between blood pressure changes and core organ perfusion. The timing of blood pressure changes during the development of other types of shock, such as distributive shock, is controversial. This is mainly because the factors that cause hypoperfusion in diseases other than hypovolemia are more complex. These factors include toxins in the bloodstream and interruption of sympathetic nerve regulation—conditions that are not easily measured or completely predictable.

Abnormal heart rate, blood pressure, and respiratory rate usually require clinical correlation. Initial numerical values may not reflect the child's true cardiovascular status. Trends in vital signs or persistent vital sign abnormalities, however, are good indicators of cardiovascular status. Tables 3-4, 3-6, and 3-7 list the wide range of normal respiratory rates, heart rates, and blood pressures in children of different ages. These wide ranges of normal vital signs make these numbers difficult to interpret without a history and physical assessment, especially when the values are normal or high. *Sustained* high respiratory rate and heart rate may indicate a real cardiovascular problem. *When respiratory rate, heart rate, or blood pressure is low using proper technique, be careful, because there is probably a serious problem in oxygenation, ventilation, and/or perfusion.*

Hypovolemic shock

Hypovolemia (loss of fluid) is the usual cause of shock in children in the out-of-hospital setting. The most common cause of hypovolemia is bleeding from blunt injuries such as falls or vehicle collisions with the child as a pedestrian, bicyclist, or passenger. Vomiting and diarrhea from gastroenteritis is a second common cause.

The signs and symptoms of hypovolemic shock vary with the amount and timing of fluid loss. There are both **compensated** and **decompensated** shock states. Compensated and decompensated shock represent different stages, or degrees, of hypovolemic shock.

Early (compensated) shock

Signs of compensated shock are tachycardia and peripheral "clamping down," or vasoconstriction. Vasoconstriction causes the signs of abnormal circulation to skin: poor skin color (pallor or mottling), dry and cool skin temperature, delayed capillary refill time, and decreased pulse strength. A cold environment or hypothermia may cause vasoconstriction, which mimics poor perfusion. Systolic blood pressure is normal in compensated shock.

In the compensated stage of hypovolemic shock, appearance may seem normal, or the child may appear slightly restless or not interactive. In a child with gastroenteritis and fever, the appearance may be abnormal because of sleepiness, listlessness, or loss of activity. Sometimes, high temperature may cloud accurate interpretation of appearance.

Late (decompensated) shock

In decompensated shock, perfusion is profoundly affected because compensatory mechanisms have failed. Increased heart rate and peripheral vasoconstriction are no longer able to maintain perfusion of core organs. Appearance is abnormal because of inadequate brain perfusion. The child will be restless, agitated, and inconsolable, or lethargic and poorly responsive. Hypotension, or low blood pressure for age, develops when there is about a 25% blood volume loss. Other late signs are effortless tachypnea and significantly increased heart rate. If not reversed, decompensated shock will lead to cardiopulmonary failure, with bradycardia and respiratory failure, and then to cardiopulmonary arrest.

The timing of blood pressure changes during the development of hypoperfusion in non-hypovolemic shock, such as distributive shock, is controversial.

There are many causes of shock, including acute blood or volume loss, poor intake, infection or congenital cardiovascular abnormalities.

Evaluating the presenting complaint

On arrival, find out about the presenting complaint. Key questions include the onset of illness, presence of fever, frequency and amount of fluid losses (vomiting and diarrhea), past history of cardiovascular problems, and if the child has been injured. In children with mild distress who are not in shock, there is usually time to get a more complete SAMPLE history later, as part of the focused history.

Cardiovascular Assessment

The PAT

Use the PAT for quick initial assessment of circulation. As outlined in Chapter 3, the PAT evaluates appearance, work of breathing, and circulation to skin.

Appearance

First, assess the child's appearance by careful listening and looking. A child with decreased core circulation may have signs of poor brain perfusion, including:

- lethargy
- poor eye contact
- weak cry
- decreased motor activity
- diminished interactiveness with caregivers, the prehospital professional, and the environment (Figure 5-1).

Sometimes the child will be restless and inconsolable. Appearance, however, is *not* a very accurate sign of circulatory problems. Abnormal appearance may be caused by many different things, such as poor oxygenation/ventilation, head trauma, hypothermia, drugs, or fever, as well as cardiovascular problems. Assessing appearance is a good way to tell if the child is ill, but not a good way to identify what the physiologic problem is.

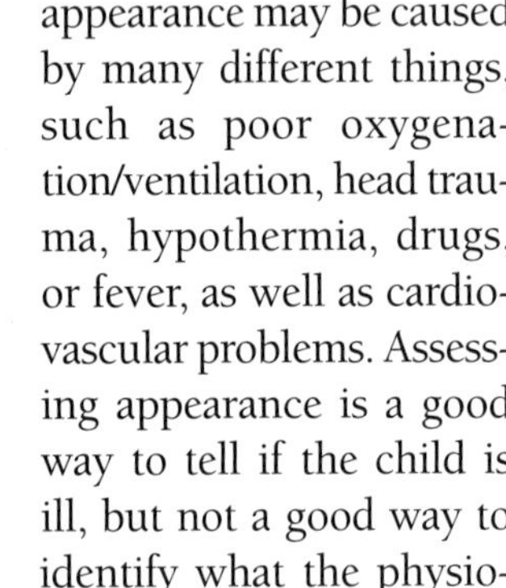

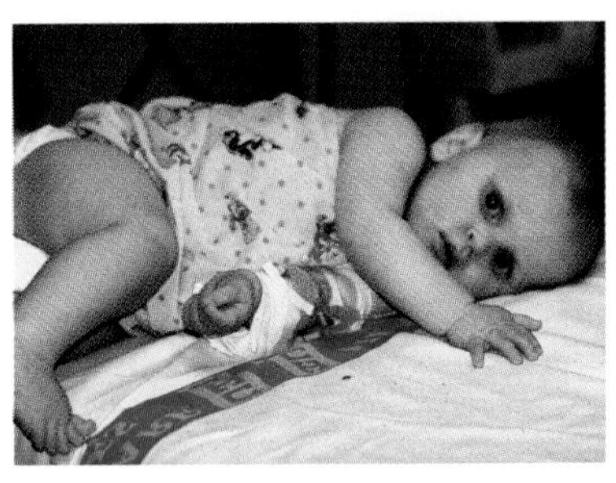

Figure 5-1 A child with decreased core circulation will have an abnormal appearance. This dehydrated child has listlessness, poor motor activity, and decreased interactiveness.

Work of breathing

Next, assess work of breathing. If circulation to vital organs is decreased, the child's respiratory rate will increase. Effortless tachypnea is a common, but nonspecific sign of decreased circulation. Retractions, grunting, flaring, and abnormal airway sounds, on the other hand, reflect respiratory distress and failure, and are not common in shock.

Circulation to skin

After assessing appearance and work of breathing, assess circulation to skin by looking at skin color. The child may have abnormal color because of clamping down of skin circulation, which causes mottling, pallor, and cyanosis.

The ABCDEs

After the PAT, perform the hands-on ABCDE components of the initial assessment. There are four parts to the "C" or circulation step:

1. Heart rate
2. Pulse quality
3. Skin temperature and capillary refill time
4. Blood pressure

Heart rate

First measure heart rate by feeling a pulse for 30 seconds, then doubling the number. A normal heart rate is between 60 and 160/min, depending on the child's age, as noted in Table 3-6. The radial or brachial areas are good places to take the measurement in infants and children. The carotid pulse is acceptable in older children and adolescents, but it is hard to feel in infants. If a pulse is difficult to feel, determine heart rate by listening to the heart sounds with a stethoscope placed on the medial side of the nipple.

Pulse quality

Presence of a strong central pulse (carotid, brachial, femoral) with a strong peripheral pulse (radial) suggests a good blood pressure. A strong central pulse with a weak peripheral pulse may indicate early shock or another problem such as **hypothermia**. *If a brachial pulse is not palpable, consider the child to be hypotensive.*

Skin temperature and capillary refill time

The next part of the cardiovascular assessment is evaluating skin signs. Check skin temperature at the kneecap or forearm. Normal skin temperature is warm. Then determine capillary refill time by pressing firmly on the soft skin. Capillary refill time should be less than 2 to 3 seconds in a child who is not cold (Figures 5-2a and 5-2b). Acute volume loss and hypoperfusion will cause clamping down of peripheral circulation, which will show up as cool skin and delayed capillary refill time. Capillary refill time is a good test for circulation in children. The prehospital professional can become comfortable with the technique and interpretation of the key findings by practicing on every child.

larized and functions as a noncollapsible vein. Needle insertion into this space is quick, simple, effective, and usually safe. Complications are infrequent and usually minor. For a step-by-step explanation of this procedure, see page 279.

The transport decision: Stay or go?

After completing the initial assessment and beginning general treatment when appropriate, the prehospital professional must decide whether to go or stay on scene. If the PAT and ABCDEs are normal and the child has no history of serious illness or injury mechanism, no anatomic abnormalities, and no pain, the child does not usually require urgent treatment or immediate transport. Take the time to get a focused history and perform a focused exam and a detailed examination on the scene if possible.

On the other hand, if the child has a serious mechanism of injury, a physiologic or anatomic abnormality, severe pain, or if the scene is not safe, transport immediately. With such patients, do the additional assessment and attempt specific treatment on the way to the hospital, if possible.

The transport decision is sometimes difficult in a child with a suspected cardiovascular problem who needs vascular access. If the child is in compensated shock and has a palpable brachial pulse or normal blood pressure, immobilize (if the child is injured), manage the airway and breathing, control hemorrhage, and transport immediately. Attempt vascular access for specific treatment on the way to the ED.

If the child is in decompensated shock, the prehospital professional has several options, depending on the clinical condition of the child, the local EMS system regulations, the prehospital professional's comfort level, and the time to the nearest ED. If the child is injured, always transport immediately. If the child is ill with abnormal appearance and hypotension, considering attempting vascular access once on scene, then transporting.

Additional assessment

If the child is stable and there are no immediate safety concerns for the child or prehospital professional, conduct the focused history and focused and detailed exams on scene. Use the SAMPLE mnemonic (Table 5-1) to recall important features of the focused cardiovascular history. Use age-appropriate approaches to gain the child's trust and speak directly to her. Ask the caregiver to add to the child's history. Obtain the history from the caregiver if the child is too young to speak or is unable to cooperate.

After the focused history, perform a focused exam of the heart, peripheral circulation, and the abdomen. Then, do a detailed anatomic exam of the entire body, as outlined in Chapter 3.

Perform an ongoing assessment of all children with cardiovascular problems while on the way to the ED. The child's status may change during transport, so observe and document any physiologic trends. Use the PAT to monitor effective perfusion and watch respiratory rate, heart rate, blood pressure, and pulse oximetry. Keep the child in shock on a cardiac monitor. Be prepared to increase the level of respiratory and cardiovascular support, if the child worsens or fails to respond.

Summary of Cardiovascular Assessment

The PAT provides a good first cardiovascular evaluation. Abnormal appearance, normal work of breathing, and poor circulation to skin suggest a possible perfusion problem. The ABCDEs—pulse quality, skin temperature, and capillary refill time—complement the PAT and will help identify the type and degree of physiologic insult to circulation. Conventional vital signs—heart rate, blood pressure, and respiratory rate—when used with the rest of the initial assessment, can also be helpful in cardiovascular assessment. These vital signs, however, can sometimes be misleading and must be correctly obtained and interpreted for age. Trends in vital signs, or persistence in

Table 5-1 SAMPLE Components in a Child with Cardiovascular Problems

Component	Explanation
Signs/Symptoms	Onset of volume loss Presence of vomiting or diarrhea Quality of vomitus or stool
Allergies	Known allergies History of anaphylaxis
Medications	Exact names and dosages of ongoing medications Use of laxatives or antidiarrheal medications Potential exposure to other medications or drugs Timing and doses of analgesic/antipyretics
Past medical problems	History of heart problems History of prematurity Prior hospitalizations for cardiovascular problems Immunizations
Last food or liquid	Timing of the child's last food or drink, including bottle or breast feedings
Events leading to the injury or illness	Travel Fever history Symptoms in family members

abnormal vital signs, are more accurate indicators of real physiologic problems than mild vital sign abnormalities on initial assessment.

Distributive Shock

In true distributive shock, the child has decreased vascular muscle tone (peripheral **vasodilatation**), not a change in circulating blood volume. This loss of vascular tone is relative hypovolemia and causes decreased perfusion (hypoperfusion) to vital organs. Patients with distributive shock may also have hypovolemia, such as in the septic patient with poor intake and water losses from vomiting, diarrhea, and fever.

The most common cause of distributive shock with hypovolemia is sepsis, especially in children under 2 to 3 years of age. Other causes of distributive shock without hypovolemia are anaphylaxis, chemical intoxication with drugs that decrease vascular tone (e.g., beta blockers, barbiturates), or spinal cord injury (above T-6) with interruption of spinal sympathetic nerves to muscle walls of peripheral arteries.

Assessment

Signs of distributive shock indicate that the patient has low peripheral vascular resistance and decreased organ perfusion. These signs may vary with the specific cause, as noted in the descriptions of the three major types of distributive shock (Table 5-2). The progression of physical signs in distributive shock is not as predictable as in hypovolemic shock. In late distributive shock, the findings are indistinguishable from findings in late shock from any cause: abnormal appearance from poor brain perfusion and hypotension.

Major types of distributive shock

Sepsis

Sepsis occurs when any type of infection, usually bacterial or viral, overwhelms the body's defense

Table 5-2 Types of Shock in Children

Shock Type	Physiologic Insult	Common Causes	Treatment
Hypovolemic	Volume loss	Hemorrhage Gastroenteritis (vomiting, diarrhea) Burns	Rapid transport IV fluid boluses
Distributive	Decreased vascular tone	Sepsis Anaphylaxis Drug overdose Spinal cord injury	Rapid transport Fluid administration Epinephrine for anaphylaxis Dopamine for septic shock
Cardiogenic	Heart failure	Congenital heart disease Cardiomyopathy Dysrhythmia Overdose	Rapid transport Cautious fluid administration, 10 ml/kg Consider a vasopressor like dopamine

system and causes generalized breakdown in core organ function. Distinctive signs of early distributive shock from sepsis are warm skin, tachycardia, and bounding pulses. A septic child's appearance will be abnormal and may include listlessness, lethargy, decreased interactiveness, restlessness, and poor consolability. Fever, poor feeding, vomiting, diarrhea, and fussiness also may be present.

Ill children usually like to be held and cuddled. If a child with a fever does not want to be held but is more comfortable when left alone, the child may have **paradoxical irritability**. This may be a sign of sepsis or meningitis.

Sometimes, a petechial rash or ecchymosis is present on the skin of a septic child. If an ill-appearing child has a rash, check to see if it blanches. Place one finger on each side of the spot and pull in opposite directions. If the spot goes away, it is not petechial. If the spot does not go away, it may be petechial and another sign of sepsis.

Anaphylaxis

Anaphylaxis is a major allergic reaction that involves a generalized system attack. The airways and vascular system are the main sites of this often life-threatening reaction. The most common cause is an insect sting from a common bumblebee or fire ant. A child in anaphylactic shock will have hypoperfusion as well as additional signs such as stridor and/or wheezing, with increased work of breathing. The child will also have altered appearance with restlessness and agitation and sometimes a sense of impending doom. **Hives**, an intensely itchy skin rash, may be present as well (Figure 5-4).

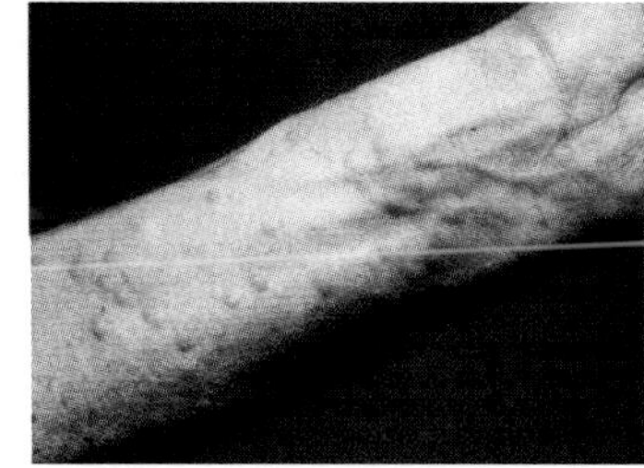

Figure 5-4 Hives suggest an allergic reaction and may or may not be present with anaphylaxis.

Spinal shock

Spinal shock usually results from a mechanism of injury that involves the back, neck, or both. The child has motor paralysis. There is a loss of autonomic support of circulation. Hence, she may not demonstrate a tachycardic response to actual or relative hypovolemia. These patients will be both hypotensive and bradycardic.

Specific treatment of distributive shock

The primary difference between treatment of distributive and hypovolemic shock is the potential need for a **vasopressor agent** to improve vascular tone and heart muscle function in distributive shock. *Treat all shock conditions first with general noninvasive treatment.* Administer

100% high-flow oxygen and put the poorly responsive child with shock in a head-down position.

ALS Advanced LIFE support

Treatment of decompensated distributive shock

Attempt vascular access on scene once. Deliver fluid boluses, up to 60 ml/kg of a crystalloid solution in 20 ml/kg boluses on the way to the ED. If the child has lost protective airway reflexes or has refractory shock, support ventilation with BVM or endotracheal intubation.

If cardiovascular instability (hypotension, markedly increased heart rate, and poor responsiveness) persists after volume therapy with 60 ml/kg of crystalloid, try a vasopressor agent (dopamine or epinephrine). *Do not administer a vasopressor agent if you suspect untreated hypovolemia.*

Treatment of anaphylaxis

A child with anaphylaxis requires special treatment with epinephrine and with a beta agonist if bronchospasm is present. Unlike a simple allergic reaction, anaphylaxis has important and dangerous cardiovascular effects.

Epinephrine is an excellent drug for treatment of anaphylaxis. Its "alpha" and "beta" properties have two important effects: (1) constriction of the blood vessels to help counter the vasodilation of anaphylaxis, and (2) opening up the airways to help reverse the bronchospasm of anaphylaxis. For all children with allergic reactions associated with wheezing, administer epinephrine, 0.01 mg/kg (0.01 ml/kg) of 1:1000 solution (maximum 0.3 mg or 0.3 ml) subcutaneously (SQ). If a child has hypoperfusion with anaphylaxis, administer epinephrine by IV and use a maximum dose of 0.1 mg and a more dilute solution to help decrease the possibility of an adverse drug reaction. Draw up 0.01 mg/kg (0.1 ml/kg) of the 1:10,000 epinephrine solution (maximum 0.1 mg or 1 ml of the epinephrine) and dilute the solution further with 9 ml of normal saline to reduce the epinephrine concentration to 1:100,000.

Be extremely careful with IV epinephrine and double-check doses! If epinephrine is given IV to a normal patient, serious negative reactions may occur. These include coronary vasoconstriction and cardiac dysrhythmias such as **ventricular fibrillation**. Another useful drug for anaphylaxis is **diphenhydramine**, an antihistamine that helps reduce the itching. It may also help counter the vascular and lung effects in anaphylaxis. The dose is 1 mg/kg IV. Give both diphenhydramine and epinephrine in a child with anaphylaxis, and also administer nebulized albuterol if she is wheezing.

CASE STUDY 2

A 9-month-old girl has experienced vomiting and diarrhea for 3 days. The father called 911 when the infant seemed sleepy and had a bluish color. Your assessment reveals a lethargic, limp, mottled infant in a crib breathing rapidly without retractions or flaring. The brachial pulse is barely palpable. Her skin is cool and dry, and capillary refill time is greater than 3 seconds. Breath sounds are clear. The abdomen is normal, without palpable organs. Respiratory rate is 50 breaths/min, and blood pressure is 40 mm Hg/palp. Cardiac monitor shows a heart rate of 200 beats/min.

What type of shock is present?
Outline the management priorities.

Cardiogenic Shock

Cardiogenic shock is rare in children. The most likely cause is either congenital heart disease or **cardiomyopathy** from **myocarditis**. Myocarditis is a disease of the heart muscle, usually caused by a virus. A primary **dysrhythmia**, such as **supraventricular tachycardia** (SVT), may also cause cardiogenic shock. Finally, overdose with a **cardiotonic** drug, such as a **calcium channel blocker** or beta blocker, is another etiology.

Assessment

A history from the caregiver will usually reveal that the child has had generalized, nonspecific symptoms such as loss of appetite, lethargy, irritability, and sweating. There is often a history of congenital heart disease or the presence of a midline chest scar from heart surgery.

Cardiogenic shock develops from left heart failure. Impaired left heart function causes decreased core organ perfusion. On physical assessment, the child may appear abnormal—sluggish, irritable, or agitated. The cry may be weak; spontaneous motor activity and muscle tone decreased; and the color mottled or occasionally cyanotic. Heart rate is rapid; blood pressure may be high (early) or low (late). The skin is cool and wet or **diaphoretic** (not dry as with hypovolemic shock). A backup of fluid in the lungs causes increased work of breathing and inspiratory crackles.

Increased right-sided cardiac pressures are also present in cardiogenic shock. They may appear as jugular venous distention and liver enlargement (**hepatomegaly**). *Hepatomegaly is an especially useful finding in infants and toddlers.* Peripheral edema and jugular venous distension are rare in children.

Specific treatment of cardiogenic shock

If cardiogenic shock is suspected by history and/or physical assessment, give high-flow oxygen and place in a position of comfort. Transport after general noninvasive treatment.

ALS Advanced LIFE support

Treatment of cardiogenic shock

On the way to the ED, consider vascular access. Give a cautious fluid bolus of only 10 ml/kg of crystalloid, then reassess appearance, work of breathing, circulation to skin, heart rate, and blood pressure.

If there is no rhythm disturbance on the cardiac monitor, and the child remains poorly perfused after the initial fluid bolus, consider a vasopressor agent, either dopamine or epinephrine, if the transport time is long. Start vasopressors at low doses, based on per kilogram **nomograms**, then **titrate** to achieve acceptable perfusion (improved appearance and skin circulation and decreased heart rate and respiratory rate).

The major difference between treatment of hypovolemic, distributive, and cardiogenic shock is the lower amount of fluid administration and earlier consideration of a vasopressor for cardiogenic shock.

Classification of Shock States

Table 5-2 summarizes the three common types of shock in children, the usual associated physiologic insult, common causes, and specific treatment. Hypovolemic shock is usually caused by vomiting and diarrhea, or hemorrhage after injury. Always suspect sepsis, a form of distributive shock, in the infant or toddler who has fever and abnormal appearance. A petechial skin rash is a red flag for sepsis. Treatment of all shock types includes general noninvasive interventions. Consider fluids in children who are decompensated with abnormal appearance and hypotension. Vasopressor agents have a limited role.

The proper administration technique for vasopressors is unknown. The small infusion rates necessary in young children cannot be easily controlled in ambulances.

! Tip

The major goals in treatment of cardiogenic shock are the reduction in volume of fluid administration and early consideration of a vasopressor.

Dysrhythmias

Bradycardia

In children, bradycardia almost always represents hypoxia. It is a prearrest rhythm, and the prognosis is ominous if it is untreated. Immediate delivery of high-flow oxygen and assisted ventilation are essential. Untreated bradycardia will quickly cause shock, hypotension, and death. In children with asthma or respiratory distress, bradycardia means profound hypoxia. Pulse oximetry, when available, will help determine the degree of hypoxia in the field.

Congenital heart block is an extremely rare cause of bradycardia in infancy and early childhood. Drug overdose (e.g., beta blockers, calcium channel blockers, digoxin) may also cause bradycardia. Bradycardia may also result from **vagal stimulation** (laryngoscopy, suctioning, gastric tube placement). If bradycardia occurs, temporarily stop the specific procedure.

Heart rates are frequently below the normal range for age in normal school-aged children. Adolescent athletes are good examples. These patients are otherwise normal and well perfused and do not require treatment.

Assessment of the child with bradycardia

If the child has a heart rate below the range for age (see Table 3-6), evaluate carefully for signs of a real physiologic problem, such as respiratory failure or shock. The PAT and ABCDEs, along with a brief history, will establish the likely cause, the severity of the problem, and the urgency for treatment.

Be extremely careful with IV epinephrine and double-check doses!

! Tip

In children, bradycardia almost always represents hypoxia.

Treatment of bradycardia

If the child has a low heart rate and the initial assessment is normal, administer oxygen, monitor the child, and transport to the hospital. Consider vascular access on the way and do not treat further. If the child has bradycardia and an initial assessment that shows oxygenation, ventilation, or perfusion abnormalities, give 100% oxygen and transport. If she does not respond to oxygen, begin assisted ventilation by BVM. Check effectiveness of ventilation by observing for chest rise and an increase in heart rate.

In certain rare situations, chest compressions for bradycardia are necessary. If the heart rate is low (usually <60/min), with signs of poor perfusion after assisted ventilation with BVM, begin chest compressions.

ALS Advanced LIFE support

Drug therapy for symptomatic bradycardia

BVM is the primary treatment for bradycardia. If the heart rate does not rise in response to assisted ventilation, administer IV or IO epinephrine as the first-line drug. IV or IO atropine is indicated after epinephrine, but will probably not help unless congenital heart block or vagal stimulation is present.

Before administering vasopressor drugs, always assess for mechanical problems with oxygen delivery. Specifically check for disconnected oxygen tubing, poor mask seal, airway obstruction, inadequate chest rise, endotracheal tube blockage, or malposition. Other causes of bradycardia, from hypoxia or ischemia, are pneumothorax, hypovolemia, cardiomyopathy, poisoning, or increased intracranial pressure.

PROCEDURE 14

Endotracheal Administration of Drugs

If neither IV nor IO access is available for giving drugs during a resuscitation, the endotracheal route is a good alternative for at least four pediatric drugs: lidocaine, atropine, naloxone, and epinephrine. While endotracheal drugs are probably not as effective as IV or IO drugs, they can help improve the chances of successful resuscitation while IV or IO access is established. The best technique for endotracheal drug delivery is not known. For a step-by-step explanation of this procedure, see page 281.

Tachycardia

Tachycardia may be a nonspecific sign of fear, anxiety, pain, or fever and may not represent serious injury or illness. Tachycardia may also be a sign of a life-threatening problem such as hypoxia or hypovolemia. Most tachycardia in children is **sinus tachycardia** and may require fluid administration but not specific treatment.

Assessment of the child with tachycardia

Tachycardia must be assessed in conjunction with the PAT and ABCDEs. As in the assessment of bradycardia, interpret heart rate based on knowledge of the normal range for age (see Table 3-6). Always ask about a history of congenital heart disease and check for midline chest scars from cardiac surgery.

Table 5-3 distinguishes sinus tachycardia from other cardiogenic causes of tachycardia, particularly supraventricular tachycardia (SVT) and ventricular tachycardia (VT).

Specific treatment of tachycardia

If the child presents in shock with tachycardia, determine appropriate treatment by examining two variables on the rhythm strip:

1. Heart rate
2. Width of the **QRS complex**

If the child has a narrow QRS tachycardia (<0.08 seconds), and the heart rate is variable and less than 220 beats per minute, the cause is usually sinus tachycardia from noncardiac conditions (e.g., hypoxia, hypovolemia, fear, pain). No specific cardiac treatment of the tachycardia is needed. Instead, treat with fluids, oxygen, splinting, analgesia, or sedation as indicated.

ALS Advanced LIFE support

Specific treatment of SVT

If the QRS is less than 0.08 seconds, and the rate is not variable and is greater than 220 beats/min, consider SVT as the likely etiology. In a stable child, consider a vagal maneuver first. Ice to the face (if available) evokes the "**diving reflex**" and is a powerful vagal maneuver in infants and toddlers. Place crushed ice in a plastic bag, glove, or washcloth and apply firmly over the mid-face (cheeks, nose, and mouth) for approximately 15 seconds, until the rhythm changes or the patient's condition dictates immediate cessation of the procedure (Figure 5-5). Do not occlude the nose (to allow breathing) and provide constant reassurance to the child. Other vagal maneuvers (carotid sinus massage or valsalva) are also safe. Only attempt the vagal maneuver once.

Then, if the heart rate does not change to sinus, give adenosine at 0.1 mg/kg rapid IV or IO push and follow with a 2–5 ml bolus of normal saline. Repeat dose of 0.2 mg/kg once if necessary. Maximum single dose is 12 mg or 0.3 mg/kg.

If a child with suspected SVT is in shock or is unconscious, administer adenosine prior to electrical countershock if vascular access is possible within 30 seconds. If there is no vascular access, and the child is unconscious, immediately administer synchronized electrical countershock at 0.5 to 1.0 joules/kg as a starting electrical charge. Then double to 2 joules/kg, then again to 4 joules/kg, if ineffective. If the synchronized mode does not work or is ineffective, switch to the asynchronized mode (**defibrillation**).

Avoid specific treatment for rapid heart rates. Most tachycardia in children is sinus tachycardia and does not require dysrythmia treatment.

Controversy

Ice to the face for SVT is a controversial field procedure. It has not been evaluated for efficacy or safety in the out-of-hospital setting.

Wide complex tachycardia

If the child is conscious and has a QRS greater than

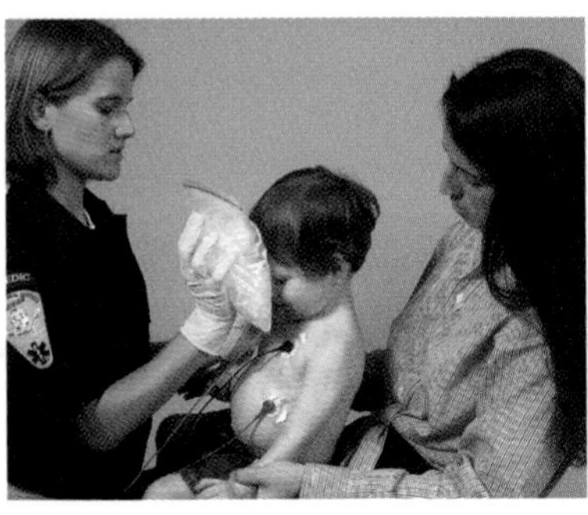

Figure 5-5 Placing a bag of ice on a child's face elicits the "diving reflex" and may convert SVT to sinus rhythm.

Table 5-3 Distinguishing Pediatric Sinus Tachycardia, Supraventricular Tachycardia (SVT), and Ventricular Tachycardia (VT)

Feature	Sinus Tachycardia	Supraventricular Tachycardia	Ventricular Tachycardia
History	Fever Volume loss Hypoxia Pain	Congenital heart disease Known SVT Nonspecific symptoms (e.g., poor feeding, fussiness)	Serious systemic illness
Heart rate	<220 beats/min	>220 beats/min, (often 240–300 beats/min)	>150 beats/min
Respiratory rate	Variable	Constant	Variable
QRS interval	Narrow, <0.08 sec	Narrow, <0.08 sec	Wide, >0.08 sec
Assessment	Hypovolemia Hypoxia Painful injury	CHF may be present	CHF may be present
Possible treatments	Fluids Oxygen Splinting Analgesia/sedation	Vagal maneuvers Adenosine Synchronized electrical countershock	Synchronized electrical countershock Amiodarone Lidocaine

0.08 seconds and a heart rate greater than 150 beats/min, consider ventricular tachycardia as a likely cause. Transport and attempt an IV en route if perfusion is normal. Be sure to ask the caregiver if the child has had heart disease or heart surgery because sinus tachycardia with a conduction abnormality (**bundle branch block**) may look like VT. These cases are quite rare.

If the child has VT and is unconscious and/or in shock, immediately administer synchronized electrical countershock. Use the same electrical charge as recommended for SVT. Then administer amiodarone, 5 mg/k over 20-60 min or lidocaine, 1mg/kg bolus, then 20-50 ug/kg/min.

Controversy

An important controversy involves transport of pediatric cardiopulmonary arrest victims. Recent studies indicate that if children in cardiopulmonary arrest fail out-of-hospital ALS, they probably will not survive.

Electrical Countershock

When a child's heart deteriorates into ventricular tachycardia or fibrillation, there is usually a severe systemic insult—such as profound hypoxia, ischemia, electrocution, or myocarditis. When the child is pulseless and has ventricular fibrillation perform a electrical asynchronized countershock (defibrillation) as quickly as possible with the appropriate technique. If a child has SVT or VT and shock, use synchronized countershock. For a step-by-step explanation of this procedure, see page 283.

Other pediatric dysrhythmias

Dysrhythmias are rare in children. Dysrhythmias that are common in the adult population (e.g., ventricular ectopy) occur in children only in unusual circumstances (hypoxia, congenital heart defects, after cardiac surgery, after defibrillation).

Summary of Dysrhythmias

Cardiac rhythm disturbances are rare in children. Bradycardia almost always means hypoxia and is often a prearrest state. Tachycardia may be SVT, VT, or sinus tachycardia. Children can develop heart rates greater than 200 beats/min because of stimuli such as hypoxia or pain, so carefully evaluate the cardiac rhythm before treating specifically. Other types of adult dysrhythmias, such as VT or ventricular ectopy, are uncommon in children.

Cardiopulmonary Arrest

Causes

Pediatric cardiopulmonary arrest is almost always the result of lack of oxygen or perfusion from one of many noncardiac causes. In contrast to adults, cardiopulmonary arrest in children usually follows a primary respiratory arrest. Shock is the second common pathway to cardiopulmonary arrest.

Most cardiopulmonary arrests occur in infancy and are caused by sudden infant death syndrome (SIDS). Myocardial infarction, a frequent cause of cardiac arrest in adults, is extremely unusual in young children.

The most common cause of cardiac arrest in toddlers and children is blunt trauma from vehicle-related injuries and falls. Survival from cardiac arrest depends on several factors: time before the start of basic life support (BLS), time to advanced life support (ALS), and presenting rhythm.

Assessment in cardiopulmonary arrest

A child in cardiopulmonary arrest is unresponsive, apneic, and pulseless. The cardiac monitor will show a cardiopulmonary arrest rhythm, usually asystole or bradyasystole (asystole or a slow rhythm, <20–30 beats/min with wide QRS complexes). Pulseless electrical activity or VF may be present. SVT and VT are rare causes of cardiopulmonary arrest.

Asystole or bradyasystole in most cases reflects profound hypoxia and ischemia. Pulseless electrical activity may represent a variety of ischemic, hypoxic, hypothermic and traumatic insults. Some pulseless electrical activity may arise from low-flow states with blood pressures too low to record in the out-of-hospital setting. VF most often occurs in a child older than 2 years from myocarditis, poisoning, electrocution, drowning, or hypoxia.

Specific treatment of cardiopulmonary arrest

Priorities of cardiopulmonary arrest management are early airway management, chest compressions, BVM ventilation or endotracheal intubation, IV or IO needle insertion with rapid administration of epinephrine, and/or electrical countershock/defibrillation.

Prehospital cardiopulmonary arrest treatment requires good BLS skills.

Cardiopulmonary Resuscitation (CPR)

CPR encompasses the basic procedures for sustaining critical oxygenation, ventilation, and perfusion recommended by the American Heart Association. The pediatric techniques are slightly modified from the adult technique to reflect known differences in cardiopulmonary arrest between age groups. Furthermore, there are specific differences between infants and children, including number of rescuers, placement of hands and fingers, rates of ventilation, and rates and depth of chest compressions. For a step-by-step explanation of this procedure, see page 286.

Resuscitation Tape

Treatment of infants and children in the out-of-hospital setting is difficult because children of different ages require different-sized equipment, different doses of medications, and different amounts of fluids. The pediatric resuscitation tape uses length as a valid marker of size-specific equipment and medication needs. It is portable, easy to use, and applies to all out-of-hospital equipment and medications. For a step-by-step explanation of this procedure, see page 290.

Figure 5-6 and Table 5-4 summarize ALS therapy with electrical countershock and medications for cardiopulmonary arrest. An important controversy is the role of "high dose" epinephrine. Many protocols allow administration of 0.1 mg/kg of epinephrine for subsequent doses if the dose of 0.01 mg/kg is not successful. This higher dose is unproven in humans and may be harmful.

Deciding which pediatric cardiopulmonary arrest patients require hospital transport is another important controversy. Recent studies indicate that if children in cardiopulmonary arrest fail out-of-hospital resuscitation with BLS and ALS, they will not survive. Patients who are victims of hypothermia or drowning, or who have ingested massive amounts of sedative-hypnotic drugs (e.g., barbiturates) may have more chance of survival and deserve extended treatment before death is declared.

Some children may undergo limited field resuscitation attempts, which sometimes can be stopped before transport in keeping with local EMS death-in-the-field policies. Studies indicate that survival in unwitnessed out-of-hospital cardiopulmonary arrest is rare. When resuscitation is terminated, communicating with the caregivers is important (Figure 5-7), as explained in Chapter 11. Moreover, advise grief counseling for parents and family.

Cardiopulmonary arrest in children is associated with high provider stress, and critical incident stress debriefing may be helpful for prehospital professionals after such a tragedy.

Summary of Cardiopulmonary Arrest

Cardiopulmonary arrest is a rare event in the overall population but not uncommon in out-of-hospital pediatrics. Survival is unlikely, but attention to airway, CPR, and epinephrine delivery are key interventions. Sometimes, for children with VF or pulseless VT, electrical countershock is indicated. In all cases of cardiopulmonary arrest, grief counseling for the caregivers and critical incident stress debriefing for the prehospital professionals are recommended.

Figure 5-7 Communication with the caregivers and family is imperative after the death of a child.

CASE STUDY 3

A distraught mother calls 911 because her child is blue. You find a 4-month-old boy cyanotic, pulseless, and apneic. There is no history of illness or injury. The infant had been put down for a nap 1 hour previously, and the mother could not wake him up. Cardiac monitor shows asystole.

Outline management priorities.

Discuss termination of resuscitation in the field.

Figure 5-6 Treatment of Pediatric Cardiopulmonary Arrest

Determine pulselessness.
Begin CPR. Check rhythm.

Asystole/Pulseless Electrical Activity

1. **Consider endotracheal intubation.**
2. **Obtain IV or IO access.**
3. **Administer epinephrine.**

   If IV/IO administration
   - Use 1:10,000 solution
     At 0.01mg/kg (0.1ml/kg)

   If endotracheal instillation
   - Use 1:1000 solution (except newborns)
     At 0.1 mg/kg (0.1 ml/kg)
   - In newborns use 0.03 mg/kg (0.3 ml/kg) of 1:10,000
4. **Repeat epinephrine every 3-5 min.**
5. **Consider and treat specific causes:**
   - Hypovolemia
   - Hypothermia
   - Cardiac tamponade
   - Tension pneumothorax

Ventricular Tachycardia/Ventricular Fibrillation

1. **Defibrillate up to three times:**
   - 2 joules/kg
   - 2-4 joules/kg
   - 4 joules/kg
2. **Consider endotracheal intubation.**
3. **Obtain IV or IO access.**
4. **Administer epinephrine.**

   If IV/IO administration
   - Use 1:10,000 solution
     At 0.01mg/kg (0.1ml/kg)

   If endotracheal instillation
   - Use 1:1000 solution (except newborns)
     At 0.1 mg/kg (0.1 ml/kg)
   - In newborns use 0.03 mg/kg (0.3 ml/kg) of 1:10,000
5. **Defibrillate** with 4 joules/kg 30-60 sec after each epinephrine dose, every 3-5 min.
6. **Administer antidysrhythmic drugs:**
   - Amiodarone: 5 mg/kg IV/IO bolus or
   - Lidocaine: 1 mg/kg IV/IO bolus

Table 5-4 Drugs for Treatment of Pediatric Cardiopulmonary Arrest

Drug	Indication	Dose	Comment
Amiodarone	VT/VF	5 mg/kg IV/IO	Maximum dose is 15 mg/kg/day
Epinephrine 1:10,000 (1mg/10ml)	Asystole/PEA VT/VF	IV/IO Administration: 0.01 mg/kg = 0.1 ml/kg	In newborns, use the 1:10,000 epinephrine solution for ET instillation at 0.03 mg/kg = 0.3 ml/kg
Epinephrine 1:1000 (1mg/ml)	Asystole/PEA VT/VF	ET instillation: 0.1 mg/kg = 0.1 ml/kg	• Dose for ET administration is 10 times IV/IO dose, except in newborns. • Use 1:1000 epinephrine solution for ET instillation in children
Lidocaine 1% or 2% (10 mg/ml or 20 mg/ml)	VT/VF	• 1 mg/kg IV/IO bolus Infusion at 20-50ug/kg/min • 2-10 mg/kg for ET administration	• ET dose is not established. • Use 2-10 times IV/IO dose.

CHAPTER RESOURCES

Case Study Answers

See page 79

This child has septic or distributive shock. The rash is an ominous sign and means aggressive treatment is necessary to save the child's life. The appropriate first interventions are oxygen, shock positioning, and BVM ventilation.

ALS Advanced LIFE support Establish IV or IO access on scene. Transport and deliver 20 ml/kg fluid boluses to a maximum of 60 ml/kg while on the way to the ED. Consider giving a vasopressor agent, either dopamine or epinephrine, after fluid administration if the transport time is long. Endotracheal intubation may be necessary after BVM ventilation.

This case also shows the universal precautions. The child probably has a communicable, infectious disease. Direct specific questions about exposures and prophylactic treatment to your infection control personnel.

See page 88

Based on the history and physical assessment, this child has late or decompensated hypovolemic shock. The priorities for management include oxygen, shock positioning, and BVM ventilation with high-flow oxygen.

ALS Advanced LIFE support Establish IV or IO access on scene. Transport and deliver crystalloid at 20 ml/kg boluses to 60 ml/kg while on the way to the ED. This child will require large fluid volumes, based on the physical assessment. If there is no response (such as improved appearance, capillary refill time, decreased heart rate, and improved blood pressure) to the first line of interventions, consider septic or distributive shock. Further treatment for this child includes endotracheal intubation and potential vasopressor support with dopamine or epinephrine.

CHAPTER RESOURCES

See page 94

This child has asystole—a rhythm that is unlikely to respond to any treatment. The arrest was unwitnessed, which suggests a prolonged downtime, but since no **rigor mortis** is present, attempt CPR and BVM.

ALS Advanced LIFE support Consider endotracheal intubation. Insert an IO or IV line. Measure him with a resuscitation tape to determine appropriate drug doses and equipment size. Give epinephrine either down the ET tube, or through the IO or IV line, whichever is in place first. Administer epinephrine as per local EMS protocol. If asystole continues, contact medical oversight to consider termination of resuscitation on scene.

If resuscitation is stopped, activate grief counseling for the family and offer critical incident stress debriefing for all involved prehospital personnel.

Suggested Educational Resources

1. American Academy of Pediatrics and the American College of Emergency Physicians. *Textbook for APLS: The Pediatric Medicine Course.* 3rd ed. Elk Grove Village, IL: American Academy of Pediatrics and American College of Emergency Physicians; 1998.
2. American Heart Association. *Textbook of Pediatric Advanced Life Support.* Dallas, TX: American Heart Association; 1997.
3. Dieckmann RA, Vardis R. High-dose epinephrine in pediatric out-of-hospital cardiopulmonary arrest. *Pediatrics* 1995; 95(6): 901–913.
4. Sirbaugh PE, Pepe PE, et al. A prospective, population-based study of the demographics, epidemiology, management, and outcome of out-of-hospital pediatric cardiopulmonary arrest. *Annals of Emerg Med* 1999; 33(2): 174–184.
5. Young K, Seidel JS. Pediatric cardiopulmonary resuscitation: A collective review. *Annals of Emerg Med* 1999; 33(2): 195–205.

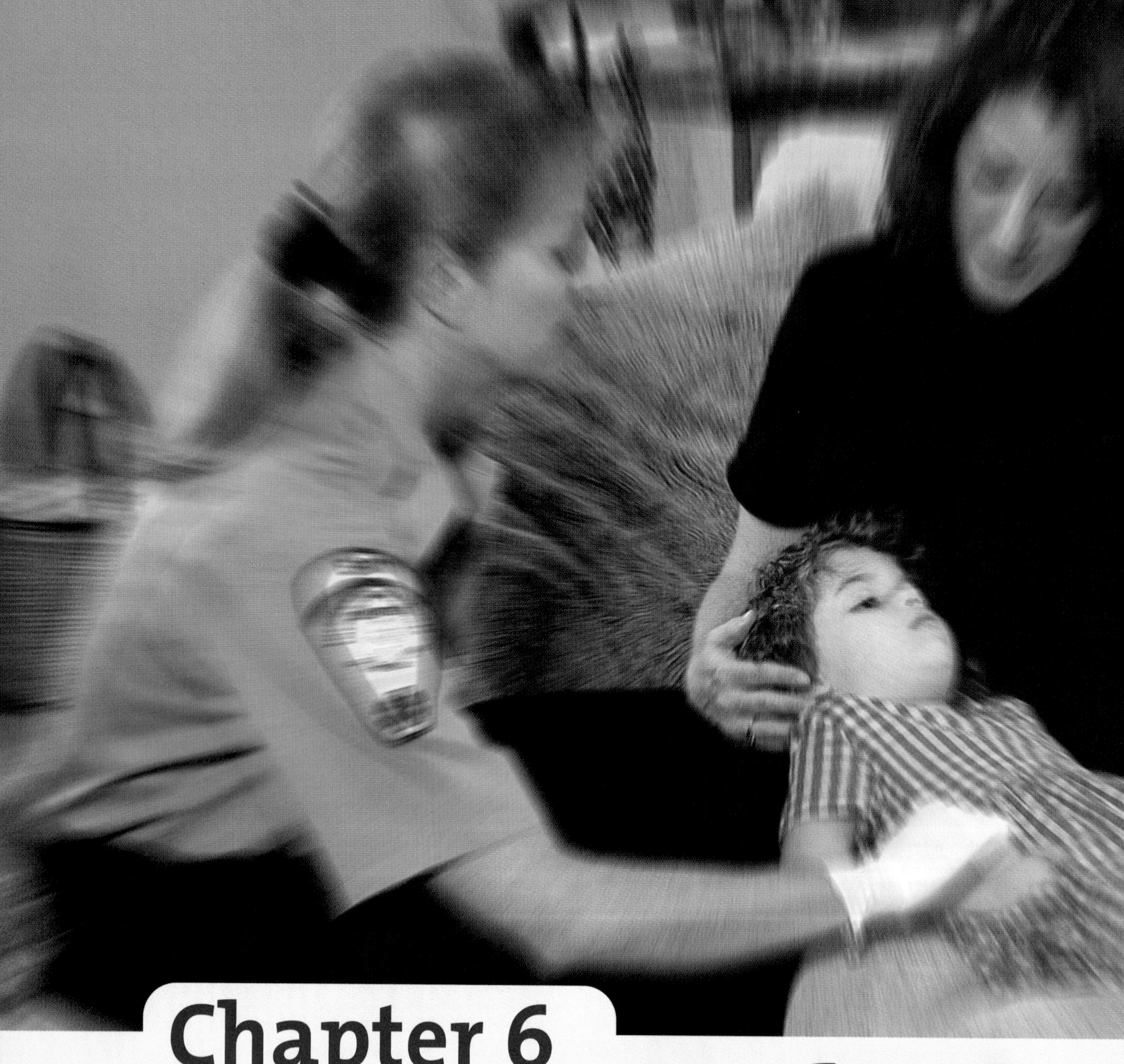

Chapter 6 Medical

Learning Objectives

1. Describe the major types of seizures.
2. Compare the advantages and disadvantages of rectal and IV diazepam for status epilepticus.
3. Discuss the association of fever and serious disease.
4. Distinguish the common causes of altered level of consciousness in infants and children, and outline management.
5. Describe signs and symptoms of hypoglycemia and hyperglycemia, and outline management.
6. Apply appropriate assessment and treatment techniques to case studies presenting patients with seizures and other medical emergencies.

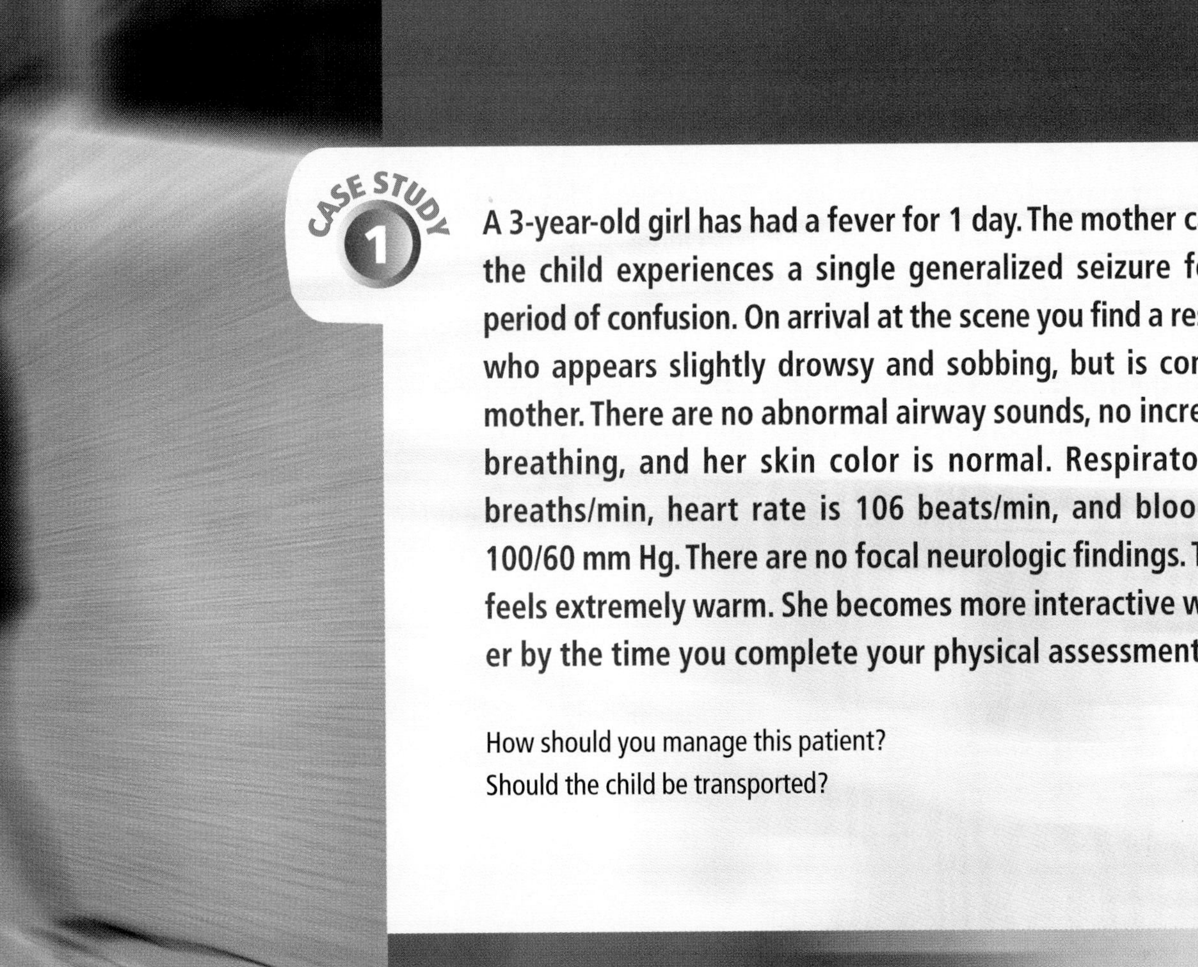

A 3-year-old girl has had a fever for 1 day. The mother calls 911 when the child experiences a single generalized seizure followed by a period of confusion. On arrival at the scene you find a responsive child who appears slightly drowsy and sobbing, but is consoled by her mother. There are no abnormal airway sounds, no increased work of breathing, and her skin color is normal. Respiratory rate is 24 breaths/min, heart rate is 106 beats/min, and blood pressure is 100/60 mm Hg. There are no focal neurologic findings. The youngster feels extremely warm. She becomes more interactive with the mother by the time you complete your physical assessment.

How should you manage this patient?
Should the child be transported?

Emergencies

Introduction

Approximately half of all pediatric 911 calls are illness, or "medical," complaints. Compared to injured patients, children with illnesses usually have more serious conditions and are more difficult to assess and treat. This chapter reviews three common out-of-hospital pediatric medical emergencies: seizures, fever, and altered level of consciousness.

Respiratory illness and seizures are the two most common out-of-hospital pediatric medical emergencies. Fever is a common complaint but by itself is not an emergency. However, fever is often associated with illnesses; such as bronchiolitis, sepsis, or seizures; in infants and preschool-aged children. Altered level of consciousness is a less common pediatric emergency but can be a sign of a serious or life-threatening medical emergency. Altered level of consciousness requires immediate treatment to prevent brain injury or death.

Accurately assessing a child with an illness includes an approach to history taking and physical examination that is appropriate for the age of the child, as discussed in Chapter 2. Communicating with the child and family is essential for good clinical care, establishment of trust, and development of comfortable interactions with children.

Seizures

Seizures are common in childhood. About 5% of children will have at least one seizure by the age of 6 years. Seizures cause much fear and agitation for caregivers and bystanders. The common **generalized tonic-clonic seizure** involves abnormal rhythmic movements of the face, eyes, and skeletal muscles. Most seizures in children are generalized seizures, but there are many other less frequent forms as well, with a wide range of physical findings. **Epilepsy** is a chronic condition involving recurrent seizures that occur over time, sometimes without any known provoking factors.

Febrile seizures

Most pediatric seizures are due to fever alone, which is why they are called **febrile seizures**. This type of seizure is a generalized tonic-clonic seizure in children between 6 months and 5 years of age who have a fever. Febrile seizures will not usually cause any brain injury. *A febrile seizure cannot be diagnosed in the field because other serious causes of fever and seizures, such as meningitis, must be ruled out.* While 30% of all childhood seizures are febrile seizures, there are many other causes of seizures. These include trauma, hypoxia, hypoglycemia, infection, ingestion, bleeding into the brain, metabolic disorders, and congenital neurologic problems. Also, children with epilepsy who do not receive their antiseizure or anticonvulsant medication are another common group who seize and require care by prehospital professionals.

Most febrile seizures are short lived (less than 15 minutes). Because the cause of seizures with fever cannot be determined in the field, *transport all children with seizures or make sure there is a physician evaluation of the child.* A fever with a seizure is not the same as a febrile seizure.

Status epilepticus

Status epilepticus is either (1) a series of two or more seizures without recovery of consciousness, with the child unable to carry on verbal communication between the seizures, or (2) a continuous seizure more than 20 to 30 minutes long. Status epilepticus is a serious neurologic emergency that carries the risk of brain injury or death. Early treatment may stop the convulsion with fewer drugs and less need for major interventions such as endotracheal intubation. A prolonged seizure of less than 20 minutes in length may also have serious consequences, including progression to status epilepticus.

During status epilepticus, the risk of brain injury depends mostly on the *cause* of the seizure, not the *length* of the seizure. This is also true for prolonged seizures. Hypoxia is the most important complication of seizures, and is usually the cause of brain injury when that occurs. Hypoxia is usually preventable by simply opening and clearing the airway and administering oxygen. In most cases, a brief seizure in a child is not life threatening and has no long-term effects. Only when a physician determines the cause of the child's seizure can the family be informed about risk of recurrence, possible brain injury, and treatment. The prehospital professional rarely has sufficient data in the field to provide such information.

Classification of seizures

The type of physical movements during the seizure provide a way to classify seizures, as shown in Table 6-1. The main difference is whether the seizure involves the entire body (generalized) or only one part of the body (focal or partial), and, in partial seizures, whether consciousness is preserved (simple) or impaired (complex).

Partial seizures with loss of consciousness (**complex partial seizures**) can become generalized seizures. The movements that might accompany partial seizures include sudden jerking of one arm or leg, or one side of the body, or lip smacking. The child may also describe a strange taste, feeling, or visual disorder (**aura**).

Table 6-1 Classification of Seizures

Type	Description
Generalized	
Tonic-clonic (grand mal)	Trunk rigidity and loss of consciousness, with sudden jerking of both arms and/or both legs; may be only tonic (rigidity), or clonic (jerking)
Absence (petit mal)	Brief loss of awareness without any abnormal movements; the child may appear to be staring
Partial (focal)	
Simple	Focal motor jerking, without loss of consciousness; may be sensory, autonomic, or psychic, without motor jerking
Complex	Focal motor jerking, with loss of consciousness; sometimes there is secondary generalization to a tonic-clonic seizure

Complications

Seizures may cause hypoxia from airway obstruction, aspiration, or inadequate ventilation. A second concern is brain injury from long seizure times in a child with a serious underlying cause such as infection, intoxication, or hemorrhage. Another less significant risk for the child who experiences a febrile seizure is *seizure recurrence*. The child may seize again during the same febrile illness, or during a subsequent febrile illness.

Status epilepticus may occur as the child's first seizure. Children under 3 years of age tend to have acute causes of status epilepticus, such as hypoxia, infection, or toxins. On the other hand, children over 3 years of age who

Do not treat absence or simple partial seizures because they will not cause brain injury.

When to treat a seizure is a matter of debate. Although most seizures will stop spontaneously and do not need any treatment, some untreated children will go on to the dangerous condition of status epilepticus. The best practical approach is to treat if the child is seizing on arrival of the prehospital professional.

present with status epilepticus tend to have chronic causes (e.g., epilepsy and inadequate anticonvulsant treatment). If the child has a serious underlying illness as the cause of status epilepticus, the longer the seizure, the greater the risk of brain injury.

Assessment and Treatment of the Actively Seizing Child

If a child is actively seizing when the prehospital professional arrives, there are several essential steps:

1. *Open the airway.*

   Managing the airway is the most important initial action. Table 6-2 summarizes the important steps in airway management.

ALS Advanced LIFE support

Airway

Do not attempt intubation during a convulsion. It is usually unnecessary and is almost always impossible during the active seizure. Complications are common.

2. *Calm caregiver's fears.*

   Assure the caregiver that the seizure will stop and inform them that certain procedures and medications may be necessary. Do not try to diagnose or give a reason for the seizure.

3. *Get key information.*

   Ask if the child has a previous diagnosis of epilepsy, how the seizure began, and when it started.

4. *Immobilize the spine of trauma patients.*

   Think about possible spinal injury if the seizure came after a head injury.

5. *Assist ventilation if the child is cyanotic or has a pulse oximetry reading below 90% while on 100% oxygen by nonrebreathing mask or blow-by.*

   A reliable oxygen saturation is difficult to obtain during the seizure. Be careful not to overreact when the pulse oximeter is simply not recording accurately.

   Use an appropriate-sized BVM device and 100% oxygen. BVM may not be effective during the seizure. Keep suctioning.

Controversy

The best position in which to place the child during a seizure is controversial. Supine position may increase aspiration risk but allows easy airway and breathing management. Lateral decubitus position provides some protection against aspiration but makes it more difficult to give oxygen and aid breathing.

Tip

Airway and ventilatory support are key aspects of seizure management.

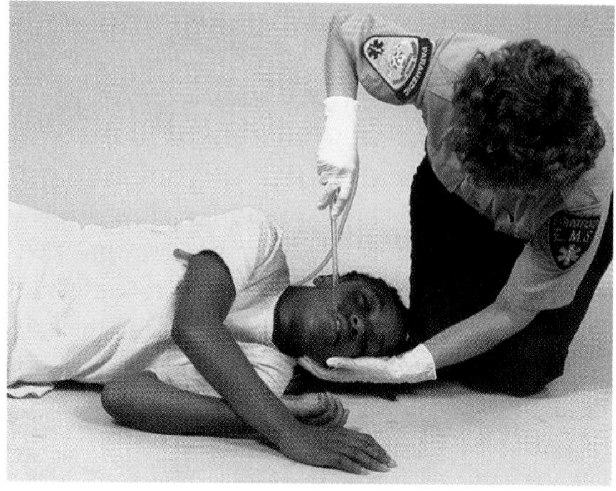

Figure 6-1 Position the head to open the airway, place the child in the lateral decubitus position, and clear the mouth of vomitus with suction.

Table 6-2 Initial Airway Management in Seizing Children

Position the head to open the airway.
Clear the mouth with suction.
Consider the lateral decubitus position if the child is actively vomiting and suction is inadequate to comfortably control the airway (Figure 6-1).
Provide 100% oxygen by nonrebreathing mask or blow-by.
Consider a nasopharyngeal airway. (Oropharyngeal airways are seldom required.)
Loosen tight clothing and ensure that the head is not striking anything hard.

Treatment of hypoglycemia

6. *Consider hypoglycemia.*

Quickly assess serum glucose with a bedside dipstick. Check the glucose level and follow standard dextrose administration guidelines for treatment of hypoglycemia if indicated (Table 6-3).

Seizure treatment with anticonvulsants

7. *Give the child diazepam or another benzodiazepine.*

The **benzodiazepine** drugs are excellent first-line anticonvulsants. Common drugs in this class are diazepam, midazolam, and lorazepam. Lorazepam requires refrigeration and is usually not available to prehospital professionals. *In most cases, if the child is seizing when the prehospital professional arrives, give diazepam rectally or IV.* IM midazolam is a possible alternative.

8. *Watch closely for apnea or respiratory depression.*

Be prepared to use BVM ventilation for respiratory depression after administering a benzodiazepine drug. Do BVM ventilatory support first because some children will experience brief periods of respiratory depression after benzodiazepine administration that will subside with BVM only. Most children do not need endotracheal intubation.

9. *If the patient is hemodynamically unstable or continues to seize after the initial anticonvulsant is administered, secure an IV or IO line.*

Keep the IV or IO line open with a chrystalloid solution. Most seizing children do not require vascular access in the field.

10. *Transport the child.*

When the seizure stops, or if the seizure continues after treatment with a benzodiazepine drug, transport. Perform the focused history and exam and the detailed exam, if possible, on the way to the hospital. During transport do ongoing assessment. Keep the patient on a cardiac monitor and a pulse oximeter, if available.

Table 6-3 Dextrose Administration Guidelines During Seizures

Indications
• Infant and child with glucose level <60 mg%
• Newborn with glucose level <40 mg%
Treatment
• Child <2 years old Give D25W, 2–4 ml/kg IV or IO bolus (Dilute D50W 1:1 with sterile water or normal saline)
• Child >2 years old Give D50W, 1–2 ml/kg IV or IO bolus
• If there is no IV or IO line, give glucagon 1.0 mg, IM.
Newborn with glucose level <40 mg%
• Give D10W, 2–4 ml /kg/bolus (1 part D50W, 4 parts sterile water or normal saline) IV or IO

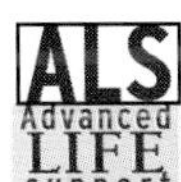

Dilemmas in benzodiazepine administration

Unfortunately, the prehospital professional will not know the cause of a seizure in any individual child. Treat all children with prolonged seizures who are still seizing on arrival the same way—with a benzodiazepine drug like diazepam. The disadvantage of drug treatment with diazepam is respiratory depression, especially if the seizure is prolonged and if the patient is already on **phenobarbital** or an oral benzodiazepine. Be ready to support breathing.

The exact glucose value requiring treatment is controversial. Each child may have a different threshold for symptomatic hypoglycemia. Consider glucose treatment for any child with altered level of consciousness and a bedside glucose of less than 80 mg%, and consider not treating a normal child with a bedside glucose over 60 mg%.

Never insert an oral airway into the mouth of a seizure patient who is regaining consciousness.

Always give oxygen to a child who is having a seizure or who is postictal.

Rectal (PR) diazepam is effective, safe, and easy. Use 0.5 mg/kg/dose PR with a lubricated syringe. Repeat at 0.25 mg/kg every 10 to 15 minutes × 3. The maximum single dose is 10 mg. The PR dose will take 2 to 5 minutes to work.

IV diazepam is an effective treatment for status epilepticus or prolonged seizures. The IV diazepam dose is 0.1–0.2 mg/kg (up to 4 mg). Give at the slow infusion rate of 1 mg per minute. IV diazepam may cause respiratory depression, especially with rapid IV push. Start with 0.1 mg/kg. Do not give diazepam IM because it is not well absorbed and is irritating to muscle tissue. Consider half the normal dose of diazepam if the child is on phenobarbital or has received other benzodiazepines in the previous few hours.

Diazepam begins to work quickly, but its anticonvulsant action does not last long, a serious limitation in long field or transport times. Another dose of diazepam (or another anticonvulsant medication, if available) may be necessary within 10 to 20 minutes if the drug is given.

IM midazolam is another medication for seizure control for a patient without IV access. The dose is 0.1 mg/kg IM. It will take about 15 minutes to work, with a full effect in 30 to 60 minutes. Because it has different absorption when given in the muscle, it can last for 2 to 6 hours and usually does not need to be repeated in the ambulance. The seizure will stop in most children within 10 to 15 minutes after giving a benzodiazepine rectally, IV, IO, or IM.

Rectal diazepam

Cannulating a peripheral vein in a child often slows down delivery of essential ALS drugs, especially in infants and toddlers. The rectum is an effective alternative route for emergency drug administration. Diazepam is a lipid soluble benzodiazepine that is reliably absorbed through the rectum and will terminate most seizures without further treatment. For a step-by-step explanation of this procedure, see page 291.

Calm parents' fears about the seizure, but do not diagnose or provide them uncertain information about the cause of the seizure or chance of recurrence.

Assessment of the Postictal Child

Usually the child's seizure is already over when the prehospital professional arrives. This postictal state is characterized by abnormal appearance with sleepiness, confusion, irritability, and decreased interactiveness that may last from minutes to hours.

Perform the initial assessment. Generally after the initial assessment, you will continue on scene with the focused history and physical exam and the detailed exam. Some examples of a stable postictal patient are the child with a previous diagnosis of epilepsy who experiences a brief grand mal seizure or a child under age 3 years with fever and a possible febrile seizure. The postictal child may return to a more normal level of alertness, muscle tone, and interactiveness in 15–30 minutes. The ABCDE evaluation in the field is important, and knowledge of an improving neurologic state is extremely helpful in the ED.

Sometimes, the cause of the seizure is unknown, and the child is at risk for recurrent seizures, or the child may experience a long postictal state (more than 30 to 60 minutes). Such children may have a serious underlying illness. Transport and do the focused history and physical exam and the detailed exam, if possible, on the way to the hospital. Table 6-4 lists worrisome circumstances, when the postictal child may need immediate transport and specific treatment urgently in the ED. If the child has had a seizure after closed head injury, always immobilize the **cervical** spine, as discussed in Chapter 8.

If the postictal patient has a previous diagnosis of epilepsy, during the focused history ask the name and dosage of medications and when the last dose was given. Inquire when the last

Table 6-4 Worrisome Circumstances with the Postictal Child

Posttraumatic seizure
Postingestion seizure
Seizure and hypoxia
Seizure in a neonate (<4 weeks of age)
First seizure in a child >6 years
More than one seizure
Seizure time >5 min

blood levels were obtained and whether the levels were adequate. Find out the duration of the convulsion and ask for a description of the motor activity, including where it started, how it progressed, and how long the child was conscious. From this information, determine the type of seizure (e.g., generalized or partial, or partial with secondary generalization). Ask carefully about head trauma. Consider the possibility of an ingestion or overdose.

Allay the caregiver's fears. If the child has had his first seizure, the caregiver may be extremely worried, frightened, or panicky. Use this opportunity to provide education regarding seizures.

Summary of Seizures

Seizures are common in children, and frightened caregivers frequently call 911 to assist in managing this problem. Usually the seizure has stopped before ambulance arrival, in which case the tasks include only assessment of the postictal child and transport to the hospital with no treatment.

Sometimes the child is seizing on arrival and requires medical management. The treatment includes opening and clearing the airway, giving oxygen, then, if ALS, administering a benzodiazepine medication, usually diazepam. Rectal diazepam stops most seizures in children. Effective alternatives are IV diazepam and IM midazolam. The benzodiazepine medications often cause temporary respiratory depression, which requires BVM support without endotracheal intubation, in most cases.

Fever

Children can run high fevers in response to either bacterial or viral infections. High fever (>40°C or 104°F) can be due to minor illness such as a cold or serious problems such as pneumonia, meningitis, or infections of the blood. Fever in a child usually makes the caregivers worry.

! Tip

Fever does not cause brain damage.

Fever is a sign of infection, rather than a problem itself. Body

CASE STUDY 2

You respond to a call about a child with fever. The baby-sitter states that the 2-year-old boy has had vomiting, fever, and lethargy over the past 2 days. The child began a generalized tonic-clonic seizure while waiting for the ambulance, and is seizing when you arrive. Respiratory rate is 50 breaths/min, and blood pressure cannot be obtained during the seizure. Cardiac monitor shows a heart rate of 180 beats/min. There is no sign of trauma.

Outline management priorities.

What are the advantages of treating this child on scene?

temperature less than 105°F is not harmful to the child, but any temperature elevation may be associated with bacterial infection. Fever does not cause brain damage.

Determine the presence of fever by history and field evaluation. Knowing the exact level of temperature rise, however, will usually not change field management.

Assessment

The initial assessment will help determine the severity of the child's illness and the urgency for treatment. If the initial assessment is normal, take a focused history and perform a focused physical exam. Ask about important signs and symptoms of infection. These will be different depending on the type and source of infection, but can include symptoms such as chills, **malaise**, poor feeding, **lethargy**, vomiting, diarrhea, abdominal pain, stiff neck, headache, and irritability. Ask about other diseases because children that may be immune deficient (e.g., patients with **sickle cell disease**, cancer, human immunodeficiency virus [HIV], or post-organ transplantation) require a higher concern about serious infection with any fever.

Blip

Never use ice, cold water, fans, or alcohol baths to cool a feverish child.

Signs of infection that are often present with fever are tachycardia, tachypnea, nasal congestion, cough, and respiratory distress. Fever may make the child appear sicker than he really is. The more ominous signs include a bulging fontanelle (<18 months of age), stiff neck, paradoxical irritability, seizures, prolonged capillary refill time, or a petechial rash, as described in Chapter 5. After the focused examination, if the child has no physiologic abnormalities, do the detailed examination to look for possible sources of infection or other physical signs of infection.

Age and fever

In addition to signs and symptoms, the age of a child is important in assessing the significance of fever. A fever in an infant less than 4 weeks old may be the only indication of sepsis or serious bacterial infection. A feverish infant this young will require cultures and other diagnostic tests, as well as **antibiotics**, in the ED. The symptoms of serious bacterial infection in a young infant may be vague and nonspecific, such as fussiness, poor feeding, and sleepiness. Signs of serious infection in this age group (infants <4 weeks of age) include pallor and abnormal appearance. In the first few days of life only, **jaundice** may be a sign of serious bacterial infection.

Also, a high fever (>102.2°F), in a child under 3 years old may indicate a bacterial infection. This age group appears more likely to have bacterial illness than older children.

Management

Management of fever in the child who has a normal initial assessment includes preventing transmission of disease to the prehospital professional. Also, if the child is older than 3 months, consider beginning simple cooling measures when the temperature is above 101.2°F, to make him feel better. The management steps include:

1. Use body substance precautions to diminish disease transmission.
2. Cool the feverish child by undressing him, but do not allow him to get hypothermic. Do not use cold water, fans, ice, or alcohol baths to lower temperature.
3. Transport, and be aware of possible seizures or decompensation from sepsis.
4. Explain to the caregiver that fever alone is not dangerous to the child.

Summary of Fever

Fever is a response to any type of infection. It is rarely a problem by itself. The age of the child and other associated signs and symptoms are important in determining probability of serious illness. In most cases, simple cooling measures and transport are the primary actions for the prehospital professional.

Altered Level of Consciousness

Altered level of consciousness is an abnormal neurologic state. In this state, the child may behave inappropriately for his age by being less alert, less interactive, inconsolable, non-distractable, or unresponsive to things going on around him. Altered level of consciousness can reflect many states of appearance—from irritability to unresponsiveness. Sometimes, all the caregiver will say is that his child is "not acting right." It is important to believe him.

A mnemonic—AEIOUTIPPS (remember: the five vowels in the alphabet [AEIOU], followed by tips [TIPPS])—recalls many of the severe causes of altered level of consciousness (Table 6-5).

Assessment

To assess neurologic status quickly, use the PAT and the disability component of the hands-on ABCDEs. These two parts of the initial assessment will evaluate both cortical and brain stem functions, as described in Chapter 3. A child with altered level of consciousness always has an abnormal appearance. The specific abnormal state might be better described as unresponsiveness, **hypotonia**, weak cry, **ataxia**, falling down, inability to walk, personality change, listlessness, or combativeness. In the initial assessment of a child with altered level of consciousness, pay attention to the presence of any odors that may help determine the cause (e.g., hydrocarbons or ethanol on the child's breath or clothes).

During the ABCDEs, determine a level of consciousness with the AVPU scale. AVPU is a quick way to determine level of consciousness in both ill and injured children. It categorizes motor response based on simple responses to two different stimuli (voice and pain). Although it is not proven to be accurate in children, it is a familiar neurologic categorization system to most prehospital professionals and may have some usefulness in pediatrics.

Finally, observe **motor activity**, and check the pupils. In the assessment of motor activity, watch for purposeful and symmetric movement of extremities, seizures, **posturing**, or **flaccidity**. In the assessment of pupils, check size (small or large), equality, and response to light. Pupils may have abnormal size or reactivity in the presence of drugs, ongoing seizures, hypoxia, or approaching **brain stem herniation**.

Also, look for an identifying bracelet or other obvious information source about important medical history, such as diabetes (Figure 6-2).

Table 6-5 AEIOUTIPPS: Possible Causes of Altered Level of Consciousness

Alcohol
Epilepsy, endocrine, electrolytes
Insulin
Opiates and other drugs
Uremia
Trauma, temperature
Infection
Psychogenic
Poison
Shock, stroke, space-occupying lesion, subarachnoid hemorrhage

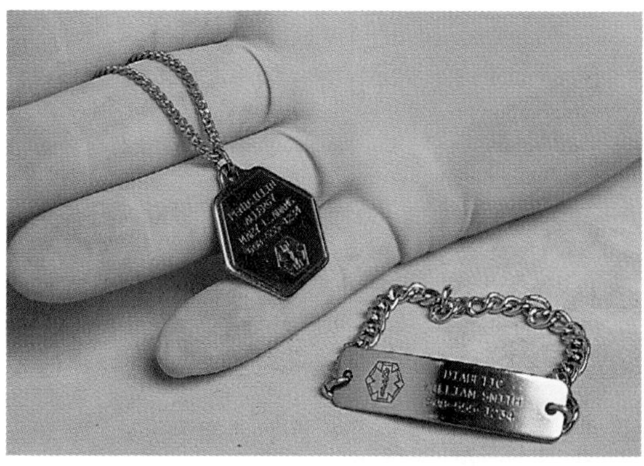

Figure 6-2 In a child with altered level of consciousness, look for a bracelet with his medical history.

Management

Assume that every child with an altered level of consciousness and no trauma history has suffered hypoxia, ischemia, or a metabolic insult like hypoglycemia. First stabilize the ABCs.

1. *Open the airway.*

In the sluggish or semicomatose patient, suction the inside of the mouth. The patient may have airway obstruction from secretions or vomitus. If there is no **gag reflex** or if the patient is totally unresponsive, position the head and insert an oropharyngeal or nasopharyngeal airway. Keep the spine immobilized if there is a suspicion of head or neck injury.

! Tip

There are many causes of altered level of consciousness, but management must focus on the ABCDEs.

2. *Ensure adequate breathing.*

Patients with altered levels of consciousness may have inadequate breathing despite apparent respiratory movements. Administer 100% oxygen by nonrebreathing mask. Do BVM ventilation with 100% oxygen if the patient is cyanotic, has oxygen saturation less than 90% on 100% oxygen by nonrebreathing mask, or if he is breathing ineffectively.

ALS Advanced LIFE support

Treatment of altered level of consciousness

Consider endotracheal intubation to protect the airway and to avoid aspiration. Ventilate the patient with suspected brain injury but do not hyperventilate (see Chapter 8). Place the patient on a cardiac monitor and a pulse oximeter.

3. *Safeguard circulation.*

Get venous access and obtain a venous specimen for **serum glucose** measurement. Keep the infusion rate at a To-Keep-Open (TKO) rate unless the child is in shock. Reassess the child's level of consciousness.

4. *Perform a quick bedside blood glucose test.*

Administer oral glucose to a child with diabetes who is conscious and has a gag reflex. If a bedside glucose test shows hypoglycemia (<40 mg% in a newborn, <60 mg% in a child), give an IV glucose bolus or IM **glucagon** as outlined in Table 6-3.

5. *In the child with altered level of consciousness and depressed respirations, give naloxone.*

The naloxone dose is 0.4 mg in an infant or child, or 2 mg in an adolescent IV, IM, IO, or per endotracheal tube. Use caution when giving naloxone to a newborn because naloxone may cause seizures in babies of narcotic-addicted mothers. **Narcotic** overdose is an unlikely cause of altered level of consciousness in a young child, but is an important consideration in teenagers. Constricted pupils are a universal finding in pure opiate overdoses, but may occur when the child has taken other drugs concurrently.

Hypoglycemia

Hypoglycemia is a low-blood-sugar or serum-glucose concentration less than 40 mg% in a newborn, or less than 60 mg% in a child. The common causes of pediatric hypoglycemia are lack of food, insulin imbalance in a diabetic, **transient** neonatal hypoglycemia, and intoxication (alcohol or other drugs). The most frequent scenario for out-of-hospital hypoglycemia is a child with known diabetes who uses too much insulin, exerts himself excessively, or delays a meal. Hypoglycemia can also be a part of the metabolic imbalance created by generalized organ failure during serious illness. Therefore, evaluate any acutely ill-appearing child for hypoglycemia, especially if the child has abnormal appearance or altered level of consciousness.

Initial assessment

Signs and symptoms of hypoglycemia in the infant and young child can be hard to detect, especially in younger infants. The changing signs and symptoms are noted in Table 6-6. Mild hypoglycemia may cause vague symptoms such as hunger, irritability, and weakness, and signs such as agitation, tachypnea, and tachycardia. Symptoms of moderate hypoglycemia usually reflect the increasing influence of extra catecholamine

Table 6-6 Signs and Symptoms of Hypoglycemia

Mild	Moderate	Severe
Hunger, irritability, weakness, Agitation, tachypnea, tachycardia	Anxiety, blurred vision, stomachache, headache, dizziness Sweating, pallor, tremors, confusion	Seizure, coma

release as the body attempts to compensate for lack of sugar to the tissues. Appearance becomes abnormal and level of consciousness becomes impaired. The signs of severe hypoglycemia are dramatic changes in level of consciousness (e.g., seizures, coma), when blood sugar is dangerously low.

Management

If a diabetic patient is physiologically stable and cooperative and the signs and symptoms suggest hypoglycemia, allow him to attempt oral glucose replacement. Give 0.5–1.0 g/kg of sugar. There is 20 g of glucose in 13 ounces of cola or orange soda and in 12 ounces of orange juice or apple juice.

ALS Advanced LIFE support

Treatment of hypoglycemia

Treat hypoglycemia if the child has altered level of consciousness and quick bedside blood glucose testing is less than 40 mg% in a newborn or less than 60 mg% in a child, as outlined in Table 6-3. Children have different tolerances to hypoglycemia, so a child may be alert and cooperative while having blood sugar levels between 40 to 50 mg%. Give this child oral glucose or allow him to breastfeed.

For the physiologically unstable patient with altered level of consciousness, give IV or IO glucose immediately. Give oral glucose or allow breastfeeding when he becomes alert and cooperative. Repeat IV or IO doses as needed if appearance or behavior changes.

If there is no IV access give glucagon 1 mg IM. Repeat in 20 minutes as needed. Glucagon will provide a temporary increase of the glucose level as long as there are liver stores of **glycogen** (concentrated glucose). This method of glucose replacement may not work in the newborn, who is best treated by breastfeeding.

Transport

After giving IV or IO dextrose or IM glucagon, reassess. Watch for return to normal appearance and behavior. If the child with altered level of consciousness does not return to normal in a few minutes, transport immediately and attempt to do additional assessment on the way to the ED. If the child returns to normal, consider doing additional assessment on scene, along with giving oral glucose.

Signs and symptoms of hypoglycemia can be nonspecific.

Additional assessment

Do a focused history when possible. Ask key questions, such as:

- How quickly did the symptoms progress?
- Does the patient have diabetes or any other known illness?
- Was any medication or food given?
- Is it possible the child was exposed to drugs or alcohol?
- If the patient is a diabetic, has there been a recent change in medication or meals?
- Is this the first episode? If not, how often does this happen?

- If the patient is a newborn, has the mother received prenatal care?
- Has the mother had any medical problems with the pregnancy?
- Is the mother a diabetic?
- What is the newborn being fed and how often?

After the focused history, perform a focused and detailed exam. Reassess. If the child has diabetes and received too much insulin, and if there are no physiologic or anatomic abnormalities on reassessment, consider contacting medical oversight. In some EMS systems, if the child's physician is available to evaluate the child with the caregiver, the child may not have to be transported to the ED.

Summary of Altered Level of Consciousness

There are many causes of altered level of consciousness in children. The caregiver may be the best judge of changed behavior or altered level of consciousness, especially in the infant or

CASE STUDY 3

A frantic 12-year-old boy calls 911 when he finds his 4-year-old sister unconscious. On your arrival at the scene, the boy says that his sister had a few minutes of whole body shaking movements. Grandma tells you that the child was recently diagnosed with diabetes mellitus and has been taking insulin. The girl appears disoriented. She is breathing effectively without abnormal airway sounds or increased work of breathing. Her skin is pale. Respiratory rate is 30 breaths/min, heart rate is 140 beats/min, and blood pressure is 98/68 mm Hg. Her rapid bedside glucose test is 40 mg%.

What are the possible causes of the altered level of consciousness?
What are the treatment possibilities?

toddler. The assessment must address the ABCs and especially consider reversible causes such as hypoglycemia.

Hyperglycemia

Hyperglycemia is an elevated blood sugar. Associated changes include dehydration and often **ketoacidosis**—a condition of too much acid production from breakdown of fat. Hyperglycemia and ketoacidosis usually occur in a diabetic who has not taken his insulin or followed his diet.

Assessment

There are no specific field findings that determine hyperglycemia. While the quick bedside glucose test will show a high reading, it is not very accurate in the high range. Early symptoms include increased thirst, increased urination, and weight loss. Late signs and symptoms include weakness, nausea, vomiting, abdominal pain, fruity odor on breath, tachypnea, tachycardia, hyperventilation, and poor skin circulation.

Management

Treat the ABCDEs based on the physical assessment. Transport.

ALS Advanced LIFE support

Treatment of dehydration

Establish an IV or IO line and give 10 to 20 ml/kg of normal saline if there are signs of dehydration or shock.

CHAPTER RESOURCES

Case Study Answers

See page 99

The child is physiologically normal and requires assessment on scene and probably no field treatment. As you manage the child, allay the caregiver's fears. Use the opportunity to provide the caregiver with education regarding seizures and fever. Take a focused history. The story suggests a possible febrile seizure.

Transport all children with a history of seizure activity to the hospital because it is impossible to "diagnose" a febrile seizure in the field. However, this child deserves on-scene evaluation before transport. There are many causes of seizures, including serious infections such as meningitis. Because the child is probably still febrile, perform simple cooling methods. *Do not give cold water or alcohol baths or sponge to lower temperature; these methods can lead to shivering and actually increase the body temperature.* Reassess the patient frequently and prepare for another seizure.

See page 105

Open and manage the airway with suction and positioning. Administer 100% oxygen by nonrebreathing mask. If there is a history of trauma to the head or neck, immobilize the head and cervical spine. If there is no trauma, place the patient in the sniffing position and use the jaw thrust maneuver to maintain the airway. If respirations are too shallow or irregular or if oxygen saturation is less than 90%, assist ventilation with appropriate-sized BVM device. Insert an oropharyngeal or nasopharyngeal airway.

Use a length-based resuscitation tape to determine drug doses, as described in Procedure 17.

ALS Advanced LIFE support Rapidly assess the serum glucose with a bedside dipstick. If the glucose level is less than 60 mg%, establish an IV and give D50W 1.0 ml/kg by IV bolus. If there is no IV, give glucagon IM 1.0 mg.

Give rectal diazepam 0.5 mg/kg then 0.25 mg/kg/dose PR every 15 minutes × 3 if seizures continue. Alternatively, consider IV diazepam or IM midazolam. Try to stay on scene and transport after the seizure stops. Early drug treatment will probably make the seizure easier to stop. Also, it is much simpler to transport a child who is not actually seizing. In most cases, seizures will stop after 5 minutes and one dose of diazepam. Consider placing an IV line on the way to the hospital, but this may not be necessary. Attach the child to pulse oximetry, if available, and a cardiac monitor.

CHAPTER RESOURCES

See page 110

A 4-year-old diabetic child with altered level of consciousness will usually be hypoglycemic. However, you must consider other serious causes such as head injury; hypoxia; alcohol, drugs, and other intoxicating agents; and infection.

Give the child oral glucose if she is able to cooperate.

Quickly assess the serum glucose with a bedside dipstick if oral glucose does not work. Because the glucose level is less than 60 mg% give D50W 1.0 ml/kg IV bolus. If there is no IV, give glucagon IM 1.0 mg. Recheck glucose level in 5 minutes if the child does not return to normal.

Transport the child immediately if there is no response to glucose. If she returns to normal, complete the additional assessment on scene, then transport to an ED. In some EMS systems, if the child returns completely to normal and if the child's physician is available to consult with the family, transport may not be necessary.

Suggested Educational Resources

1. AAP Provisional Committee on Quality Improvement. Practice parameter: The neurodiagnostic evaluation of the child with a first time simple febrile seizure. *Pediatrics* 1996;97:769.
2. Albano A, Reisdorff EJ, Wiegenstein JG. Rectal diazepam in pediatric status epilepticus. *Am J Emerg Med* 1989;7:168–172.
3. Dieckmann RA. Rectal diazepam for prehospital pediatric status epilepticus. *Ann Emerg Med* 1994;23(2):216–223.
4. Hirtz DG. Febrile seizures. *Pediatr Rev* 1997;18:5.
5. Vining EPG. Pediatric seizures. *Emerg Med Clin North Am* 1994;12:973.

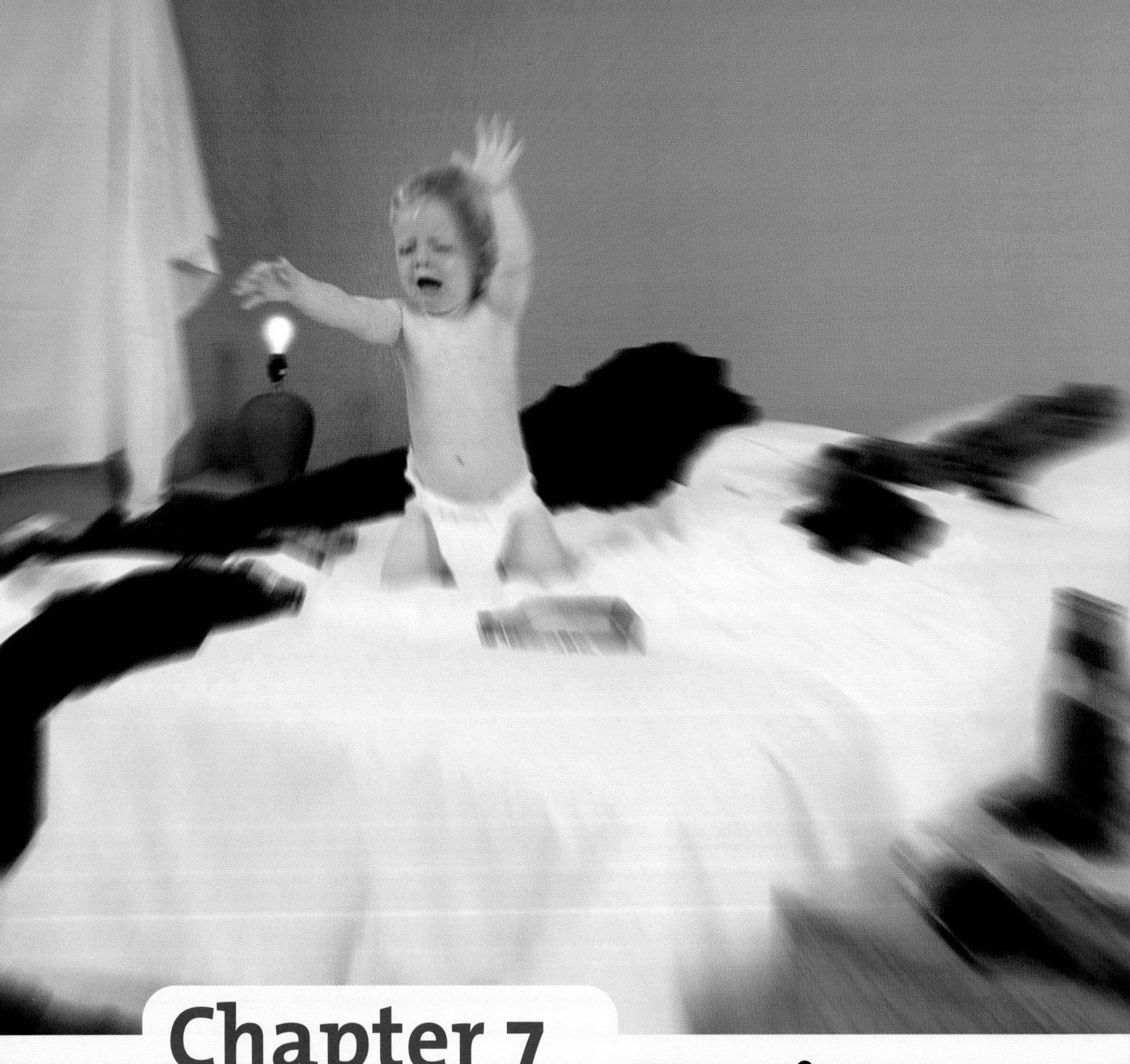

Chapter 7 Toxic

Learning Objectives

1. Distinguish age-related differences in toxic exposures.
2. Describe the physical assessment of the child with a suspected toxic exposure.
3. Discuss the risk assessment of the child with a suspected toxic exposure.
4. Explain the management possibilities for toxic exposures.
5. State the role of the regional poison control center in assessment and treatment of toxic exposures.
6. Apply appropriate assessment techniques and treatment plans to case studies presenting patients with toxic ingestion.

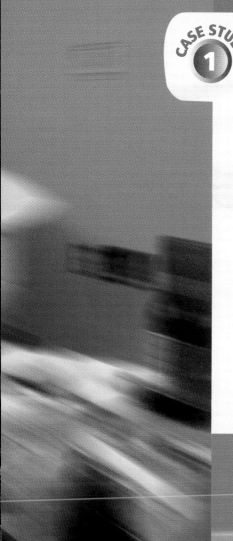

CASE STUDY 1

A 911 caller from a crime-ridden part of town requests assistance for a young child in the next apartment who is reportedly acting "goofy" and screaming. On arrival you find an 18-month-old boy wandering around in a cluttered room. There is drug paraphernalia on the floor. The mother is agitated, pacing, and acting in a hostile manner. The mother states that the child had been well until an hour ago, when he started to act strangely and speak in a bizarre way.

The child appears to be agitated. He is running around, will not interact with you or the mother, and shows no interest in verbal or physical play. His speech makes no sense. Work of breathing and circulation to skin are normal. Respiratory rate is 25 breaths/min, heart rate is 120 beats/min, and blood pressure is 115/80 mm Hg. His pupils are dilated. On the way to the ED, he has a brief, grand mal seizure.

What are the key aspects of the scene size-up and physical assessment?
Outline transport and management priorities.

Exposures

Introduction

A toxic exposure is an ingestion, inhalation, injection, or application of any substance that causes illness. It includes unintentional poisoning (such as a toddler who ingests gasoline or a caregiver's medication), recreational exposure (such as an adolescent who smokes cocaine), and exposure to hazardous materials (such as a school child who inhales a spilled, toxic chemical).

Toxic exposures are a common pediatric out-of-hospital complaint, but rarely result in death. In 1996, there were 21 deaths in children under 6 years of age, out of 1,137,295 reported exposures (Table 7-1). For every poisoning death of a child less than 5 years of age, there are 80,000 to 90,000 ED visits and 30,000 hospitalizations. Iron is the leading cause of childhood poisoning deaths, followed by tricyclic antidepressants. Activated charcoal, a substance for intestinal decontamination after toxic ingestions, is available for oral administration to children. However, it is usually not necessary to give charcoal in the out-of-hospital setting.

The regional poison center is a valuable resource to the prehospital professional for every child with a toxic exposure. Most poison centers work closely with EMS systems.

www.PEPPsite.com

Age-Related Differences

Children make up 70% of all toxic exposures. Eighty percent of childhood poisonings occur in children younger than 5 years of age. The toddler is a fearless, adventuresome, curious individual with a big appetite (Figure 7-1). She will put anything that fits into her mouth, no matter how bad it tastes. In a toddler, there is usually only one poison involved, and the exposure is usually small and unintentional.

> **! Tip**
>
> The poison center has a key role in community prevention and treatment of toxic exposures.

Toxic exposures in the school-aged child or adolescent, on the other hand, are often intentional, either as a recreational experiment or as a suicide gesture or attempt. She may be influenced by peer pressure or under emotional or psychosocial stress. In this age group, intentional ingestions lead to more ED visits and hospital admissions than unintentional exposure. Unlike the young child, adolescents usually ingest large quantities of substances. The inges-

Table 7-1 Toxicologic Cases, 1996

Reported cases	2,155,952
Patients <3 years	847,539 (39%)
Patients <6 years	1,137,295 (53%)
Total patients <20 years	1,446,533 (67%)
Fatalities <20 years	74

Litovitz TL, Smilkstein M, Felberg L, et al. 1996 annual report of the American Association of Poison Control Centers Toxic Exposure Surveillance System. *Am J Emerg Med* 1997;15:447–500.

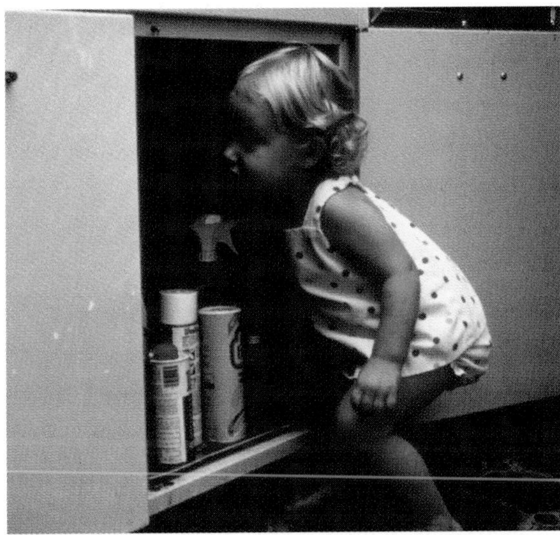

Figure 7-1 A toddler is adventurous and has a big appetite. She will try to taste or swallow almost any substance.

tion or inhalation of two or more substances is common (called **polypharmacy**). Often the adolescent requires both medical and psychosocial treatment.

The adolescent can also present legal problems because of such issues as **consent for care** and refusal of transport. Any adolescent who makes a suicide attempt or gesture, regardless of how trivial it may seem, must be transported to the ED, even if the child refuses. In some cases, law enforcement must become involved in scene management and transport.

Hazardous materials exposures can occur at any age. In such exposures, there are often multiple patients.

Common substances responsible for serious poisonings in children

Most poisonings occur in the home. Table 7-2 lists common substances responsible for serious poisonings.

Summary of Age-Related Differences

Most toxic exposures are minor and involve household products. The most common patient is the toddler who unintentionally ingests a single agent in small quantity. The second commonest patient is the adolescent who uses recreational drugs and may have polypharmacy. Serious exposures in children involve analgesics, carbon monoxide, and common adult medications, while serious exposures in adolescents involve analgesics and recreational drugs.

Prearrival Preparation and Scene Size-Up

Sometimes, at the time of dispatch, the toxin has already been identified by the caregiver, the poison center, or another health professional. In such cases, immediately contact medical oversight or the poison center, depending on local EMS protocol. They will help clarify the toxicity of the agent and priorities in assessment and treatment. In other cases, where the dispatch involves a toddler or adolescent with a sudden change in behavior, consider a toxic exposure.

On arrival, first perform the scene size-up. Note if there are possible toxins in the area or on the patient's clothes or skin that

! Tip

Most patients with toxic exposures are toddlers or preschool-aged children. There is usually only one poison involved and the exposure is usually small and unintentional.

Table 7-2 Common Substances Responsible for Serious Toxic Exposures

Children	Adolescents
Acetaminophen	Acetaminophen
Antidepressants	Amphetamines/ Stimulants
Carbon monoxide	Antidepressants
Ethanol/Other alcohols	Carbon monoxide
Iron	Ethanol/Other alcohols
Salicylates	Barbiturates
Smoke	Iron
Over-the-counter cold preparations	Narcotics
	Phenothiazines
	Inhalants

can be hazardous to the patient or the prehospital professional. If so, immediately decontaminate the area, assess the scene, and treat. Medical oversight may need to call the poison center or other public health agency to find out what the risks are and how to proceed if this information is not already known. If there is a possible toxin or hazardous material, secure the scene (close off the area) and minimize the risk of toxic exposures through the skin or lungs.

Next, look over the surrounding area. Take bottles, containers, plastic bags, suspicious substances, plants, or syringes to the ED.

If the caregiver refuses to let a poisoned child be transported to the hospital, ask medical oversight to talk to the caregiver over the telephone or radio. If this does not work, request assistance from law enforcement personnel.

Never forget about toxic hazards on scene. Watch out for absorbable toxins and protect skin and eyes by using gloves and other protective gear.

The adolescent who makes a suicide attempt or gesture, regardless of how trivial it may seem, must be transported to the ED, even if the child refuses.

Assessment of the Child with a Possible Toxic Exposure

Initial assessment

After the scene size-up and environmental evaluation for toxins, assess the child. Use age-appropriate techniques to approach the patient, as outlined in Chapter 2, and conduct a complete assessment, as described in Chapter 3.

History is the best tool for assessment in pediatric poisoning. It is usually more accurate than physical evaluation for determining the specific type of toxic exposure. In the first few minutes, the important questions are the identity of the agent, when the exposure occurred, and the amount of the agent involved in the exposure.

Special considerations in the ABCDEs

After the PAT, do the hands-on ABCDEs and immediately treat any physiologic abnormalities. Special elements of the physical assessment that may help identify the type of poison include: breath odor, vital signs, pupillary size, temperature and moisture of skin, and presence or absence of bowel sounds. Also, look for stains and powders on the skin or clothes.

Airway

Clear, maintain, and control the airway in the child with a suspected toxic exposure who has altered level of consciousness. This may happen in a child exposed to a **sedative hypnotic** drug, such as alcohol, a benzodiazepine, or a barbiturate. Beware of the child who has ingested a **caustic** agent such as **lye**. This child may have severe burns of the esophagus and present with **dysphagia** and signs of upper airway obstruction. In the comatose or unresponsive patient, always consider the other common causes of altered level of consciousness, such as a head or cervical spine injury or hypoglycemia from alcohol. Immobilize the spine if head, neck, or spinal injury is suspected.

Breathing

Give 100% supplemental oxygen by a nonrebreathing mask if there is altered level of consciousness, respiratory distress, or a history of exposure to a toxic substance known to cause breathing problems. One example of this type of toxic exposure would be **hydrocarbon** inhalation. Pulse oximetry is generally useful but is not accurate for some toxic exposures. For example, carbon monoxide poisoning usually gives a normal oxygen saturation reading in a child with severe hypoxia. Sedative hypnotic drugs may decrease respiratory rate, and **sympathomimetic agents**, such as cocaine, amphetamines, **phencyclidine**, marijuana, and hashish may increase respiratory rate.

Circulation

If the child has eaten or swallowed a possible cardiopulmonary toxin, place her on a cardiac monitor to watch for dysrhythmias. Drugs such as beta blockers digoxin or calcium channel blockers may decrease the heart rate, while sympathomimetic agents or anticholinergic agents, such as **scopolamine** or jimson weed, may increase heart rate.

Disability

Altered level of consciousness is a common effect of many different chemical exposures. Recreational drug use with sedative hypnotics depresses the central nervous system (CNS). Sympathomimetic drugs may stimulate the CNS and cause excitement, agitation, paranoia, or hallucinations. Tricyclic antidepressants may cause seizures or coma.

Exposure

Undress the child and look for evidence of toxic exposure to the eyes and skin. Many substances, such as hydrocarbons, irritate the eyes. Other toxic substances, such as **hydrochloric acid**, irritate the skin. **Organophosphate insecticides** enter through the skin and can cause a severe **cholinergic crisis** with **miosis**, **salivation**, abdominal cramping, and bradycardia.

Bring bottles, containers, plastic bags, suspicious substances, plants, or syringes to the ED.

Initial management of toxic exposures

After the initial assessment, determine the need for treatment and transport of the poisoned child by combining the physical assessment with a risk assessment. The physical assessment is a way to determine the child's physiological stability and

CASE STUDY 2

You respond to a call for an unconscious 4-year-old girl. The parents report that, on arriving home, they found the child unconscious and lying supine on the living room floor. A babysitter was watching TV and had not checked on the girl for about 1 hour. She had been playing normally in the kitchen when last seen.

The child is unresponsive to verbal or painful stimuli. Work of breathing is normal, but the skin looks pale. Her pupils are dilated. Respiratory rate is 20 breaths/min, heart rate is 130 beats/min, and blood pressure 90/60 mm Hg. You note red stains around the mouth and on her clothes. There is an open bottle of red wine next to the patient. Bedside glucose determination is 40 mg/dl.

Outline management priorities.
Should you give activated charcoal?

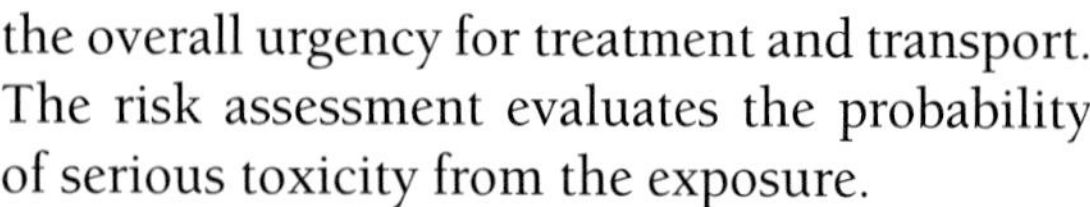

the overall urgency for treatment and transport. The risk assessment evaluates the probability of serious toxicity from the exposure.

Risk assessment

Assess the chances of serious toxicity from the following five pieces of information:

1. Identity of the agent involved and its lethality, usually through consultation with medical oversight or the poison center
2. Amount of the poison ingested, in milligrams (mg)
3. Child's weight
4. The per-kilogram amount of poison in the exposure, in mg/kg
5. Time since the exposure

Common toxic agents such as aspirin, acetaminophen, or iron have predictable physiologic effects that are determined by how much of the drug was taken, time since exposure, and amount of drug per kg. By collecting information and evidence at the scene, the prehospital professional serves an important role in later ED testing and treatment.

! Tip

In suspected toxic exposures, perform risk assessment to determine the chances of serious toxicity.

? Controversy

If the child is stable and has a history of a single small ingestion of a harmless agent, some EMS systems allow the transport to be canceled after agreement from medical oversight. However, this is controversial because ED evaluation may identify other concerns or possible complications.

Sometimes the prehospital professional's risk assessment determines that a child has had a lethal exposure, although the child is physiologically stable. Indeed, in a small child, one ingested pill of some common medications can kill. Table 7-3 lists potentially dangerous agents where a tiny toxic exposure (e.g., one pill) may be fatal to a toddler.

The transport decision: Stay or go?

After the initial assessment, primary treatment, and risk assessment, consider whether to transport immediately, doing additional assessment and treatment on the way to the ED, or to stay on the scene. If the results of the physical assessment and the risk assessment show that the child is normal after only a single small ingestion of a harmless agent, consider canceling transport after appropriate consultation with medical oversight or the poison control center. This is controversial, however, because some EMS systems consider hospital transport necessary in all toxic exposure cases. Other systems allow the poison center to manage minor ingestions exclusively over the telephone.

If the physical assessment indicates that the child has any physiologic abnormality, or if the risk assessment indicates that the toxic exposure is potentially harmful, transport and do additional assessment on the way to the ED, if possible. Symptoms of toxicity are different depending on the substance involved. A

Table 7-3 One Pill Can Kill

Medicine	Lethal Dose
Camphor	One tsp of oil
Chloroquine	One 500-mg tab
Clonidine	One 0.3-mg tab
Glyburide	Two 5-mg tabs
Imipramine	One 150-mg tab
Lindane	Two tsp of 1% lotion
Diphenoxylate/atropine	Two 2.5-mg tabs
Propranolol	One or two 160-mg tabs
Theophylline	One 500-mg tab
Verapamil	One or two 240-mg tabs

child without symptoms may have ingested a lethal dose of a substance.

For example, ingestions of iron and acetaminophen, two common household over-the-counter medicines, may be extremely dangerous but cause no early symptoms. History from the scene is critical to the management in the ED.

Additional assessment

After the initial assessment, if the child has a normal physical assessment and is asymptomatic, and if the risk assessment indicates no serious toxicity, do additional assessment on scene with the focused history and exam and the detailed exam. Sometimes, this additional assessment can also be done on the way to the ED. Table 7-4 lists important history in a suspected toxic exposure, presented in the standard SAMPLE format. During the initial assessment and the risk assessment, the prehospital professional will have already obtained some of the SAMPLE history.

Summary of Assessment of the Child with a Possible Toxic Exposure

Every child with a toxic exposure needs a careful physical assessment and risk assessment. The physical assessment includes all of the features of the standard assessment, with an emphasis on the history—which is usually the most important part of the evaluation. Preparation begins on the way to the scene with dispatch information about the age of the patient and type and potential toxicity of exposure. Preparation then continues with the scene size-up and environmental assessment.

Most pediatric poisonings do not require treatment in the field.

After the physical assessment, the risk assessment will help determine if there might be serious toxicity based on what

Table 7-4 The Pediatric SAMPLE for Toxic Exposures

Component	Explanation
Signs/Symptoms	Time of suspected exposure Behavior changes in child Emesis and exact nature of vomitus
Allergies	Known drug reactions or other allergies
Medications	Identity of suspected toxin Amount of toxin exposure (count pills or measure volume) Pill or chemical containers on scene Exact names and doses of prescribed medications
Past medical problems	Previous illnesses or injuries
Last food or liquid	Timing of the child's last food or drink Type and time of home treatment (such as ipecac)
Events leading to the exposure	Key events leading to the exposure Type of exposure (inhaled, injected, ingested, or absorbed through the skin) Poison center contact

type of toxin was involved, the amount of the toxin, the weight of the child, and the time since the exposure. The risk assessment gives important information about expected physiologic effects, need for treatment, and timing of transport. The poison center often plays a key role in helping decide about treatment and transport.

Toxicologic Management

The prehospital professional has three possible options for toxicologic management of serious, or potentially lethal, exposures: (1) decontamination, or removal or reduction of toxicity of the poison; (2) enhancement of elimination, or increasing the speed of removal of the toxin; or (3) antidote administration to reverse the actions of the poison directly.

Decontamination

After the treatment and transport decision, consider decontamination. There are several ways to decontaminate, depending on the toxin and the type of exposure.

Skin

If there is a chance that the poison was **absorbed** through the skin, remove the child's clothing. The prehospital professional must protect her own skin and eyes by using gloves and protective gear. Flood the skin with large amounts of water, and then wash it well with soap and water.

Eyes

Immediately wash out the eyes if there has been direct eye contact. **Alkali** burns with caustic agents such as lye are the most dangerous. Flush the eyes for 20 minutes using normal saline or water. Attach IV tubing to the bag of normal saline and flush the eye with the end of the IV tubing. If this is not possible, hold the patient's head under the sink and pour water into the eye from a pitcher or glass. When the eyes are the main point of exposure, continue flushing during transport if possible.

Do not give ipecac to a child with a suspected ingestion.

Gastrointestinal decontamination

Dilute any **acid** or alkali ingestions by asking the alert patient to drink an 8-ounce glass of milk. **Ipecac** may have been given in the home by the caregiver. Make note of this and the time it was given. *The vomiting induced by ipecac does not usually remove significant amounts of ingested toxins from the stomach.* It is not known how effective and safe ipecac is when given to the out-of-hospital patient. Ipecac's usefulness is limited even in the home, and it is not recommended for use in children by prehospital professionals (Figure 7-2). Ipecac is not available to prehospital professionals in many EMS systems.

Activated charcoal. *Most high-risk toddlers and preschool children do not require any out-of-hospital treatment.* In cases where gastrointestinal decontamination is necessary, consider using activated charcoal. Activated charcoal is made from burned wood products. Its surfaces are "activated" by steam or chemical treatment, so the material can **adsorb** other substances. It is a nonabsorbable binding agent. Activated charcoal has no odor or taste, but it can have a granular consistency that children do not like. The biggest problem with field use of activated charcoal is the difficulty in getting children to take

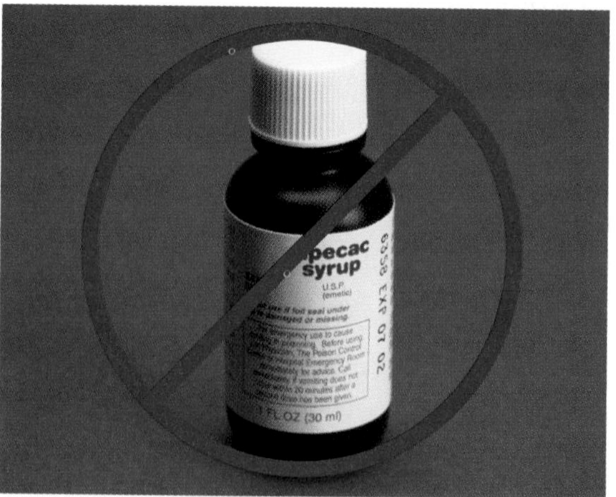

Figure 7-2 Ipecac has no role in prehospital professional treatment of pediatric poisoning.

it. In addition, it can stain and create a mess in the ambulance, so be careful handling it. It is uncertain how valuable activated charcoal is when used out-of-hospital, so carefully weigh the risks and benefits in each case.

The activated charcoal dose is 10 times the mass of the ingested substance. However, because the actual amount of ingested material is usually not known, use 1 g/kg of the child's body weight. Activated charcoal begins working immediately. It adsorbs the ingested toxins in the stomach and small bowel and reduces bloodstream absorption of the toxins. *Even a swallow may help, so it is usually worth the effort to get a child to at least try it if the risk assessment indicates possible toxicity.* Some agents are not adsorbed by activated charcoal, as noted in Table 7-5.

ALS Advanced LIFE support

Administration of activated charcoal The child must be stable and cooperative to receive activated charcoal. Because young children or adolescents may not want to drink the activated charcoal, some EMS systems use a nasogastric tube as an alternative method of delivery if the ingestion is potentially serious or lethal. *Delivery of activated charcoal by nasogastric tube can be dangerous and must be reserved for highly unusual circumstances where transport time is long and risk assessment shows severe toxicity.*

Never force a child to take activated charcoal because it will probably not be successful and may do harm. Two pediatric deaths from activated charcoal aspiration into the lungs occurred in 1996. In both cases, the actual poisoning was trivial, and the activated charcoal was unnecessary. Try to get the child to take a drink through a straw by asking nicely and using gentle urging. Consider adding a flavoring agent to make the mixture more acceptable to drink, then transport the child. Flavoring activated charcoal with a ground-up chocolate bar or another familiar flavor or adding activated charcoal to chocolate milk may help in getting the child to ingest it, especially if transport time is long. This technique has not been studied in the out-of-hospital setting, but appears to have some promise.

Table 7-5 Toxins Poorly Adsorbed by Activated Charcoal

Toxins
Simple ions
Iron
Lithium
Cyanide
Simple alcohols
Ethanol
Methanol
Strong acids or bases

Table 7-6 summarizes activated charcoal and guidelines for use.

Enhancement of elimination

Sorbitol is a cathartic that is mixed with many commercial activated charcoal preparations. Cathartics have been promoted to clear the bound toxin from the gut and help speed up elimination. The effectiveness of cathartics has not been proven. Sorbitol is not an approved drug in most EMS systems. Prehospital professionals may think they are giving pure activated charcoal when the preparation actually is a mixture of activated charcoal and sorbitol. *Sorbitol may cause nausea, vomiting, abdominal discomfort, and significant diarrhea in children. Therefore never use a cathartic in children.*

The biggest problem with field use of activated charcoal is the difficulty getting children to take it, so consider using a flavoring agent.

Do not give activated charcoal to an uncooperative child unless there is a potentially lethal ingestion and long transport time.

Antidotes

Consider any known antidotes if the toxic agent is identified. Antidotes are

Table 7-6 Activated Charcoal: Guidelines for Use

Product Information	A highly adsorbent, harmless, tasteless material made from wood pulp (Figure 7-3)
Indication	To limit amount of drug absorbed by the body in most toxic ingestions (i.e., for intestinal decontamination) Repeated doses may enhance the elimination process.
Technique	Mix 1 g/kg patient weight with water to form a slurry. If the quantity of ingested substance is known, give 10 times the ingested dose of toxin by weight. Administer orally (or by nasogastric tube in rare situations). Consider adding a flavoring agent.
Contraindications	Loss of gag reflex Altered level of consciousness Unwillingness voluntarily to take the drug Corrosive substance ingestion, unless other toxins have also been ingested
Adverse Effects	Constipation or intestinal bezoar (large foreign-body mass in gut) Pulmonary aspiration Diarrhea and dehydration may occur in young children given a combined cathartic (e.g., sorbitol) and activated charcoal.
Remarks	Will not bind alcohols, heavy metals (iron, lead), lithium

Sorbitol may cause nausea, vomiting, abdominal discomfort, and diarrhea in children and therefore should not be used in pediatric patients.

rarely indicated because out-of-hospital exposures to reversible agents are unusual in pediatrics. Table 7-7 lists the few commonly available antidotes for several uncommon chemical exposures.

Summary of Toxicologic Management

Most children with toxic exposures do not require treatment of any kind in the field. Occasionally, after consultation with medical oversight about a normal child with a history of a harmless unintentional single ingestion, consider cancellation of ED transport. In other circumstances, when physical assessment and risk assessment together show physiologic instability or possible toxicity, treatment is indicated. After managing the

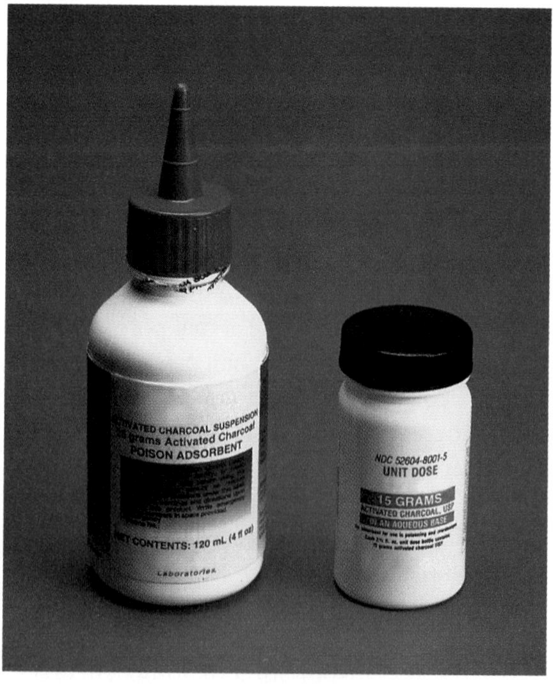

Figure 7-3 Activated charcoal is a treatment option for potentially serious ingestions.

ABCDEs, consider toxicologic management by decontamination or, in special situations, administering an antidote. Attempt decontamination whenever possible. This usually means washing the skin, flushing the eyes, or beginning gastrointestinal decontamination with activated charcoal. Activated charcoal is a useful binding agent for most, but not all, ingestions. As a general rule, do not administer activated charcoal to an uncooperative child. Sorbitol is contraindicated in children, and antidotes are rarely helpful because most pediatric exposures do not involve drugs or toxins with reversible actions.

Table 7-7 Common Antidotes

Poison	Antidote
Organophosphate	Atropine
Potassium Tricyclic antidepressants	Bicarbonate
Opiates	Naloxone

Role of the Poison Center

Involve the regional poison center whenever possible. In most EMS systems, contact with the poison center happens through medical oversight. Sometimes, the caregiver has already contacted the poison center and the 911 system is notified after that. An additional advantage of involving the poison control center is that they often have the capability to follow up with continuing reassessment by telephone.

Remember to educate the family or caregiver on poisoning prevention if circumstances allow, as discussed in Chapter 1.

The value of activated charcoal for out-of-hospital treatment of ingestions is unproven. While the drug has a possible advantage of early binding of toxins in the gut, there are important complications such as aspiration.

! Tip

Poison control centers have the capability to follow up with continuing reassessment by telephone.

CASE STUDY 3

It is spring in the countryside. You respond to a 911 call initiated by a local farmer, who is caring for two neighbor girls who suddenly became sick and agitated. On arrival you find two 12-year-old girls complaining of abdominal cramps, sweating, drooling, and muscle weakness. One of the girls begins vomiting. The initial assessment is similar in both patients. Work of breathing is increased, with audible wheezing and retractions. Skin appears pale. Pupils are small, and some muscle twitching is present. The respiratory rate, heart rate, and blood pressure are elevated for both girls.

Discuss decontamination procedures for the patients as well as for others at the scene.
Is there any specific treatment for this toxic exposure?

CHAPTER RESOURCES

Case Study Answers

See page 115

The PAT indicates a child with abnormal appearance, normal work of breathing, and normal circulation to skin. This physiologic state suggests a CNS or **systemic** process, such as hemorrhage from head trauma, drug intoxication, a generalized infection, or a metabolic abnormality such as hypoglycemia. The scene size-up and environmental assessment strongly suggest a drug exposure and possibly an unsafe situation.

The risk assessment is limited. The mother's behavior suggests intoxication with a sympathomimetic drug such as cocaine or amphetamines, but the exact exposure will be difficult to determine in the field. Take containers, plastic bags, suspicious substances, or plants to the ED.

On the way to the hospital the patient has a seizure. The initial priority is to clear, maintain, and control the airway and supply oxygen. Reassess. If the child's convulsions restart and continue for 5 minutes, the condition probably needs treatment with a benzodiazepine drug.

ALS Advanced LIFE support **Drug treatment for prolonged seizures**
Treat with a benzodiazepine—either diazepam or midazolam. Give rectal diazepam 0.5 mg/kg/dose through a lubricated syringe or give IV midazolam 0.1 mg/kg IM. During transport, frequently reassess and monitor response to treatment.

At the ED, write down clear and legible notes on the prehospital record, including the observed environmental conditions and the mother's behavior, and make sure that someone will make a report to the child protective services agency.

See page 119

The physical assessment shows an unresponsive child with normal work of breathing and abnormal circulation to skin. The bedside glucose determination suggests hypoglycemia. Suction the mouth and nose, place a nasopharyngeal airway, and give oxygen. Anticipate possible aspiration.

Treatment of hypoglycemia
Place the child on a cardiac monitor. Make sure there is vascular access and administer 1.0 ml/kg of 50% dextrose in water. If attempts to get access fail, give glucagon, 1.0 mg IM. The child should immediately respond to dextrose.

Do not administer activated charcoal. First, it may be aspirated if the child has no gag reflex or is not intubated, and the substance is given by mouth or nasogastric or orogastric tube. Second, activated charcoal does not adsorb alcohol—the suspected toxin in this case. Alcohol is well

CHAPTER RESOURCES

known to cause hypoglycemia in young children. Because this is a toddler, it is probably a single-substance ingestion of alcohol.

Perform a risk assessment. Ask the caregivers when the ingestion took place, how much ethanol was in the bottle before the ingestion, what medications are in the home, if they contacted a poison control center, and if the patient has any allergies or chronic medical or psychiatric problems. By knowing the amount of alcohol ingested, the weight of the child, and the time since the ingestion, you can estimate the expected level of intoxication. This calculation, or risk assessment, can be done with the help of the poison control center or medical oversight or both.

Transport the patient and all possible poisons immediately to the ED. It is probably ethanol ingestion because of the clinical condition of the little girl and the environmental evidence. There is no specific antidote for ethanol toxicity.

See at page 131

Assess the scene. Are there toxins in the environment or on the patient's clothes or skin that can be hazardous to the prehospital professional? If so, contact the appropriate authority. Reduce the risk of toxic exposure to yourself and other scene personnel.

Pay careful attention to breathing. Give supplemental oxygen. One of the girls is vomiting. Protect her airway from aspiration with suction. Do not induce vomiting because of the danger of abrupt respiratory arrest and seizures.

ALS Advanced LIFE support

Treatment of organophosphate poisoning

If there is a possibility of prolonged patient transport time, consider using atropine, 0.01 mg/kg. Atropine is a direct antidote for organophosphate poisonings.

Protect your own skin by using gloves and other protective clothing. Explain to the patient and caregiver that you will need to remove the child's clothes. Flush the skin with large amounts of water. Wash the skin, hair, and under the nails well with soap and water. Flush exposed eyes with large amounts of warm water or saline.

Suggested Educational Resources

1. American Academy of Clinical Toxicology and European Association of Poison Centres and Clinical Toxicologists. Joint Position Statements on Gastrointestinal Decontamination. *Clin Toxicol* 1997;35:695–762.

2. Dieckmann, RA. Toxic Exposures. In: Seidel JS, Henderson DP. *Prehospital Care of Pediatric Emergencies.* Boston, MA: Jones and Bartlett Publishers; 1997: 122–129.

3. Koren G. Medications which can kill a toddler with one tablet or teaspoon. *Clin Toxicol* 1993; 31(3):407–413.

4. Litovitz TL, Smilkstein M, Felberg L, et al. 1996 annual report of the American Association of Poison Control Centers Toxic Exposure Surveillance System. *Am J Emerg Med* 1997;15:447–500.

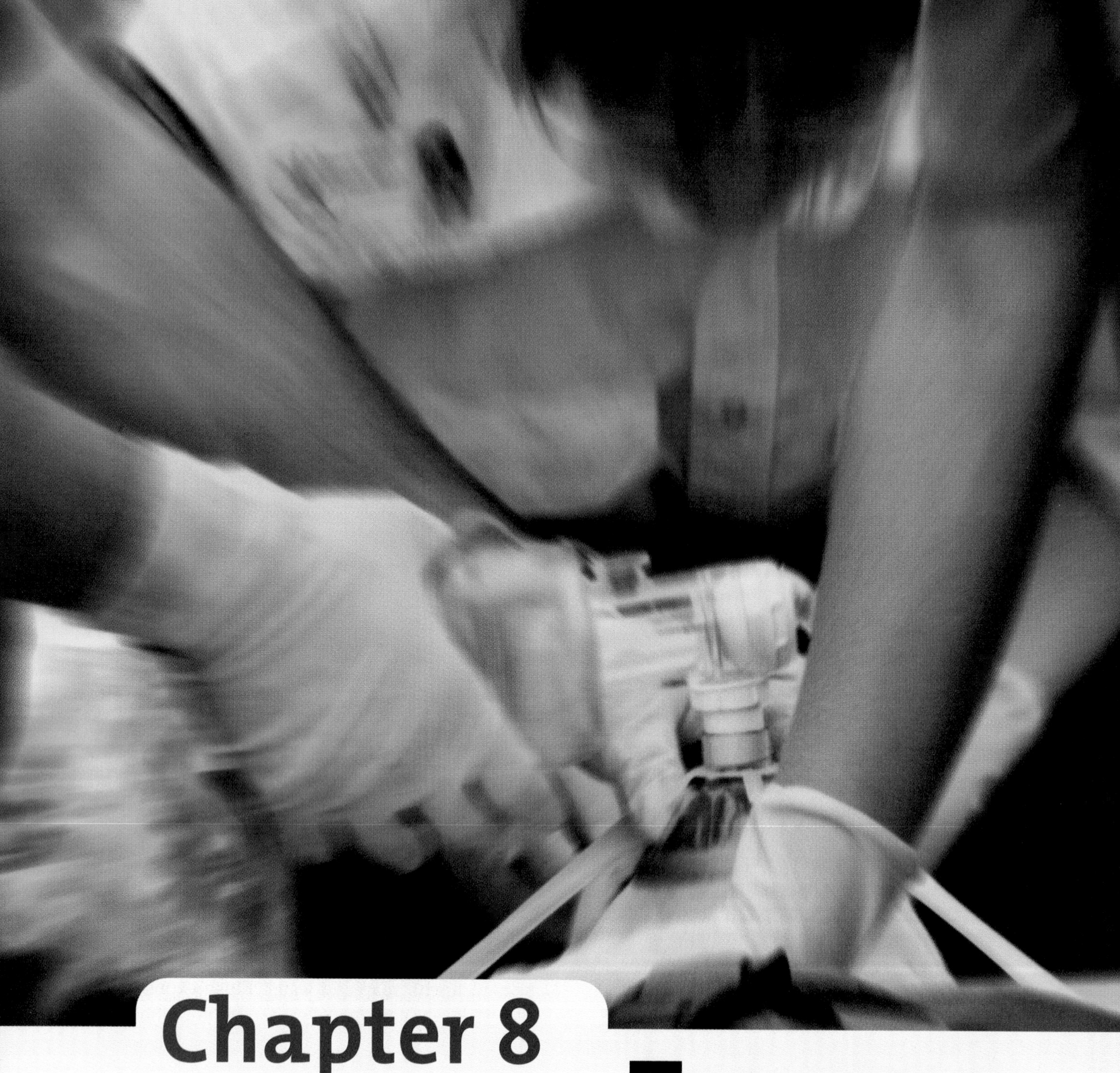

Chapter 8 Trauma

Learning Objectives

1. Explain the unique anatomic features of children that predispose them to injuries.
2. Sequence the initial assessment of the injured child.
3. Integrate the essential trauma interventions in the ABCDEs.
4. Distinguish different approaches in airway management of injured children.
5. Discuss assessment and treatment of pediatric burn patients.
6. Describe priorities in managing a child and family in a multicasualty incident.
7. Apply appropriate assessment techniques and treatment plans to case studies presenting a variety of trauma situations.

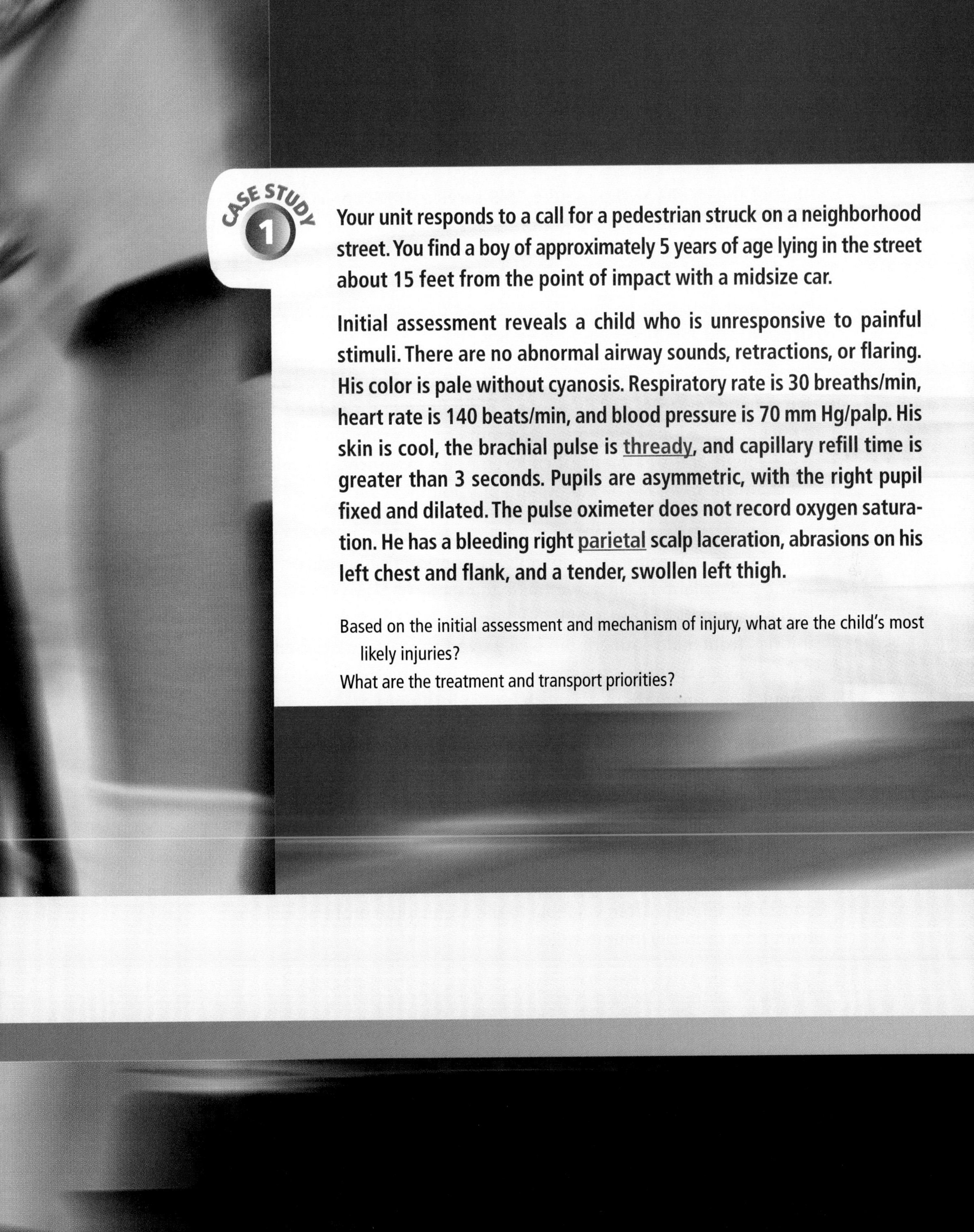

Your unit responds to a call for a pedestrian struck on a neighborhood street. You find a boy of approximately 5 years of age lying in the street about 15 feet from the point of impact with a midsize car.

Initial assessment reveals a child who is unresponsive to painful stimuli. There are no abnormal airway sounds, retractions, or flaring. His color is pale without cyanosis. Respiratory rate is 30 breaths/min, heart rate is 140 beats/min, and blood pressure is 70 mm Hg/palp. His skin is cool, the brachial pulse is thready, and capillary refill time is greater than 3 seconds. Pupils are asymmetric, with the right pupil fixed and dilated. The pulse oximeter does not record oxygen saturation. He has a bleeding right parietal scalp laceration, abrasions on his left chest and flank, and a tender, swollen left thigh.

Based on the initial assessment and mechanism of injury, what are the child's most likely injuries?

What are the treatment and transport priorities?

Introduction

Half of the children who require EMS services have an acute injury. Fortunately, the most common injuries are minor problems, such as lacerations, burns, mild closed head injuries, and extremity fractures. In these cases, the role of the prehospital professional is straightforward: perform a scene size-up, assess for physiologic or anatomic problems, and transport to the ED. Treatment usually entails only wound care, immobilization, and splinting when necessary.

Multisystem trauma, in contrast, provides the prehospital professional with great challenges and rewards, and demands a disciplined and child-specific approach. Usually, principles of adult trauma management can be effectively and safely applied to the assessment and treatment of children, with modifications related to differences in mechanisms of injury, anatomy, and physiologic response.

Between infancy and adulthood, injuries are the most common cause of death. Most injuries are unintentional. However, intentional injuries, primarily child maltreatment and violent assaults, are the leading mechanisms of traumatic death in infants and are a significant cause of injury and death in children and adolescents. Intentional injuries from maltreatment are easily overlooked, as discussed in Chapter 12. About 80% to 90% of pediatric trauma involves a blunt mechanism. This differs from the adult population, where there is a much higher incidence of penetrating injuries. Handgun injuries, however, are on the rise in children and are now the most common cause of penetrating injuries in adolescents.

The emotional response of prehospital professionals to an injured child can be intense. They often see the patient as a friend or relative and can be impaired in their professional duties. Experience and education will help the prehospital professional develop an efficient and emotionally neutral approach. Critical incident stress debriefing is often valuable to the prehospital professional after treating a seriously injured child.

www.PEPPsite.com

Fatal Injury Mechanisms

Table 8-1 summarizes the most frequent fatal mechanisms of injury in children and adolescents. Vehicular trauma (including automobile occupant, pedestrian, and bicyclist injuries) is the leading specific mechanism in all age groups. Drowning is the second leading cause. House fire is a significant cause of death, especially in the eastern United States. Falls are common but rarely cause major injury unless the length of the fall is greater than the child's height.

Table 8-1 Leading Mechanisms of Injury-Related Death

1 to 4 years old	5 to 15 years old
Vehicular trauma	Vehicular trauma
Drowning	Drowning
House fires	Homicide
Homicide	House fires
Falls	Gunshot wounds

Unique Anatomic Features of Children: Effect on Injury Patterns

Head

Children seriously injure their heads more than any other body part. The severity of head injury usually determines the patient's outcome.

Until early school age (5 years old), the head takes up a large percentage of overall body mass and surface area when compared to adults. Since the head is large in proportion to the body, it functions like the heavy end of a lawn dart, becoming the lead point in a fall (Figure 8-1).

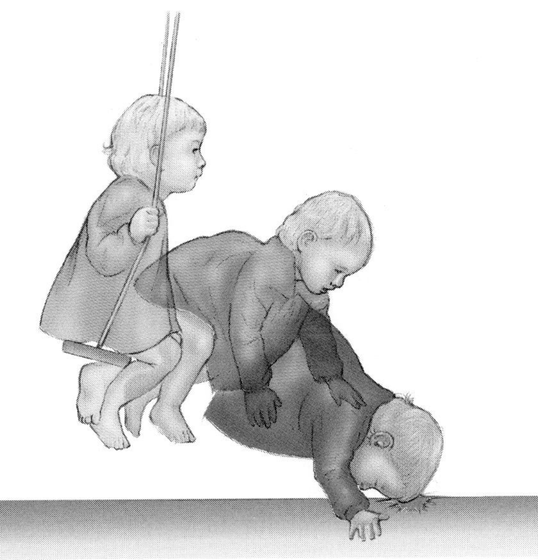

Figure 8-1 The head is usually the lead point in a fall and acts like a lawn dart.

Spinal column

As a group, children do not suffer many fractures or dislocations of the bones of the spinal column.

When fractures of spinal bones do occur, the event typically involves a high-energy mechanism (e.g., motor vehicle crash) with axial loading of the **spine** or extreme **flexion** or extension. Traumatic spinal cord injury, or disruption of the central nerve pathways themselves, is also rare in children, although spinal cord injury does occur without spinal bone injury.

Tip

Injuries cause almost half the deaths among children from 1 to 4 years of age and outrank all other causes of death combined among older children and adolescents.

The most common cervical spine injuries in children occur at the level of the high cervical spine, where the weaker neck muscles cannot brace against sudden movement of the heavy head. In reality, most children with high cervical injury are in full arrest on the scene, and they have usually been subjected to a severe **acceleration-deceleration mechanism** involving a motor vehicle crash or a long fall.

The most common lower spine injuries occur in the mid- to lower **thoracic** spine. Mechanisms include direct blows, falls, or spinal **compression** during a motor vehicle crash from improperly placed seat belts.

Chest

The ribs of the child are mainly **cartilage** and are softer than those of the adult. As a result, the **chest wall** is flexible and does not fracture easily. For this reason, rib fractures and **flail chest** are uncommon in younger children. The chest wall of children is not very muscular, so they do not have the soft-tissue protection from injury that is present in adolescents and adults (Figure 8-2). Any forces from impact may be transferred directly to the internal organs. Therefore, be vigilant with the child who is struck or hit hard in the chest and suspect possible injuries to the lungs and heart. Contusions and **abrasions** of the

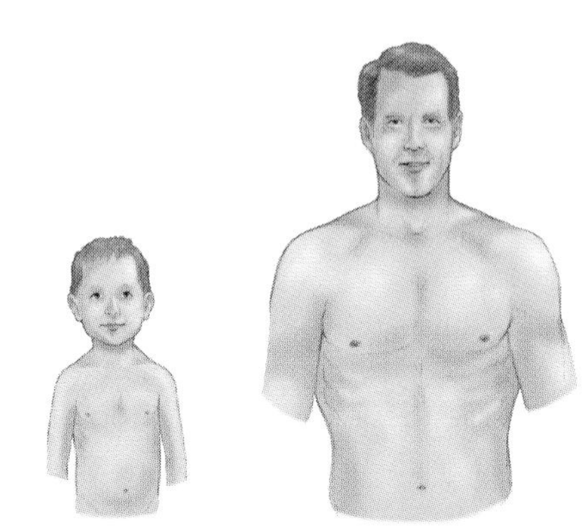

Figure 8-2 The child's chest wall is not well muscularized, so it lacks the soft tissue protection from injury that is present in adolescents and adults.

! Tip

If penetration of the chest wall, back, or high abdomen is present, look for tension pneumothorax.

chest wall may indicate internal injuries. On the other hand, a symmetrical, nontender chest wall does not rule out internal injuries.

Pulmonary contusions, or bruises to the lung tissue, are the most common form of serious lung injuries in children. They require an X ray to diagnose and cannot be identified in the field. A child who sustains blunt chest trauma and has hypoxia or respiratory distress may have a pulmonary contusion. Moreover, because the child's chest is small, blunt or penetrating trauma to the chest and back, between the nipple line and the lowest ribs, may affect both the chest and the abdomen. The diaphragm can rise as high as the nipple line during full expiration and can flatten to the level of the lowest ribs during full inhalation (Figures 8-3a and 8-3b).

Penetrating chest trauma may cause serious problems in oxygenation and ventilation. When the chest wall, back, or high abdomen is penetrated, look for **tension pneumothorax** and **sucking chest wounds**. These injuries are rare in children but must be recognized because they may require specific immediate life-saving treatment in the field.

Abdomen

The **abdomen** is often the site of serious blood loss in pediatric patients and is the most common site of injury causing shock.

The solid organs of the upper abdominal cavity are the liver, **spleen**, and kidneys. These organs are disproportionately larger and more exposed than in adults and are poorly protected by the child's softer ribs and relatively underdeveloped abdominal muscles (Figure 8-4). Though injured less commonly than the solid organs, the hollow organs of the abdomen, especially the stomach, small bowel, and bladder, may also be injured.

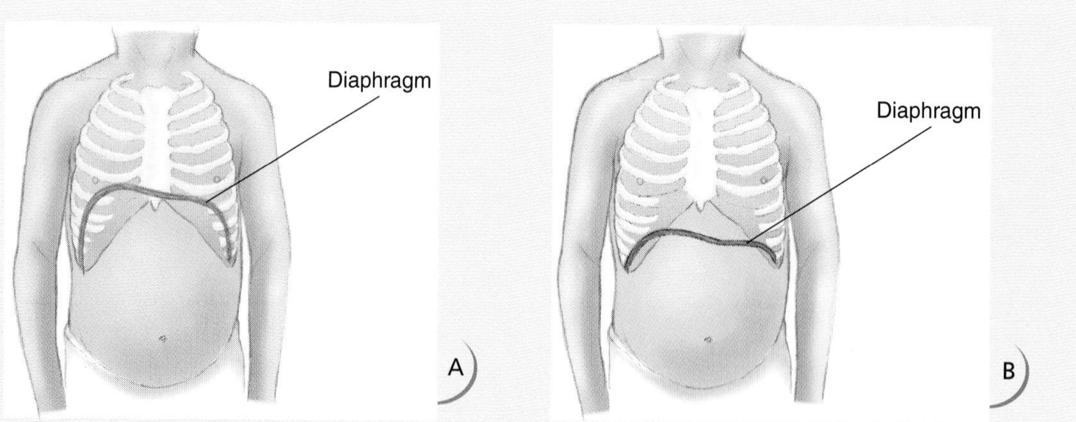

Figure 8-3 The diaphragm can rise as high as the nipple line during full expiration (A) and can flatten to the level of the lowest ribs during full inspiration (B). Therefore, injuries to the abdomen may occur after trauma to a large area of body surface.

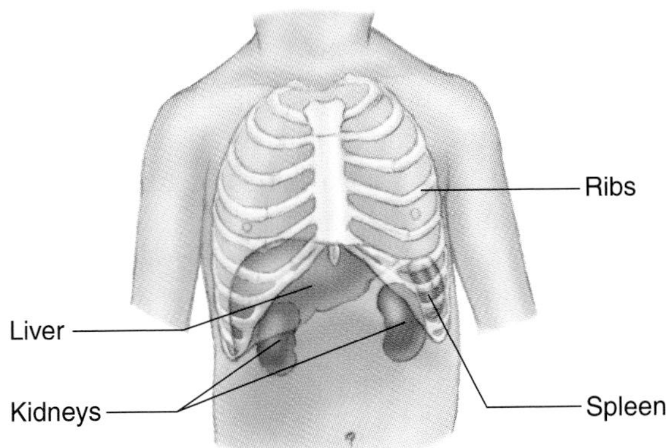

Figure 8-4 The solid organs of the upper abdominal cavity are disproportionately larger and more exposed in children than in adults and are poorly protected by their softer ribs and relatively underdeveloped abdominal muscles.

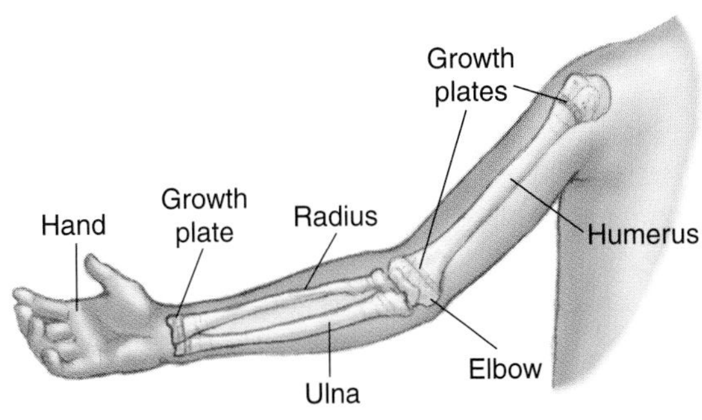

Figure 8-5 The growth plates at the ends of children's bones are easily fractured.

Because of the smaller size of the younger child's **pelvis** relative to other anatomic parts, pelvic injuries are less common. When the child reaches adolescence, the pelvis has adult characteristics and pelvic fractures become more frequent.

Assume that every child with a serious trauma mechanism has a life-threatening abdominal injury. Many children with abdominal injury have no immediate signs and may not complain of pain. Fear, young age, or other distracting injuries may hide signs and symptoms.

When present, signs include growing abdominal distention or rigidity, tenderness, abdominal wall contusions or abrasions, and hemodynamic instability. **Serial examinations**, or repeated examinations, may improve the accuracy of abdominal assessment.

Extremities

Children's bones are more flexible and not as well protected by muscle and soft tissues as the bones of adults. They are especially vulnerable to fractures at the weak, cartilaginous growth plates at the ends of the bones (Figure 8-5). Minor fractures through only one side of the bone (often called **greenstick fractures**) are common and may have minimal clinical signs. Suspect a fracture whenever there is point tenderness or limited range of motion, even when there is not much swelling or tenderness and no deformity.

The most serious complications of extremity injuries are **neurovascular** problems and blood loss into the soft tissues at the fracture site. Blood loss may be severe in long-bone fractures (e.g., fractures of the femur) or in pelvic fractures. The symptom usually associated with serious extremity injuries is pain. Pain is frequently underestimated and undertreated in children!

The abdomen is the most frequent site of injury causing shock. Serial examinations greatly improve the accuracy of assessment of abdominal injury.

Never overlook the possibility of solid organ injury when there has been blunt injury because fear, young age, or other distracting injuries may mask signs and symptoms.

Skin

The skin provides temperature regulation. Children have more skin surface area in relation to their overall size and weight than adults do. Because of this, heat loss from the skin is rapid. Even without injuries that damage the skin, injured children are at increased risk for hypothermia, or cooling of core organs. Hypothermia will jeopardize organ function. The signs and symptoms of hypothermia can be the same as those of hypovolemia and hypoperfusion. To avoid hypothermia, especially in a preschool-aged child, use simple methods (such as lights and warm blankets) to reduce heat loss. Turn up the heat in the ambulance.

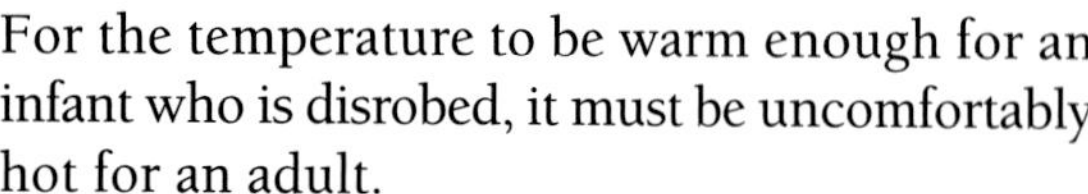

For the temperature to be warm enough for an infant who is disrobed, it must be uncomfortably hot for an adult.

Mechanism of Injury: Effect on Injury Patterns

The different mechanisms of injury in children and the unique anatomic features of children together produce predictable patterns of injury. Because penetrating injuries are uncommon and because the head (when compared to the rest of the body) is larger in childhood, injured children often have blunt injuries primarily involving the head. These are termed closed head injuries. If the energy of impact is severe and involves the entire body, the child may have a pattern of **multisystem trauma** involving the head, chest, abdomen, and long bones.

! Tip

Suspect a fracture whenever findings include point tenderness or limited range of motion.

Table 8-2 lists the common mechanisms of pediatric injury and the associated patterns of injury. Figure 8-6 illustrates the typical injury sequences in children.

Assessment of the Injured Child

The initial steps in assessing the injured child follow the approach for all children outlined in

Table 8-2 Common Mechanisms and Associated Patterns of Pediatric Injury*

Mechanism of Injury	Associated Patterns of Injury	
Motor vehicle crash (child is passenger)	UNRESTRAINED:	Multiple trauma, head and neck injuries, scalp and facial lacerations
	AIR BAG:	Head and neck, facial and eye injuries
	RESTRAINED:	Chest and abdominal injuries, cervical and lower-spine fractures (Figure 8-6a)
Motor vehicle crash (child is pedestrian)	LOW SPEED:	Lower-extremity fractures
	HIGH SPEED:	Chest and abdominal injuries, head and neck injuries, lower-extremity fractures (Figure 8-6b)
Fall from a height	LOW:	Upper-extremity fractures
	MEDIUM:	Head and neck injuries, upper- and lower-extremity fractures
	HIGH:	Chest and abdominal injuries, head and neck injuries, upper- and lower-extremity fractures (Figure 8-6c)
Fall from a bicycle	WITHOUT HELMET:	Head and neck injuries, scalp and facial lacerations, upper-extremity fractures
	WITH HELMET:	Upper-extremity fractures (Figure 8-6d)
	HITTING HANDLEBAR:	Internal abdominal injuries

*Adapted from *Teaching Resource for Instructors in Prehospital Pediatrics (TRIPP),* 1998 Version 2.0, Center for Pediatric Emergency Medicine (CPEM), New York, NY.

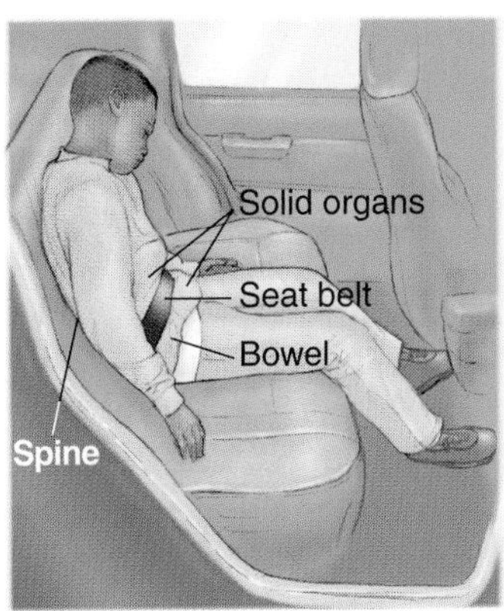

Figure 8-6a A restrained child in a motor vehicle crash may have a lap belt injury involving the solid organs, the bowel, and the spine.

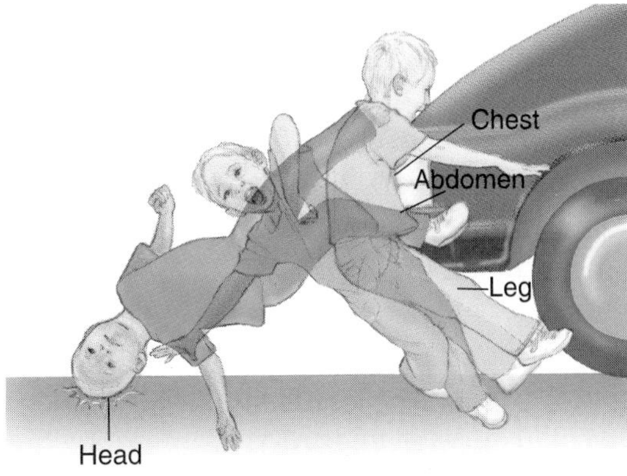

Figure 8-6b Children frequently sustain multisystem injuries involving the head, chest, abdomen, and leg.

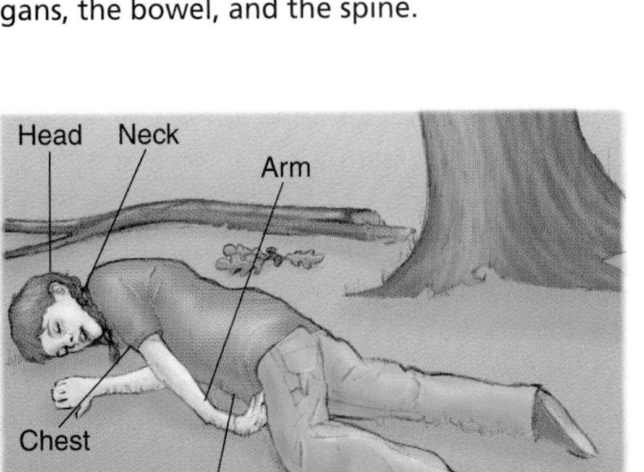

Figure 8-6c A fall from height frequently involves injury to the head and neck, chest, abdomen, and the extremities.

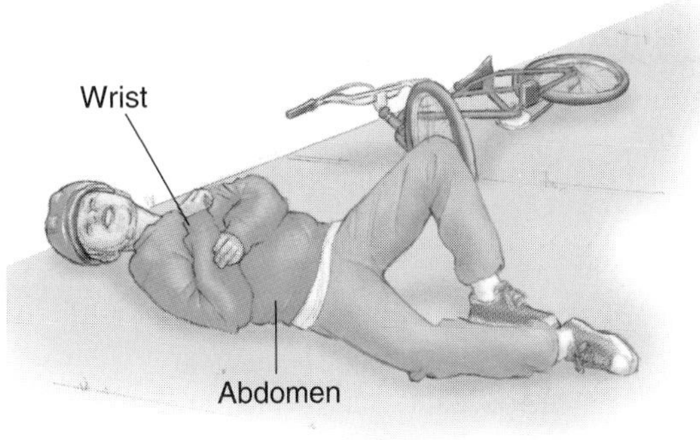

Figure 8-6d A fall over the handlebars of a bike may result in injuries to the abdomen and extremities.

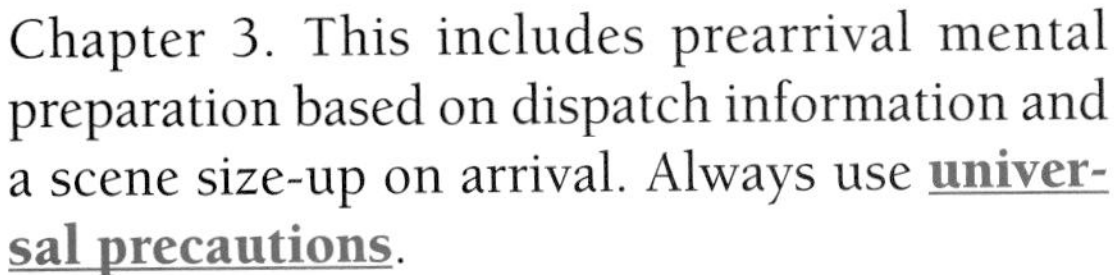

Chapter 3. This includes prearrival mental preparation based on dispatch information and a scene size-up on arrival. Always use **universal precautions**.

Most pediatric trauma patients have only minor injuries. These patients are stable and need a complete on-scene assessment before transport. This on-scene evaluation includes (1) initial assessment using the PAT and the hands-on ABCDEs, (2) a focused history, (3) a focused physical exam, and (4) a detailed exam. The most difficult challenge comes when there is a child with multisystem injuries who needs a prioritized, efficient on-scene approach to assessment and treatment, and rapid transport to the ED.

The PAT

The PAT helps with the initial assessment of type of physiologic disturbance, severity of injury, and determination of urgency of treatment. The PAT is a rapid way to evaluate physiologic status as well as to determine the amount of pain. The PAT involves assessment of appearance, work of breathing, and circulation to skin.

! Tip

Likely causes of abnormal appearance in a pediatric trauma patient are closed head injury; hypoxia; hemorrhage; and pain from fractures, burns, and soft tissue injuries.

Appearance

Appearance reflects brain function, which may be abnormal due to **primary brain injury** (caused by direct trauma to the brain tissue itself), **secondary brain injury** (caused by an indirect insult to the brain tissue from a low supply of blood or oxygen), or pain. The most likely causes of abnormal appearance in a pediatric trauma patient are closed head injury; hypoxia; hemorrhage; and pain from fractures, burns, and **soft-tissue injuries**.

Toxins may also cause abnormal appearance, but are uncommon causes of poor responsiveness in the preschool and school-aged trauma patient. However, toxins—most often recreational drugs—are an important possibility in the adolescent. Table 8-3 lists common causes of abnormal appearance in injured children.

Table 8-3 Common Causes of Abnormal Appearance in Injured Children

Category of Injury	Examples
Primary brain injuries	Closed head injury Brain edema Concussion Contusion Intracranial hematoma Intracranial hemorrhage Penetrating brain injuries
Secondary brain injuries	Hemorrhage with hypoperfusion Liver laceration Long-bone fracture Pelvis fracture Splenic rupture Hypoxia Aspiration of gastric contents Inadequate breathing Pulmonary contusion Smoke inhalation Tension pneumothorax
Pain	Burns Fractures Soft-tissue injuries
Toxins	Alcohol Amphetamines Carbon monoxide Cocaine and crack Marijuana Sedative-hypnotics

Work of breathing

Work of breathing is increased by injuries that affect the airway or the child's capacity to breathe. Table 8-4 summarizes causes of increased work of breathing in pediatric trauma patients. Shock can sometimes cause effortless tachypnea, a way of blowing off carbon dioxide in the blood that collects when there is a lack of perfusion to cells and tissues.

Listen for abnormal airway sounds, such as stridor or change of speech, which are important signs that might mean upper airway obstruction, as discussed in Chapter 3. Wheezing reflects lower airway irritation and bronchospasm. This may occur from inhalation of small particles or harmful substances, such as hot gases and vaporized toxins. Grunting indicates decreased gas exchange at the level of the air sacs, such as with pulmonary contusion. After listening, look for retractions and nasal flaring to further assess for hypoxia.

Table 8-4 Injury Causes of Increased Work of Breathing

Cause	Examples
Airway injuries	Hematomas of the tongue, mouth, or neck Penetrations into the upper airway Smoke and hot gas inhalation
Chest injuries	Pulmonary contusion Sucking chest wound Tension pneumothorax
Abdominal injuries	Injury to the diaphragm
Shock	Liver laceration Long-bone fracture Pelvis fracture Splenic rupture

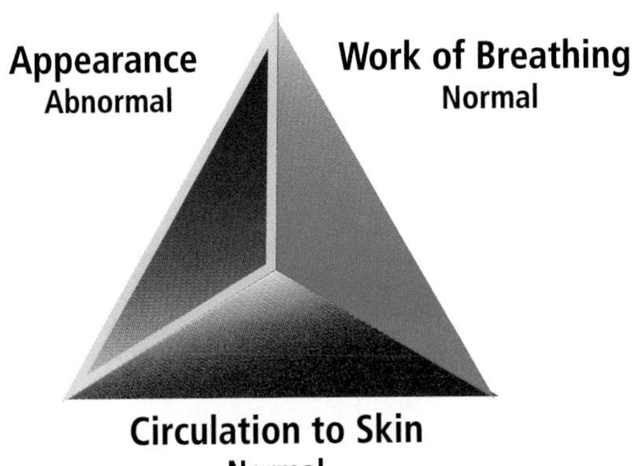

Figure 8-7 A patient with closed head injury has abnormal appearance, but normal work of breathing and normal circulation to skin.

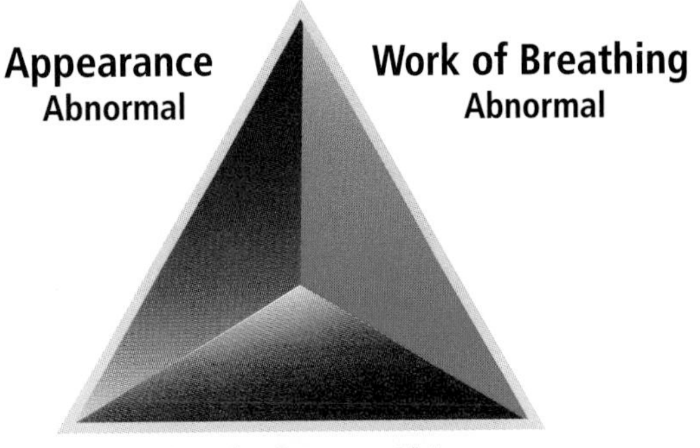

Figure 8-8 A patient with multiple system injury has abnormal appearance, abnormal work of breathing, and abnormal circulation to skin.

Circulation to skin

Circulation to skin reflects the amount of blood flowing through the blood vessels to the skin and mucous membranes. If skin color is abnormal in a child who is not cold, it may mean hypovolemia and hypoperfusion. The cause of hypoperfusion and shock is usually blood loss from intraabdominal bleeding. In newborns and young infants, because their cranial sutures have not fused and blood can build up inside the skull, intracranial bleeding can occasionally cause shock. Large body surface area burns will cause rapid loss of fluid through the skin and, over time, hypovolemia.

Figure 8-7 and Figure 8-8 show the PAT findings for the two most common patterns of major pediatric trauma: closed head injury and multisystem injury.

The ABCDEs

The ABCDEs are the second component of the initial trauma assessment. The trauma ABCDEs have a special focus on spinal precautions and control of blood loss.

The pediatric initial assessment, including the PAT and ABCDEs, does not require any specialized equipment and must be rapid. Treat each physiologic problem with a specific intervention, as the problem is identified in the ABCDE sequence. Table 8-5 lists the key features of the pediatric trauma ABCDEs and possible special trauma interventions.

Airway

Airway is always the first priority. Trauma victims are more likely to have airway problems because there might be obstruction by soft tissues, bleeding, **emesis**, edema, or foreign objects. Closed head injury, sometimes in combination with recreational drug use, may cause loss of protective airway reflexes or reduce effectiveness of breathing.

Sometimes the choice of specific interventions to open and maintain the airway depends

Table 8-5 Pediatric Trauma ABCDEs

Element of Assessment	Special Interventions
Airway	Modified jaw thrust maneuver Spinal immobilization
Breathing	Needle thoracostomy Dressing to sucking chest wound Assisted ventilation
Circulation	External hemorrhage control Shock position Splinting of fractured extremity Volume resuscitation
Disability	Oxygenation with nonrebreathing mask
Exposure	Body temperature maintenance

upon the field evaluation of the possibility of spinal injury. Because preschool-aged children are often unable to provide a reliable history of weakness, numbness, or spinal pain, mechanism of injury alone is often the primary indication for spinal immobilization in infants, toddlers, or preschool-aged children. Consider spinal injury in any child with any of the following findings in assessment of physiology, anatomy, history, or mechanism of injury:

- altered level of consciousness
- signs or symptoms of weakness or numbness
- physical evidence of trauma to the head or spine
- spinal pain
- a mechanism of injury involving the head or spine

Never let concern for spinal injury compromise appropriate management of the child's airway.

If the child has any of the physiologic, anatomic, history, or mechanism of injury findings for possible spinal injury, carefully immobilize the entire spine while managing the airway. Unstable cervical spine injuries, although uncommon in children, can kill quickly. Other spine injuries can cause devastating disabilities. However, never let concern for spinal injury affect appropriate management of the child's airway.

Actions. If airway obstruction is present, use a modified jaw-thrust maneuver combined with manual spinal in-line stabilization (Figure 8-9) to establish and maintain airway patency. Insert an **airway adjunct** if the child is unable to maintain an open airway. Use suction to clear any fluid or a Magill forceps to remove foreign bodies from the mouth, nose, or upper airway. Be prepared to turn the child on his side and suction if he vomits, to prevent aspiration of stomach contents. Quickly but carefully logroll the patient if vomiting occurs before he is secured to a spine board (Figure 8-10). Use spinal immobilization to hold the patient in place so that there is no spinal movement when the backboard is turned (Figure 8-11).

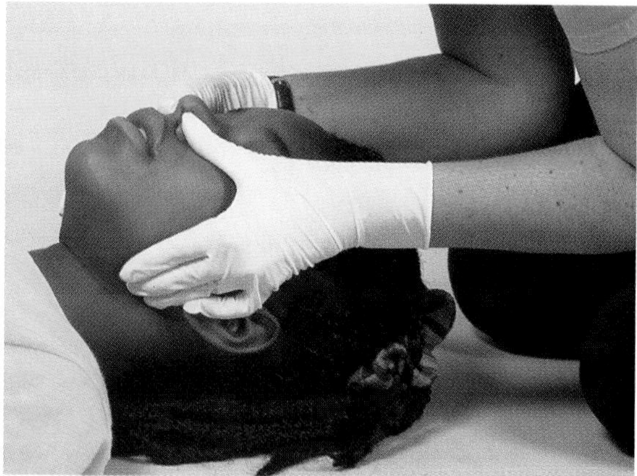

Figure 8-9 If airway obstruction is suspected in a child with possible spine injuries, use the modified jaw thrust maneuver combined with manual spinal in-line stabilization.

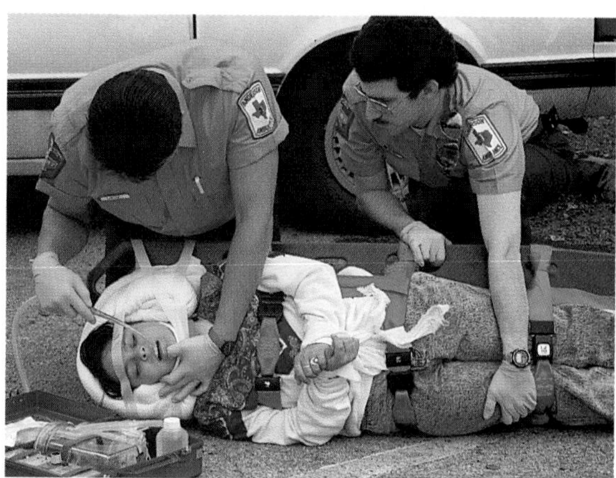

Figure 8-10 Log roll the patient as a unit if vomiting occurs before he is secured to a spine board.

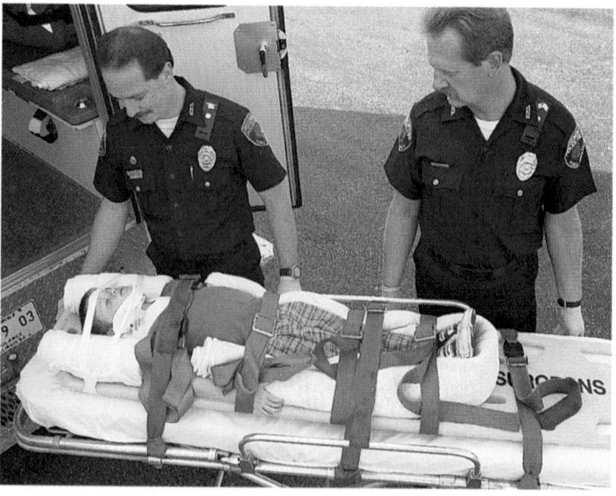

Figure 8-11 Spinal immobilization must secure the body so that there is no spinal movement when the backboard is turned.

Spinal Immobilization

The spinal column is made of 33 articulating bones, and its structure changes significantly during childhood growth. The age of the child, the developmentally appropriate behaviors, and the physical state of spinal growth are important factors in the incidence and types of pediatric spinal injuries. Cervical spine injuries are the most dangerous, but whenever the mechanism of injury, signs, or symptoms suggest possible spinal injury, immobilize the entire spine. For a step-by-step explanation of this procedure see page 293.

Breathing

Breathing is the second priority. Injuries to the airway, chest wall, lungs, or abdomen, as well as gastric distention due to air swallowing, may negatively affect breathing. Head and cervical spine injuries will sometimes depress the brain's instinct to breathe or diminish the protective airway reflex. Pulmonary aspiration of gastric contents is a common and potentially serious complication of head injuries. Aspiration will cause extreme hypoxia and increased work of breathing.

Look for soft-tissue or penetrating injuries of the chest or back. Listen for quality and symmetry of breath sounds with the stethoscope. Feel the chest wall for **crepitus**, pain, or instability. Use pulse oximetry to assess the degree of hypoxia, especially when there is no change of skin color.

Actions. If breathing is inadequate, position the child and assist ventilation. Pull the jaw into the mask. Pushing the mask onto the face to make a seal may cause cervical spine flexion. The E-C clamp technique (Figures 8-12a, 8-12b, 8-12c, and 8-12 d) will help with proper hand placement for good mask-to-face seal. Consider inserting an airway adjunct to help maintain an open airway.

Give 100% oxygen through a nonrebreathing mask or BVM. There is no nonrebreathing mask size for infants, so use a properly fitted oxygen mask on these patients. Airway management for the trauma patient is similar to airway management for the ill patient. Provide assisted ventilation with BVM, based on respiratory effort and level of neurologic disability. Use the "squeeze-release-release" timing technique to keep the right breathing rate. Allow a brief pause between each breath to minimize the chance of gastric distention. The AVPU score and pupillary reactions are the best guides for rate of ventilation in the **comatose** child, as outlined in Table 8-6.

> **! Tip**
>
> Pulmonary aspiration of gastric contents is a common and potentially serious complication of head injuries.

Case Study 2

A neighbor calls 911 about a 2-year-old boy who has fallen from an open third-story window onto a patch of grass. On scene, you find a boy who is alternating between crying and sleeping. He will not interact or fix gaze with you. He has no abnormal airway sounds, retractions, or flaring. His color is pink. Respiratory rate is 25 breaths/min, heart rate 130 beats/min. Skin is warm with capillary refill time of 2 seconds. Blood pressure cannot be obtained on one attempt. You find no other obvious injuries.

What is this child's greatest threat to life?
Is endotracheal intubation indicated on scene?

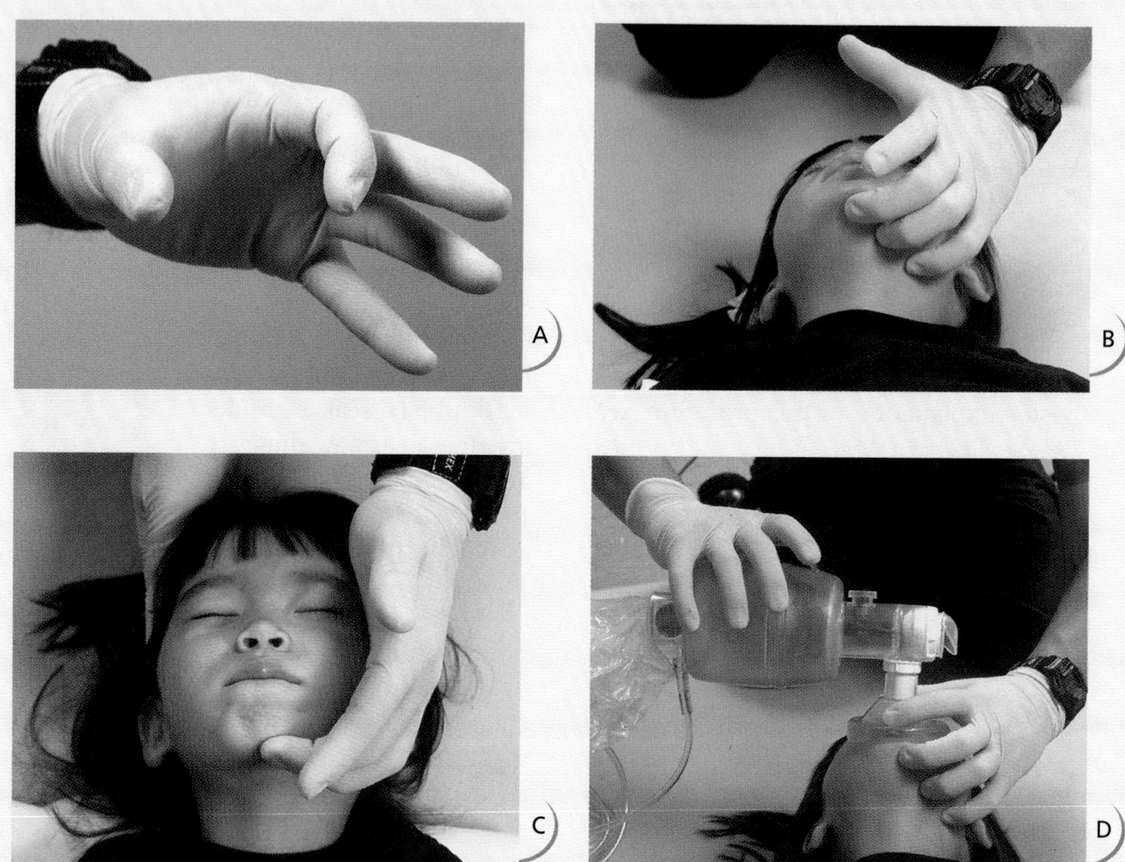

Figure 8-12 The E-C clamp technique will facilitate proper hand placement for good mask-to-face seal (A) Hand displaying E-C shape (B) Fingers resting on bony ridge of jaw (C) Fingers positioned to hold mask (D) BVM in place

Treating penetrating chest injuries, sucking chest wounds, impaled objects, and tension pneumothorax in pediatrics is the same as in adults. Cover sucking chest wounds with an **occlusive dressing**, such as a petrolatum gauze, taped on three sides (Figure 8-13). This technique will allow trapped air to escape while helping to prevent the entrance of air and development of tension pneumothorax. Do not remove impaled objects.

! Tip

If a patient with penetrating chest trauma also has respiratory distress, hypoxia, and hypoperfusion, perform needle decompression to treat possible tension pneumothorax.

ALS Advanced LIFE support

Management of tension pneumothorax

If a patient with penetrating chest trauma also has respiratory distress, hypoxia, and hypoperfusion, perform **needle decompression** to treat possible tension pneumothorax.

Needle decompression may also be necessary in the child with blunt chest injury. If the child has serious blunt chest-wall injury and respiratory distress, especially if he worsens with assisted ventilation, consider needle thoracostomy. In this situation, the child has a small pneumothorax, and positive pressure

Table 8-6 Ventilation Rates in Closed Head Injury

Patient Category		Rate of Ventilation
A	Alert	None
V	Responsive to Verbal	Normal for age,* usually none
P	Responsive to Pain	
	Pupils equal	Normal for age
	Both pupils fixed and dilated	Above normal rate,** until pupils constrict
	Pupils asymmetric	Above normal rate, until pupil constricts
U	Unresponsive	
	Pupils equal	Normal for age
	Both pupils fixed and dilated	Above normal rate, until pupils constrict
	Pupils asymmetric	Above normal rate, until pupil constricts
	Child posturing	Above normal rate, until posturing stops

* 30 breaths/min for infants; 20 breaths/min for toddlers and children
** 35 breaths/min for infants; 25 breaths/min for toddlers and children

ventilation quickly increases the air pressure in the **pleural space**. The tension on the lung and major vascular structures worsens and severely hampers ventilation and circulation.

The same deterioration after positive pressure ventilation can also occur in the child with an apparent minor wound of the chest or back. This wound may be a penetration into the pleural space with a small pneumothorax. Therefore, use positive pressure ventilation cautiously and properly and consider needle thoracostomy only when the child has respiratory distress and hypoperfusion.

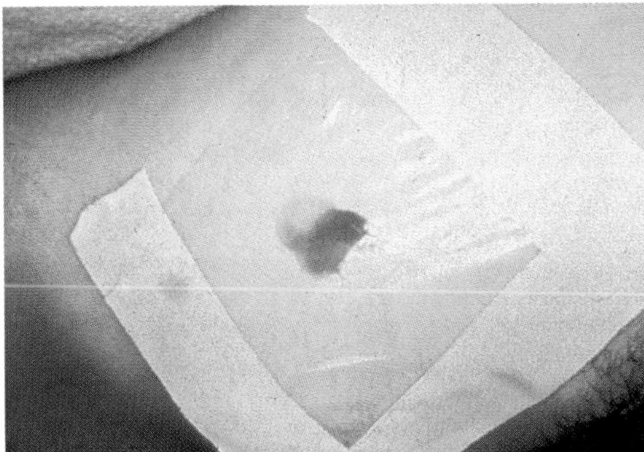

Figure 8-13 Cover sucking chest wounds with an occlusive dressing such as a petrolatum gauze taped on three sides.

Needle Thoracostomy

When the mechanism of injury, signs, and symptoms suggest tension pneumothorax in a child, create an opening between the pleural space and the atmosphere to immediately reduce elevated air pressure. This will help reexpand the lung, improve venous return, and restore cardiopulmonary function. For a step-by-step explanation of this procedure see page 298.

Management of gastric distention with nasogastric/orogastic tube

Assisted ventilation or crying often causes air swallowing and gastric distention. Nasogastric (NG) or orogastric (OG) intubation, if available, may improve assisted or unassisted ventilation by decreasing the upward pressure on the diaphragm caused by the distended stomach, and by reducing the probability of emesis. If possible, insert an

NG tube after endotracheal intubation of a comatose patient. **Contraindications** for NG intubation include midfacial trauma and suspected **basilar skull fracture** (raccoon's eyes, Battle's sign, or suspected CSF rhinorrhea or otorrhea). In these cases, perform OG intubation. Weigh the benefits of gastric decompression against the possible complications of airway compromise (which may result from vomiting and aspiration or tube misplacement into the trachea).

! Tip

Evaluate heart rate continuously. Tachycardia may be a response to pain, fear, cold, or anxiety, but a trend of rising heart rate suggests ongoing blood loss.

Continuous blood pressure measurements are rarely useful and waste time that could be better spent on assessment and treatment.

? Controversy

Volume resuscitation in pediatric trauma is controversial. Recent studies suggest that rapid administration of crystalloid fluids to adult patients with internal bleeding may worsen outcome, after penetrating injury.

Circulation

Multisystem pediatric trauma more often involves abnormalities of the airway and breathing than the circulation. However, circulation may be impaired in the trauma patient because of external or internal bleeding, compression of vessels, pneumothorax, spinal injury, or pump failure due to cardiac injury or **tamponade**. When assessing perfusion, make sure the child is warm, or skin signs may be inaccurate. Evaluate heart rate continuously. Tachycardia may be due to pain, fear, cold, or anxiety, but a trend of rising heart rate suggests ongoing blood loss. Blood pressure is *not* a good indicator of hypovolemia and hypoperfusion. *Consider attempting to take blood pressure once in children less than 3 years of age or omit this step altogether in this young age group if time is crucial.* Make sure the blood pressure cuff size is correct.

Controversies in volume resuscitation of the pediatric trauma patient

The indications, technique, and rate of **volume resuscitation** for blood flow support of the pediatric trauma patient are controversial. Recent studies suggest that rapid use of crystalloid fluids may worsen outcome in adult patients with internal bleeding from penetrating injury. In this circumstance, volume resuscitation may increase perfusion, which in turn increases the rate of bleeding. Dislodgment of a clot may also be a factor. In addition, there is concern that progressive **hemodilution** of red cells remaining in the circulation may further decrease oxygen carrying capacity.

Do not use **military anti-shock trousers** (MAST) in children. The leg compartments may cause ischemia to the lower extremities and the abdominal compartment may limit breathing. In adults, MAST do not appear to improve outcome from multiple trauma; no controlled studies in children are available at this time. A possible indication for the MAST is hypotension with a clinically unstable pelvic fracture. In this situation, the MAST may stabilize the pelvis fracture and help limit internal bleeding.

Actions. If the child has signs of decompensated shock, stop any visible external bleeding with direct pressure on the wound. Use sterile gauze compresses, and follow universal precautions. Splint any extremities with obvious deformity. Apply oxygen and place the child in the head-down position for transport.

Begin transport when the airway is properly secured, ventilation is good, and the child is fully immobilized.

Volume resuscitation

If the child has decompensated shock or significant active blood loss, obtain vascular access and start volume resuscitation on the way to the ED. Look first for peripheral IV sites in the arms or external jugular area. Attempt to secure two lines. Rarely, IO needle insertion is indicated, but only when IV cannulation fails and the child has decompensated shock and is unconscious.

Use isotonic crystalloid (Ringer's lactate or normal saline). Administer 20 ml/kg, or

10 ml/lb. Infuse boluses using a pressurized system or the pull-push method, with an in-line, three-way stopcock and a large syringe (Figures 8-14a and 8-14b). Repeat 20 ml/kg boluses as needed to improve appearance and stabilize vital signs.

Never delay transport in an effort to establish vascular access. Only about one third of crystalloid remains in the vessels after administration, and crystalloid has no useful oxygen carrying capacity. The time it takes to give crystalloid on scene will never make up for the ongoing loss of red blood cells that occurs with untreated internal bleeding.

Disability

Disability refers to brain or spinal cord trauma. Children may have primary or secondary brain injuries, or both.

Primary brain injury includes brain hemorrhage, brain swelling, or **axonal shearing**. The common pathway from these types of brain injury is increased intracranial pressure. Untreated, the downward spiral of increased intracranial pressure leads to **brain herniation**, **brain death**, and cardiorespiratory arrest. Primary brain injury is not preventable.

Secondary brain injury results from systemic hypoxia and/or hypoperfusion, usually after injuries to the chest and abdomen. Secondary brain injury can also increase intracranial pressure enough to cause brain herniation. The combination of primary and secondary brain injury is the most devastating set of circumstances. *Secondary brain injury may be preventable with good field and hospital care.*

There is also a particularly harmful form of repetitive brain injury that may be difficult to detect during physical assessment, which results from intentional shaking of an infant. It is termed **shaken baby syndrome** (or shaken infant syndrome) and is explained in Chapter 12.

Assess the degree of neurologic disability from injury with the AVPU scale (see Table 3-8). This scale may be more accurate in children with injury rather than illness, although it has not been validated in either group of children. Disability is not the same as abnormal appearance in the PAT, but they go hand in hand. An injured child may have an abnormal appearance for

Blip

Military anti-shock trousers (MAST) may be dangerous in children. They may cause ischemia to the lower extremities or limit ventilation.

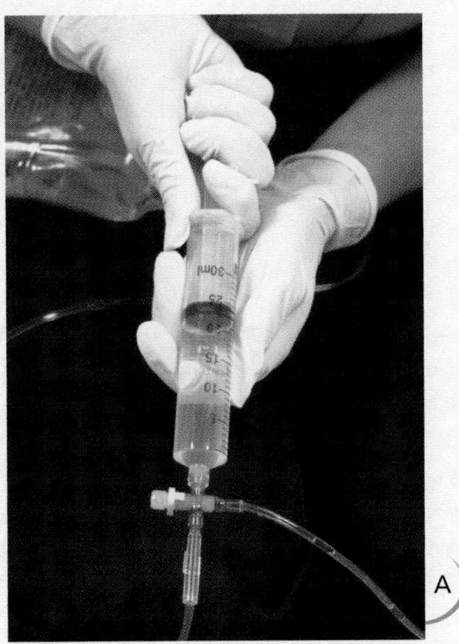

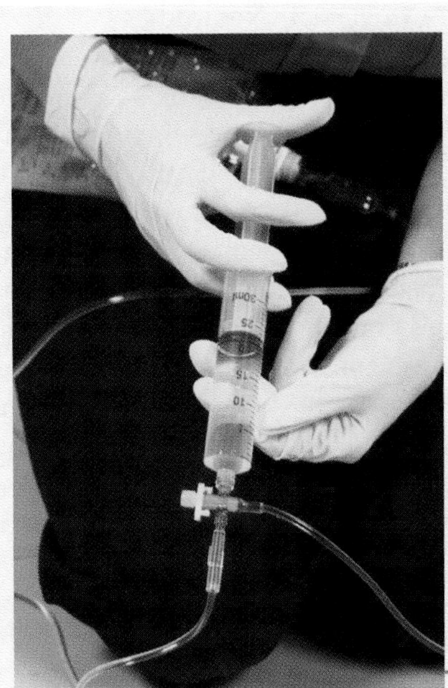

Figure 8-14 Infuse boluses using a pressurized system or the pull-push method with an in-line three-way stopcock and a large syringe. (A) Pull fluid bolus into syringe after turning stopcock off to patient; (B) Push fluid bolus into patient after turning stopcock off to IV bag.

many reasons other than brain or spinal cord injury. For example, he may have pain, hypoxia, or intoxication. Abnormal appearance can signal serious medical or traumatic disorders. The AVPU scale, in contrast, is a more useful tool to assess degree of severe brain injury. AVPU will usually be normal or "A" in mild to moderate injury. The child with an abnormal AVPU assessment often has a critical problem involving either primary or secondary brain injury, or both.

Assessing disability also includes looking for abnormal positioning and seizures, and checking for pupil size, symmetry, and **reactivity**. The pupils provide important information about the structure and function of the brain and help determine airway management in comatose patients.

! Tip

Use assisted ventilation to maintain oxygenation and to avoid carbon dioxide retention in pediatric trauma patients with AVPU scale scores of P or U.

? Controversy

The rate of ventilation in comatose patients is controversial. No one has studied enough children with serious closed head injury to know at what point the benefit of hyperventilation and reduction of cerebral blood flow to decrease intracranial pressure outweighs the associated risk of brain ischemia.

Actions. In pediatric trauma patients with AVPU scores of P or U, use assisted ventilation to keep good oxygen levels and to avoid carbon dioxide retention. The rate of ventilation in such patients is controversial. No studies are available on children suffering serious closed head injury to help decide when the benefit of hyperventilation outweighs the associated risk of brain ischemia. One approach bases the decision process on the AVPU scale, the pupil size, and responsiveness, as outlined in Table 8-6.

If the patient with closed head injury has signs of severe brain injury (P or U on the AVPU scale) or has possible brain herniation (P or U on the AVPU scale and **asymmetric** pupils or posturing), watch ventilation rate carefully. Ventilate the brain-injured child who has **dilated** or asymmetric pupils, or who is posturing at an above-normal rate. Use a rate that is 5 breaths/min *more* than the normal rate for age—35 breaths/min in an infant less than 1 year old, or 25 breaths/min in a child older than 1 year. When the pupils constrict or the posturing stops, resume the normal rate for age.

In all children, avoid unnecessary hyperventilation. Carbon dioxide levels determine brain blood flow, and overly aggressive ventilation will rapidly blow off carbon dioxide, produce dramatic reduction in perfusion, and may cause secondary brain injury.

ALS Advanced LIFE support

Management of elevated intracranial pressure

Do not give fluid to the well-perfused patient with isolated head injury. In the presence of head injury and hypovolemia, however, fluid administration is necessary for maintenance of brain perfusion. *The injured brain hates ischemia*! **Mannitol** may be useful to maintain brain perfusion in the child with asymmetric pupils or posturing, but it is available in only a few EMS systems. Only use mannitol in children with normal perfusion.

Exposure

Exposure *is* the last step in the initial assessment. Good exposure allows full assessment of the child's entire anatomy, including the extremities. Quickly examine the back during the immobilization procedure for soft-tissue or penetrating injuries. Assess circulation and neurologic function **distal** to obvious or suspected extremity injuries. Although not usually life threatening, complicated extremity injuries (such as open fractures of the humerus or femur) may cause significant physical handicaps and may contribute to death.

Actions. Keep the child warm while he is exposed, to avoid hypothermia. Consider placing a cap fashioned from bandages over the child's head to decrease heat loss (**Figure 8-15**).

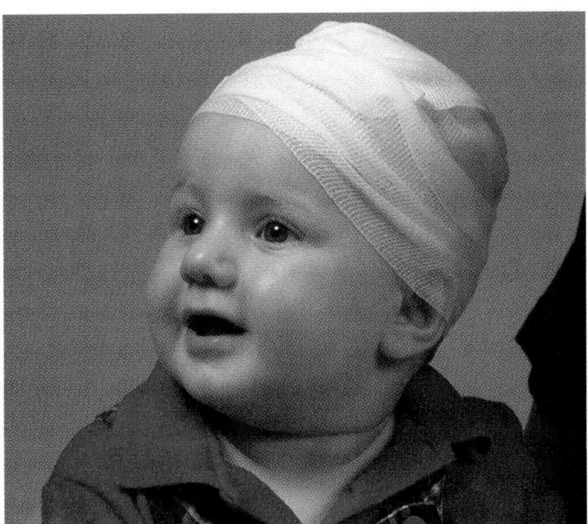

Figure 8-15 To decrease heat loss, fashion a cap from bandages to place over the head.

Summary of the Initial Trauma Assessment and Management

Children experience predictable mechanisms of injury and have vulnerable anatomic parts, such as the head and abdomen, that are most likely to be injured. These expected features of pediatric trauma allow the prehospital professional to anticipate injury patterns, especially closed head injuries and abdominal injuries. The initial trauma assessment combines the PAT and the ABCDEs in an ordered sequence to identify abnormal physiology and to intervene appropriately. Like the assessment of the ill child, the trauma assessment of a child is different from that of the adult. The child's airway is small and easily obstructed, the lungs are vulnerable to contusion, and the solid organs and long bones are more exposed to blunt injury and hemorrhage. The prehospital professional's primary role in multisystem trauma is to ensure an open airway, assist ventilation, and minimize secondary brain injury. Work to avoid hypoxia and hypotension. Short time on scene and rapid transport to the ED are overriding priorities for all children with more than simple minor injuries. Vascular access and volume resuscitation are secondary tasks that may only be considered on the way to the hospital.

Special Airway Considerations in Pediatric Trauma

Severely head-injured children with neurologic disability often require field interventions to

- protect the airway and prevent aspiration
- improve or control ventilation
- improve or control oxygenation

Endotracheal intubation has long been considered the best method for airway management in this setting. Under the constraints of the out-of-hospital environment, however, endotracheal intubation is not always the optimal management tool. Optimal airway management includes consideration of both the risks and benefits of all interventions. Choose the safest and most functional airway management technique under any given set of circumstances. For example, the optimal field airway management for a combative head injury may consist of oxygen delivery by nonrebreathing mask or BVM ventilation, neutral positioning, and constant readiness to reposition and suction in case of emesis.

Under the constraints of the out-of-hospital environment, endotracheal intubation is not always the optimal management tool.

Do not attempt blind nasotracheal intubation in children.

Prehospital factors that might change airway management decisions include the following:

- risk of increasing intracranial pressure (by increasing the child's combativeness or inducing gagging during procedures)
- ability to access the airway
- length of on-scene and transport times
- personnel availability and experience

- capability to perform rapid sequence induction (RSI) for intubation

Table 8-7 lists the factors that the prehospital professional must consider to choose the optimal airway management approach for each patient.

ALS Advanced LIFE support

Advanced airway management of the pediatric trauma patient

If a severely injured child needs endotracheal intubation, the preferred path is orotracheal, with manual neutral stabilization of the cervical spine at the same time (see Procedure 10). Although blind nasotracheal intubation causes less cervical spine motion in the adult, it is more difficult in the child because of the front location of the **larynx** and the possible complication of **adenoidal** bleeding. Do not attempt blind nasotracheal intubation in any child younger than 8 years of age.

Rapid sequence induction (RSI) for pediatric endotracheal intubation, with sedatives and paralyzing drugs, is standard practice in many EDs and is available in a limited number of EMS regions. Its effectiveness, safety, and feasibility are controversial. Further study is required to determine its indications as a widely available prehospital tool for out-of-hospital pediatric airway management.

Table 8-7 Factors Influencing Optimal Airway Management Decisions

Factors Favoring BLS (BVM)
Combativeness, strong gag reflex
Presence of trismus (spasm of jaw muscles)
Short on-scene and transport times
Factors Favoring ALS (Endotracheal Intubation)
Unresponsive child
Absent gag reflex
Inability to ventilate with BVM
Apnea, poor muscle tone, no gag
Long extrication or transport time
Limited personnel available to assist during transport
Availability of RSI procedure

RSI= rapid sequence induction for intubation.

The Transport Decision: Stay or Go?

Controversy

Rapid sequence induction for pediatric endotracheal intubation, with sedatives and paralyzing drugs, is standard practice in many EDs and is available in a limited number of EMS regions. Its effectiveness, safety, and workability are controversial.

After the initial assessment and the appropriate on-scene interventions, consider the timing for transport. Immediately transport every pediatric trauma patient who has any abnormal physiologic or anatomic findings, severe pain, or a serious mechanism of injury. Pediatric trauma patients who have no physiologic or anatomic problems, no complaints of severe pain, and no serious mechanism of injury usually do not need immediate transport. Examples of injuries in stable patients include minor extremity cuts or abrasions, small burns, and joint pain without swelling or tenderness. These children can usually undergo additional on-scene assessment using the focused history and physical exam and detailed physical exam. If the scene size-up suggests circumstances that could be dangerous to the child or prehospital professional, transport immediately. Potentially dangerous conditions that would warrant immediate transport and completion of assessment in the ambulance include nearness to fire or toxins, threatened violence, angry bystanders or caregivers, and suspected child maltreatment.

Table 8-8 SAMPLE History in Pediatric Trauma

Component	Explanation
Signs/Symptoms	Time of event Nature of symptoms or pain Age-appropriate signs of distress
Allergies	Known drug reactions or other allergies
Medications	Timing and size of last dose Timing and dose of analgesic/antipyretics
Past medical problems	Prior surgeries Immunizations
Last food or liquid	Timing of the child's last food or drink, including bottle or breast feeding
Events leading to the injury	Key events leading to the current incident Mechanism of injury Hazards at scene

Additional assessment

Perform the focused history and physical exam and the detailed physical exam in the field only if the pediatric trauma patient is physiologically normal and the conditions are safe. Otherwise, address these components of the assessment in the ambulance while on the way to the ED, if possible. The focused history and detailed physical exam are not necessary in physiologically unstable patients. For these patients, support of the airway, breathing, circulation, and disability are paramount, and the focused history and detailed physical exam may divert the prehospital professional from the primary responsibility to support vital functions.

When obtaining the focused history, use the SAMPLE template, as outlined in Chapter 3. Focus only on points likely to affect initial trauma assessment and interventions. Table 8-8 provides a SAMPLE template oriented to pediatric trauma patients.

The detailed physical examination is a head-to-toe or (in infants, toddlers, and preschool-aged children) toe-to-head, front-to-back complete physical examination of the patient. This exam uses the traditional assessment tools of observation, palpation, and auscultation as outlined in Chapter 3. The focused and detailed physical exams focus primarily on anatomic problems.

Once the child is on the way to the ED, do ongoing reassessments, especially with patients with abnormal physiology. This includes serial evaluations of the PAT, ABCDEs, pulse oximetry, vital signs, heart rate and rhythm on the cardiac monitor, anatomic problems, and response to treatment. Be sure to monitor and treat pain, if possible.

Summary of the Transport Decision

After the initial assessment, make the decision about transport. The children that are appropriate for on-scene additional assessment—with the focused history and physical exam and detailed exam—are stable patients in safe scene circumstances. Most injured children are stable. All other patients deserve immediate ED transport with continuation of assessment on the way to the ED. The SAMPLE mnemonic will help in getting the focused history from the child or caregiver or both. Do ongoing assessment of all injured patients.

Immobilization and Splinting

Indications for spinal immobilization of children are the same as for adults. Almost all moderate-to-severe pediatric trauma involves the head, so most injured children with more than minor injuries are likely to need spinal immobilization. Immobilize the neck using a properly sized pediatric extrication collar and a head immobilizer, when available. Otherwise, use properly secured towel rolls and tape (see Procedure 19).

Preschool-aged children may not be able to locate or inform the prehospital professional of the presence of neck or back pain. Fear and other painful injuries may hide the pain. The small child's large head may require modification of immobilization procedures. For example, placing a thin (1-inch) layer of padding beneath a child's body from shoulders to hips before securing the child to the spine board (Figure 8-16) will help to properly align the airway and the spinal column.

! Tip

Almost all moderate to severe pediatric trauma involves the head, so most injured children with more than minor injuries are likely to need spinal immobilization.

The spine doesn't stop at C-7, and spinal immobilization is not complete unless the entire body is secured. Secure the patient against all axes of motion on the spine board. Near-vertical positioning may be necessary during extrication. Secure the patient against **lateral** movement by padding along the sides of the body to eliminate all space between the patient and the straps.

Avoid chin straps and other immobilization aides that might impair ventilation. Leave room for chest expansion during breathing when tightening chest straps or flaps. Make sure cervical collars do not change or have the potential to change neutral position or to compress the airway. Ensure that immobilization equipment does not interfere with assessment and access to the patient. Well-immobilized children sometimes fight less than those who are poorly immobilized. This may be because of a "swaddling" effect, or a feeling of security, or it may simply take too much energy to fight secure restraints. Also, reassure the immobilized child and offer relaxation or distraction techniques to minimize discomfort.

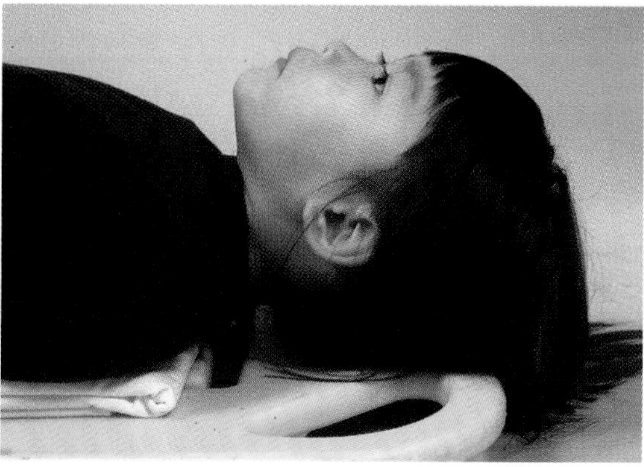

Figure 8-16 Keep the airway and spine in a neutral position by placing a layer of padding beneath the child's body from shoulders to hips before securing the child to the spine board.

Splinting deformed or painful extremities is also an important prehospital intervention. Splinting has many important functions: pain control, hemorrhage reduction, and preservation of neurovascular function. For example, by placing the bone in an anatomic position, the **femur** splint will help minimize severe blood loss from femur fractures. Unless the extremity shows neurovascular compromise or unless there is severe pain, splint bones that may be fractured or dislocated in an "as is" position. Leave exposed bone out, in order to avoid introducing further contamination by forcing fractured bone fragments back under the broken skin (Figure 8-17).

Restraint of Children During Transport

Make sure all persons riding in an ambulance are appropriately restrained. Secure injured children with possible spinal injury in a supine posi-

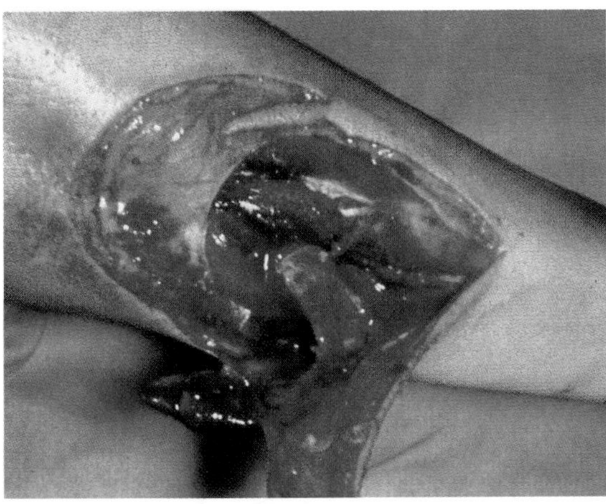

Figure 8-17 Leave exposed bone out. Do not attempt to reduce open fractures, unless circulation is absent.

tion on a spine board, and secure the board to the gurney. If the child has mild to moderate trauma without possible spinal injury, use EMS system guidelines for age-appropriate restraint. An older child can be restrained in a captain's chair. Allow a family member to remain within view or speaking distance of the child, but never compromise the child's treatment or the safety of anyone in the vehicle.

A controversial issue for pediatric transport is the appropriate use of a child restraint seat in the ambulance. Child restraint seats that have been in a car crash may be damaged and unsafe. However, standard child restraint seats that have not been subject to any potentially damaging forces may have a role in transport of children with minor injuries. The most effective, safe, and feasible techniques for securing the seat to the ambulance and the child to the seat are not known.

Pediatric Burn Patients

The assessment and management priorities for the burn patient are the same as for any other trauma patient. Make sure the scene is safe before approaching the child. Always consider the possibility of exposure to hazardous materials and carbon monoxide gas, and use protective measures. Get technical help, if available, from authorities on hazardous materials.

Assess the scene for risk factors for airway and breathing. Important considerations in fire and smoke exposures include the following:

- enclosed space
- heavy smoke
- fumes
- steam
- hot vapors
- chemical hazards
- explosions with blunt or penetrating injury

Assess the patient for signs of smoke or particle inhalation and thermal burns of the airway. Give 100% oxygen for suspected carbon monoxide poisoning in children with abnormal appearance or altered level of consciousness, or in any children exposed to fire or smoke in an enclosed space. Anticipate hidden injuries (especially abdominal) from a fall or a blast injury.

Transportation of injured infants in child restraint seats is controversial. Uninjured children or children with minor injuries may safely be transported in undamaged child restraint seats.

Make a quick estimation of burned body surface area. A modified anatomic map of children of different ages gives an approximation of burned body surface area, as shown in Figures 8-18a, 8-18b, and 8-18c. If such a map is not available, use the "rule of palms," which states that the patient's palm = 1% of body surface area (Figure 8-19). The percent of burned body surface area is therefore roughly equal to the number of patient palm-sized areas burned.

Although most burns are unintentional, assess all burn patients not only for the extent of their burns but also for risk factors for intentional injury. **Scald** and **contact burns** are common in children and are frequent findings in child maltreatment victims, as explained in Chapter 12. A suspicious pattern of burn, especially a "glove" or "stocking" distribution (Figure 8-20), a scald burn (Figure 8-21), or an unbelievable story are possible signs of intentional injury.

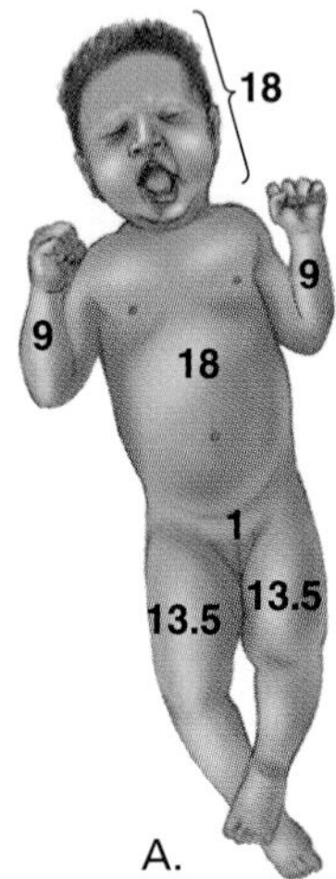

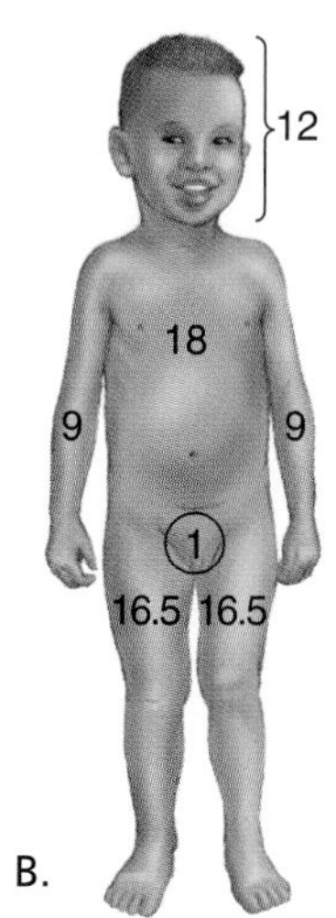

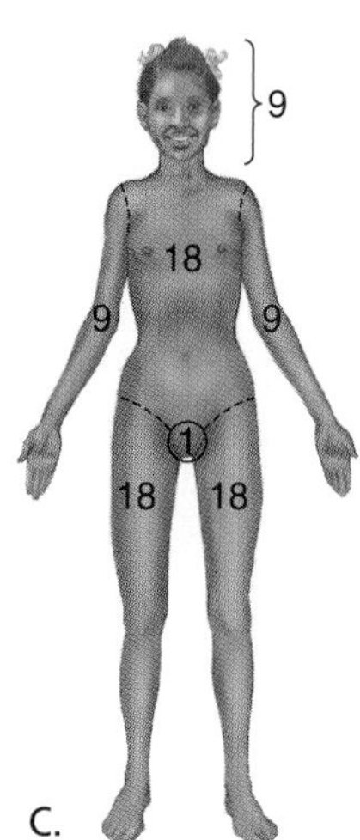

Figure 8-18 A modified anatomic map of children of different ages gives an approximation of involved body surface area for calculation of extent of burn. (A) Infant (B) Child (C) Adolescent

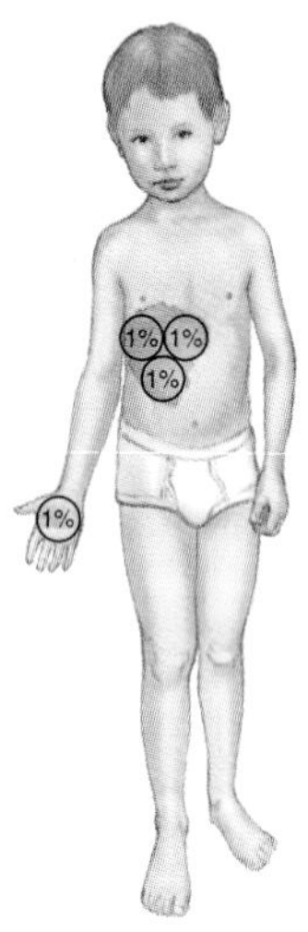

Figure 8-19 The palm is approximately 1% of the body surface area.

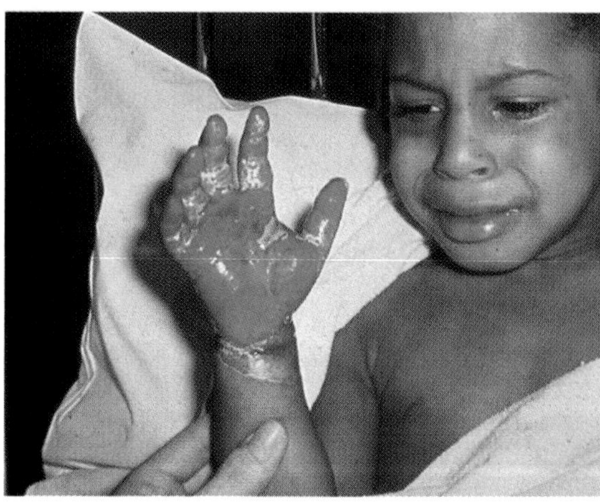

Figure 8-20 Consider intentional injury with a suspicious pattern of the burn, especially a "stocking" or "glove" distribution.

Management of burns

Remove any burning clothes. Give 100% oxygen to all patients with more than small, localized scalds or contact burns. High-flow oxygen therapy is the only field treatment for suspected carbon monoxide poisoning. Because of the risk of hypothermia, do not flush or wet burned areas unless necessary to decontaminate or stop the burning process. Cover burned areas with clean dry sheets or nonstick **dressings**. Covering helps to reduce pain by minimizing exposure

Do not apply ointments or creams to burn areas.

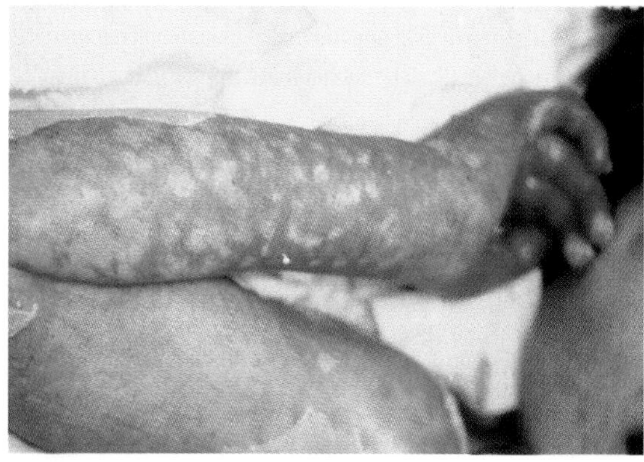

Figure 8-21 Scald burns are extremely painful and require analgesia in the field.

to air currents. Do not apply ointments or creams to burn areas.

ALS Advanced LIFE support

Advanced airway management of the pediatric burn patient

Consider early endotracheal intubation in any patient exposed to a fire in an enclosed space with a suspected inhalation injury to the airway. Such patients may have abnormal airway sounds, abnormal positioning, and respiratory distress or failure. Singed or burned nasal hairs and carbonaceous, coughed-up mucus may also mean there is airway injury and signal an unstable airway. Also, airway injury or aspiration of particulate matter during smoke inhalation may cause bronchospasm. If wheezing is present, give a bronchodilator, either SQ epinephrine or inhaled albuterol.

Pharmacologic management of the pediatric burn patient

Try to establish at least one IV line in patients with moderate to severe burns greater than 5% body surface area. Insert IV and IO catheters through a burn site if no other site exists, for fluid resuscitation. Give 20 ml/kg rapid boluses for signs of hypovolemia. Provide analgesia and sedation early and titrate to effect.

Pain management and sedation

Fear and pain in children are frequently ignored or misinterpreted. Pain management is an important out-of-hospital priority, especially in long transport circumstances. Infants and young children experience the same degree of pain as older children and adults; they just can't express it in words.

Pain and anxiety are different things and require different treatments. Treat pain with an analgesic drug, such as a narcotic like morphine or fentanyl. Treat anxiety with a sedative drug, such as a benzodiazepine like diazepam or midazolam. For example, a child with continued pain after immobilization of an isolated extremity fracture (Figure 8-22) needs morphine to control the principal problem, which is pain. Narcotics such as morphine are pain killers, but also provide some sedation. On the other hand, a child who is anxious and has extreme psychomotor agitation, such as a child bucking an endotracheal tube, needs a sedative such as diazepam because anxiety is the problem, not pain.

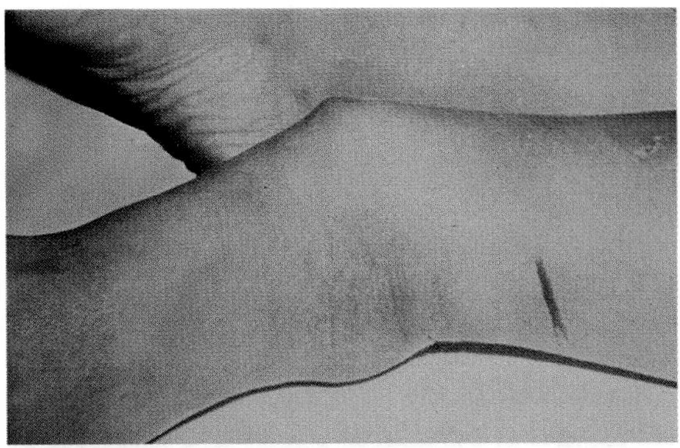

Figure 8-22 Isolated extremity fractures require anagelsia in the field unless there is severe blood loss or possible abdominal injury.

Pain and anxiety are different things and require different treatments.

IV analgesics such as morphine are most appropriate in hemodynamically stable trauma patients with burns or with isolated long-bone fractures or dislocations. If serious blood loss or bleeding is suspected, or if assessment suggests hypoperfusion, avoid narcotics because they may contribute to hypotension. This is a big concern in a child with possible abdominal injury. Consider sedative drugs when transporting an awake, intubated child or a child who has received neuromuscular blocking agents (paralytics) during RSI to help with endotracheal intubation. Benzodiazepine drugs can also

Avoid narcotics in the multiple trauma patient because they may contribute to hypotension.

Analgesia and sedation in out-of-hospital pediatrics has not been evaluated for effectiveness and safety. Pain relief is desirable, but not if it causes hypoperfusion.

Table 8-9 ALS: Pharmacologic Management of Pain and Anxiety

Pain	
Morphine sulfate	Dose: 0.05–0.10 mg/kg IV (max 2.0 mg/dose). Use 0.05 mg/kg dose in infant younger than 6 mos May repeat every 5–10 min at half the initial dose as needed
Fentanyl	Dose: 1.0 µg/kg May repeat every 5 min at half the initial dose to a maximum of 3.0 µg/kg
Anxiety	
Diazepam	Dose: 0.1 IV (max 2.0 mg/dose) or 0.5 mg/kg PR (max 10.0 mg/dose) May repeat every 15 min at half the initial dose as needed
Midazolam	Dose: 0.05 mg/kg May repeat every 5 min at half the initial dose as needed

contribute to hypotension, so give them only to patients who are hemodynamically stable.

Table 8-9 lists common medications to treat pain or anxiety in a hemodynamically stable child after consultation with medical oversight as per local EMS protocol.

All IV sedatives and narcotics will cause respiratory depression. Give by slow IV push over 3 to 5 minutes. Give supplemental oxygen to all children receiving these medications. Place the child on a cardiac monitor and use pulse oximetry when available. Be ready to begin positive pressure ventilation with bag-valve-mask if the child develops respiratory depression. Naloxone (0.1 mg/kg/dose to a maximum single dose 2.0 mg IV/IO/SQ/ET) may temporarily reverse respiratory depression due to narcotic administration. Treat circulatory compromise with IV fluid boluses.

! Tip

If multiple victims from one family are being taken to different facilities, try to give information on the locations of all family members to each receiving hospital.

Multicasualty Incidents Involving Children

Multicasualty events include more than one victim. Witnessing a serious injury or death of a family member is a psychologically devastating event. If multiple victims from one family are being taken to different facilities, try to give information on the location of all family members to each receiving hospital.

Provide uninjured children with a safe place to stay. If the caregiver cannot identify a relative or family friend, transfer the care of uninjured children to a community service agency or law enforcement officer. When possible, keep brothers and sisters and friends together. Tell the children if their parents have been injured, but reassure them that their parents are being cared for. Don't lie or mislead them, but try not to communicate a bad prognosis or death of a parent at the scene, where proper support personnel are not available.

If a child is to be transported without a caregiver, give the caregivers the child's destination in writing and notify accompanying law enforcement or public service personnel. Ensure that all family members know the destination of each family member.

In natural disasters such as floods, hurricanes, fires, or earthquakes, there may be many immediate blunt or minor injuries to children. Injuries are also common in the immediate postdisaster period when the community is in an upheaval. The most common early injuries include lacerations and contusions. Burns and chemical exposures may increase with the use of kerosene lamps and stoves, generators, and open-flame sources.

Critical incident stress debriefing for all personnel may be important following a multicasualty incident or disaster involving children.

In multicasualty incidents, attempt to keep siblings and friends together.

CASE STUDY 3

You respond to the scene of a house fire just as firefighters bring out a 7-year-old boy on a stretcher. You learn that the fire followed an explosion in the garage. The child was found in the hallway leading to the garage, which is now in smoke and flames.

The boy is crying. He is dazed and disoriented but tells you he is in a lot of pain. He has intercostal retractions but no audible abnormal airway sounds or flaring. You cannot determine his skin color because of soot-burned clothes and charred skin. Respiratory rate is 50 breaths/min, heart rate 136 beats/min, and blood pressure is 95/60 mm Hg. Bilateral wheezes are present on auscultation. The brachial pulse is strong and capillary refill time is 2 seconds. He has approximately 8% body surface area second- and third-degree burns over his face, anterior trunk, and abdomen. Pulse oximetry is 92% on room air.

What are the likely causes of this child's physiologic abnormalities?
What are your treatment and transport priorities?

CHAPTER RESOURCES

Case Study Answers

See page 129

Based on the PAT and initial assessment, the child has respiratory failure and shock and has a critical closed head injury. He is multiply traumatized and immediate resuscitation is necessary to save his life and salvage his brain. Respiratory failure may be caused by a pulmonary contusion. Shock in this patient is most likely due to abdominal bleeding. The femur fracture and scalp laceration may cause further blood loss. The asymmetric pupils and AVPU score of U suggest rapidly increasing intracranial pressure from primary brain injury due to brain hemorrhage or edema, with possible impending brain herniation. In addition, the hypotension and ischemia may be causing secondary brain injury.

Assess the airway and immobilize the entire body. Be prepared to suction and position the body to protect the airway if vomiting occurs. Insert an airway adjunct with the head held in a neutral position with the spine. Administer high-flow oxygen with a face mask and do BVM positive pressure ventilation at a rate that constricts the right pupil to the size of the left pupil. Then maintain ventilation at that rate. Control scalp bleeding with direct pressure.

Quick transport is crucial. Do not prolong time on scene. Focused history and exam and detailed physical exam will not be possible because of the critical nature of the patient and overwhelming need for airway, breathing, and circulation support. Apply a traction splint if possible on the way to the hospital.

ALS Advanced LIFE support Consider endotracheal intubation. Attempt at least one IV during transport and give 20 ml/kg of **isotonic** fluid rapidly. Reassess and repeat boluses at 20 ml/kg up to 60 ml/kg as needed to improve blood pressure and decrease heart rate. If an IV cannot be started, attempt IO needle insertion. Check neurovascular status distal to the possible fracture site before and after immobilization.

Notify the hospital early during transport and provide status updates as needed to assist the ED in preparation for the patient.

See page 139

Because of the mechanism of injury and obvious neurologic disability, you expect that this child has a critical closed head injury that will likely be the most important threat. You must also assume this child has a spinal injury due to the height of the fall. The initial assessment does not suggest airway injury, respiratory distress or failure, or shock. However, the mechanism is significant, so anticipate abdominal injuries.

Immobilize the child. Watch for vomiting. Do not delay transport to get a definitive airway by endotracheal intubation. The optimal airway management in this patient involves only BLS interventions. Give high-flow oxygen through a face mask. Be prepared to assist ventilation with BVM as needed.

Consider endotracheal intubation during transport if the child's worsens and does not respond to BVM.

Consider the possibility that the child's injuries represent maltreatment. Survey the scene for any unusual reactions or circumstances if this does not delay or interfere with patient treatment and rapid transport. Remember that confrontation and accusation delay care and transport of the child.

CHAPTER RESOURCES

See page 153

This child has abnormal appearance and altered level of consciousness, possibly from hypoxia, carbon monoxide poisoning, or closed head injury. The assessment also shows increased work of breathing and airway injury. This is probably due to smoke irritation or thermal and chemical injuries to the airway and lungs. Blunt chest injury from the blast may also have caused pulmonary contusion. While he does not have clinical signs of shock, anticipate possible chest and abdominal injuries.

Give 100% oxygen by non-rebreathing mask, immobilize the entire spine, and ensure an adequate airway with suction. Pulse oximetry shows oxygen saturation, but it will not help assess carbon monoxide poisoning. Extinguish active burn sites and cover the boy with a clean sheet.

Do not delay transport. Ventilate by BVM with humidified warmed oxygen if respiratory distress worsens. Avoid hypothermia.

ALS Advanced LIFE support Endotracheal intubation is not indicated here unless stridor or respiratory failure develops and transport time is long. Administer inhaled beta agonist or SQ epinephrine for bronchospasm, using a 1:1000 formulation and a dose taken from the length-based resuscitation tape. Attempt IV access during transport. IO access is an option if peripheral venous access is unsuccessful and the child develops decompensated shock. Give 20 ml/kg of crystalloid by rapid boluses. Consider analgesia with IV morphine for pain, per local EMS protocol or medical oversight if ongoing assessment does not indicate hypoperfusion.

Determine destination and transport as quickly as possible to an appropriate ED for care of pediatric burns and multiple system trauma.

Suggested Educational Resources

1. Foltin G, Tunik M, Cooper A, eds. *Teaching Resource for Instructors of Prehospital Pediatrics*. New York: Center for Pediatric Emergency Medicine; 1998.

2. Lockert-Jackson and Associates. *Pediatric Trauma: Emergency Medical Update* [videotape]. Winslow, WA: Lockert-Jackson and Associates; 1992. (36 minutes).

3. Luten, RC. *Pediatric Advanced Life Support: PALS Plus* [videotape]. St. Louis, MO: American Safety Video Publishers, a division of Mosby; 1992. (35 minutes).

4. McSwain N, ed. Initial care and resuscitation of the injured child. In: *PHTLS, Basic and Advanced Pre-Hospital Trauma Life Support*. 3rd ed. St. Louis: Mosby Lifeline; 1994: 310–331.

5. Romig L. Assessment of the traumatized child. *Emergency* Sept. 1993:35–38.

6. Simon J, Goldberg A. Pediatric trauma. In: *Prehospital Pediatric Life Support*. St. Louis: C.V. Mosby; 1989: 70–81.

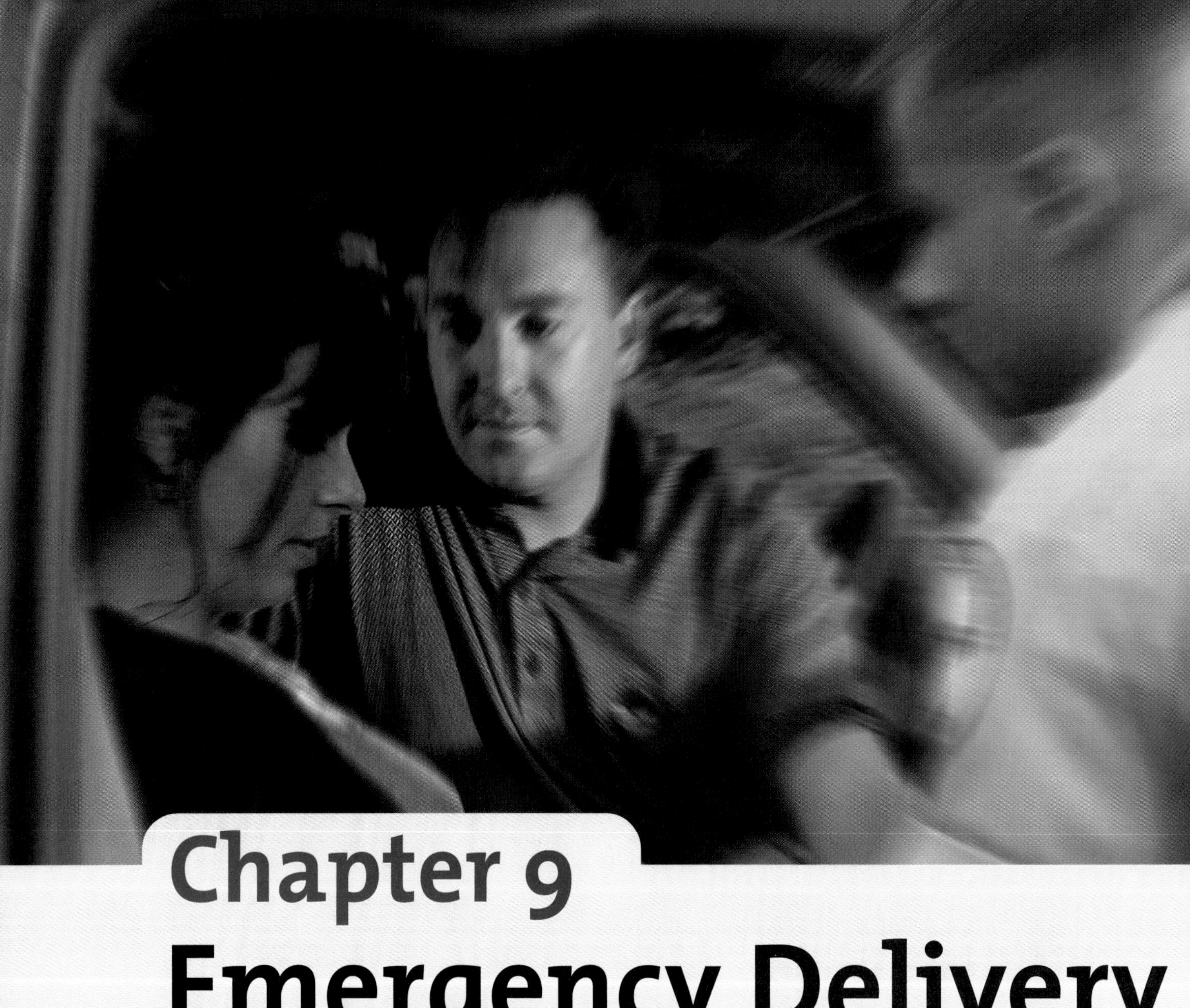

Chapter 9
Emergency Delivery Stabilization

Learning Objectives

1. Differentiate when to transport a laboring woman and when to prepare for delivery in the field.
2. Describe how to prepare for a delivery, perform a delivery, and do postdelivery care.
3. Discuss treatment for presence of meconium.
4. Explain the indications and technique for ventilatory assistance in a newborn.
5. Distinguish which newborns require vascular access for drug and fluid administration.
6. Apply appropriate assessment techniques and treatment plans to case studies presenting a woman in labor.
7. Apply appropriate assessment techniques and treatment plans to case studies presenting a newborn in distress.

You are called to a bowling alley where a 23-year-old woman is in labor. Her husband tells you that her water broke about 1 hour ago, their car broke down, and they have been unable to find transportation to the hospital.

What questions and physical findings will help you decide whether to transport or perform the delivery on scene?

If you decide to deliver on scene, what preparation is necessary?

and Newborn

Introduction

Although most deliveries occur without complications, there are many risks in the out-of-hospital setting. The probability of death or lifelong brain injury is much higher when the child is born after a spontaneous, out-of-hospital delivery compared to a controlled, in-hospital delivery. The treatment during an infant's first few minutes after birth may make a great difference in the quality of her life. The child born in an emergency is more likely to be preterm, which increases the risk of complications. Problems in management or technical factors in the delivery and immediate newborn care that are controllable through better education and skills development also play a role. Emergency delivery can be challenging to the prehospital professional. The presence of two patients—the mother and the newborn infant—adds another dimension to this challenge.

www.PEPPsite.com

Triage of the Patient in Labor

The safest place for the laboring mother and the baby is in a delivery room of a hospital or treatment center. Sometimes, however, this is not possible, and labor is fully in progress when 911 is activated. Emergency delivery in a moving vehicle is dangerous. When treating a woman in labor, the prehospital professional must first decide through appropriate triage whether to transport the mother to an ED or to prepare for an out-of-hospital delivery.

A special problem is an emergency delivery with multiple births—twins, triplets, or births with even more than three babies. Multiple births are more likely to involve preterm infants, who may require more resuscitation or care after delivery. Sometimes the mother does not know that there is more than one baby. In these situations, use the rules for triage of mothers with single births and consider calling for a second ambulance.

In order to properly triage the laboring patient, ask two simple questions and then perform a brief physical assessment of the mother's **perineum**. This information will tell whether delivery is imminent (Table 9-1).

Two questions

First, get a good history from the woman and/or partner about the number and type of prior deliveries. Typically, after active labor begins, it takes longer for first-time mothers to become fully **dilated** and longer to deliver once they

Table 9-1 Determining If Delivery Is Imminent

Questions
Is this your first delivery? If you have delivered before, how long was the labor?
Do you feel the "urge to push"?
Physical findings
Is the child's head crowning?
Is the head or scalp visible at the perineum during contractions?

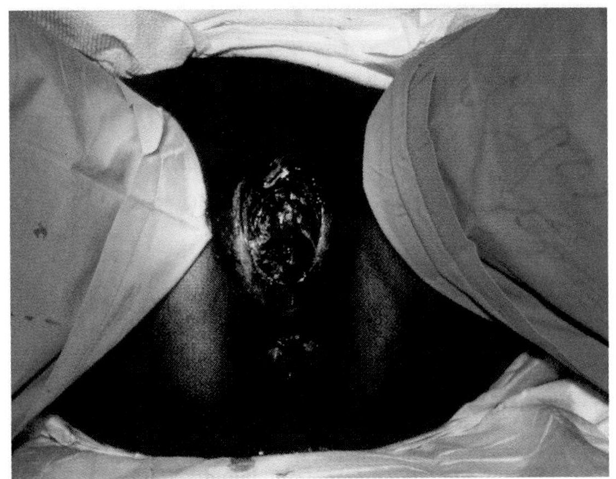

Figure 9-1 Use the presence or absence of crowning to help decide whether to transport or prepare for delivery.

are fully dilated. Therefore *establish if this is her first delivery.* For women who have delivered previously, ask how long their previous labor was. A history of short labor with prior pregnancies may repeat itself.

Second, ask the mother if she has an "urge to push." Most women experience this feeling at the end of labor. It is a sign that delivery is near, usually within 30 to 60 minutes. This is not always the case, though. Sometimes the laboring woman feels this urge before she is fully dilated. *In general, if the mother has the urge to push, the delivery will take place within an hour in first pregnancies, but within 30 minutes in second, third, or later pregnancies.*

Assessment of the perineum

Next, perform a brief physical assessment of the perineum to get the rest of the important information for triage. Look for **crowning**—the visible appearance of the fetal head at the **vaginal introitus** (Figure 9-1). Crowning is a sign that delivery is near.

If the child's head is not immediately visible, look at the mother's perineum during a contraction and note if the head becomes visible. *If the infant is crowning or if the baby's head is visible at the perineum with contractions, prepare for delivery unless the transport time is extremely brief (less than 5 minutes).*

Breech deliveries

Four percent of term deliveries are **breech** deliveries, where the first part to come out of the mother is not the head. Inspection of the perineum will not show crowning, but another anatomic part such as the feet or buttocks. In this situation, transport immediately to the nearest ED. Breech deliveries are complicated, and it is better immediately to begin the trip to the ED and risk a delivery in the ambulance than to prepare to deliver the baby at the scene.

Avoid doing an emergency delivery in a moving ambulance.

The "urge to push" experienced by most women at the end of labor is a sign that delivery is near, usually within 30 to 60 minutes.

Summary of Triage of Patient in Labor

The responses to the two questions (first delivery? feeling urge to push?) and the visual assessment of the perineum will provide the important information about field triage of a laboring woman. Look for crowning and estimate time to the hospital to decide whether to transport or prepare for delivery. Breech births are especially difficult and require immediate transport. If delivery is near in multiple-birth situations, plan to deliver on scene and call for another ambulance.

Preparation for Delivery

Resuscitation-oriented history

Many factors in the mother's medical history will affect the outcome of the baby and help predict the need for newborn resuscitation. However, once the decision has been made to deliver on scene, only three questions are pertinent for the immediate safety of the baby (Table 9-2).

1. *Do you have twins or multiple* **fetuses***?*

   If twins or multiple newborns are expected, prepare for more than one delivery. This may mean finding extra equipment, preparing an additional warm environment, and planning the management of the first baby while delivering the second. This may require calling for a second ambulance.

2. *When are you due to deliver?*

   A significant number of out-of-hospital deliveries will be preterm (less than 36 weeks' **gestation**), and the earlier the expected delivery date, the greater the chances of delivering a depressed newborn. *Knowing the due date is important for preparing the right resuscitation equipment.* The most important equipment is for airway management and breathing support. Make sure there are masks sized for preterm infants less than 30 weeks' gestation. Have a size 0 **laryngoscope** blade and endotracheal tubes in sizes 2.5 and 3.0 ready as well (Figure 9-2).

3. *What color is the amniotic fluid?*

   Greenish color in the **amniotic fluid** is a sign of fetal passage of **meconium**, which is fetal stool. Meconium release by the fetus may indicate intrauterine stress, especially hypoxia. Meconium is a sign of two possible problems: a depressed newborn or airway obstruction. Thick meconium can clog the airway of the newborn. Aggressive suctioning of the baby's mouth and oropharynx before delivery of the body may prevent meconium aspiration and respiratory distress.

! Tip

Meconium might indicate two possible problems: a depressed newborn or airway obstruction.

Table 9-2 Resuscitation-Oriented History: Three Essential Questions
1. Do you have twins or multiple fetuses?
2. When are you due to deliver?
3. What color is the amniotic fluid?

Assembling equipment

If the triage decision is to deliver on scene, get the appropriate equipment ready. Table 9-3 lists the essential ambulance equipment that is best organized in a portable **obstetric** pack for vaginal delivery.

Warming the environment

Avoiding hypothermia is an important part of newborn management. Before delivery, make the room or ambulance as warm as possible. *Turn up the heat until it is uncomfortable for an adult!* Turn off the air conditioning. Air blowing across the newborn can lead to heat loss, so turn off all fans. If the setting allows, consider having a family member warm towels in the dryer in anticipation of the delivery.

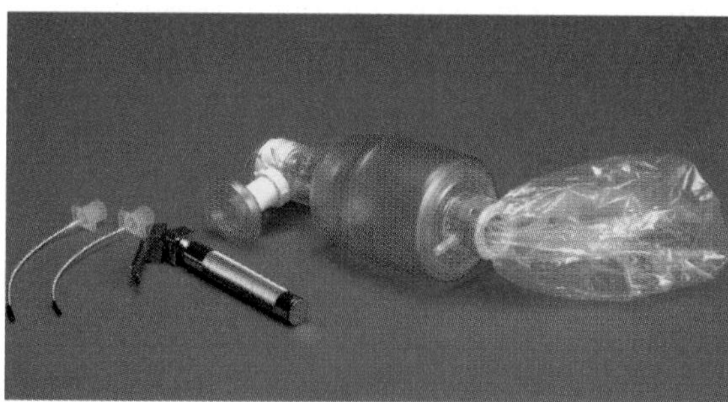

Figure 9-2 Special equipment for premature infant resuscitation: Mask, size 0 laryngoscope blade, and endotracheal tubes sizes 2.5 and 3.0.

Table 9-3 Contents of a Portable Obstetric Pack for Vaginal Delivery

Contents
1 sterile disposable scalpel or scissors
3 disposable towels
1 receiving blanket
1 sterile disposable bulb syringe
2 sterile umbilical clamps or ties
1 large plastic bag with twist tie (to store the placenta)
2 plastic lined underpads
1 disposable plastic apron, mask, and protective eyewear

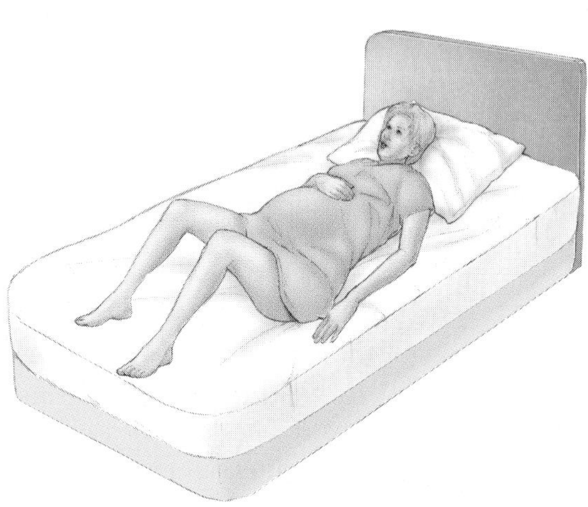

Figure 9-3 A safe position for the delivery is with the mother lying supine on one side of a bed, with the plan to allow her to deliver the baby onto the bed with minimal handling.

Positioning the mother

Although it is a medical emergency for the patient and the family, the delivery of a baby is also a personal and highly emotional event. Plan ahead how to position the mother for the delivery and tell her the plan, but *let her stay in a comfortable position and keep her covered until the time of the actual delivery*.

A safe position for the delivery is lying supine (mother on her back) on one side of a bed. Allow her to deliver the baby onto the bed with minimal handling (Figure 9-3). However, suctioning the baby's mouth and nose before delivery of the body is difficult with the mother in this position because most infants are born face down. For most deliveries, this is not a concern and suctioning the infant is possible after delivery of the body. Another technique is placing an object, such as a catalog or a stack of folded towels, under the mother's buttocks. This will raise her enough to allow oropharyngeal suctioning of the baby.

Another safe position is the **Sims position**, in which the mother lies on her side with her back toward the attendant and her knees drawn toward her chest (Figure 9-4). In this position,

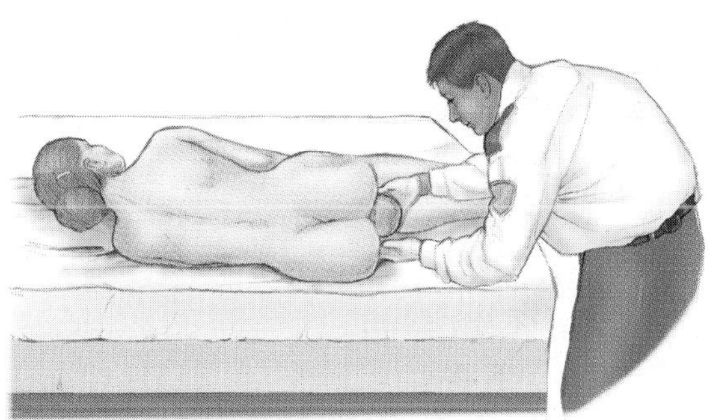

Figure 9-4 The Sims positions has the mother on her side with her back toward the attendant and her knees drawn toward her chest. This position allows for easy suctioning.

the infant's head is easy to reach for suctioning before delivery. This is a big help in deliveries complicated by meconium-stained amniotic fluid where complete suctioning of the infant's mouth and oropharynx before delivery of the body is crucial. In this position, the mother's perineum is still over the bed, so delivery onto the bed with minimal handling is still possible.

A third position to consider, in situations where oropharyngeal suctioning is necessary, is with the woman lying supine and positioned sideways on the bed, with each foot on a separate chair and her perineum at the edge of the bed (Figure 9-5). After the baby's head is delivered, this position provides enough space to suction the mouth and nose before delivering the body. The disadvantage of this position is the lack of a supportive surface under the perineum, so that the prehospital professional must actually "catch" the baby.

! Tip

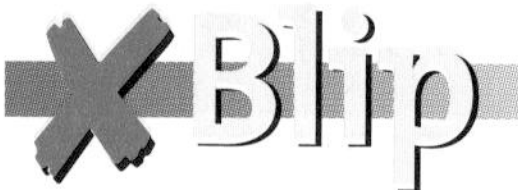

A large number of out-of-hospital deliveries will be preterm, and the need for resuscitative efforts rises with the number of days of prematurity.

Blip

Do not interfere unnecessarily with the delivery process.

Selecting a clean delivery surface

Select a surface that is as clean as possible to conduct the immediate care of the child. Make sure everyone involved in the child's care has washed her hands and has several pairs of gloves.

Vaginal Delivery

Performing the delivery

Most babies deliver themselves and need no assistance at all, especially if the laboring mother is lying supine or in a Sims position in bed. *Do not interfere unless necessary. Try to control the delivery so that nothing happens too abruptly.*

Use the following sequence for all deliveries:

1. Allow the mother to push the head out of the vaginal opening.
2. Next, with one finger, feel the infant's neck for the **umbilical cord** (Figure 9-6). If it is there, gently lift it over the baby's head. Do not pull hard on the cord because it may lead to **avulsion** of the cord with severe hemorrhage.
3. If the woman is delivering in bed, let the delivery proceed without intervention. Place

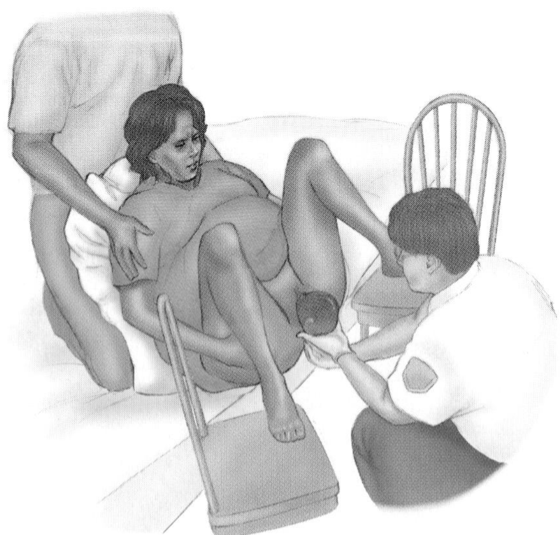

Figure 9-5 Alternate delivery position. The woman is perpendicular to the bed with each foot on a separate chair and her perineum at the end of the bed.

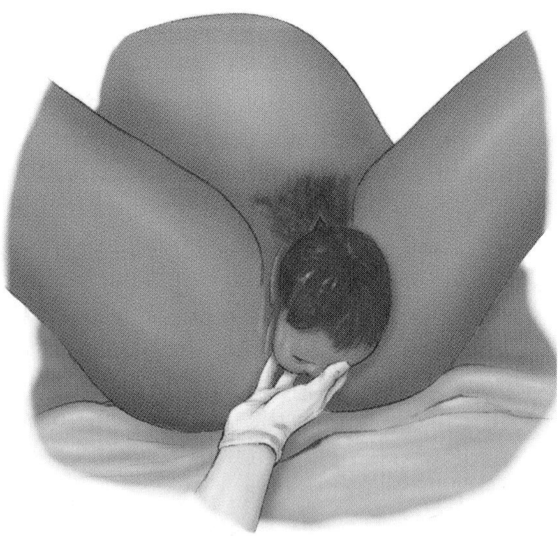

Figure 9-6 Ensure the umbilical cord is not wrapped around the baby's neck.

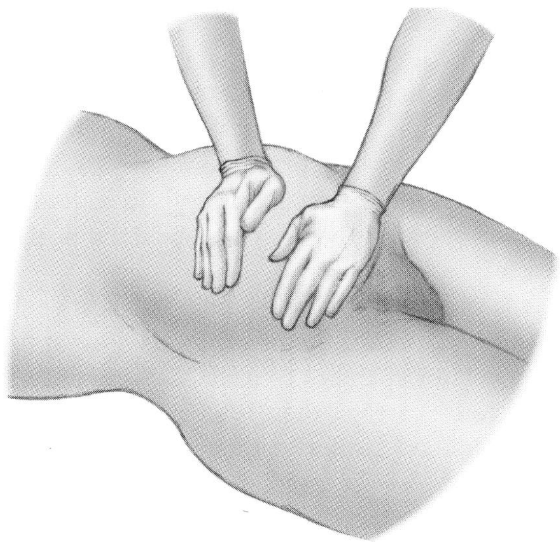

Figure 9-11 To massage the uterus, place one hand with fingers fully extended just above the mother's pubic bone and use your other hand to press down into the abdomen and gently massage the uterus until it becomes firm.

ALS Advanced LIFE support

Treatment of postpartum hemorrhage

In the mother who continues to bleed after the placenta is delivered and has dizziness, pallor, tachycardia, or low blood pressure, begin crystalloid replacement. Give 1 to 2 liters over 30 to 45 minutes during transport. A blood transfusion may be necessary in the hospital.

Summary of Vaginal Delivery

Delivery is a natural process that usually does not require active intervention. However, delivery of an infant is not a common procedure in the out-of-hospital setting, so the level of anxiety for both the laboring patient and the prehospital professional is often high. Review the steps for performing a vaginal delivery while on the way to the scene. Have the proper equipment ready, control the temperature of the environment, and position the mother to help childbirth and early newborn care. If the child has meconium-stained amniotic fluid, carefully suction the nose and mouth before delivering the shoulder. Control postpartum bleeding with uterine massage and encouragement of breast feeding.

Immediate Care of the Newborn

Although most term babies are healthy and need little treatment, follow a well-organized plan for assessment and immediate care of all babies. Table 9-4 lists the five essential steps to care for *every* newborn in every setting. *Most term newborns will not require any ALS interventions.*

Dry and warm the baby

At birth the baby is covered in amniotic fluid and can lose a lot of heat through **evaporation** unless the child is immediately dried. Heat loss drastically increases the amount of oxygen the infant needs. Thoroughly dry every infant, healthy or depressed. This will take no more than 5 to 10 seconds.

Do not use direct oral suction on a catheter or endotracheal tube to get rid of meconium. The risk of infection is too great to the operator, and there is no advantage over standard suction techniques.

Perform the initial steps of drying, suctioning, and positioning on all infants, whether active or depressed.

Table 9-4 Organized Approach to Assessment and Care of Newborns

Dry and warm the baby.
Clear the airway.
Assess breathing.
Assess heart rate.
Assess color.

Clear the airway

The newborn's head is larger than an older child's or adult's compared to its overall body size, which leads to flexion of the neck in a supine position. This may cause airway **occlusion**. Avoid this by extending the head slightly to place the airway in a neutral position. Repeat nasopharyngeal suctioning to make sure there is an open airway.

Assess breathing

Next, assess breathing. Most babies will be crying, and this is proof of breathing. Breathing effort may be slightly irregular in normal newborns. Gasping or grunting are usually signs of increased work of breathing and respiratory distress.

If the baby does not have any visible breathing, she is **apneic** and requires immediate treatment. Apnea in newborns presents in two forms: primary apnea or secondary apnea. **Primary apnea** will reverse with simple touch stimulation and suctioning. **Secondary apnea** will not reverse without assisted ventilation. If the baby is apneic or has gasping respiration after drying and suctioning, further stimulation is not likely to improve ventilation. Assume the infant has secondary apnea and begin BVM ventilation with 100% oxygen, as discussed in Depressed Newborn Resuscitation below.

! Tip

Assist ventilation in an infant with a heart rate less than 100 beats/min with BVM because the respiratory effort is not enough.

If the baby is not breathing or has gasping respiration after drying and suctioning, the infant has secondary apnea and BVM is necessary.

A special situation occurs when the prehospital professional encounters a child with respiratory depression after an abrupt delivery by a narcotic-addicted mother. Do not give naloxone to the child because the drug may cause seizures in the baby. Assist ventilation with BVM and follow the guidelines for care of a depressed newborn, as described below.

Assess heart rate

In newborns, low heart rates are usually due to hypoxia, not primary cardiac disease. The crying, active baby has an adequate heart rate. Assess heart rate carefully in a baby who is not active or who requires assisted ventilation. This means either listening to the heart with a stethoscope or palpating the base of the umbilical cord (Figure 9-12). A quick way to do this is to count the number of beats over 6 seconds and multiply this number by 10.

Treat heart rates of less than 100 beats/min with BVM, even if the breathing is normal. In most infants with bradycardia, BVM improves heart rate to greater than 100 beats/min immediately and no further treatment is necessary, as discussed in Depressed Newborn Resuscitation below.

Assess color

Assessing skin color in newborns has several unique features. **In utero**, the infant depends on placental delivery of oxygen, and, compared to adults, the fetal oxygen concentrations are very low. The fetus has several ways to live and grow in this low-oxygen environment. When the infant is born and has not begun to breathe air, she may appear cyanotic. This is normal until she begins spontaneous breathing.

If the baby has cyanosis, determine if the bluish color is central (on the trunk and face) or peripheral (limited to the hands and feet). This difference will help with decision making and therapy. If **central cyanosis** is present, admin-

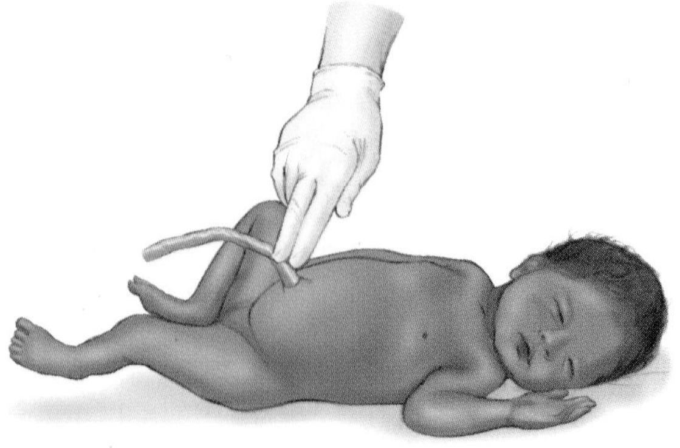

Figure 9-12 Feel for a pulse at the base of the umbilical cord.

ister oxygen because true hypoxia is present. Apply free-flow oxygen directly to the infant's face. Place the oxygen tubing into a face mask, set the flow rate at 5 liters/min, and hold the mask loosely over the baby's face.

Peripheral cyanosis, limited to the hands and feet, is also termed acrocyanosis. This is a common finding in newborns through the first 24 to 48 hours of life and requires no therapy.

Using the PAT in newborns

After performing the initial five steps for care of all newborns, use the PAT for continued evaluation of overall cardiopulmonary status. The only adjustment from the standard PAT is in the evaluation of newborn appearance. Because the newborn has not developed interactive behavior, the important components of appearance are muscle tone, spontaneous motor activity (movement), and cry. Table 9-5 compares the PAT and the adapted newborn PAT for assessment of appearance.

Apgar score

All hospitals and some EMS systems use the **Apgar score** for newborn assessment. This score measures the baby's overall cardiopulmonary and neurologic function at 1 and 5 minutes of life, then every 5 minutes thereafter in the unstable baby. *Do not use the Apgar score to guide resuscitation. It is a measure of the effectiveness of interventions.*

Depressed Newborn Resuscitation

Depressed newborn resuscitation refers to the series of interventions used to stimulate spontaneous breathing. When the baby remains depressed after drying, warming, and clearing the airway, begin resuscitation.

Use the following sequence:

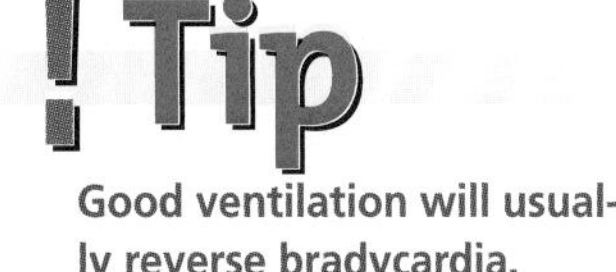

Good ventilation will usually reverse bradycardia.

1. Dry infant and place on her back in a warm environment.
2. Suction her mouth and nose.
3. Position the head slightly extended.
4. Assess breathing. If absent or irregular, do BVM ventilatation with 100% oxygen at 40 to 60 breaths per minute.
5. Assess heart rate. If less than 100 beats/min, do BVM ventilation (Figure 9-13).
6. Assess heart rate after 30 seconds of ventilation. If less than 60 beats/min, proceed with chest compressions at 120 compressions/min. Continue BVM.
7. Continue positive pressure ventilation until heart rate is above 100 beats/min and spontaneous breathing is present.

Table 9-5 PAT Adapted for Assessment of Newborn Appearance

PAT Element	Newborn PAT Element	Explanation of Newborn PAT Element
Tone	Tone	Does the baby have spontaneous movement? Is the child vigorous? Limp? Not moving?
Interactiveness	Reactivity	Does the baby respond to drying and suctioning?
Consolability	Not developed	—
Look/Gaze	Not developed	—
Speech/Cry	Cry	Is the baby's cry strong and loud? Weak? Absent?

Endotracheal intubation and epinephrine administration

Check heart rate after 30 seconds. If less than 60 beats/min, prepare for endotracheal intubation and administration of epinephrine: 0.1-0.3 ml/kg of a 1:10,000 solution (0.01 to 0.03 mg/kg), diluted with 1 to 3 ml of normal saline.

Continue chest compressions and give repeated doses of epinephrine every 3 to 5 minutes until heart rate is above 60 beats/min.

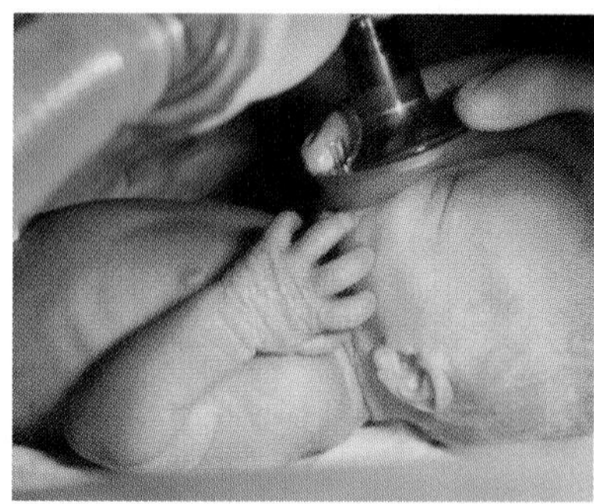

Figure 9-13 Using a bag-valve-mask on a neonate

The inverted pyramid

The inverted pyramid (Figure 9-14) shows the need for interventions in depressed newborns. Basic life support (BLS) is usually all that is required during deliveries and therefore makes up the broad top areas of the inverted pyramid. In contrast, ALS interventions such as chest compressions, intubation, and medication administration are rarely required and make up the smaller lower areas of the pyramid.

The benefit of meconium removal to prevent respiratory distress in newborns may have been overstated in earlier literature. The real need for complete removal of meconium from the airways is still not well known.

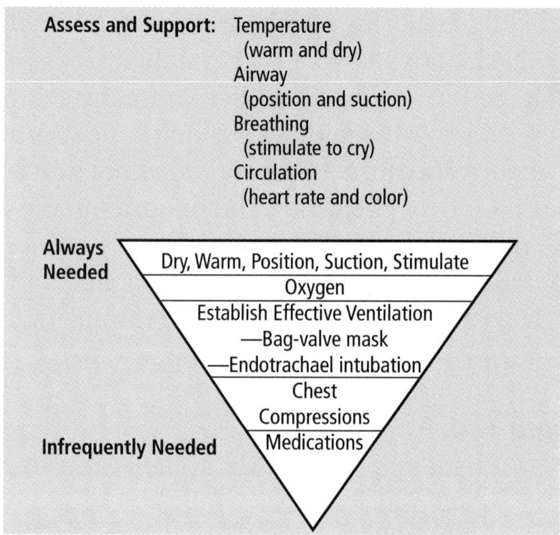

Figure 9-14 Guidelines for neonatal resuscitation as recommended by the American Heart Association

Reproduced with permission. © *Pediatric Advanced Life Support*, 1997. Copyright American Heart Association.

Meconium aspiration

A child born through thin meconium, who appears active and without respiratory distress, needs only routine oral and nasal suctioning and standard newborn care. On the other hand, a child born with meconium staining who has respiratory distress needs additional suctioning of the mouth and nose to limit aspiration of sticky meconium. Even when meconium is present, focus on oxygenation and ventilation of the baby. *In the patient with respiratory failure or apnea, remove meconium quickly, then begin providing adequate oxygenation and ventilation.*

In EMS systems where a meconium aspirator is available, this device may speed up the removal of meconium from the trachea in a neonate with respiratory distress. However, this has not been studied in the prehospital setting and its ability to improve outcomes is not known.

Shock

Shock at birth may be due to **asphyxia** and **acidosis** or, less commonly, blood loss at the time of delivery. Signs and symptoms of shock include abnormal appearance (lethargy, hypotonia), abnormal color (pallor, mottling), tachycardia, and prolonged capillary refill time. However, these are nonspecific signs and may also represent hypothermia or acidosis or both.

Treatment of shock

If the patient is in shock or cardiopulmonary arrest, consider the intraosseous route for fluid and drug delivery. Give 10 to 20 ml/kg of normal saline. (Table 9-6)

Summary of Depressed Newborn Resuscitation

The typical newborn response to hypoxia is apnea and bradycardia. Therefore, the primary treatment is to reverse hypoxia with immediate BVM ventilation. If the child does not improve, chest compressions and endotracheal intubation may be needed on the scene before transport. Shock is rare and is most commonly seen after resuscitation or following asphyxia. Hypovolemia is an uncommon cause of shock in the newborn, but the first-line treatment for shock is volume replacement. Therefore, transport immediately and attempt an IV or IO on the way to the hospital.

ALS Advanced LIFE support

Vascular access

Vascular access is not usually needed in newborns because problems are almost always respiratory, where airway and ventilation management are the primary treatments.

Get vascular access only for fluid delivery or for administration of essential medications. IV access sites include the peripheral veins in the **antecubital fossa** and the **saphenous veins** just anterior to the **medial malleolus** at the ankle. Treat a hypovolemic newborn like an acute trauma patient with life-threatening blood loss who needs blood products. *If access is needed due to bleeding, transport immediately and attempt IV or IO access on the way to the hospital.*

When there is no IV or IO access, give resuscitation medications such as epinephrine through the endotracheal tube. Do *not* give other solutions, such as sodium bicarbonate or dextrose, through the endotracheal tube because these solutions are damaging to the lungs.

Umbilical catheterization by prehospital professionals is a controversial procedure. While this route of vascular access in experienced hands is effective and quick, the prehospital professional rarely needs it and serious complications can occur. For EMS systems using umbilical venous catheterization, consider giving all medications and solutions this way. Do not place the umbilical catheter in too far, but place it to a depth where blood return is first seen. This will help keep the catheter out of the **portal venous system** and avoid complications of vasopressor drugs entering the liver. *Never delay the transport of a newborn with severe blood loss to start an umbilical line.*

Treat a hypovolemic newborn like an acute trauma patient with life-threatening blood loss.

Medications that can be given through the endotracheal route are the same in newborns as in adults: epinephrine and naloxone.

Table 9-6 Fluid Boluses in Neonatal Shock and Hypoglycemia

	Shock	Hypoglycemia	
Infant	Saline Dose	10% Dextrose Dose	Maintenance IV
Very preterm (<27 weeks)	10–20 ml	2–4 ml	4 ml/hr
Preterm (28–35 weeks)	20–40 ml	4–8 ml	8 ml/hr
Near term (>35 weeks)	30–60 ml	6–12 ml	12 ml/hr

Stabilization for Transport

The active term infant requires no intervention or electronic monitoring during transport. Restrain the mother appropriately and allow her to hold the baby during transport. Encourage her to breast feed the active infant if she so chooses. This may prevent hypoglycemia and promote maternal-infant bonding, uterine contractions, and decreased uterine bleeding. Provide a warm environment in the ambulance.

Transport of the compromised neonate

Monitoring

After resuscitation, reassess the status of the infant throughout transport. Place cardiac leads in the same position as in an adult. A heart rate between 120 and 160 beats/min is normal in a newborn. If heart rate decreases, follow the procedures for depressed newborn management.

Attach pulse oximetry monitors for oxygen saturation on a finger or toe. Saturations between 90% and 100% are normal. Although **hyperoxia** (high oxygen saturation) may occur, it is better to ensure good oxygenation during transport by giving a high concentration of oxygen than to allow hypoxia to occur because of concern about too much oxygen.

! Tip

Encourage the mother to breastfeed the active, vigorous infant.

Hypothermia

Hypothermia happens quickly in newborns. Oxygen demand triples when skin temperature drops 1 degree. Signs of hypothermia are similar to shock. Keep the baby warm during transport. Have a small knit cap available to place on the infant's head. Turn the heat on in the ambulance even at the risk of discomfort to the mother and crew. Place the baby on the mother's bare chest (skin-to-skin contact) and cover both of them to improve the infant's temperature.

ALS Advanced LIFE support

Transport of the compromised neonate: Hypoglycemia

The depressed newborn or prematurely delivered baby is at risk for hypoglycemia. Hypoglycemia is unlikely in the first 30 minutes. If transport times are longer than this, measure a bedside glucose at approximately 30 minutes after birth or immediately in any baby who has a drastic change in activity.

Following the resuscitation of an infant, expect hypoglycemia due to stress. Do not wait for hypoglycemia to present, but rather attempt an IV while transporting and begin

CASE STUDY 3

A panicky male calls 911 to report that his wife just gave birth to a child unexpectedly. You arrive at the scene where a woman has just delivered a baby in her apartment. The umbilical cord is still attached. The baby is a small male infant and appears quite premature. He is blue, limp, and lifeless, and has no respiratory effort.

Discuss the management of the child.

What is the role of vascular access?

10% dextrose in water at 4 ml/kg per hour as an infusion. Use an IO for treatment of documented hypoglycemia if an IV cannot be established, but do not start an IO for **prophylaxis** of hypoglycemia. When neither an IV nor an IO can be started during true hypoglycemia, give glucagon IM. Glucagon may not work in newborns because the baby may not have any glycogen stores to break down.

Treat the baby if the rapid glucose determination is less than 40 mg/dl. If the infant is active, in no respiratory distress, and has a **suck reflex**, allow her to breast feed or offer her 20 to 30 ml of 5% dextrose by mouth. Otherwise, establish an IV and administer 10% dextrose (1 ml of 50% dextrose in water with 4 ml normal saline), 2 to 4 ml/kg push, followed by 4 ml/kg per hour infusion, as shown in Table 9-6.

Oxygen therapy

The active, vigorous baby is most likely *not* cyanotic and will not need oxygen administration. However, the depressed infant or one that needed resuscitative efforts requires oxygen. Give oxygen by face mask at 1 to 2 liters/min if the baby is spontaneously breathing.

Do not burn the child's thin, sensitive skin with a commercial heat production device. Place a towel between the skin and the device.

CHAPTER RESOURCES

Case Study Answers

See page 157

First decide whether to transport the mother to the nearest hospital or to prepare for delivery of the newborn. Ask if this is a first pregnancy and if the mother feels the urge to push. If the mother feels the urge to push, then examine for the presence of crowning.

If you decide to deliver at the scene, obtain a resuscitation-oriented history. Are twins present? What is the due date? What color was the amniotic fluid when membranes ruptured? These questions will assist you in preparation. Prepare the obstetric delivery pack, familiarize yourself with the equipment, and make sure all necessary equipment is present. Warm the environment and get clean, dry towels to use to dry the baby. Get or make a cap to place over the child's scalp to reduce heat loss from the head. Find a clean delivery surface for the baby.

See page 164

If time allows, review the procedure for a vaginal delivery while on the way to the scene. On arrival, first plan for appropriate positioning of the mother. Place the women in supine or Sims position, because vigorous oropharyngeal suctioning prior to delivery is not usually necessary. Discuss the position with the patient ahead of time so that she understands the plan for delivery.

Clear amniotic fluid implies there is no meconium. Meconium is released by the fetus in conditions of stress. While the presence of clear fluid does not rule out the possibility of a depressed newborn, it is a reassuring sign and increases the chances of an active child that will need only the five steps of standard newborn care.

See page 170

The baby is in acute distress and needs immediate intervention. Thoroughly dry the baby, position him on his back, and suction the mouth and nose. Tie or clamp the umbilical cord at 3 inches and 4 inches from the baby and cut it. At this point, if the infant is still not breathing, do BVM ventilation with 100% oxygen at 40 to 60 breaths/min. After 30 seconds of assisted ventilation, reassess the heart rate. If the heart rate is less than 60 beats/min, begin chest compressions at 120 compressions/min.

ALS Advanced LIFE support

Endotracheal intubation and epinephrine administration

If the infant does not respond to these efforts with improvement in tone, color, and heart rate within 30 seconds, have one member of the team prepare for intubation and

continued

administration of epinephrine. To do it most effectively, cardiopulmonary resuscitation requires three individuals, one to assist ventilation, one to administer chest compressions, and one to prepare for intubation and possible administration of medications. If only two prehospital professionals are present, as is frequently the case, get help from another adult to perform chest compressions.

Vascular access

Vascular access is not usually needed for newborn resuscitation. Most depressed newborns require only simple techniques—drying, warming, and clearing the airway. Occasionally BVM assissted ventilation is indicated, and, infrequently, endotracheal intubation. The endotracheal tube is also a good way to deliver epinephrine if required.

It is rare to treat a baby who is depressed; does not respond to standard care, BVM, and endotracheal intubation; and requires vascular access for drugs or fluids. In such a case, insert an IO needle and give drugs and fluids this way. The IO technique is fast, simple, and usually effective in newborns, infants, toddlers, and young children. Umbilical vessel cannulation is not available in most EMS systems, is usually unnecessary, and may cause complications in inexperienced hands.

Umbilical vessel cannulation is commonly used as a means of drug and fluid administration during newborn resuscitation in hospitals. Because the prehospital professional has rare, if any, opportunity to perform this procedure, maintaining the skill is difficult. Therefore, the value of umbilical vessel cannulation as a field skill, over the simple IO procedure, is questionable.

Suggested Educational Resources

1. American Academy of Pediatrics and American Heart Association. *Textbook of Neonatal Resuscitation.* 3rd ed. Elk Grove Village, IL: American Academy of Pediatrics and American Heart Association; 1994.
2. American Academy of Pediatrics, American College of Obstetricians and Gynecologists. *Guidelines for Perinatal Care.* 4th ed. Elk Grove Village, IL: American Academy of Pediatrics; 1997.
3. MacDonald HM, Mulligan JC, Allen AC, Taylor PM. Neonatal asphyxia. I. Relationship of obstetric and neonatal complications to neonatal mortality in 38,405 consecutive deliveries. *J Pediatr.* 1980;96(5):898-902.
4. Kattwinkel J, Niermeyer S, et al. An advisory statement from the pediatric working group of the international liaison committee on resuscitation pediatrics. Pediatrics 1999;103:e56.

Chapter 10

Children with Care Needs

Learning Objectives

1. Discuss important modifications of field assessment techniques for children with special health care needs (CSHCN).
2. Distinguish the special transport considerations with CSHCN.
3. State the complications of tracheostomy tubes, central venous lines, gastrostomy tubes or gastric feeding tubes, and ventriculoperitoneal shunts, and outline management.
4. Apply appropriate assessment techniques and treatment plans to case studies presenting a variety of emergency situations involving CSHCN.

You are called to the scene of a 3-year-old girl with numerous underlying medical problems who has lost her gastrostomy tube.

On arrival, the father says that the child has cerebral palsy, with spasticity and a seizure disorder. The gastrostomy tube was needed because she had problems swallowing. The tube is the only way to feed her and give her medications. It fell out this morning as the father was cleaning it. The child takes carbamazepine for her seizures and received her morning dose. She usually gets her feedings at night and the father reports no trouble with the tube feedings last night.

Your assessment shows a happy child who is in a special chair and is unable to walk or talk. She has no abnormal airway sounds or increased work of breathing. Her skin is pink. Heart rate is 90 beats/min, respiratory rate is 20 breaths/min, and blood pressure is 85 mm Hg/palp. You cannot straighten her arms. There is a well-healed opening on her upper abdomen, with a small amount of yellow drainage.

How you can assess this child?
Describe treatment and transport approaches.

Special Health

Introduction

Children with special health care needs (CSHCN) are a diverse group of patients who frequently need out-of-hospital emergency assessment and treatment. This high user group includes children with ongoing physical, developmental, or learning disabilities and children with chronic medical conditions. Many CSHCN were either born prematurely or have suffered closed head injury and have chronic problems with their nervous system, lungs, brain, or kidneys. Examples of acquired conditions include cerebral palsy or posttraumatic epilepsy. Other CSHCN have congenital problems such as cyanotic heart disease or spina bifida.

Technology-assisted children (TAC) are a subgroup of CSHCN who depend on medical devices for their survival. Common devices include tracheostomy tubes, home ventilators, indwelling central venous lines, feeding tubes, pacemakers, and ventriculoperitoneal shunts.

Today CSHCN are surviving longer and often live at home. They need emergency medical care more frequently than children without special health care needs. Because of their abnormal baseline status, CSHCN pose unique problems in field assessment and treatment. Therefore, prehospital professionals must recognize common types of CSHCN, know modifications in assessment, and understand management of frequent problems.

www.PEPPsite.com

Assessment of CSHCN

Modifications

Begin evaluation of CSHCN with standard pediatric assessment techniques adjusted to the child's developmental age, rather than his chronological age. With TAC, do not become distracted by their specialized equipment. Care for the child, not the machinery. Caregivers may be extremely helpful in figuring out the baseline status of CSHCN or in operating or troubleshooting the equipment. Ask for assistance from the caregiver!

Blip

Do not become distracted by the specialized equipment used by TAC. Care for the child, not the machinery.

The assessment of CSHCN has the following important modifications:

1. Baseline status: Ask the caregivers what "normal" is for their child. They will know his baseline better than any medical record.
2. Rely on the caregivers' opinions: What do they think is wrong? In what ways is the child "not acting right"?
3. If the child is physiologically stable, take a focused history on scene. Caregivers usually know the child's medical history, health problems, medications, medical devices, and current complaints. They are also aware of what approaches work best, as well as the child's typical responses and behaviors.

4. The child may be slow to answer questions or may be unable to talk. Use a patient approach to the stable child and begin by talking directly to the child, rather than to his caregiver.
5. Communicate with the child using developmentally appropriate language, gestures, and techniques, as discussed in Chapter 2.
6. If a caregiver is not present, find out if the child has a form or card with information about his medical problem, normal vital signs, medications, and other important medical data. Figure 10-1 is an example of such a form developed by the American College of Emergency Physicians and the American Academy of Pediatrics. Several states recommend that CSHCN carry information cards, such as Wisconsin's Child Alert 10-33, New Mexico's ChUMS (Children's Updated Medical Summary), and New Hampshire's SKIPS (Special Kids Information Program).
7. Look for a Medical Alert bracelet.
8. The normal baseline vital signs for a CSHCN may be "out of the normal range" compared to a child of the same age who does not have special health care needs. Standard vital signs may have limited value in assessment of CSHCN. Pay more attention to the PAT and observations from the caregiver.
9. Do not assume that a child with a physical disability is cognitively impaired. Many children with cerebral palsy, for example, have **spasticity** but do not have cognitive abnormalities. Discreetly ask the caregiver about the child's normal level of functioning, understanding, and interactions.
10. Be polite and professional. Listen to the parents and take their concerns seriously. Families of CSHCN often have had a lot of experience with the medical system. If most of their experience has been positive, they will view the prehospital professional as an ally. However, if they have had bad experiences with the medical system, they may be suspicious or aggressive.
11. Keep in mind the amount of stress caregivers of a CSHCN may be experiencing.

Pediatric assessment triangle

The PAT is a good way to look and listen for signs that will help figure out the type of physiologic problem and the urgency for treatment of a CSHCN. However, because CSHCN often have altered baseline, there are several limitations and modifications to the PAT.

Approach the developmentally delayed child using techniques appropriate to his developmental level, not his age in years.

Appearance

Although the child's overall appearance reflects the adequacy of oxygenation, ventilation, perfusion, and CNS status, this

Emergency Information Form for Children With Special Needs

Last name:

American College of Emergency Physicians® | American Academy of Pediatrics

Date form completed By Whom	Revised	Initials
	Revised	Initials

Name:	Birth date: Nickname:
Home Address:	Home/Work Phone:
Parent/Guardian:	Emergency Contact Names & Relationship:
Signature/Consent*:	
Primary Language:	Phone Number(s):
Physicians:	
Primary care physician:	Emergency Phone:
	Fax:
Current Specialty physician: Specialty:	Emergency Phone:
	Fax:
Current Specialty physician: Specialty:	Emergency Phone:
	Fax:
Anticipated Primary ED:	Pharmacy:
Anticipated Tertiary Care Center:	

Diagnoses/Past Procedures/Physical Exam:	
1.	Baseline physical findings:
2.	
3.	Baseline vital signs:
4.	
Synopsis:	
	Baseline neurological status:

*Consent for release of this form to health care providers

Figure 10-1 ACEP/AAP CSHCN Form

is the part of the PAT that will differ the most in CSHCN. The underlying medical problem may cause an abnormal muscle tone, such as the increased tone and spasticity in a child with cerebral palsy. There may be decreased interactiveness, a common behavioral state in a child with brain damage or developmental delay. Look or gaze is helpful because most CSHCN can recognize their caregiver by looking or by voice. A CSHCN may be unable to speak, but the strength and quality of his cry may be a useful sign of health or distress. For example, a high-pitched cry in a child with a VP shunt may mean obstruction.

Asking the caregiver about the child's baseline, and about what is different, is the best way to assess the child's appearance accurately.

! Tip

Assess appearance by asking the caregiver about the child's baseline.

Do not assume that a child with a physical disability is mentally impaired. Many children with cerebral palsy, for example, have spasticity but not cognitive abnormalities.

Work of breathing

Many CSHCN are likely to have respiratory problems. Children with chronic pulmonary disease such as **bronchopulmonary dysplasia** (BPD), often have rapid respiratory rates and increased work of breathing. When such children have a fever or experience an added respiratory illness or injury such as pneumonia or chest trauma, they have less reserve. Therefore, work of breathing in these patients increases rapidly with any acute illness or injury.

Children with BPD or congenital heart disease are much more likely to develop respiratory infections, especially from respiratory syncytial virus (RSV), in the winter. They can decompensate quickly. CSHCN who have developmental delay and neurologic problems are at high risk for aspiration, pneumonia, and respiratory failure. Once again, ask the caregiver about the child's normal baseline breathing (e.g., respiratory rate, breath sounds) and what is different.

Assess abnormal breath sounds (stridor, wheezing, or grunting) from across the room. Some "abnormal" airway sounds may be normal for a CSHCN. For example, a child with a tracheostomy tube usually has noisy breathing, and an infant with BPD may have slight expiratory wheezing.

Abnormal positioning, such as tripoding and head bobbing, are important visual signs of increased work of breathing and hypoxia and usually indicate serious breathing problems. For the child who usually has mild retractions, the degree or location of retractions will provide clues to increased work of breathing. For example, the baseline retractions may be mild and only subcostal, but are now severe and also suprasternal. Nasal flaring is not usually a baseline condition because this sign suggests significant hypoxia that is rarely permitted in children at home.

Circulation to skin

The skin color may be abnormal in CSHCN, such as in infants with cyanotic congenital heart disease, chronic lung disease, cancer, or liver failure. A child with cyanotic congenital heart disease or chronic lung disease may have bluish lips and mucous membranes, nail beds, and extremities. A child with cancer may appear pale, whereas the skin of a child with liver disease may appear yellow. Ask a caregiver to describe the child's baseline color.

Adaptations in the ABCDEs

After performing the PAT, complete the initial assessment by adjusting the evaluation of the ABCDEs to the child's baseline.

Airway

Open and maintain the airway. Keeping an open airway may be more difficult with the CSHCN. The child may have poor muscle tone and head control, or copious **secretions**. Getting, and then keeping, the right head position may require several maneuvers: a shoulder roll to correctly position the head in a neutral axis with the airway, and a chin lift or jaw thrust to open the airway. Always have suction available and use it frequently.

Tracheostomy care
A child with a tracheostomy has an artificial airway that is easily blocked by secretions or by dislodgment of the device. The tracheostomy section of this chapter addresses specific management techniques in these children.

Breathing

Count the respiratory rate. Listen to the lungs for **bilateral** air movement and abnormal chest sounds. Listening may not give accurate results in the CSHCN who cannot sit still or who has noisy breathing. Also, obtain pulse oximetry and compare to baseline. Keep the child in a position of comfort. Give supplemental oxygen to any CSHCN with increased work of breathing or increased respiratory rate by blow-by, face mask, or BVM. For CSHCN, the caregiver may know the best way to give oxygen to the child. For infants or children already on home oxygen, increase the flow rate. For a patient with a tracheostomy tube, place the oxygen directly over the tube or **stoma**.

Bronchodilator administration
If a CSHCN has a history of breathing problems or uses bronchodilators at home, give a bronchodilator when wheezing is present.

Circulation

Assess heart rate, pulse quality, skin temperature, and capillary refill time. These are not usually different in CSCHN and require no modifications in interpretation. If the child's age is 3 years or less, consider obtaining a blood pressure but the value may be hard to obtain and hard to interpret in this age group. Attempt to measure blood pressure in all children over 3 years of age. Tachycardia is a common baseline finding in CSHCN, and by itself does not indicate shock. To evaluate heart rate and blood pressure, assess with the other key characteristics of circulation, as outlined in Chapter 3.

Bradycardia is not usually a normal feature of CSHCN. It is a sign of hypoxia or inadequate brain perfusion. Suspect hypoxia in a child with BPD or other chronic cardiopulmonary condition who has a HR below normal for chronologic age. Suspect increased intracranial pressure in a child with a VP shunt.

Management of shock in CSHCN is no different than for normal children. Standard management includes oxygen, positioning, and BVM support as needed.

Treatment of shock
A child in shock needs volume replacement. The CSHCN has the same fluid requirements as a normal child. If the patient is injured, transport immediately and attempt vascular access. Give 20-ml boluses of crystalloid on the way to the ED. If the child is ill, and if he has compensated shock, transport and attempt access and fluid administration on the way. If the ill child has decompensated shock, make one attempt at vascular access on scene, if possible. Because a CSHCN may be more difficult to assess accurately, and because vascular access is often troublesome, always transport a child with suspected shock as soon as possible.

! Tip

The normal baseline vitals for a CSHCN may be different or "out of the normal range" for a child of that age.

Bradycardia is not usually a normal finding in CSHCN.

Disability

The CSHCN often has an abnormal baseline neurologic status. Assess neurologic status by looking at appearance as part of the PAT, and establishing level of consciousness with the AVPU mnemonic. Compare the findings to the child's baseline. In the assessment of motor activity, assess purposeful movement, symmetrical movement of extremities, seizures, posturing, or flaccidity. Treat altered level of consciousness,

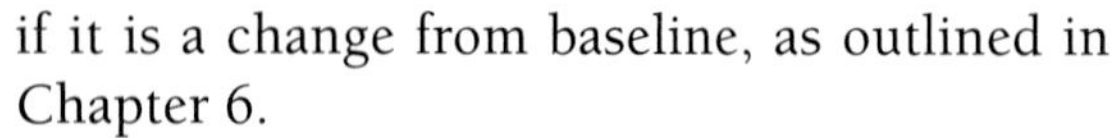

if it is a change from baseline, as outlined in Chapter 6.

Exposure

Be sure to inspect the child's entire body, but respect his modesty. Do not allow the child to become cold. Many CSHCN have minimal body fat and can become hypothermic quickly.

Summary of Assessment of CSHCN

Listen carefully to the caregiver when assessing CSHCN. Ask about the child's baseline status: What is "normal" for this child? Such children may present a confusing picture, with unexpected behaviors, communication difficulties, extensive medical histories, and complicated equipment. The child's neurologic status is often abnormal. If the caregiver is not present, look for sources of baseline information, such as a medical information card or Medical Alert bracelet. Use standard assessment techniques and developmentally appropriate approaches modified by baseline comparisons, to evaluate and manage acute problems.

Blip

Do not allow caregivers to hold children on their laps during transport.

Transport

Table 10-1 lists key principles of transport of CSHCN. Always restrain children in the ambulance. Do not allow caregivers to hold children on their laps. The type of restraint device to use and the method of securing the device in the ambulance are both controversial issues.

In general, if the child is critically ill or injured, restrain the child on his back on a secured gurney. Try to use a backboard for spinal immobilization if the child has suffered an injury to the head or if he has a spinal injury. Check with the caregiver about positioning and availability of any special car seat. In some children, the supine position may compromise the airway due to too much secretion, poor tone, or anatomic abnormalities. A specially designed car seat may be the best option.

Many CSHCN have supplemental oxygen and oxygen delivery equipment. Transport this equipment with them to the ED.

Summary of Transport

CSHCN often have special transport considerations. Make sure the child is safely restrained in the ambulance. This may require using a special seat. Be as creative as possible in achieving safety, but do not compromise airway or breathing. Address the issue of transport with the caregiver and bring all equipment to the ED.

Technology-Assisted Children

Technology-assisted children (TAC) have devices that may malfunction at home. The most common devices are **tracheostomy tubes**, ventriculoperitoneal (VP) shunts, **indwelling central venous catheters**, and **feeding tubes**. Equipment malfunction can cause a range of

Table 10-1 Principles of Transport of a CSHCN

1. Transport a CSHCN who is on home oxygen with the oxygen. If the child has no respiratory distress, continue the same rate of oxygen flow.
2. Transport a child on a home ventilator with the ventilator if there are no equipment problems. If there is a concern about the ventilator, provide assisted ventilation via BVM or endotracheal tube.
3. If the child has poor muscle control, or increased muscle tone, immobilize the child as needed in a position that is comfortable for him. If he has a special seat, wheelchair, or other equipment (e.g., feeding pump, suctioning device) transport these items to the ED.

problems. Some malfunctioning may have minor or no immediate effects, such as loss of a feeding tube or clotting of an indwelling central venous catheter. Other malfunctioning may cause serious physiologic effects, such as respiratory distress from loss of a tracheostomy tube or intracranial pressure elevation from obstruction of a VP shunt.

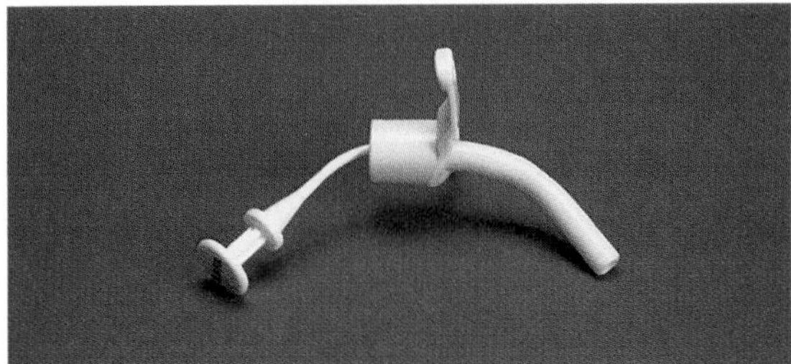

Figure 10-2 A tracheostomy tube

Tracheostomy tubes

A tracheostomy is a surgical opening (stoma) in the front of the neck into the trachea. A tracheostomy tube (sometimes called a "trach tube") is an artificial airway passed through this opening that allows the child to breathe (Figure 10-2). Infants and children may have a tracheostomy for several reasons, as noted in Table 10-2.

There are several types of tracheostomy tubes, and they come in many sizes. The size is written on the wings or flanges of the tube. The size and name (indicating type of tube) are also on the box. The inner and outer diameters are often on the wings as well (Figure 10-3). The most common pediatric tube sizes are 2.5 mm to 10.0 mm (sizes 000–10). All tracheostomy tubes have a standard outer opening or hub outside the neck so a BVM can be attached. For some tubes, an adapter may be needed to make this connection.

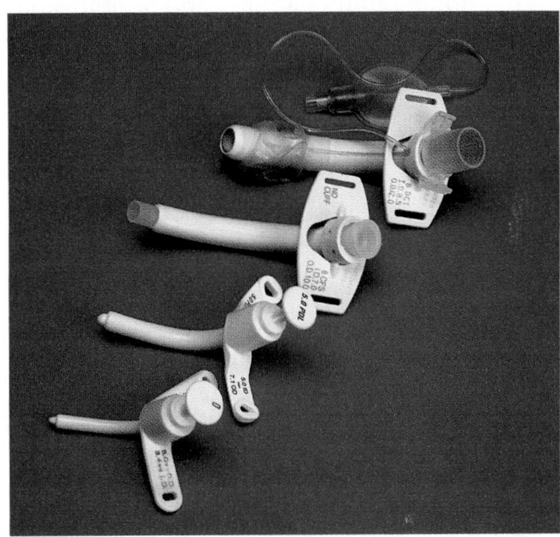

Figure 10-3 Sizes and inner and outer diameters are often written on the wings of tracheostomy tubes.

Types of tracheostomy tubes

The main types of tracheostomy tubes are fenestrated, double lumen and single lumen (Figure 10-4). Tubes can also come with or without a cuff. These cuffs can be filled with air or foam. All

Table 10-2 Indications for a Tracheostomy

1. To bypass an obstruction in the upper airway due to trauma, surgery, or a birth defect
2. To allow clearance of secretions
3. To provide long-term mechanical ventilation of children with chronic respiratory problems, injuries to the lungs, major central nervous system deficits, or severe muscle weakness

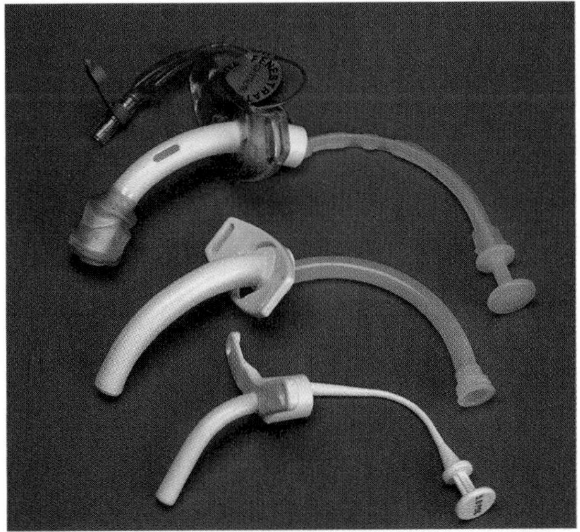

Figure 10-4 Fenestrated, double lumen, and single lumen tracheostomy tubes (top to bottom).

tubes have an **obturator**, which is a solid plastic guide placed inside the tube to make insertion easier. Use the obturator to clear the tube of secretions in an emergency if a suction catheter is not available.

A single lumen tracheostomy tube has one hollow tube or cannula for both airflow and suctioning of secretions. Uncuffed, single lumen tubes are usually for neonates, infants, and young children. A double lumen tube has both a hollow outer cannula and a removable (also hollow) inner cannula. Remove the inner cannula for cleaning, and keep it in place to provide mechanical ventilation. Never remove the outer cannula unless the entire tube must be replaced.

A fenestrated tube has holes (fenestrations) for air to flow upward through the vocal cords and mouth. This lets the child talk and breathe naturally. Fenestrated tubes have a decannulation plug attached to the outer cannula that blocks airflow through the stoma. If the child cannot breathe through his nose or mouth, remove this plug, so breathing is possible through the stoma. In addition, many fenestrated tubes also have a hollow inner cannula that must be in place for mechanical ventilation.

! Tip

The most common complication of a child with a tracheostomy tube is respiratory distress due to obstruction of the tube.

Oxygen delivery and assisted ventilation through a tracheostomy tube

A child with a functioning tracheostomy tube can receive oxygen by the blow-by method or by BVM ventilation:

1. *Blow-by oxygen.* Place a stoma mask or pediatric face mask a short distance above the tracheostomy tube or stoma and give oxygen at 10–15 liters/min.
2. *BVM to tracheostomy tube adapter.* Attach a BVM device directly to the outer end of the tracheostomy tube (Figure 10-5).

For a child who has a stoma (surgical opening in the neck) but no tracheostomy tube, or when a tube cannot be reinserted, apply a seal with a mask over the stoma and ventilate through the stoma; *or* block the stoma with a **sterile** gauze and finger, and ventilate with a mask to the mouth or mask to the mouth and nose technique. Begin BVM as needed.

Tracheostomy complications: Obstruction

Obstruction of the tracheostomy tube is a life-

CASE STUDY 2

A distraught mother calls 911 because her 4-month-old son is having trouble breathing. On arrival, the mother tells you that the infant was 2 months premature at birth and required endotracheal intubation right after delivery. He stayed in the hospital for 2 months with the tube in his mouth for breathing problems. Since he has been home he always breathes fast, but today the respiratory rate is higher than usual, and he will not take his bottle. He is on no medications.

The infant is crying and restless and has grunting. There are supraclavicular, intercostal and subcostal retractions and nasal flaring. His skin is dusky. Respiratory rate is 70 breaths/min, heart rate is 88 beats/min, and blood pressure is not obtained. Pulse oximetry is 86%.

What are the key historical points?
Outline the assessment and management priorities.

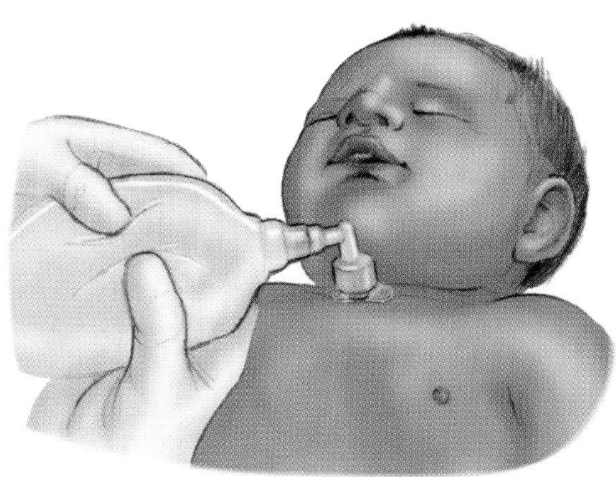

Figure 10-5 BVM device attached directly to the external end of the tracheostomy tube.

threatening emergency for CSHCN. Obstruction can be due to secretions, incorrect insertion (tube malposition), or mechanical problems with the tube. Obstruction causes respiratory distress and failure.

Assessment. When a child has an obstructed tracheostomy tube, the chest is not rising and the child cannot breathe on his own. The PAT shows poor appearance, increased work of breathing, and cyanosis in cases of respiratory failure. The ABCDEs will further indicate poor air movement and bradycardia.

Treatment: Clearing an obstructed tube. To clear an obstructed tracheostomy tube, follow these steps:

1. Position the child's head with a roll under the shoulders. Ensure that the outer opening of the tube is clear.
2. Check that the tube is in the proper location. It should be against the neck, and the obturator should not be in place.
3. If the child has a fenestrated tube, remove the decannulation plug.
4. If none of these maneuvers work, suction the tube with a suction catheter.

Treatment: Suctioning a tracheostomy tube. If efforts to clear the obstruction are unsuccessful, suction the tracheostomy tube using the following procedure (Figures 10-6a and 10-6b):

1. Ask the caregiver if they have suction catheters, equipment, and supplies. If so, use these. Otherwise choose a suction catheter small enough to pass through the tube. (A size 1.0, (or 3.0-mm), tube will take a size 6 to 8 French catheter.) The caregiver may know the right size catheter. If equipment is not immediately available, insert the obturator to try to clear the obstruction.
2. If using a portable suction machine, set it to 100 mm Hg or less.
3. Give oxygen (over the tracheostomy tube) with a mask, then loosen secretions by placing up to 1.0 to 2.0 ml of normal saline into the tube.
4. Insert the suction catheter approximately 2 to 3 inches into the tube. If the child begins

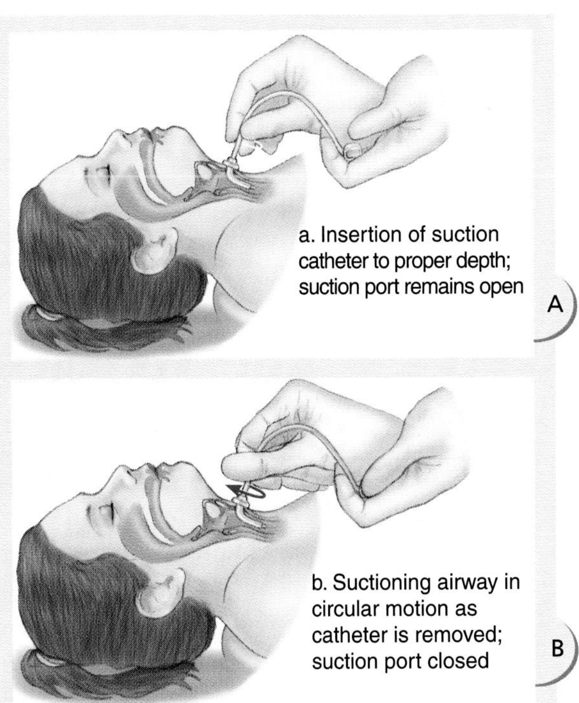
a. Insertion of suction catheter to proper depth; suction port remains open
A
b. Suctioning airway in circular motion as catheter is removed; suction port closed
B

Figure 10-6 (A) Insertion of suction catheter to proper depth; suction port remains open. (B) Suctioning airway in circular motion as catheter is removed; suction port is closed.

to cough, the catheter is through the tube and into the trachea, and the depth of insertion is correct. Do not use suction while inserting the catheter, and *never force the catheter.*

5. Cover the suction port (hole) and suction for 3 to 5 seconds, while slowly removing the catheter. Never suction for longer than 10 seconds. Always monitor the child's heart rate and color during this procedure. Stop suctioning immediately if the heart rate begins to drop or the child becomes blue.
6. If the obstruction is removed, and the child can breathe on his own, do not suction further. If additional suctioning is needed, apply oxygen (by blow-by or direct ventilation) and repeat steps 3 to 5.

Replacing a tracheostomy tube
Treatment of a tracheostomy problem usually requires simple techniques to establish a patent airway, such as suctioning or removal of the old tracheostomy tube and replacement with a new tube. Occasionally it is impossible to ventilate a child through an existing tracheostomy tube because of decannulation or complete obstruction. Under these conditions, the prehospital professional must place a new tracheostomy tube to save the child's life. For a step-by-step explanation of this procedure, see page 300.

Central venous catheters

Many children receive nutritional support or medications at home through a **central venous catheter**. This includes children with poor weight gain due to gastrointestinal or liver problems, children with cancer who require chemotherapy, and children with infections who are receiving antibiotics at home.

! Tip

The most common complication in a TAC with a partially implanted central venous catheter is a broken or dislodged catheter.

Most central venous catheters require a surgical incision, but some can be placed **percutaneously** or through intact skin. They can enter through the skin of the chest, neck, or groin, but the internal end usually lies in or near the **superior vena cava** or right **atrium**. Some are single-lumen lines. Others are double lumen, with two separate external openings, but only one internal opening or port.

Types of catheters

Central venous catheters may be inserted into the external jugular, subclavian, or cephalic veins (Figure 10-7). The skin entry site for the catheter is usually on the chest or arm. These are **partially implanted devices**.

Totally implanted devices are catheters attached to totally implanted injection ports or reservoirs. The catheter is in a central vein, such as the superior vena cava. Instead of coming out of the skin, as in partially implanted catheters, the end is attached to a reservoir (dome or port) that is in a subcutaneous pocket, usually on the chest. Therefore, there are no external parts visible, just a bulge or bump where the device rests.

Complications of central venous catheters

Dislodged or broken catheter. Table 10-3 lists common complications of central venous catheters. The most common problem with the

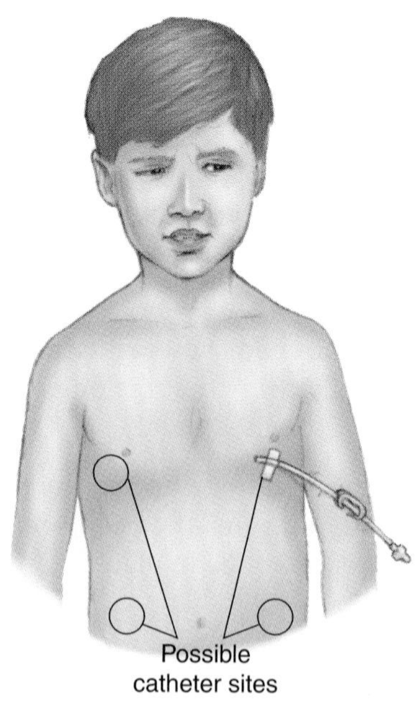

Figure 10-7 Possible insertion sites for a central intravenous catheter

partially implanted devices is a broken or dislodged catheter. Check the site for bleeding. If the catheter is in place, but there is bleeding from the entry site, apply direct pressure with a sterile gauze. If the catheter has been completely pulled out, and there is bleeding, apply direct pressure with a sterile gauze.

If the bleeding is from the catheter and the catheter is in place, inspect the catheter and its end. If a cap is missing, replace the cap, if possible.

Clamping a leaking central venous catheter
If the child is bleeding through a hole or cut in the catheter, clamp the exposed end. The caregiver usually has a clamp available, but if this has been misplaced, wrap the tips of a **hemostat** with gauze and apply to the catheter. If no hemostat is available, open the emergency delivery kit and use an umbilical clamp. If there has been bleeding, estimate the amount of blood loss. Provide appropriate fluid therapy if there are signs of poor perfusion or shock. Do not use the central venous catheter.

Infection at catheter site. Infection can occur at the site where a partially implanted catheter enters the skin or in the pocket where a totally implanted device is placed. Signs of infection are redness, tenderness, swelling, warmth, or yellow discharge (pus) from the site.

The child can also have a blood infection with fever, chills, and shock. In this case, treat for septic shock, as described in Chapter 5. If the line is possibly infected, do not use it for vascular access.

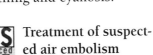

Table 10-3 Common Central Venous Catheter Complications

Dislodged or broken catheter
Infection at catheter site
Problems with accessing or flushing the catheter (obstruction)
Air embolism
Medical problems related to infusion

Obstruction. A problem with accessing or flushing the catheter is an indication of obstruction. This complication can occur with all types of catheters. All that is required is patient assessment and transport. The major concern is a child who depends on hyperalimentation (IV nutrition) for calories and glucose. If the line is malfunctioning, and the child has not received any nutrition, his blood glucose may be low.

Treatment of hypoglycemia
Perform a quick fingerstick check of the blood sugar if there are signs or symtoms of hypoglycemia and treat with IV dextrose or IM glucagon if the blood sugar is low, as described in Chapter 6.

Air embolism. This complication can occur if air accidentally gets into a central venous catheter when the line is being flushed or if the catheter breaks. Symptoms of air embolism include shortness of breath, chest pain, and coughing. Assessment will show increased work of breathing and cyanosis.

If the indwelling central venous catheter site appears infected, do not use it for vascular access.

The main complication of feeding tubes is dislodgment.

Treatment of suspected air embolism
Clamp the catheter, provide the child with oxygen, place the child on his left side in the head-down position, and transport to the ED.

Medical problems related to infusion. Because of the various fluids and medications delivered through central venous catheters, several medical problems can develop. These include allergic reactions, abnormal heart rate or rhythms, or respiratory problems. Treat the appropriate problem, and bring the fluids that were being infused to the ED for analysis.

Feeding tubes

A feeding tube (also called a gastrostomy tube) supplies nutrition and medications to CSHCN who are unable to eat by mouth. A feeding tube allows the child to take in enough calories for adequate growth and nutrition.

Types of feeding tubes

Feeding tubes go through the nose (nasogastric [NG]) or, occasionally, through the mouth (orogastric [OG]) and into the stomach or small intestine (nasojejunal [NJ], orojejunal [OJ]). These tubes are usually long catheters that are taped in place on the child's face (Figure 10-8). Another type of feeding tube goes directly into the stomach from an external site on the abdomen. There are several names for this type: **G-tube**, **button tube**, or **percutaneous endoscopic gastrostomy** (PEG) tube.

! Tip

In a child who depends on hyperalimentation for calories and glucose, if the line is malfunctioning and the child has not received any nutrition, his blood glucose may be low.

Complications of feeding tubes

The main complication of a feeding tube is dislodgment. The child may have aspirated fluid if a feeding tube has come out. Perform an assessment, paying special attention to the work of breathing and chest auscultation.

Treatment. If an implanted tube (G-tube) comes out, check the site for bleeding and apply direct pressure with a sterile dressing. If the insertion site around the implanted tube appears irritated or infected (the skin appears red, warm, or swollen), apply a sterile dressing to the site.

Whenever a tube dislodges or there is evidence of infection, transport the child to the ED. If the child was on an infusion of fluid or medication, ask the caregiver to disconnect the pump (infusion device) and transport it with the child.

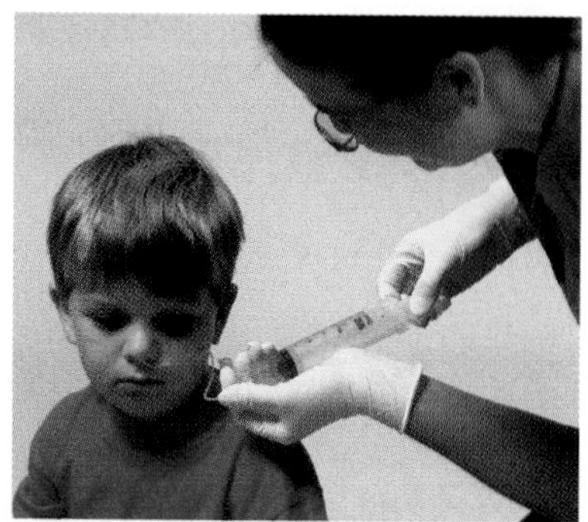

Figure 10-8 Nasojejunal catheter taped in place on the child's face.

ALS Advanced LIFE support

Removing a feeding tube

If the NG or OG tube appears to be in place but the child is having respiratory difficulty, ask the caregiver to check its position. If position cannot be confirmed, remove the tube.

VP shunts

A ventriculoperitoneal (VP) shunt is a device that drains excess cerebrospinal fluid from the brain. It usually runs from a ventricle (in the brain) under the skin, then down the neck into the **peritoneum** of the abdomen or into the heart (Figure 10-9). Its path (or track) can usually be felt on one side of the head and down the neck until the track reaches a scar on the chest wall or abdomen. A VP shunt helps a child with **hydrocephalus** maintain normal brain pressure. The hydrocephalus may be due to a congenital problem or to an acquired condition such as bleeding, trauma, or infection.

Complications of VP shunts

The major complications with a VP shunt are obstruction and infection. The most common complication is a shunt obstruction and malfunction. Table 10-4 lists key questions to ask during assessment to evaluate the severity of the complaint and the urgency for treatment.

Assessment of a child with a possible VP shunt obstruction or infection

Symptoms of a VP shunt obstruction are the same as those of increased intracranial pressure and include headache, lethargy, sleepiness, irritability, nausea, or vomiting, or trouble walking. Fever is usually a sign of a shunt infection or an **intercurrent** illness, but can occur with a shunt malfunction alone. Signs of a VP shunt obstruction are abnormal appearance, high-pitched cry, seizures, or altered level of consciousness.

A child with a shunt infection may have a fever, headache, feeding difficulty, or altered behavior. Signs of a shunt infection include abnormal appearance, altered level of consciousness, and septic shock.

Treatment

Make sure the child has a clear airway and effective breathing. Supply supplemental oxygen and transport the patient. If the child has bradycardia, irregular respirations, and elevated blood pressure (**Cushing's triad**), there is increased intracranial pressure and herniation is imminent. Begin BVM ventilation, and rapidly transport.

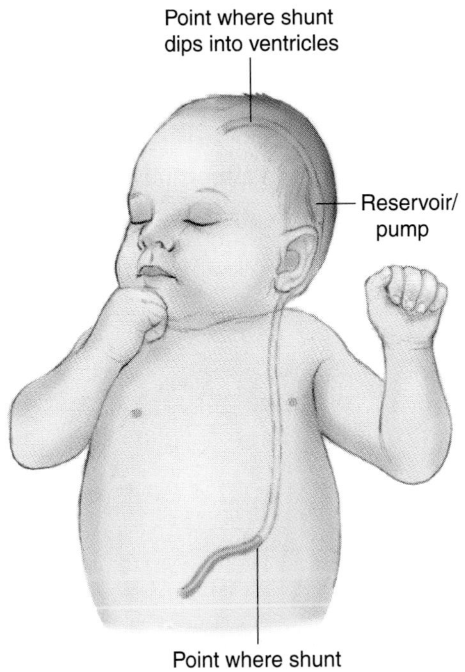

Figure 10-9 A VP shunt directs cerebrospinal fluid from a ventricle in the brain to the skin and then down the neck to either the abdomen or the heart.

Table 10-4 Key Questions for Suspected VP Shunt Malfunction
When was the VP shunt placed?
Is the child acting the same as the last time there was a shunt problem (obstruction)?
Has the child had a fever?
Has the child complained of a headache, vomiting, or nausea?

ALS Advanced LIFE support

Hyperventilation for suspected increased intracranial pressure

If BVM is not effective, attempt endotracheal intubation. Hyperventilation is a treatment for children with impending or frank herniation. However, the role of hyperventilation in treating out-of-hospital intracranial pressure elevation from hydrocephalus is not well understood. Hyperventilation, through rapid carbon dioxide reduction and vasoconstriction, will reduce brain perfusion. On the other hand, overly aggressive ventilation may dangerously decrease perfusion and cause brain ischemia. If a child with a VP shunt has signs of impending or frank herniation, treat with mild hyperventilation at a rate of 5 breaths/min more than normal rate for age (35 breaths/min in an infant, 25 breaths/min in a child). This is the same treatment as outlined for traumatic brain injury in Chapter 8.

The best method of hyperventilation for out-of-hospital intracranial pressure elevation from hydrocephalus is controversial. Beware of aggressive ventilation that may dangerously decrease perfusion and cause brain ischemia.

Summary of Technology-Assisted Children

TAC may encounter many challenging problems with their equipment. The prehospital professional must be familiar with the basic purpose, design, and common complications of tracheostomy tubes, central venous catheters, feeding tubes, and VP shunts. Always ask the caregiver about the equipment and transport all devices and infusions with the child to the ED.

CASE STUDY 3 **You respond to a call from the father of a 10-year-old girl with a VP shunt saying his daughter complains of a headache and has been vomiting for 4 hours.**

The patient tells you that she has a VP shunt for hydrocephalus. She woke up with a headache this morning and vomited once. She still has the headache, but denies other complaints. Her father tells you that this is the way she usually presents when she is having trouble with her shunt. The last time this happened, approximately 1 year ago, she needed an operation.

The girl is sitting in a chair and appears alert and interactive. There are no abnormal airway sounds. Work of breathing and skin color are normal. Respiratory rate is 18 breaths/min, heart rate is 96 beats/min, and blood pressure is 110/70 mm Hg.

Outline assessment techniques.
Should this child be transported?

Case Study Answers

See page 175

Assess the child by asking her father what her normal baseline is, both in terms of vital signs and level of activity and interactiveness. Ask him if this is how his daughter is normally, or if there have been any changes, and, if so, what is different?

Examine her gastrostomy opening to check for bleeding. If there is bleeding, apply pressure with a sterile gauze. If there is no bleeding, cover with a sterile gauze to prevent gastric fluid (the yellow drainage) from irritating the surrounding skin.

Ask her father if she requires special positioning or a chair for comfort. Ask the father to assist you as you place the patient on the gurney for transport. If she has a special chair, bring that with you to the ED. If she does not have a special chair, consider placing the child in a child restraint seat for ambulance transport.

See page 182

The child is at high risk because of prematurity, young age (4 months), history of chronic respiratory disease since birth, and present history of abnormal behavior (will not take bottle). Changes in behavior are important indicators of system distress in CSHCN. Because he already has baseline rapid breathing, assume he has limited reserve and will quickly decompensate.

The child has increased work of breathing, and his restlessness (abnormal appearance) indicates early respiratory failure. Vital signs and pulse oximetry are consistent with respiratory failure. The slow heart rate of 88/min indicates severe hypoxia.

Give supplemental oxygen by nonrebreathing mask. Assisted ventilation may be necessary to prevent progression to cardiopulmonary arrest. Provide BVM ventilatory support if appearance does not improve or if bradycardia continues. Transport to ED.

Consider endotracheal intubation if BVM does not improve color, HR and oxygen saturation

See page 188

The patient's PAT and vital signs are normal for a 10-year-old. Vomiting and a headache are signs of a VP shunt malfunction. However, her normal appearance and interactive state indicates that there is no impending herniation.

Place her on a cardiac monitor and transport to the hospital. Look for changes in PAT and vital signs. If she has rapid decrease in appearance, especially interactiveness, if her heart rate begins to drop, or if her respiratory pattern becomes irregular, begin BVM ventilation.

Suggested Educational Resources

1. Center for Pediatric Emergency Medicine (CPEM). Teaching Resource for Instructors in Prehospital Pediatrics (TRIPP). Version 2.0 New York: Center for Pediatric Emergency Medicine; 1998.
2. Rushton DB, Witte M. *Children with Special Health Care Needs, Technology Assisted Children.* Salt Lake City: Primary Children's Medical Center; 1998.

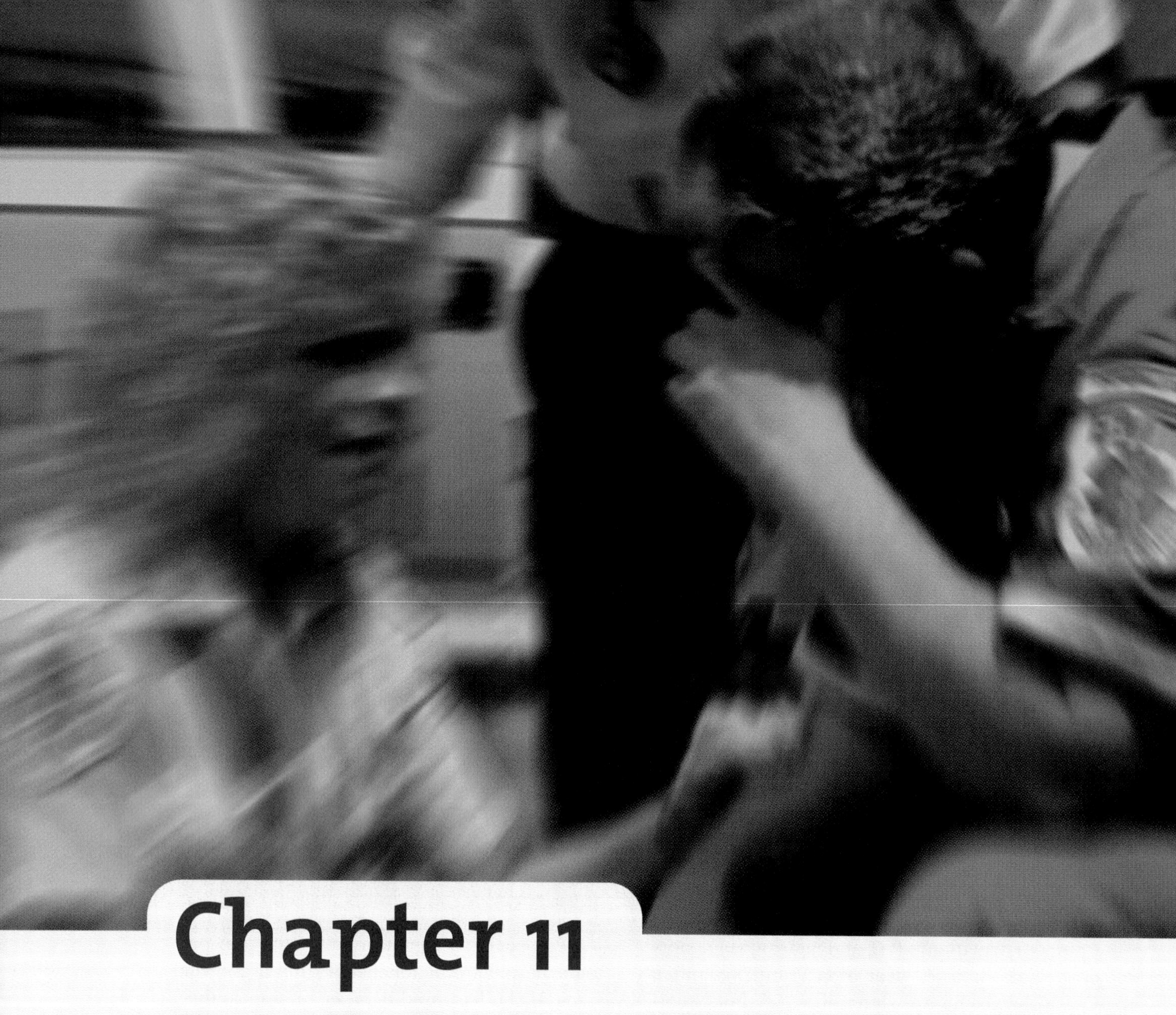

Chapter 11
Sudden Infant (SIDS) and Death

Learning Objectives

1. Describe the common clinical presentation and risk factors for SIDS.
2. Discuss the actions of the prehospital professional in the setting of suspected SIDS.
3. Discuss responses of the family to the death of an infant or child.
4. Interpret responses of prehospital professionals to the death of an infant or child.
5. Describe community resources for support after the unexpected death of an infant or child.
6. Apply appropriate action steps to case studies that involve the death of an infant or child.

CASE STUDY 1

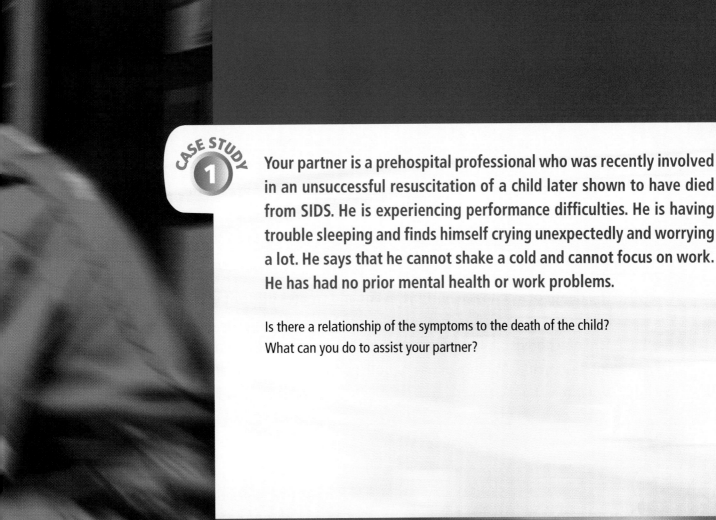

Your partner is a prehospital professional who was recently involved in an unsuccessful resuscitation of a child later shown to have died from SIDS. He is experiencing performance difficulties. He is having trouble sleeping and finds himself crying unexpectedly and worrying a lot. He says that he cannot shake a cold and cannot focus on work. He has had no prior mental health or work problems.

Is there a relationship of the symptoms to the death of the child?
What can you do to assist your partner?

Death Syndrome of a Child

Introduction

Sudden infant death syndrome (SIDS) and the death of a child are among the most difficult patient care experiences for the prehospital professional. SIDS is the leading cause of infant death between 1 month and 1 year of age and the third leading cause of infant mortality in the United States. The causes of SIDS are not known.

The death of a child is a horrible event and creates difficult emotional issues for the caregivers as well as for the prehospital professional. The infant may be in the care of a parent, child care provider, or baby-sitter at the time of death and may not be at home. Absence of one or both parents may complicate field management and interactions at the scene.

www.PEPPsite.com

Definition of SIDS

SIDS is the unexpected death of an infant who is otherwise healthy. In 1989, the National Institute of Child Health and Human Development (NICHD) revised the definition of SIDS as follows: "the sudden and unexpected death of an infant under one year of age which remains unexplained after a thorough postmortem evaluation, including performance of a complete autopsy, examination of the death scene, and review of the clinical history." As this definition makes clear, SIDS cannot be diagnosed at the scene or in the ED.

! Tip

SIDS is the leading cause of infant death from age 1 month to 1 year.

Common Clinical Presentation

When the prehospital professional arrives on the scene of a suspected SIDS death, the history is usually that of a healthy infant between 1 and 6 months of age who was put to bed shortly after a feeding and then was found dead in bed. Often, there is a history of a recent cold. The caregivers may have checked on the infant at intervals and found nothing out of the ordinary, and they did not hear sounds of struggle. The face and **dependent** portions of the body may have reddish-blue mottling, a condition called postmortem lividity. **Lividity** is caused by venous blood pooling in the dependent side of the body. There may be some blood-tinged discharge from the mouth.

Table 11-1 External Appearance of SIDS Victims
Cold skin
Frothy or blood-tinged fluid in the mouth and nose
Lividity or dark, reddish-blue mottling on the dependent side of the body
Normal hydration and nutrition
Rigor mortis
Vomitus (uncommon)

Table 11-2 Risk Factors for SIDS
Formula feeding (possible)
Prematurity and low birth weight
Prone sleeping position and, to a lesser extent, side-sleeping
Soft, bulky blankets or comforters
Soft objects, such as pillows, that trap air or gases in a baby's sleeping area
Soft sleeping surfaces
Tobacco smoke exposure (especially during pregnancy, but also after birth)
Young maternal age

Table 11-1 lists the common signs of SIDS. Some signs differ, depending on how long the infant has been dead. Some cases of SIDS will not show any of these signs.

Epidemiology and Risk Factors

SIDS is the leading cause of death in infants between 1 month and 1 year of age. There are nearly 3000 SIDS cases per year in the United States. It occurs most frequently between 2 and 4 months of age. Approximately 90% to 95% of all SIDS cases are babies less than 6 months of age. SIDS occurs more often in males (60% to 70%) and more frequently in the winter months in all areas of the country.

Sometimes a sudden, unexpected infant death is not caused by SIDS, and the medical examiner can identify a specific illness or injury as the cause. This occurs in approximately 5% of suspected SIDS deaths. This group includes deaths caused by child maltreatment, as discussed in Chapter 12. On the scene, the prehospital professional cannot determine the true cause of death in an infant. Therefore, do not think suspiciously about the caregiver; instead, *treat every caregiver like a grieving parent.* Never discuss on the scene the possibility of maltreatment as a possible cause of death. However, be sure to note details of the death scene and record observations in the patient care report. To help identify deaths that may not be due to natural causes, document any observations in the scene size-up, physical assessment, or focused history that seem atypical or inconsistent with SIDS. For example, dangerous or unclean home conditions, bruises or burn marks on the child's body, or a changing or implausible story are possible red flags for child maltreatment that require explicit documentation, as discussed in Chapter 12.

The typical SIDS scenario is an apparently healthy baby, usually less than 6 months of age, found dead in bed after having been seen alive a short time before.

Never discuss child maltreatment as a possible cause of death on the scene.

Although the causes of SIDS are unknown, there are a number of risk factors, which are noted in Table 11-2.

Summary of SIDS

SIDS is the most common cause of infant death. It is unpredictable and silent. The underlying cause is not known. The prehospital professional cannot "diagnose" SIDS in the field, and the emergency physician cannot diagnose SIDS in the ED. To determine the cause of death, an

Table 11-3 Pros and Cons of Transporting Suspected SIDS Infants

PROS	CONS
ALS capability in ED	Caregiver concern about infant's body
Facilitation of autopsy	Disruption of scene investigation by medical examiner
More medical personnel to manage infant and caregivers	High costs in dollars, personnel, and equipment
Physician involvement in management	Possible violation of family's culture
Religious services	Removal of family from familiar setting
Social services for grief counseling	Transport liabilities, especially ambulance crashes and adverse bystander reactions

autopsy must be performed. There are, however, common clinical signs and important risk factors, which may be helpful in identifying possible SIDS cases.

Actions in Suspected SIDS

Clinical interventions

The prehospital professional's first actions when SIDS is suspected must always be the assessment and treatment of the baby. Immediately begin resuscitation, using standard treatment protocol, unless the infant meets local EMS system criteria for death in the field. In most SIDS cases, the baby has easily recognizable signs of death, and no interventions or resuscitation are indicated.

The transport decision: Stay or go?

After assessing the child's cardiopulmonary status, begin CPR if there is a detectable heart rate and other signs of life. If resuscitation is started and the child responds, transport as soon as medically appropriate, as discussed in Chapter 5.

! Tip

In all cases of cardiopulmonary arrest, immediately begin resuscitation, using standard treatment protocol, unless the infant meets local EMS criteria for death in the field.

If the infant is already dead upon the prehospital professional's arrival at the scene or the initial response to CPR is unsuccessful, consider not transporting the infant for autopsy until after the scene investigation is complete. Notify medical oversight when there is uncertainty. Table 11-3 lists the pros and cons of transporting suspected SIDS infants. Because the prehospital professional cannot distinguish a child with SIDS from any other child in cardiopulmonary arrest, use standard principles of treatment and transport for children in cardiopulmonary arrest, as discussed in Chapter 5.

ALS Advanced LIFE support

Value of transport after failed ALS in cardiopulmonary arrest

The value of immediate or delayed hospital transport when a child does not respond to resuscitation is controversial. It is extremely unlikely that the ED will offer more successful medical interventions for cardiopulmonary arrest than an ALS prehospital professional can provide at the scene. The chances of neurologic survival of a child in the ED, after failed ALS in the field, are almost zero.

Sometimes, the child will meet the EMS system's death-in-the-field criteria or resuscitation will not be successful, but grief counseling is not available at the scene. In this situation, consider transporting the baby to the hospital in a controlled transport mode (no lights or siren) with the caregiver, if possible. Encourage the caregiver to hold or touch the baby on scene. Before leaving the scene to transport a dead infant to an ED, write down and tell the name and address of the hospital to family and friends.

Support of caregivers

The prehospital professional's emotional support of the caregivers is extremely important. When possible, have one person stay with the caregiver to explain and comfort. Let family or caregivers stay with the child, and do not separate them even during transport. Be clear that the child is dead and do not attempt to say this in obscure language, such as "your child has left us" or "she has gone to a better place." Avoid unnecessary remarks that intend to comfort the caregiver, such as "You can always have other children," "I know how you feel," or "You will get over this in time." Table 11-4 suggests specific ways to communicate with caregivers when there is an unexpected death of a child.

Table 11-4 Communicating about an Unexpected Death of a Child

Use the child's name.
Show empathy and express condolences.
Ask questions in a nonjudgmental manner.
Never become hostile or angry.
Use a calm and directive voice.
Be clear with instructions and answers to questions.
Provide explanations to the caregivers about treatment and transport.
Repeat statements when necessary.
Reassure caregivers that there was nothing they could have done.
Allow the caregiver to accompany the baby if possible.

Do not obscure the fact that the child is dead by using kind but ambiguous language.

Summary of Actions in Suspected SIDS

When faced with an infant in cardiopulmonary arrest, begin or continue CPR according to the local EMS system policies on death in the field. In some EMS systems, policy will permit withholding or discontinuing resuscitation and focusing on the important tasks of talking to the family and helping them with their grief. Figure 11-1 provides a typical sequence of events for when there is a suspected SIDS cases. Table 11-5 lists the responsibilities of the medical examiner and local health department in a case of suspected SIDS.

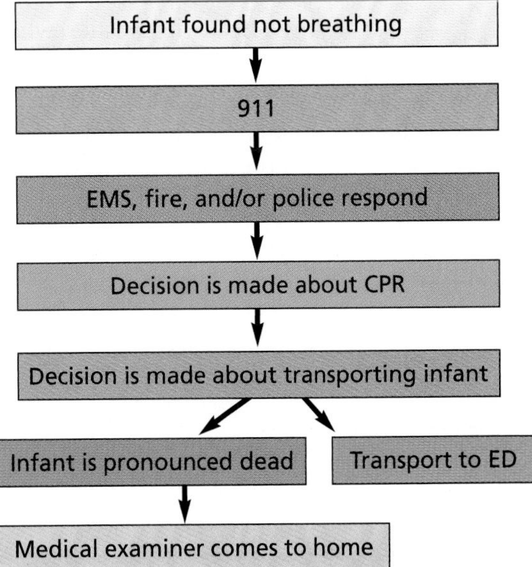

Figure 11-1 Flowchart of what to do in suspected SIDS cases.

Information Collection

History

Get a focused history at the scene if the child is not transported to the ED. Refrain from asking judgmental or leading questions. Table 11-6 gives examples of key questions to ask. Always ask the baby's name at the beginning of the interview and

Table 11-5 Medical Examiner and Local Health Department Responsibilities in Suspected SIDS Cases

Medical Examiner's Responsibilities	Local Health Department's Responsibilities
Performs death scene investigation	Provides information and counseling
Performs autopsy	Referral information for peer support
Notifies local health department	Provides information to state program
Notifies state program	Periodic follow-up
Signs death certificate	Community education (with peer group)
Notifies parents of cause of death	

use her first name in all discussions with the caregiver.

Scene size-up

Perform a scene size-up and note findings carefully. These are often important pieces of information for the medical examiner and medical experts who later review the entire case. Look at the location of the infant on arrival at the scene (e.g., in the crib or bed, on the floor). If the infant has been moved, investigate the location where death occurred and document whether or not she was in her own crib, the nature of the sleeping surface, and whether she was sharing a crib or bed (and with whom). Also describe the covering blankets or comforter (soft, thick) and note whether the blanket was over the face.

Document the sleep position when placed down for sleep and when discovered (prone, side, or supine). Check for the presence of other objects in the area where the infant was found, especially pillows or other soft or bulky items. Note any unusual conditions such as high room temperature or odors in the air. Look for street drugs or medications and bring all medications, if possible.

Blip

Refrain from asking judgmental or leading questions that suggest that the caregiver may be at fault for the infant's death.

Ask the name of the child and use it.

Table 11-6 Key Questions in Focused History

What happened?
Who found the infant* and where?
What did the caregiver do?
Has the infant been moved?
What time was the infant last seen alive?
Had the infant been sick?
Was the infant receiving any medications?

*When asking these questions, use the infant's name (rather than "the infant").

Documentation

Document all findings in the history, patient assessment, treatment, and scene size-up completely and accurately on the patient care record. Failure to fully document can result in unnecessary investigations or significant emotional stress to the caregiver and prehospital professional.

Potential Responses to an Infant Death

Caregiver's response

The prehospital professional is often the first official person on the scene following the discovery of the dead infant. Responses of the caregiver to the sudden and unexpected death of an infant are not predictable and may vary from numb silence to violent hysteria. Common reactions include denial, anger, hysteria, withdrawal, intense guilt, or no visible response. The caregiver may or may not accept that the infant is dead or that resuscitation is not possible. The caregiver may cling to the hope that the prehospital professional can do something to save the infant, even though the child is obviously dead.

The caregiver may make demands of the prehospital professional, which could include one or more of the following:

- Repeated questions
- Request to not start care or to stop resuscitation efforts
- Request to be alone with the infant
- Request for the cause of death
- Interference with care
- Insistence on continuation of care

When the caregiver or family makes such demands, maintain a calm, clear, and professional approach. Keep explanations simple. Follow EMS system protocol for death in the field and maintain an empathetic and nonjudgmental attitude. Enlist the assistance of family members or friends.

If the prehospital professional does not attempt to resuscitate the infant and is waiting at the scene for the medical examiner, attempt to gather the family's support network (Figure 11-2).

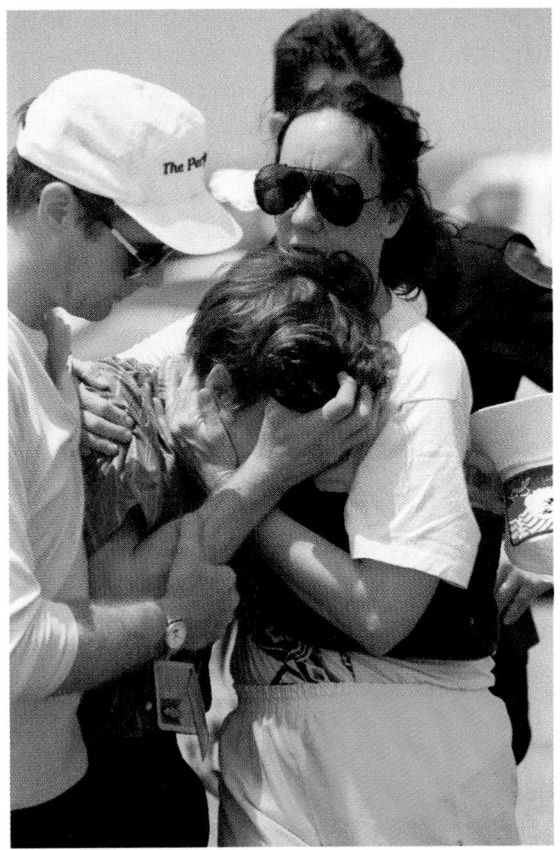

Figure 11-2 Caregivers can react to the death of a child in many ways. Attempt to gather the family's support network.

This may involve calling friends, relatives, clergy, or public agencies to help care for other children at home. If the scene is a child care setting, consider calling law enforcement to assist with other children and to contact the child's caregivers or the caregivers of other children in the provider's care.

Responses of the caregiver to the sudden and unexpected death of an infant are not predictable and may vary from numb silence to violent hysteria.

Prehospital professional's response

The role of the prehospital professional in the setting of unexpected infant or child death is difficult. After death is declared, comfort the parents. Never blame. Offering sensitive support to the family and gathering accurate information in a nonthreatening manner helps ease the future

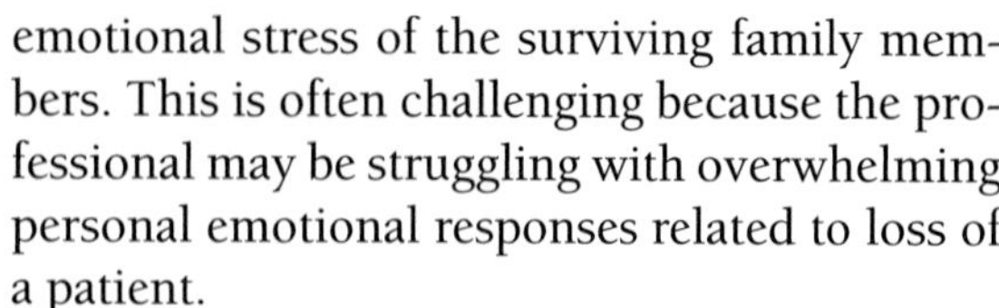

emotional stress of the surviving family members. This is often challenging because the professional may be struggling with overwhelming personal emotional responses related to loss of a patient.

Sometimes there are cultural or language differences between the prehospital professional and the caregiver. There may be unfamiliar rituals and behaviors, in how death is regarded or in how grief is expressed. This presents another important challenge to the professional. Cultural diversity must be respected in order to have useful communication with the caregiver. When cultural or language differences arise, attempt to find an interpreter to explain and translate.

Do not be alarmed by cultural differences in coping with death.

! Tip

Unexpected death of an infant or child is one of the most stressful experiences for the prehospital professional.

Responses of the prehospital professional to the sudden and unexpected death of an infant may include one or more of the following:

- Anger or blame
- Identification with the caregiver
- Withdrawal
- Avoidance of the caregiver
- Self-doubt (if resuscitation is attempted and baby does not recover)
- Sadness and depression

Table 11-7 Responses of Prehospital Professionals That May Interfere with Communicating with Caregivers after Unexpected Death

Expecting tearful and hysterical responses
Being unable to believe that the caregiver did not initiate CPR
Distrusting a caregiver who has decided the infant is dead and does not want CPR
Misunderstanding the mourning and grief behaviors of persons of different cultures or religious beliefs

The prehospital professional may have unrealistic expectations of how the caregiver should behave and respond, or may believe that the caregiver was responsible for the baby's death.

CASE STUDY 2

You are dispatched to a home where a father has called 911 to report that his 3-month-old son is blue and not breathing. The father is inconsolable. He states that the mother is out of town and that he last saw the child when he put him to sleep 10 hours ago.

You find a cold, blue, stiff, apneic child. The mouth has slightly frothy secretions, but there is no other evidence of injury or physical abnormality. The cardiac monitor shows asystole.

What are your key medical actions?
How should you deal with the father?

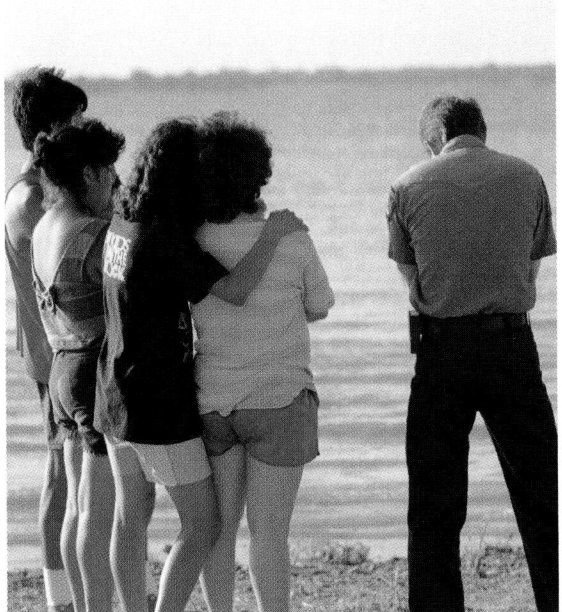

Figure 11-3 Stress is an unavoidable part of a prehospital professional's job. The death of a child can be agonizing.

Table 11-8 Signs and Symptoms of Critical Incident Stress

Anger and irritability
Changes in eating habits
Changes in sleeping patterns
Depression
Excessive alcohol consumption
Inability to concentrate
Mood changes and emotional instability
Physical illness
Recurring dreams or frightening images
Withdrawal

These feelings can become obstacles to communication. Table 11-7 outlines common obstacles to communication with the bereaved caregiver and family.

Critical Incident Stress

Stress is an unavoidable part of the prehospital professional's job. The death of a child may be the most stressful situation in the prehospital professional's career (Figure 11-3). Recognizing stress is a key part of successfully coping with stress and maintaining a healthy mental attitude. Table 11-8 lists the frequent signs and symptoms of stress.

There are many ways to decrease the impact of stress related to the death of an infant or child. Critical incident stress debriefing (CISD) may be an important technique for helping cope with the emotional toll of SIDS and unexpected infant or child death. Ensure that CISD is available to all prehospital professionals after any highly stressful experience. Other techniques to help decrease stress include the following:

- Talk to field supervisors and experienced prehospital professionals to share feelings.
- Exercise, plan leisure time, and limit overtime hours. Maintain a well-balanced lifestyle outside of work.
- Seek support from a CISD professional or from a SIDS or infant death specialist at the local or state health department.
- Read about stress management and SIDS and unexpected death of a child.
- Get adequate rest and eat a balanced diet.
- Avoid excessive alcohol or drugs.
- Write a personal journal.

! Tip

CISD may be an important technique for coping with the emotional toll of SIDS and unexpected infant or child death.

? Controversy

The value and appropriate timing of CISD is not known. While the prehospital professional will suffer predictable stress after death of a child in her care, how and when such intervention should occur, has not been studied.

- Obtain religious or peer counseling.
- Request professional psychological assistance.

Community resources

Community resources available to caregivers and to prehospital professionals to help them cope with the unexpected death of a child include the following:

- Local support groups
- Local public health departments
- National SIDS Alliance (1-800-221-SIDS)
- Professional counseling

Controversy

Risk reduction and risk counseling are important community prevention activities. Further research must help define the appropriate educational role of the prehospital professional at the scene of an injury or death.

Risk reduction activities and risk counseling

In addition to seeking assistance from community resource groups, prehospital professionals can also play a key role in educating parents in the community on the ways to decrease the risks of SIDS. This includes distribution of the American Academy of Pediatrics "Back to Sleep" brochures and active support of their recommendation to place babies on their backs to sleep. Although side-sleeping is several times safer than prone sleeping, the risk of SIDS for the side-sleeping position is still double the risk of the supine position. Prehospital professionals can participate in community risk reduction by advocating for firm, flat mattresses in safety-approved cribs and avoidance of soft or bulky blankets or comforters and overheating.

Support of campaigns against cigarette smoking is also important. Recent research shows that the risk of SIDS doubles among babies exposed to cigarette smoke after birth, and triples for those exposed both during pregnancy and after birth. As for all infants, encouragement of breastfeeding is a useful action because formula feeding is probably a risk factor for SIDS.

Prehospital professionals can also become involved in local or state child fatality review teams. These teams meet and discuss the trends

CASE STUDY 3

A frightened neighbor hears screaming and chanting next door and calls 911. You arrive and the neighbor states that she fears her neighbors are drug dealers and have killed their newborn child.

You enter the next apartment and find a chaotic scene involving many people. A motionless infant is lying on the living room floor. The caregiver speaks no English and gestures to the body. The assessment reveals a well-developed child of about 3 to 6 months of age, with lividity and rigor mortis. The child is cyanotic, apneic, and unresponsive. There are no signs of injury on the body. The cardiac monitor shows asystole.

What facts suggest that this case may be SIDS? Child abuse?
Is transport indicated?

in communities on infant and child deaths. They often review all sudden and unexpected deaths in children less than 2 years of age in order to improve the accuracy of SIDS as a diagnosis versus other natural causes and versus nonnatural causes, especially child maltreatment.

Summary of Information Collection, Responses at the Scene, and Critical Incident Stress

Death of a child is an emotional event for everyone. When a baby's death is managed at the scene, there are many challenges to the prehospital professional. Use a supportive and nonjudgmental approach. Expect complex caregiver responses; these will vary with the individual, with possible cultural differences. Gather information and complete documentation on scene that will help establish cause of death and identify possible risk factors in the environment. Recognize that a critical incident stress response is common for the prehospital professional and seek assistance. Consider involvement in community SIDS risk reduction campaigns.

Prehospital professionals can play a key role in educating parents in the community on the ways to decrease the risk of SIDS.

CHAPTER RESOURCES

Case Study Answers

See page 191

Coping with unexpected death in children is one of the most stressful professional experiences you will encounter. It is common for health care providers to experience significant personal sadness and depression over SIDS experiences. It is important to recognize stress reactions in order to do something about them. Talk to your peers and supervisors. Seek assistance from local SIDS groups, religious counselors, or mental health professionals. A formal critical incident stress debriefing with qualified personnel is sometimes valuable both to review medical care and to reduce feelings of self-blame and helplessness.

See page 198

In most EMS systems, the child would meet death-in-the-field criteria and would not require any resuscitation attempt. If you are uncertain about whether resuscitation is indicated, begin CPR and call medical oversight to clarify treatment options. Do not transport dead children to the ED with lights and sirens. This is an important public safety issue because of the potential danger to ambulance occupants and bystanders during a lights-and-sirens transport.

In this setting, provide a direct and calm explanation to the parent that the child is dead. Get the child's name and use it. Do not ask questions in a way that suggests blame. Use a controlled and supportive dialogue with the father. If the child is not transported, try to get grief counseling for the parent, contact the medical examiner from the scene, and consider critical incident stress debriefing for yourself and your partner. Gather family support resources.

See page 200

The child has physical findings that suggest SIDS. There are no signs of physical injury. Remember that your assessment and documentation must be factual. The different cultural background of the family does not mean the child was abused. You must treat the family in a nonjudgmental manner and be highly respectful of cultural issues. If home grief counseling by an appropriate provider is not available, consider transporting the infant to the hospital for further investigation, psychosocial intervention, and grief counseling. Because of the language and cultural differences, on-scene information collection and counseling might be difficult. No medical treatment is indicated unless local EMS policy requires CPR on all lifeless children independent of assessment. Consider critical incident stress debriefing.

Suggested Educational Resources

1. American Academy of Pediatrics. Positioning and Sudden Infant Death Syndrome (SIDS): Update. AAP Task Force on Infant Positioning and SIDS. *Pediatrics* 1996;98 (6):1216–1218.
2. Back KJ. Sudden, unexpected pediatric death: Caring for the parents. *Pediatr Nurs* 1991;17 (6):572–575.
3. Brooks JG, ed. Sudden infant death syndrome. *Pediatr Ann* 1995;24:345–383.
4. Horchler JN, Morris RR. *The SIDS Survival Guide: Information and Comfort for Grieving Family and Friends and Professionals Who Seek to Help Them.* 2nd ed. Hyattsville, MD: SIDS Educational Services, Inc.; 1997.
5. Krous HF and the International Standardized Autopsy Protocol Committee of the Global Strategy Task Force. Instruction and reference manual for the international standardized autopsy protocol for sudden unexpected infant death. *J SIDS and Infant Mortality* 1996;1:203–246.

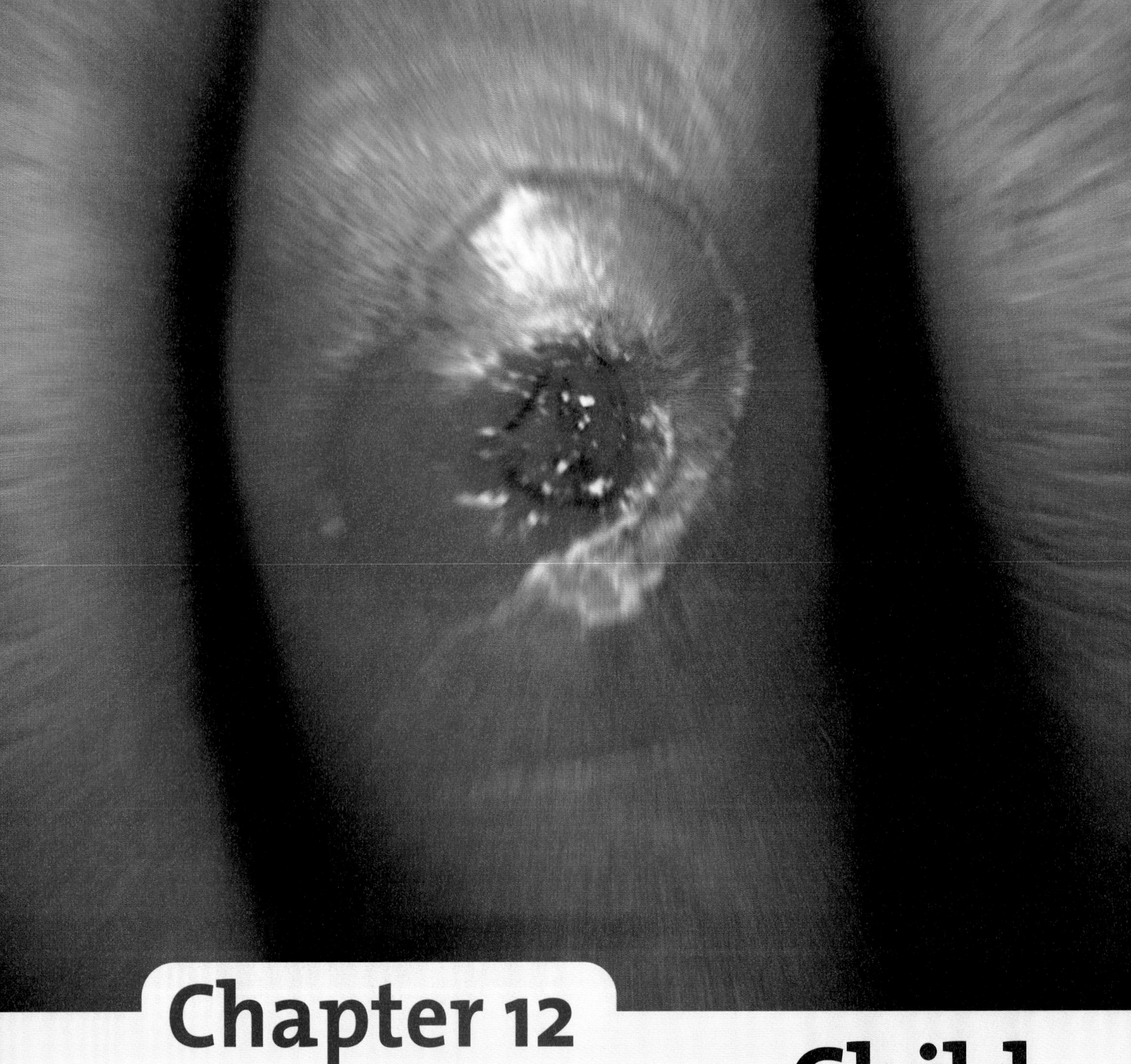

Chapter 12

Child

Learning Objectives

1. Discuss the role of child protection services (CPS) in management of suspected child maltreatment.
2. Distinguish features in the history and physical assessment, and in the child's and caregiver's behaviors, that may suggest child maltreatment.
3. Describe appropriate communication with caregivers of suspected victims of maltreatment.
4. Discuss the prehospital professional's legal responsibility to document and report suspected child maltreatment.
5. Apply appropriate assessment techniques and action steps to case studies that present situations that may involve child maltreatment.

A baby-sitter calls 911 because a child has a fever. You enter a tidy apartment and the baby-sitter leads you to a cramped bedroom to examine a crying 8-month-old infant boy in a crib.

Your assessment reveals a thin, malnourished-looking boy who is crying. He follows readily, fixes gaze, grasps an offered tongue blade, and has a pink color. There are no retractions, and circulation to skin is normal. A small circular burn is present on the child's hand. The baby-sitter states that the baby has a fever and she just ran out of formula.

What are your initial management priorities?
What is your role legally?

Maltreatment

Introduction

Prehospital professionals must know when to suspect child maltreatment. They are likely to care for victims of maltreatment and can have a vital role in recognition and, sometimes, in delivery of emergency medical care. Prehospital professionals also provide valuable scene documentation and reporting of suspected cases of maltreatment. These actions are important to protect and treat vulnerable children and to break the cycle of maltreatment in communities.

Unfortunately, child maltreatment is common. It is a leading cause of death in infants less than 6 months old. Physical abuse and neglect are often visible and easily detectable, but sexual abuse, emotional abuse, and neglect may not be clinically obvious. The prehospital professional's role in management of these conditions is more limited.

Some children who die from maltreatment are known to local child protection services, the legal organizations set up in every community to monitor, manage, and prevent child maltreatment. These deaths are sometimes preventable. Abused or neglected children have a high probability of being maltreated again. Early recognition is important to prevent future injury or death.

www.PEPPsite.com

Background

In 1997, child protection services (CPS) organizations in the United States received 3,195,000 reports of suspected maltreatment. There were 1,015,000 confirmed victims. The death rate among victims is high, with three children dying every day from maltreatment. Many survivors are negatively affected for life, both physically and psychologically, and may themselves become abusive or neglecting caregivers. Children who suffer long-term effects from neglect are not as well documented, but their numbers are large. Table 12-1 lists some of these long-term complications.

Younger children are at higher risk for fatal abuse and neglect than older children. Most maltreated children who die are less than 5 years old and over one third are under 1 year of age. Approximately half of these deaths happen to children known to CPS agencies as current or prior clients.

Child maltreatment involves risk factors and lapses in child protection at the individual, family, community, and society levels. No geographic, ethnic, or economic setting is free of child maltreatment. In fact, the incidence rates are similar for urban, suburban, and rural communities. There is no typical family situation. Children from low-income families are, however, more likely to suffer maltreatment than are children from higher-income families. Child maltreatment has also been connected to drug and alcohol abuse, teen pregnancy, teen suicide, and chronic truancy.

Table 12-1 Possible Complications of Maltreatment

Criminal behavior beginning in young adulthood
Death
Low self-esteem and underachievement
Permanent physical or neurologic damage
Poor school performance
Poor social bonding
Psychological disorders or psychiatric symptoms
Retarded growth and development
Social withdrawal
Substance abuse
Suicidal tendencies
Vulnerability to further abuse

A perpetrator of child maltreatment can be any person who has care, custody, or control of the child. This includes the child's parent, teacher, baby-sitter or child care staff person, relative, institution staff person, bus driver, playground attendant, caregiver, or boyfriend or girlfriend of the caregiver.

Children learn from their parents. A child who has been raised in a home where violence is a response to frustration will, as an adult, tend to react violently. Such a child does not learn skills necessary for controlling anger or frustration. In the same way, a parent who lacks self-esteem or maturity cannot teach these characteristics to a child. Without significant outside influences, the child is likely to become an adult who thinks like his parent. When this happens, the cycle of maltreatment continues unchanged. Adults tend to repeat the actions and attitudes that they learned as children.

Maltreatment happens for many different reasons. Rarely does the prehospital professional have the information to be certain of maltreatment in the field. However, there are many clues in the environment, in the behavior of the child and caregiver, in the history from the caregiver, and in the physical condition of the child. These clues must cause the prehospital professional to be suspicious. Recognizing and reporting suspected child maltreatment is one of the best ways the prehospital professional can prevent childhood injury.

Definition of Child Maltreatment

Child maltreatment is a general term that includes all types of abuse and neglect.

Types of maltreatment

Physical abuse

Physical abuse occurs when a person intentionally inflicts, or allows to be inflicted, injury to a child under 18 years of age or to a mentally disabled child under 21 years of age, which causes or results in risk of death, disfigurement, or distress. Injury associated with child maltreatment can be physical or emotional.

Emotional abuse

Emotional abuse occurs when there is an ongoing and consistent pattern of behavior that interferes with the normal psychological and social development of a child.

Sexual abuse

Sexual abuse occurs when an older child or adult engages in sexual activities with a dependent, developmentally immature child or adolescent for the older person's own sexual excitement or for the enjoyment of other persons (as in child pornography or prostitution).

In most cases of sexual abuse, the perpetrator is an adult who knows the child and is often living under the same roof.

When adults with poor coping skills are faced with stressful situations, child maltreatment may result in a cycle of maltreatment.

Few of the incidents involve the stranger that children are warned about. Sexual abuse usually does not occur as a single incident. It does not always involve violence and physical force. The perpetrator may use the power of adult–child authority or the parent–child bond instead of force or violence. Therefore, it is often not detectable by the prehospital professional in a single encounter.

Child neglect

Child neglect occurs when a child's physical, mental, or emotional condition is harmed or in danger because the caregiver has failed to supply basic necessities. Other forms of child neglect include a caregiver's misuse of drugs or alcohol and child abandonment. Neglect is the failure to act on behalf of a child. Neglect involves child-rearing practices that are inadequate or dangerous. It is an act of omission. Neglect may not have visible signs, and it usually occurs over a period of time (Figure 12-1).

! Tip

Abuse represents an action against a child (commission). Neglect represents a lack of action for the child (omission).

Neglect may be physical or emotional. **Physical neglect** is a failure to meet the requirements basic to a child's physical development, such as supervision, housing, clothing, medical attention, nutrition, and support. Some social service agencies subdivide this category into more specific acts of omission, such as medical neglect, lack of proper supervision, or educational neglect. **Emotional neglect** is failure to provide the support or affection necessary to a child's psychological and social development.

Abuse versus neglect

The difference between abuse and neglect is that abuse represents an action against a child whereas neglect represents a lack of action for the child. Abuse is an act of commission; neglect is an act of omission. In abuse, a physical or mental injury is inflicted on a child. In neglect, there is a failure to meet the basic needs of the child for adequate food, supervision, shelter, guidance, education, clothing, or medical care. Abuse may be directed toward only one child in the family, whereas neglect usually involves all the children in the family.

Summary of Background and Definitions of Child Maltreatment

Child maltreatment is common in all communities. These conditions often involve repetition of dysfunctional behaviors through generations to create a cycle of maltreatment. Physical abuse is the most obvious form of maltreatment and can often be suspected during a physical assessment. The prehospital professional has a valuable role in the assessment, treatment, and reporting of child maltreatment in the community.

Child Protection Services

he CPS agency is a community legal organiza- .on responsible for protection, rehabilitation, nd prevention of child maltreatment. CPS has the egal authority to temporarily remove children at isk for injury or neglect from the home and to secure foster placement. CPS is responsible for initial investigations of suspected maltreatment. They must make complicated and important decisions about the maltreatment accusations, remove children from home and place into foster care at times, and provide services for abusive and neglectful families. Table 12-2 lists the initial actions

Please place this sticker over Figure 12-1 on page 208.

Table 12-2 Initial CPS Actions

1. When a report of child abuse or neglect is received, either from a health professional or a law enforcement agency, the protocols of the receiving agency determine the timing and scope of the initial response.
2. The facts are reviewed to determine if a home visit is appropriate and, if so, which members of the team will be involved.
3. The CPS caseworker assesses risk to the child, the family's ability to provide safety, and supportive resources available to the family.
4. After the investigation and assessment, a reported incident is determined to be founded, unfounded, or unable to determine because of lack of information.

Table 12-3 Duties of the Prehospital Professional in Suspected Maltreatment

Recognition of suspicious circumstances in the scene size-up
Physical assessment of the child
Assessment of the behavior of the child and caregiver
Performance of the detailed anatomic exam, when appropriate
Communication with the caregiver and family
Careful documentation and reporting

of the CPS when a report is filed. Law enforcement also investigates the facts and determines who is responsible for maltreating the child.

The CPS staff are trained to help families under stress. It is not the duty of the prehospital professional to scold, criticize, or judge caregivers or to intervene in issues of dysfunctional parenting or suspected maltreatment. Recognize that the community has organized services in place to manage these complex issues.

Duties of the Prehospital Professional

The prehospital professional has an extremely important role at the scene. CPS and health professionals in the ED rely on the scene size-up and documentation of suspected child maltreatment. Table 12-3 lists the prehospital professional's duties in suspected maltreatment cases.

Scene size-up

First, ensure that the scene is safe for the child and for the prehospital professionals. Then, carefully document the scene conditions that might support suspicion of maltreatment. Child maltreatment is so serious that it must be considered in every injury case. It must also be considered in illness cases with suspicious circumstances in the environment, behavior of the child or caregiver, history, or physical exam. Look for unsanitary or dangerous home conditions such as visible guns or drug paraphernalia or an unsafe care situation.

! Tip

Consider child abuse in every injury case, as well as in illness cases with suspicious circumstances in the environment, behavior of the child or caregiver, history, or physical exam.

Initial assessment

If the scene is safe, perform an initial assessment of the child, as outlined in Chapter 3, and give appropriate medical care. If an infant with suspected maltreatment has an abnormal appearance (e.g., listlessness, impassiveness, inconsolability, weak cry) or altered level of consciousness (abnormal response to verbal or painful stimuli), but normal work of breathing and skin circulation, consider the child to have a possible serious physiologic problem, such as a brain injury or toxic/metabolic abnormality.

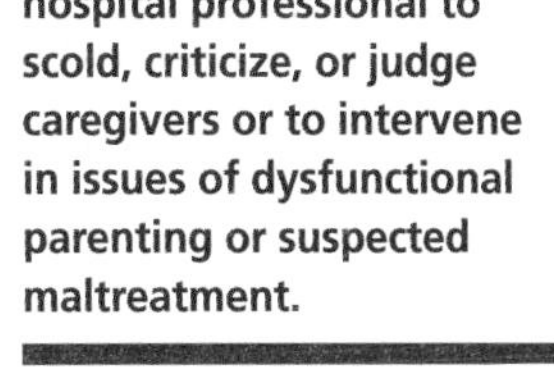

Blip

It is not the duty of the prehospital professional to scold, criticize, or judge caregivers or to intervene in issues of dysfunctional parenting or suspected maltreatment.

One cause of abnormal appearance in a child who has possibly been maltreated is shaken baby

Table 12-4 Focused History: Questions and Evaluation Considerations

Questions	Considerations
How did the injury occur?	Is the caregiver's explanation plausible? Do the physical conditions at the scene support the alleged mechanism of injury?
When did it happen?	Was there a long delay before 911 was notified? Does the injury appearance match the time frame?
Who witnessed the event?	Do all of the caregivers' or witnesses' stories match? Was there adequate supervision?
What is the child's medical history?	Are there preexisting psychosocial, developmental, or chronic problems?
Does the child have a physician?	When was the last visit? Does the physician know the child?

! Tip

After assessing a stable child for whom there is concern of maltreatment, always transport the child to the ED.

(or shaken infant) syndrome. (Figure 12-2). Shaken baby syndrome involves diffuse intracranial hemorrhages, usually from violent shaking of the child. The signs, symptoms, and physical findings in shaken baby syndrome vary depending on the amount of trauma to the brain. These range from mild lethargy and irritability to seizures, coma, or death. The long-term brain injuries from shaken baby syndrome are high. Seizures, learning disabilities, and other neurologic handicaps are common. In about 20% of cases, the child dies. While shaken baby syndrome can never be diagnosed by the prehospital professional, it can be suspected in some cases.

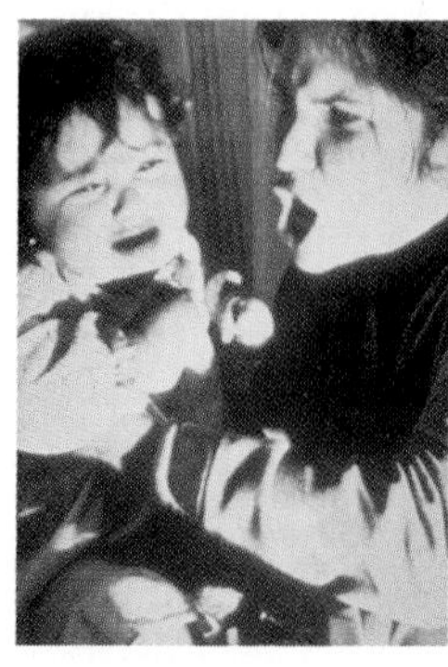

Figure 12-2 Shaken baby syndrome is a distinct medical condition that involves intracranial bleeding from violent shaking.

The transport decision: Stay or go?

After the initial assessment and initiation of medical treatment, consider immediate transport, when appropriate. If a child with suspected maltreatment has a physiologic abnormality or a serious anatomic abnormality, begin transport. If the scene is unsafe for the child or prehospital professional, transport and do additional assessment on the way to the ED.

Additional assessment

After the initial assessment, do an additional assessment if the child is stable and the scene is safe. Take a careful history, using the questions suggested in Table 12-4. *Do not ask questions in an accusatory way or the interview may become useless or even threatening.* Pay close attention to, and take notes on, the caregiver's answers. Evaluate the caregiver's responses to the questions for indications of possible maltreatment. Consider the developmental and age-appropriate capabilities of the child. Make note of inconsistency or evasiveness in providing the details of the event. One of the most important signs of inflicted injury is a discrepant history—a description of an injury that does not match the circumstances (Figure 12-3). Another sign of possible inflicted injury is a caregiver's history that changes.

If the injury is described as an "accident" or as unintentional, attempt to find out how it hap-

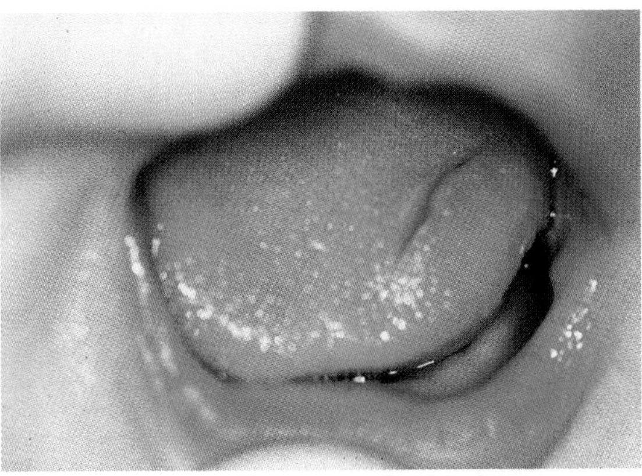

Figure 12-3 A caregiver's history of a child biting his tongue is not believable in an infant who has no teeth. This discrepant history suggests inflicted injury.

Table 12-5 Child Behaviors That May Suggest Maltreatment

Avoids caregiver
Story is different from caregiver's
Constantly seeking food or favors
Does not look at caregiver for assurance
Wary of physical contact

pened. For example, if the caregiver reported that the child fell, determine the distance, the stopping surface, and the initial reactions of the child. This information from the scene may be the most accurate of all for the ED staff, CPS agency, and law enforcement.

Assessing the child's behavior

Although some forms of maltreatment are difficult to detect, there are often clues in the child's behavior. Children will often send messages that suggest maltreatment. These clues may be in the form of "acting out" or behaviors that reflect the child's attempt to cope with or hide the maltreatment. Children tend to act as barometers of the family environment. Behavioral indicators are more difficult to detect and interpret than physical indicators. Table 12-5 lists unusual child behaviors that may suggest maltreatment.

Consider the nature of the supervision and the behavior of the child. To a child, the fear of the unknown may be more frightening than the maltreatment itself. Therefore, any direct questioning of a child may have variable results. The child may also resist assessment. Children often will try to hide their injuries in an attempt to protect the abuser, especially if the perpetrator is a caregiver. The child may feel that the punishment received was deserved or that the perpetrator will be punished or taken from the home if the maltreatment is discovered. The child may believe that he will be removed from the home if the maltreatment is reported. In the same way, other family members may try to protect an abusive caregiver or pretend that the maltreatment is not occurring.

When maltreatment occurs within a home, it does *not* mean that strong bonds do not exist between family members. Fear of severe punishment or breakup of the family unit may prevent the reporting of maltreatment by other members of the household. Sexual abuse is often accompanied by threats of violence or retaliation. The child may be made to feel responsible for the abuse and any corrective and disruptive action. Many children simply do not believe that anyone will believe them or listen to them if they report the abuse.

Often, children will send messages through their behavior that suggest maltreatment .

Sometimes the child's abnormal circumstances or behavior are obvious. The patient may be abandoned or unsupervised, or he may have an inappropriate caregiver—such as another child or an impaired adult. The child may be developmentally delayed or may demonstrate behavior showing distress, such as inconsolability or constant crying.

Assessing the caregiver's behavior

The behavior of the caregiver toward the child and toward the prehospital professional can suggest possible maltreatment. Common characteristics among caregivers of maltreated children are isolation, poor self-concept, immaturity, lack of parenting knowledge, and lack of interpersonal skills. They may not have the skills to interact in a competent way with the prehospital professional. These characteristics may show through in "red flag" behaviors, noted in Table 12-6. However, a caregiver who does not show any of these characteristics and appears pleasant and appropriate may still be maltreating a child.

Even if "red flag" behaviors are detected, the prehospital professional should never confront a caregiver with suspicions of maltreatment because such an approach at the scene will only confuse and delay care and potentially endanger the child. Confrontation may also create a hostile and dangerous situation for the prehospital professional. Instead, note the presence of alcohol or drugs and document quotations from the caregiver that show incompetence or possible misinformation, inconsistency, or evasiveness. Watch interactions among the caregivers and document them if they seem noteworthy.

Blip

Never confront a caregiver with suspicions of maltreatment; such an approach at the scene will only confuse and delay care and potentially endanger the child.

Table 12-6 "Red Flag" Caregiver Behaviors

Aggressiveness or defensiveness when asked about problems concerning their child
Apathy
Bizarre or strange conduct
Little or no concern about the child
Overreaction to child misbehavior
Not forthcoming with events surrounding injury

Detailed physical exam

The prehospital professional will often find suspicious findings in the detailed physical exam of the child. Most maltreated children will not have **acute** injuries or illnesses that affect cardiopulmonary or neurologic physiology. Therefore, the anatomic exam is especially useful. The detailed exam may reveal the suspicious patterns and physical findings of child abuse.

Physical findings that suggest inflicted injury include the following:

- Bruises of different ages located on the face, ears, neck, back, thighs, genitalia, or buttocks (Figure 12-4)
- Facial bruises from slapping (Figure 12-5)

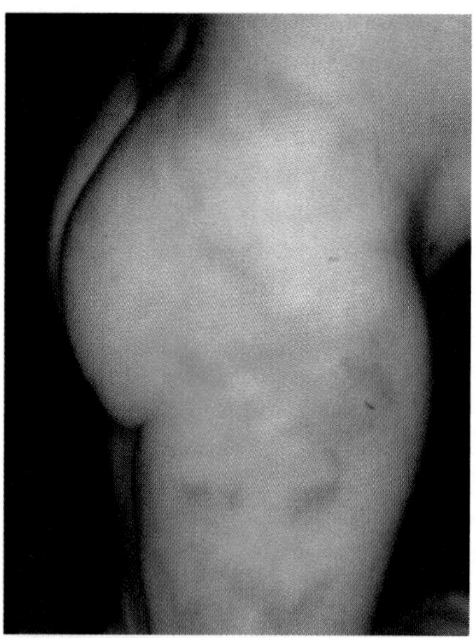

Figure 12-4 Bruises of different ages suggest physical maltreatment.

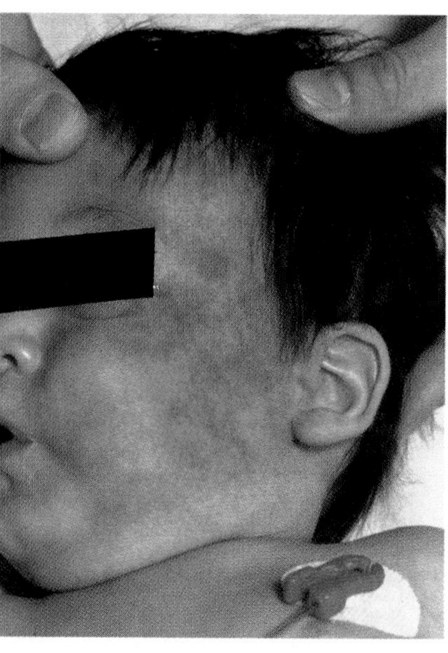

Figure 12-5 The face is a common target for physical abuse.

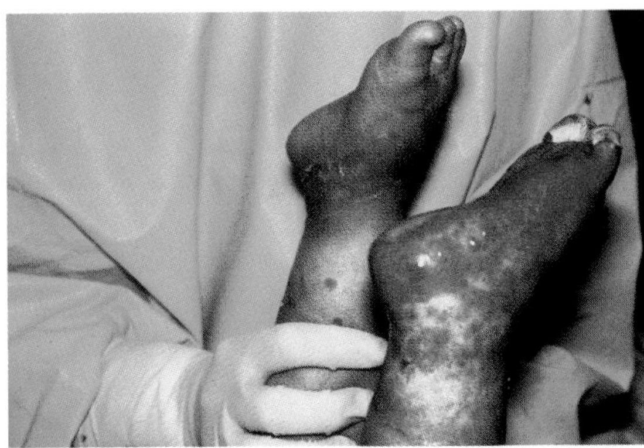

Figure 12-6 Stocking/glove burns of the hands and feet in the infant or toddler are almost always inflicted injuries.

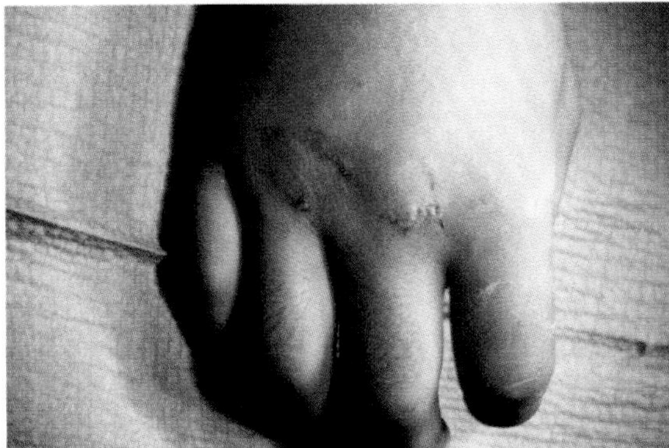

Figure 12-8 A human bite wound has a characteristic appearance.

- Stocking/glove scald burns from immersion into hot water (Figure 12-6)
- "Donut" burns from immersion into a tub or sink (Figure 12-7)
- Human bites (Figure 12-8)
- Cord bruises (Figure 12-9)

An important physical indicator of maltreatment is the presence of bruising in developmentally inappropriate anatomic areas. For example, bruises on the elbows, knees, shins, or forehead are common in preschoolers. They occur after the normal bumps and falls experienced by children of this age. However, these bruises in an infant who is not yet mobile may suggest inflicted injury. The presence of bruises or cuts on a child does not necessarily mean maltreatment. The older the child, the greater his ability to do things that might result in injury. Bruises on the back, thighs,

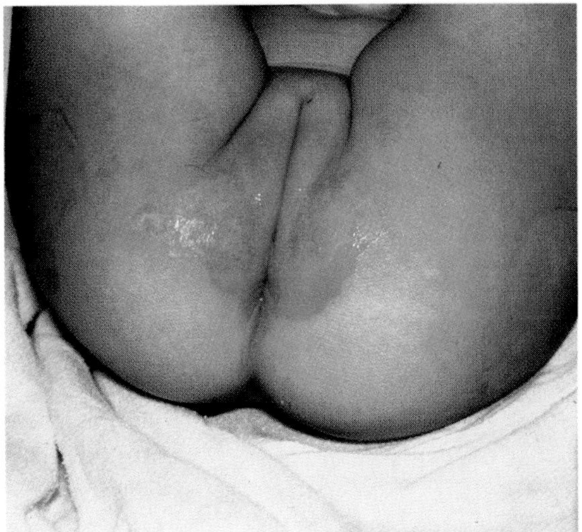

Figure 12-7 A donut burn occurs when a child is held in a hot bath and the area in contact with the cooler porcelain is spared.

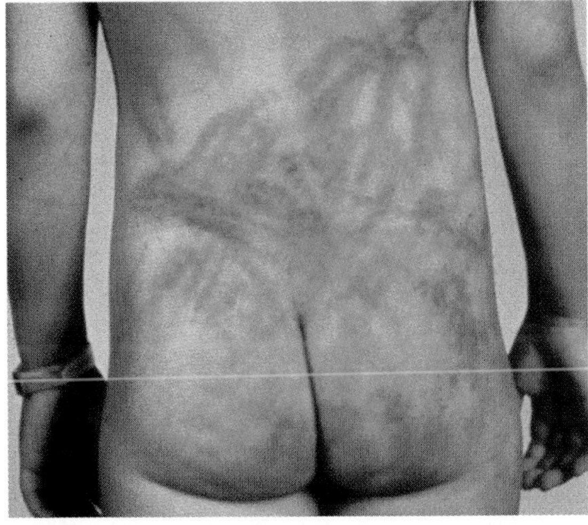

Figure 12-9 Cord bruises are a commonly inflicted injury in children.

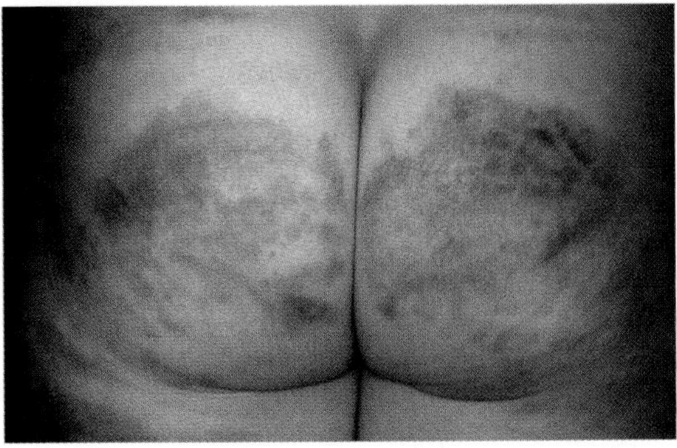

Figure 12-10 Bruises on the buttocks are usually inflicted injuries.

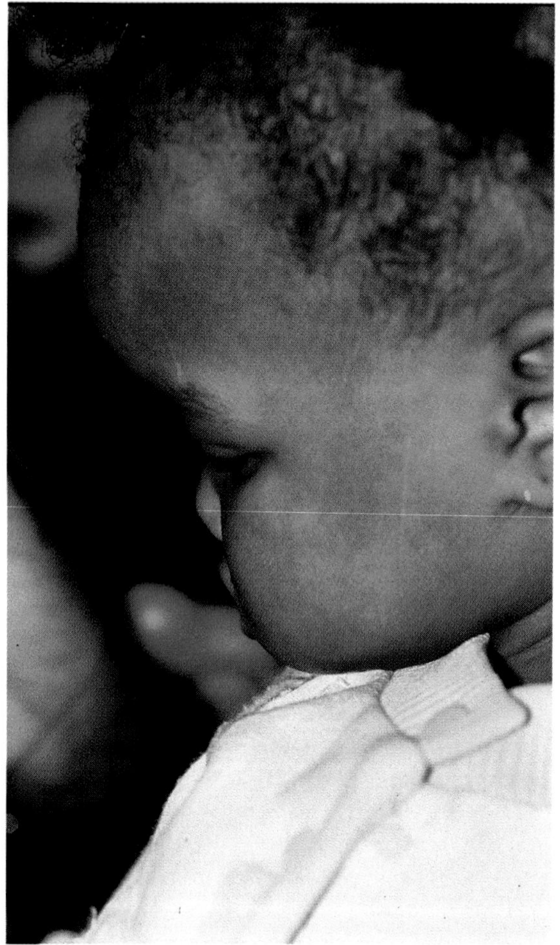

Figure 12-11 Mongolian spots are a defect in pigmentation and can be easily mistaken for bruises.

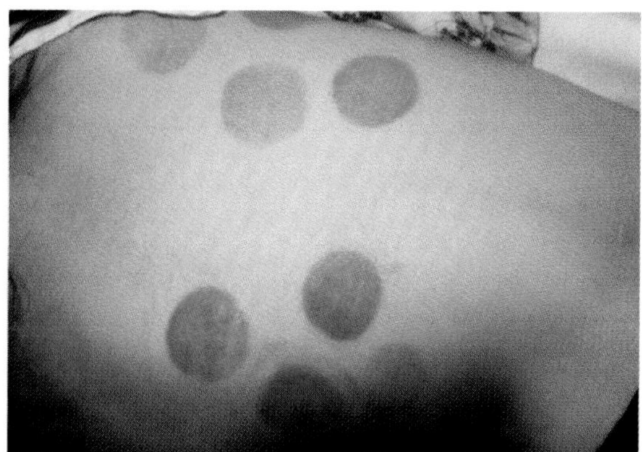

Figure 12-12 Cupping is the cultural practice of placing warm cups on the skin to pull out illness from the body. The red, flat, rounded skin lesions are often more intensely red at the borders.

buttocks, face, or backs of the legs are more likely to be inflicted (Figure 12-10). Suspect any injury in an infant as possibly inflicted.

Deceptive skin signs masquerading as abuse

Sometimes, physical findings may suggest inflicted injury, but are deceptive. For example, mongolian spots on dark-skinned patients can be easily mistaken for bruises (Figure 12-11). These spots are benign patches of abnormal pigmentation. Certain disease states such as leukemia or hemophilia can also produce skin

CASE STUDY 2

911 is called for a "child vomiting." You respond to a private home, where you find two agitated parents, insisting that their child be taken immediately to the hospital. Your assessment shows a 4-year-old girl, dressed, crying, scared, and lying on her bed. She will not engage or make eye contact. There are no abnormal airway sounds or signs of increased work of breathing. Her color is pale. The parents explain that she was previously healthy and suddenly became ill an hour ago.

The focused and detailed exams show an occipital hematoma, chest tenderness, and multiple bruises of varying ages on the legs and buttocks. During the physical exam, the father berates you to hurry up and take the child to the hospital.

What are the red flags for maltreatment?
What are your medical and legal responsibilities?

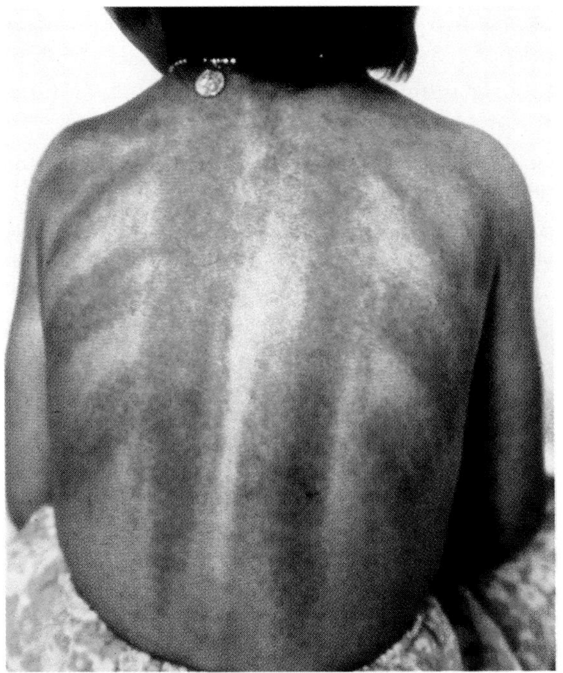

Figure 12-13 Rubbing hot coins, often on the back, produces rounded and oblong red, patchy, flat skin lesions.

findings that appear to be bruises. For these reasons, distinguishing intentional injuries can be difficult, and physical exam is rarely conclusive in the field.

Another benign skin finding that masquerades as abuse is the pattern of lesions produced by several cultural rituals intended to treat illness. The most common of these patterns are associated with Asian practices called **cupping** (Figure 12-12) and **coin rubbing** (Figure 12-13). These superficial lesions have distinctive rounded edges. Caregivers of these children can explain the purpose for such practices—information that can help distinguish these inflicted injuries that are intended to help from inflicted injuries that are intended to harm.

Summary of Assessment in Suspected Maltreatment

The prehospital professional is in a unique position to recognize indicators of possible child maltreatment. The initial principles of field care are the scene size-up, careful physical assessment for physiologic abnormalities and for anatomic patterns of inflicted injuries. Additional assessment and identification of "red flag" child and caregiver behaviors are sometimes extremely important to later maltreatment investigations. The diagnosis of child maltreatment is rarely possible in the field. All cases require a complete investigation by the community CPS agency.

Communication with the Child and Caregivers

Communicate with the child in an age-appropriate manner. When assessing a stable child for whom there is concern of maltreatment, transport the child to the safe environment of the ED for full evaluation as soon as possible.

Communication with the caregiver in suspected maltreatment is a challenging task for the prehospital professional. The prehospital professional may wish to find out "what really happened" or to express anger at the caregiver, but it is important not to do this. Do not accuse. Bring objective information to the ED where there is appropriate medical and CPS intervention. *Remain nonjudgmental.* Caregivers who have maltreated their children may be caught up in a web of **psychosocial** or economic stressors. When confronted, caregivers often respond either defensively or with severe anger.

The on-scene role of law enforcement in suspected child maltreatment is controversial. In most cases, it is prudent to transport a child to the ED for physician and CPS evaluation. Occasionally, the prehospital professional must call law enforcement assistance for protection or to ensure transport.

Sometimes a caregiver may refuse to cooperate in further assessment, decline transport, or attempt to leave. These are significant behaviors to document. Also, the prehospital professional must decide how to proceed when the caregiver refuses care of the child. In most cases, immediately contact law enforcement to assist with the scene. Never

Never attempt to physically restrain a caregiver or a child whose caregiver insists on leaving.

attempt to physically restrain a caregiver or a child whose caregiver insists on leaving. These are law enforcement matters, and the prehospital professional must never endanger himself or his coworkers. Whenever possible, notify medical oversight when the scene situation is confusing but not dangerous. The oversight physician can attempt to speak directly with the caregiver to ask permission for treatment and transport.

Medicolegal Duties

Documentation

When documenting history and physical assessment on the ambulance record, describe objective findings; do not alter the facts or add personal feelings. This approach will be much more useful for physicians treating the child in the ED and for the CPS agency, and will be more powerful as a legal document. The facts will speak for themselves in court. Subjective statements written on the ambulance record may make the document inadmissible in court. For example, write, "palms show 1 centimeter circular burn" instead of "cigarette burn to hand." Use objective, clear, specific terminology. Place in quotation marks any statements from caregivers that the prehospital professional wishes to record (e.g., father states that "child climbed into hot bathtub.")

! Tip

Document physical findings objectively. The facts will speak for themselves in court.

? Controversy

The duty of the prehospital professional to report directly to CPS about suspected child maltreatment is variable and controversial. Ideally, the report should come from ED staff, but some states require an additional report from the prehospital professional.

Duty to report

In some states prehospital professionals must legally report suspicion of child maltreatment as **mandated** reporters. This means they are protected from being liable for false allegations. Therefore, if objective evidence raises the possibility of abuse, there is a moral and legal duty to report it; it does not mean the prehospital professional has absolute proof of inflicted injury. The report then requires an appropriate investigation by the local CPS agency. In other states, the duty of the prehospital professional is to ensure that a report is filed. An agreement from the ED staff to report will usually suffice.

Although no law can forbid the filing of civil or criminal charges, most state laws protect the reporter of suspected child maltreatment from any decision or award in a lawsuit. Any person participating in making a report of suspected child maltreatment or neglect is immune from civil or criminal liability if the reporting is in good faith.

The identity of the person who reports maltreatment is also protected under most state laws. Every report of suspected maltreatment is confidential. Administrative rules that govern the receipt of child maltreatment reports specifically prohibit the CPS worker from identifying the reporter. A report of suspected child maltreatment is not an attempt to harm or punish a family, but an attempt to help the child.

On the other hand, failure to report suspicion of child maltreatment may result in legal action against the prehospital professional. These laws are designed to protect the child. Even in states where they are not legally required to report, the prehospital professionals' important role in identifying possible child maltreatment is widely recognized. In all 50 states, physicians and nurses are mandated reporters. Therefore, if the health professional ignores the written, objective, recorded findings of the prehospital professional, criminal and civil liability against the physician and nurse may result.

Summary of Communication and Medicolegal Duties

When child maltreatment is suspected, the prehospital professional often faces a challenging scene situation. Communication with the child may be difficult, and interactions with the caregiver may be frustrating and sometimes hostile. A professional, nonjudgmental approach is necessary. Document conditions in the environment, the child's and caregiver's behavior, the history, and relevant physical findings that may suggest maltreatment. The prehospital professional has a moral and legal duty to report suspected cases of maltreatment and is protected from legal action for an allegation that proves false.

Anyone making a report of suspected child maltreatment is safe from civil or criminal liability as a result of such action if the reporting is done in good faith.

CASE STUDY 3

911 is notified by a neighbor in a suburb that an infant is injured. On arrival at the scene, you find the mother in her home sobbing and a 7-month-old infant girl crying but lying still. Mother states that the child climbed onto a table and fell off, hurting her leg. The child appears distressed and is poorly consolable by the mother. The child does not want to interact and will not fix gaze. She has no abnormal airway sounds, retractions, or flaring. Her skin is pink. The chest and abdomen are normal. There are a few bruises on the buttocks. Extremity exam shows a tender, swollen right thigh with normal distal perfusion.

What is the red flag in this situation?
What interventions are needed?

CHAPTER RESOURCES

Case Study Answers

See page 205

Except for a bandage on the burn, there is no need for any other immediate medical management. However, transport of the child to the hospital is key. Document all findings carefully and objectively. Your field care record may be a key legal document. No one else may ever see the home conditions as clearly as you. Provide scene observations and share concerns about neglect to the emergency nurse and physician. Ensure that the ED staff will make a report to the CPS agency, or file a report yourself.

See page 214

An inconsistent story to explain obvious injuries in a patient with other old injuries and a volatile scene situation are strong signs of maltreatment. The child is physiologically stable, but transport her to the ED as soon as possible. Exercise a calm response to the father's behavior. Do not confront him with your suspicions. Consider giving him something to do, such as carrying an oxygen tank to the ambulance. Ask the parents to meet you at the hospital. Do additional assessment on the way.

Document carefully the important conditions at the scene, the child's and father's behavior, the history, and the physical evaluation. On arrival at the ED and after patient care responsibility has been transferred, discuss your concerns with the emergency physician and make sure there will be a CPS referral. In some states, you must file a CPS report yourself.

CHAPTER RESOURCES

See page 217

There is an important problem with the mother's history: a 7-month-old does not have the motor skills to climb, so the bruises may be inflicted. Moreover, the abnormal behavior of the child is worrisome. Examination of the leg indicates a potential fracture. This story and assessment suggest maltreatment. After the initial assessment, begin transport because the child's abnormal appearance may indicate a brain injury. Get additional history, and do a focused and detailed exam on the way to the ED.

Splint the leg. Provide analgesia if possible. Document the scene size-up, the child's and mother's behaviors, and the history. Put statements from the mother in quotations. On arrival at the ED, discuss findings with the physician and make sure the CPS agency will be notified, or file the report yourself.

Suggested Educational Resources

1. American Academy of Pediatrics. *A Guide to References and Resources in Child Abuse and Neglect.* Elk Grove Village, IL: American Academy of Pediatrics; 1998.
2. Prevent Child Abuse America. *Child Abuse and Neglect Statistics.* Chicago, IL: Prevent Child Abuse America; April 1998; www.childabuse.org/facts97.html accessed 10/15/99.
3. Wang CT, Daro D. *Current Trends in Child Maltreatment Reporting and Fatalities: The Results of the 1997 Annual Fifty-State Survey.* Chicago, IL: National Committee to Prevent Child Maltreatment; 1998.

Chapter 13

Medicolegal

Learning Objectives

1. Explain the rationale for pediatric-specific protocols, policies, and procedures in EMS systems.
2. Differentiate between direct and indirect medical oversight for pediatric out-of-hospital care.
3. Discuss the doctrine of "implied consent" in the out-of-hospital treatment and transport of a minor.
4. Describe the prehospital professional's responsibilities when a child or guardian refuses transport or care.
5. Decide how to manage situations involving legal considerations presented in case studies.

You are called to a high school to manage a teenager with a possible overdose. The school nurse introduces you to a distraught but otherwise normal 15-year-old girl, who was seen taking a large number of Tylenol tablets 2 hours ago after a fight with her boyfriend. She now denies any ingestion and refuses care or transport.

What rights does the teenager have to refuse care and transport?
What methods of persuasion can you use?

Considerations

Introduction

An integrated EMS-EMSC continuum requires both specific clinical services for children and operational systems to organize, monitor, and improve such services. Most of this book addresses how to provide clinical care to children effectively and safely in the out-of-hospital setting. This chapter discusses operations—the essential but less dramatic side of the EMS-EMSC continuum. Operations are the administrative backbone of the EMS system. They are the policies, procedures, and protocols that embody the medicolegal authority and medical oversight for field pediatric practices and provide the written directives to tell the prehospital professional what to do.

Rationale for Protocols, Policies, and Procedures

The goal of operations is to manage day-to-day field care with performance standards that have been set up by the EMS system. Performance standards are reflected in education and training, as well as in protocols, policies, and procedures. Protocols outline specific treatment guidelines for common illnesses and injuries. **Policies** and **procedures** reflect the **medicolegal** expectations of the community for out-of-hospital care, quality management, and system accountability. These forms of regulation consist of clear, written directives to guide prehospital professionals. Protecting children's needs requires constant surveillance of EMS operations. Because of this, pediatric-specific protocols, policies, and procedures are necessary tools for a comprehensive EMS system.

> **! Tip**
>
> Protocols outline specific clinical treatment guidelines for common illness and injury conditions.

State statutes and a state EMS authority usually have basic requirements for local EMS systems, provide a guide for regulation, and establish EMT scope of practice. Local policies, procedures, and protocols may be very different from one EMS system to the next. **Mutual aid agreements** between bordering geographic areas are especially useful for EMS-EMSC systems because resources, equipment, and personnel for specialized care are not distributed evenly. Indeed, specialized trauma care and critical care centers for children are usually only available at major hospitals in large urban areas; in some states, no specialized centers exist for children at all.

Definitions

Protocols define field treatments, or the order and type of medical interventions for specific illness and injury conditions. They give the appropriate pharmacologic options, including drug doses, routes of delivery, and methods of administration. Most EMS systems have out-of-hospital pediatric advanced life support (ALS) illness and trauma treatment protocols (Figure 13-1). Appropriate treatment protocols for out-of-hospital basic life support (BLS) personnel, as well as for first responders and other non-ALS personnel, are also important to comprehensive EMS systems, but are not yet widely available.

Policies are medicolegal operational standards to guide prehospital professionals. They are intended to help with decision making in difficult or legally sensitive pediatric field situations such as:

- consent for care or transport
- refusals
- death in the field
- triage
- hospital destination
- child maltreatment

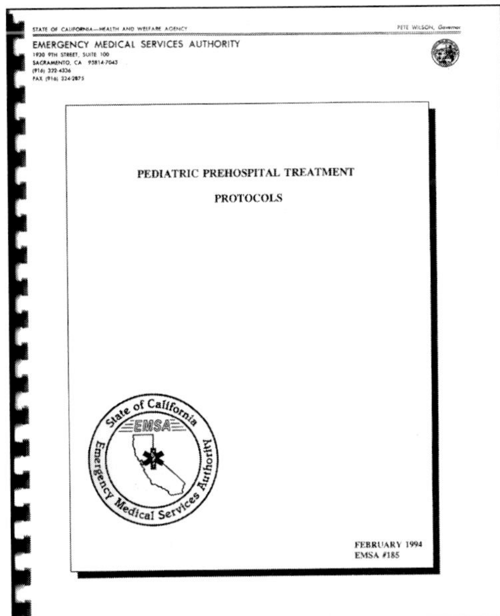
STATE OF CALIFORNIA—HEALTH AND WELFARE AGENCY PETE WILSON, Governor

EMERGENCY MEDICAL SERVICES AUTHORITY
1930 9TH STREET, SUITE 100
SACRAMENTO, CA 95814-7043
(916) 322-4336
FAX (916) 324-2875

PEDIATRIC PREHOSPITAL TREATMENT

PROTOCOLS

State of California EMSA Emergency Medical Services Authority

FEBRUARY 1994
EMSA #185

Figure 13-1 A policies and procedures book outlines EMS field treatments for children.

Policies usually explain how the prehospital professional should handle certain situations, not what to do medically. Procedures describe the sequence of actions in medical protocols or in medicological policies.

Medical oversight is the medicolegal physician support for the prehospital professional's practice. It is how physicians and EMS officials supervise field practice. Medical oversight includes direct and indirect methods.

Medical oversight for pediatrics

> **! Tip**
>
> **Policies and procedures reflect the medicolegal expectations of the community for out-of-hospital care, quality management, and system accountability.**

On-line (direct) medical oversight

On-line or **direct medical oversight** refers to the communication between the prehospital professional and medical oversight by telephone or radio. This form of oversight is required by some local EMS systems for many or all cases involving children under 18 years of age (Figure 13-2) because decisions about pediatric ALS treatment (e.g., IVs, drug routes, and doses), triage, scene control, and transport are often difficult. Table 13-1 lists possible problems or issues in pediatric field practice that often need on-line physician input or direct medical oversight, with examples of specific field scenarios.

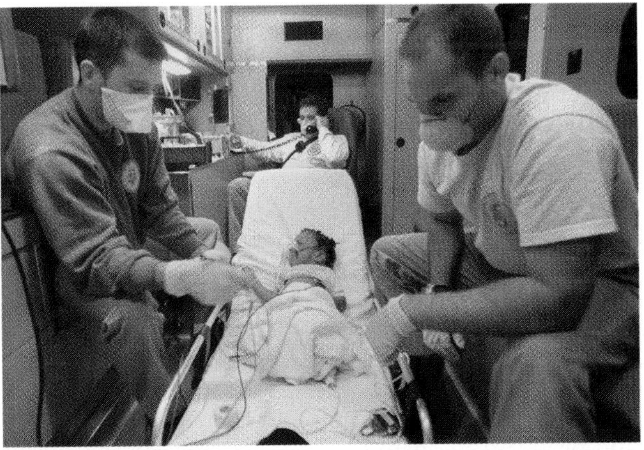

Figure 13-2 Direct medical oversight can be extremely helpful when the prehospital professional confronts medical and legal problems with children.

Table 13-1 Possible Pediatric Issues Needing Direct Medical Oversight

Pediatric Issue	Possible Scenario
Type of field treatment	IV or rectal diazepam for status epilepticus
Hospital destination	Appropriate ED for infant trauma patient
Specialized scene control	Hazardous materials exposure in school
Transport	Requirement for ED care after minor poisoning

Off-line (indirect) medical oversight

Off-line or **indirect medical oversight** involves both prospective and retrospective medical oversight. Prospective indirect oversight requires planning for expected educational and operational requirements within the prehospital professional's scope of practice. Retrospective indirect oversight requires setting up specific ways to review individual and overall system performance against expectations or standards of care. It provides individual and system accountability and ensures appropiate care. Pediatric care within EMS requires unique applications of indirect medical oversight.

Table 13-2 gives common examples of how indirect oversight sets up and monitors different types of policies, procedures, and protocols for children.

Table 13-2 Indirect Medical Oversight

Examples of Prospective Oversight
Pediatric BLS and ALS ambulance equipment/drugs
Pediatric out-of-hospital treatment protocols
Skills training Airway foreign body removal Endotracheal intubation IO needle insertion Rectal diazepam
Pediatric-specific policies Hospital destination Triage Transport Refusal of care Suspected SIDS Maltreatment
Examples of Retrospective Oversight
Review of compliance with treatment, triage, and transport policies
Review of success, failure, and complications of pediatric procedures and patient outcomes
Epidemiologic data on types of pediatric illness and injury
Review of ED or hospital capabilities for the care of children

Summary of Rationale for Protocols, Policies, and Procedures

Pediatric-specific guidelines for operations in EMS systems—as defined in protocols, policies, and procedures—help set standards for care of children that recognize differences from adults. Medical oversight is especially important in out-of-hospital services to families and children because of the unusual circumstances that often arise medically and legally.

Treatment Protocols

Table 13-3 lists some common EMS pediatric treatment protocols. These vary among states and EMS regions, but they are becoming more similar as EMSC becomes more uniformly implemented nationwide.

Table 13-3 Examples of Pediatric Treatment Protocols

Airway obstruction
Allergic reaction/anaphylaxis
Altered level of consciousness
Bradycardia
Burns
Cardiopulmonary arrest
Hypoperfusion or shock
Neonatal resuscitation
Seizures
Respiratory distress
Tachycardia
Toxic exposures
Trauma

Table 13-4 Pediatric Out-of-Hospital Policies and Procedures

Consent
Refusal of care or transport
Physician on scene
Resuscitation
Sudden infant death syndrome
Hospital destination
Child maltreatment
Sexual assault

Pediatric Policies and Procedures

Table 13-4 lists EMS policies and procedures that have the most significance for pediatrics. The field policies with the most frequent application to pediatric care are **consent**, refusal of care or transport, hospital destination, and child maltreatment.

Consent

If there is one overriding legal principle that governs medical care, it is the requirement for consent. Without the individual's consent no one may be touched, treated, or transported. **Minors** (children under 18 years old), however, present a special problem because by law they do not have the legal ability to give consent. Therefore, in most states, a parent or legal guardian must give consent before a minor can be medically treated or transported. If, however, there is a life- or limb-threatening pediatric emergency in a location where there is no legal guardian present, the prehospital professional may proceed with the appropriate medical treatment and then transport, based on the **emergency exception rule**.

The emergency exception rule is more commonly known as the doctrine of **implied consent**. For minors, this doctrine means that if a medical emergency is possibly serious and there is no way to get consent from the child's legal guardian, then the prehospital professional can presume consent and proceed with appropriate treatment and transport. This presumption is based on the concept that if the legal guardian knew the possible severity of the emergency she would consent to medical treatment of the child. Any time a minor is treated without consent, the burden of proof that the

Never withhold medically necessary treatment of a minor because of absence of a legal guardian.

Controversy

The most frequent medicolegal controversy in pediatric out-of-hospital care is consent. The authority of the prehospital professional to act is unclear in many emergency situations involving children. EMS systems vary in the level of authority they allow their prehospital professionals in such cases.

emergency actions were necessary falls on the prehospital professional—who must clearly document on the child's record the nature of the medical emergency and the reason the minor required immediate treatment and/or transport.

If possible, contact on-line medical oversight for assistance when consent is unclear or if there is a confrontation on scene. Before transporting a minor, if the guardian is unavailable and cannot be notified, give information about the destination ED to the most responsible person on scene, to be passed on to the legal guardians.

! Tip

Get police assistance when an impaired or intoxicated guardian refuses care or transport of an ill or injured child.

Never confront the caregiver with accusations, moral judgments, or threats.

Refusal of care or transport

Guardian refusal

A special situation occurs when the prehospital professional is faced with a child or a legal guardian who refuses care or transport. The child's legal guardian may legally refuse care if she is alert, oriented, and mentally competent. If the child has a life- or limb-threatening condition and the guardian refuses care or transport, first notify medical oversight, if possible, so that the physician can speak directly to the legal guardian.

If you believe a minor has a life- or limb-threatening emergency and the legal guardian is refusing to give consent for medical treatment even after physician contact, notify the police. The prehospital professional alone cannot force the guardian to consent to medical care and may need to withhold treatment and transport.

In situations where the guardian is intoxicated or otherwise impaired, the approach will depend on local EMS policy. When a legal guardian suffers from diminished judgment, law enforcement officers may place a minor in **temporary protective custody**. If necessary, have medical oversight speak to law enforcement officers to explain the need for treatment and transport.

While temporary protective custody may allow the prehospital professional to transport a minor to a medical facility for purposes of medical evaluation, it does not give the prehospital professional the right medically to treat a minor. Only when there is a serious medical emergency can a prehospital professional medically treat without consent.

Never confront the caregiver with accusations, moral judgments, or threats when difficult scene circumstances develop. This approach will only aggravate the situation and will not help the child.

CASE STUDY 2

You respond to the scene of a chaotic street carnival. A bystander called 911 because a 15-month-old girl has been inadvertently burned by a street performer. You find a crying but alert child with extensive thermal burns over her face, chest, and legs. The child has no abnormal airway sounds, retractions, or flaring. Circulation to skin is normal. The father is grossly intoxicated and insists that the child does not need medical care.

Can the father withhold consent?

What is the best approach to ensure appropriate care of the child?

Child refusal

Children who are either legally emancipated or mature may give consent for medical treatment and transport. These laws vary from state to state. In most states, **emancipated minors** are over 14 years old and have been formally declared adults by the court. **Mature minors** do not have the formal legal status of emancipated minors, but have similar legal characteristics: married, pregnant, on active-duty status in the armed service, or 15 years or older and living separate and apart from their guardians. In most states, these children have the legal rights to give consent for treatment or to refuse it. Table 13-5 lists the legal circumstances in which pediatric patients can give or refuse consent for medical care and transport.

If a child is not an emancipated or a mature minor, then she has no legal capacity either to give consent or to refuse medical care. If such a child says she refuses medical care or transport, the statement has no legal authority.

There are many unclear or confusing issues facing the prehospital professional in consent and refusal cases. Every case needs careful scene management, notification of medical oversight if available, and accurate documentation in the prehospital record. Regardless of whether the child has the right legally to give or withhold consent, it is always prudent to try to get the child's agreement to treat and transport (Figure 13-3). This approach respects the personal dignity and self-determination of the patient and minimizes confrontation.

A child cannot legally refuse care or transport.

Local EMS policy on consent should clearly define the following:

- who can refuse ambulance transport, based on state law
- the process for field evaluation, consultation, and documentation
- the method for enlisting police and medical oversight when the patient or guardian is dangerous and refuses transport, and when a child has a life-threatening problem and the guardian is refusing transport

Table 13-5 Pediatric Patients Able to Refuse Care and Transport

Patient has a competent legal guardian on scene who is refusing to consent OR Patient is an emancipated minor or a mature minor, which gives her the right to grant or refuse consent
Characteristics of emancipated or mature minors:
Married
Pregnant
Active-duty status in the armed service
15 years or older, living separate and apart from parent
14 years or older and emancipated by declaration of Superior Court
AND patient is not on a psychiatric hold
AND patient demonstrates competency to refuse

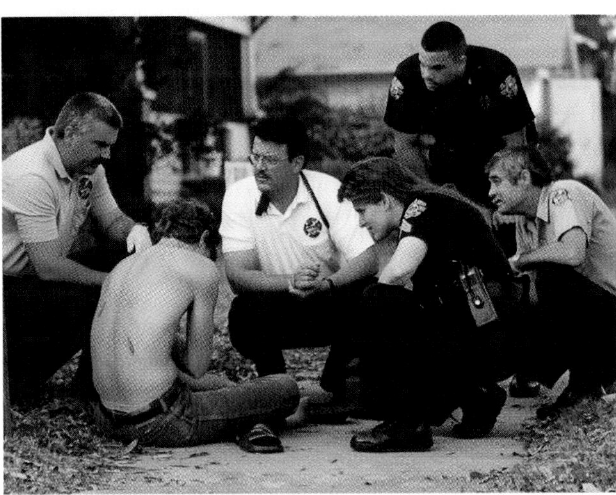

Figure 13-3 Attempt to get consent with adolescents who do not want to go to the ED.

Summary of consent

Laws strictly protect the rights of patients to accept or reject medical care. Children pose special problems in interpretation of consent when an ambulance is summoned and a guardian is not present or is present but possibly unfit. EMS systems should provide clear protocols based on state law to guide the prehospital professional and/or medical oversight.

Physician on scene

Because all out-of-hospital care happens under the authority of EMS medical oversight, prehospital professionals cannot usually carry out orders from other physicians, even the patient's private physician, unless specifically authorized by medical oversight or the medical director of the EMS agency. This policy is often controversial. Medical oversight may either allow the on-scene physician to assist prehospital professionals or transfer total authority to the on-scene physician. If the on-scene physician takes responsibility for treatment, she must usually accompany the child to the ED.

! Tip

Every case of unclear consent or refusal needs careful scene management, notification of medical oversight if available, and accurate documentation in the prehospital record.

Resuscitation

Sometimes resuscitation attempts for children in cardiopulmonary arrest are ineffective or unnecessary, as discussed in Chapter 11 on SIDS and death of a child. Resuscitation policy should define circumstances when cardiopulmonary resuscitation must be initiated, when it may be withheld, and when it may be stopped. For pediatric cases, the policy must take a medically conservative approach, but allow appropriate withholding of resuscitation to focus on grief management and family interactions.

Suspected sudden infant death syndrome (SIDS)

The actions of the prehospital professional are especially important to caregivers of SIDS victims and may have a big influence on grief responses and psychological and social adjustments. EMS systems should have, as part of educational and training requirements for field personnel, a formal training program for SIDS. Local EMS procedure should clearly establish the responsibility of the prehospital professional at death scenes regarding care of the body, notification of coroner, and interaction with caregivers.

Hospital destination

The hospital destination policy for children must define the following components:

1. Field triage criteria (which patients with what conditions go where)
2. Designated receiving hospitals
3. Specialized pediatric centers

Ideally, integrated EMS-EMSC systems have pediatric standards for all EDs. Some EMS systems may also have specialized pediatric centers (general trauma centers with pediatric capability, pediatric critical care centers, or pediatric trauma centers). These specialized centers are also part of the overall community hospital configuration and may be primary receiving facilities for certain pediatric patients.

For a child, the appropriate ED may be different from the ED appropriate for an adult. In some EMS systems, a child may meet multiple special care criteria (for example, the severely burned patient may meet ED, trauma, and burn center triage criteria). The destination policy must give prioritization for such cases as part of prospective indirect medical oversight, or establish that medical oversight will make all complex triage decisions. In most cases, take the child to the ED the legal guardian chooses, unless hospital destination policy requires an alternative facility.

Child maltreatment

Education of prehospital professionals in identifying possible maltreatment is an essential component of initial education and continuing medical education in pediatrics, as outlined in

Chapter 12. A procedure for reporting suspected cases of maltreatment and for appropriate patient transport to an ED is an important component of every EMS system.

Sexual assault

This policy should ensure that sexual assault victims are initially evaluated in a careful, knowledgeable, and respectful way by prehospital professionals and that they are transported to an ED where there are experienced clinicians, with appropriate **ancillary** and follow-up services. This service requires a high level of pediatric expertise in the ED.

If the on-scene physician takes authority, she must usually go along with the child to the ED.

? Controversy

The role of the child's private physician in scene care of a child with an emergency is controversial. The prehospital professional must abide by local EMS system policy, but the precise limitations in providing assistance to an on-scene physician are sometimes unclear. Always act in the best interests of the child when the policy is confusing.

Summary of Pediatric Policies and Procedures

EMS systems should provide clear guidelines for common problems involving children. Issues requiring direction through policy or medical oversight (or both) include physician on scene, resuscitation, suspected SIDS, hospital destination, maltreatment, and sexual assault.

CASE STUDY 3

You are called to a pediatrician's office because a 12-month-old male is in respiratory distress. The infant appears lethargic and fatigued. There is audible wheezing with retractions and flaring. Circulation to skin is normal. You administer blow-by oxygen and begin albuterol by a handheld nebulizer placed in the bottom of a cup. The pediatrician insists that the child be taken to a hospital 20 miles away, which is closest to the family's home, rather than to the nearest ED.

Can the private physician direct the prehospital professional to a hospital destination out of area?

What is the best approach to care of the infant?

CHAPTER RESOURCES

Case Study Answers

See page 221

Unless a legal guardian gives consent to treat and transport the child, this is a difficult scene situation. There are three issues that may provide the legal authority to treat and transport. First, the child's guardian may have given the school a signed release for consent, and that would permit you to treat and transport. Second, if the ingestion of Tylenol may be lethal, this would be a life-threatening situation where the doctrine of implied consent might apply. Last, taking the Tylenol may be construed as attempted suicide and, in most states, a suicidal person may be transported to a medical facility for psychiatric evaluation against her will.

As a practical matter, respect the girl's dignity but be firm that transport to an ED is necessary. Try to establish rapport and do not be judgmental. If a friend or counselor is available, try to get assistance in persuading the teenager to agree to care and transport.

See page 226

Usually, a competent father can legally withhold consent for care and treatment of his child. However, this impaired guardian may not be able to refuse.

First, try to get the father to consent to care and transport. Second, call medical oversight to allow direct communication from the physician to the father. Next, if these gentle approaches fail, call the police for assistance. In most cases, the police will either get the father to consent or they will take temporary custody and direct you to transport the patient to an ED for evaluation. If, while examining the patient, you believe that the patient is suffering from a life-threatening emergency, and can support that conclusion in documentation, then treat the patient under the doctrine of implied consent.

CHAPTER RESOURCES

See page 229

You must follow the hospital destination policy of your EMS system. A private physician is not a legal source of medical oversight to prehospital professionals. In most cases, the child must be transported to the closest ED approved to care for children.

Whenever there is a physician on scene, contact medical oversight for guidance and direct consultation between physicians. In some EMS regions, if the pediatrician goes with the child in the ambulance, medical oversight may allow transport to an ED that is not the closest facility.

Suggested Educational Resources

1. Barkin RM. Pediatrics in the Emergency Medicine Services System. *Pediatr Emerg Care.* 1990;6:72–77.
2. Dieckmann RA, ed. *Pediatric Emergency Care Systems. Planning and Management.* Baltimore, MD: Williams & Wilkins; 1992.
3. Roush WR, ed. *Principles of EMS Systems.* Dallas, TX: American College of Emergency Physicians; 1994.
4. Seidel JS, Henderson DP, eds. *Emergency Medical Services for Children: A Report to the Nation.* Washington, DC: National Center for Education in Maternal Health; 1991.
5. Selbst SM. Medical Legal Issues in Prehospital Pediatric Emergency Care. *Pediatr Emerg Care.* 1998;4(4):276–78.
6. Selbst SM, Korin JB. The Medical Record. In: *Preventing Malpractice Lawsuits in Pediatric Emergency Medicine.* Dallas, TX: American College of Emergency Physicians; 1999; 46–53.

Procedures

Radio Reporting

Introduction

Gathering and organizing pertinent information about children to report to other prehospital professionals, medical oversight, and the receiving ED requires pediatric terms. Clear, concise communication helps ensure an orderly flow of out-of-hospital tasks: describing children and their clinical problems accurately to medical oversight personnel; informing the receiving ED personnel about incoming patients; and making an effective transfer of information about the patient's assessment and care. Each EMS region has unique requirements for radio reporting to medical oversight and to the receiving ED. Sometimes, the reporting is not by radio, but via telephone or another form of real-time communication. The local EMS agency should have a reporting or communications protocol that specifically addresses on-line medical oversight and ED notification requirements for children.

In addition to the spoken presentation and format for radio reporting, another important part of reporting is documentation. Each EMS agency has its own form that tells not only the clinical facts but also the necessary information for billing and for detailed incident or system analysis.

Rationale

A logical and descriptive format for presentation of key information about ill or injured children is essential for everyday field practice. It promotes the cost-efficient use of communications equipment and time on local airwaves. Proper radio reporting also integrates efforts from all emergency care professionals—prehospital professionals, nurses, and doctors—and helps ensure that vital data is transmitted completely and concisely. Pediatric-specific reporting techniques will assist appropriate age-related modifications in assessment, treatment, triage, and transport.

Preparation

The prehospital professional should prepare for and practice radio reporting about children. It is helpful to have a radio reporting format that is agreed on by the EMS agency, medical oversight, and the ambulance providers. The desired format can be printed on small pads as a checklist. This may help in the flow and understanding of patient information during situations when the prehospital professional has multiple tasks and when the environment or equipment make communicating difficult. Such notes may be useful not only during transport but also when transferring care at the ED.

Indication

Use good radio reporting procedure in any radio, telephone, facsimile (fax), personal, or other communication with medical oversight, the receiving ED, or other prehospital providers regarding on-scene or inbound pediatric emergency patients (**Figure P1-1**). Good reporting technique is also indicated for chart documentation.

Contraindication

The only relative contraindication to appropriate radio reporting is the child with a physiologic abnormality requiring constant hands-on care. This situation may make it difficult for the prehospital professional to communicate fully with a receiving ED or medical oversight while on the way to the ED. In most cases, a coworker, such as a partner, can assist with notifying the ED that a distressed child is on the way, although complete reporting of patient assessment, treatment, and response to treatment may not be possible. There are no contraindications to accurate reporting through chart documentation.

Equipment

Equipment requirements vary depending on the EMS system. Equipment may include telecommunications equipment, computerized real-time data transmission, or video. The patient care record is essential, as are other assessment worksheets in some EMS systems.

Possible Complications

1

Using incorrect, deceptive, or unclear terminology, or failing to distinguish the pediatric report from the more frequent adult-oriented report, may confuse medical oversight and delay preparation by the receiving ED.

Do not give long radio reports when there is a distressed child in the ambulance.

! Tip

Report the patient's assessment using the PAT.

? Controversy

Using the PAT as the basis for reporting, especially in an adult-oriented EMS system, may confuse nurses and doctors if they are not educated in the use of the PAT for describing children. Out-of-hospital and in-hospital personnel must all be familiar with the PAT as an assessment tool for communication about children.

Procedure

1. State child's age, gender, and estimated body weight. Using the patient's name is generally not pertinent to treatment, triage, or transport, so do not use names in the radio report. Emergency medical channels are easily monitored, and omitting the patient's name protects her identity and medical confidentiality.
2. Give the child's chief complaint.
3. Provide in one sentence the mechanism of injury or history of illness, and state pertinent past medical history (usually none or brief).
4. Summarize the assessment and establish the level of severity and urgency for treatment using the Pediatric Assessment Triangle (PAT). Address all three elements of the triangle, using appropriate descriptive words and terms, as listed in Table P1-1.

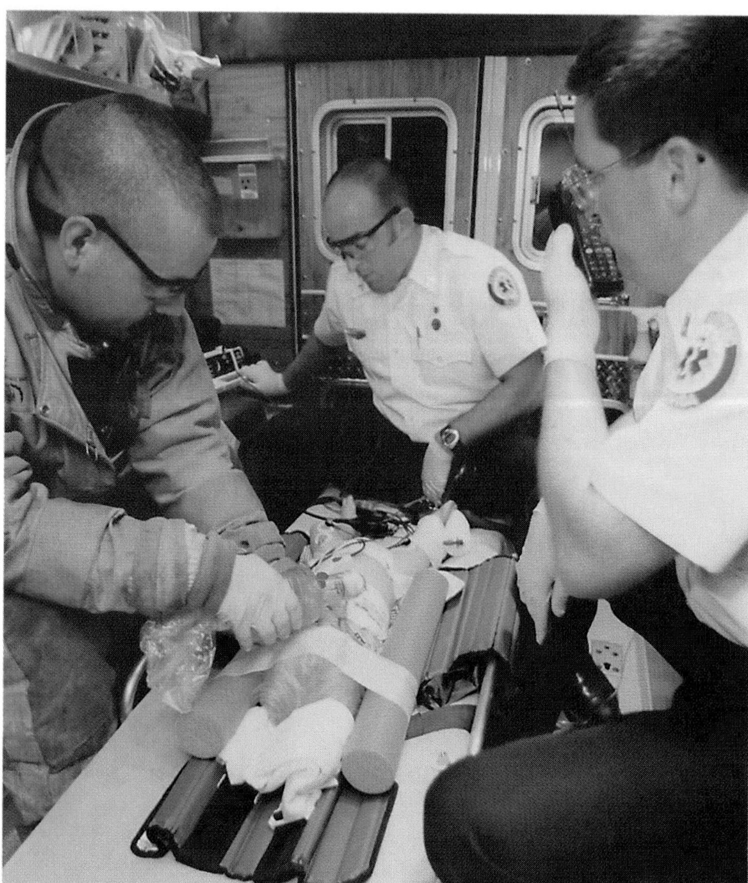

Figure P1-1 Use pediatric-specific reporting in any radio, telephone, fax, or other communications with medical oversight, the receiving ED, or with other prehospital professionals.

Table P1-1 Examples of Pediatric-Specific Terminology for PAT

Appearance (use TICLS mnemonic to recall individual features)
Tone Active, vigorous, good muscle tone Limp, listless, motionless, will not sit or walk **Interactiveness** Alert, interactive, attentive, playful Restless, agitated, screaming **Consolability** Consolable or distractible by caregiver, comfortable Cannot be consoled **Look/Gaze** Fixes gaze, maintains good eye contact Will not engage or make eye contact **Speech/Cry** Strong cry, normal speech Weak cry, cannot speak
Work of breathing
Apneic Abnormal positioning (sniffing position, tripoding) Abnormal airway sounds (snoring, stridor, wheezing, grunting) Retractions (supraclavicular, intercostal, subxiphoid) Nasal flaring
Circulation to skin
Pink, good color Mottled, dusky Pale Cyanotic

Avoid focusing on vital signs.

Do not contact the receiving ED or medical oversight until you are prepared to give accurate patient information.

5. Report any abnormalities in the ABCDEs. Avoid focusing on vital signs.
6. State treatment and response, using the PAT.
7. Estimate time of arrival and state the proposed receiving ED.
8. Request agreement from medical oversight with interventions and request additional orders as per local EMS protocol.
9. Repeat medical oversight orders to confirm understanding.
10. Table P1-2 is a sample pediatric reporting template.

Table P1-2 Sample Pediatric Reporting Template

We are [on scene] or [en route to (name of ED)] with a [state age in days, weeks, months, or years as appropriate] [state boy or girl] patient weighing [state approximate body weight in kilograms].		
CC	The patient's chief complaint is [state chief complaint in one or two words].	
HPI	State brief history of present illness/injury.	
PMH	State brief, pertinent, medical history (*note:* usually there is none).	
PAT	Appearance	Describe the patient's appearance using descriptive terms.*
	Work of breathing	Describe the work of breathing using descriptive terms.
	Circulation to skin	Describe the circulation to skin using descriptive terms.
INITIAL ABCDEs ASSESSMENT	Summarize key findings from the ABCDEs. Avoid emphasis on vital signs.	
TX	Report the treatment and the patient's response. Use these elements as the basis for ongoing assessment: the PAT, the ABCDEs, repeating vital signs in children over 3 years of age, and reassessing of positive anatomic findings in distressed children who have received the focused and detailed exams.	
ETA	Our ETA to [state receiving ED] is _____ minutes. Do you have any advice or questions? [Request additional orders as per local protocol at this point.]	

*See Table P1-1 for examples of pediatric-specific descriptive terminology.

Oxygen Delivery

Introduction

Hypoxia in the infant or child causes cardiopulmonary distress and may lead to organ failure. Careful assessment of the child's cardiopulmonary status includes standard physical assessment techniques and pulse oximetry. A normal pulse oximetry reading is 95% or greater. A pulse oximetry value of less than 95% oxygen saturation on room air is an indication for supplemental oxygen. A value less than 90% with the child on 100% oxygen by nonrebreathing mask is also an indication for ventilatory support. Hypoxia is usually easy to treat. Rapid intervention may slow or reverse cardiopulmonary distress or failure and avoid the need for ventilatory support. While respiratory disease is usually the cause of hypoxia in children, other conditions such as hypovolemic shock, severe poisonings, or seizures may also produce hypoxia from ischemia or inadequate ventilation.

There are different procedures for giving oxygen to children that vary the amount of actual oxygen supplementation. Use an oxygen delivery technique that matches the child's clinical condition, age, and need for oxygen. For example, give oxygen by nasal cannula or simple mask to the child in no or mild distress who has an open airway. Give oxygen via nonrebreathing mask or BVM to the child with moderate to severe respiratory distress. Rarely, a critical child requires endotracheal intubation for positive pressure ventilation and oxygen administration. When supplemental oxygen does not improve the child's condition, consider other complicating factors, such as a pulmonary disorder (inadequate gas exchange such as pneumonia), a circulatory disorder (inadequate blood flow such as hypovolemic shock), or, rarely, a toxicologic disorder (such as carbon monoxide poisoning).

Be creative in delivering oxygen to young children. Under some circumstances, giving blow-by oxygen may avoid agitating the child and increasing his distress.

Rationale

A child's immature anatomy and physiology make respiratory distress and failure common pediatric emergencies. When apnea or hypoventilation occur, hypoxia develops quickly. Therefore, give oxygen to any child with clinical signs of cardiopulmonary distress or failure, or with a history suggesting possible abnormalities in gas exchange. Children seldom have a condition where excess oxygen turns off their respiratory drive, so it is better to overtreat with oxygen than to undertreat.

Indications

- Respiratory distress
- Pulse oximetry less than 95% on room air
- Respiratory failure
- Partial upper-airway obstruction
- Partial lower-airway obstruction
- Worsening of chronic lung disease
- Status epilepticus
- Overdose
- Shock from any cause
- Multiple trauma
- Any condition possibly causing decreased oxygen delivery to tissues
- Smoke inhalation
- Carbon monoxide poisoning

Contraindications

There are few absolute contraindications to oxygen delivery to a child who may be hypoxic. There are, however, rare relative contraindications to certain oxygen delivery techniques that do not match the child's clinical condition. For example, oxygen delivery by nonrebreathing mask may be relatively contraindicated in a child with a mild worsening of chronic lung disease (e.g., cystic fibrosis, bronchopulmonary dysplasia) who depends on hypoxia for ventilatory drive. Oxygen has proper doses and routes of administration for maximum benefit, minimum toxicity, optimal feasibility, and reasonable cost.

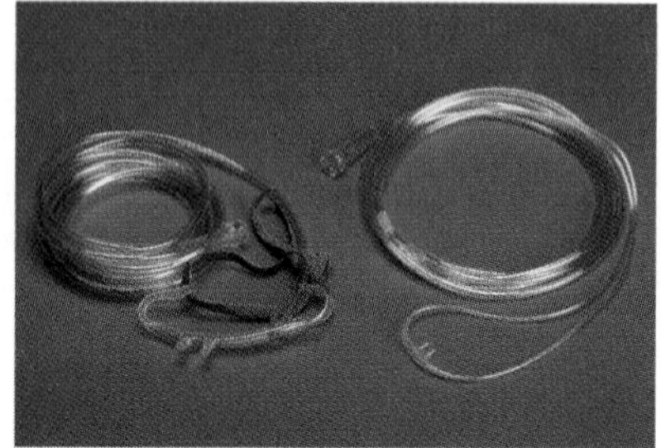

Figure P2-1 Infant and pediatric nasal cannula

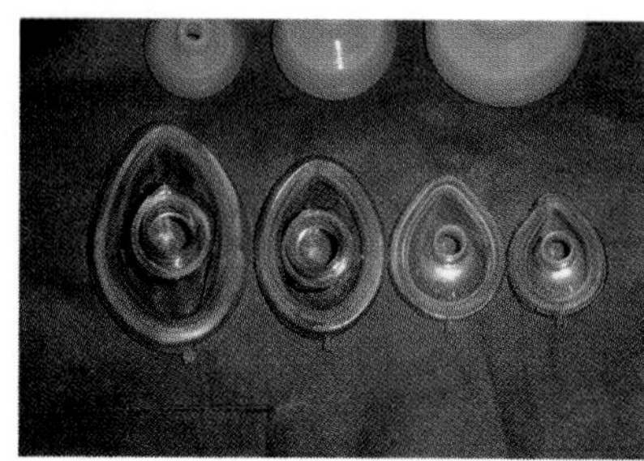

Figure P2-2 Pediatric mask sizes

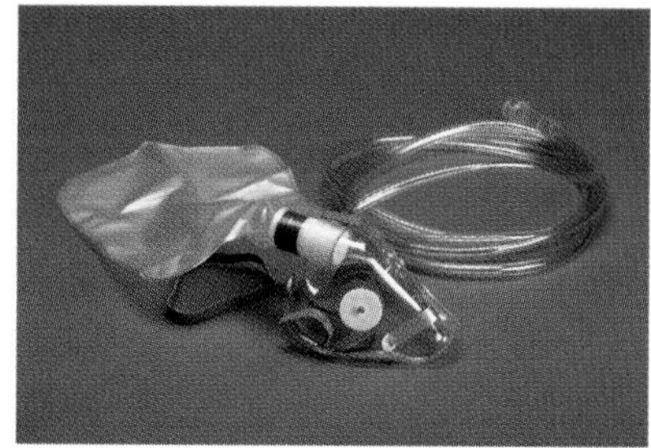

Figure P2-3 Pediatric nonrebreathing mask

Equipment

Infant and pediatric nasal cannula (Figure P2-1)
Pediatric mask sizes (Figure P2-2)
Pediatric nonrebreathing mask (Figure P2-3)
Oxygen connecting tubing
Oxygen source

Possible Complications

Injury, if the pressurized tank is punctured or a valve breaks off

Potential for fire, because oxygen supports combustion

Respiratory arrest if high concentrations of oxygen are given to the child with chronic lung disease (rare)

Agitation and worsening of hypoxia, if delivery technique is overly aggressive

Hypothermia in an infant under 6 months of age with an endotracheal tube in place, who receives cool, unhumidified oxygen for more than 30 minutes

The appropriate oxygen delivery technique is based on the child's condition, age, and need for oxygen.

Preparation

1. Connect the pressure regulator and flow meter to the oxygen source. Turn on the tank.
2. Match the correct oxygen delivery device with the patient assessment (child's condition, age, and need for oxygen) (Table P2-1).

Procedure

1. Explain to the child and family why oxygen is needed and how the device works. Use developmentally appropriate language. Table P2-2 suggests methods to ease anxiety in the child who does not want to cooperate with oxygen delivery.
2. For blow-by oxygen using a paper cup, punch a hole in the bottom of the cup and insert the tubing through the hole (see Figure 4-2). Placing stickers on the cup or drawing smiley faces may decrease the child's anxiety.
3. Allow the child to remain in a position of comfort, which may be sitting on the caregiver's lap. In the ambulance, the child must be safely restrained.
4. To apply a mask, select the correct size. The mask should extend from the bridge of the nose to the cleft of the chin (Figure P2-4). Avoid placing pressure on the eyes.
5. Place the mask over the child's head, starting from the nose downward. Squeeze the nose clip and adjust the head strap.
6. To apply a nasal cannula, curve the plastic prongs back into the nostrils. Loop the tubing around the ears (Figure P2-5).
7. For blow-by oxygen, instruct the caregiver to hold the tubing or paper cup close to the child's face to maximize oxygen delivery (see Figure 4-5).

Table P2-1 Oxygen Delivery Technique and Patient Assessment

Device	Flow Rate	Concentration Delivered	Considerations
Nasal cannula	1 to 6 liters/min	Up to 44%	Low-flow system Least restrictive Slowly start flow of oxygen after cannula is secured to avoid frightening child May help to tape cannula to child's cheeks Use in infants who are obligatory nose breathers or if there is difficulty in obtaining a correct-size mask
Simple mask	6 to 10 liters/min	35% to 60%	Low-flow system Infant, pediatric, and adult size masks are available Use minimum flow rate to flush the mask
Non-rebreathing mask	12 to 15 liters/min	60% to 90%	High-flow system Consists of face mask and reservoir bag with a valve on the exhalation port to prevent drawing in room air during inhalation and a valve between the reservoir bag and mask to prevent exhalation of air into the reservoir bag Use in spontaneously breathing patients who require highest concentration of oxygen available (children with respiratory distress and shock) Make sure the flow rate keeps the reservoir bag inflated With a snug fit, delivers highest oxygen concentration available by mask Pediatric and adult masks are available Partial rebreather masks are indicated in neonates and infants who cannot overcome valve resistance
Blow-by	6 to 10 liters/min	Depends on flow rate and proximity to face	Indicated for infant or young child requiring oxygen who will not tolerate mask on the face Start oxygen flow through simple mask, corrugated tubing, or oxygen tubing threaded through the bottom of a cup Hold the delivery device as close to the child's nose and mouth as tolerated

Reprinted with permission from: Emergency Nurses Association. Respiratory distress and failure. Adapted from "*Emergency Nursing Pediatric Course, Provider Manual*". Park Ridge, IL: 1999.

2

The amount of oxygen to give routinely to children with chronic lung disease is unknown and probably differs for each individual. In some children, oxygen delivery may have the unexpected effect of worsening hypoxia. If the child has a history and assessment suggesting acute hypoxia and increased work of breathing, give oxygen but be ready to assist ventilation with BVM.

! Tip

An oxygen mask may frighten a child.

Do not force the child to lie down because it may increase the child's anxiety and agitation.

Table P2-2 Methods to Gain Child's Cooperation for Oxygen Delivery

Allow the child to hold the mask prior to placing it on his face.
Allow the child to feel the flow of oxygen prior to placing the mask on his face.
Describe the mask in appealing terms, such as a "space mask" or "Santa Claus beard."
If the child struggles, consider using the blow-by technique to avoid agitation and increasing the oxygen demands. Placing stickers or drawing smiley faces on the cup may decrease the child's anxiety.

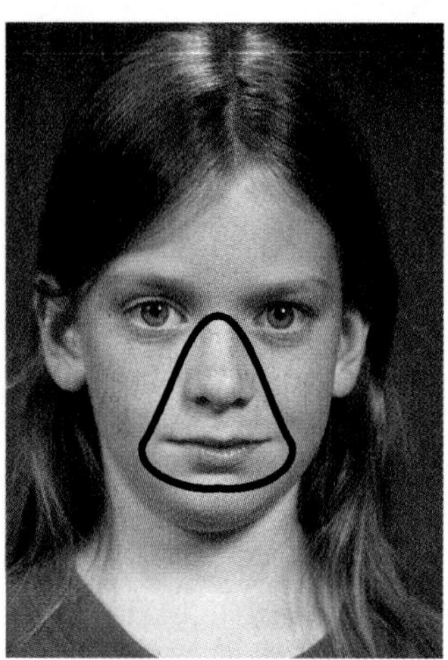

Figure P2-4 A proper size mask extends from the bridge of the nose to the cleft of the chin.

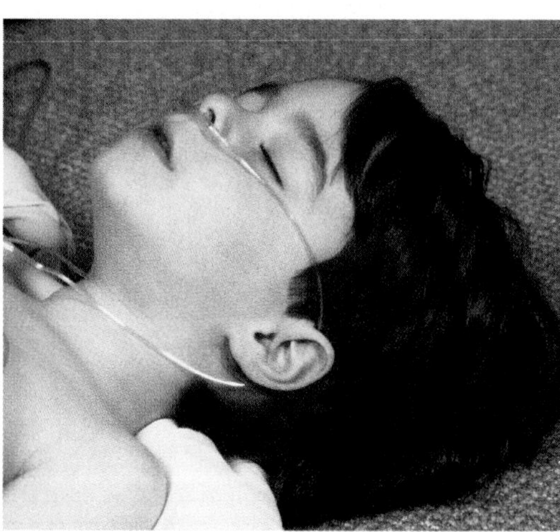

Figure P2-5 Place the nasal cannula with the plastic prongs curving back into the nostrils. Loop the tubing around the ears.

Suctioning

Introduction

Children of all ages are prone to airway obstruction from secretions, vomitus, pus, blood, edema, and foreign bodies. In newborns, airway obstruction from amniotic fluid, meconium, and blood is a common and potentially critical problem that is usually treatable with suction alone. In infancy and childhood, conditions such as closed head injury or status epilepticus may cause loss of airway protective reflexes and put the child at risk for loss of airway patency from aspiration or airway obstruction. Children needing endotracheal intubation often have diseases or trauma associated with fluid in the endotracheal tube, airways, or air sacs; this fluid must be removed to ensure adequate oxygenation and ventilation. Children with tracheostomy tubes may get fluids or foreign bodies in the tubes, which must be evacuated.

Rationale

Suctioning is a basic technique to maintain an open airway. Children have tiny airways that are easily obstructed. The type of suction device and suctioning procedure to use depends on the child's age and clinical problem (Table P3-1). Bulb syringes remove thin secretions from newborns or infants, but do not permit deep suctioning. Suction catheters remove thin secretions from the mouth, nose, or throat, and are useful in all age groups. Suction catheters are also necessary for endotracheal tube suctioning. Large-bore rigid suction catheters are useful in infants and children (not newborns) to remove thick secretions, vomitus, pus, blood, or particulate matter from the mouth.

Figure P3-1 Bulb syringe

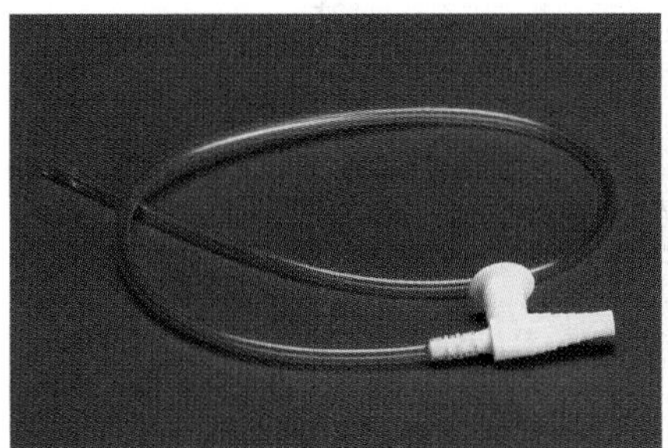

Figure P3-2 Suction catheter

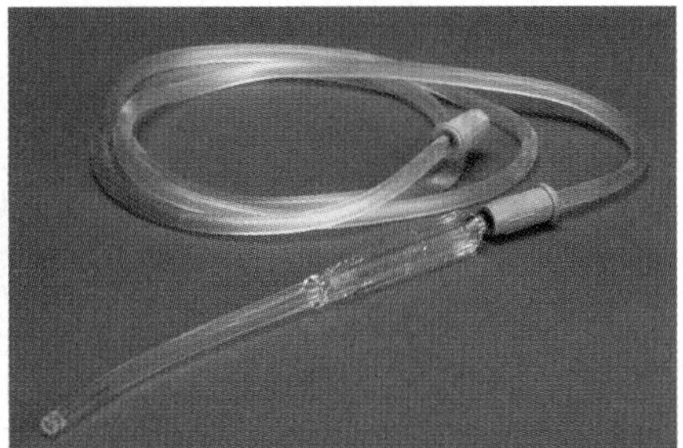

Figure P3-3 Rigid tip catheter

Indications

All newborns

Infants or children with fluids or foreign bodies in the nasopharynx or oropharynx

Intubated patients with fluids or foreign bodies in the tubes

Patients with tracheostomy tubes with fluids or foreign bodies in the tubes

Contraindications

Children with complete airway obstruction and suspected airway foreign body, prior to seeing the airway with laryngoscopy

Intubated children with increased intracranial pressure and approaching herniation

Equipment

Bulb syringes, one- and two-piece types (Figure P3-1)

Endotracheal suction catheters, sizes 8 to 12 French (Figure P3-2)

Feeding tubes, size 5 or 7 for small infants

Large-bore rigid suction catheter (Figure P3-3)

! Tip

In suspected foreign body aspiration, look at the airway prior to suctioning.

Possible Complications

Injury to the mouth, airway, or lung

Gagging, vomiting

Aspiration of stomach contents

Hypoxia from prolonged suctioning

Pushing foreign body into trachea with suction device

Increased intracranial pressure

Do not suction beyond your direct vision, to avoid causing gagging, vomiting, and possible aspiration.

Suction for less than 5 seconds, but use enough time to remove secretions.

The size of the suction catheter (F) is equal to twice the calculated ET tube size (mm).

Preparation

1. Select appropriate suction device based on clinical condition or type of obstruction and age. If there is no functioning negative pressure or suction source (vacuum outlet, battery-powered or electric portable suction, or hand-powered portable suction), use a bulb syringe for thin secretions.
2. Make sure the suction device is operational.
3. Determine correct catheter size with the pediatric **resuscitation tape**. The suction catheter should be smaller than the nostril. An easy formula to determine suction catheter size (F) is to double the ET size (mm).
4. Open catheter package.
5. Connect suction tubing or rigid suction catheter to connecting tubing and suction source.
6. Set suction force to maximum (80–120 mm Hg).
7. Maintain sterile technique.

Procedure

Oro/nasopharyngeal suctioning with bulb syringe

1. Squeeze the bulb away from the infant to remove air.
2. Suction the mouth, then the nose.
3. Open the mouth and insert the syringe tip at the side of the mouth, then advance the syringe to remove thin secretions (Figure P3-4a). Avoid inserting the syringe tip into the deeper soft tissues at the back of the mouth. Do not use a two-piece bulb syringe in the mouth because it may come apart.
4. Lift the nostril slightly and suction the nose. Insert the syringe tip straight back into the nostril or at a right angle to the face (Figure P3-4b).

Oro/nasopharyngeal suctioning with suction catheter

1. Suction the mouth, then the nose.
2. Open the mouth and advance until the tip touches secretions.
3. Block the side port and begin suctioning. Do not do deep suctioning beyond what is in direct vision.
4. Remove catheter with twisting motion.
5. Insert the catheter into the nostril, never beyond the angle of the jaw.
6. Block the side port to begin suctioning when the tip touches secretions.
7. Remove the catheter with a twisting motion.
8. Never suction longer than 5 seconds.

Endotracheal suctioning with suction catheter

1. Ask partner to hyperventilate the patient 5 to 6 times.
2. With thumb off the side port, insert suction catheter through endotracheal tube and down the trachea until resistance is met.
3. Apply suction off and on by placing thumb over the side port while withdrawing and twisting catheter (maximum 5 seconds).
4. Irrigate catheter with normal saline.
5. Ask partner to hyperventilate 5 to 6 times.
6. Repeat, as necessary.

Oropharyngeal suctioning with large-bore rigid suction catheter

1. Open the mouth and advance catheter until it touches secretions.
2. Close the side port or turn on suction to begin suctioning.
3. Remove the catheter with a twisting motion.
4. Do not suction more than 5 seconds.

Table P3-1 Suction Technique Based on Age and Type of Obstructing Material

Newborns	Bulb syringe or suction catheter
Infants and children with thin secretions	Bulb syringe or suction catheter
Newborns, infants, and children with endotracheal tube	Suction catheter
Infants and children with thick secretions or particulate matter	Large-bore suction catheter

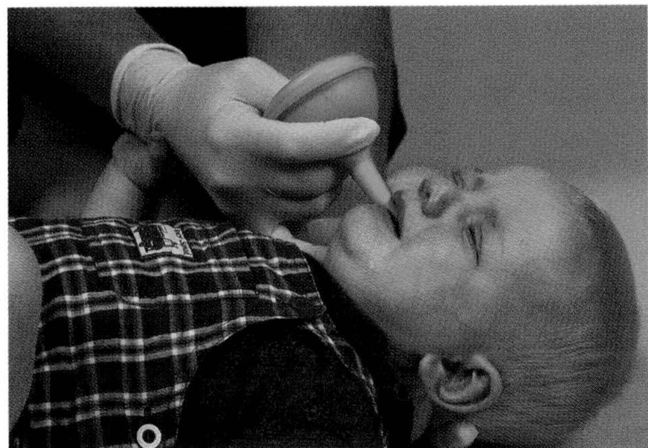

Figure P3-4a Using a bulb syringe in an infant's mouth

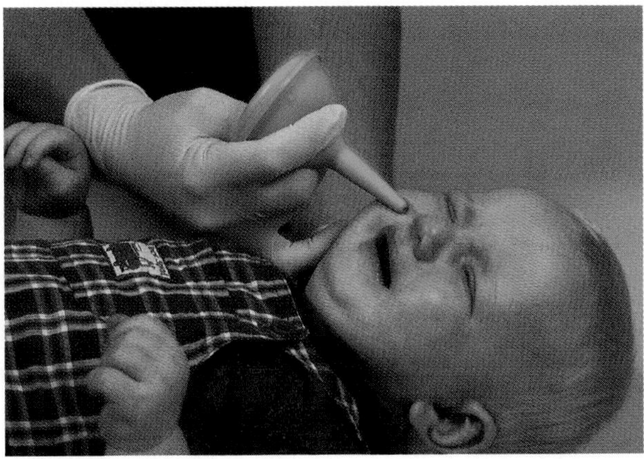

Figure P3-4b Using a bulb syringe in an infant's nose

Airway Adjuncts: Oropharyngeal and Nasopharyngeal Airways

Indications

Respiratory insufficiency

Airway obstruction

Seizures

Contraindications

OP Airway

Conscious patient with gag reflex

Unconscious patient who may have ingested a caustic or petroleum product

NP Airway

Age less than 1 year

Nasal obstruction

Possible basilar skull fracture

Major nasofacial trauma

Equipment

Nasopharyngeal airways (Figure P4-1)

Oropharyngeal airways (Figure P4-2)

An NP airway is useful in maintaining an open airway during an active seizure.

Introduction

An oropharyngeal (OP) or nasopharyngeal (NP) airway **adjunct** is often helpful to maintain an open airway for optimal ventilation. Sizing is important; improperly-sized OP or NP airways may cause further obstruction. The prehospital professional must know when to use an OP or NP airway adjunct, how to determine the proper size, and how to insert the adjunct safely and effectively.

Rationale

Opening the airway of a small infant or child by positioning alone, with the head-tilt/chin-lift maneuvers or jaw thrust, may not keep the tongue from obstructing the airway. Adequate ventilation often requires placement of airway adjuncts. They are easy to insert and may markedly improve airway patency. Adjuncts may immediately improve the child's spontaneous ventilation. In addition, they may allow more effective BVM ventilation, reduce gastric inflation, and avert the need for endotracheal intubation.

Preparation

1. Position patient's airway:

   Medical patient

   - Perform the head-tilt/chin-lift maneuver to open the airway. Avoid **hyperextension** of the neck because it may cause airway obstruction.
   - Use a towel under the shoulders of an infant or small child to get neutral airway position.

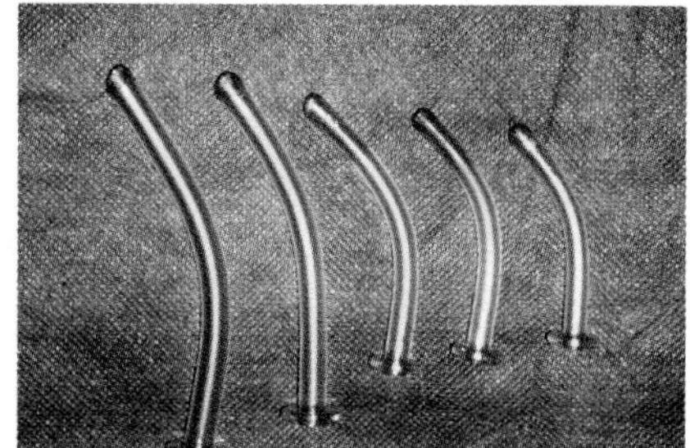

Figure P4-1 Different sizes of NP airways

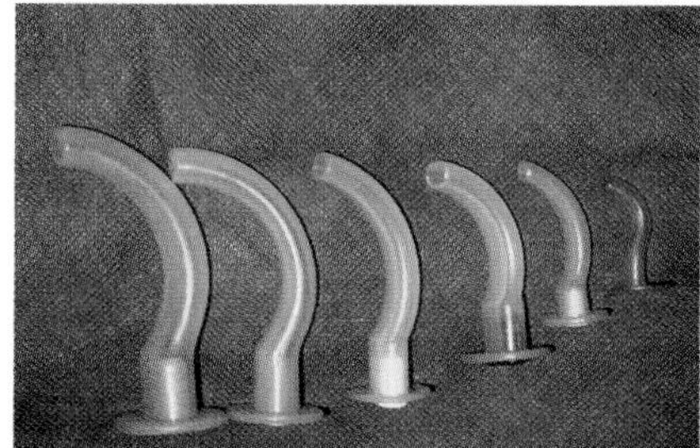

Figure P4-2 Different sizes of OP airways

Trauma patient

- Use the modified jaw thrust maneuver with in-line spinal stabilization to open the airway.

2. Select the proper-sized adjunct:

OP Airway

- Use resuscitation tape (see Procedure 17) OR
- Measure the device on the patient:
  - Place OP airway next to face with the **flange** at the level of the central **incisors**, and the bite block segment parallel to the hard **palate** (Figure P4-3).
  - The tip of the appropriate-size OP airway should reach the angle of the jaw.

NP Airway

- Use resuscitation tape (see Procedure 17) OR
- Measure the device on the patient:
  - The outside diameter of the NP airway should be less than the diameter of the nostril.
  - Place the NP airway next to the face and measure from the tip of the nose to the **tragus** of the ear (Figure P4-4).
  - Adjust movable flange (if present) up or down to get appropriate length.

Procedure

OP Airway Insertion

1. Depress tongue with a tongue blade (if available).

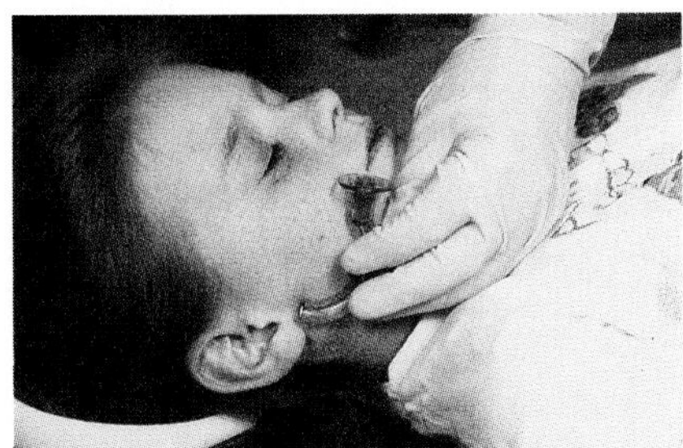

Figure P4-3 Place an OP airway next to the face, with the flange at the level of the central incisors and the bit block segment parallel to the hard palate.

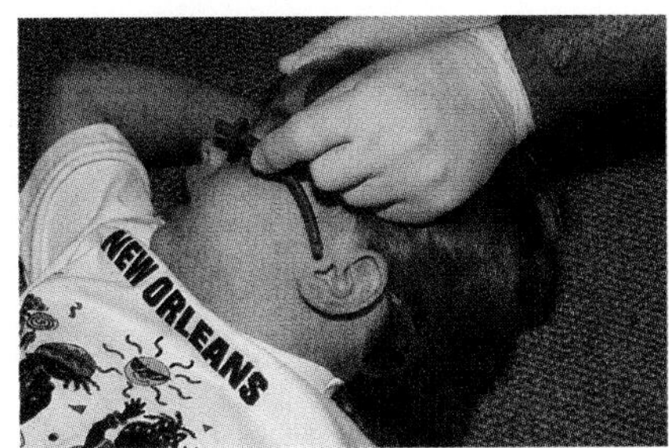

Figure P4-4 Place the NP airway next to the face and measure from the tip of the nose to the tragus of the ear.

Controversy

The use of airway adjuncts in facial trauma is controversial. If the child has an open fracture of the craniofacial bones, the device could penetrate into the brain and cause further brain injury or hemorrhage. The devices must be used cautiously or not at all in the setting of *severe* bony injury.

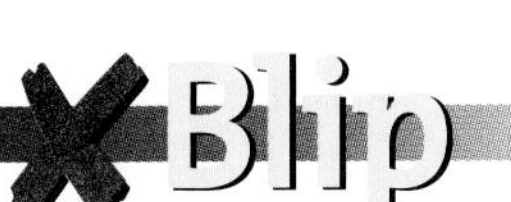

Never attempt to insert an OP airway in a conscious child.

Possible Complications

OP Airway

If OP airway is too small, the tongue may get pushed back into the pharynx, obstructing the airway (Figure P4-8)

If OP airway is too large, it may obstruct the larynx

Pharyngeal bleeding

Laryngospasm

Vomiting

NP Airway

Adenoidal tissue laceration

Pharyngeal bleeding

Obstruction of tube with fluids or soft tissues, causing airway obstruction

If an NP airway is too long, vagal stimulation or esophageal entry with gastric distention may occur

Laryngospasm

Vomiting

Do not insert an OP airway that is too small, or it will push the tongue back and obstruct the airway.

If the left nostril is selected for the NP airway, rotate the device 180 degrees in order to line up the bevel with the airway.

2. Place OP airway down into mouth until flange rests against lips.
3. If a tongue blade is not available, point the OP airway tip toward the roof of the mouth and depress the tongue with the curved part of the OP airway (do not scrape the palate).
4. Insert OP airway until flange is against lips; gently rotate 180 degrees into position. Flange should be resting against lips (Figure P4-5).

NP Airway Insertion

1. Lubricate NP airway.
2. Insert with **bevel** toward **septum** (center of nose).
3. Advance tip along floor of nasal cavity.
4. If using the right nostril, advance until flange is seated against outside of nostril. The tip should be in the nasopharynx (Figure P4-6).
5. If using the left nostril, begin inserting the airway with the curvature upward until resistance is felt (about 2 cm), then rotate the device 180 degrees and advance until flange is against outside of nostril (Figure P4-7).

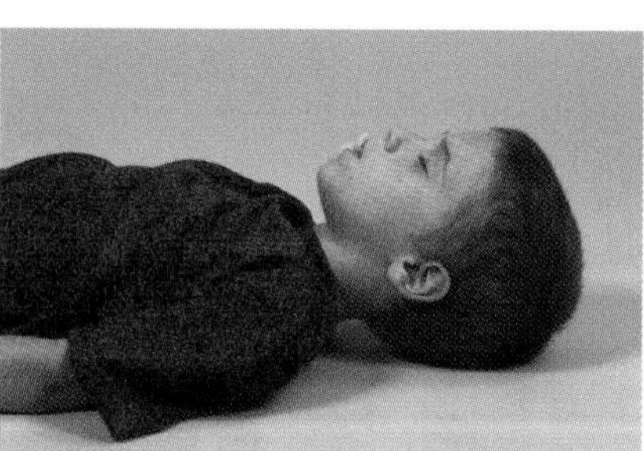

Figure P4-5 The flange of the OP airway should be resting against the lips.

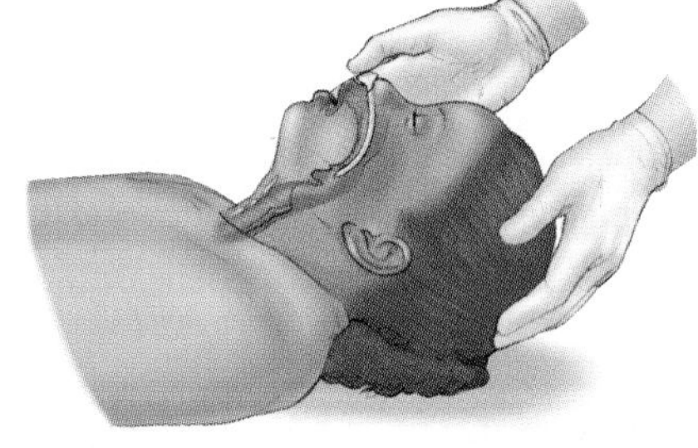

Figure P4-6 If using the right nostril, advance the NP airway until the flange is seated against the outside of the nostril. The tip should be in the nasopharynx.

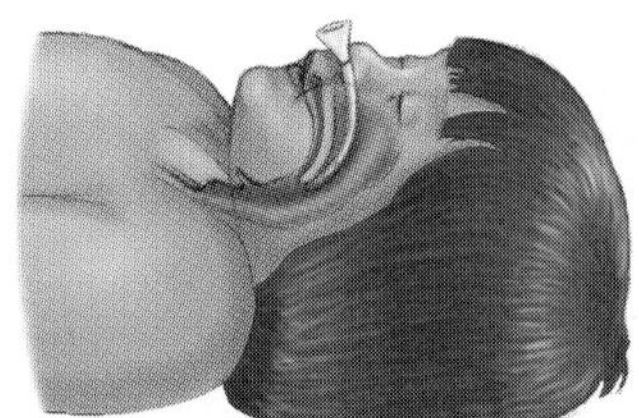

Figure P4-7 If using the left nostril, begin inserting the NP airway with the curvature upwards until resistance is felt (about 2 cm), then rotate the device 180° and advance until the flange is against the outside of the nostril.

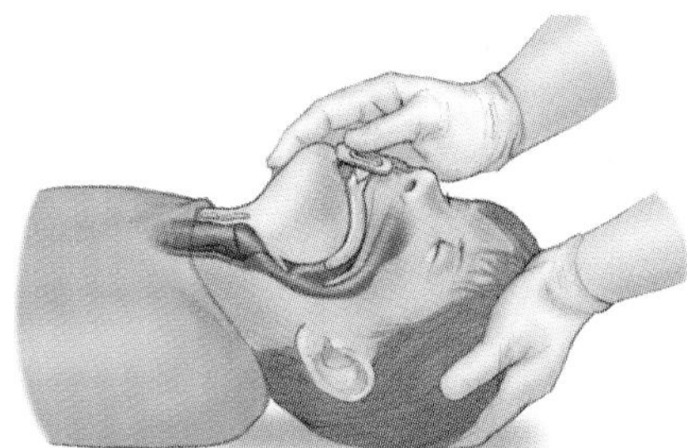

Figure P4-8 If the OP airway is too small, the tongue may be pushed into the pharynx, obstructing the airway.

Foreign Body Obstruction

Introduction

Foreign body obstruction of the airway is a common cause of brain injury and death in toddlers and preschool children, who place objects in their mouths as part of the exploratory behavior normal for these age groups. The infant or child with a completely obstructed airway poses the ultimate medical challenge because a moment's delay can be devastating or fatal. Although it is important when treating a patient with foreign body obstruction to begin with basic maneuvers to clear the airway, more advanced techniques may be necessary.

Indications

Complete airway obstruction

Severe partial airway obstruction and respiratory failure

Contraindication

Partial airway obstruction with maintenance of the airway

Equipment

Laryngoscope and straight blades (Miller sizes 1 and 2)
Pediatric Magill forceps (**Figure P5-1**)
BVM devices (infant and pediatric)

Rationale

In the setting of complete airway obstruction, prehospital professionals can make the difference between life and death. Immediate removal of an airway foreign body can often be achieved using basic life support (BLS) procedures, yet every year children suffer grave injury and death because of failure to use basic clearance maneuvers. Sometimes, the foreign body is deeper in the airway or embedded in tissue, so that basic maneuvers are unsuccessful. In such cases, using Magill forceps and direct laryngoscopy may be the only option for removal.

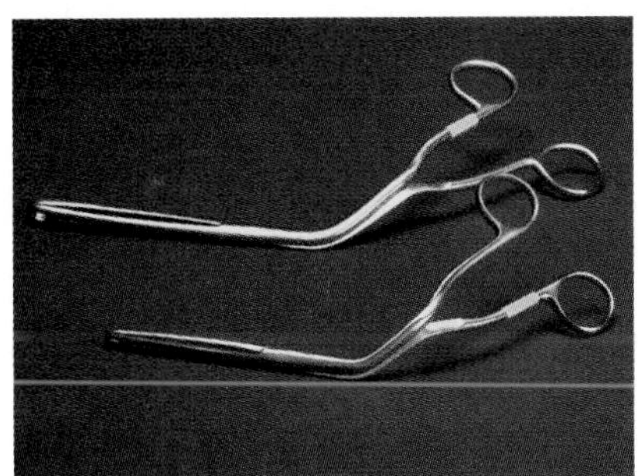

Figure P5-1 Magill forceps, adult and pediatric sizes

Preparation

1. Place an unconscious child in a supine position. Place an unconscious infant in a prone position.
2. Attempt BLS maneuvers first (see Procedure below).
3. Attach appropriate-size straight blade to laryngoscope handle.
4. Ensure light is working on laryngoscope blade.
5. Test suction device.

Procedure

BLS Maneuvers

Conscious patient (airway is completely obstructed, and patient is unable to speak, cry, or make noise)

- *Younger than 1 year*: Give 5 back blows (see Figure 4-6a), then 5 chest thrusts (see Figure 4-6b). Reassess, repeat.

Possible Complications

Hypoxia

Foreign body is pushed farther into airway

Laryngeal and tracheal injury

Teeth and mouth injury

Do not perform blind finger sweeps, which may push the foreign body further into the airway.

Attempt BLS maneuvers before using Magill forceps.

- *Older than 1 year*: Give 5 abdominal thrusts with child standing (see Figure 4-7a).

Unconscious patient

1. Open airway with the head-tilt/chin-lift or modified jaw thrust maneuver.
2. Attempt to ventilate.
3. Use obstructed airway maneuvers appropriate for age:
   - *Younger than 1 year*: Give 5 back blows with the infant in a prone position, then 5 chest thrusts with the infant in a supine position. Reassess, repeat.
   - *Older than 1 year*: Give 5 abdominal thrusts with the child supine (see Figure 4-7b).
4. If the foreign body is visible, remove it. *Do not use blind finger sweeps.*

Move to advanced life support (ALS) maneuvers if BLS maneuvers fail.

ALS Advanced LIFE support

Laryngoscopy and Magill forceps

1. Grasp laryngoscope handle.
   - Hold laryngoscope in left hand.
   - Use trigger-finger technique (Figure P5-2).
2. Open mouth by using thumb pressure on chin.
3. Insert pediatric laryngoscope blade into mouth.
4. Lift tongue with blade.
5. Exert gentle traction upward along the axis of the laryngoscope handle at a 45-degree angle. *Do not use teeth or gums for leverage.*
6. Advance blade.
7. Watch the tip until foreign body is visible. *Do not go past vocal cords.*
8. Use suction to improve visibility and maintain airway.
9. Remove object.
   - Grasp closed Magill forceps in right hand.
   - Insert Magill forceps into mouth, tips closed.
   - Open forceps and move tips around foreign body.
   - Grasp foreign body and remove while looking directly at it.
   - Look at the airway and make sure it is clear of foreign bodies or debris.
   - Remove laryngoscope blade.

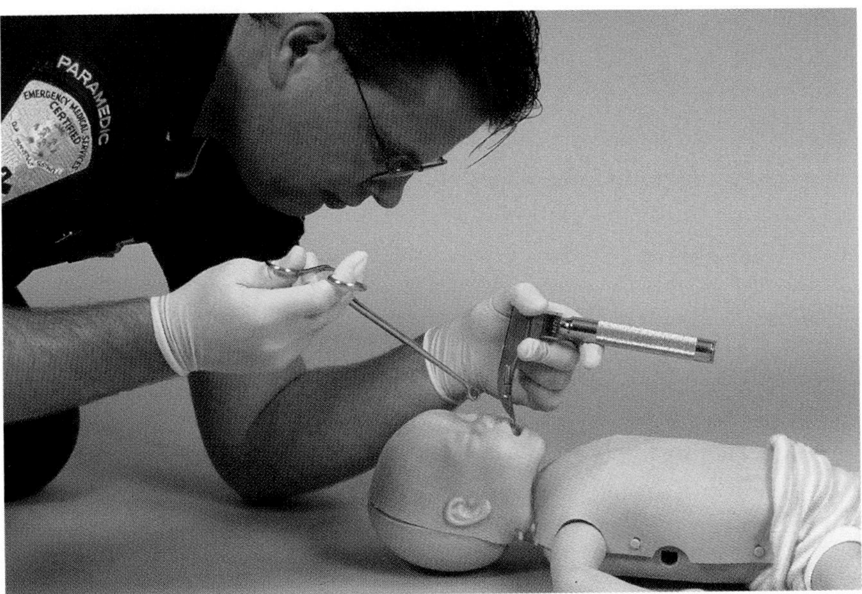

Figure P5-2 Insert Magill forceps into the mouth with the tips closed.

Suctioning may push the foreign body farther into the airway, so look at the airway before suctioning.

Repeat BLS procedures if no foreign body is seen by direct laryngoscopy.

There is no universal procedure to maintain airway patency after removal of an airway foreign body. Each case is unique. Endotracheal intubation may not be necessary if the child is breathing effectively without stridor at rest.

10. After removal of foreign body:
    - Reassess respiratory status.
    - Use suction if needed.
    - Attempt to ventilate if the child does not breathe spontaneously.
11. Return to BLS maneuvers if no foreign body is seen by direct laryngoscopy.

Bronchodilator Therapy

Indication

Wheezing

Contraindication

Known sensitivity to bronchodilator drugs

Equipment

Inhalation therapy (Nebulizer)

An oxygen-powered nebulizer that aerosolizes the liquid bronchodilator to small particle size that can reach the alveoli

Oxygen source

Mask or mouthpiece with liquid reservoir

Bronchodilator drugs

Albuterol solution (5 mg/ml solution for inhalation)

Other inhaled bronchodilators include terbutaline, metaproterenol, and isoetharine

Inhalation therapy (MDI)

MDI, mask and spacer

Bronchodilator drugs

Albuterol MDI (90 micrograms [µg] per puff)

Subcutaneous therapy

Tuberculine (TB) or 3-ml syringe

25- or 27-gauge needle

Bronchodilator drugs

Epinephrine (1:1000 or 1 mg/ml)

Another injectable bronchodilator is terbutaline (1 mg/ml)

Avoid injectable drugs in cooperative, wheezing patients. The procedure is painful and is no more effective than inhaled bronchodilators.

Give an uncooperative child subcutaneous epinephrine.

Introduction

Wheezing from bronchospasm is one of the most common out-of-hospital pediatric problems. Children who are wheezing are in acute respiratory distress and are often anxious, agitated, and uncooperative. The prehospital professional must use a developmentally appropriate approach with the child and caregiver when giving general noninvasive respiratory care and using bronchodilator medications. The caregiver can help by holding, soothing, and supporting a scared child. One way to give **aerosolized** bronchodilators is with an oxygen-powered nebulizer. Another way is the metered dose inhaler (MDI), although this inhalation technique has not been studied in the out-of-hospital setting. If the child is uncooperative or unable to use inhaled bronchodilator therapy, subcutaneous (SQ) drug delivery is another possibility.

Rationale

Early bronchodilator therapy, on the scene and on the way to the ED, helps immediately open airways, relieve respiratory distress, and improve oxygen delivery. Inflammation and edema of small airways develop quickly if wheezing and bronchospasm are untreated. Early bronchodilator therapy may reduce the need for more aggressive hospital therapy, shorten ED and hospital times, and decrease chances of complications or death. Continuous inhalation treatment with a nebulized beta agonist is the best initial approach with severe respiratory distress.

Preparation

Inhalation therapy

1. Have the caregiver hold the child on his lap. An older child can sit alone.
2. Have the child in an upright position of comfort.
3. Explain what is happening. Most children need only inhalation bronchodilator therapy by oxygen-powered nebulizer or with an MDI.

Subcutaneous therapy

1. Position the child on the caregiver's lap or straddling the caregiver's leg.
2. Expose the thigh or **deltoid** area for injection (see Procedure 7).

Procedure

Inhalation therapy

1. If the child can cooperate, deliver nebulized bronchodilator through a mouthpiece.
   - Child weighing less than 15 kg: Albuterol (5 mg/ml) at 2.5 to 5.0 mg (0.5–1.0 ml), diluted to 3 ml with normal saline
   - Child weighing more than 15 kg: Albuterol (5 mg/ml) at 5 to 10 mg (1–2 ml) diluted to 3 ml with normal saline
2. Alternatively, nebulize the bronchodilator and have the caregiver hold the mask to the child's face.
3. Tape two tongue blades together to make a nose clip to help breathing through the mouthpiece (Figure P6-1).
4. If a MDI is used, attach spacer and mask when the child is too young or unable to trigger aerosol effectively (see Figure 4-9).
5. Monitor respiratory rate, heart rate, and pulse oximetry during therapy.

Subcutaneous therapy

1. If the child cannot cooperate with inhalation therapy, give epinephrine by SQ injection. Use 0.01 mg/kg or 0.01 ml/kg of 1:1000 solution with a maximum of 0.3 mg or 0.3 ml. Use one of two anatomic locations:
   - Lateral aspect of deltoid in upper arms (older child)
   - Anterior thigh
2. Inject the medication into the SQ area of the skin.

Figure P6-1 A noseclip can help the child breathe through the mouthpiece.

Possible Complications

Anxiety

Dizziness

Dysrhythmias

Headache

Hypertension

Nausea

Palpitations

Restlessness

Tachycardia

Tremors

Vomiting

The role of the MDI in out-of-hospital bronchodilator therapy is not known. While ED studies have shown that the MDI is as effective as inhaled drugs for most children, and it has not been studied in the out-of-hospital setting. MDI with mask and spacer, however, can probably deliver an adequate bronchodilator dose to most children older than 6 months of age.

Use bronchodilators for all infants and children who are wheezing from any cause.

Intramuscular and Subcutaneous Injections

Indication

Administration of medications when vascular access is not possible or practical

Contraindications

Poor perfusion

Availability of alternative effective routes: oral, inhalation, IV, or IO

Equipment

Tuberculin or 3-ml syringe
22- or 25-gauge needle
- 1-inch to 1½-inch for IM injection

25- or 30-gauge needle
- ⅝-inch for SQ injection

Select the injection site based on age, anatomic considerations, and volume of medication to be given.

Avoid injecting close to a major nerve because it may cause nerve damage.

Introduction

The intramuscular (IM) or subcutaneous (SQ) route is acceptable for giving several important medications to children. These medications include epinephrine, diphenhydramine, and morphine sulfate. The IM or SQ routes have limitations, but when inhalation, IV, or IO delivery of medication is not possible, IM or SQ administration may be lifesaving.

Rationale

IM or SQ administration allows the medication to absorb slowly but steadily. IM medications are absorbed more quickly than are SQ medications. The advantages of IM and SQ techniques are easy delivery and high safety. The disadvantages are poor patient acceptance and delayed effect. Avoid IM or SQ medications in patients with low perfusion because absorption is unpredictable. Sometimes, in situations involving a child with low venous pressures, such as in anaphylaxis, IM or SQ is an excellent first choice for delivery while vascular access is attempted.

The SQ route (for example, for epinephrine in bronchospasm) has few complications because it avoids contact with tendons, nerves, and blood vessels. The IM route may result in nerve damage, particularly if the injection is in the buttocks of an infant or small child.

Preparation

1. Explain the procedure using developmentally appropriate terminology. Avoid using the word *shot* because the child may associate this with being shot by a gun. Be honest and tell the child it will hurt but be over as quickly as possible. Describe the needle stick as a pinch or a bee sting.
2. Select the medication, reaffirm if the child is allergic to any medications.
3. Select the appropriate syringe and needle. Keep needles out of the child's sight.

   Needle length for IM injection

   - For the **ventrogluteal** or **dorsogluteal** sites, use a needle slightly longer than one-half of the distance between the thumb and finger when the skin at the injection site is grasped.

- For the deltoid and **vastus lateralis** sites, use a 1-inch needle if the skin is grasped. If the muscle is stretched, use a ⅝-inch needle.

Needle length for SQ injection

- Use the smallest needle size (25- or 30-gauge) with a ⅝-inch length.

4. Cleanse the top of the medication vial with an alcohol wipe or open the **ampule**.
5. Withdraw the appropriate volume of medication, based on the child's mg/kg dose. Calculate the dose or obtain from a length-based resuscitation tape (see Procedure 17). Expel all but 0.1 ml of air from the syringe.
   - The maximum volume SQ is 0.5 to 1.0 ml.
   - The maximum volume IM is:

     2.0 ml in older children

     1.0 ml in small children and older infants

     0.5 ml in small infants
6. Select the appropriate injection site (Table P7-1 and Figures P7-1, P7-2a, P7-2b, and P7-2c). Consider the following factors:
   - The volume of medication
   - The condition of the muscle
   - The type of medication
   - The child's ability to be properly positioned
7. Position and secure the child. Consider letting the caregiver hold the child in one of the following ways:
   - Have the child sit on the caregiver's lap, facing to the side. Put one of the child's arms around the caregiver's waist and have the caregiver hold the child close to her chest. The caregiver can hold the child's arm or legs (Figure P7-3).
   - Position the child straddling the caregiver's lap, sitting chest to chest. Tell the caregiver to hug the child. The caregiver can help to hold an arm or leg (Figure P7-4).

Possible Complications

Abscess (rare)

Cellulitis

Damage to blood vessel, nerve, or tendon

Redness or swelling at the site

Adverse reaction to the medication

Put pressure on the site after the needle is removed, and massage the area to increase absorption.

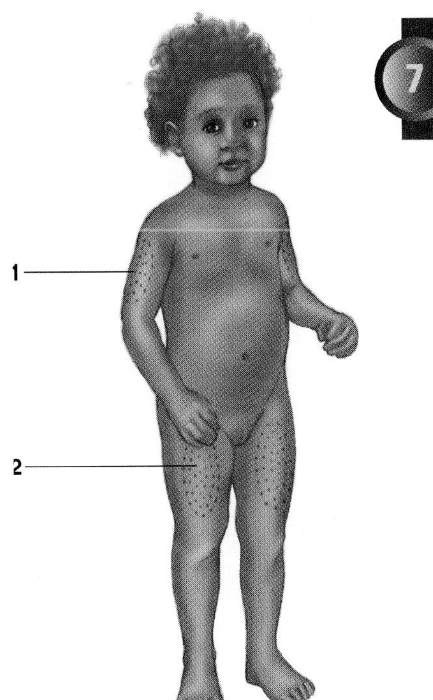

Figure P7-1 Appropriate sites for SQ injections. 1) deltoid site; 2) anterior thigh site

Table P7-1 Appropriate Sites for IM and SQ Injections

Site	Indications	Landmarks	Considerations	Disadvantages
Vastus lateralis muscle: Largest muscle group in children under 3 years of age (Figure P7-2a)	Use in infants and small children Preferred site for all ages	Palpate the greater trochanter and the knee joint; divide the distance into thirds Use middle third for injection site	Can be used for SQ or IM injections	Thrombosis of the femoral artery More painful than deltoid or gluteal sites
Ventrogluteal muscle: Large muscle with few nerves and blood vessels (Figure P7-2b)	Use in children over 3 years of age	Have the child lie on his side and bend the upper leg forward in front of the lower leg Palpate greater trochanter and anterior and posterior iliac crests Place palm over greater trochanter with fingers open in a V shape pointing toward iliac crests Inject into center of the V shape	Well-defined landmarks to identify the site	None
Dorsogluteal site (Figure P7-2c)	Use in children over 3 years of age	Have the child lie on his stomach and rotate his legs and toes inward Palpate greater trochanter and posterior iliac spine; draw an imaginary line between these two points Inject lateral and above the imaginary line	In an older child, larger volumes of medication (2 ml) can be injected because the muscle mass is larger	Contraindicated in children under 3 years of age and those who have not been walking for at least 1 year Medication may inadvertently be given SQ in older child with a large muscle mass Do not damage the sciatic nerve, which tracks out from the lower lumbar spine and goes underneath the gluteal muscles

Site	Indications	Landmarks	Considerations	Disadvantages
Deltoid	Use for small volumes of medication. Used in children 18 months of age and older	Palpate the shoulder and go two finger-breadths below Give the injection in the upper third of the muscle	Usually used for SQ injections Faster absorption rate than gluteal site Fewer side effects from the injection and less painful site	May damage the radial nerve in young children Because of the limited muscle mass, only small volumes of medication can be injected

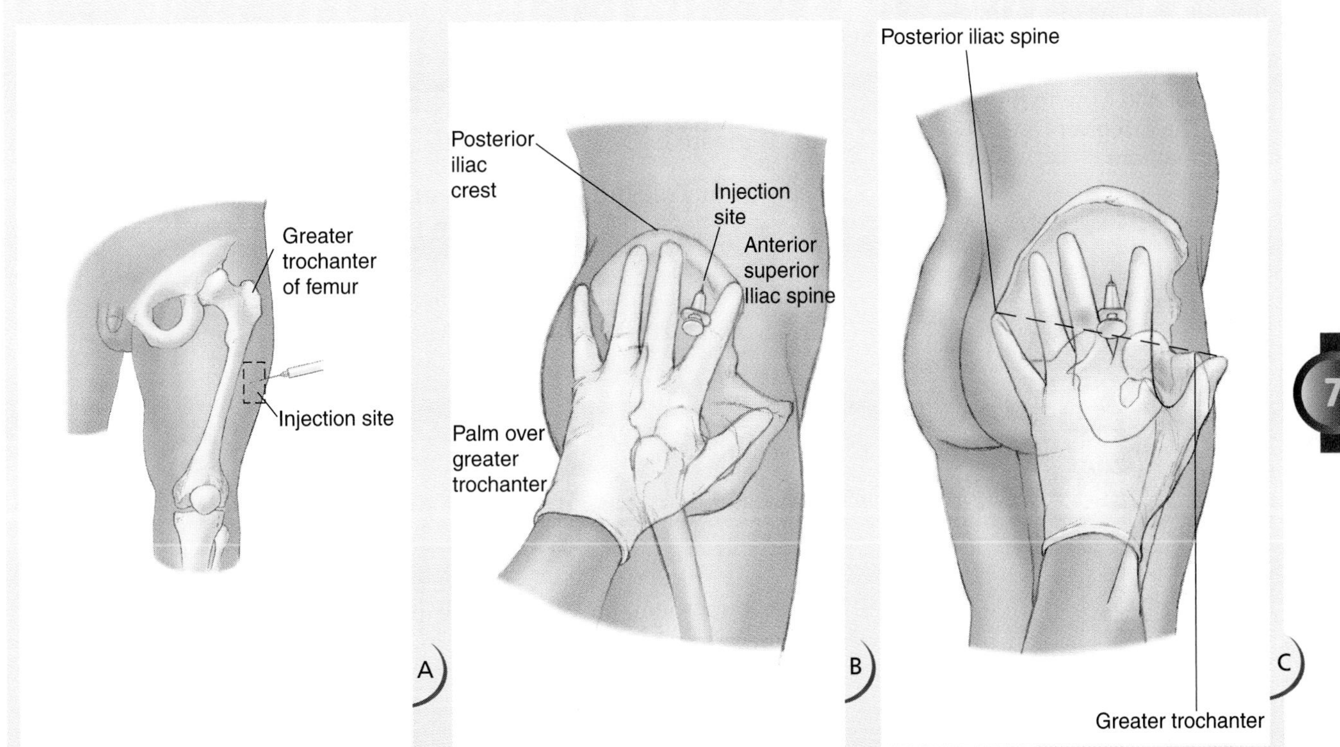

Figure P7-2 Appropriate sites for IM injections.

7

! Tip

Ask the child to relax the muscle to decrease the pain.

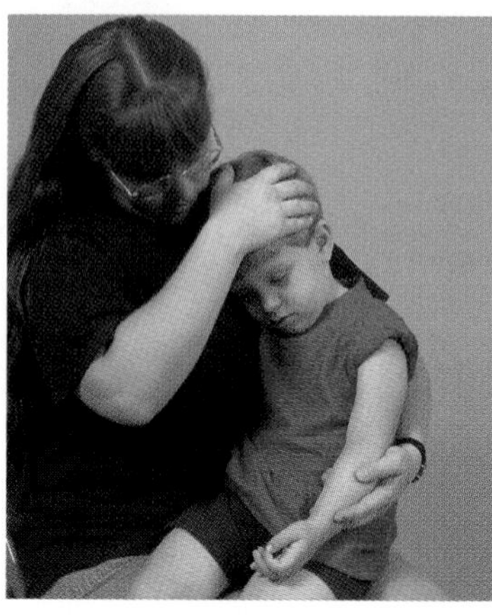

Figure P7-3 Have the child sit on the caregiver's lap, facing to the side. Put one of the child's arms around the caregiver's waist and have the caregiver hold the child close to her chest. The caregiver can hold the arm or legs.

Figure P7-4 Position the child straddling the caregiver's lap, sitting chest to chest. The caregiver can hold the arm or leg.

Some experts believe that the dorsogluteal site should not be used until the child has been walking for at least one year.

Procedure

Injection

IM injections (Figure P7-2)

1. The vastus lateralis site is preferable. Use the ventrogluteal or dorsogluteal sites if the thigh muscle is not accessible in children over 3 years.
2. Stretch the skin and insert the needle at a 90-degree angle.
3. Release the skin and pull back on the plunger to aspirate for blood.
4. If no blood appears, inject the medication. If blood appears, remove the syringe and start the procedure again.
5. Gently massage the area after the needle is removed.

SQ injections (Figure P7-1)

1. Use the area over the deltoid or anterior thigh.
2. Gently grasp the skin and insert the needle at a 45-degree angle.
3. Insert the needle into the SQ area of the skin (Figure P7-5).
4. Release the skin and pull back on the plunger to aspirate for blood.
5. If no blood appears, inject the medication. If blood appears, remove the syringe and start the procedure over.

After the injection

1. Praise the child.
2. Apply an adhesive bandage to the site.
3. Dispose of the syringe.
4. Write down the name of the medication, dosage, route, time, and any effects.

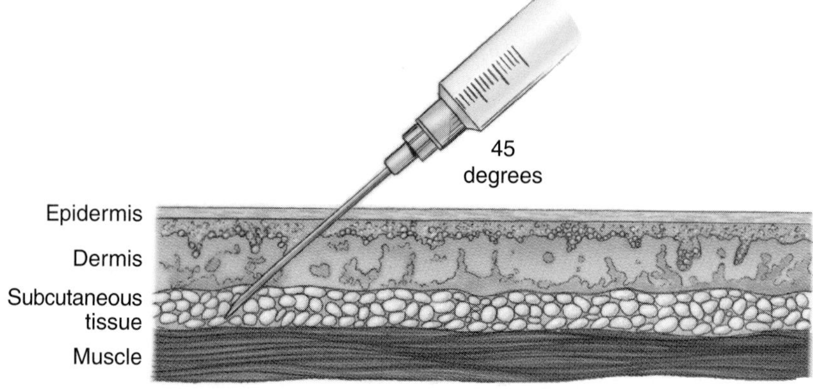

Figure P7-5 A subcutaneous injection is below the dermis and above the muscle.

Bag-Valve-Mask Ventilation

Introduction

Bag-valve-mask (BVM) ventilation is a way to deliver assisted ventilation to a child in respiratory failure. Sixty to ninety-five percent oxygen can be given effectively and safely by choosing a well-fitted mask, connecting the oxygen reservoir to a supplemental oxygen source at 15 liters/minute, disabling the pop-off valve, and bagging at an age-appropriate rate.

Indications

Apnea or respiratory arrest

Respiratory failure

Cyanosis

Oxygen saturation (SaO_2) less than 90% despite administration of 100% oxygen by nonrebreathing mask

Contraindication

Complete airway obstruction

Equipment

Transparent masks with inflatable rim, sizes neonate through adult (**Figure P8-1**).

Self-inflating resuscitator (bag), at least 450 ml volume

Rationale

Assisted ventilation is a way to provide adequate oxygenation and ventilation to a child who is unable to breathe adequately on his own. While the technique does not provide the definitive airway control that endotracheal intubation does, in many cases BVM ventilation will be the best technique for assisting ventilation during resuscitation and transport. BVM ventilation is one of the prehospital professional's most useful skills in pediatric out-of-hospital care.

Preparation

1. Measure the mask on the patient. The mask should extend from the bridge of nose to the cleft of the chin, avoiding compression of the eyes (see Figure P2-4). The right size mask will have a small volume, to minimize dead space and to prevent rebreathing of expired carbon dioxide. Transparency allows the rescuer to observe the child for cyanosis of the lips and for emesis.
2. Select an appropriate resuscitator bag: While a small child can be safely and effectively ventilated using a big bag, a small bag will not work for a large child. Pediatric tidal volume is approximately 8 ml/kg. The bag should have a volume of 450 to 750 ml. An adult bag (1200 ml) is okay for larger children or adolescents.
3. If a pop-off valve is present, block it to permit higher inspiratory pressures and achieve chest rise (**Figure P8-2**).
4. Connect one end of oxygen tubing to the oxygen device and the other end to the flow meter, set to 15 liters/minute.

Figure P8-1 Transparent adult, child, infant, and neonate masks

Possible Complications

Hypoxia

Barotrauma

Gastric distention

Emesis and aspiration

The relative value of BVM versus endotracheal intubation in respiratory failure is not known. BVM may be as good as endotracheal ventilation in the out-of-hospital setting in children with acute illness or injury.

Avoid hyperextension of the neck, which may cause airway obstruction or spinal injury.

8

Pull the jaw into the mask, instead of pushing the mask into the face.

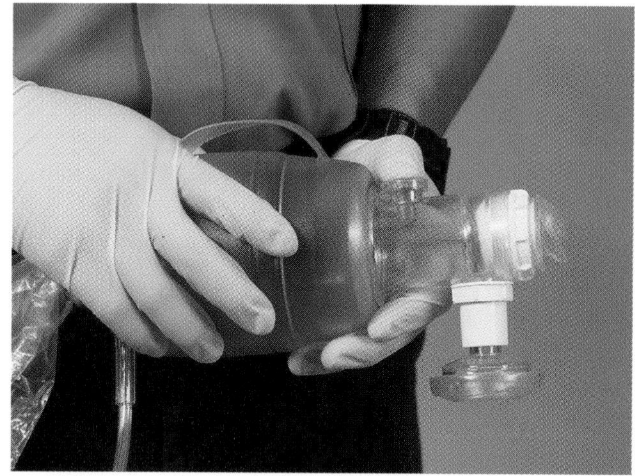

Figure P8-2 If a pop-off valve is present, occlude it to permit delivery of higher inspiratory pressures.

Procedure

1. Open airway.
   - *Medical* patient: Use head-tilt/chin-lift maneuver.
   - *Trauma* patient: Use jaw thrust with in-line manual stabilization.
2. Ensure neutral positioning (sniffing position).
   - Because infants and toddlers have large heads, place a small roll under the shoulders to achieve the sniffing position.
   - Avoid hyperextension of the neck because this may cause airway obstruction or spinal injury.
   - Insert appropriate airway adjunct if airway patency cannot be maintained with chin lift/jaw thrust maneuver (see Procedure 4).
     - Use an oropharyngeal (OP) airway if the patient does not have a gag reflex, OR
     - Use a nasopharyngeal (NP) airway if the patient is more than 1 year of age and has an active gag reflex.
3. Begin ventilation.

BVM ventilation using one-rescuer technique

a. Apply the mask to the face and get an airtight seal using the E-C clamp technique (see Figure 8-12).

b. Pull the child's jaw into the mask, instead of pushing the mask into the face, to establish a seal. Failure to provide a tight seal may result in delivery of lower oxygen concentrations or an inadequate volume of air.

c. Avoid placing pressure on soft tissues under the chin because this may compress the airway.

d. Squeeze bag with the dominant hand, watching for chest rise. Squeeze the bag only until the chest rise is visible, then release. Say, "Squeeze, release, release" during ventilation to achieve the correct inspiratory volume and to allow for expiration.

Child: 20 squeezes/minute

Infant: 30 squeezes/minute

e. Assess effectiveness of ventilation:

- Look for adequate bilateral rise and fall of chest.
- Auscultate for lung sounds at the midaxillary line bilaterally.
- Monitor oxygen saturation.

The two-rescuer technique is preferable in a trauma patient or if the one-rescuer technique does not get a good seal.

A bag less than 450 ml will not generate enough inspiratory pressure to ventilate a large child.

BVM using two-rescuer technique

The two-rescuer technique is preferable in trauma patients or if the one-rescuer technique does not create an effective seal.

a. First rescuer applies the mask to the face and maintains a seal.

- *Medical patient:* Hold the mask to the face with the thumb and index fingers of both hands; use the other fingers to perform a chin lift.
- *Trauma patient:* Perform a jaw thrust maneuver, lifting the jaw into the mask with both hands, while maintaining in-line manual stabilization.

b. Pull the child's jaw into the mask, instead of pushing the mask into the face, to establish a seal.

c. Avoid placing pressure on soft tissues under the chin because this may compress the airway.

d. Second rescuer ventilates (Figure P8-3).

4. Avoid gastric distention.

a. Watch the abdomen for signs of enlargement during ventilation.

b. If this happens, reposition the airway, and observe chest rise carefully—squeeze the bag only until the chest *starts* to rise.

c. If BVM is to be continued during transport, consider placement of an orogastric or nasogastric tube for gastric decompression (see Procedure 9).

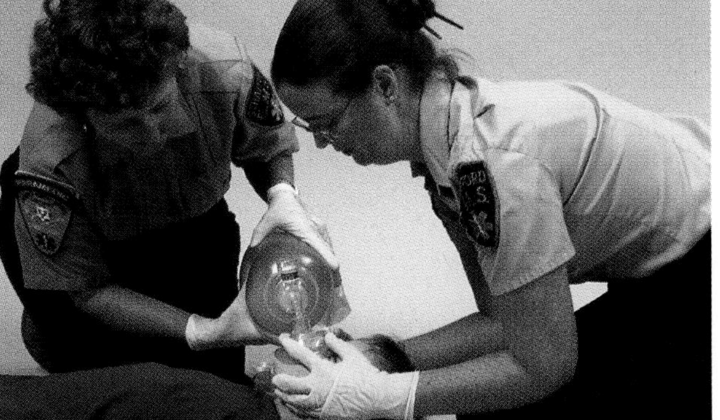

Figure P8-3 Two-rescuer BVM technique

Orogastric and Nasogastric Intubation

Indication

Abdominal distention associated with assisted ventilation

Contraindications

NG and OG intubation

Unconscious child with poor or no gag reflex and unsecured airway. In this case, do endotracheal intubation first to decrease risk of vomiting and aspiration.

Caustic ingestions. In a child who has ingested a caustic substance, there is a risk of esophageal damage with passage of the tube.

NG intubation

Perform OG intubation to avoid intracranial passage of the NG tube when the child has any of the following findings: severe head or facial trauma, as indicated by midfacial injuries, nasal bleeding, or clear nasal secretions.

Infants with nostrils too small to accommodate the tube. OG intubation is preferred for infants younger than 6 months of age.

Equipment

Gastric tube: A double-lumen sump tube is the best device for removing stomach contents (**Figure P9-1**).
30- to 60-ml syringe with funnel-tipped adaptor for manual removal of stomach contents through tube
Mechanical suction
Adhesive tape
Non-petroleum lubricant

Do not peform gastric intubation on an unconscious patient because she is at risk for aspiration.

Introduction

Gastric intubation has many purposes, such as cleaning out the stomach and giving activated charcoal after a toxic ingestion, evaluation and treatment of gastrointestinal hemorrhage, and gastric **decompression** in cases of **bowel** obstruction or distention from assisted ventilation. In the out-of-hospital setting, gastric intubation has only one indication: decompression of the stomach during assisted ventilation. The tube may be placed into the stomach through the nose (nasogastric [NG] intubation) or through the mouth (orogastric [OG] intubation).

Rationale

During assisted ventilation, it is common to inflate the stomach, as well as the lungs, with air. Gastric inflation with air slows downward movement of the diaphragm and decreases tidal volume—making ventilation more difficult and necessitating higher inspiratory pressures. In addition, inflation of the stomach with air increases the risk that the patient will vomit and aspirate. Gastric intubation with an NG or OG tube decompresses the stomach and makes assisted ventilation easier.

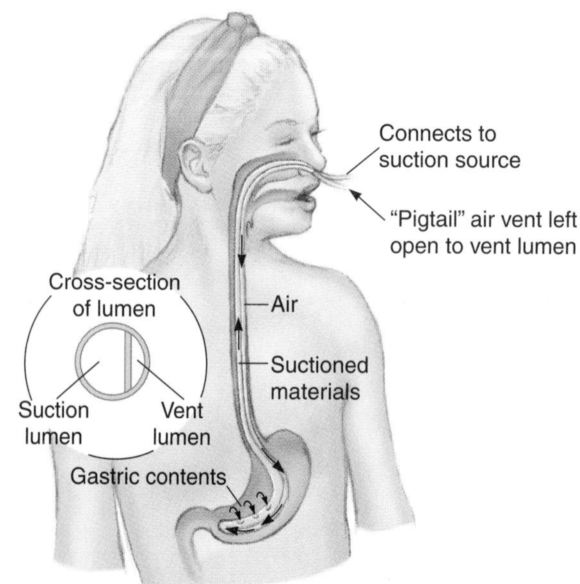

Figure P9-1 Double lumen sump tube

Preparation

1. Select the proper size tube. Sizing techniques are outlined in Table P9-1.
2. Measure the tube on the patient. The length of the tube should be the same as the distance from the lips or tip of the nose (depending on if the route OG or NG is used) to the left ear PLUS the distance from the left ear to the left upper quadrant of the abdomen, just below the **costal margin** (Figure P9-2).
3. Mark this length on the tube with a piece of tape. When the tip of the tube is in the stomach, the tape should be at the lips or nostrils.
4. Place the patient in a supine position.
5. Assess the gag reflex. If the patient is unconscious and has a poor or no gag reflex, perform endotracheal intubation before gastric intubation.
6. In a trauma patient:
   a. Maintain in-line stabilization of the cervical spine if a neck injury is possible.
   b. Choose the orotracheal route if the patient has severe head or facial trauma or has serious midfacial injuries.
7. Lubricate the end of the tube.

Possible Complications

Placement of the tube into the trachea with hypoxia

Vomiting and aspiration of stomach contents

Airway bleeding/obstruction

Passage of tube into brain

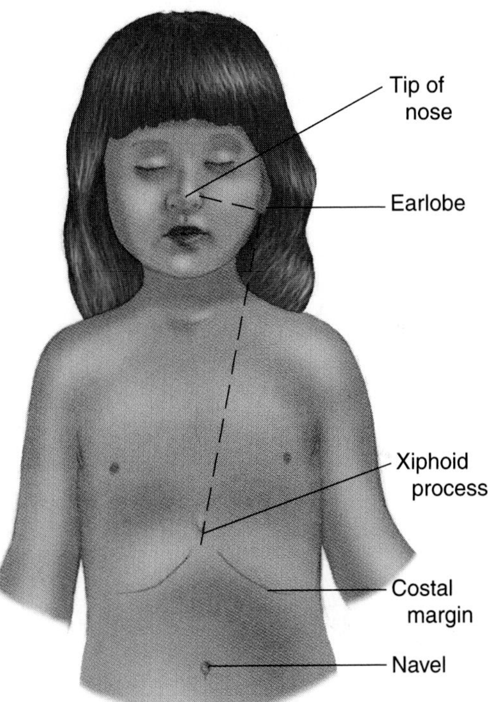

Figure P9-2 Technique for measuring the distance to pass the NG tube

Procedure

NG intubation

1. Pass the tube gently through the nostril, directing the tube straight back. *Do not angle the tube superiorly.*
2. If the tube does not pass easily, try the opposite nostril, or a smaller tube. *Never force the tube.*

Table P9-1 Methods for Determining NG/OG Tube Size
1. Refer to a length-based resuscitation tape (see Procedure 17).
2. Select a tube size that is the same as the size of the patient's nostril, through which it should pass with minimal resistance.
3. Use a tube size twice the endotracheal (ET) tube size (a child who needs a 5.0-mm ET tube needs a 10.0 French NG or OG tube)

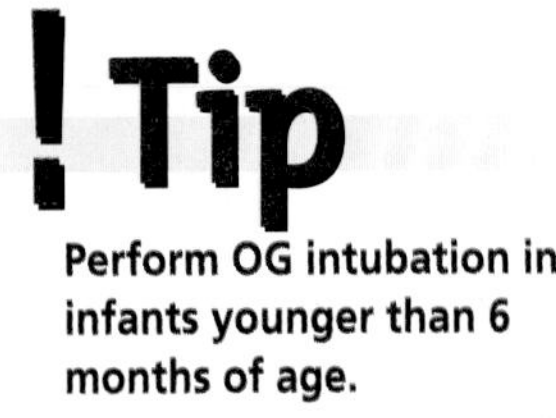

Perform OG intubation in infants younger than 6 months of age.

The value of NG and OG insertion is unproven. Although these procedures are routine in EDs, no studies have tested the benefit of easier ventilation against the potential complications of hypoxia from tracheal intubation or aspiration of stomach contents.

Talking or crying during the procedure is a good indication that the gastric tube is not in the trachea.

Never use force to pass an NG tube.

3. If NG passage is unsuccessful, use the OG approach.

OG intubation

1. Insert the tube over the tongue, using a tongue blade if necessary to help insertion.
2. Advance the tube into the hypopharynx, then insert rapidly into the stomach.
3. If coughing, choking, or change in voice occurs, immediately remove the tube. It may be in the trachea.

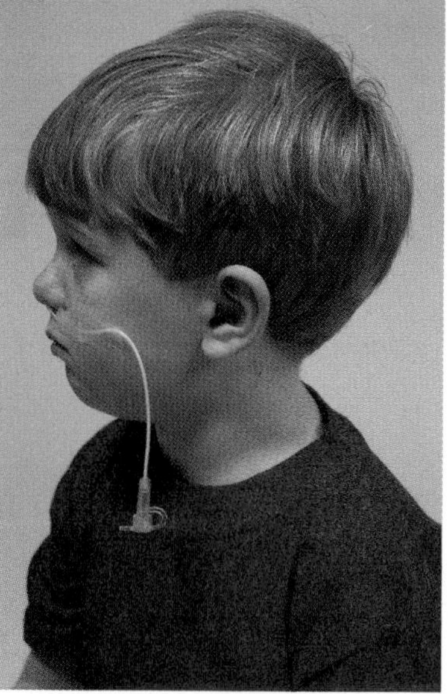

Figure P9-3 Proper method for taping an NG–OG tube.

Check placement of NG or OG tube

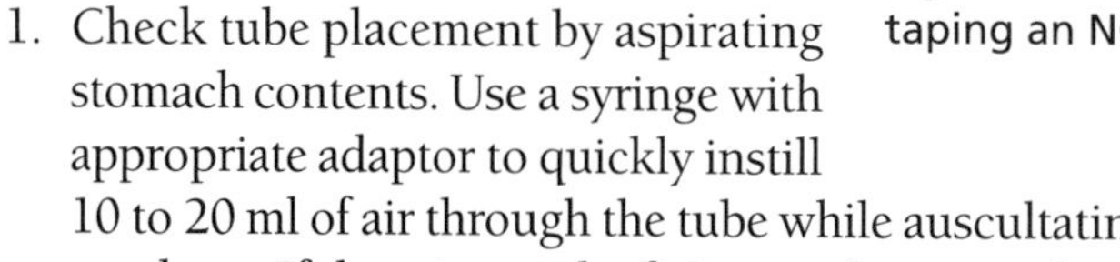
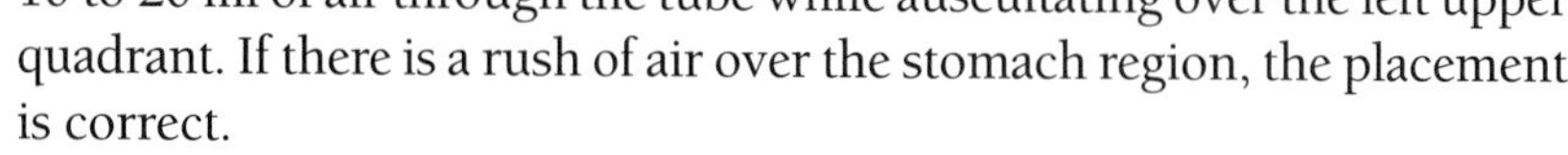

1. Check tube placement by aspirating stomach contents. Use a syringe with appropriate adaptor to quickly instill 10 to 20 ml of air through the tube while auscultating over the left upper quadrant. If there is a rush of air over the stomach region, the placement is correct.
2. If correct placement cannot be verified, remove the tube.

3. Secure the tube to the bridge of the nose or to the cheek, using adhesive tape (Figure P9-3).
4. Aspirate air from stomach, using a 30- to 60-cc catheter-tipped syringe, or connect to mechanical suction at low, continuous, or intermittent setting.

Endotracheal Intubation

Introduction

Endotracheal intubation (ETI) is a time-honored, lifesaving procedure for some critical patients, but it has important modifications and pitfalls in children. There are several anatomic considerations that make the pediatric airway different from the adult airway:

- The child's vocal cords are more anterior and superior.
- The tongue is larger.
- The mandible and oral cavity are smaller.
- The diameter and length of the trachea are less.
- The soft tissues are more fragile.

Performing the procedure quickly and safely in the field can be tricky. Inappropriate or unsuccessful intubation attempts may result in hypoxia or injury to the child's airway.

Indications

Respiratory or cardiopulmonary arrest

Respiratory failure

Inability to maintain patent airway

Loss of protective airway reflex

Need for prolonged hyperventilation

Need for endotracheal administration of resuscitative medications

Contraindications

Permanent tracheostomy (relative)

Good response to BVM and short transport time (relative)

Anatomic abnormalities that would probably prevent successful intubation (large tongue hematoma, massive facial injuries) (relative)

Rationale

Successful ETI allows optimal oxygenation and ventilation, provides a tube for medication delivery, and decreases the risk of aspiration and loss of airway control. A properly placed and secured endotracheal tube is a good tool for managing critical patients, but the procedure can take a long time, and there are frequent and serious complications.

The value of performing ETI in children in the out-of-hospital setting is controversial. More studies are necessary to define which groups of children will benefit from this procedure, in light of the well-known risks of hypoxia, esophageal intubation, tube dislodgment, and airway injury, as well as transport delay.

Preparation

1. Make sure oxygen delivery equipment is connected to an oxygen source.
2. Select an appropriately sized endotracheal tube (**Tables P10-1** and **P10-2**) for oral ET intubation.
3. For a properly selected uncuffed ET tube:
   - Allow a minimal air leak. The absence of an air leak may indicate excessive pressure at the cricoid cartilage.
4. For a properly selected cuffed ET tube:
   - For a cuffed ET tube under size 6 mm, do not test or inflate cuff.
   - For cuffed ET tube size 6 mm and over, check cuff for leaks, maintaining aseptic technique, as follows:

     Inflate cuff with appropriate volume of air.

     Remove syringe.

Equipment

Uncuffed ET tubes in pediatric sizes (2.0–5.0) (**Figure P10-1**), in addition to cuffed adult sizes (6.0–8.0)
Pediatric laryngoscope with fresh batteries
Pediatric laryngoscope blades, curved (sizes 2–4) and straight (sizes 0–4) (**Figure P10-2**)
Light bulb
Large-bore rigid suction catheter
Suction catheters, sizes 5–12 French
Pediatric stylets
Water-soluble lubricant
Oropharyngeal airways
Pediatric bag-valve device, at least 450 ml volume
Pediatric face masks
Adhesive tape
Skin adhesive
Pulse oximeter
Oxygen source
Device for confirmation of tracheal ET placement

Possible Complications

Aspiration of stomach contents

Dislodgment of ET tube from trachea

Esophageal intubation

Hypoxia

Increased intracranial pressure

Laryngeal, tracheal, pharyngeal, or esophageal injury

Teeth and mouth injury

Vocal cord injury

Feel cuff for integrity.

Deflate cuff.

Leave syringe with appropriate volume of air attached to the tube.

5. Attach blade to laryngoscope handle, and make sure the light works.
6. Test the large-bore rigid suction catheter.
7. Insert stylet into ET tube, stopping the stylet at least 1 cm from the end of the ET tube.
8. Bend the ET tube into gentle upward curve. In some cases, bend the tube into the shape of a hockey stick.
9. Lubricate tube with a water-soluble lubricant.
10. Prepare device for confirmation of tracheal ET placement (see Procedure 11).
11. To predict correct ET tube position at gum line, either:
    - Check resuscitation tape, OR
    - Calculate ET position with formula:
      gum line position (in cm) = ~3 × tube size
12. Have partner prepare for:
    - ongoing patient assessment
    - providing time counts for ventilation rates
    - watching monitors (heart rate, pulse oximetry)
    - handling suction devices
    - handling ET tube
    - applying gentle cricoid pressure
    - stabilizing neck, if child has possible spinal trauma
13. Position patient (avoid hyperextension or hyperflexion of neck).
    - Medical patient: Place the child in the "sniffing" position (**Figure P10-3a**).
    - *If spinal trauma is possible*: Place the child in neutral position with in-line manual stabilization (**Figure P10-3b**).

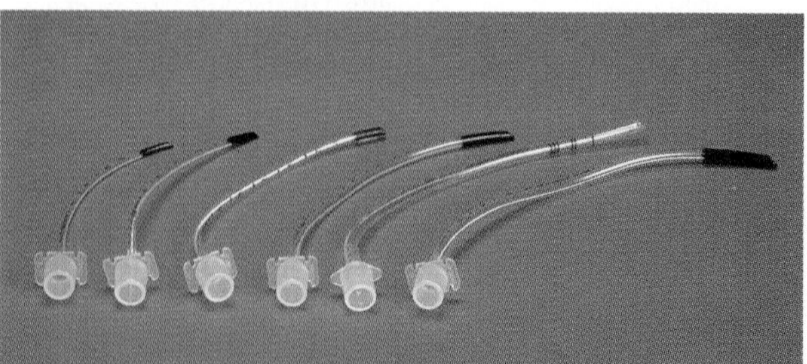

Figure P10-1 Uncuffed ET tubes in pediatric sizes 2.5, 3.0, 3.5, 4.0, 4.5, and 5.0

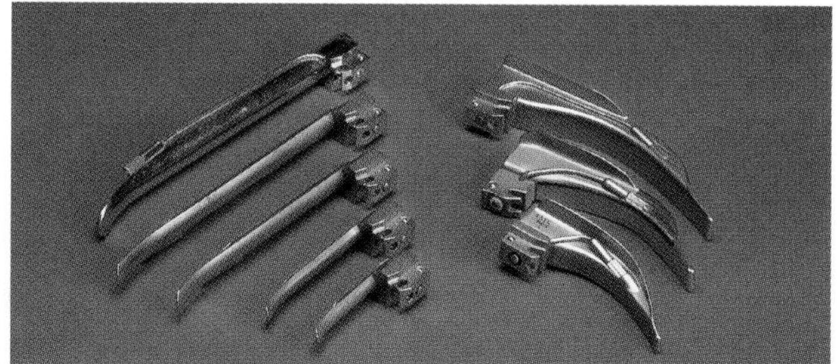

Figure P10-2 Pediatric laryngoscope blades; blades (0, 1, 2, 3, 4) and curved blades (2, 3, 4)

Table P10-1 Suggested Endotracheal Tube and Suction Catheter Sizes

Age	ETT Size (mm)	Suction Catheter Size (French)
Premature newborn	2.0–2.5	5
Newborn	3.0–3.5	6–8
6 months	3.5	8
12–18 months	4.0	8
3 years	4.5	8
5 years	5.0	10
6 years	5.5	10
8 years	6.0	10
12 years	6.5	10
16 years	7.0–8.0	12

Beware of inadequate spinal immobilization during intubation attempts in trauma patients.

! Tip

Make sure proper equipment is available and functioning prior to intubation attempt.

Table P10-2 Selecting ET Tube Size

Remembering numbers

Newborns and infants:

Preterm infants: 2.0- or 2.5-mm tube

Term newborns or small infants: 3.0- or 3.5-mm tube

Infants 6–12 months: 3.5-mm tube

Infants 12–18 months: 4.0-mm tube

For Children >1 year:

Use the resuscitation tape (see Procedure 17).

OR

The diameter of the ET tube is approximately the same size as the child's fingernail on the fifth finger.

OR

$$\text{Size} = \frac{\text{(age in years)}}{4} + 4$$

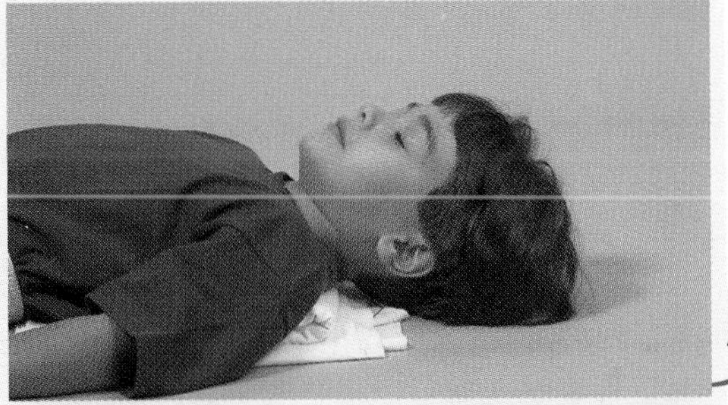

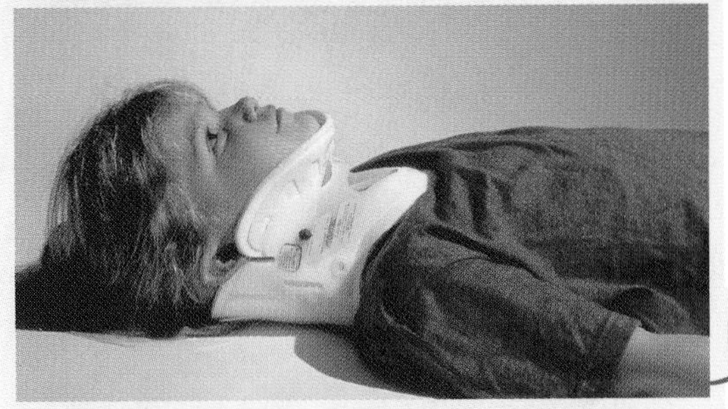

Figure P10-3 (A) Place the medical patient in sniffing position for endotracheal intubation. (B) Place the trauma patient in neutral position to avoid injury of the spine.

Maintain gentle cricoid pressure until appropriate tube location is confirmed.

Blip

Never assume the ET tube is in the trachea unless you see the tube passing through the vocal cords.

Procedure

Insert oral ET tube

1. Have partner oxygenate and ventilate patient 5 to 6 times with BVM and 100% oxygen, at a rate of one ventilation every 2 seconds. Say "squeeze, release, release" to reinforce proper rate.
2. Grasp laryngoscope in left hand.
3. Ask partner to stop ventilating and begin timing, giving 20 to 30 second counts.
4. Open mouth by applying thumb pressure on chin; remove OP airway if present.
5. Have partner apply gentle cricoid pressure (**Sellick maneuver**) to prevent **gastric reflux** (Figure P10-4).
6. Hold laryngoscope in "trigger finger" position.
7. Insert pediatric straight laryngoscope blade into mouth (Figure P10-5).
8. Lift tongue with blade.
9. Exert gentle traction upward along the axis of laryngoscope handle at a 45-degree angle (Figure P10-6). *Do not use teeth or gums to gain leverage.*
10. Advance blade straight along tongue. Continue looking at ET tube tip, until tip is just beyond epiglottis (Figure P10-7).
11. If there is difficulty seeing the vocal cords:

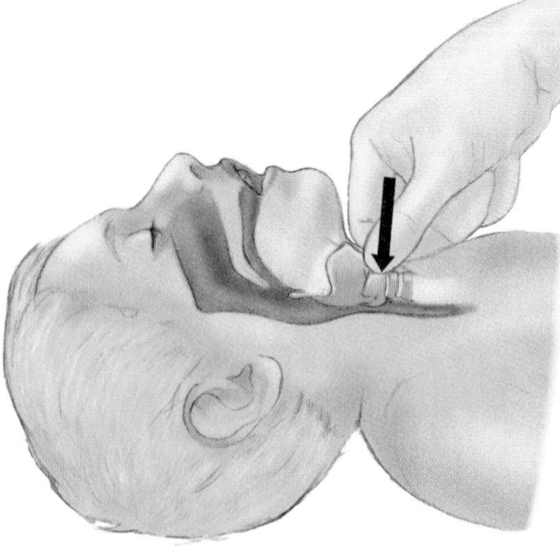

Figure P10-4 Cricoid pressure occludes the esophagus to prevent gastric reflux.

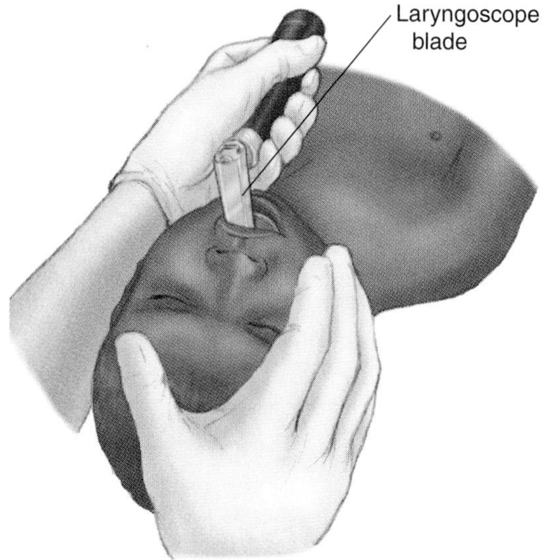

Figure P10-5 Insert the pediatric straight laryngoscope blade into the patient's mouth.

- Advance or retract laryngoscope blade.
- Modify amount of cricoid pressure (Sellick maneuver).
- Remove vomitus, blood, other fluids, or particulate matter with rigid, large-bore suction device.

12. If gastric reflux appears near, increase cricoid pressure or stop laryngoscopy attempt.
13. Continue to look at vocal cords and suction.
14. Remove large solid matter with pediatric Magill forceps.
15. Insert ET tube.
    - Hold tube in dartlike fashion with right hand and insert tip of tube from right corner of mouth down between vocal cords (**Figure P10-8**). Do not insert tube in channel of laryngoscope blade because this blocks the view of the vocal cords.
    - Watch the endotracheal tube go through the vocal cords.
    - Advance tube until vocal cord marker on ET tube is situated beyond vocal cords.
    - Look for centimeter marking on endotracheal tube in relation to the gum line.
16. Remove laryngoscope blade, holding ET tube in place.
17. Remove stylet from ET tube.

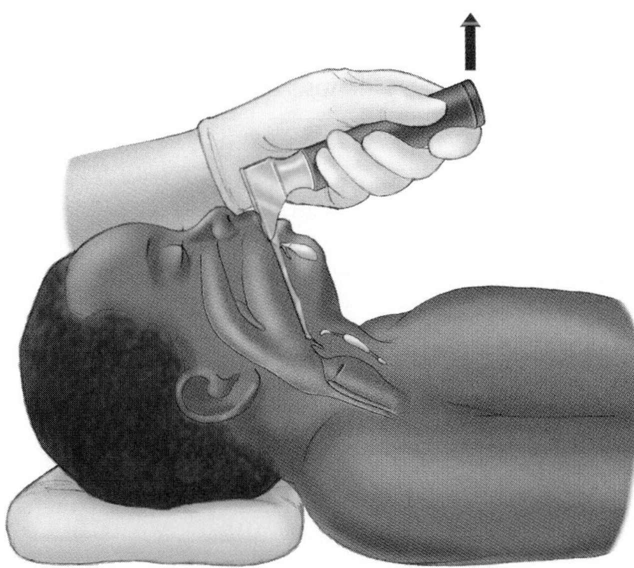

Figure P10-6 Place gentle traction upward along the axis of the laryngoscope handle at 45°.

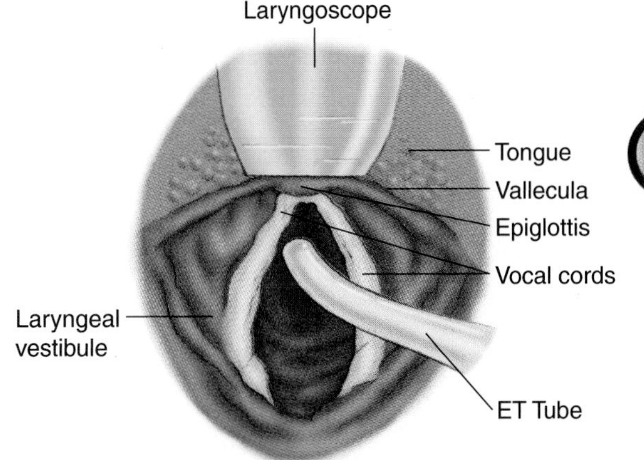

Figure P10-7 View of normal anatomic landmarks for advancing the ET tube using straight blade

18. Inflate cuff with pilot balloon. (If cuffed ET tube is under size 6 mm, do not inflate balloon.)
    - If cuff was inflated, remove syringe and check "pilot" balloon for inflation.
    - Maintain tube position by holding ET against upper lip.
    - If large amount of fluid is evident in ET tube, use a suction catheter to clear the airway.
    - Have partner maintain ET tube position and ventilate patient with bag-valve device.
19. Record tube position on permanent record.
    - Use centimeter mark at teeth or gum line.
    - Mark on ET tube with indelible pen.
20. Assess correct position in trachea.
    - Do general patient evaluation (appearance, heart rate, pulse oximetry).
    - Look for bilateral chest rise.
    - Make sure there is no bubbling, gurgling sounds in epigastric area indicating air-water interface (check for 2 breaths).
    - Auscultate for bilateral lung sounds at the midaxillary line, third intercostal space (check for 2 breaths on right then 2 breaths on left).
    - Use device to confirm tracheal positioning (see Procedure 11).
21. Place tape around tube.
    - Reassess proper location of tube and make sure the patient is stable.
    - Give ventilation instructions to partner.

! Tip

Chest rise is the best indication of correct tracheal placement of the ET tube.

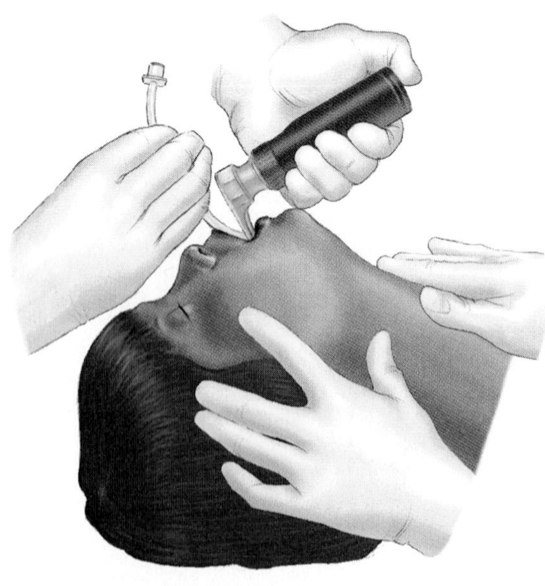

Figure P10-8 Advance the endotracheal tube from the right corner of the mouth past the vocal cord and into the trachea.

Secure ET tube

1. Insert correctly-sized oral airway (see Procedure 3) as bite block, and make sure ET tube is not compressed. Do not use a Hudson bite block in pediatric patients.
2. Carefully hold the ET tube in place while the second rescuer tapes.
3. Use cloth tape as per local EMS protocols.
4. Wrap one end of tape around the tube (avoid overlapping tape if possible) two times, close to the patient's mouth (Figures P10-9a and P10-9b).
5. Bring tape around patient's neck. Use special precautions for trauma patients.

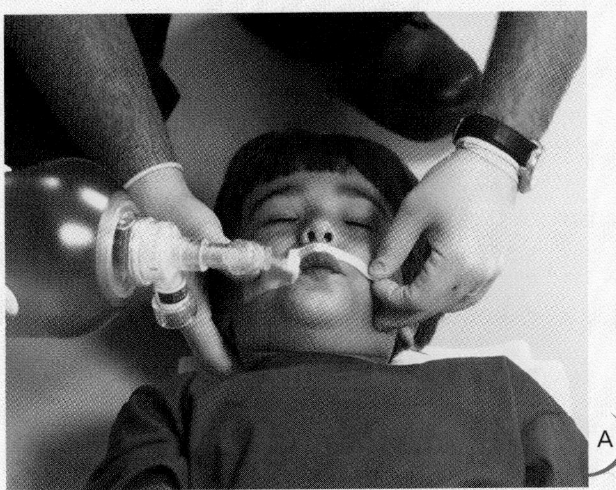

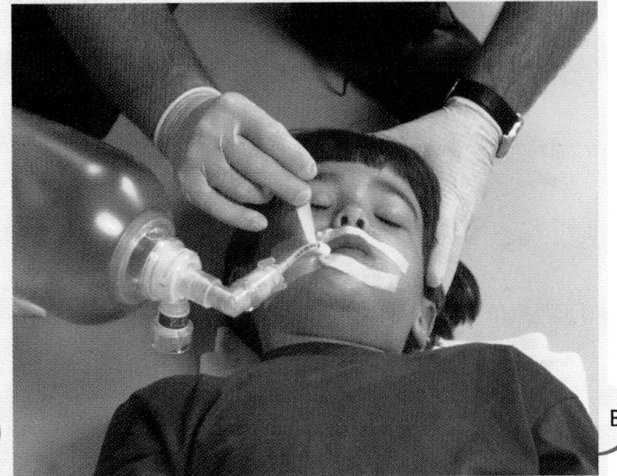

Figure P10-9 Secure the endotracheal tube by taping it close to the patient's mouth.

6. Bring tape up to opposite side of face and wrap around the tube twice, crimping end of tape so it can be easily removed (Figure P10-10).

Reconfirm tube placement

1. Recheck to make sure there is no bubbling, gurgling noise in epigastric area (air-water interface) for 2 breaths.
2. Reassess breath sounds bilaterally at the midaxillary line, third intercostal space (2 breaths on right, then 2 breaths on left).
3. Take extra care handling an ET tube in a pediatric patient because it can be easily dislodged.
4. Reassess after patient is in ambulance (and after change of position or change in patient status).
5. Report and record findings.

Tip

Always reassess tube location after patient movement or when there is a change in patient status.

Indications for tube removal

Immediate tube removal

1. No chest rise with ventilation
2. Presence of epigastric gurgling sounds
3. Failure to confirm tracheal placement with detection device (see Procedure 11)
4. Vomitus in ET tube

Postresuscitation extubation

This is *rarely* indicated in the field. All three situations must be present.

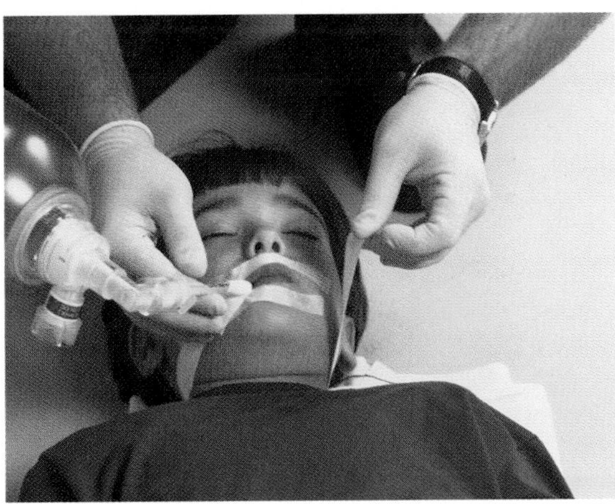

Figure P10-10 Reinforce the tape around the child's neck.

1. Spontaneous breathing with adequate rate and tidal volume
2. Conscious patient
3. Coughing and gagging with inability to maintain oxygenation and ventilation

Extubation procedure

1. Ensure rigid large-bore suction device is functioning.
2. Suction oropharynx.
3. Turn patient on left side.
4. Deflate cuff completely (if cuff is inflated).
5. Remove ET tube quickly at end-inspiratory phase, while suctioning.

Confirmation of Endotracheal Tube Placement

Introduction

Performing pediatric endotracheal intubation (ETI) in the out-of-hospital setting may be difficult or impossible even for experienced prehospital professionals. Confirming position of the endotracheal (ET) tube in the trachea is a major challenge because esophageal intubation is a common and dangerous complication of ETI. Currently there are three methods to confirm placement of the ET tube:

1. Clinical assessment
2. Use of end-tidal carbon-dioxide detection device
3. Use of esophageal aspiration bulb or syringe

Rationale

A properly positioned ET tube makes it possible effectively to oxygenate and ventilate children with critical illnesses or injuries. Esophageal placement of an ET tube, on the other hand, is usually harmful or fatal. Moreover, if the child is moved, a correctly placed ET tube may easily dislodge from the trachea to the esophagus. Delayed detection may result in hypoxia. Clinical assessment of placement of the ET tube is inaccurate, especially in infants and small children. Often, there is a lot of noise in the surrounding area (family members, loud music next door, traffic), that may make it hard to hear breath sounds. Or, breath sounds may be transmitted from the esophagus or stomach throughout the chest of a child and mislead the listener. Fortunately, several mechanical adjuncts are available to supplement clinical assessment and help confirm correct ET tube placement in the trachea.

Indication

Endotracheal intubation

Contraindications

An esophageal aspiration bulb or syringe cannot be used in a child weighing less than 20 kg

An adult carbon-dioxide detector device cannot be used in a child weighing less than 15 kg

Equipment

Stethoscope
Esophageal detector bulb or syringe (Figure P11-1) OR Colorimetric end-tidal carbon dioxide detector device (Figure P11-2)

Do not use an esophageal detector bulb or syringe if the child weighs less than 20 kg.

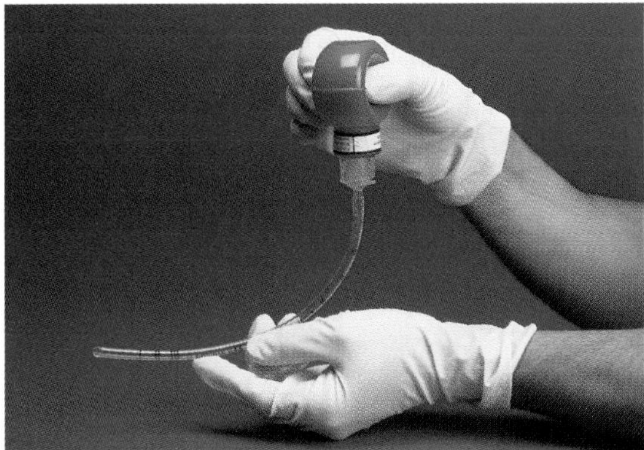

Figure P11-1 Aspiration bulb

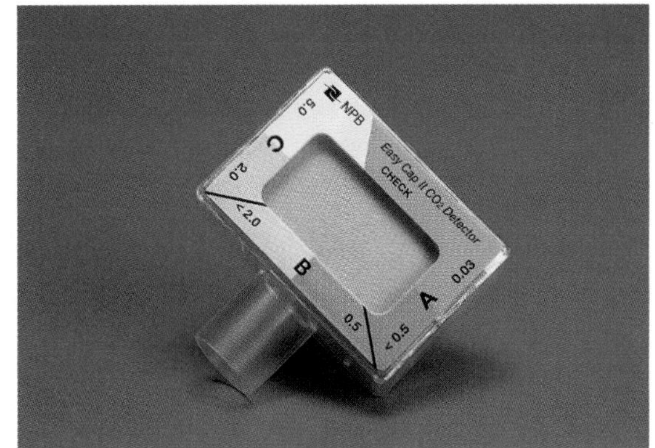

Figure P11-2 Carbon dioxide detector device

Possible Complications

A faulty device or misinterpretation of results of carbon-dioxide detector or esophageal detector device may result in incorrect ET tube placement or incorrectly removing an ET tube that was correctly placed.

Rebreathing carbon dioxide may cause hypercarbia in an infant weighing less than 15 kg if an adult-sized detector is left in-line.

If the child weighs less than 15 kg, use a pediatric device. If the child weighs 15 kg or more, use an adult device.

Do not remove the ET tube just because breath sounds are heard in the stomach. They may be transmitted sounds from the lungs.

Preparation

1. Intubate the infant or child with a correctly sized ET tube (see Procedure 10).
2. Determine weight of the patient.
3. Suction any fluid from the ET tube.

Esophageal detector (aspiration) bulb or syringe

1. Remove esophageal detector bulb or syringe from packaging.

Carbon dioxide detector

1. Determine correct size of the carbon dioxide detector.
   - Use a pediatric device if the child weighs less than 15 kg.
   - Use an adult device if the child weighs 15 kg or more.
2. Check the expiration date on the carbon dioxide detector package.
3. Remove the carbon dioxide detector from its packaging.
4. Inspect the carbon dioxide detector prior to use for:
   - bright purple color
   - dryness

Procedure

Clinical assessment

1. Look for bilateral rise and fall of the chest.
2. Remove ET tube if there is no chest rise with assisted ventilation.
3. Listen for breath sounds over the stomach (Figure P11-3).
   - If gurgling is present (like a straw in milk), the ET tube is in the esophagus.
   - If breath sounds only are present in the stomach, continue your assessment and do not remove the tube unless there is noticeable gastric distention with ventilation.
4. Listen for breath sounds in the right midaxillary line, then in the left midaxillary line.
   - If breath sounds are equal, secure the tube.
   - If breath sounds are greater on the right side than on the left side, then the tube may be in the right mainstem bronchus. Slowly pull back the ET tube until breath sounds are equal.

Esophageal detector bulb or syringe

1. Attach the device to the end of the ET tube.
2. Aspirate slowly over 3 to 5 seconds (Figure P11-4).
3. If resistance is felt, then the ET tube is in the esophagus. Remove it.
4. If air is aspirated, the ET tube is in the trachea. Secure it.

Carbon dioxide detector device

1. Attach the device to the end of the ET tube (Figure P11-5) and attach the other end to the bag-valve device.
2. Begin ventilation.
3. Observe the carbon dioxide detector for color change *during exhalation*. Read only after a total of *six breaths*.
4. Check the color and act accordingly (Table P11-1 and Figure P11-6).
5. Regardless of whether the ET tube is in the trachea the carbon dioxide detector will change to a purple color when 100% oxygen is

Remove the carbon dioxide detector from the ET tube if ET drugs are given because a wet detector may not show a correct color change from purple to yellow.

If the child is dead no color change will occur, even if placement is correct, because there is no carbon dioxide being produced.

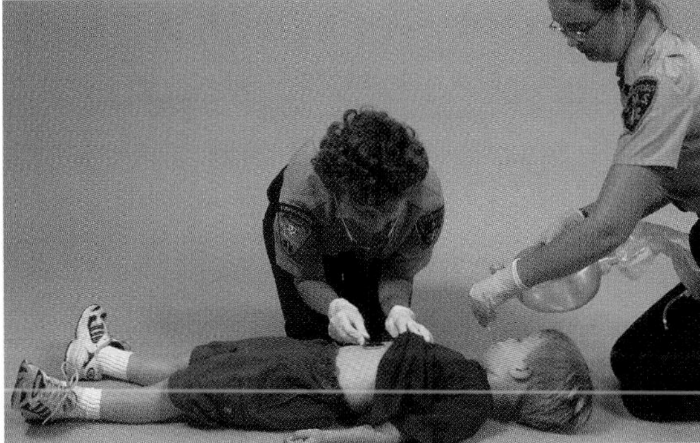

Figure P11-3 Listening for breath sounds over the stomach.

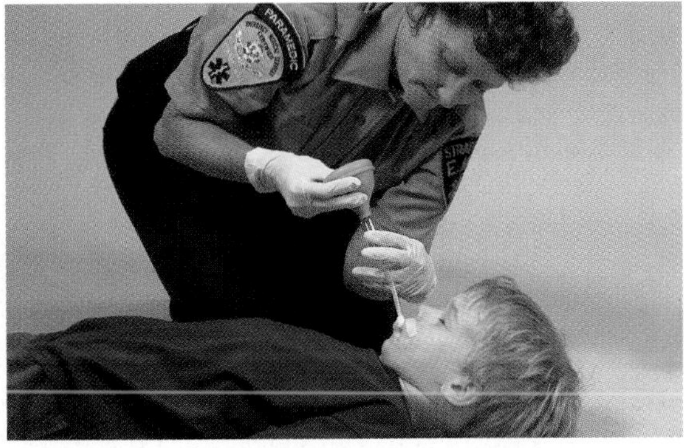

Figure P11-4 Using the aspiration device

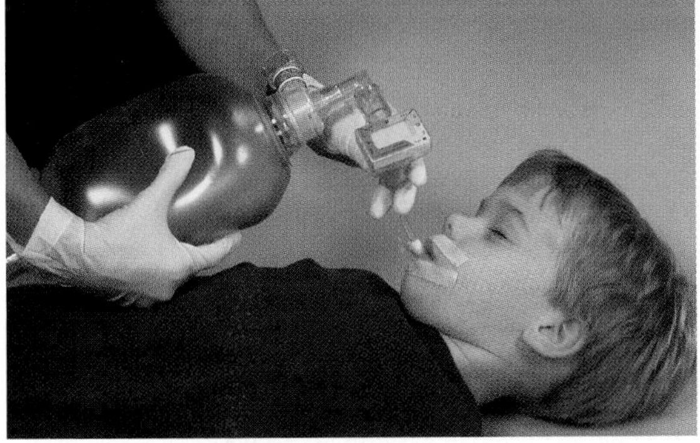

Figure P11-5 Using the carbon dioxide detector

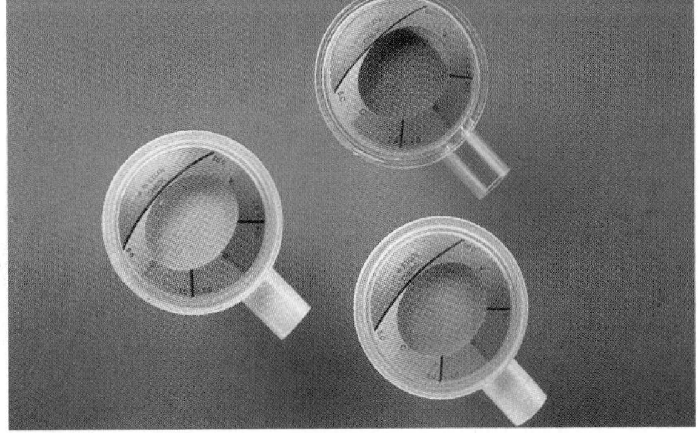

Figure P11-6 The carbon dioxide detector will change in a patient with a pulse from purple to tan to yellow. In a patient without a pulse, or when the ETT is in the esophagus, the carbon dioxide detector will not change color and will remain purple.

An important controversy is whether a carbon dioxide detector or esophageal detector (aspiration) bulb or syringe is better. There is not enough data on efficacy, safety, and feasibility to clearly support one technique alone.

squeezed through the bag and ET tube into the lungs. The color on exhalation is the one to pay attention to because the color in the expiratory phase of breathing reflects carbon-dioxide production.

6. Do not use an adult carbon-dioxide detector on a patient weighing less than 15 kg because the adult device has too much dead space and an infant can rebreathe carbon dioxide if it is left in line.
7. Leave the carbon-dioxide detector in line for transport unless the transport time exceeds 60 minutes.
8. Document observations and interventions.

Table P11-1 Use of Colorimetric Carbon Dioxide Detector in ET Tube Placement

Color	Patient with Pulse	Patient without Pulse
Yellow	Yes—tube correctly placed Leave tube in place and secure it	Yes—tube correctly placed Leave tube in place and secure it
Tan	Think about it Ventilate six more times (while reassessing tube placement) Reassess detector for color change. If still tan, leave tube in place and secure Attempt to correct any possible cause of low perfusion or low carbon dioxide	Think about it Ventilate six more times (while reassessing tube placement) Reassess detector for color change. If still tan, leave tube in place and secure Attempt to correct cause of low perfusion or low carbon dioxide
Purple	Problem—tube incorrectly placed Extubate Ventilate with BVM Reintubate	Problem—tube may be incorrectly placed, or the child is dead and not producing measurable amounts of carbon dioxide Look at vocal cords with laryngoscope If tube is incorrectly placed: Extubate Ventilate with BVM Reintubate If tube is between vocal cords, and vocal cord marker is below vocal cards: Leave tube in place Check adequacy of CPR Proceed with ALS protocol

11

Intravenous Access

Introduction

Establishing intravenous (IV) access is a time-honored method of fluid and drug administration. However, unlike the situation with an adult, securing IV access in a pediatric patient is often difficult or impossible in the out-of-hospital setting. Fortunately, the majority of pediatric patients do not require IV access before ED arrival and many out-of-hospital medications do not require an IV route for administration.

Rationale

IV access makes it easier to give medications and provides a route for fluid therapy in illness or injuries where there is possible blood or fluid loss. IV delivery is the gold standard for giving medications because it permits rapid and predictable onset of action for most important drugs. The indications for IV access must be carefully weighed against common complications and risks associated with the procedure. These include diversion from airway and breathing management, possible delays to ED care, and pain to the child. Also, there is a risk to the prehospital professional from exposure to bloodborne pathogens. However, in certain children, such as the critically ill child with shock, IV therapy in the field can be lifesaving.

Preparation

1. Assemble the equipment. Select the appropriate IV solution and tubing.
   - Inspect the solution for cloudiness, expiration date, leakage, or contamination.
   - Use microdrip IV tubing for giving medication.
   - For fluid administration, use a macrodrip.
   - Spike the fluid bag with the tubing, clamp the tubing, squeeze the drip chamber until it is half full, open the clamp, and flush the tubing.
   - Select the appropriate catheter, depending on need for fluid volume. Use a smaller catheter when only medications are indicated.
2. Prepare the child and family for the procedure. Use developmentally appropriate language to explain the procedure.
3. Select the site.
   - The scalp is an excellent site in newborns.
   - The best sites in the infant are the hands, antecubital fossa, and saphenous vein at the ankle or feet (**Figure P12-1**). The **dorsum** (back) of

Indications

Cardiopulmonary arrest

Shock

Cardiac dysrhythmia

Illness or injury possibly requiring immediate IV drug or fluid administration

Contraindications

Availability of another reliable administration route

Brief transport time

Consider vascular access on the way to the ED in the following situations:

- Multisystem injury
- Compensated shock
- Cardiogenic shock
- Newborn with circulatory depression from hypovolemia

Equipment

IV catheters, 14- to 24-gauge
IV tubing (macrodrip or microdrip)
IV solution
Rubber band or elastic band tourniquet
Adhesive tape or occlusive dressing
Gauze pad
Pediatric arm board

Never delay transport in any critically injured infant or child; consider IV attempts on the way to the hospital.

Possible Complications

Pain

Infiltration: Look for pain or edema at the site, inability to infuse fluids, or lack of blood return. Discontinue IV and insert at another site.

Hypothermia from giving too much room-temperature fluid to an infant

Skin infection

Thrombophlebitis

Inadvertent fluid overload

Catheter shear

Inadvertent arterial puncture

Controversy

Few children require IV access in the field or on the way to the ED. Injured children must always be transported before attempting IV access. For ill children, especially if there is a short transport time, it is controversial which ones need IV access, and whether IV access should be attempted on scene or on the way to the hospital.

If IV access is for giving medication only, use microdrip tubing. For giving fluid, use macrodrip tubing.

the hand is a good site in chubby infants. To access that site, grasp the child's hand with the fingers closed and flex the wrist downward.

- In toddlers and older children, potential sites are the hands and antecubital areas. Use the child's nondominant extremity if possible. The external **jugular** veins are good sites (Figure P12-2).

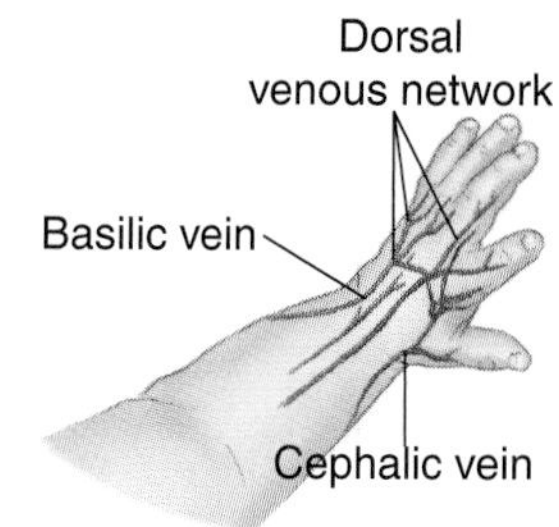

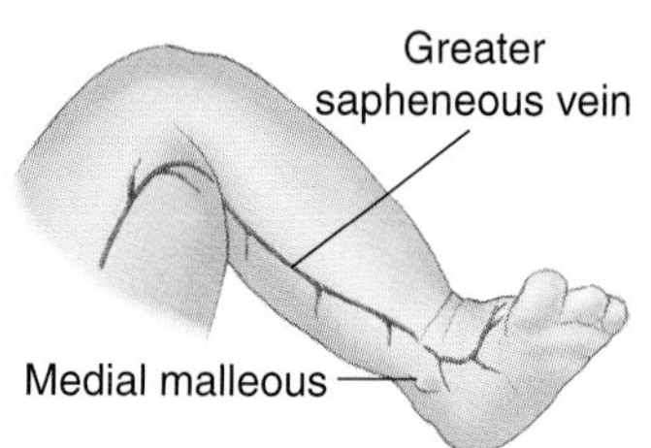

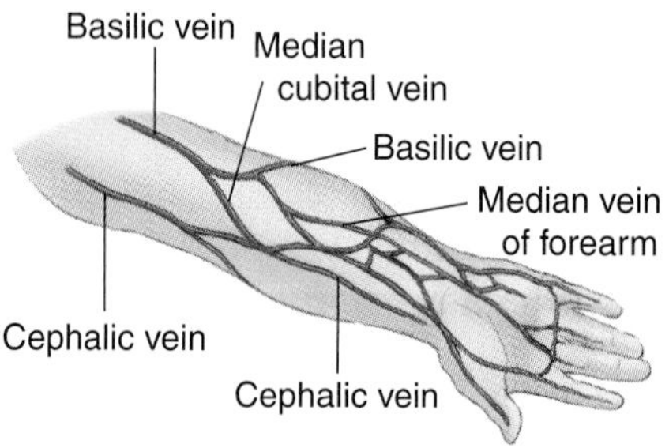

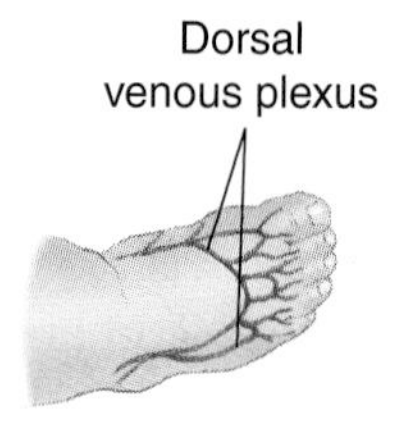

Figure P12-1 The best IV sites in infants are the hands, antecubital fossa, the saphenous veins at the ankle, and the feet.

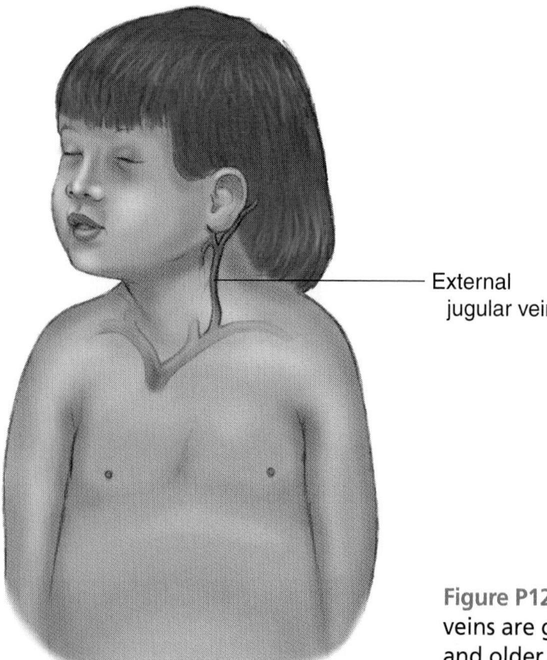

Figure P12-2 The external jugular veins are good IV sites in toddlers and older children.

- Avoid inserting the catheter over a joint.
- Consider the antecubital fossa when fluid boluses are required because veins that are more distal in the forearm or hand are usually smaller.
- Hand veins are often mobile under the skin and may move with contact with the catheter.

4. Position the patient supine, or in the caregiver's lap if the child is under school age (Figure P12-3). Secure the child's legs to avoid kicking. For external jugular cannulation, place the child in a slight head-down position (Figure P12-4). The caregiver can help hold the child and immobilize the insertion site.
5. Apply the rubber band or tourniquet proximal to the entry site. Do not make it too tight. The tourniquet should not block arterial flow. If it is necessary to make the vein more visible, do the following:
   - Place the extremity in a dependent position.
   - Tap or massage the site.
   - Ask the older child to clench and unclench his fist.
6. Cleanse the site with antiseptic solution.

Position the child and secure the site before beginning the procedure.

Do not use words like "stick" or "needle" when describing the procedure to the child. Instead, consider an explanation such as, "I will be putting a soft tube into your arm to give your veins a drink."

Procedure

1. Insert the needle:
   - Stabilize the vein by pulling the skin taut distally from the insertion site.

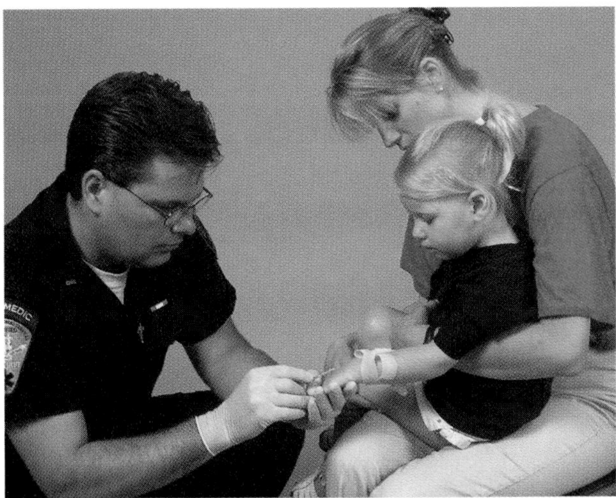

Figure P12-3 Place the child in the supine position or in the caregiver's lap. Secure the child's legs to avoid kicking.

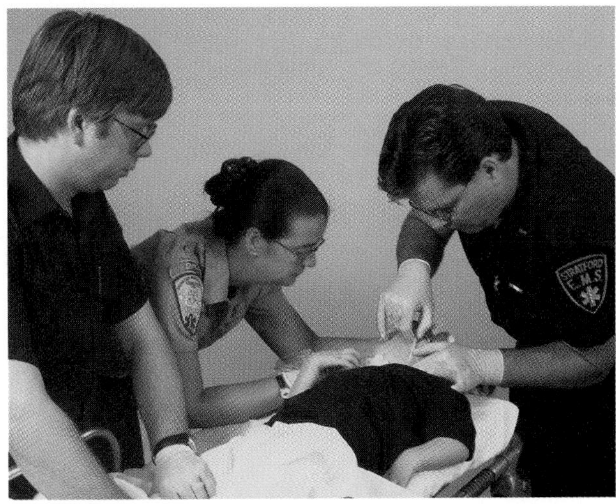

Figure P12-4 For external jugular cannulation, place the child in a slight head-down position.

Be careful not to secure the tape too tightly to immobilize the extremity, as this will block blood flow in the vein.

Reward and comfort the child after the procedure.

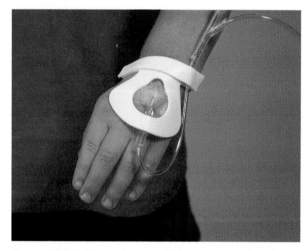

- Insert the catheter through the skin with the bevel up, at a 30-degree angle. Insert the catheter slowly; blood return may be delayed for a few seconds.
- When there is a flashback of blood, advance the catheter into the vein and then remove the needle. Never pull the catheter back over the needle because this may cause shearing of the catheter tip.
- Release the tourniquet.
- Compress the vein proximal to the site to prevent blood loss through the catheter while connecting the tubing. It is also helpful to position a gauze pad under the catheter at this time. Connect the tubing to the catheter.

2. Stabilize the catheter with tape or occlusive dressing. Avoid placing an excess amount of tape or gauze over the site because it obstructs the view of the site. Use a clear medicine cup or other device to protect the site while allowing access and visualization (Figure P12-5).

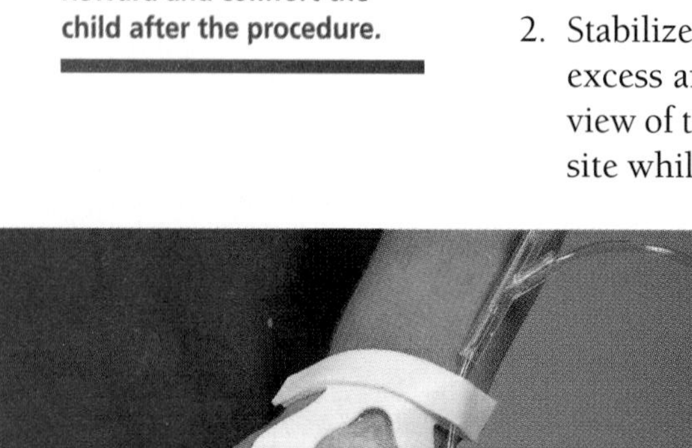

Figure P12-5 Use a clear medicine cup or other device to protect the site while allowing access and visualization.

3. Immobilize the extremity. Be careful not to apply the tape too tightly, as this will block the flow of blood through the vein.
4. Monitor the solution drip rate to avoid giving too much or too little fluid.
5. Dispose of the needle.

Troubleshooting

1. If the fluid is not infusing properly, assess the following:
   - Make sure the tourniquet has been released.
   - Make sure the child's arm is not bent.
   - Make sure the tape is not too tight.
   - Make sure the tubing is not kinked.
   - Make sure the clamp is open.
   - Lower the fluid bag below the extremity and assess for a backflow of blood into the tubing.
   - Raise the fluid bag higher if possible.
2. If none of the above measures are effective, discontinue the IV and restart in another site.

Intraosseous Needle Insertion

Introduction

Establishing vascular access is often difficult or impossible during life-threatening emergencies in infants and young children. The intraosseous (IO), intramedullary, or marrow route for the delivery of resuscitation fluids and medications has been used for over 50 years in children and adults. Many studies have confirmed that the intraosseous space is an excellent route for medications and fluids. The primary technical problem is successfully piercing the bony **cortex** (outer layer of the bone) in older children. The bones of neonates and infants are usually soft and the intraosseous space is relatively large, so needle insertion is easy in children of these younger age groups. Good equipment, preparation, and effective technique are especially important for success.

Indication

Severe illness or injury requiring immediate drugs or fluids, when IV access is impossible or unlikely to be successful

Contraindications

Available secure IV line

Lower-extremity deformity in same bone as insertion site

Equipment

14- to 16-gauge IO needles (**Figure P13-1**)
Alcohol swab for cleaning the skin
Normal saline and IV tubing
10-cc syringe
Stopcock (optional)

Rationale

Using an IO needle to give drugs or fluids is an excellent alternative to cannulating peripheral veins. The IO space is highly vascularized and functions as a noncollapsible vein. Needle insertion into this space is quick, simple, effective, and usually quite safe. There are several possible sites, but the easiest location is the proximal tibial. The IO space is suitable for infusion of almost all parenteral medications, crystalloid fluids, or blood products—which are quickly absorbed from small veins of the bone into the central circulation. Complications are usually minor and infrequent.

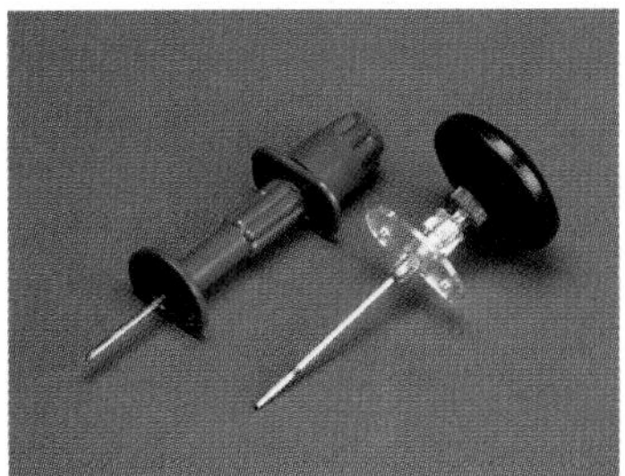

Figure P13-1 IO needles

Preparation

1. Place the patient in the supine position.
2. Put a small towel roll under the knee.
3. Prepare the skin over the insertion site.

Procedure

1. Use the flat surface of the proximal medial tibia, medial to the tibial **tuberosity** on the flat side of the bone (Figures P13-2a and P13-2b).
2. Introduce the IO needle in the skin, directed away from the growth plate or pointing toward the foot.
3. Pierce the bony cortex with a firm, twisting motion. Use a back-and-forth twisting motion to enter the marrow space. Do not push hard on

There is no data that compares intraosseous infusions of fluids and medications to IV administration. While intraosseous access is easy, quick, and safe, it is painful in a conscious child and therefore is only practical in a critically ill or injured child.

Possible Complications

Compartment syndrome

Failed infusion

Growth plate injury

Bone infection

Skin infection

Bony fracture

When placing the IO needle, use firm pressure and a twisting motion.

Insert the IO needle gently. Too much force may push the needle all the way through the bone and into the soft tissues.

the needle. A "pop" may be felt as the needle passes through the bony cortex and into the marrow cavity.

4. Remove the stylet and aspirate marrow contents. Keep any bone marrow aspirate for glucose check or for other tests in the ED. Sometimes marrow cannot be aspirated.
5. Confirm correct placement by infusing 10 ml of normal saline without resistance.
6. Attach IV line to the hub, or to a stopcock, and infuse fluids or drugs directly into intraosseous space.
7. Secure the needle to the overlying skin with tape.
8. Monitor the calf to ensure that there is no swelling to indicate leakage of fluid.

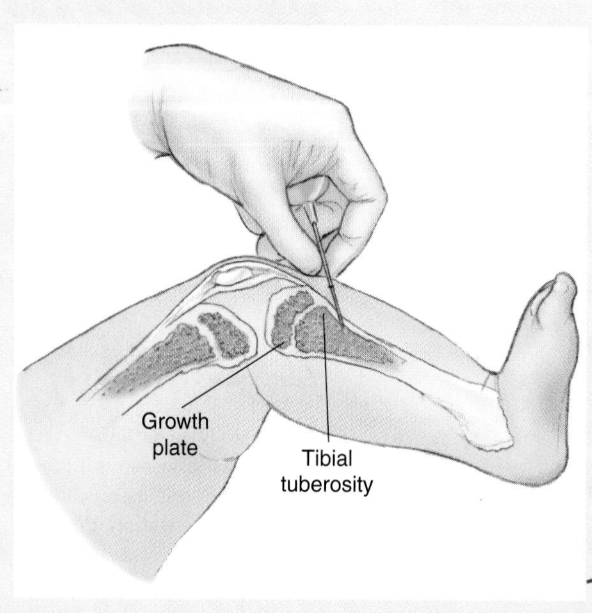

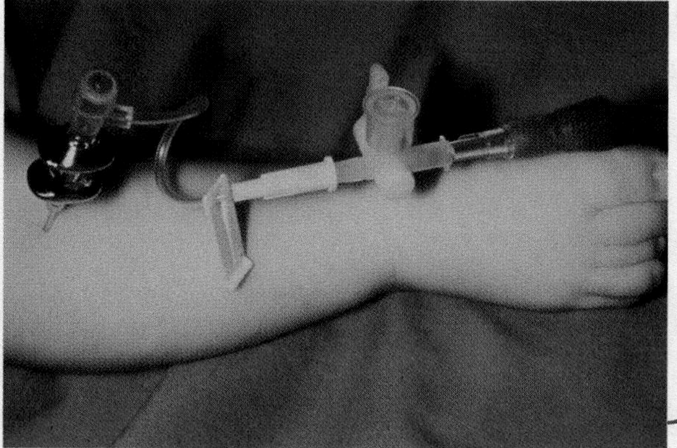

Figure P13-2 (A) An IO needle in the proximal tibial tuberosity (B) An IO needle in the proximal tibia of an unconscious infant in shock

Endotracheal Drug Delivery

Introduction

The ability of the airways of the lungs to absorb medicines has been recognized for over a century. Giving medication through an endotracheal tube is a simple alternative to IV or IO drug delivery in a cardiopulmonary resuscitation. The airways are well vascularized and can absorb certain emergency medications. Drug dosages and dilutions in endotracheal (ET) delivery may be different from IV or IO administration.

Indications

Cardiopulmonary resuscitation

Lack of IV or IO access

Contraindication

Functioning IV or IO access

Equipment

ET tube
Long catheter (feeding tube, suction catheter, nasogastric [NG] tube, or umbilical catheter)
Catheter size (in French units): approximately 2 times ET tube size (in mm) (**Table P14-1**)
Desired drug/diluent mixture
Normal saline or sterile water
Bag-valve device
Use 1 to 3 ml of diluent in infants, and 5 to 10 ml in older children. Use a minimum of 1 to 3 ml of diluent to ensure distribution and a maximum of 1.0 ml/kg (to approximately 30 ml total dose) to prevent problems with gas exchange in lungs.

Rationale

If neither IV nor IO access is available for giving drugs during cardiopulmonary resuscitation, the ET route is a good alternative for four pediatric drugs: lidocaine, atropine, naloxone, and epinephrine. The absorption, blood levels, onset, and duration of action are different with each drug. ET doses are unique for each agent, and are higher than IV or IO doses because absorption is not as good. While ET drugs are probably not as effective as IV or IO drugs, they can help improve the chances of successful resuscitation while IV or IO access is established.

Endotracheal drug administration is a potential route for medications during early phases of resuscitation.

Preparation

1. Intubate the patient.
2. Stabilize and secure the ET tube.
3. Preoxygenate and ventilate.

Procedure

1. Draw the calculated drug dose into a syringe (**Table P14-2**).
2. Dilute the medication with the proper diluent (diluting agent, either normal saline or sterile water.)
3. Insert tip of small feeding tube or catheter past distal tip of ET tube (**Figure P14-1**). (This step is optional)
4. Instill solution directly into the trachea, or ET tube.
5. Follow with injected air to clear tubing.
6. Ventilate 5 times with bag-valve device to disperse the solution into the entire lung.
7. Repeat medications if indicated.

Never give sodium bicarbonate by the ET tube.

It is unknown whether direct instillation of drugs into the trachea is better than instillation into the ET tube.

Possible Complications

Hypoxia

Hypercarbia

Pneumonitis

Tracheal injury

Adverse side effects of drug itself

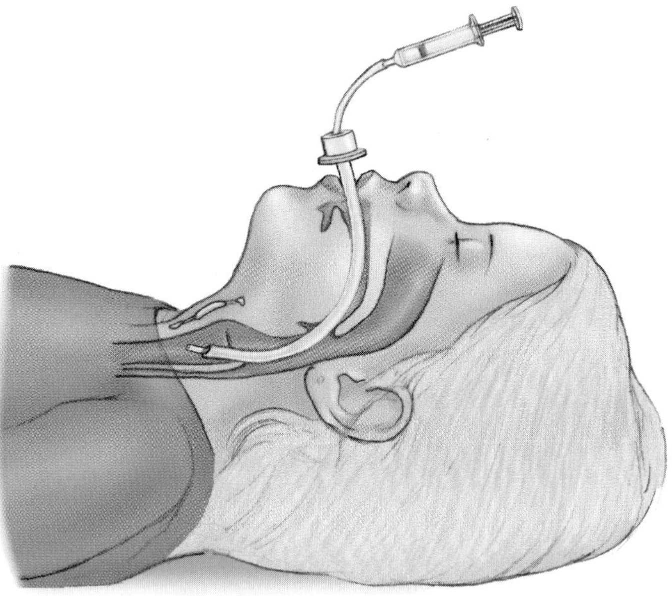

Figure P14-1 Inject drugs directly into the trachea through a feeding tube or other long catheter.

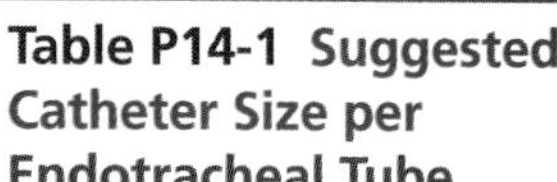

Table P14-1 Suggested Catheter Size per Endotracheal Tube

ET Tube Size (mm)	Catheter Size (Fr)
2.5	5
3.0	6
3.5–4.5	8
5.0–6.5	10
7.0	12

Table P14-2 The LANE Mnemonic: Suggested Medications and Doses via ET Tube Route

ET Tube Medications	IV Doses	ET Tube Dosages*	Diluent
Lidocaine, 1% or 2% (10 or 20 mg/ml)	1 mg/kg	2–10 mg/kg (same dose)	Sterile water
Atropine (0.1 mg/ml)	0.02 mg/kg	0.04 mg/kg (2 times IV dose)	Normal saline
Naloxone (1.0 mg/ml)	0.1 mg/kg	2–4 mg total dose	Normal saline
Epinephrine (1:1000) (1.0 mg/ml)	0.01 mg/kg	0. 1 mg/kg (10 times IV dose)	Normal saline
For newborns (1:10,000) (0.1 mg/ml)	0.01mg/kg	0.03 mg/kg (3 times IV dose)	Normal saline

*These doses are based on animal studies and are approximations.

Tip

IV and IO are better routes of drug administration than ET tube.

Controversy

The absorption and extent of central delivery of drugs given via ET tube is not known and dose recommendations have not been validated by scientific studies on children.

Electrical Countershock

Introduction

Electrical **countershock** for **tachydysrhythmias** has long been part of adult emergency care and is one of the most effective treatments for sudden cardiac arrest from ventricular dysrhythmias. However, in children, ventricular dysrhythmias are rare, especially in infants, and pediatric supraventricular tachycardia (SVT) is usually treatable with medical therapy. For these reasons, pediatric electrical countershock is not often indicated. However, when a child develops ventricular fibrillation or pulseless ventricular tachycardia, electrical countershock may be lifesaving. Also, electrical countershock may resuscitate a child in shock with SVT. Use the **synchronized** mode initially when there is SVT or ventricular tachycardia with a pulse, and the **asynchronized** mode for ventricular fibrillation or ventricular tachycardia without a pulse.

Indications

Ventricular fibrillation

Pulseless ventricular tachycardia

SVT with shock and no vascular access rapidly available

Ventricular tachycardia with shock and unresponsiveness with pulse and no vascular access rapidly available

Atrial fibrillation or atrial flutter with shock

Contraindication

Conscious patient with good perfusion

Equipment

Standard defibrillator
Newer models feature lower power outputs to deliver lower energy countershocks
Automatic External Defibrillator (>8 yrs)

Rationale

When a child's heart deteriorates into ventricular tachycardia or fibrillation, there is usually a severe systemic insult such as profound hypoxia, ischemia, electrocution, or myocarditis. Death may result if treatment is delayed. SVT, in contrast, is usually a more stable cardiac rhythm. When the child is pulseless and has ventricular fibrillation or ventricular tachycardia, perform electrical asynchronized countershock (defibrillation) as quickly as possible with the appropriate technique or use an automated external defibrillator (AED) if the child is over 8 years or 25 kg. If a child has SVT or ventricular tachycardia and shock, use synchronized countershock. Do not attempt to perform electrical countershock on a child with SVT who is well perfused.

Do not deliver countershock to a conscious child with SVT or ventricular tachycardia unless the child is in shock and has no IV or IO access rapidly available for medical treatment.

Preparation

1. Open airway and ventilate by BVM while assembling equipment for electrical countershock.
2. If child is pulseless, begin closed-chest compressions.
3. Select the proper paddles size. Use the 8-cm adult paddles if these will fit on the chest wall; otherwise, use the 4.5-cm pediatric paddles (**Table P15-1**).
4. Prep paddles or skin **electrodes** with electrode jelly, paste, or saline-soaked gauze pads, or use self-adhesive defibrillator pads. Do not let jelly or paste from one site touch the other and form an "electrical bridge" between sites, which could result in ineffective defibrillation or skin burns.

Possible Complications

Ineffective delivery of countershock because of failure to charge, improper positioning on the chest, incorrect paddle size, or improper conduction medium

Burns on the chest wall

Failure to "clear" before voltage discharge, leading to electrical shock of a team member or bystander

Tachydysrhythmia

Bradycardia

Myocardial damage or necrosis

Cardiogenic shock

Embolic phenomena

For a child with ventricular fibrillation or pulseless ventricular tachycardia, use the asynchronized mode.

Automated external defibrillators (AEDs) may be used in childern > 8 yrs (>25 kg) with pulseless ventricular tachycardia or fibrillation.

Failure to firmly apply paddles to the chest wall will decrease effective delivery of charge.

Table P15-1 Paddle Size

Use the largest paddles that will fit!
8-cm adult paddles (Use in children over 12 months of age or weighing more than 10 kg) On anterior chest wall, or Anterior-posterior
4.5-cm pediatric paddles (Use in infants up to 12 months of age or weighing less than 10 kg) on the anterior chest wall

5. Establish appropriate electrical charge (Table P15-2).
6. Select synchronized or asynchronized mode.
7. Properly charge pack and stop chest compressions.

Procedure

1. Apply the paddles directly to the skin. Place one paddle on the anterior chest wall on the right side of the sternum inferior to the clavicle and the other paddle on the left midclavicular line at the level of the **xiphoid process** (Figure P15-1).
2. As another option, use the anterior-posterior position (Figure P15-2).
3. Clear the nearby area to avoid shocking someone. Announce, "I am going to shock on three. One, I am clear. Two, you are clear. Three, everybody is clear."
4. Begin recording rhythm.
5. Deliver the countershock with firm pressure.
6. Assess the patient for evidence of **reperfusion** and check the monitor for the rhythm.
7. If the first electrical shock is unsuccessful, deliver additional electrical countershocks as per EMS protocol.
8. Give specific dysrhythmia treatment with epinephrine, lidocaine, or other drugs, as per EMS protocol.
9. Treat bradycardia or other dysrhythmias.

Table P15-2 Appropriate Electrical Charge for Countershock

Dysrhythmia	Mode	Charge
Ventricular fibrillation Ventricular tachycardia without a pulse	Asynchronized (defibrillation)	2 joules/kg, then 4 joules/kg, then 4 joules/kg, as needed. Then 4 joules/kg 30–60 seconds after each dose of epinephrine.
Ventricular tachycardia with pulse SVT Atrial fibrillation and atrial flutter with shock	Synchronized	0.5–1.0 joule/kg. Repeat as needed.

The preferred paddle location in children is controversial and no study in humans has compared the two techniques. Anterior chest wall placement has the advantage of a supine child and easier airway management. Anterior-posterior placement may allow larger paddles and more effective delivery of the charge.

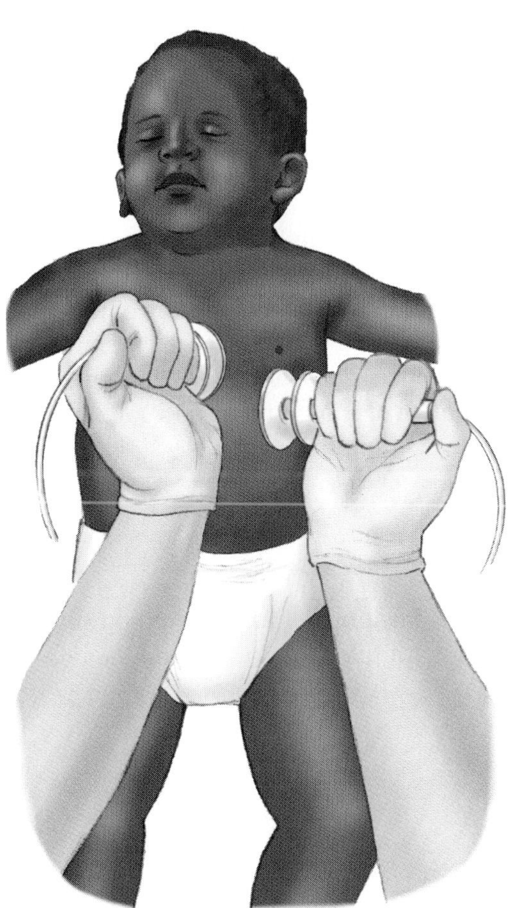

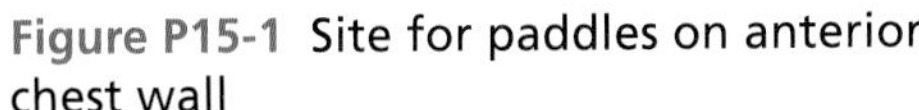

Figure P15-1 Site for paddles on anterior chest wall

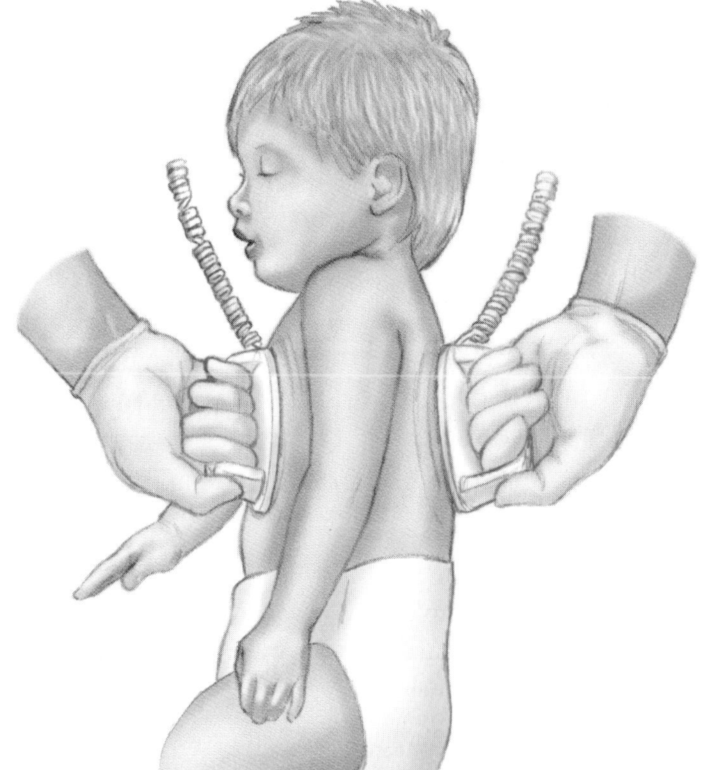

Figure P15-2 Site for paddles with child on side and paddles placed anterior-posterior

Cardiopulmonary Resuscitation

Indications

Newborn, infant, or child of any age who is apneic and pulseless

Newborn with a heart rate less than 60 beats/min and not improving after standard newborn care

Infants and children with a heart rate less than 60 beats/min and shock

Contraindication

Newborn, infant, or child with effective perfusion (palpable central or peripheral pulse)

Equipment

Mouth-to-mask device (Figure P16-1)
Bag-valve-mask (BVM) device, infant or child (see Procedure 8)
Airway adjuncts (see Procedure 4)
Appropriate mask sizes (see Procedure 2)

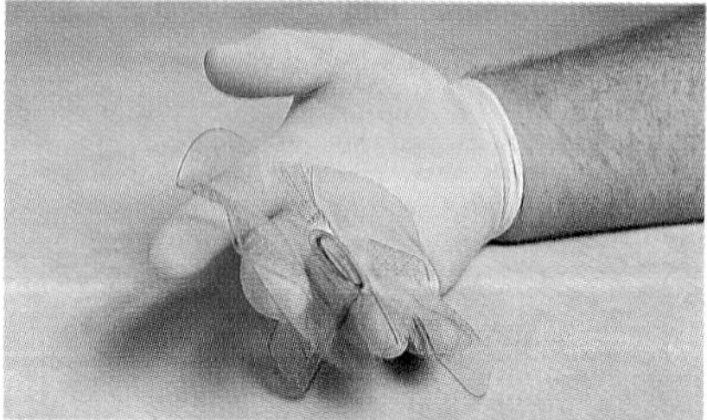

Figure P16-1 Mouth-to-mask device

The value of CPR in children is unproven for any condition except drowning. There are no available studies to compare the effectiveness of different types of ventilation or compression techniques.

Introduction

Cardiopulmonary arrest (CPA) occurs when a patient's heart and lungs stop functioning. In children, CPA usually begins as a primary respiratory arrest. This is in contrast to adults, in whom CPA or "sudden death" is almost always a primary cardiac event that occurs with onset of ventricular fibrillation and an abrupt change in the heart's electrical activity. Because cessation of effective breathing is the precipitating factor in pediatric CPA, airway management and ventilation are to children in CPA what defibrillation is to adults. Cardiopulmonary resuscitation (CPR) refers to basic airway management, artificial ventilation, and chest compressions to provide oxygen and circulation to core organs—the heart, brain, and lungs. In children, CPR has been shown to improve survival from drowning, and it may also benefit patients in CPA from other causes.

Rationale

CPR encompasses the basic procedures for sustaining critical oxygenation, ventilation, and perfusion recommended by the American Heart Association. The pediatric techniques are slightly modified from the adult techniques to reflect the known differences in CPA between age groups. Furthermore, there are specific differences between infants and children, including number of rescuers, placement of hands and fingers, rates of ventilation, and rates and depth of chest compressions.

Preparation

1. Position a child on a hard surface. Position an infant on a hard surface or on the forearm of the rescuer with the hand supporting the head.
2. Call for a second rescuer.

Procedure

1. Assess responsiveness.
2. If unresponsive, assess breathing.

Assess breathing

1. Open airway using either the head-tilt/chin-lift maneuver (medical patient) or jaw thrust maneuver (trauma patient) to achieve a neutral position.

2. If spinal injury is possible, have a second rescuer maintain manual spinal immobilization.
3. Look, listen, and feel for signs of breathing.
4. Remove any obvious obstructions, such as loose teeth or vomitus.

Ventilation rate

1. If no breathing, begin mouth-to-mask ventilation (Figure P16-2), or perform BVM ventilation with 100% oxygen. Give two initial effective breaths and observe chest rise. If possible, have a second rescuer apply gentle cricoid pressure to help reduce gastric distention.
2. If breaths do not expand the chest, reposition the head and attempt again. If breaths are still ineffective, suction the mouth with a bulb syringe or flexible suction catheter (newborns) or a large-bore rigid suction catheter (infants and children) and attempt breaths again.
3. If breaths now expand the chest, assess pulse.
4. If pulse is present, but the victim is still not breathing, continue ventilations (one every 2 seconds in newborns; one every 3 seconds for infants and children age 8 years and younger; one every 5 seconds for children older than 8 years).
5. Slowly repeat "squeeze…release…release" to time BVM ventilation rate.
6. Use the E-C clamp technique to achieve a good mask seal and watch for adequate chest rise to ensure effective ventilation.

Compression rate

1. Check central pulse.
   - Newborn: umbilical cord stump or listen to **precordium**
   - Infant: brachial pulse (see Figure 3-11) or femoral pulse
   - Child: carotid pulse
2. If pulse is absent or if heart rate is less than 60 beats/min, with shock or poor peripheral perfusion, begin chest compressions.
   - Newborn: 3 compressions: 1 ventilation
   - Infant and child: 5 compressions: 1 ventilation
3. Use proper compression technique, compression-ventilation ratio, depth of compression, and compression-release ratio (Tables P16-1 and P16-2).

   Finger or hand placement

   - Newborn/infant (<12 months): Use two or three fingers on the **sternum** just below the

Possible Complications

Coronary vessel injury
Diaphragm injury
Hemopericardium
Hemothorax
Interference with ventilation
Liver injury
Myocardial injury
Pneumothorax
Rib fractures
Spleen injury
Sternal fracture

Manipulation of the head to keep the airway in a neutral position is essential for effective ventilation.

Avoid gastric distention by using slow breaths to make the chest rise visibly, and by gentle cricoid pressure.

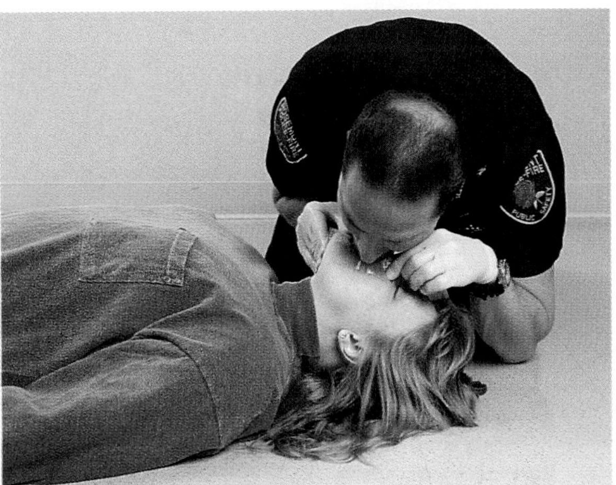

Figure P16-2 Mouth-to-mask CPR

A potential problem when using the thumbs for chest compression with the fingers encircling the back is restriction of ventilation if more than the thumbs and fingertips are touching the chest and back.

In newborns, the better compression method is with two thumbs encircling chest.

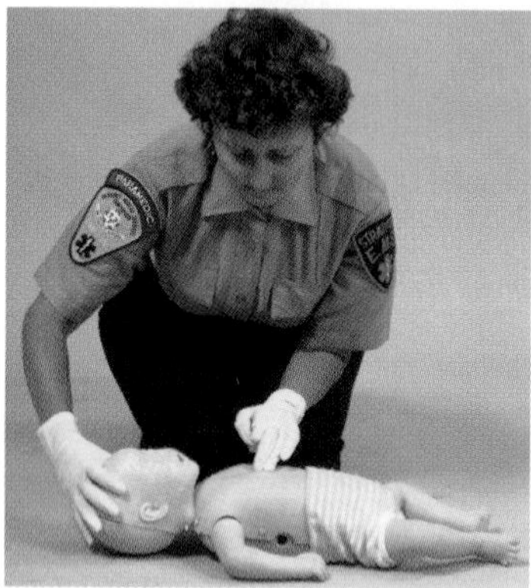

Figure P16-3 Use two fingers on the sternum just below the intermammary line.

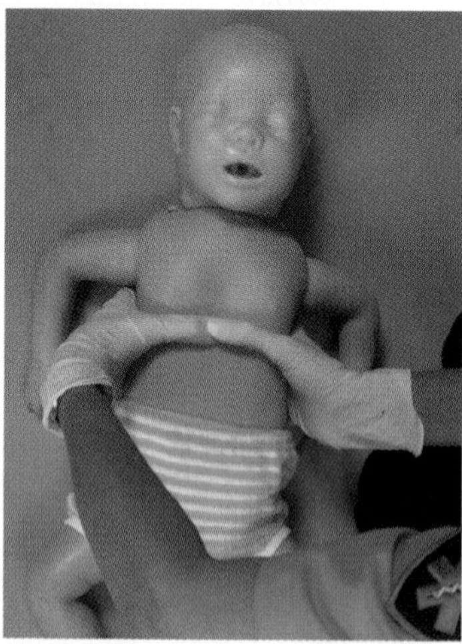

Figure P16-4 Encircle the chest and use thumbs just below the intermammary line.

Table P16-1 Delivered Compression-Ventilation Ratios per Minute*

Age	Rate of Compressions	Rate of Ventilations	Compression-Ventilation Ratio
Newborn (< 1 month)	120	30	3:1
Infant (1–12 months)	100	20	5:1
1–8 years	100	20	5:1
Over 8 years			
One rescuer	80–100	10–12	15:2
Two rescuers	80–100	12	5:1

*The rate of compressions and the actual number of compressions delivered per minute are different. The *rate of compressions* refers to the timing of compressions when they are being performed, and the rate does not account for pauses for breathing. *Delivered compressions* are the actual number of compressions delivered per minute after accounting for breathing. The ratios are calculated from the timing rates, not the delivered rates.

intermammary line (Figure P16-3), with the other hand supporting the spine. *Or*, encircle the chest and use thumbs just below the intermammary line (Figure P16-4) with the fingers supporting the spine. The 2-thumb encircling chest method is preferred.

- Child (1 to 8 years old): Use the heel of one hand on the sternum above the xiphoid process (Figure P16-5).
- Child (>8 years): Use the heel of both hands on the sternum above the xiphoid process.

Compression rates

These are the timing rates for single rescuers, not the actual number of compressions delivered each minute because of pauses for ventilations and reassessments.

- Newborn: At least 120 compressions/min
- Infant: 100 compressions/min
- 1–8 years: 100 compressions /min
- 8 years: 80 to 100 compressions /min

Depth of compressions

The depth of chest compressions should be approximately one third to one half the depth of the chest. Compressions should be deep enough to produce a palpable brachial, femoral, or carotid pulse.

- Newborn: 0.50 to 0.75 inch
- Infant: 0.5 to 1.0 inch

Table P16-2 Parameters for BLS Resuscitation in Children

Age	Compressions (min)	Ventilations (min)	Depth (in.)	Hand Placement for Compression
Newborn (< 1 month)	120	30	1/3 to 1/2 the depth of the chest	2 fingers at midsternum, 1 finger below nipple line, or 2 thumbs at midsternum with hands encircling chest (preferred)
Infant (1–12 months)	100	20	0.5–1.0	2 fingers at midsternum, 1 finger below nipple line, or 2 thumbs at midsternum with hands encircling chest
1–8 years	100	20	1.0–1.5	3 fingers or heel of 1 hand at midsternum, 2 fingers above xiphoid process
Over 8 years			1.5–2.0	Heel of both hands at midsternum, 2 fingers above xiphoid process
One rescuer	80–100	10–12		
Two rescuers	80–100	12		

- 1–8 years: 1.0 to 1.5 inches
- Over 8 years: 1.5 to 2.0 inches

Compression-release ratio The compression-release ratio is 1:1, which means that the time when there is no pressure on the chest should be as long as a compression.

4. Coordinate ventilations with compressions: Allow 1.0 to 1.5 seconds for 1 ventilation after every 5 compressions.
5. Use the two-rescuer technique when possible (Figure P16-6).
6. Reassessment: Check pulse after approximately 1 minute or after every 20 compression-ventilation cycles.

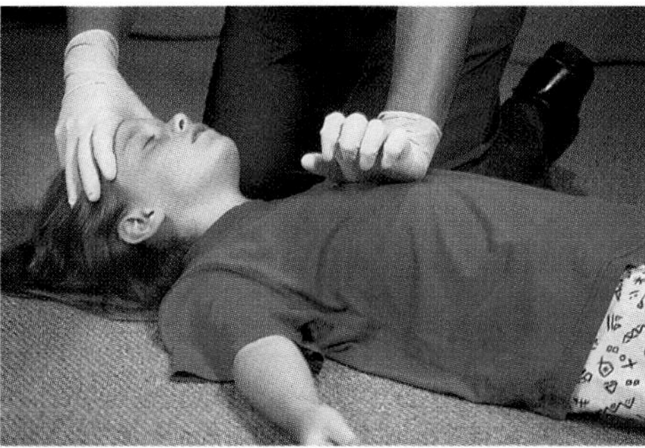

Figure P16-5 In a child 1–8 years old, place heel of the hand on the mid-sternum 2 fingers above the xiphoid process.

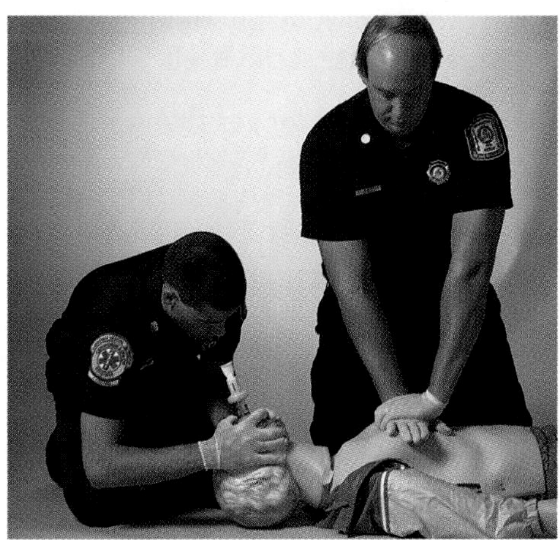

Figure P16-6 Two-rescuer technique

A common problem in the transition from one-rescuer to two-rescuer child CPR is the lack of coordination between ventilations and compressions.

Do not use mechanical devices to compress the sternum of a child.

Continuously assess effectiveness of CPR by ensuring chest rise and feeling for a palpable pulse.

Resuscitation Tape

Indication

Children requiring equipment, medication, or fluids, weighing from 3 to 34 kg body weight

Contraindications

Premature infant weighing less than 3 kg

Child older than 10 to 12 years of age or weighing more than 34 kg body weight (use adult equipment and drug dosages)

Equipment

Pediatric resuscitation tape

Possible Complications

None

Store the tape in a place that is easily accessible, such as the pediatric equipment kit.

There are several different brands of length-based pediatric resuscitation tapes; these have not been compared for speed, accuracy, or safety.

Measuring to the child's toes (instead of heel) will add a number of kg to the estimated weight and may result in equipment sizes that are too large or drug doses that are excessive.

Introduction

The pediatric resuscitation tape or length-based resuscitation tape is a simple and effective tool to measure lengths and to determine approximate weights in children. In addition, the tape provides appropriate equipment sizes and drug doses by lengths and by weights.

Rationale

Treatment of infants and children in the out-of-hospital setting is difficult because children of different ages require different sizes of equipment, doses of medications, and volumes of fluids. Mistakes are common when selecting appropriate equipment and medications in critical pediatric emergencies without the benefit of an accurate weight. The pediatric resuscitation tape uses length as a valid marker of size-specific equipment and medication needs. It is portable, easy to use, and applies to all out-of-hospital equipment and medications.

Preparation

1. Place the patient in a supine position.
2. Extend the patient's legs.

Procedure

1. Measure child's length—from head to heel—with the tape.
2. Note and say weight in kilograms that corresponds to the child's measured length at the heel.
3. If the child is longer than the tape, use adult equipment and medication doses.
4. From the tape, identify appropriate equipment sizes.
5. From the tape, identify appropriate medication doses.

Rectal Diazepam Administration

Introduction

Rectal drug administration is a well-known delivery technique in children and is useful for many medications, including antipyretics and **anticonvulsants**. The only rectal medication approved in most EMS systems is diazepam for pediatric status epilepticus. Status epilepticus is a major pediatric medical emergency that may benefit from quick treatment. Although the first priority is airway and breathing, additional therapy may include medication to terminate the seizure. In most cases intravenous, intramuscular, or intraosseous drug administration is not necessary because rectal diazepam is probably as effective and has no added complications.

Indication

Status epilepticus

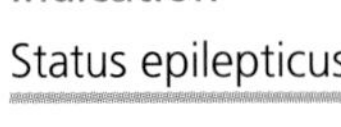

Contraindications

Newborn age (a month or less) (relative)

Recent rectal surgery (e.g., for Hirschsprung's disease, imperforate anus) (relative)

Equipment

Lubricant
Tuberculin syringe, or 14- to 20-gauge over-the-needle catheter with 3- to 5-ml syringe
IV solution of diazepam
Tape (optional)

Rationale

Establishing IV or IO access is often time consuming and may delay delivery of essential advanced life support (ALS) drugs, especially in infants and toddlers. The **rectum** is an effective alternative route for emergency drug administration. The rectum is highly **vascularized** (Figure P18-1), and certain drugs are quickly absorbed through the lining or mucosa. Diazepam is a lipid-soluble benzodiazepine that is reliably absorbed through the rectum and will terminate most seizures without further treatment. It will take a few minutes longer to stop the seizure after rectal administration of diazepam as compared to IV diazepam. Occasionally, as with the IV diazepam preparation, more than one dose of rectal diazepam is necessary because of the drug's short duration of action.

The rectal dose of diazepam is 0.5 mg/kg, or five times the intravenous dose, to a maximum dose of 10 mg. Onset of action for rectal diazepam is slower.

The relative effectiveness and safety of rectal diazepam versus intramuscular midazolam are not known.

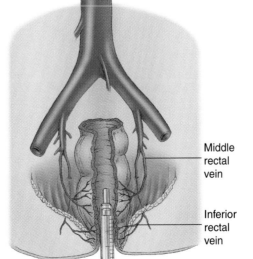

Preparation

1. Use the pediatric resuscitation tape to determine the weight of the child (see Procedure 17), or establish the patient's weight from information provided by the caregiver.
2. Draw up the calculated dose of IV medication into a disposable tuberculin syringe or 3- to 5-ml syringe.

Figure P18-1 Anatomy of the human rectum

Possible Complications

Respiratory depression

Administration that is too high with inadequate serum level

Rectal tearing

Administration of diazepam too high into the rectum may decrease its anticonvulsant effect, because the drug may be absorbed differently and broken down more quickly in the liver.

18

The most serious potential complication of rectal diazepam is respiratory depression, which is usually from the drug, but may be from the prolonged seizure, or the underlying cause of the seizure.

3. Lubricate the syringe or catheter:
   a. If using the tuberculin syringe as the administration device, remove needle and apply lubricant to the tip of the syringe.
   b. If using a 3- to 5-ml syringe (or tuberculin syringe, to draw up medication only), remove needle, attach over-the-needle catheter (plastic portion only), and lubricate catheter.

Procedure

1. Position the patient in the decubitus position, knee-chest position, or supine position (**Figure P18-2**) with a second prehospital professional or the caregiver holding the legs apart.
2. Carefully introduce the syringe or over-the-needle catheter approximately 5 cm (2 inches) into the rectum.
3. Inject the solution into the rectum. Remove the syringe.
4. Hold buttocks closed for 10 seconds.
5. Tape buttocks closed (optional).

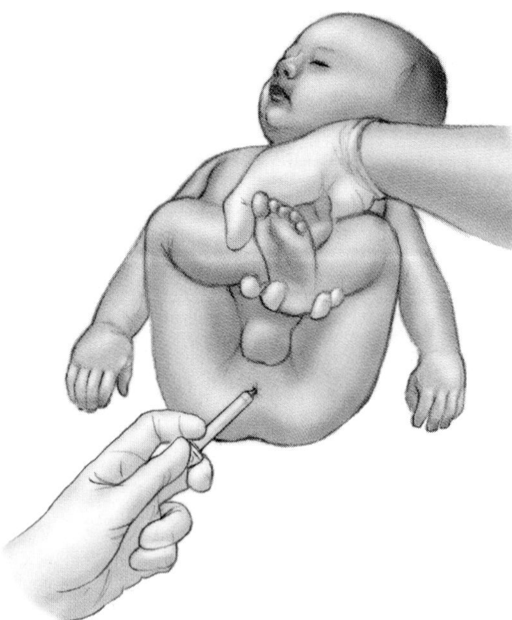

Figure P18-2 Expose the rectum by lifting the legs, then insert the syringe.

Spinal Immobilization

Introduction

Spinal injury may be subtle or difficult to recognize because of altered level of consciousness, distracting injuries, or lack of obvious signs. Failure to recognize potential spinal injury can lead to death or permanent disability. Spinal immobilization is therefore essential for every child who sustains a suspicious mechanism of injury (where the head, neck, or spine may be involved), who has pain or tenderness of the spine, or who has signs or symptoms of weakness or loss of sensation.

Rationale

The spinal column is made of 33 articulating bones, and its structure changes significantly during childhood growth. The age of the child and the physical state of spinal growth are important factors in the incidence and types of pediatric spinal injuries. Whenever the mechanism of injury, signs, or symptoms suggests possible spinal injury, the entire spine must be immobilized. This is best performed with the patient supine on a rigid spine board and in a neutral, in-line position. In field situations where

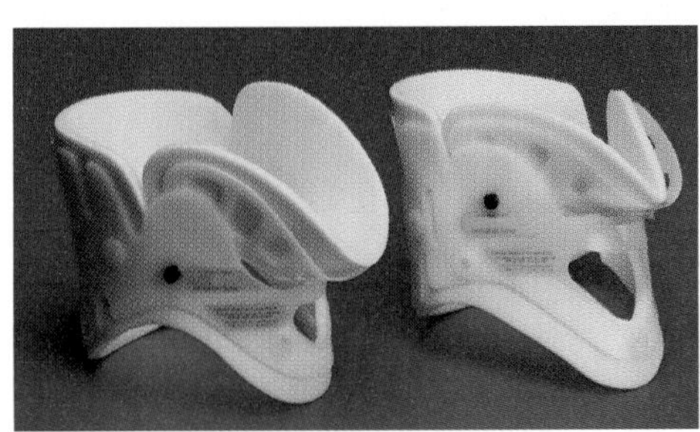

Figure P19-1 Rigid cervical collars in pediatric sizes

Figure P19-2 Head cushions from a cervical immobilization device

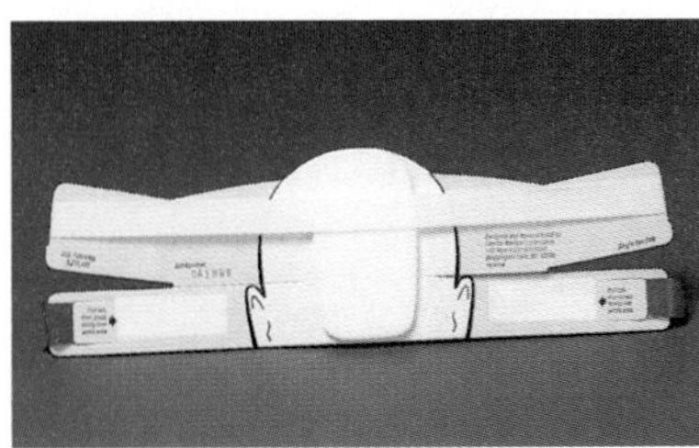

Figure P19-3 Cervical immobilization device

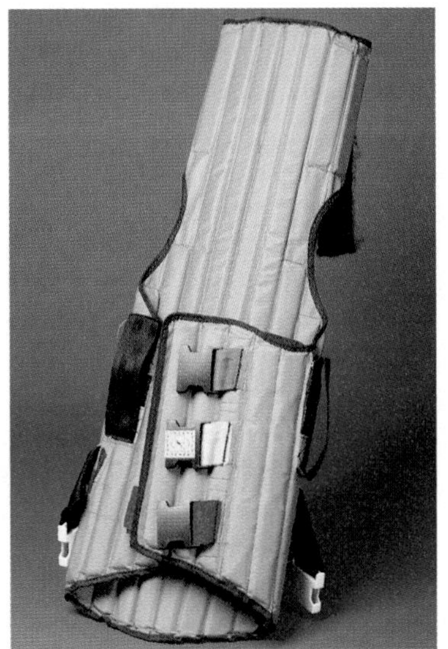

Figure P19-4 Vest-type device

Indications

Any significant mechanism of injury above the clavicles, including the head, neck, face, or axial spine

Acute weakness or loss of sensation after an injury

Pain or tenderness to the neck or spine

Deformity to the neck or spine

Altered level of consciousness after an injury

Contraindications

The combative child is a relative contraindication because forceful restraint of a combative child with spinal or head injury can worsen the injury.

If the risks of agitation and increased spinal movement from full spinal immobilization are greater than the benefits, consider more acceptable but less definitive immobilization options, and document circumstances clearly.

Equipment

Long spine board
Padding materials (blankets, towels)
Rigid cervical collars in pediatric sizes (**Figure P19-1**)
Straps with fastening device
Wide tape (2-inch or 3-inch)

Optional equipment
Head cushions from a cervical immobilization device (CID) (**Figure P19-2**)
Commercial pediatric immobilization device (**Figure P19-3**)
Vest-type immobilization device (**Figure P19-4**)

Possible Complications

Airway obstruction

Impairment of ventilation

Obscuring hemorrhage or other injuries

Spinal injury from improper technique

Back pain

Reassure nervous children that the immobilization is only temporary, but it is necessary. Try distraction.

Do not use sandbags or weighted material because of the risk of injury in the event of movement.

Controversy

The indications for long-board spinal immobilization of infants and toddlers are unknown. Infants and young children cannot verbally communicate symptoms such as weakness, numbness, or pain, so the threshold for immobilization must be lower than for the older child. However, restraining a conscious child on a long board will cause pain and agitation in a short time.

this immobilization technique is not possible, maintain the anatomic stability of the entire spinal column as carefully as possible, and use age-specific considerations in approaching the child to minimize spinal movement.

Preparation

1. If the child is unstable or the environment is unsafe, quickly remove the patient onto the long spine board using manual spinal stabilization techniques.
2. If the depth of the patient's head is greater than that of the torso, arrange padding on the board to keep the entire lower spine and pelvis in line with the cervical spine and parallel to the board (Figure P19-5). This padding must cover the entire surface of the long spine board from the patient's shoulders to the hips.
3. Prepare the child and caregiver for the procedure by explaining actions. Make a game of it for an alert, cooperative child.

Procedure

Initial manual immobilization

1. Gently align the head and neck into a neutral position similar to the "sniffing position" (Figure P19-6). Do not force neutral position if there is resistance to movement, crepitus, or increased spinal pain.
2. Have an additional rescuer(s) restrain other body parts as needed to reduce motion.
3. Have a second rescuer apply a size-appropriate rigid cervical collar (Figure P19-7). Evaluate the neck area that will be covered by the cervical collar. Determine the appropriate size with the manufacturer's recommendations. If the correct-size cervical collar is unavailable, skip to the next step.
4. Transfer the patient as a unit onto a spine board or alternate immobilization device that is long enough to support the patient's full length (Figure P19-8). Perform the clinical assessment of the patient's back, buttocks, and breath sounds during the logroll process. Be prepared to treat injuries.
5. After placing the child on the board, pad all open spaces under the patient before securing the patient to the board.

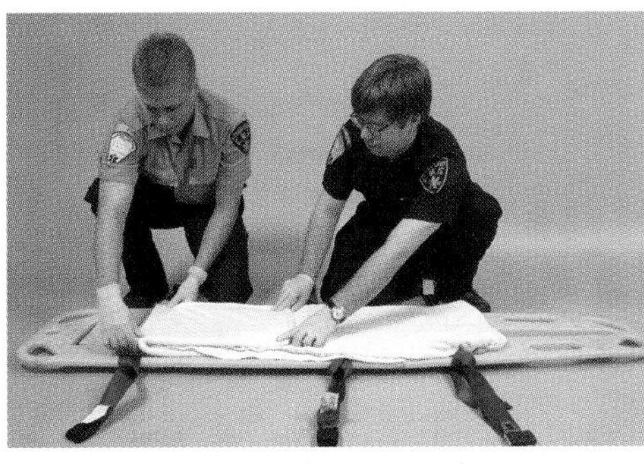

Figure P19-5 If the depth of the patient's head is greater than that of the torso, arrange padding on the board to keep the entire lower spine and pelvis in line with the cervical spine and parallel to the board.

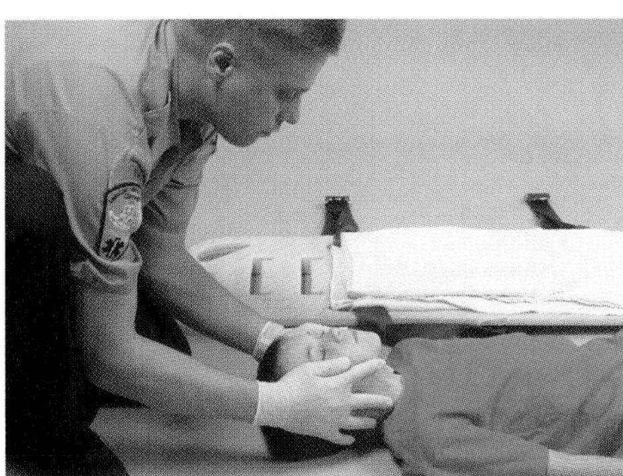

Figure P19-6 Align the head and neck in a neutral cervical-spine position similar to the sniffing position for airway.

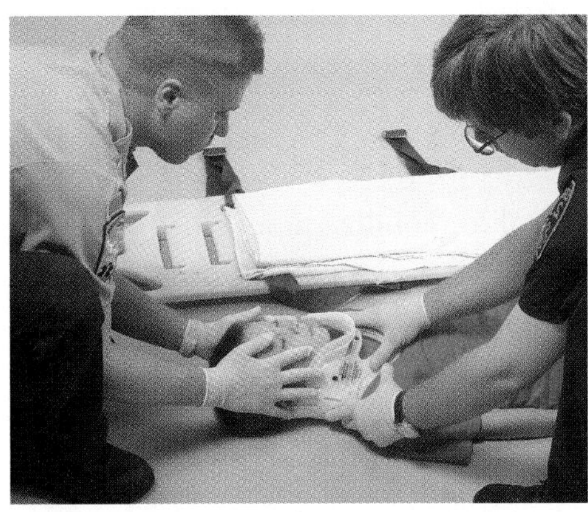

Figure P19-7 Have the second rescuer apply a size-appropriate rigid cervical collar.

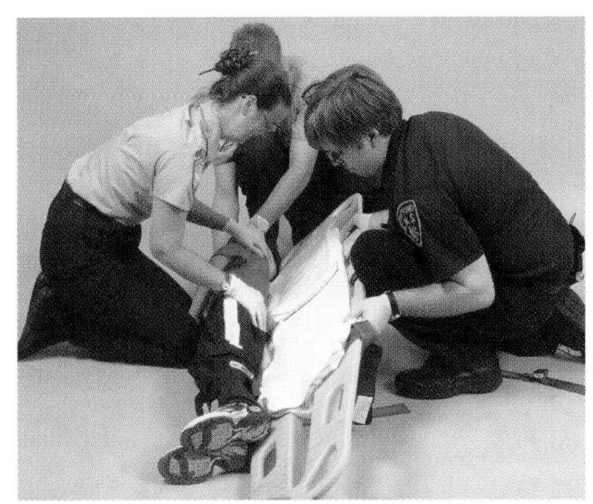

Figure P19-8 Transfer the patient as a unit onto a spine board or alternate immobilization device that is long enough to support the patient's full length.

Securing a patient to an immobilization device

1. Secure the patient's body to the board while manually maintaining the neutral alignment of the head and neck.
2. To secure against lateral movement, pad along the patient's sides to the edge of the board, especially along the pelvis and legs (Figure P19-9).

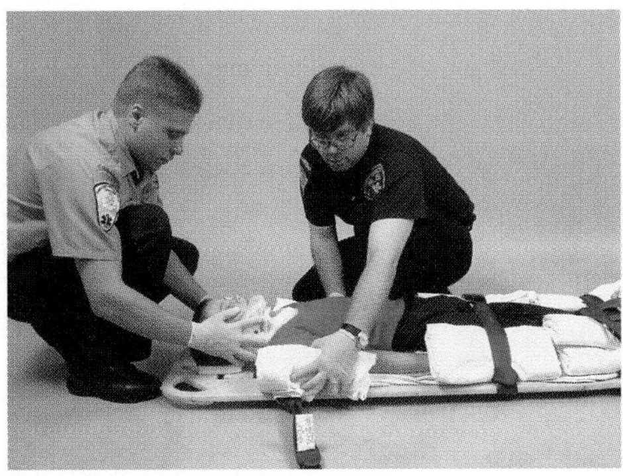

Figure P19-9 To secure against lateral movement, pad along the patient's sides to the edge of the board, especially along the pelvis and legs.

Pad the patient to make the child as wide as the board.

Do not accept the labeled sizes for cervical collars ("pediatric" or "infant"). Measure each patient individually.

The effectiveness and safety of the vest-type immobilization device is controversial. The device is supposed to provide added restraint to a long spine board, but risks and benefits are not established.

Assign one rescuer to in-line neck immobilization of a combative child.

Never place tape across the child's neck, as this may obstruct the airway.

3. Stabilize the cervical spine by using blanket rolls, or blocks from the CID, to restrict lateral head motion and rotation and to prevent upward motion of the shoulders (Figure P19-10). Do not pad the young child's head because the large **occiput** will flex the neck and bend the airway out of neutral position.
4. Secure against axial shifts if the board needs to be tilted (going down stairs, fitting into a small elevator, or for elevating the head in cases of head injury).
5. Place straps across the patient at the level of the **axilla**, pelvis, and legs. Do not place straps over the abdomen or use straps to impair movement of the diaphragm.
6. Further secure the head with tape directly over the patient's eyebrows (Figure P19-11). Avoid chin straps that may complicate airway maintenance in case of emesis.

Pediatric immobilization using a vest-type immobilization device

1. Perform the steps for initial manual immobilization.
2. Remove the vest device from its case. Open the head and body flaps. If the child's legs are longer than the device, place the device on a long spine board.
3. If padding is required to keep the child in neutral position, place it on the device.

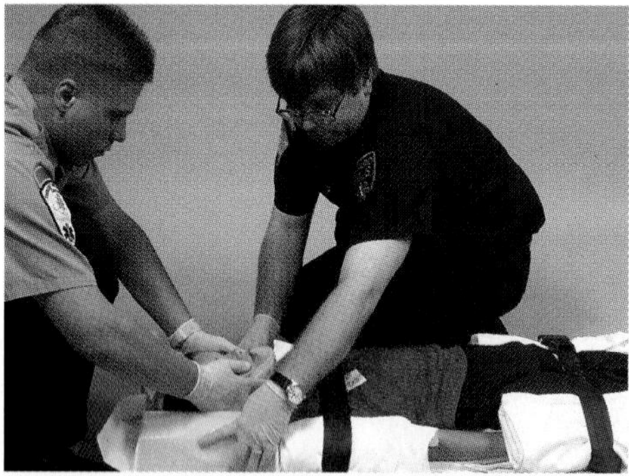

Figure P19-10 Stabilize the cervical-spine by using blanket rolls, or blocks from a cervical immobilization device, to block lateral head motion and rotation, and to prevent upward motion of the shoulders.

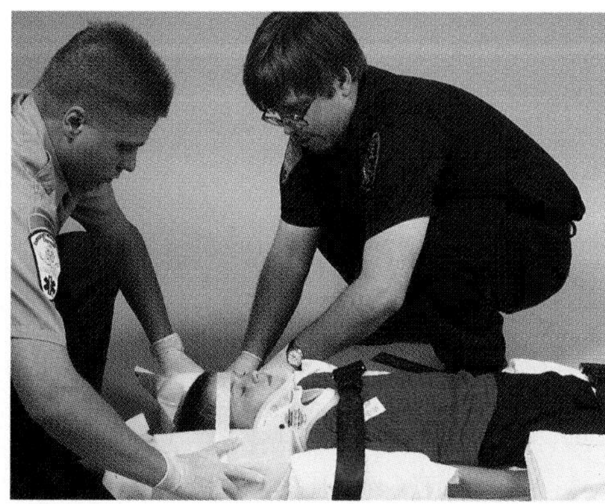

Figure P19-11 Secure the head by using tape directly above the patient's eyebrows.

4. Using standard techniques (logroll, pivot onto board), move the patient as a unit onto the device.
5. Lift the body flaps up and fold them inward on themselves along the lateral sides of the patient. This will ensure that the abdomen and chest are not restricted.
6. Secure the body flaps across the patient's trunk with tape or the attached straps. Make sure not to restrict the child's diaphragm or breathing.
7. Lift the head flaps up along the child's head, then fold the flaps down to the side so that the top edges are even with the child's forehead.
8. Place a strap across the child's forehead, connecting it across both sides of the head flaps (Figure P19-12).
9. Secure the immobilized child to a long spine board using the techniques above.

When using tape, use the longest strips possible to maximize adhesive surface and security.

Never release manual neck stabilization until the entire spine is properly immobilized.

Releasing and monitoring immobilization

1. Do not release manual head and neck stabilization until the entire spine is properly immobilized.
2. Reassess airway, breathing, and circulation for possible compromise due to immobilization technique.
3. Assess the patient's distal neurologic status before and after immobilization.

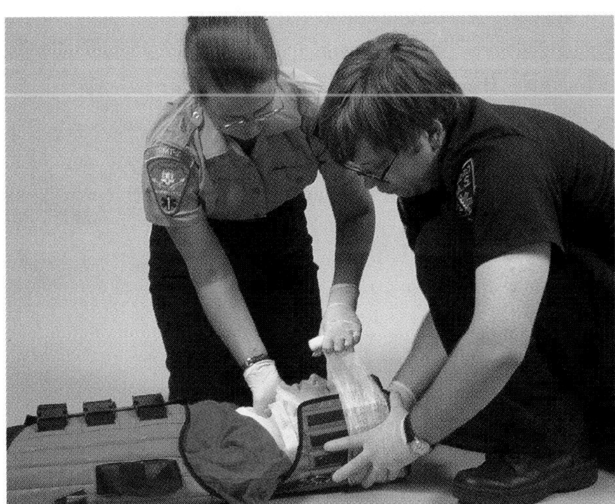

Figure P19-12 Using the vest type device, place a strap across the child's forehead, connecting it across both sides of the head flaps.

Needle Thoracostomy

Indications

Penetrating chest-wall injury in a child with respiratory distress and hypoxia

Blunt chest-wall injury in a child with respiratory distress and hypoxia that worsens with assisted ventilation

Contraindication

History of a severe bleeding disorder such as hemophilia (relative)

Equipment

14- or 16-gauge over-the-needle catheter

30-ml syringe

Povidone-iodine solution

The frequency of tension pneumothorax after blunt chest-wall injury is not known, and the indications for needle thoracostomy in this out-of-hospital situation are controversial.

Feeling for a midline trachea and listening for breath sounds are inaccurate ways to assess for pneumothorax in an infant or young child.

Suspect a tension pneumothorax when a child with chest injury worsens with assisted ventilation.

Introduction

A pneumothorax occurs when air gets between the two pleural membranes of the lung, a potential space that is empty under normal breathing conditions. Tension pneumothorax develops when the air in the pleural space has enough pressure to shift the internal contents of the chest and impair function of the lungs, heart, and great vessels. Reduction in blood return to the heart and diminished cardiopulmonary function will result in shock and cardiopulmonary arrest if the tension pneumothorax is untreated. The child with tension pneumothorax has usually had positive pressure ventilation in the field and will have physiologic abnormalities on assessment, with evidence of increased work of breathing and hypoxia. Classical adult physical findings, such as a shifted trachea or diminished breath sounds on the affected side, may not be detectable in an infant or child. If cardiac output is severely impaired by the tension pneumothorax, the child will also exhibit shock.

Rationale

When the mechanism of injury, signs, and symptoms suggest tension pneumothorax in a child, create an opening between the pleural space and the atmosphere to immediately reduce elevated air pressure. This will help reexpand the lung, improve venous return, and restore cardiopulmonary function. The easiest method for creating a communication between the pleural space and the outside atmosphere is by producing an open pneumothorax. The technique requires inserting a large-bore needle into the pleural space and leaving it open to the air. This procedure is more frequently indicated after penetrating injury than blunt injury.

Preparation

1. Position the child supine.
2. Raise the arm above the head on the affected side, and have the caregiver or second rescuer hold it.
3. Select the site (Figure P20-1).
   - second intercostal space at the midclavicular line OR
   - fourth intercostal space at the anterior axillary line

4. Before preparing the site, count the ribs *twice* to ensure proper site location. The nipple is usually at the fourth intercostal space.
5. Prepare the site with providone-iodine solution.

Possible Complications

Open pneumothorax

Hemothorax

Diaphragm penetration

Bowel penetration

Hemopericardium

Coronary vessel injury

Procedure

1. Attach the needle, with stylet in place, to the syringe.
2. Insert the needle through the skin at 60-90 degrees and advance until the tip hits a rib.
3. Advance the needle over the top of the rib margin (Figure P20-2).
4. Push the needle tip into the pleural space. A slight "pop" is usually felt when the needle pierces the outside pleural membrane, or parietal pleura.
5. Pull back the plunger of the needle to aspirate air.
6. Remove the syringe and stylet and leave the catheter in the pleural space, anchored in the chest wall.
7. Monitor work of breathing, circulation to skin, heart rate, respiratory rate, and blood pressure.
8. Consider doing contralateral needle thoracostomy if the child does not improve.

Do not insert the needle under the rib margin because the vessels and nerves there are easily injured.

20

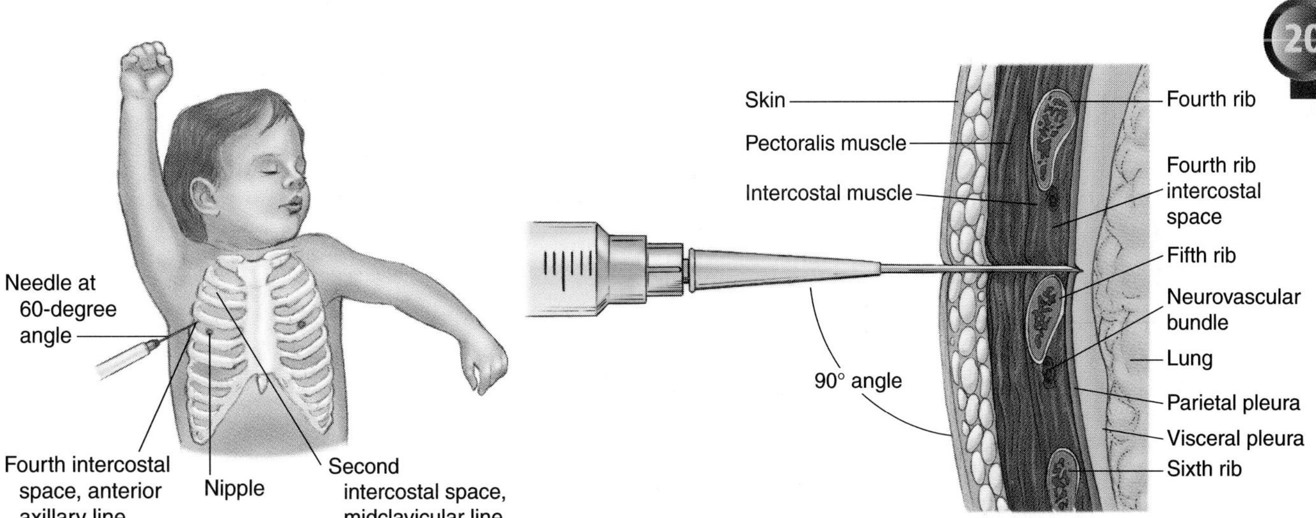

Figure P20-1 Position the child with arm raised and identify entry sites.

Figure P20-2 Insert the needle over the top of the rib margin in the fourth intercoastal space (pictured) at the anterior axillary line, or in the second intercostal space at the midclavicular line.

Removing and Replacing a Tracheostomy Tube

Indications

Decannulation

Obstruction

Contraindications

Inadequately sized tract or stoma for insertion of a new tracheostomy tube; in this case, insert an endotracheal tube

Lack of a replacement tracheostomy tube or appropriately sized endotracheal tube

Equipment

Suction device
Sterile suction catheters
Oxygen
Bag-valve-mask, standard pediatric and adult mask sizes
Tracheostomy cannulas, appropriately sized for patient (see Figure 10-4)
Endotracheal tubes, standard pediatric, and adult sizes
Laryngoscope handle with blades
Tape or tracheostomy ties
Gauze pads
5- or 10-ml syringe
Water-soluble lubricant
Scissors
Sterile saline
Stethoscope

Talk to the caregiver about the size and type of tracheostomy tube and about known problems with the stoma or tube.

Introduction

Children with tracheostomy tubes are increasingly common in the out-of-hospital setting. Most of these children live at home and have trained caregivers. Rarely, a tracheostomy tube problem occurs with a technology-assisted child (TAC) and 911 is activated.

Rationale

Treatment of a tracheostomy tube problem usually requires simple techniques, such as suctioning or removal of the old tube and replacement with a new tube. Partial airway obstruction from clogging of the old tube may not be relieved by suctioning alone, or it may be impossible to ventilate a child through an existing tracheostomy tube because of **decannulation** or complete obstruction. Under these conditions, the prehospital professional must place a new tracheostomy tube to save the child's life.

Preparation

1. Ask the caregiver if there are any special problems with the child's trachea or special requirements involving the child's tracheostomy.
2. Ask the caregiver if a replacement tracheostomy tube is available.
3. Speak directly to the child about what to expect and attempt to enlist her cooperation.

Procedure

Removing an old tracheostomy tube

1. Position the child with the head and neck hyperextended to expose the **tracheostomy** site.
2. Apply oxygen over the mouth and nose, and occlude (close off) the stoma or tracheostomy tube (Figure P21-1).
3. If the existing tube has a cuff, deflate it:
   - Connect a 5- to 10-ml syringe to the valve on the pilot balloon.
   - Draw air out until the balloon collapses.
   - Cutting the balloon will not deflate the cuff.
4. Cut or untie the cloth ties that hold the tracheostomy tube in place.

5. Withdraw the tracheostomy tube using a slow, steady, outward and downward motion.
6. Assess airway for patency and adequate ventilation.
7. Provide oxygen and ventilation through the stoma as needed.

Replacing the tracheostomy tube

Insert a tracheostomy tube of the same size and model whenever possible. If this is not available, use a smaller tube or an endotracheal tube of the same outer diameter as the tracheostomy tube.

1. If the tube uses an insertion obturator, place this in the tube. If the tube has an inner and outer cannula, use the outer cannula and obturator for insertion.
2. Moisten or lubricate the tip of the tube (and obturator) with water, sterile saline, or a water-soluble lubricant.
3. Hold the device by the flange (wings) or hold the actual tube like a pencil.
4. Gently insert the tube with an arching motion (follow the curvature of the tube) posteriorly then downward. Slight traction on the skin above or below the stoma may help (Figure P21-2).
5. Once the tube is in place, remove the obturator, attach the bag, and attempt to ventilate. If the tube uses an inner cannula, insert to allow mechanical ventilation with a bag-valve device.
6. Check for proper placement by watching for bilateral chest rise, listening for equal breath sounds, and observing the patient. Signs of improper placement include lack of chest rise, unusual resistance to assisted ventilation, air in the surrounding tissues, and lack of patient improvement.

Possible Complications

Creation of a false lumen

Subcutaneous air

Pneumomediastinum

Pneumothorax

Bleeding at insertion site

Bleeding through tube

Right mainstem intubation with endotracheal tube

If unable to reinsert a tracheostomy tube, use a similarly sized endotracheal tube.

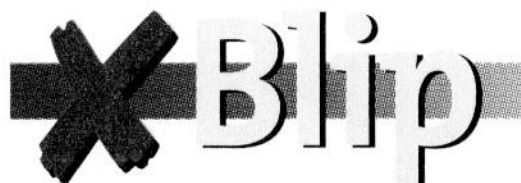

Do not force a large tracheostomy tube through a new stoma site.

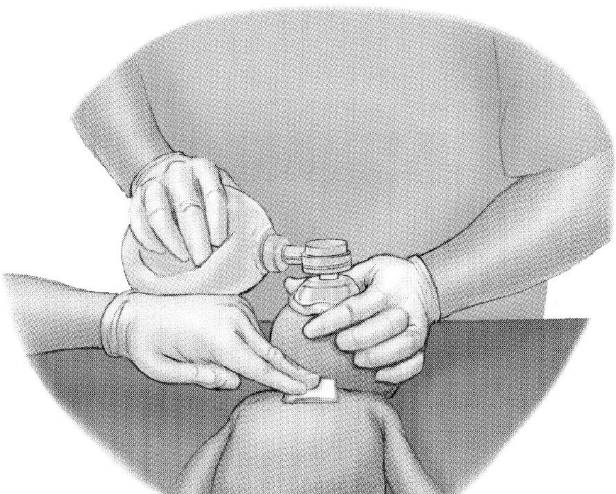

Figure P21-1 Apply oxygen over the mouth and nose, and occlude the stoma or tracheostomy tube.

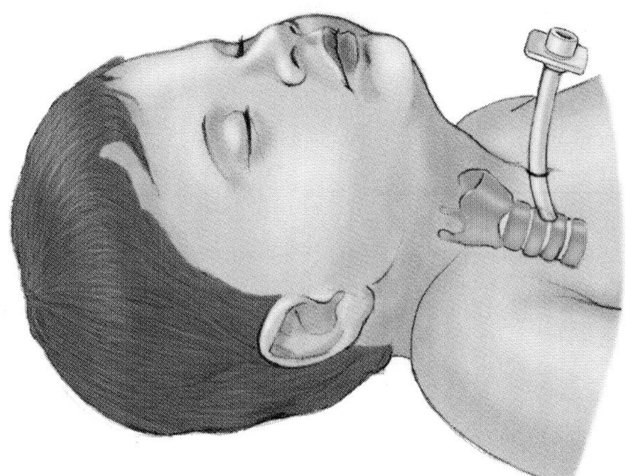

Figure P21-2 Gently insert the tube with an arching motion (follow the curvature of the tube) posteriorly then downward. Slight traction on the skin above or below the stoma may help.

Do not advance an endotracheal tube too far through the stoma.

Keep the suction catheter close at hand.

7. If the tube cannot be inserted, withdraw the tube, administer oxygen, and ventilate as needed.
8. Use a smaller-size tracheostomy tube for the second attempt.
9. If still unsuccessful with a smaller tracheostomy tube, insert an endotracheal tube through the stoma.
   - Check the length of the original tracheostomy tube, note the markings on the endotracheal tube, and advance it to the same depth as the original tube.
   - The inserted portion of the endotracheal tube will be approximately half the distance needed for oral insertion.
   - Do not advance the tube too far, or it may go into the right mainstem bronchus.
10. If still unsuccessful, use a suction catheter as a guide (**Figure P21-3**).
    - Insert a small, sterile suction catheter through the tracheostomy tube.
    - Without applying suction, insert the suction catheter into the stoma.
    - Slide the tracheostomy tube along the suction catheter and into the stoma, until it is in the proper position.
    - Remove the suction catheter.
    - Assess ventilation through the tracheostomy tube.
11. If still unsuccessful, consider orotracheal intubation or transport the patient with ventilation through the stoma using a stoma mask or newborn mask, or through bag-valve mask over the nose and mouth while covering the stoma with a sterile gauze.
12. After proper placement, cut the ends of the tracheostomy ties or tape diagonally (allows for easy insertion), pass through eyelets (openings) on the flanges, and tie around the patient's neck, so that only a little finger can pass between the ties and the neck.

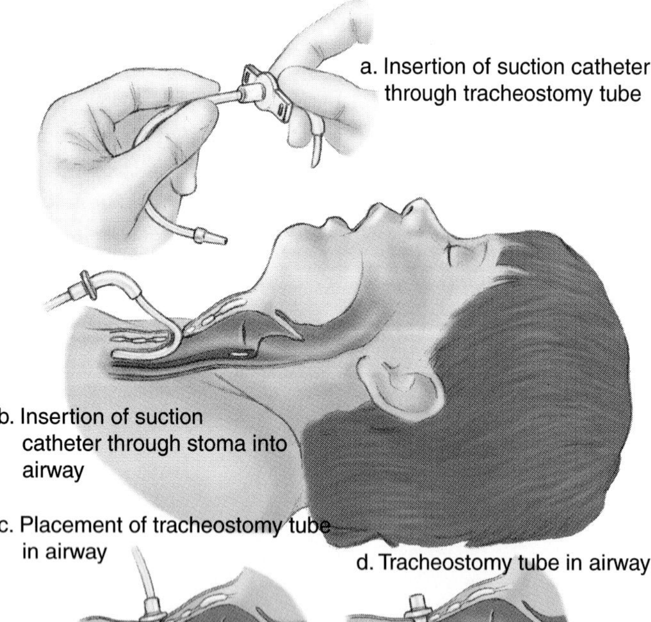

Figure P21-3 If still unsuccessful, use a suction catheter as a guide.

Appendices

Appendix 1

Community Outreach and Education

Introduction

Chapter 1 touches on the prehospital professional's responsibility to help prevent and treat injury and disease. Deciding where to begin can often be an overwhelming process. This appendix will introduce a number of ideas and resources to help get you started. Whether your outreach efforts involve the local, state, or national levels, increasing awareness and knowledge among parents, children, and caretakers will ultimately make a significant difference.

Suggested Educational Outreach Activities

Study the statistics

A good first step in any outreach effort is to look at the numbers and assess the situation. What is the most common cause of injury or death in your community? Once you have determined which areas need the most work, consider the various approaches and the best audiences to address when designing prevention activities. Statistics help to convince others of the need to develop programs on a particular issue. They also help to evaluate whether your work is making an impact in your community. Local indicators can come from a number of sources, such as hospital emergency departments, police records, and government agencies.

Develop a relationship with schools

Contact local schools to determine what injury and violence prevention programs are available to their students. Volunteer to help develop or implement additional injury prevention programs that address the most frequent causes of injury. Are teachers and administrators prepared for emergencies? Create programs that instruct teachers on emergency preparedness, and on how to communicate important health and safety messages to their students.

Become a community educator

Investigate opportunities for making presentations at parenting courses, community colleges, hospitals, schools, YMCAs, health clubs, public libraries, and youth groups. Keep in mind that the most effective learning takes place when people are doing things, not just listening and watching. Offer hands-on workshops on subjects such as first aid, bicycle safety, correct use of child restraint seats, or disaster prevention. Find out which topics are in greatest demand for various audiences.

Collaborate with local organizations

Call your local chapter of the American Academy of Pediatrics (AAP) to find out if there are pediatricians in your area who would be willing to work with you on educational outreach projects. Generate support from local businesses to build corporate partnerships and raise in-kind contributions or "give-aways" for public events.

Become a spokesperson and advocate

Once you have identified an important safety concern in your community, educate and involve the community by getting the message out. Submit news releases, letters to the editor, and opinion/editorials to local newspapers, newsletters, or magazines. Develop media contacts and volunteer to do radio or television interviews. Use your role as a health care expert to advocate for regulatory changes when appropriate. Organize a town forum or assemble a panel of experts in your community to work together to build awareness of the issue and to effect change. The Office of Public Relations at the AAP offers speaker's kits with slides on childhood injury and violence prevention. They can be ordered by calling (800) 433-9016.

Organize a health and safety fair

A public event such as a fair provides an opportunity to involve local organizations in sending important health and safety messages to a large number of parents, grandparents, caregivers, and children. It is an effective way for people to learn more about the resources available in their community. More information on how to plan a health and safety fair can be found on the AAP website (www.aap.org) under "Advocacy."

Organize a poster contest

Invite schools and youth groups to consider a specific health or safety issue carefully by asking children to develop a poster that presents an effective awareness or prevention message. Make arrangements to exhibit the posters in a public location and offer a prize or special recognition to the winner.

AAP Publications Resource List

The American Academy of Pediatrics publishes materials that can assist in your education and prevention efforts. The materials listed below can be purchased from the AAP's Department of Marketing and Publications by calling (800) 433-9016. Many AAP policy statements and educational materials can also be downloaded free from the AAP website (www.aap.org).

Parent education brochures

A Parent's Guide to Water Safety

Alcohol: Your Child and Drugs

Allergies in Children

Child Sexual Abuse

Choking Prevention and First Aid

Cocaine: Your Child and Drugs

Family Shopping Guide to Car Seats

How to Help Your Child with Asthma

Inhalant Abuse: Your Child and Drugs

Keep Your Family Safe from Firearm Injury

Playground Safety

Protect Your Child from Poison

Raising Children to Resist Violence

Substance Abuse

Surviving: Coping with Adolescent Depression and Suicide

The Teen Driver

Toy Safety

Your Child and the Environment

Fact sheets

About Bicycle Helmets

Air Bag Safety

Baby-Sitting Reminders

Bicycle Safety: Myths and Facts

Choosing the Right Bicycle for Your Child

Home Water Hazards for Young Children

Infant Furniture: Cribs

Infant Sleep Positioning and SIDS

Lawn Mower Safety

Life Jackets and Life Preservers

One-Minute Car Seat Safety Check-Up

Pool Safety for Children

Prevent Shaken Baby Syndrome

Protect Your Child...Prevent Poisoning

Protect Your Home Against Fire

Safe Bicycling Starts Early

Safety Tips for Home Playground Equipment

Safe Driving...A Parental Responsibility

The Child as Passenger on an Adult's Bicycle

Tips for Getting Kids to Wear Helmets

Water Safety for Your School-Age Child

When Your Child Needs Emergency Medical Services

Videos

Caring for Your Newborn: A Parent's Guide for the First 3 Months

Mastering Asthma: A Family's Guide to Understanding and Living with Childhood Asthma

Portrait of Promise—Preventing Shaken Baby Syndrome

Safe Active Play: A Guide to Avoiding Play Area Hazards

Internet resources

The Internet is an excellent resource for health- and safety-related information. Many organizations and government agencies provide statistics, product recall lists, grant information and safety tips for consumers. The following list of resources is only a sampling of the range of pertinent information available. Visit the AAP website (www.aap.org) for links to these resources.

AAA Foundation for Traffic Safety

Agency for Health Care Policy and Research, Department of Health and Human Services

American Burn Association

American College of Emergency Physicians—Injury Prevention

American Heart Association

American Public Health Association (APHA), Injury Control and Emergency Health Services Section

Centers for Disease Control and Prevention

Department of Health and Human Services

Consumer Product Safety Commission

Food and Drug Administration

Injury-Free Coalition for Kids

Maternal and Child Health Bureau

National Center for Health Statistics

National Center for Injury Prevention and Control

National Fire Protection Association

National Highway and Transportation Safety Administration, Auto Safety Hotline

National Injury and Violence Prevention Resource Center

National Institutes of Health

National Program for Playground Safety

National Safe Kids Campaign

National Safety Council

Prevention Online, Substance Abuse and Mental Health Services Administration

World Health Organization

Appendix 2

Pediatric Survey for State EMS Systems

Regulation and policy

1. Does your state have specific EMSC legislation?

2. Do you believe EMSC legislation is warranted?

3. Does the legislation provide for additional EMS funding for EMSC?

4. Has the legislation resulted in any measurable changes?

5. If your state does not have an EMSC bill, are you working on preparing such legislation?

6. Does your state have a permanent EMSC, pediatric advisory committee, or task force?

7. How are the EMSC advisory committee members selected?

8. If your state does not have an EMSC advisory committee, is there representation by a pediatric expert on your EMS advisory committee?

Resource management

1. Does your state have an EMS plan?

2. Does your state's EMS plan specifically address pediatrics?

3. If not, is there a separate state EMSC plan?

4. Does your state have an EMS administrator specifically assigned to EMSC? What percent of his or her time is devoted to EMSC?

5. What models or templates, if any, do your state use for planning, implementing, and evaluating EMSC standards, guidelines and recommendations?

Human resources and training

1. Do you use the recommended pediatric content in the NHTSA-MCHB (National Highway Transportation Safety Association–Maternal and Child Health Bureau) basic national standard curriculum for EMT-B education?

2. If not, what curriculum is used? How many hours of pediatric education are required for EMT-Bs?

3. Do you intend to use the recommended pediatric content in the NHTSA-MCHB intermediate and advanced national standard curriculum for EMT-Is and EMT-Ps?

4. If not, what curriculum will be used?

5. How many hours of pediatric education are required for EMT-Is and EMT-Ps?

6. How many hours, if any, of pediatric education are required for other out-of-hospital providers, as part of their primary training curriculum for initial certification/licensure?

7. What curricula are used?

   a. Dispatchers

   b. First responders

   c. Mobile intensive-care nurses

8. Does your state require pediatric continuing education (CE) courses for out-of-hospital providers? How many hours per year are required for each provider group?

9. If not, how does your state ensure that CE addresses children?

10. Does your state recommend or require any special pediatric life support course for either initial out-of-hospital provider education or CE; e.g., the Pediatric Education for Prehospital Professionals (PEPP) Course, the California Pediatric Airway Project, the Training Resource for Instructors in Prehospital Pediatrics (TRIPP), or Pediatric Advanced Life Support (PALS)?

Transportation

1. Do your BLS units have pediatric equipment that meets guidelines published in *Prehospital Emergency Care*, vol. 1, no. 4 (October), 1997?

2. Do your ALS units have pediatric equipment that meets guidelines published in *Prehospital Emergency Care*, vol. 1, no. 4 (October), 1997?

Facilities

1. Does your state have standards, guidelines, or recommendations for emergency department preparedness in pediatrics?

2. Is there a recommended system for categorization or selection of different levels of pediatric facilities?

3. Are pediatric capabilities of emergency departments in any of your local EMS systems verified, monitored, or evaluated? How?

4. Does your state have standards, guidelines, or recommendations for pediatric medical and trauma field triage protocols?

5. Does your state have standards, guidelines, or recommendations for interfacility consultation and/or secondary transfer of children to higher-level centers?

6. Does your state have standards, guidelines, or recommendations for pediatric interfacility transport providers?

7. Does your state have standards, guidelines, or recommendations for pediatric critical care centers?

8. Does your state have standards, guidelines, or recommendations for pediatric rehabilitation?

9. Does your state have standards, guidelines, or recommendations for transfer to or designation of pediatric rehabilitation facilities?

Communication

1. Does your state recommend or have template examples of pediatric dispatch protocols?

2. If not, are there specific pediatric considerations within general dispatch protocols?

Public information, education, and prevention

1. Does your state recommend or require out-of-hospital providers to have specific education in childhood illness and injury prevention?

Medical direction

1. Does your state recommend or have template examples of out-of-hospital BLS and ALS pediatric field treatment protocols for use by local EMS agencies and providers? Which ones?

2. Does your state recommend or have template examples of out-of-hospital pediatric policies and procedures (e.g., consent, suspected abuse, or neglect) for use by local EMS agencies and providers? Which ones?

Apgar score A system of scoring a newborn's physical condition at one minute and five minutes after birth. The heart rate, respiration, muscle tone, response to stimuli, and color are each rated 0, 1, or 2. The maximum total score is 10.

apnea A temporary cessation of breathing.

asphyxia A condition caused by insufficient oxygen.

aspiration The process of sucking in. Foreign bodies may be aspirated into the nose, throat, or lungs on inspiration.

assessment Evaluation.

asthma A disease caused by increased responsiveness of the tracheobronchial tree to various stimuli. The result is paroxysmal constriction of the bronchial airways. Clinically, there is severe dyspnea accompanied by wheezing.

asymmetric Without symmetry.

asynchronized Untimed; in electrical countershock, the asynchronized mode (defibrillation) will be delivered at a time unrelated to the cardiac cycle.

asystole Cardiac standstill; absence of contractions of the heart.

ataxia Defective muscular coordination, especially that manifested when voluntary muscular movements are attempted.

atrium One of two (right and left) upper chambers of the heart. The right atrium receives blood from the vena cava and delivers it to the right ventricle, which, in turn, pumps blood into the blood vessels of the lungs. The left atrium receives blood from pulmonary veins and delivers it to the left ventricle, which, in turn, pumps blood into the body.

atropine sulfate A anti-cholinergic agent that counteracts effects of parasympathetic stimulation. Effects include tachycardia, dry mouth and skin, blurred vision, and loss of bowel sounds.

aura A subjective sensation preceding a paroxysmal attack; in epilepsy the aura may precede the attack by several hours or only by a few seconds.

auscultate To listen.

auscultation The process of listening for sounds within the body.

autonomic Self-controlling; functioning independently; related to the autonomic nervous system.

avulsion A tearing away of a part or structure.

axial Situated in or pertaining to an axis, such as the spine.

axilla The armpit.

axonal shearing A tearing of axons or nerve sheaths, caused by a blunt mechanism, to produce severe brain injury.

bacteria A common type of germ, treatable with antibiotics, causing disease.

barbiturates A family of sedative–hypnotic drugs usually taken by mouth and frequently used as recreational substances.

barotrauma Any injury caused by a change in the atmospheric pressure.

baseline A known or initial value with which subsequent observations can be compared.

basilar Pertaining to the base of the skull.

basilar skull fracture A fracture into the base of the skull, sometimes associated with brain hemorrhage or brain injury.

belly breathing Abdominal muscles are the main muscles used to breathe; this type of breathing is normal in infants because their chest wall is thin and weak.

benzodiazepine A family of sedative–hypnotic drugs usually taken by mouth and frequently used as recreational substances.

beta agonists Chemicals that excite the beta receptors of certain cells; one important effect is relaxation of smooth muscles of the airways in children with wheezing.

beta blockers Chemicals that block beta receptors; these chemicals are commonly used to reduce the work of the heart in patients with heart disease.

bevel A surface slanting from the horizontal or vertical.

bezoar A hard mass of entangled material sometimes found in the stomachs and intestines.

bicarbonate A chemical that increases ph or alkalinity.

bilateral Pertaining to, affecting, or relating to two sides.

bile A secretion of the gall bladder into the intestine to help digestion.

blunt (trauma) A mechanism of injury in which force occurs over a broad area and the skin is not usually broken.

bolus A single dose.

bowel The intestine.

brachial Pertaining to a main artery and vein of the arm.

brady A prefix indicating slow.

bradyasystole A heart rhythm on the cardiac monitor that is either asytole or very slow with wide QRS complexes, less than 20–30 beats per minute.

bradycardia A slow heartbeat.

brain death Cessation of brain function.

brain herniation Forceful shifting of the brain contents through a bony opening because of increased pressure in one compartment of the brain, usually resulting in cardiopulmonary arrest.

brain stem The stemlike part of the brain that connects the cerebral hemispheres with the spinal cord.

breech A newborn presentation that is not the head, usually the buttocks.

bretyllium A type of anti-dysrhythmic drug, useful for ventricular tachycardia.

bronchi The two main branches leading from the trachea to the

3. Does your state allow or mandate the following out-of-hospital pediatric ALS field skills?
   a. Endotracheal intubation
   b. Administration of paralytic agents to facilitate endotracheal intubation?
   c. Intraosseous infusion
   d. Rectal diazepam
   e. Needle thoracostomy
4. Is there a mechanism for concurrent and retrospective review of out-of-hospital pediatric care?

Trauma systems

1. Does your state have standards, guidelines, or recommendations for pediatric trauma centers or other designated pediatric trauma care facilities?
2. Does your state have standards, guidelines, or recommendations for pediatric trauma care within general trauma centers?

Evaluation

1. Does your state have an EMS data collection system that allows assessment of pediatric care by numbers, types of problems, field interventions, and ED outcomes?
2. Is there a specific pediatric component to your state's EMS quality improvement plan?

Appendix 3

Commonly Used Acronyms and Prefixes

Acronym List

AAP American Academy of Pediatrics
ALS advanced life support
BDP bronchopulmonary dysplasia
BLS basic life support
BVM bag-valve-mask (ventilation)
CE continuing education
CERT community emergency response teams
ChUMS Children's Updated Medical Summary
CID cervical immobilization device
CISD critical incident stress debriefing
CNS central nervous system
CPA cardiopulmonary arrest
CPR cardiopulmonary resuscitation
CPS child protective services
CSF cerebrospinal fluid
CSHCN children with special health care needs
ED emergency department
EMSC emergency medical services for children
ET endotracheal
ETI endotracheal intubation
ETT endotracheal tube
HIV human immunodeficiency virus
ICU intensive care unit
IM intramuscular
IO intraosseous
IV intravenous
MDI metered-dose inhaler
MICN mobile intensive care unit
NG nasogastric (tube)
NHTSA National Highway Traffic Safety Administration
NICHD National Institute of Child Health and Human Development
NP nasopharyngeal
OG orogastric (tube)
OP oropharyngeal
PAT pediatric assessment triangle
PR rectal
RSI rapid-sequence induction
RSV respiratory syncytial virus
SIDS sudden infant death syndrome
SKIPS Special Kids Information Program
SQ subcutaneous
SVT supraventricular tachycardia
TAC technology-assisted children
TRIPP Training Resource for Instructors in Prehospital Pediatrics
VP ventriculo-peritoneal (shunts)
VT ventricular tachycardia

Prefix List

brady slow
broncho related to the bronchi
cardio pertaining to the heart
gastro denoting the stomach
hydro pertaining to water or to hydrogen
hyper above, excessive, or beyond
hypo less than, below, or under
inter in the midst, between
intra within
naso pertinent to the nose
neuro pertinent to a nerve, nervous tissue, or nervous system
oro denoting the mouth
psycho indicating relationship to the mind or mental processes
sub under, beneath, in small quantity, less than normal
vaso a vessel, as in a blood vessel

Glossary

abdomen The anatomic portion of the anterior trunk below the ribs and above the pelvis; it contains the stomach, lower part of the esophagus, small and large intestines, liver, gall bladder, spleen, pancreas, and bladder.

abdominal Pertaining to the abdomen.

abrasion A portion of skin or of a mucous membrane scraped away as a result of injury.

abscess A localized collection of pus.

absorb To take in, suck up, or imbibe.

abuse Injure.

acceleration-deceleration injury A type of injury caused when a moving body part, such as the head, stops suddenly on impact with another object.

acetaminophen A synthetic drug with antipyretic and analgesic actions similar to aspirin, used in patients with sensitivity to aspirin. Trade names for acetaminophen include Tylenol and Datril.

acid A corrosive substance with low ph.

acidosis Excessive acidity of body fluids due to an accumulation of acids (as in diabetic acidosis or renal disease) or an excessive loss of bicarbonate (as in renal disease).

acrocyanosis Cyanosis of the extremities; acrocyanosis of the hands and feet may be normal in the infant within the first hour after birth.

activated charcoal Very fine powder prepared from soft charred wood that is highly adsorbent; it is often used in treating people who have ingested poisons.

acute Sharp, severe, with rapid onset.

adenoidal Lymphoid tissue in the back of the mouth and oropharynx.

adolescent A young man or woman between the ages of 10 and 18 years.

adsorb Attachment of a substance to the surface of another material, such as poison to activated charcoal.

aerosol A solution in the form of a mist, often a drug, for inhalation.

agent Something that causes an effect; thus, bacteria that cause a disease are said to be agents of the specific disease. An injury agent is the energy causing the damage, such as thermal energy from a burn.

agonist A substance that stimulates or activates.

airway adjunct An artificial device to maintain an open airway.

albuterol A bronchodilator used in inhalation treatments.

alcohol A class of organic compounds that includes rubbing alcohol (methanol) and drinking alcohol (ethanol)

alkali A strong base with a high ph, usually corrosive to tissues.

alveoli The air sacs of the lungs in which the exchange of oxygen and carbon dioxide takes place.

amniotic fluid The liquid or albuminous fluid contained in the amnion. This fluid is transparent and almost colorless. The liquid protects the fetus from injury, helps maintain an even temperature, prevents formation of adhesions between the amnion and the skin of the fetus, and prevents conformity of the sac to the fetus.

amphetamine "Speed"; a drug of abuse that is related to epinephrine.

ampule A small glass conta that can be sealed and its tents sterilized.

analgesic A drug that relie pain.

anaphylaxis A severe forr hypersensitivity reaction produces dangerous phy ic changes, such as bron chospasm, shock, and hi

anatomic Relating to the a my or structure of an org

ancillary Something that a another action or effect b not essential to the accon ment of the action.

antecubital fossa The triar area lying anterior to and the elbow, bounded medi the pronator teres and la by the brachioradialis mu

anterior Before or in front anatomical nomenclature refers to the ventral or ab nal side of the body.

antibiotic Any of a variety natural or synthetic subs that inhibit growth of, o destroy, bacteria that are responsible for infectiou diseases.

anticholinergic Pertaining agent that blocks parasyn thetic nerve impulses; eff include tachycardia, dry and skin, blurred vision, loss of bowel sounds.

anticonvulsant Agent that vents or relieves convuls

antidote A substance that tralizes poisons or their

antipyretic An agent that fever.

anxiety A feeling of apprel sion, worry, uneasiness, dread.

apathy Indifference; insen lack of emotion.

lungs, providing the passageway for air movement.

bronchus One of the two large branches of the trachea.

bronchiolitis Inflammation of the bronchioles by a virus.

bronchoconstriction Narrowing of the bronchial tubes.

bronchodilator A drug that helps open the airways to improve air movement and reduce wheezing.

bronchopulmonary dysplasia Iatrogenic chronic lung disease that develops in premature infants following a period of intensive respiratory therapy.

bronchospasm Abnormal narrowing with obstruction of the lumen of the bronchi due to spasm of the smooth muscles.

bundle branch block A defect in the heart's electrical conduction system in which there is a failure of conduction down one of the main branches of the bundle of His.

button tube A type of gastrostomy tube.

BVM ventilation Assisted ventilation with a bag-valve-mask device.

calcium channel blockers A family of drugs used in adults with heart disease that helps reduce the speed of conduction through the heart and the overall work of the heart.

cannulate To introduce a cannula through a vein or passageway.

capillary Any of the minute blood vessels carrying blood and forming the capillary system.

carbon monoxide A colorless, tasteless, odorless poisonous gas that gives no warning of its presence; it is produced as the result of imperfect combustion and oxidation.

cardiomyopathy Disease of the myocardium, especially due to primary disease of the heart muscle.

cardiopulmonary arrest Sudden cessation of functional ventilation and circulation.

cardiotonic Affecting the heart.

cardioversion Electric shock therapy used to terminate cardiac dysrhythmias.

cartilage A specialized type of dense connective tissue, softer than bone, that is common in the skeletons of children.

catecholamine A family of chemicals in the body, such as epinepherine and norepinephrine, that tend to speed up or excite target tissues, especially in the heart, lungs, and muscles.

cathartic A purgative agent for the bowel.

catheter A tube passed into the body for evacuating or injecting fluids.

caustic Corrosive and burning; destructive to living tissue.

central cyanosis Slightly bluish, grayish, or dark purple discoloration of the skin (on the trunk and face) due to presence of hypoxia.

central line A venous access device inserted into and kept in a deep vein in order to maintain a route for administering fluids and medicines, or for gaining access to the heart to obtain information about pressures in the venous circulation.

central venous catheter Catheter inserted into the vena cava to permit intermittent or continuous monitoring of central venous pressure and to facilitate obtaining blood samples for chemical analysis.

cerebral Pertaining to the brain.

cerebral cortex The higher brain; the source of the senses, thinking, feeling, and voluntary movement.

cerebral palsy A nonprogressive paralysis resulting from developmental defects in brain or trauma or hypoxia at birth.

cerebrospinal fluid A water cushion protecting the brain and spinal cord from physical impact.

cervical Of, pertaining to, or in the region of the high spine.

chain of survival A community-based survival strategy for sudden cardiopulmonary arrest.

chest wall The musculoskeletal framework of the chest.

chicken pox (varicella) An acute viral disease with mild constitutional symptoms (headache, fever, malaise) followed by an eruption appearing in crops and characterized by macules, papules, and vesicles.

child abuse The intentional infliction of physical or emotional damage to a child.

child maltreatment A general term applying to all forms of child abuse and neglect.

child neglect Failure by those responsible for caring for a child to provide for the child's nutritional, emotional, and physical needs.

child protective services (CPS) This agency is the community legal organization responsible for protection, rehabilitation, and prevention of child maltreatment and neglect. CPS has the legal authority temporarily to remove from home children at risk for injury or neglect and to secure foster placement.

cholinergic Pertaining to nerve endings that liberate acetylcholine and are involved in physiologic processes with smooth muscle, such as in the gut, bladder, lungs, and heart.

chronic Of long duration.

circulation Perfusion; process of moving blood, oxygen, nutrients, carbon dioxide, and cellular waste throughout the body via arteries, arterioles, capillaries, venules, and veins.

clavicles The collarbone; a bone, curved like the letter *f*, that articulates with the sternum and scapula.

closed-head injury Injury usually associated with trauma in which the brain has been injured, but the skin has not been broken and there is no obvious bleeding.

cognitive Mental; relating to mental capacities.

colorimeter Instrument for measuring intensity of color, especially one for determining the amount of carbon dioxide in expired air.

comatose In a condition of coma.

compartment syndrome Any condition in which structures such as nerves and blood vessels are being constricted in a space, usually by blood or edema.

compensated shock The early stage of shock, while the body can still compensate for reduced perfusion of core organs.

complex partial seizure A partial or focal seizure with loss of consciousness.

compression A squeezing together; state of being pressed together.

concussion A brain injury causing any type of altered state of consciousness.

conduction The process by which a state of excitation is transmitted to the fibers of the nervous system or muscle systems.

congenital Present at birth.

congenital heart block A type of abnormal electrical conduction through the heart that results in slowing of the heart rate.

consent The granting of permission by the patient for an act to be carried out by another person, such as permission for a medical procedure to be performed by a professional.

constipation Infrequent defecation with passage of unduly hard and dry fecal material.

contact burn A thermal burn from direct contact with a hot object, fluid, or gas.

contraindications Any symptom or circumstance indicating the inappropriateness of a form of treatment.

contusion An injury in which the skin is not broken; a bruise.

coping strategies Methods of handling stress.

corrosive Producing corrosion or destruction of tissue.

cortex The outer layer of an organ or bone.

costal margin The inferior edge of the rib cage.

countershock (electrical) The application of an electric current to the heart directly or indirectly in order to treat a dysrhythmia.

crackles Discrete, noncontinuous lung sounds.

crepitus The noise or feel of gas in soft tissues.

cricoid cartilage The lowermost cartilage of the larynx; it is shaped like a signet ring, the broad portion or lamina being posterior, the anterior portion forming the arch.

croup A childhood disease characterized by edema of the upper airways with barking cough, difficult breathing, and stridor.

crowning Stage in delivery when the fetal head presents at the vaginal opening.

crystalloid A neutral fluid that has the salt composition of bodily fluid.

culture Growth of microorganisms or living tissue cells in special media.

Cushing's triad Simultaneous bradycardia, irregular respirations, and elevated blood pressure that occurs with brain herniation.

cyanosis Slightly bluish, grayish, slatelike, or dark purple discoloration of the skin due to presence of hypoxia.

cyanotic heart disease A type of congenital heart disease with a right to left shunt resulting in partially oxygenated blood in the systemic circulation.

cyclic antidepressants A type of antidepressant drug that may cause coma, seizures and conduction disturbances if taken in an overdose.

cystic fibrosis An inherited disease of exocrine glands affecting the pancreas, respiratory system, and apocrine glands; it usually begins in infancy and is characterized by chronic respiratory infection, pancreatic insufficiency, and increased electrolytes in sweat.

decannulation The removal of a tube.

decompensated shock The late stage of shock, when blood pressure is low and perfusion to core organs inadequate.

decompensation Failure of heart to maintain adequate circulation.

decompression The removal of pressure, as from gas in the stomach.

decontamination The process of removing a poison.

decubitis The side-down position.

defibrillation An electrical therapy for stopping fibrillation of the heart.

defibrillator An electrical device that produces defibrillation of the heart; it may be used externally or in the form of an automatic implanted defibrillator.

DeLee trap A type of simple suction device.

deltoid The muscle that covers the shoulder prominence.

dependent Lower region of the body; the part closest to the ground.

depression A hollow or lowered region.

developmental disability *See learning disability.*

dextrose A simple sugar.

diabetes mellitus A metabolic disorder in which the ability to metabolize sugar is impaired, usually because of a lack of insulin.

diaphoretic In a state of excessive perspiration.

diaphragm The muscle separating the chest from the abdominal cavity, which allows breathing.

diazepam An anti-anxiety, sedative–hypnotic drug.

dilation Expansion, enlargement.

diluent An agent that dilutes the substance or solution to which it is added.

diphenhydramine An antihistamine drug for treating allergic reactions or anaphylaxis.

diptheria An acute infectious disease of childhood characterized by fever, upper airway obstruction, and respiratory distress.

direct medical oversight On-line, real-time supervision of the prehospital professional's practice by base hospital physicians or nurses.

distal Farthest from the center.

distention Inflation, enlargement.

diving reflex Submersion of the face and nose in water to produce a vagal reaction; used to terminate an important dysrhythmia of childhood called supraventricular tachycardia.

doctrine of implied consent A legal foundation through which a prehospital professional can justify treatement of a minor without consent in the case of a serious medical emergency.

documentation A written recording of events.

dorsogluteal An anatomic area just behind the hip.

dorsum The back or posterior surface of a part.

dressings Protective covering for diseased or injured parts.

dysphagia Inability to swallow or difficulty in swallowing.

dysrhythmias Abnormal, disordered rhythm.

edema A local or generalized collection of tissue fluid.

effortless tachypnea Tachypnea, without the signs of increased work of breathing; this represents the child's attempt to blow off extra carbon dioxide to correct the acidosis generated by poor perfusion.

electrode A conductor for electrical impulses.

electrolytes The chemical components of a body solution.

emancipated minor Person legally under age but recognized by the state as having the legal capacity to consent for self (usually over 14 years of age).

embolic Pertaining to or caused by embolism.

embolism Obstruction of a blood vessel by foreign substances or a blood clot.

emergency exception rule *See doctrine of implied consent.*

emotional abuse The intentional infliction of emotional harm to a child.

emotional neglect The intentional omission of emotional support to a child.

empathy The objective awareness of and insight into the feelings, emotions, and behavior of another person.

EMS–EMSC continuum The linked community services set up to prevent and treat childhood emergencies. The continuum includes prevention, the primary physician, out-of-hospital care, hospital care, and rehabilitation.

encephalitis Inflammation of the brain.

endocrine An internal secretion.

endotracheal intubation A method of intubation in which an endotracheal tube (ETT) is placed through a patient's mouth, directly through the larynx between the vocal cords, and into the trachea, to open and maintain an airway.

environment The surroundings, conditions, or influences that affect an organism or an injury.

epigastric Pertaining to the abdominal area below the sternum.

epigastrium Abdominal area below the sternum.

epiglottis A thin, leaf-shaped structure located immediately posterior to the root of the tongue that prevents food and secretions from entering the trachea.

epiglottiditis Inflammation of the epiglottis.

epilepsy A condition of recurrent seizures.

esophagus A muscular canal that carries food from the pharynx to the stomach.

ethanol An alcohol used for recreational purposes.

epinephrine Adrenalin; a powerful chemical that stimulates the sympathetic nervous system, and causes the "fight or flight" reaction.

evaporation Change from liquid to vapor.

exhalation The process of breathing out.

extremity The hand or foot.

extubate To remove a tube, as an edotracheal tube.

febrile Feverish; pertaining to a fever.

feeding tube A tube placed into the stomach through the mouth, nose, or skin.

femoral Pertaining to the thigh bone or femur.

femur The thigh bone.

fetal-placental transfusion The transfusion of blood from the baby to the placenta, leading to a decrease in the infant's blood volume. This can occur if the baby is held higher than the uterus or womb prior to clamping the cord.

fetus A human or mammal in an early form of intrauterine development.

fever Elevation of temperature above the normal range, usually over 38 degrees centigrade or 100.5 degrees Fahrenheit.

flaccid Limp or absent muscular tone.

flail chest An unstable condition of the chest wall due to two or more fractures on each affected rib resulting in ineffective breathing.

flange A wing that projects above the main structure.

flaring The exaggerated opening of the nostrils during labored inhaling that indicates increased work of breathing and moderate to severe hypoxia.

flexion The act of bending.

fontanelle A soft spot lying between the cranial bones of the skull of a fetus or infant.

fracture A break through bone.

gag reflex The protective reflex that keeps food, fluid, or secretions from getting into the trachea.

gastric distention Enlargement of the stomach with air.

gastric reflux Regurgitation of stomach contents into the esophagus.

gastric tube A tube directly into a patient's stomach, allowing removal of gas, blood, and toxins, or instillation of medications and nutrition.

gastroenteritis Inflammation of the stomach and intestinal tract.

gastrostomy tube A feeding tube placed directly through the wall of the abdomen used in patients who cannot ingest liquids or solids.

generalized tonic-clonic seizure (grand mal) Sudden jerking of both arms and/or both legs, with trunk rigidity and loss of consciousness.

general trauma center A hospital designated as a specialty center for trauma patients of all ages.

gestation The length of time from conception to birth.

glottis The sound-producing apparatus of the larynx, consisting of two vocal folds.

glucagon A hormone that has the property of increasing the concentration of sugar in the blood.

glucose Sugar.

glycogen Stored sugar.

grand mal (seizure) *See generalized tonic-clonic seizure.*

greenstick fracture A fracture involving only part of the outer layer or cortex of a bone.

grunting A short, low-pitched sound at the end of exhalation, present in children with moderate to severe hypoxia; it reflects poor gas exchange because of fluid in the lower airways and air sacs.

Heimlich maneuver Technique for pushing in the epigastrum to remove a foreign body from the trachea or pharynx, where it is preventing flow of air to the lungs.

hematoma A swelling or mass of blood (usually clotted) confined to a organ, tissue, or space and caused by a break in a blood vessel.

hemodilution A reduced relative concentration of red blood cells in the circulation blood volume.

hemodynamic Relating to the circulation of blood through the body.

hemopericardium Accumulation of blood around the heart muscle in the pericardial sac.

hemorrhage Bleeding.

hemostat Instrument clamp; in its closed position it squeezes tissues or vessels and arrests the flow of blood.

hemothorax Blood in the pleural cavity caused by rupture of blood vessels, usually due to chest trauma.

hepatomegaly Enlargement of the liver.

herniation The process of tissue pushing through a small opening, such as when the brain under pressure pushes through a small opening in the bone with resulting severe injury or death.

Hirschsprung's disease A congenital bowel disorder where an area of the large intestine lacks smooth muscle to propel bowel contents. The colon above the inactive area of the sigmoid dilates and there is chronic constipation, abdominal distention, and fecal impaction.

hives Wheals; an itchy rash caused by contact with or ingestion of an allergic substance or food.

host The organism acted upon in an injury or illness process.

hydrocarbon A basic organic compound made up only of hydrogen and carbon.

hydrocephalus The increased accumulation of cerebrospinal fluid within the ventricles of the brain.

hydrochloric acid A powerful and corrosive aqueous solution of hydrogen chloride (HCl).

hyperalimentation The enteral or parenteral infusion of a solution that contains sufficient amino acids, glucose, fatty acids, electrolytes, vitamins, and minerals to sustain life, maintain normal growth and development, and provide for needed tissue repair.

hypercarbia Increased amount of carbon dioxide in the blood.

hyperextension Extreme or abnormal extension.

hyperflexion Extreme or abnormal flexion.

hyperglycemia An increase of blood sugar levels, as in diabetes mellitus.

hyperoxia Increased oxygen in the blood.

hyperventilation Increased minute volume which results in a lowered carbon dioxide level (hypocapnia) and decreased brain perfusion.

hypocarbia Decreased carbon dioxide in the blood, usually from an excess rate of ventialtion.

hypoglycemia Low sugar in the blood.

hypoperfusion Inadequate circulation

hypopharynx The lowermost portion of the pharynx, or back of the mouth, which leads to the larynx and esophagus.

hypotension Decrease of systolic and diastolic blood pressure below normal for age, representing decompensated shock.

hypotensive Denoting low blood pressure.

hypothermia Having a body temperature below normal range.

hypotonia Reduced muscular tension.

hypoventilation Reduced minute volume, either from reduced rate and/or depth of breathing.

hypovolemia Diminished blood volume.

hypoxia Inadequate oxygen.

hypnotic Pertaining to sleep or sedation.

immobilization The making of a part or limb immovable.

imperforate (anus) Without an external opening.

implied consent A type of consent in which a patient who is unable to give consent is given treatment under the legal assumption that he or she would want treatment if thinking in a normal way.

incisors The cutting teeth; the four front teeth in each jaw.

indirect medical oversight Offline physician or nurse support for the prehospital professional's practice. This type of oversight can be in either a prospective (before) or retrospective (after) form.

indwelling catheter A tube left in place.

infant A fetus from time of birth through one year of age.

infection The state or condition in which the body or a part of it is invaded by a pathogenic agent (microorganism or virus) that, under favorable conditions, multiplies and produces injurious effects.

inflammation The non-specific immune response to any type of bodily injury such as from a foreign body, ischemia, physical trauma, ionizing radiation, electrical energy, or extreme temperature.

infusion A liquid substance introduced into the body for therapeutic or diagnostic purposes.

ingestion The process of taking a material (particularly a toxic substance) into the gastrointestinal tract.

inhalation Act of drawing breath or gas into the lungs; inspiration.

injection The forcing of a fluid into a vessel or cavity intramuscularly or under the skin.

insecticides A poisonous agent used to exterminate insects.

insulin A hormone secreted by the pancreas that lowers blood sugar.

intercostal Between the ribs.

intercurrent Intervening.

intermammary Between the breasts.

internal Within the body.

intervention A therapeutic action.

intoxication The state of being intoxicated, especially of being poisoned by a drug or toxic substance.

intracranial Within the cranium or skull.

intramedullary Within the marrow cavity of a bone; intraosseous.

intraosseous Within the marrow cavity of a bone; intramedullary.

intravenous Within or into a vein.

in utero Within the uterus.

ipecac An oral medicine to induce vomiting; this medicine is no longer recommended for use by prehospital professionals.

ischemia Deficiency of blood supply.

isotonic A solution which has the same tonicity as bodily fluid, for example, normal saline or plasmalyte.

jaundice A condition characterized by yellowness of skin, whites of eyes, mucous membranes, and body fluids due to deposition of excess bilirubin in the blood (hyperbilirubinemia).

joule A measure of electrical energy; work done in one second by current of one ampere against a resistance of one ohm.

jugular Pertaining to the throat area, such as the jugular vein.

jugular veins *External,* receives the blood from the exterior of the cranium and the deep parts of the face. It lies superficial to the sternocleidomastoid muscle as it passes down the neck to join the subclavian vein. *Internal,* receives blood from the brain and superficial parts of the face and neck. It is directly continuous with the transverse sinus, accompanying the internal carotid as it passes down the neck, and joins with the subclavian vein to form the innominate vein.

ketoacidosis Acidosis due to an excess of ketone bodies, usually from either diabetes mellitus or starvation.

kyphosis An exaggeration or angulation of the normal posterior curve of the spine, with resultant humped appearance of the back.

laceration A wound or irregular tear of the flesh.

laryngoscope An instrument for examining the larynx.

laryngoscopy An examination of the interior of the larynx.

laryngospasm A spasm of the laryngeal muscles.

larynx The enlarged upper end of the trachea, below the root of the tongue, that contains the vocal cords.

lateral Pertaining to the side.

lateral decubitus position The position with the patient on his or her side.

learning disability Inability or defect in ability to learn.

lethargy Listlessness; weakness.

lidocaine A drug used for local wound anesthesia and to treat ventricular dysrhythmias such as ventricular tachycardia or ventricular fibrillation.

lithium A medicine used for certain psychiatric disorders.

lividity Dark skin discoloration, as from venous pooling and lack of circulation.

lumen The open space within an artery, vein, intestine, or tube.

lye Corrosive, alkaline cleaning liquid.

macrodrip A type of fluid infusion technique suitable for large volumes.

malaise Discomfort, uneasiness, or generalized ill feeling, often indicative of infection.

malleolus The protuberance on both sides of the ankle joint, the lower extremity of the fibula being known as the lateral malleolus and lower end of the tibia as the medial malleolus.

maltreatment *See child maltreatment.*

mandible The horseshoe-shaped bone forming the lower jaw.

mannitol A strong sugar solution used as an osmotic diuretic to draw out abnormal free water, such as for reduction of water in the brain to decrease cerebrospinal fluid pressure.

marrow The soft tissue occupying the inside space of long bones.

mature minor A person without the formal legal status of an emancipated minor, but having similar characteristics: married, pregnant, on active-duty status in the armed service, or 15 years or older and living separate and apart from his or her guardians. This person has the legal right to give consent for treatment as well as the legal right to refuse.

meconium The bowel contents of a fetus. The presence of meconium in amniotic fluid means the fetus may have suffered some type of stress, such as hypoxia, and may be depressed and need to be resuscitated.

medial Pertaining to the inner side.

medicolegal Related to medical jurisprudence or forensic medicine.

meningitis Inflammation of the membranes of the spinal cord or brain.

mental retardation A state of below-normal intellectual function.

metabolic Pertaining to the body's metabolism or internal chemistry.

microdrip A type of fluid infusion technique suitable for small volumes.

midaxillary (line) Imaginary vertical line drawn through the middle of the axilla (armpit), parallel to the midline.

midfacial Pertaining to the middle of the face.

military anti-shock trousers A garment designed to put pressure on the lower extremities and abdomen in order to squeeze blood from the peripheral vessels so as to increase core organ circulation.

minor A person not of legal age and thus requiring consent from a legal guardian for medical or surgical care.

minute ventilation The volume of air exchanged per minute. [minute ventilation = tidal volume × respiratory rate]

miosis Abnormal contraction of pupils.

mongolian spots Blue-gray areas of discoloration of the skin caused by abnormal pigment, not by trauma or bruising.

mortality Death.

motor activity Muscle use.

mottling A condition of abnormal skin circulation, caused by vasoconstriction or inadequate circulation.

mucosa A mucous membrane.

mucous membranes The membranes lining passages communicating with the air, such as the mouth, bowel, and lungs.

multisystem trauma Injury involving more than one organ system, such as combined injury to the chest, abdomen, and brain.

muscular dystrophy A congenital condition involving weakness and atrophy of muscles.

mutual aid agreement An agreement between two or more communities to assist each other when a disaster or medical event exceeds the resources of a single system.

myocardial infarction The death of part of the heart muscle caused by partial or complete occlusion of one or more of the coronary arteries.

myocarditis Inflammation of the myocardium.

naloxone A drug that reverses the effects of narcotic drugs.

narcotic An opiate drug that produces analgesia and sedation, as well as euphoria when used for recreational purposes.

nares The nostrils.

nasal cannula An oxygen delivery device in which oxygen flows through two small, tube-like prongs that fit into the patient's nostrils.

nasofacial Pertaining to the nose and face.

nasogastric (tube) A tube inserted through the nose into the stomach.

nasopharyngeal Pertaining to the pharynx and nose.

nasopharynx The part of the pharynx situated above the soft palate and behind the nose.

nausea An unpleasant sensation usually preceding vomiting.

nebulization The production of small particles such as a spray or mist from a liquid.

nebulizer An apparatus for producing a fine spray or mist.

necrosis Death of tissue.

needle decompression The removal of air from a closed space, such as from the pleura.

neglect *See child neglect.*

neurologic Pertaining to the nervous system.

neurovascular Concerning both the nervous and vascular systems.

nomograms A representation by graphs, diagrams, or charts of the relationship between numerical variables.

obstetric Pertaining to the process of giving birth.

obstetrics The branch of medicine that concerns the care of women during pregnancy, childbirth, and the immediate postpartum period.

obturator An inner stabilizing structure that gives stiffness to a hollow tube, to allow insertion or clearing of an obstruction.

occipital Concerning the back part of the head.

occiput The back part of the skull.

occlusion The closure of a passage.

occlusive dressing A dressing that covers completely.

offline medical oversight *See indirect medical oversight.*

online medical oversight *See direct medical oversight.*

operations Administrative processes.

opiates *See narcotics.*

oral By mouth; a medication delivery route.

organophosphate (insecticides) A type of poison with cholinergic properties, used as an insecticide.

orogastric tube A tube inserted through the mouth into the stomach.

oropharynx The part of the pharynx lying between the soft palate and upper portion of the epiglottis.

oropharyngeal (airway) Firm airway tube that is inserted into the mouth of an unconscious patient to prevent the flaccid tongue from blocking the airway.

otorrhea Discharge from the ear.

pain A sensory and emotional experience associated with actual or potential tissue damage.

palate The horizontal structure separating the mouth and the nasal cavity; the roof of the mouth.

pallor Lack of color; paleness.

palpable Perceptible, especially by touch.

palpate To examine by touch.

palpitation A rapid or throbbing pulsation, as an abnormally rapid throbbing or fluttering of the heart.

paradoxical irritability A marker for possible serious pediatric illness, consisting of a particular type of irritability where attempts to console further distress the child.

paralytic agents Drugs used to completely paralyze a patient's muscles, in order to assist in endotracheal intubation.

parenteral Denoting any medication route other than oral or rectal, such as intravenous, subcutaneous, intramuscular, or transmucosal.

parietal Pertaining to, or forming, the outer wall of a cavity; the upper and lateral parts of the skull.

partial implanted device An indwelling line that is partially implanted under the skin and partially exposed above the skin.

patency The state of being freely open.

pathology Study of the nature and cause of disease.

pediatric critical care center A type of specialized center for children with advanced resources for care of critically ill children.

pediatric trauma center A type of specialized center for children with advanced resources for care of critically injured children.

pelvis The bony structure formed by the innominate bones, the sacrum, the coccyx, and the ligaments uniting them.

penetrating Entering through the skin.

percutaneous endoscopic gastrostomy A type of feeding tube inserted into the stomach with the aid of an endoscope and then pulled through a stab wound made in the abdominal wall.

percutaneously Through the skin.

peritoneum The serous membrane reflected over the viscera and lining the abdominal cavity.

perineum The structures occupying the pelvic floor.

peripheral cyanosis Slightly bluish or dark purple discoloration of the skin (on the hands and feet only) due to presence of abnormal amounts of reduced hemoglobin in the blood.

perfusion Blood circulation.

peritoneal (shunt) Concerning the peritoneum.

petechiae Small, purplish, nonblanching spots on the skin that appear in certain severe fevers and are indicative of possible sepsis.

pharynx Passageway for air from nasal cavity to larynx and food from mouth to esophagus.

phencyclidine (hydrochloride) A hallucinogen, referred to as PCP or angel dust. Moderate doses cause elevated blood pressure, rapid pulse, increased skeletal muscle tone, and, sometimes, myoclonic jerks.

phenobarbital A hypnotic, long-acting sedative and anticonvulsant.

phenothiazines An anti-psychotic drug.

physical abuse *See child abuse.*

physical neglect *See child neglect.*

physiological Concerning body function.

physiology The vital functions of the core organs.

placenta The spongy structure attached to the uterus of mammals through which the fetus derives its nourishment.

pleura The serous membrane that enfolds both lungs and is reflected upon the walls of the thorax and diaphragm.

pleural fluid Fluid in the pleural space, which may be blood or another liquid associated with infection or inflammation.

pleural space The space between the parietal and visceral layers of the pleura.

pneumomediastinum Air or gas in the mediastinal tissues.

pneumonia An inflammation of the lungs caused primarily by bacteria, viruses, and chemical irritants.

pneumothorax A collection of air in the pleural cavity, which if under pressure may cause severe physiologic changes with poor venous return and inadequate cardiac output.

policies Medicolegal operational standards to guide prehospital professionals intended to help with decision-making in difficult or legally sensitive field situations

polypharmacy An ingestion involving more than one drug.

portal venous system The special venous drainage system that takes blood from the intestines to the liver.

posterior Toward the rear or caudal end; opposed to anterior.

posteriorly From the back, from behind, or from underneath.

postictal state The confused state of a patient after having a seizure.

positive pressure ventilation Assisted ventilation.

postmortem lividity In the deceased, a condition in which the face and dependent portions of the body have a reddish-blue mottling caused by venous blood pooling in the affected areas.

postpartum After childbirth.

post-traumatic epilepsy A seizure disorder that occurs after a closed-head injury.

posturing Abnormal positioning after a brain injury.

potassium An important body chemical and possible poison that may cause serious problems with the heart if present in excessive amounts in the blood stream.

preschooler A child three to five years old.

preterm Pertaining to events occurring prior to the 37th week of gestation.

primary brain injury A type of injury from direct trauma to the brain, including contusion, hemorrhage, and hematoma.

procedure A physical intervention.

prognosis The prediction of the course and end of a disease, and the estimate of chance for recovery.

prone Lying horizontal with face downward.

prophylaxis Prevention.

protocol A step-by-step process for treatment.

providone-iodine solution An antiseptic solution.

proximal Nearest the point of attachment, center of the body, or point of reference; opposite of distal.

psychogenic Of mental origin.

psychosocial Related to both psychological and social factors.

psychosomatic Pertaining to the relationship of the mind and body.

pulmonary Concerning or involving the lungs.

pulmonary contusion A bruise of the lung.

pulmonary edema A build-up of fluid in the lungs.

pulse The fluid wave of blood traveling through the arteries as a result of each heartbeat.

pulse oximeter A device to measure oxygen saturation in the blood.

pulse pressure The difference between the systolic and the diastolic pressure.

pupillary Concerning the pupil.

purpuric Pertaining to bruising of the skin.

pus The liquid product of inflammation, generally yellow in color.

QRS complex The electrical shape of a major portion of the heart rhythm on the cardiac monitor, representing venticular electrical activity.

racemic Including all isomers of a drug, such as epinephrine.

reactivity The capacity for reacting to a stimulus.

rectal Pertaining to the rectum.

rectum The lower part of the large intestine, about 5 inches long, between sigmoid flexure and the anal canal.

recurrence A return of symptoms after a period of quiescence, as in recurrent fever and yellow fever.

reflux A return or backward flow.

rehydration Restoration of fluid volume in a person who has been dehydrated.

reperfusion The reinstitution of blood flow to an area that was ischemic.

respiratory Pertaining to respiration.

respiratory arrest Cessation of spontaneous respirations.

respiratory distress An abnormal physiologic condition of hypoxia identified by increased work of breathing. The physical signs of increased work of breathing represent the patient's attempt to make up for decreased gas exchange, and to maintain oxygenation and ventilation.

respiratory failure A state of respiratory decompensation when the infant or child wears out his or her compensatory mechanisms for hypoxia, and can no longer maintain oxygenation and ventilation.

resuscitation tape A device for correlating a child's length with recommended drugs and equipment.

retractions Physical drawing in of the chest wall between the ribs that occurs with increased work of breathing.

retropharyngeal Behind the pharynx.

rhinorrhea Thin watery discharge from the nose.

rigor mortis The stiffness that occurs in dead bodies.

rupture A breaking apart of an organ or tissue.

salicylates Different forms of aspirin.

saline Containing or pertaining to salt.

salivation The act of secreting saliva.

saphenous veins Two superficial veins, the great and small, passing up the leg.

scald A burn to skin or flesh caused by moist heat and hot vapors, as steam.

school-aged children Children between the ages of six and ten years.

sciatic nerve The largest nerve in the body, arising from the sacral plexus on either side, passing from the pelvis through the greater sciatic foramen, down the back of the thigh, where it divides into tibial and peroneal nerves.

scoliosis The lateral curvature of the spine.

secondary brain injury A brain injury from systemic hypoxia and hypoperfusion, usually after multiple injuries to the chest and abdomen. It can also increase intracranial pressure enough to cause brain herniation.

secretion The process of producing liquid materials into the blood or body cavities.

sedative An agent that relaxes.

sepsis A pathological state, usually in a febrile patient, resulting from the presence of invading microorganisms or their poisonous products in the bloodstream.

septic shock Shock from infection, involving hypotension and signs of inadequate organ perfusion.

septum A wall dividing two cavities.

serum glucose The level of blood sugar.

sexual abuse Rape, sexual assault, or sexual molestation. The active person in this may be male, female, adult, or child, and the abused person may be of the same or opposite sex of the abuser.

shaken baby syndrome A syndrome seen in abused infants and children. The patient has been subjected to violent, whiplash-type shaking injuries inflicted by the abusing individual. This may cause coma, convulsions, and increased intracranial pressure due to tearing of the cerebral veins with consequent bleeding into the subdural space.

shock A clinical syndrome in which the blood flow and oxygen delivery are inadequate for normal organ function.

shunt A tube that diverts excess cerebrospinal fluid from the brain to the abdomen.

sickle cell disease A hereditary disease characterized by abnormal clumping together of deformed red blood cells. The patients have painful crises, anemia, infection-risks, and other serious complications.

Sims position A semi-prone position with the patient on her side, with her opposite knee and thigh drawn well up to facilitate delivery of a baby.

sinus tachycardia Rapid heart rate in a child with normal conduction.

slurry A thin, watery mixture.

sniffing position An upright position in which the patient's head and chin are thrust slightly forward to keep the airway open; the child appears to be sniffing.

soft-tissue injuries Injuries to the skin, fat, muscles, ligaments, and tendons.

sorbitol A cathartic agent used to increase bowel activity; it is contraindicated in children.

spacer A device to facilitate inhalation of bronchodilator drugs that does not require timing of inhalation with discharge of the drug from the canister.

spasticity Increased tone or contractions of muscles causing stiff and awkward movements.

spinal cord An ovoid column of tissue averaging about 44 cm in length, flattened anteroposteriorly, extending from the medulla to the 2nd lumbar vertebra in the spinal canal.

spine The vertebral column.

spleen The major abdominal organ involved in the production and destruction of red blood cells and immune cells. It is filled with blood and can hemorrhage after injury.

splinting Fixation with a splint.

status epilepticus A state of continuous seizures or multiple seizures without a return to consciousness for 30 minutes.

sterile Free from living microorganisms.

sternum The narrow, flat bone in the median line of the thorax in front. It consists of three portions distinguished as the manubrium, the gladiolus, and the ensiform or xiphoid process.

stoma An opening in the neck that connects the trachea directly to the skin.

stopcock A valve that regulates the flow of fluid from a container.

stress Forces that disrupt equilibrium or produce strain.

stridor A harsh sound during inspiration, high-pitched due to partial upper airway obstruction.

stylet A slender, solid, or hollow plug of metal for stiffening or clearing a cannula or catheter.

subarachnoid Below or under the arachnoid membrane and the pia mater of the covering of the brain.

subcostal Beneath the ribs.

subcutaneous Beneath or to be introduced beneath the skin.

subdural hemorrhage Beneath the dura mater.

subglottic Beneath the glottis.

substernal Situated beneath the sternum.

subxiphoid Below the xiphoid process of the sternum.

sucking chest wound An open or penetrating chest-wall wound through which air passes during inspiration and expiration.

suck reflex A primitive reflex of the newborn.

suction The act of sucking up.

sudden infant death syndrome (SIDS) The completely unexpected and unexplained death of an apparently well infant.

superior vena cava One of the two largest veins in the body that carries blood from the upper extremities, head, neck, and chest into the heart.

supine Lying on the back with the face upward.

supraclavicular Located above the clavical.

suprasternal Above the sternum.

supraventricular tachycardia An abnormal heart rhythm with a rapid, narrow QRS complex rate.

symmetry Correspondence in shape, size, and relative position of parts on opposite sides of a body.

sympathomimetic Adrenergic; producing effects resembling those resulting from stimulation of the sympathetic nervous system, such as effects following the injection of epinephrine.

symphysis pubis The injunction of the pubic bones on midline in front; the bony eminence under the pubic hair.

symptomatic Of the nature of or concerning a symptom.

synchronism Simultaneous occurrence of acts or events.

systemic Pertaining to a whole body rather than to one of its parts; somatic.

tachycardia Rapid heart rate.

tachydysrhythmia Abnormal, rapid heart rhythm.

tachypnea Rapid respiration.

tamponade Compression of tissues.

temporary protective custody When a legal guardian suffers from diminished judgement, law enforcement officers may place a minor in some form of *temporary protective custody.* While this may allow the prehospital professional to transport a minor to a medical facility for purposes of medical evaluation, it does not give the prehospital professional the right medically to treat a minor.

tension pneumothorax An accumulation of air or gas in the pleural cavity that progressively increases and causes serious hemodynamic changes.

terbutaline (sulfate) An effective bronchodilator.

tertiary care Sophisticated care available only at a referral hospital with a high level of medical capabilities.

thermoregulation Heat regulation.

thoracentesis Surgical puncture of the chest wall for removal of pleural fluids.

thoracic Pertaining to the chest or thorax.

thoracostomy Resection of the chest wall to allow drainage of the chest cavity.

thready Weak.

tidal volume The amount of air that is exchanged with each breath.

titrate To regulate flow or administration of a drug to attain a desired effect.

toddler A child between the ages of one and two years.

totally implanted device A catheter totally implanted and not visible to the eye.

tourniquet Any constrictor used on an extremity to facilitate venipuncture or intravenous injections.

toxic exposure An ingestion, inhalation, injection, or application of any substance that causes illness. It includes accidental poisoning (such as the toddler who ingests a household cleaner, detergent, bleach, or other toxin), recreational exposure (such as the adolescent who smokes cocaine), and hazardous materials exposure (such as a school-aged child who inhales a spilled toxic chemical).

trachea A cylindrical cartilaginous tube from the larynx to the bronchial tubes. It extends

3. Does your state allow or mandate the following out-of-hospital pediatric ALS field skills?
   a. Endotracheal intubation

   b. Administration of paralytic agents to facilitate endotracheal intubation?

   c. Intraosseous infusion

   d. Rectal diazepam

   e. Needle thoracostomy

4. Is there a mechanism for concurrent and retrospective review of out-of-hospital pediatric care?

Trauma systems

1. Does your state have standards, guidelines, or recommendations for pediatric trauma centers or other designated pediatric trauma care facilities?

2. Does your state have standards, guidelines, or recommendations for pediatric trauma care within general trauma centers?

Evaluation

1. Does your state have an EMS data collection system that allows assessment of pediatric care by numbers, types of problems, field interventions, and ED outcomes?

2. Is there a specific pediatric component to your state's EMS quality improvement plan?

Appendix 3

Commonly Used Acronyms and Prefixes

Acronym List

AAP American Academy of Pediatrics

ALS advanced life support

BDP bronchopulmonary dysplasia

BLS basic life support

BVM bag-valve-mask (ventilation)

CE continuing education

CERT community emergency response teams

ChUMS Children's Updated Medical Summary

CID cervical immobilization device

CISD critical incident stress debriefing

CNS central nervous system

CPA cardiopulmonary arrest

CPR cardiopulmonary resuscitation

CPS child protective services

CSF cerebrospinal fluid

CSHCN children with special health care needs

ED emergency department

EMSC emergency medical services for children

ET endotracheal

ETI endotracheal intubation

ETT endotracheal tube

HIV human immunodeficiency virus

ICU intensive care unit

IM intramuscular

IO intraosseous

IV intravenous

MDI metered-dose inhaler

MICN mobile intensive care unit

NG nasogastric (tube)

NHTSA National Highway Traffic Safety Administration

NICHD National Institute of Child Health and Human Development

NP nasopharyngeal

OG orogastric (tube)

OP oropharyngeal

PAT pediatric assessment triangle

PR rectal

RSI rapid-sequence induction

RSV respiratory syncytial virus

SIDS sudden infant death syndrome

SKIPS Special Kids Information Program

SQ subcutaneous

SVT supraventricular tachycardia

TAC technology-assisted children

TRIPP Training Resource for Instructors in Prehospital Pediatrics

VP ventriculo-peritoneal (shunts)

VT ventricular tachycardia

Prefix List

brady slow

broncho related to the bronchi

cardio pertaining to the heart

gastro denoting the stomach

hydro pertaining to water or to hydrogen

hyper above, excessive, or beyond

hypo less than, below, or under

inter in the midst, between

intra within

naso pertinent to the nose

neuro pertinent to a nerve, nervous tissue, or nervous system

oro denoting the mouth

psycho indicating relationship to the mind or mental processes

sub under, beneath, in small quantity, less than normal

vaso a vessel, as in a blood vessel

Glossary

abdomen The anatomic portion of the anterior trunk below the ribs and above the pelvis; it contains the stomach, lower part of the esophagus, small and large intestines, liver, gall bladder, spleen, pancreas, and bladder.

abdominal Pertaining to the abdomen.

abrasion A portion of skin or of a mucous membrane scraped away as a result of injury.

abscess A localized collection of pus.

absorb To take in, suck up, or imbibe.

abuse Injure.

acceleration-deceleration injury A type of injury caused when a moving body part, such as the head, stops suddenly on impact with another object.

acetaminophen A synthetic drug with antipyretic and analgesic actions similar to aspirin, used in patients with sensitivity to aspirin. Trade names for acetaminophen include Tylenol and Datril.

acid A corrosive substance with low ph.

acidosis Excessive acidity of body fluids due to an accumulation of acids (as in diabetic acidosis or renal disease) or an excessive loss of bicarbonate (as in renal disease).

acrocyanosis Cyanosis of the extremities; acrocyanosis of the hands and feet may be normal in the infant within the first hour after birth.

activated charcoal Very fine powder prepared from soft charred wood that is highly adsorbent; it is often used in treating people who have ingested poisons.

acute Sharp, severe, with rapid onset.

adenoidal Lymphoid tissue in the back of the mouth and oropharynx.

adolescent A young man or woman between the ages of 10 and 18 years.

adsorb Attachment of a substance to the surface of another material, such as poison to activated charcoal.

aerosol A solution in the form of a mist, often a drug, for inhalation.

agent Something that causes an effect; thus, bacteria that cause a disease are said to be agents of the specific disease. An injury agent is the energy causing the damage, such as thermal energy from a burn.

agonist A substance that stimulates or activates.

airway adjunct An artificial device to maintain an open airway.

albuterol A bronchodilator used in inhalation treatments.

alcohol A class of organic compounds that includes rubbing alcohol (methanol) and drinking alcohol (ethanol)

alkali A strong base with a high ph, usually corrosive to tissues.

alveoli The air sacs of the lungs in which the exchange of oxygen and carbon dioxide takes place.

amniotic fluid The liquid or albuminous fluid contained in the amnion. This fluid is transparent and almost colorless. The liquid protects the fetus from injury, helps maintain an even temperature, prevents formation of adhesions between the amnion and the skin of the fetus, and prevents conformity of the sac to the fetus.

amphetamine "Speed"; a drug of abuse that is related to epinephrine.

ampule A small glass container that can be sealed and its contents sterilized.

analgesic A drug that relieves pain.

anaphylaxis A severe form of hypersensitivity reaction that produces dangerous physiologic changes, such as bronchospasm, shock, and hives.

anatomic Relating to the anatomy or structure of an organism.

ancillary Something that assists another action or effect but is not essential to the accomplishment of the action.

antecubital fossa The triangular area lying anterior to and below the elbow, bounded medially by the pronator teres and laterally by the brachioradialis muscles.

anterior Before or in front of. In anatomical nomenclature, it refers to the ventral or abdominal side of the body.

antibiotic Any of a variety of natural or synthetic substances that inhibit growth of, or destroy, bacteria that are responsible for infectious diseases.

anticholinergic Pertaining to an agent that blocks parasympathetic nerve impulses; effects include tachycardia, dry mouth and skin, blurred vision, and loss of bowel sounds.

anticonvulsant Agent that prevents or relieves convulsions.

antidote A substance that neutralizes poisons or their effects.

antipyretic An agent that reduces fever.

anxiety A feeling of apprehension, worry, uneasiness, or dread.

apathy Indifference; insensibility; lack of emotion.

Apgar score A system of scoring a newborn's physical condition at one minute and five minutes after birth. The heart rate, respiration, muscle tone, response to stimuli, and color are each rated 0, 1, or 2. The maximum total score is 10.

apnea A temporary cessation of breathing.

asphyxia A condition caused by insufficient oxygen.

aspiration The process of sucking in. Foreign bodies may be aspirated into the nose, throat, or lungs on inspiration.

assessment Evaluation.

asthma A disease caused by increased responsiveness of the tracheobronchial tree to various stimuli. The result is paroxysmal constriction of the bronchial airways. Clinically, there is severe dyspnea accompanied by wheezing.

asymmetric Without symmetry.

asynchronized Untimed; in electrical countershock, the asynchronized mode (defibrillation) will be delivered at a time unrelated to the cardiac cycle.

asystole Cardiac standstill; absence of contractions of the heart.

ataxia Defective muscular coordination, especially that manifested when voluntary muscular movements are attempted.

atrium One of two (right and left) upper chambers of the heart. The right atrium receives blood from the vena cava and delivers it to the right ventricle, which, in turn, pumps blood into the blood vessels of the lungs. The left atrium receives blood from pulmonary veins and delivers it to the left ventricle, which, in turn, pumps blood into the body.

atropine sulfate A anti-cholinergic agent that counteracts effects of parasympathetic stimulation. Effects include tachycardia, dry mouth and skin, blurred vision, and loss of bowel sounds.

aura A subjective sensation preceding a paroxysmal attack; in epilepsy the aura may precede the attack by several hours or only by a few seconds.

auscultate To listen.

auscultation The process of listening for sounds within the body.

autonomic Self-controlling; functioning independently; related to the autonomic nervous system.

avulsion A tearing away of a part or structure.

axial Situated in or pertaining to an axis, such as the spine.

axilla The armpit.

axonal shearing A tearing of axons or nerve sheaths, caused by a blunt mechanism, to produce severe brain injury.

bacteria A common type of germ, treatable with antibiotics, causing disease.

barbiturates A family of sedative–hypnotic drugs usually taken by mouth and frequently used as recreational substances.

barotrauma Any injury caused by a change in the atmospheric pressure.

baseline A known or initial value with which subsequent observations can be compared.

basilar Pertaining to the base of the skull.

basilar skull fracture A fracture into the base of the skull, sometimes associated with brain hemorrhage or brain injury.

belly breathing Abdominal muscles are the main muscles used to breathe; this type of breathing is normal in infants because their chest wall is thin and weak.

benzodiazepine A family of sedative–hypnotic drugs usually taken by mouth and frequently used as recreational substances.

beta agonists Chemicals that excite the beta receptors of certain cells; one important effect is relaxation of smooth muscles of the airways in children with wheezing.

beta blockers Chemicals that block beta receptors; these chemicals are commonly used to reduce the work of the heart in patients with heart disease.

bevel A surface slanting from the horizontal or vertical.

bezoar A hard mass of entangled material sometimes found in the stomachs and intestines.

bicarbonate A chemical that increases ph or alkalinity.

bilateral Pertaining to, affecting, or relating to two sides.

bile A secretion of the gall bladder into the intestine to help digestion.

blunt (trauma) A mechanism of injury in which force occurs over a broad area and the skin is not usually broken.

bolus A single dose.

bowel The intestine.

brachial Pertaining to a main artery and vein of the arm.

brady A prefix indicating slow.

bradyasystole A heart rhythm on the cardiac monitor that is either asytole or very slow with wide QRS complexes, less than 20–30 beats per minute.

bradycardia A slow heartbeat.

brain death Cessation of brain function.

brain herniation Forceful shifting of the brain contents through a bony opening because of increased pressure in one compartment of the brain, usually resulting in cardiopulmonary arrest.

brain stem The stemlike part of the brain that connects the cerebral hemispheres with the spinal cord.

breech A newborn presentation that is not the head, usually the buttocks.

bretyllium A type of anti-dysrhythmic drug, useful for ventricular tachycardia.

bronchi The two main branches leading from the trachea to the

from the 6th cervical to the 5th dorsal vertebra, where it divides at a point called the carina into two bronchi, one leading to each lung.

tracheitis An inflammation of the trachea.

tracheostomy Operation of incising the skin over the trachea and making a surgical wound in the trachea in order to permit an airway during tracheal obstruction.

tracheostomy tube A tube inserted into the trachea in children who cannot breathe or maintain a clear airway on their own.

tracheotomy Tracheostomy.

tragus Cartilaginous projection in front of the exterior meatus of the ear.

transient Not lasting; of brief duration.

tremor A quivering.

triage The screening and classification of sick, wounded, or injured to determine need for medical and nursing manpower, equipment, and facilities.

tricyclic antidepressant *See cyclic antidepressant.*

tripoding An abnormal position to keep the airway open; it involves leaning forward onto two arms stretched forward.

trismus Tonic contraction of the muscles of mastication.

trochanter Either of the two bony processes below the neck of the femur.

tuberculin syringe Smallest volume syringe with tiny needle useful for injection of small volumes of fluid.

tuberosity An elevated round process of bone.

umbilical catheterization Placing a cannula into the umbilical artery or vein.

umbilical cord The attachment connecting the fetus with the placenta.

uremia Toxic condition associated with renal insufficiency.

uterus An organ in the female reproductive system for containing and nourishing the embryo and fetus from the time the fertilized egg is implanted to the time of birth of the fetus.

vagal Pertaining to the vagus nerve and cholinergic nervous stimulation.

vagal stimulation Provoking a cholinergic neurologic response.

vagina A musculomembranus tube that forms the passageway between the cervix uteri and the vulva.

vaginal introitus The vaginal opening.

varicella *See chicken pox.*

vascular Pertaining to or composed of blood vessels.

vascular access Cannulation of a vein or artery.

vascularized An anatomic area with many blood vessels.

vasoconstriction Decrease in the caliber of blood vessels.

vasodilatation Dilatation of blood vessels.

vasomotor Pertaining to the nerves having muscular control of the blood vessel walls.

vasopressor agent A drug that increases vascular tone and increases blood pressure.

vastus lateralis A muscle on the upper thigh suitable for intramuscular injection.

ventilation Exchange of air between the lungs and the air of the environment.

ventilation-perfusion mismatch A pathologic state where the oxygen going into the lungs is not mixing appropriately with the blood circulating through the lungs.

ventilator A mechanical device for artificial ventilation of the lungs.

ventriculoperitoneal (VP) shunt A cannula that directs cerebrospinal fluid from a ventricle in the head/brain, to the skin, then down the neck to either the abdomen or heart.

ventricular ectopy Abnormal ventricular heart rhythm.

ventricular fibrillation Disorganized, ineffective twitching of the ventricles, resulting in no blood flow and a state of cardiac arrest.

ventricular tachycardia A rapid heart rhythm in which the electrical impulse begins in the ventricle (instead of the atrium), which may result in inadequate blood flow and eventually deteriorate into cardiac arrest.

ventrogluteal An anatomic area of the upper lateral thigh.

volume resuscitation Replenishing the blood volume.

vomitus Emesis.

wheezing Production of whistling sounds during expiration such as occurs in asthma and bronchiolitis.

womb Uterus; female organ for containing, protecting, and nourishing the fetus.

work of breathing An indicator of oxygenation and ventilation. Work of breathing reflects the child's attempt to compensate for hypoxia.

xiphoid process The lowest portion of the sternum; sword-shaped cartilaginous process supported by bone.

Index

Note: A *t* following a page number indicates tabular material and an *f* following a page number indicates a figure.

A

B

C

G

H

I

J

K

L

Q

R

S

Additional Credits

Chapter 1
Opener: © Craig Jackson/In the Dark Photography
1-3, 1-4 Courtesy of Ron Dieckmann, MD, 1-6 Courtesy of Robert Weibe, MD, 1-7 Courtesy of Ron Dieckmann, MD, 1-8 © Mindy E. Klarman/ Photo Researchers, Inc., 1-9 George Kochaniec/ CORBIS/Sygma

Chapter 2
Opener: Courtesy of Marianne Gausche-Hill, MD
2-1 Courtesy of Ron Dieckmann, MD

Chapter 3
Opener: Courtesy of Ron Dieckmann, MD
3-2 Courtesy of the National EMSC Slideset, 3-3, 3-4 Courtesy of Dena Brownstein, MD, 3-6, 3-8 Courtesy of the National EMSC Slideset, 3-13 Reproduced with permission from Thompson SW: Emergency Care of Children, 1990.

Chapter 4
Opener: Courtesy of Ron Dieckmann, MD
4-8, Courtesy of the National EMSC Slideset

Chapter 5
Opener: Courtesy of Ron Dieckmann, MD
5-1 Courtesy of Marianne Gausche-Hill, MD, 5-2 Courtesy of the National EMSC Slideset, 5-6 Reproduced with permission. © Pediatric Advanced Life Support, 1997. Copyright American Heart Association, 5-7 © Michael Kowal, Custom Medical Stock Photo

Chapter 8
Opener: © Craig Jackson/In the Dark Photography, 8-13 Courtesy of North Carolina EMSC Prehospital, 8-20 Courtesy of Ron Dieckmann, MD

Chapter 9
9-13 David J. Burchfield, MD, 9-14 Reproduced with permission. © Pediatric Advanced Life Support, 1997. Copyright American Heart Association

Chapter 10
Opener: Courtesy of the National EMSC Slideset
10-1 Courtesy of the AAP

Chapter 11
Opener: © Sean O'Brien, Custom Medical Stock Photo
11-2, 11-3 © Linda Gheen

Chapter 12
Opener: Courtesy of the AAP: from the Visual Diagnosis of Child Physical Abuse Slideset
12-1, 12-2 Courtesy of the National EMSC Slideset, 12-3–12-7 Courtesy of the AAP: from the Visual Diagnosis of Child Physical Abuse Slideset, 12-8–12-11 Courtesy of the AAP: from the Visual Diagnosis of Child Physical Abuse Slideset, 12-12, 12-13 Courtesy of the AAP

Chapter 13
Opener: Courtesy of the National EMSC Slideset
13-1 Courtesy of the State of California, Emergency Medical Services Authority, 13-2 © Mike Heller/911 Pictures, 13-3 © Craig Jackson/In the Dark Photography

Procedures
P1-1 © Craig Jackson/In the Dark Photography, P2-2, P4-1, P4-2, P11-6, P13-2b Courtesy of Marianne Gausche-Hill, MD

Photographs also supplied by the American Academy of Orthopaedic Surgeons and Jones and Bartlett Publishers. Several figures throughout the text were adapted from original artwork featured in Teaching Resource for Instructors in Prehospital Pediatrics (TRIPP) 1998 Version 2.1 from the Center for Pediatric Emergency Medicine, NY, NY.

PEPP Evaluation Form

Which course did you attend? _______ BLS _______ ALS

Please circle your response:	Strongly Disagree	Disagree	Agree	Strongly Agree
1. After completing the PEPP course, I have more confidence in my ability to assess and treat pediatric patients accurately.	1	2	3	4
2. I have a better understanding of when to use ALS skills and when to use BLS skills in treating a pediatric patient.	1	2	3	4
3. I plan to change the way I perform certain skills based on something I learned in PEPP.	1	2	3	4
4. I plan to purchase, or recommend the purchase of, new equipment based on something I learned in PEPP.	1	2	3	4
5. The PEPP student manual was useful in preparation for the PEPP course.	1	2	3	4
6. I plan to share with someone else the information and skills I learned.	1	2	3	4
7. The information and skills I learned in PEPP will be valuable to my practice.	1	2	3	4

8. What, if anything, will make it difficult for you to use the skills as presented in the PEPP course (please check all that apply):

_____ My organization does not provide the equipment needed to perform the skills as described in PEPP.

_____ The skills as presented in PEPP are different from the protocols in my area.

_____ I do not feel confident about my ability to perform the skills as described in PEPP.

_____ Other____

_____ There are no barriers to using the skills as presented in PEPP.

9. Please rate each portion of the course based on how useful it was to you by circling your response:

Portion of Course	Not at All Useful	Fairly Useful	Very Useful	Extremely Useful	Not Used
PEPP VIDEO	1	2	3	4	x
LECTURES					
Making a Difference	1	2	3	4	x
Child Development: Applying the Pediatric Assessment Triangle	1	2	3	4	x
Respiratory Emergencies	1	2	3	4	x
Cardiovascular Emergencies	1	2	3	4	x
Medical Emergencies	1	2	3	4	x
Toxic Exposures	1	2	3	4	x
Trauma	1	2	3	4	x
Emergency Delivery and Newborn Stabilization	1	2	3	4	x
Children with Special Health Care Needs	1	2	3	4	x
Child Maltreatment	1	2	3	4	x
SCENARIOS					
Child and Family Interaction	1	2	3	4	x
Cardiovascular Emergencies	1	2	3	4	x
Medical Emergencies	1	2	3	4	x
Trauma	1	2	3	4	x
Emergency Delivery and Newborn Stabilization	1	2	3	4	x
Children with Special Health Care Needs	1	2	3	4	x
SKILL STATIONS					
ALS Skills Station 1: Pediatric airway management	1	2	3	4	x
ALS Skill Station 2: Vascular access and spinal immobilization	1	2	3	4	x
BLS Skill Station 1: Pediatric airway management	1	2	3	4	x
BLS Skill Station 2: Spinal immobilization	1	2	3	4	x

Comments: